SECOND EDITION

REAPPRAISALS IN CANADIAN HISTORY
PRE-CONFEDERATION

C.M. Wallace

R.M. Bray

A.D. Gilbert

Laurentian University

PRENTICE HALL CANADA INC.,
SCARBOROUGH, ONTARIO

To the Memory of A.D. Gilbert

Canadian Cataloguing in Publication Data

Main entry under title:

Reappraisals in Canadian History, pre-confederation

2nd ed.
Includes index.
ISBN 0-13-447335-3

1. Canada – History – To 1763 (New France).
2. Canada – History – 1763–1867. 3. Canada – History
– To 1763 (New France) – Historiography. 4. Canada –
History – 1763–1867 – Historiography. I. Wallace,
C. M. (Carl Murray), 1932–   . II. Bray, R. M.
(Robert Matthew), 1944–   . III. Gilbert, A. D.
(Angus Duncan), 1941–1994.

FC161.R38 1996   971   C95-932485-2
F1026.R38 1996

Prentice-Hall, Inc., Englewood Cliffs, New Jersey
Prentice-Hall International (UK) Limited, London
Prentice-Hall of Australia, Pty. Limited, Sydney
Prentice-Hall Hispanoamericana, S.A., Mexico City
Prentice-Hall of India Private Limited, New Delhi
Prentice-Hall of Japan, Inc., Tokyo
Simon & Schuster Asia Private Limited, Singapore
Editora Prentice-Hall do Brasil, Ltda., Rio de Janeiro

ISBN 0-13-447335-3

Acquisitions Editor: Allan Gray
Copy Editor: Leah Johnston
Production Editor: Valerie Adams
Production Coordinator: Deborah Starks
Permissions: Marijke Leupen
Cover Design: Julia Hall
Cover Image: Frances A. Hopkins / "Canoe Party Around Campfire" (detail)
Page Layout: Arlene Edgar

1 2 3 4 5   RRD   00 99 98 97 96

Printed and bound in the U.S.A.

Every reasonable effort has been made to obtain permissions for all articles and
data used in this edition. If errors or omissions have occurred, they will be corrected
in future editions provided written notification has been received by the publisher.

We welcome readers' comments, which can be sent by e-mail to
collegeinfo_pubcanada@prenhall.com

Table of Contents

Preface

Reappraisals in Canadian History is designed for use in university-level survey courses. It is, however, neither a textbook nor a traditional reader. Each of the units in the two volumes focuses on differing or complementary interpretations of a particular historical problem. A brief introduction to each unit establishes the context for the selected readings, and suggestions for relevant additional sources are included.

The vitality in Canadian historical studies over the past two decades has been outstanding, resulting in a profusion of new periodicals and monographs. Few organizations, groups, or regions are now without a journal. This has created both opportunities and challenges in fashioning a collection such as this. Although much recent historical writing is included, we have not neglected the the important contributions of the previous generation of historians. In assembling these volumes we have consciously rejected the popular trend of trying to satisfy every region and province, every interest group, every minority, everybody. Instead we attempted to find common threads pointing to the integration of the exploding body of literature and interests. This topical approach demanded that all interests, including such disparate ones as regions, women, politics, the underclasses, and minorities, be part of the total fabric rather than segregated ghettoes.

In assembling this collection we have incurred a number of obligations. Faye Kennedy, formerly of Prentice Hall Canada, first persuaded us that there was a need for such a collection. We wish also to thank the Dean of the Faculty of Social Science and the Institute of Northern Ontario Research and Development at Laurentian University for financial assistance. Several of our students, including Ross Danaher, Michael Stevenson and James Watson, gave us logistical support. The students in HIST 1406/1407 participated cheerfully as we experimented with the classroom use of these materials in tutorials. Leo Larivière created the maps. Rose-May Demoré, our departmental secretary, responded to every call for help. Finally we must thank the dozens of historians, editors and publishers who have generously given us permission to reprint this material.

Since the publication of the first edition of *Reappraisals,* our co-editor, colleague and friend, Angus Gilbert, died of cancer. While we have made extensive changes, much of Angus' original contribution remains and we therefore dedicate this edition to his memory.

C.M. WALLACE

R.M. BRAY

Laurentian University
Sudbury, Ontario

Introduction

Canadian History and Historians

History is misunderstood more often than not. At a superficial level it appears to be one of the few immutables in an ever-changing world. That the past itself can never be altered is irrefutable, and students frequently choose history as an option at university believing that at least one subject will provide security when others mystify with unique concepts, vocabulary and content. That cozy view of history never lasts long, for as a discipline history is complex, malleable, and imprecise, subject to changing conditions and perspectives. Far from being set in cement, history is continuously being recast by each generation's need to find its own past. If R.G. Collingwood was correct, then "every new generation must rewrite history in its own way." The past that he, Winston Churchill and others found meaningful differs dramatically from that of today's leaders and their societies.

This charactersitic of history causes much confusion for students and academics alike. A psychology professor at lunch with several historians recently declared that, after she had taken world history in grade eight, further study was irrelevant. The subject, like Napoleon, was dead. One of the historians ventured the opinion that history had possibly changed more in the past twenty years than psychology. At that point she threw up her hands and left, unable to entertain such a ludicrous proposition. Yet it may be true.

That dynamic nature of the discipline of history, when compared to the permanence of past events such as the death of Napoleon, is the apparent paradox the psychology professor never unravelled. Over the past three decades a revolution has taken place in historical scholarship. In the era after the Second World War a sort of plateau, encompassing a broad consensus about the nature of the discipline, was reached. The traditional scholar worked for months or years in archives, poring over primary sources, and producing "revisionist" books or articles published in the handful of journals that all historians of Canada read. Triumphs were achieved with the discovery of new source material or a new angle on a known subject. Politics and biography were favoured, though economic, religious, military and international topics found their specialists. The overall nature of history as the study of the activities and ideas of elites, however, was rarely questioned. This view from the "court," or top-down, became the textbook version of the Canadian past, and while there were divisions over some interpretations based on ideology, religion, or even personal hostility, there was no division on what history itself was.

In Canada the small coterie of academics dominating the field included Marcel Trudel, Donald Creighton, A.R.M. Lower, W.L. Morton, Hilda Neatby, C.P. Stacey, W.S. MacNutt, Frank Underhill, Guy Frégault, and Margaret Ormsby. A younger generation of "revisionists" from the same mold was expanding the content without challenging the structures. Among them were J.M.S. Careless, Peter Waite, Margaret Prang, W.J. Eccles, Ramsay Cook, Jean Hamelin, Ken McNaught, Blair Neatby, and Jacques Monet. These people all knew each other personally, frequently comparing notes at the Public Archives of Canada, then located on Sussex Drive beside the Royal Mint in Ottawa. At the annual meetings of the Canadian Historical Association they read papers to each other, and were never short of advice. The *Canadian Historical Review*, published by the University of Toronto Press, was the final authority in English Canada, while Abbé Groulx reigned over French Canada with the *Revue d'histoire de l'Amérique française*. It was from this more or less homogeneous group that the dominant view of Canada, as presented in school textbooks, emerged. The comfortable unity of this well-written version of Canada's past permitted it to survive its generation, which many regard as the "Golden Age" of Canadian historical scholarship.

By the late 1960s, however, several younger scholars reacted against that veneration of the images of a previous generation. To them the historical imagination had been crippled by consistency. More than that, the consensus version of the past, in their view, had no relevance for the current generation. One may admire a Rolls Royce Silver Ghost, a 1955 Chevrolet, or even a Model T, the argument goes, but one must not confuse an abacus with a computer, a museum piece with modern needs.

It is the nature of history that the status quo does not survive long, and in the upheaval that characterized the whole mentality of the 1960s, several academics began to search for a more "usable past," one that abandoned the impressionistic views from the "court," and aimed at the reconstruction of a more meaningful society. The "New Social History" was the umbrella under which most of the innovations may be grouped. The dissatisfaction with a Canadian past dominated by political and economic factors led to a renovation with new methodologies, different approaches and alternate subject matter muscling in on the old-school-tie network. Subjects once ignored moved to centre stage, including work on classes and class relations, demography, literacy, the family, leisure, mobility, immigration, religion and education, though there was little cohesion among the disparate activities. Quantification and the computer found their place in the historian's baggage. *Histoire sociale / Social History*, co-sponsored by the University of Ottawa and Carleton University in 1968, eventually provided a focus and emerged as an alternate journal, though its lack of coherent editorial policy was simply a reflection of the diversity of opinion within the discipline. In a sense each historian could become a different school. The *Annales* of France, for example, were the source of inspiration for many French Canadians, while most English Canadians turned to American sociology for their models. Although there was considerable resentment over this "invasion of the barbarians" among the traditional historians, their own anecdotal approach invited criticism from those who asked different questions of sources and approached the past from new perspectives.

By the 1970s a veritable floodgate had opened. The annual meetings of the Canadian Historical Association became not one but a dozen or more fragments meeting separately. There was the ethnic group, the labour, the Atlantic, the Western, the Arctic, the Native, the women, the urban, the local, the material, the oral—the divisions were endless. Each of these had the capacity to subdivide. Labour quickly separated into the "old-fashioned" and the "New Left," with the latter winning the day and mounting its own journal, *Labour / Le Travailleur*. Each segment, in fact, launched one or more journals, such as *Urban History Review, Canadian Ethnic Studies, Polyphony, Canadian Woman Studies, Journal of Canadian Studies, B.C. Studies,* and *The American Review of Canadian Studies*. The range of topics and quality of scholarship were like the rainbow. Some, like *Acadiensis: Journal of the History of the Atlantic Region*, founded in 1971 at the University of New Brunswick, established and maintained an enviable reputation. Others have been less successful.

As a consequence of this fragmentation over recent decades, a student is faced with not one but many versions of Canadian history. This confusion may be considered an unnecessary encumbrance to those who are content with the "good old stuff," but that implies the study of a dead subject. The reappraisal is never-ending, and the challenge for the student is not to learn a few facts and dates but to sample the literature and to recognize what the authors are doing with the subject and trying to do to the reader. This requires an agile and a critical mind.

Reappraisals in Canadian History is intended to reflect this diversity of interpretation in Canadian history and to present it in such a way as to enable a student to make sense of it. This is not a "textbook" history of Canada, and makes no attempt to survey all of the main developments in that history. Nor is it simply a collection of readings, randomly selected and with little or no relationship one to another. Rather, each of the chapters is devoted to a particular historical problem and the different ways in which historians have approached that problem. In some cases their conclusions stand in sharp contradiction to each other; in others they are complementary. In every case students should attempt not merely to grasp the author's conclusions, but, of even greater importance, to understand how they were reached.

In order to do this it is useful to understand the variety of reasons that may lead different historians to reach different conclusions about what appears to be the same historical problem. In one sense, of course, there is nothing new about this. The debate over "historical relativism" is an old one, and it is now a truism that historians are influenced by the context in which they themselves live. It is, after all, hardly surprising that their view of the past is, to some degree at least, relative to their own time and place and circumstance, to their own preferences and prejudices. This may mean that they view historical evidence in a new light, or that they pose different questions of the past. It has long been accepted, therefore, that there will be differences of emphasis and interpretation, not only between different generations of historians, but also between historians of the same era.

The present fragmentation of the discipline, however, goes far beyond the traditional recognition of the relativity of historical knowledge. Implicit in it is fundamental disagreement over content and methodology, the meaning of history and its purpose. The one point on which historians do agree, however, is that not all historical interpretations are of equal validity. Certainly historians are less inclined than scholars in other disciplines to claim to have discovered any final "truths." This is understandable, given the nature of the evidence with which they deal and the problems with which they are concerned. The readings in this volume are in themselves testimony to the elusiveness of any final answers in history. Despite these limitations, historians do insist that historical scholarship can and must be subjected to critical scrutiny, that historical evidence and the use to which that evidence is put can be evaluated. The study of history at any kind of advanced level requires the development of these analytical skills, and never more so than with its current fragmentation. It is this, rather than the mastery of voluminous detail, that distinguishes the historian from the mere antiquarian. One of the purposes of this collection of readings is to assist students to develop their critical skills. Within each chapter, therefore, students should attempt to identify the interpretative thrust of each author, how the interpretation of one author differs from or complements that of another, what sources and methodologies have been employed, and, finally, how convincingly each author has based his or her interpretation on the historical evidence.

There are a number of fairly obvious points to look for. Has an author found new evidence which calls into question previous work on the subject? Is a new methodology being applied? Is anecdotal evidence, for example, being challenged by statistical analysis? Is a new type of historical evidence being brought to bear on an old problem? Is the historical problem itself being defined in an entirely new way? A very good example by way of illustration can be found in the different ways in which historians have approached the question of the nature of society in New France. In chapter 2, students will find three quite different, although complementary, portraits of that society. In one a description has been developed from the observations of contemporary observers. In another a demographic analysis of an urban area has yielded an entirely different perspective. In the third, an attempt to evaluate the position of a particular group within that society—the women of New France—the reader finds yet another focus. These three readings reflect the use of different sources, different methodologies and different questions to throw light on the same historical problem, the nature of society. In reading these articles, students must first identify these differences in approach if they are to understand and evaluate the differences in the conclusions reached by the authors.

In the pre-Confederation period of Canadian history, the student is confronted not only with conflicting interpretations but with a fragmented subject. While there is a certain unity to the history of New France, even in that era geographic barriers and differences, as well as imperial policies, meant that the St. Lawrence colony and Acadia developed in very different ways. After the Conquest, a somewhat amorphous entity labelled "British North America" contained a sometimes bewildering variety of separate colonies and territories, held together only by their common allegiance to the British Crown and their distrust of the republican experiment in the new United States of America.

The fourteen chapters in this volume are a selection from the history of New France and British North America. An attempt has been made to strike a balance between the various subjects and approaches. Although there are exceptions, generally speaking historical writing on the pre-Confederation period is more traditional and has been less influenced by the New Social History than that on the national period, perhaps because the historical sources are more intractable. The first six chapters of this volume are concerned with the history of New France. Within these chapters, however, students will encounter a wide variety of subjects. Chapters 2 and 3 deal with the social and economic development of the St. Lawrence colony, while chapter 5 contains two very contrasting views of the French military in New France. Chapter 4, on the other hand, is concerned with the tragic history of Acadia, which ended in the expulsion of most of its population. The difficult problem of the nature of the cultural interaction between Amerindian and European is considered in chapter 1, and this theme is picked up again for a later period in chapter 9, "The Fur Trade and the North West." Students should note that in both instances historians have something to learn from anthropologists, who approach this question of cultural interaction from somewhat different perspectives and employ somewhat different methodologies.

In the post-Conquest period there is even more diversity. Two chapters, 7 and 8, are concerned with interaction with the United States. The economic and geographic diversity of British North America are reflected in units on the North West, Lower Canada, and the outward-looking Atlantic colonies. In the final three units, British North America is interpreted in a less fragmented fashion, through an examination of the imperial relationship, society, and, finally, Confederation itself.

Any rigid categorization of the chapters is bound to be misleading since politics, economics, social dynamics and regional aspects pervade most studies about Canada in one way or another. The student must learn to stride through the variety, identifying the interpretations, the mind-sets, the methodologies, and the mythologies. Each chapter in this collection offers a variety of interpretations which are frequently contradictory. At the same time, each chapter has a coherence which explains something about Canada, its history and its historians. Since history is what historians say it is, the student has both the opportunity and the responsibility to identify those views and the objectives of the historians. History will continue to be misunderstood, and the student must know why.

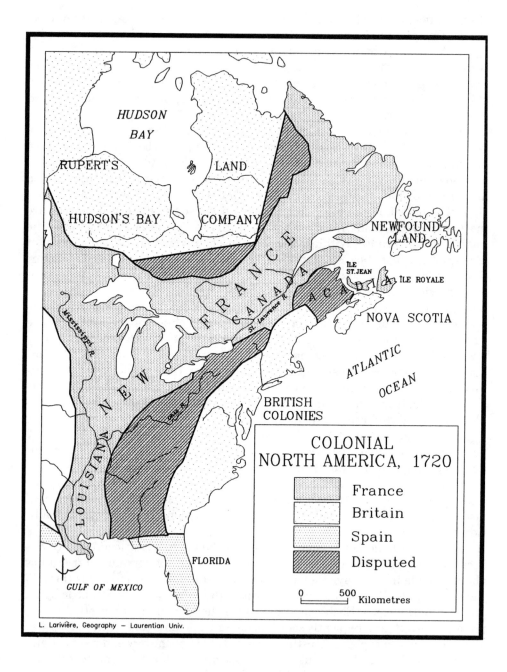

COLONIAL NORTH AMERICA, 1720

HUDSON BAY

RUPERT'S LAND

HUDSON'S BAY COMPANY

NEWFOUNDLAND

NEW FRANCE

CANADA

ACADIA

ÎLE ST.JEAN

ÎLE ROYALE

NOVA SCOTIA

Mississippi R.

St. Lawrence R.

Ohio R.

ATLANTIC OCEAN

BRITISH COLONIES

LOUISIANA

FLORIDA

GULF OF MEXICO

Legend:
- France
- Britain
- Spain
- Disputed

0   500 Kilometres

L. Larivière, Geography – Laurentian Univ.

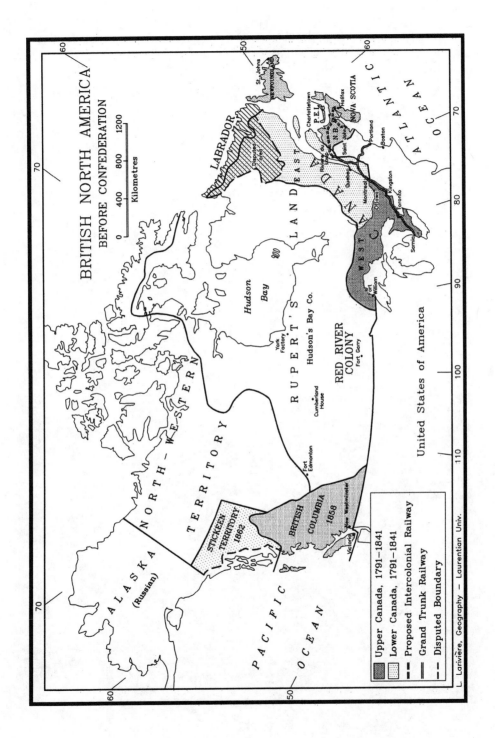

BRITISH NORTH AMERICA
BEFORE CONFEDERATION

Kilometres
0   400   800   1200

Upper Canada, 1791–1841
Lower Canada, 1791–1841
Proposed Intercolonial Railway
Grand Trunk Railway
Disputed Boundary

L. Larivière, Geography – Laurentian Univ.

ALASKA
(Russian)

NORTH–WESTERN

TERRITORY

STICKEEN
TERRITORY
1862

BRITISH
COLUMBIA
1858

New Westminster

Victoria

PACIFIC

OCEAN

Fort
Edmonton

Cumberland
House

RUPERT'S

Hudson's Bay Co.

Fort Garry

RED RIVER
COLONY

York
Factory

Hudson
Bay

LAND

EAST

WEST

Fort
William

Sarnia

Toronto

Kingston

Ottawa

Montreal

Quebec

Rivière-du-Loup

Portland

Boston

Saint John

N.B.

P.E.I.

Charlottetown

NOVA SCOTIA

Halifax

St. Johns

NEWFOUNDLAND

LABRADOR

Disputed
1825

CANADA

ATLANTIC

OCEAN

United States of America

xiii

CHAPTER
1 NATIVE-NEWCOMER INTERACTION

The "New World" the Europeans thought they had discovered in North America had in reality already been inhabited for thousands of years. The first major theme in the early history of Canada is therefore the interaction between the First Nations, or Amerindians, and the Europeans. Not surprisingly, older historical writing on this subject reflects a Eurocentric perspective, describing a process in which a barbarous and inferior culture was inevitably overwhelmed by one much more civilized and technologically advanced. This view of the Amerindian as "Savage" permeated all the literature, especially that of the influential nineteenth-century American historian Francis Parkman, whose writings defined Canada for decades.

By the 1930s, the Parkman interpretation was under attack. The first reading in this unit, "The Problem of the Iroquois," by George T. Hunt, reflects this Eurocentric approach. Nevertheless, it was hailed as a major reinterpretation of the subject when it was first published in 1940. Completely rejecting Parkman's attribution of the seventeenth-century intertribal wars to the "homicidal frenzy" of the Iroquois, Hunt suggested instead that the wars were a direct result of European-Amerindian contact and, in particular, of the relationship between the Amerindians and the fur trade. Having become totally dependent upon European technology in the form of trade goods, the Iroquois had no option other than war once their supply of beaver fur became dangerously depleted by the 1640s.

Although this emphasis on the economic importance of the fur trade to the Amerindians has been influential and was typical of the economic deterministic literature predominant before the Second World War, more recent historical writing on early Amerindian-European contact suggests that the subject is much more complex than Hunt indicated. Hunt, in turn, has therefore been attacked. In the second reading, the "Conclusion" from his *Friend and Foe:*

1

Aspects of French-Amerindian Cultural Contact in the Sixteenth and Seventeenth Centuries, Cornelius Jaenan examines the more general question of the Amerindian-European cultural relationship. Acknowledging that this interaction had a powerful effect on both parties, he suggests that the process was one in which Europeans gained, but the natives lost. Although Amerindian culture was disastrously weakened, the native peoples remained unintegrated in the developing society of New France.

For any student of this subject, the lack of historical records and voices from the Amerindians themselves places severe limitations on analysis. Hunt represented a significant advance over the Parkman indignity; Jaenan, in turn, offered a much broader view than Hunt. All historical writing, however, is representative of the era in which it is written, and that was certainly true of Parkman, Hunt and Jaenan. The final reading is from the 1990s, by Huron academic Georges E. Sioui. In "The Destruction of Huronia" from *For An Amerindian Autohistory: An Essay on the Foundations of a Social Ethic, 1992* Sioui begins with a rejection of the Hunt thesis and then offers alternative voices and views.

Suggestions for Further Reading

Axtel, James, *The Invasion Within: The Contest of Cultures in Colonial North America.* New York: Oxford University Press, 1985.

Bailey, A.G., *The Conflict of European and Eastern Algonkian Cultures, 1504–1700* (2nd ed.). Toronto: University of Toronto Press, 1969.

Dickason, Olive, "The Concept of *l'homme sauvage* and Early French Colonialism in the Americas," *Revue française d'histoire d'outre-mer*, 64, no. 234 (1977), 5–32.

_____, *The Myth of the Savage and the Beginnings of French Colonialism in the Americas.* Edmonton: University of Alberta Press, 1984.

Krech, S., *Indians, Animals and the Fur Trade: A Critique of Keepers of the Game.* Athens, Georgia: University of Georgia Press, 1981.

Johnston, Susan, "Epidemics: the Forgotten Factor in Seventeenth Century Native Warfare in the St. Lawrence Region," in *Native People, Native Lands: Canadian Indians, Inuit and Metis*, ed. B.A. Cox. Ottawa: Carleton University Press, 1987, 14–31.

Martin, Calvin, "The European Impact on the Culture of a Northeastern Algonquin Tribe: An Ecological Interpretation," *William and Mary Quarterly*, 3d. ser. XXI (January 1974), 3–26.

Martin, Calvin, *Keepers of the Game: Indian-Animal Relationships and the Fur Trade.* Berkeley, California: University of California Press, 1978.

Schlieser, K.H., "Epidemics and Indian Middlemen: Rethinking the Wars of the Iroquois, 1609–1653," *Ethnohistory*, 23, no. 2 (Spring 1976), 129–45.

Trigger, Bruce, "The French Presence in Huronia: The Structure of Franco-Huron Relations in the First Half of the Seventeenth Century," *Canadian Historical Review*, XLIX, no. 2 (June 1968), 107–41.

_____, *Natives and Newcomers: Canada's 'Heroic Age' Reconsidered.* Kingston and Montreal: McGill-Queen's University Press, 1985.

THE PROBLEM OF THE IROQUOIS

George T. Hunt

In most respects the circumstances of the contact between white man and native in North America are unique in the history of such relationships. In other centuries and in other regions, where the frontiers of superior civilizations had long been in contact with the periphera of inferior civilizations, the conditions of these frontier-peripheral areas were well-established and relatively familiar, and the process of infiltration and conquest was comparatively gradual. The Russian advance into Siberia, the French and English movement into and beyond India, the penetration of the Orient by the peddling shipmasters of the West, all these were conditioned by the fact that each civilization had already considerable knowledge of the other. In Africa the Nile Valley and the Mediterranean shore had constituted a frontier area before historic times, and even in the southern part of the African continent contacts had been more or less continuous for nearly four hundred years before actual colonization and exploitation were begun.

In North America, on the other hand, a well-advanced civilization, in which the mechanism of exploitation was already highly developed, met the Stone Age face to face, in an invasion almost simultaneously continental in extent. There had been a few premonitory invasions along the St. Lawrence River, Coronado's horsemen had retreated from the far Southwest, a few mailed footmen had floundered through southern swamps to the Great River, a few Englishmen had died at Croatan, but these tentative ventures of the sixteenth century had come to nothing. The Wars of Religion cut short the beginning made by Cartier; Texas remained virtually uninhabited; and 130 years passed before another white man glimpsed the Mississippi.

In the thirty years following 1603 the whole Atlantic seaboard swarmed with settlement. Champlain established New France at Quebec and Three Rivers; Holland built forts far up the Hudson; England was at Plymouth, in Massachusetts Bay, Virginia, and Maryland, and struggling for a foothold in Maine. The entire coast was explored and mapped. The Stone Age faced the insistent seventeenth century on a fifteen-hundred-mile front which moved swiftly and relentlessly forward. This advance was no matter of slave raids, ivory, or gold. What these white men wanted was what every native had or could get, furs or land, and the trade that was opened was a trade in which every native could take part. As a matter of fact, he was usually frantically eager to take part in it.

From *The Wars of the Iroquois: A Study in Intertribal Relations* (Madison: University of Wisconsin Press, 1967), 3–12. Reprinted by permission of the University of Wisconsin Press.

The abundance of furs and the inexhaustible market for them made North America a unique theatre of interracial contacts. On other continents the desire of traders had been for materials or products considerably less plentiful and less easily obtained by individuals, but here the ease of acquisition, the apparently limitless supply, the ready market, and the permanence of the white settlements permitted the constant participation of every native, expanded the business of trade to unprecedented proportions, and changed, almost overnight, the fundamental conditions of aboriginal economy.

If it is true that "the relations into which the Europeans entered with the aborigines were decided almost wholly by the relations which they found to exist among the tribes on their arrival,"[1] it is certainly equally true that the intertribal relations of the aborigines were in the future to be decided almost wholly by the relations existing between them and the Europeans, especially in those areas in which the fur trade was the chief factor in those relations. On the question of land, the tribes could, and often did, cooperate, and yield or resist together, but the fur trade divided them immediately into groups—those who had fur and those who had none. The great desirability of the trade goods to the Indian who had once known them became shortly a necessity, a very urgent necessity that permitted no renunciation of the trade. As new desires wakened and old skills vanished, the Indian who had fur, or could get it, survived; he who could not get it died or moved away. But whatever he did, life for him could never again be what it had been: old institutions and economies had profoundly altered or disappeared completely at the electrifying touch of the white man's trade, which swept along the inland trails and rivers with bewildering speed and wrought social revolution a thousand miles beyond the white man's habitations, and years before he himself appeared on the scene. English powder burned on the Mississippi a half century before the English cabins reached Lake Ontario,[2] and the Ottawa tribe had fought a commercial war with the Winnebago of Wisconsin, forcing French trade goods upon them, ten years before the hesitant French settlement had reached Montreal.[3] In truth, the Indian world had in many respects already vanished before the white man saw it, and it is not strange that in his great hurry he formed opinions of it that were somewhat wide of the truth. Those who wonder at the foolishness of the Indians who fought each other to extinction instead of combining to stay the white man's advance are usually the same who attribute their intertribal wars to "insensate fury" and "homicidal frenzy."[4] Tribal motives must necessarily be mysterious to the historian who ignores the social and economic metamorphosis brought about by the trade.

The area in which the fur trade was most significant was the northeastern quarter of the continent, where two great waterways led through inhospitable mountains and highlands into a region which in the seventeenth century and long thereafter teemed with fur-bearers. The St. Lawrence-Ottawa and the Hudson-Mohawk routes led to the Great Lakes and the Mississippi-Ohio country, with their innumerable tributary streams where were to be found more beaver than in any similar area in the world. Commanding both these routes lay the Huron Iroquois, composed of a half dozen consanguine tribes which with the Algonquins of the upper St. Lawrence must have represented a population of nearly 100,000. Yet after only thirty years of intermittent warfare the Iroquois proper, probably the least numerous of the tribes, never numbering more than 12,000, were in sole possession of the region east of Lake Michigan, having dispersed, incorporated, or exterminated all their neighbours; they were even credited, though somewhat mistakenly, with a shadowy empire extending west to the Mississippi, and from Carolina to Hudson Bay. As to the importance of the Iroquois, it has been said that their steady alliance with the Dutch and English of the Hudson River colony was "the pivotal fact of early American history."[5]

With intertribal relations and activities centring as they did about the tribe most active in intertribal affairs, the Iroquois, the question, why did the Iroquois do the things that they did, becomes not only pertinent but vital to an understanding of colonial history. The answers thus far given by historians are three, none of which is in the least convincing.[6] The first of these is the theory that they were possessed of an "insensate fury" and "homicidal frenzy," a theory advanced by Parkman. The second is that a superior political organization, the League of the Iroquois, produced by a superior Iroquois intellect, rendered the Five Nations invincible. This thesis was propounded by Lewis H. Morgan, who even ascribed to the Iroquois the paradoxical motive of exterminating their enemies in order to establish universal intertribal peace.[7] To these may be added a third theory, that a great supply of firearms, furnished by the greedy Dutch West India Company and unavailable to their enemies, gave rein to a natural passion for conquest and butchery, which they indulged at random but with almost unimaginable enthusiasm.

Even a cursory contemplation of the generally known facts, however, will raise further questions. If a natural superiority or an innate fury was responsible, it is curious that neither of these traits was manifest in the very closely consanguine tribes, such as the Hurons, the Erie, the Neutrals, and others which the Iroquois conquered. Neither does this thesis explain why the naturally superior and ferocious Iroquois had fled from the Algonquins of the St. Lawrence in the years preceding the coming of Champlain, and were on the defensive, stockaded in invaded territory until after 1620. Even if there had been some virtues inherent in the Iroquois blood stream, that stream had changed very early and very completely, for as early as 1656 a priest found that there were more foreigners than natives in Iroquoia, eleven different nations being represented in the country of the Seneca.[8] In 1660 it would have been hard to find 1,200 Iroquois of pure blood, according to Lalemant, who anticipated Parkman by remarking, "It may be said that, if the Iroquois have any power, it is only because they are knavish and cruel."[9] Even the casual reader feels, after reviewing the achievements of the Iroquois, that knavery and cruelty could hardly have been the mainspring of their mighty and significant labours.

With respect to the great efficiency claimed for the League, a re-examination of only a few sources leads to the conclusion that in the period of Iroquois conquest the League was little if any more effectual in achieving unanimity of action than were the loose Powhatanic and Cherokee leagues, or even the Algonquin confederacy or the Choctaw republic. Despite the bluster of Mohawk orators, there is not a single recorded instance of unanimous or anywhere near unanimous action by the League prior to 1653, and none save in peace treaties thereafter. The Mohawk orators had a way, confusing to their enemies, as they well knew, of pretending, when on their own business, to speak for the League.[10] The habit has confused historians no less. Osgood, however, has recognized that the League could at best only prevent fratricidal strife among its members.[11] In any event, that result was achieved by the other, less celebrated, confederacies with more marked success than by the League of the Iroquois. The Hurons, for instance, kept peace with their Algonquin neighbors with no organization whatever, no ties of consanguinity, no common tongue or social institutions[12]—in fact, with nothing more in common than an economic interest—while throughout a series of five wars there was no such thing as unanimity among the Five Nations. Rarely did two of the cantons combine in an attack, and then only because their commercial interests were for the time identical. Never did two cantons combine for defense. Mohawks and Onondaga both cheered the French attack upon the Seneca, and Seneca and Onondaga were steadily antipathetic to the Mohawks, who, as the eastern canton, held the Hudson River country and the Dutch trade. The Mohawks sought ceaselessly to exploit their brothers, and were at swords' points with them half the time. All that prevented a vicious intra-Iroquois war was the fact that the common interest of all three in opposing the French and the French Indians was ever greater than their conflicting interests. At that, much Iroquois blood was spilled by Iroquois, and perhaps more embassies of peace travelled within Iroquoia than from Iroquoia to foreign tribes.

If all this is true, one may ask, why has the League been so celebrated by historians, and why has it for seventy-five years been given credit for accomplishing things it did not accomplish? The most important single reason is probably Lewis H. Morgan's book *The League of the Iroquois*. Morgan was a true scholar in spirit, a conscientious observer, and a tireless worker, but he was not a historian, and he had access to few or none of the sources which could have informed him on the history of the League he so carefully observed.[13] It is perhaps not strange that when he viewed the perfected League of 1850, knowing little of Iroquois history except tradition,[14] he should have assumed that the perfection of political organization he saw then was more than two centuries old. The League as he saw it in the nineteenth century offered a plausible explanation for a hitherto unexplained phenomenon of the seventeenth century, and without critical investigation it was temptingly easy to interchange result and cause. The very excellence of his general work unfortunately perpetuated this specific error, which was widely adopted by historians.[15] To those who read the sources, however, it becomes quite clear that the League as Morgan saw it did not wage the wars of the Iroquois nor make them possible, but that in a very real sense it was the wars that made the League which he and others were privileged to examine 200 years later. The League, then, cannot be an answer to the Iroquois problem.

In the matter of armament also, the assets of the Iroquois have been overstated. The 2,000 muskets which they are credited with having possessed in 1640[16] shrink upon investigation to a possible 400, and even this is probably too generous an estimate. In that year a French prisoner testified that a "heavily armed" war band of 500 Iroquois had exactly thirty-six arquebuses.[17] The supposed greed of the Dutch West India Company is called into serious question when it is discovered that they tried desperately to stop what trade in guns there was, and that both the Company and the settlement at Beverwyck passed and attempted to enforce ordinances against it, even going so far as to ordain the penalty of death. Among the Dutch on the Hudson and Connecticut the French were as bitterly accused of trading arms to Indians as were the Dutch in the French settlements on the St. Lawrence, and the justification was as ample in the one case as in the other. Moreover, the Susquehannah, whom the Iroquois conquered, were far better provided with arms than the Iroquois, possessing even artillery in their forts.

There is no denying that these conditions, to which is attributed the Iroquois phenomenon, existed in some measure and undoubtedly had an aggregate importance, but the fact still remains that although they were paralleled elsewhere, in fact were paralleled again and again all over the continent, the phenomenon itself was unparalleled. No other tribe ever did what the Iroquois did, and yet the three theories of inherent qualities, superior organization, and superior armament fail to explain their achievements or to suggest a motive which could have driven them so far and down so hard a road.

The explanation must lie in some fundamental condition which thus far has not received the attention of the relatively few students of Iroquois history. The search should be not for the ineluctable ultimate origin, but for a general condition of Indian life, readily ascertained and recognized, from which the motivation of the Iroquois should appear to proceed inevitably. Since this general condition was peculiar in its effect upon the Iroquois, it follows that unless the Iroquois were themselves peculiar, it must have some connection with geography or climate; and when it is recalled that the rise of the Iroquois to power coincided with the spread of the white trade throughout their region and the regions beyond them, a second inference follows, namely that some peculiarity of the Iroquois position and the spread of the white trade may well have combined to produce a motivation sufficiently powerful to drive the Iroquois through a half century of bloody intertribal conflict with their brother tribesmen, the closely related peoples that almost surrounded them. The inference gains in strength when it is recalled that throughout the wars there runs ceaselessly the theme of trade and commercial arrangement, and that even the merciless Indian oratory, punctuated by gifts made in frank expectation of counter-gifts, is wound tightly about a core of commercial negotiation—of proposal and counter-proposal.

Such wars as those of the Iroquois must have had not only an insistent motivation, but also a disastrous alternative, or at least an alternative that was regarded as disastrous by those who waged them. It is quite likely that if the white trade had become a social and economic necessity to them, their position had life and death as alternatives. That position would have permitted neither compromise nor inactivity, and would explain why their wars were the first truly national intertribal wars on the continent, there being now for the first time a truly national motive. It is possible that William C. Macleod may have struck the lost chord in intertribal relations when he wrote that "the same principles of economic science apply alike to the economy of modern Germany and of the Shoshone Digger Indians, or any like economic group."[18] If the Iroquois were either facing disaster or thought that they were, they may well have turned, as do "enlightened" nations, to war. What is true is never so important, historically, as what people think is true, and while it may be convincingly reasoned, with that keen hindsight which historians often call insight, that the Iroquois would have been better off economically had they done anything other than what they did, this reasoning need not mean that the ultimate facts were clear to the Iroquois or that their motive was not (perhaps mistakenly) economic.

The thesis that when the Iroquois made war on a national scale they did so with somewhat the same ends in view as have their Christian brothers, is admittedly attractive. Such a thesis, however, requires abundant and indisputable documentary evidence, if it aspires to solve the Iroquois problem.

Notes

1. George E. Ellis, "Indians of North America," in Justin Winsor, ed., *Narrative and Critical History of America* (8 vols., Boston and New York, 1884–89), 1:283.

2. The powder was burned by the Iroquois in their assault upon the Illinois in 1680. Oswego, the first English settlement on Lake Ontario, was founded in 1726.

3. Nicolas Perrot, *Memoir on the Manners, Customs, and Religion of the Savages of North America*, translated from the French by Emma H. Blair, in her *Indian Tribes of the Upper Mississippi Valley and Region of the Great Lakes* (Cleveland, 1911), 1:293. The date is not exact.

4. Francis Parkman, *The Jesuits in North America in the Seventeenth Century (France and England in North America*, pt. 2, Boston, 1867), 434, 444, 447; John A. Doyle, *Virginia, Maryland, and the Carolinas (English Colonies in America*, vol. 1, New York, 1882), 13–14. Doyle merely remarks upon the suicidal feuds and what the Indians could have done if they had united; he does not comment on the reason for the disunity. Parkman, in his *La Salle and the Discovery of the Great West* (12th ed., Boston, 1892), 204, again ascribes their actions to "homicidal fury," though he admits that once, in 1680, "strange as it may seem," there appeared to be another motive.

5. John Fiske, *The Dutch and Quaker Colonies in America* (2 vols., Boston, 1899), 2:172. For representative opinions see Frederic L. Paxson, *History of the American Frontier* (New York, 1924), 52; Herbert L. Osgood, *The American Colonies in the Seventeenth Century* (3 vols., New York, 1907), 1:420–421; Lewis H. Morgan, *League of the Ho-dé-no-sau-nee, or Iroquois* (new edition, edited by Herbert M. Lloyd, New York, 1904), II; Parkman, *Jesuits in North America*, 447; "Governor Dongan's Report on the State of the Province," in Edmund B. O'Callaghan, ed., *Documents Relative to the Colonial History of the State of New York* (15 vols., Albany, 1853–87), 3:393; "M. Du Chesneau's Memoir on the Western Indians," *ibid.*, 9:165; Andrew M. Davis, "Canada and Louisiana," in Winsor, *Narrative and Critical History*, 45:2.

6. For a critical estimate of the literature on the subject see page 185.

7. *League of the Iroquois,* 72.

8. Reuben G. Thwaites, ed., *The Jesuit Relations and Allied Documents* (73 vols., Cleveland, 1896–1901), 43:265.

9. *Ibid.*, 45:207, 211.

10. See, for example, Kiotsaeton to the Governor, in *Jesuit Relations*, 17:253: "Onontio, lend me ear. I am the mouth for the whole of my country; thou listeneth to all the Iroquois in hearing my words"; this when he had to return to his own country to get ratification for a peace concerning only his own people. See also Grangula to La Barre, in Louis A. Lahontan, *New Voyages to North-America*, edited by Reuben G. Thwaites (2 vols., Chicago, 1905), 1:82–83, 85. There are many more examples.

11. Osgood, *American Colonies*, 2:420–422; Parkman, *Jesuits in North America*, 344; John A. Doyle, *The Middle Colonies (English Colonies in America*, vol. 4, New York, 1907), 119.

12. See below, Chapters 3 and 4.

13. When Morgan wrote his *League of the Iroquois*, the *New York Colonial Documents* were only in the process of publication, and the *Jesuit Relations* were also as yet unpublished, so he took his background from Cadwallader Colden, who probably knew less about the subject than Morgan himself. For a discussion of Colden's work see below, page 185.

14. A great deal of nonsense has been written about the reliability of Indian tradition in factual matters. Charles Eastman was a full-blood Sioux, and his *Indian Heroes and Great Chieftains* is written mainly from information obtained directly from the older people of his tribe, but George E. Hyde, after checking it with known facts, says that "it presents a spectacle of poor and distorted memory that is appalling, as nearly every date and statement of fact is incorrect." *Red Cloud's Folk* (Norman, Oklahoma, 1937), 54. See also pages viii, ix, and 60 for other cases in point. Mr. Hyde is one of the regrettably few writers in the field of Indian history who has his feet on the ground, and who deals with source material in a scientific manner.

15. It was adopted by both Parkman and Fiske, and it influenced Channing, Doyle, and Turner. The youthful Turner writes, in his doctoral dissertation, that "thus by priority in securing firearms, as well as by their remarkable civil organization," did the Iroquois rise to power, citing Morgan directly. *The Early Writings of Frederick Jackson Turner* (University of Wisconsin Press, 1938), 97.

16. Louise P. Kellogg, *The French Régime in Wisconsin and the Northwest* (Madison, 1925), 85.

17. Testimony of Marguerie, transcribed by Le Jeune, in the *Jesuit Relations,* 21:37.

18. *The Origin of the State Reconsidered in the Light of the Data of Aboriginal North America* (Philadelphia, 1924), 41–42.

CONCLUSION

Cornelius J. Jaenan

The French established contact with the Amerindians on a casual basis through the Newfoundland fisheries as early as the fifteenth century, and probably earlier. In the sixteenth century, voyages of so-called discovery and abortive colonization schemes further acquainted the French with the aborigines whom the Spaniards and Portuguese were in the process of subjugating and exploiting. Swarthy American natives were taken as curios of the New World to be displayed in various public spectacles in Western Europe, raising disquieting theological and scientific questions.

In general, the French were less involved than their neighbours in great controversies about the origins of the American aborigines, their nature, and the possible sources of their civilizations. Indeed, Frenchmen did not contact the same highly developed Amerindian civilizations as did the Spaniards in Central and South America. The French judged the Amerindians in terms of their religious beliefs and their degree of civility. Just as there was no doubt that the tribes were heathen, so there was no doubt that, in terms of the classical distinction between Greeks and barbarians, they were also barbarians. These heathen barbarians were rough and unpolished, to be sure, but views differed as to whether they were men in savage and degenerate form, the prototype of the wild man, or whether they were primitive men without benefit of religion and social institutions. Montaigne observed that "everyone calls barbarian what is his own usage." In whatever way Amerindians were viewed, the consensus was definitely that they were unpolished *sauvages*, and therefore presented a challenge to Frenchmen to civilize them and impart to them the religion, arts and culture of Europe's leading civilization.

One of the early reactions was to equate the Amerindian societies with the lost Paradise of their literary and philosophical tradition. The liberty, equality and fraternity which travellers and missionaries, at least those who tended to

From *Friend and Foe: Aspects of French-Amerindian Cultural Contact in the Sixteenth and Seventeenth Centuries* (Toronto: McClelland and Stewart, 1976), 190–97. Reprinted by permission of the author.

be critical of their own society, reported in America provided a very powerful criticism of contemporary France. The Amerindians were apparently proof that Christian Europe did not have a monopoly on goodness and rationality. Those who looked for noble savages or native utopias as a means to criticize and castigate contemporary French manners, morals and government were well served. These precursors of the eighteenth-century deists and rationalists were, however, a minority whose influence must not be exaggerated.

The French discovery of America brought together many threads to form a twisted skein of perceptions of the New World and its peoples. Theories of lost continents and prehistoric migrations, mingled with myths of concurrent creations and cataclysmic displacements of populations, these in turn being overlaid by tales of fabled isles and monstrous lands given over to the devil, fed the imaginative and beckoned the venturesome. Religious revivalism, pious mysticism and eschatological undercurrents in France raised hopes of ushering in the millenial age, of building the spiritual church and New Jerusalem in the New World. From the excitement of early contact in the sixteenth and seventeenth centuries—for the fishermen never revealed their earlier experiences or their fishing grounds—and the contradictory reports of explorers and exploiters, there emerged a dominant French view of the world and of themselves which stood in sharp contrast to the views of the Amerindians.

Although there was a strain of romantic primitivism, the dominant French view of man was that he was a changer and overseer of nature: a husbandman, a builder, an inventor, a domesticator, a civilizer. As a steward of God in his relationship to other forms of life his normal and divinely ordained role was to change and control by his arts and his technology. Frenchmen regarded their intervention in nature as purposive. The Amerindians, on the other hand, saw themselves as having a contractual or symbiotic relationship with the forces of nature. The contractual relationships of the French were to various authorities—to God, to the king, to the *seigneur*, to the religious superior, to the monopolist. Amerindians saw themselves and their tribal society as a product of nature and they acknowledged this in the names they assigned their tribes and bands. The Amerindians saw themselves as intimately dependent on nature, while the French saw themselves as superior to nature, as destined to dominate it and to bend its forces to their own objectives and aspirations. Progress in French eyes consisted of manipulating, controlling and subordinating nature and society more and more to man's initiative and enterprise. Insofar as religion and nature were intimately related, Amerindian society was more theocentric than was French society in the seventeenth century.

All in all, the French experience differed markedly from the Spanish or English encounters in day-to-day relations with the aborigines. The conceptual frameworks of all Europeans closely resembled each other, whether they classified themselves as Latins or Anglo-Saxons, as Catholics or Protestants. When the contact with Amerindians did not involve displacing the native peoples or extensive European immigration, which was the French experience as contrasted to the English and Spanish experiences, relations remained friendly. Cooperation and intercourse resulted in a certain degree of interdependence and created an impression of successful accommodation and acculturation. Such impressions were superficial observations neglecting the deeper evidences of social disorganization. The fact that the British, who had such a poor reputation in cultural contact in the Anglo-American colonies, assumed and appropriated the apparently friendly French relationship with the tribesmen after the conquest of Canada and the American Revolution suggests the need for an environmental approach to the question of culture clash. The French contact experience with the sedentary agricultural Iroquoian tribes had been less amicable than had their contact with nomadic Algonkian tribes. In the seventeenth century, the Amerindians seem to have stereotyped the Englishman as a farmer or town-dweller whose activities gradually drove the original agriculturalists deeper into the hinterland, whereas the stereotype of the Frenchman was a trader or soldier laden with baubles and brandy who asked only for furs and hospitality.

These comparatively more amicable relations between Frenchmen and Amerindians resulted in more credence being given in France to the good qualities of native life. The view that they were filthy, depraved barbarians never became a dominant and obsessive view with the French, although it was always present as an undercurrent and occasionally surfaced as in the reaction to the so-called Iroquois scourge. When goodness and virtue were accepted as possible in aboriginal societies a number of purposes might be served: those who sought the lost Paradise found in America a hope of restoring it; those who deplored the evils of sophisticated civilization found in America the noble savages; those who chafed at political oppression and bureaucratic corruption saw in America a land of freedom and opportunity; those who wearied of religious turpitude and theological strife caught a vision of the New Israel in the New World and the imminent end of the world. But those who lived and worked in New France came to believe more in the New World of their own experience than in the America invented by the metropolitan French.

Frenchmen, as a result of contact with primitive peoples, were more convinced that they stood at the pinnacle of civilization. Their society, despite some defects such as religious wars, famines, rural unrest and unemployment, and bureaucratic corruption, was an orderly, rational and Christian one, which all peoples everywhere ought to adopt and emulate if they wished to progress and elevate themselves. Although the French did not discriminate against the Amerindians on strictly racial grounds, they did by their somatic norm image consider them inferior and infantile. Native barbarism and cruelty, which must be seen in the Amerindian religious and social context to be understood, was an important factor in the literature on captivity and the creation of a stereotype of cruel savages. This literary tradition and popular stereotype were largely responsible for later discrimination against the aboriginal peoples in both Canada and the United States.

The Amerindians, for their part, had their own somatic norm image in which Frenchmen were regarded as ugly, effeminate, weak, disorganized, improvident, excitable, domineering, and quite inconsistent in applying their ideals to their everyday living. The French regarded Amerindian societies as devoid of spirituality and basic religious concepts, but it turned out that native society was as religiously oriented as European society. Indeed, many of the aspects of Amerindian life which the French were slow to comprehend—torture of captives, significance of dreams, resistance to conversion—were spiritually based. In the final analysis, it was sometimes French Catholic society that emerged as this-worldly, materialistic and superstitious. True conversion for the Amerindians meant a renunciation of their culture and a loss of their identity, a fact which the French missionaries and civil officials, without realizing the full implications of social disorganization, found quite normal because the French and Catholic qualities of their own civilization were rarely dissociated or conceived as separable.

The fact that the continent was not an empty wilderness but a populated expanse required some accommodation with its inhabitants, and some state policy of occupation. The French response to this challenge came at two levels—the spiritual and the temporal. First, the Amerindians would have to be evangelized and take their place with the Christians of France. Secondly and concurrently, they would have to be assimilated into French society by a process of Frenchification and civilization. As conversion soon proved to be a very disruptive experience in the native communities, religious conversion and cultural assimilation became more closely entwined. Unless the whole community converted and the whole apparatus of French institutions and life-style were adopted, divisions became acrimonious, reversion was likely, and social disorganization always ensued.

In their contacts the French came to sense, although they never fully comprehended or openly acknowledged, that Amerindian societies were well-integrated units. Education, for example, was fully integrated into everyday living. Therefore, French attempts to introduce formal schooling as a means of civilizing and converting the natives cut across traditional belief systems, values, institutional forms and band aspirations. No two societies could have differed more in their conceptual frameworks than did the European and Amerindian. Religion also permeated all aspects of native life, probably to a greater extent than religion permeated French life because the French, unlike the Amerindians, did not always allow their religious convictions to interfere with their economic mores, their warfare, or their personal behaviour. Because the Amerindians sought to live in tune with nature and their religious perceptions, Catholicism as a new religion could only be a disruptive innovation undermining their spiritual concepts as well as their entire way of life, their value systems, and their moral assumptions.

The French considered the Algonkian nomadic peoples as idlers and vagabonds because they were not sedentary agriculturalists or village craftsmen; conversely, the natives occasionally were only too well informed about poverty and lower-class conditions in France. Amerindian concepts of communal property, hunting territories and kinship responsibilities found no precise equivalents in French views of property rights, legal jurisdictions, contractual agreements, monopolies and sovereignty. There was no common theoretical ground for accommodation. They did not clash, however, because they remained largely isolated and separated from each other. The French towns and *seigneuries* formed a riparian colony, whereas the majority of the Amerindians, except a small number of domiciled converts resettled on reservations, inhabited the hinterlands. Because of this physical separation, there were few if any confrontations or contests about property rights or civil jurisdiction.

The French in their contacts with the natives admired their ability to grapple with problems in a resourceful manner and often abandoned their abstract speculation to adopt native ways. This utilitarianism, born of a long experience in North America, did not conform to French concepts of artisanal organization, seigneurial subservience, or military logistics, but it gradually became one of the acquired qualities that distinguished a Canadian *habitant* from a metropolitan Frenchman. The superiority of European technology had profound consequences for the Amerindians. As their hunting and warfare became more effective and their artifacts became more sophisticated, their demands grew and correspondingly their dependence on the Europeans increased both for supplies and repairs. Interdependence developed between native hunter and French trader, between native canoeman and French soldier, between native catechist and French missionary.

The French contact experience does suggest that the behavioural patterns routinized and institutionalized among the aborigines were rational, at least in the sense that they applied the best available techniques to the resources at hand in order to obtain the greatest benefit and use from them. There is also another conclusion that clearly emerges. Traditional societies cannot respond so readily to external challenges to their institutional system. Since the French were more adaptable than the Amerindians, the transfer of French institutions to North America also involved a transformation as well as a transplantation. It was the French who gained most from the cultural contacts of the seventeenth century. The French learned new techniques for building, travelling, dressing, fighting, food-gathering and survival in the wilderness. They acquired new foods and medicines. They brought new areas under their domination and new peoples in contact with their trade and religion. French society was sufficiently cohesive and stable to absorb new elements while remaining basically itself. Amerindian societies, on the other hand, often became disorganized as a result of cultural contact and too frequently exhibited the worst elements adopted from French culture.

French culture in New France, however, lacked sufficient men, materials and money to act effectively as a host society for the assimilation of the socially disorganized Amerindians. The great failure of the French in seventeenth-century

America was their inability to integrate the native peoples in appreciable numbers into a new social order, thereby overcoming the continuing stresses of cultural clash and the nefarious consequences of social disorganization. As officials of church and state came to realize by 1685, their relatively insignificant and insecure colony could not acculturate the Amerindians. The French were unable to exert the kind of social control necessary to stamp out the brandy traffic or to prevent the exodus of *coureurs-de-bois* each year to the *pays d'en haut*. They could not, therefore, hope to exert much control over the vast territories in which their traders, soldiers and missionaries lived more as guests and dependents of the natives than as representatives of a ruling power.

What was the effect of cultural differences among Amerindian tribes when contact with the French influenced their traditional way of life? All the tribes contacted by the French showed a certain traditional inertia, an adherence to their ancestral beliefs and conceptualization. To live on good terms with the different tribes the French had to accept a degree of coexistence, which meant renouncing any plan of immediate assimilation of the natives. It was essential to accommodate a certain resistance, both conscious and subconscious and rooted in native religion, on the part of the Amerindians. The aborigines developed counter-innovative techniques when they sensed that their traditional society was threatened by the French intrusion. It was in this aspect of contact that the cultural differences emerged between nomadic and sedentary tribes, and between animists and polytheists. The more advanced Amerindian cultures assimilated more rapidly than the less advanced tribes, but they were also better able to preserve their traditional belief system and social organization. It was the less advanced, northern and eastern, nomadic Algonkian-speaking tribes who were most disorganized in the face of contact and who showed the most signs of social disintegration and cultural confusion.

Numerous Amerindians became zealous Catholics, some to the point of demonstrating excessive zeal in their self-mortifications and adorations, and some of them made genuine efforts to take up French agricultural life on the reservations administered for the state by the missionary clergy. But this should not obscure the evidence that the economic and social problems arising out of French competitive pressures, the new religious divisions, the inroads of drunkenness and diseases of epidemic proportions, and the introduction of a new technology were not resolved. The converted and resettled natives were no more immune than those who continued to hold to their traditional beliefs and lifestyle. Neither conversion nor resettlement seemed to reduce appreciably the cultural conflicts that engulfed their whole society.

Assimilation meant the adoption of a new belief and value system and the setting of new limits for behaviour. It meant that actions and thoughts considered good and moral in their traditional society might be censured in French society, and that sometimes what was formerly censured might now be permissible or approved. The problems attendant on assimilation arose out of the process of change and the admixture of beliefs and values, and often resulted in the confusion of individuals and whole societies. Assimilation efforts seemed essentially to produce dislocation; they were a breaking-down process in order to reconstruct a new order. But by attacking the value system of Amerindian societies in order to replace it with a new value system, the entire integrated way of life was upset, including folklore, religion and occupational patterns. As ambiguities and inconsistencies marked the changes, it was not unusual to find rather bizarre patterns of behaviour. Personal and social demoralization seemed to be reflected in alcohol addiction which became the curse, and often the identifying characteristic, of Amerindian communities.

Acculturation is a two-way process. The French were affected by contact too. When any culture is transplanted it changes and varies, but such adaptations are more marked when the society comes into contact and into conflict with other cultures. There follows an exchange and interaction of cultures which can, theoretically, enrich or impoverish both. Cultural *métissage* results, out of which a new culture can emerge. In a limited way, this is what began to occur in New France in the seventeenth century. The Amerindian societies were undermined and disoriented in several respects, as has been shown, without at the same time being afforded an opportunity to reorganize and consolidate themselves into Euro-Amerindian cultures. The French, on the other hand, did begin to develop a distinctive Canadian culture from a French Renaissance base, which was somewhat changed in both form and spirit by the North American environment and experience, and which was greatly enriched by and made the beneficiary of the centuries-old Amerindian experience in North America.

In the French experience, as in the Amerindian, paradoxes were to be found. The highest aboriginal civilizations were those which assimilated most readily to European society, but were also those best-equipped to retain their ancestral beliefs and social structures and so resist losing their identity. In French society, the paradox was that in the seminal development of a distinctive Canadian-French culture, owing much to transplantation and to contact with the Amerindians, the efforts to mould the colony in the image of metropolitan France increased with the passing of time. The optimum condition to assert an independent identity passed in the early phase of resource exploitation, missionary dominance, and social disorganization, but as the colony grew older and stronger efforts were made to fashion it more and more in the traditional cadres of the absolute monarchy, the Gallican church, mercantilism, and seigneurialism. A result of the important contacts with the indigenous tribes of New France—contacts which absorbed much evangelical zeal, which sustained the economy, and which threatened or assured military and political survival—was a growing Canadian ethnocentrism. The colonists turned to their culture, particularly their religion, as a source of identity. There they found a sense of stability and security. As New France became more like Old France it follows that the cultural gap between French and Amerindian widened rather than closed.

THE DESTRUCTION OF HURONIA

Georges E. Sioui

In recent decades, a certain number of researchers have been critically examining George T. Hunt's theory that the Iroquois waged war for economic reasons. For Bruce G. Trigger, there is both a cultural and an economic dimension to the matter: he maintains that because the Five Nations did not possess the entrepreneurial tradition of the Wendat, they tried to increase their trading power by acquiring new hunting territories rather than trade routes.

Most recent studies, however, are closer to the older, so-called "cultural" theory advanced in the writings of Francis Parkman, which attributed the wars waged by the Iroquois on so many other Amerindians to an enmity that, under certain favourable conditions (for example, the European invasion), would lead to the annihilation of one party.

In addition, revision of the earliest Amerindian demographic data has led other investigators to explain the nature of these conflicts differently. One of these, Wichita University historian Karl H. Schlesier, in a discussion of the "legend" of Amerindian middlemen, says that "the Iroquois never attempted to become middlemen in the fur trade: neither did other Indian tribes, including the Huron or Ottawa. They all were touched by far more powerful forces than European trade goods."[1] He explains that "smallpox (the main epidemic disease brought from the Old World) emerges as the most significant among those forces. Much of the historical and ethnological literature before and after Hunt propounds biases which not only do injustice to the Iroquois, but prevent a deeper understanding of the historical truth."[2] Most authors still present what we call "the myth of economic war," attributing to Native peoples on the brink of disaster the motives, interests, and intentions of people leading a normal existence. In fact, all Amerindians were waging desperate cultural war on an invader whose pathogenic allies made his very presence a disaster.

Interpreting the Facts According to Autohistory

Louis Hall Karaniaktajeh, a Mohawk artist and philosopher from Kahnawake, sums up the Amerindian's feelings about history with bitter-sweet humour: "Twistory," he says, "is written in such a way that you think that they [the colonizers] are heroes. They're out there plundering Indian land and looting, but it's their right, their God-given right ... and the Indians are not supposed to do anything about it, they're supposed to like it; they're supposed to even help the writers of these history books to plunder them."[3]

From *For an Amerindian Autohistory: An Essay on the Foundations of a Social Ethic*, trans. Sheila Fischman (Montreal and Kingston: McGill-Queen's University Press, 1992), 39–60, 118–20. Reprinted by permission of McGill-Queen's University Press.

Of all Amerindians, the Iroquois are those who have least wanted "to help" the Europeans to "plunder" them, and for that very reason they spread terror and animosity among the first generations of Europeans to establish themselves in north-eastern North America.

"The good Hurons were destroyed by the wicked Iroquois," we were led to believe from the time we were old enough to absorb prejudices, in order to distract an entire society from the real story of the grabbing of Amerindian land.

Always bearing in mind that microbes, not men, determined this continent's history, we shall use data provided by our Amerindian autohistorical analysis to try to elucidate the circumstances that enabled Europeans to destroy the order Amerindians had established for countless generations.

In 1492, the Wendat were situated geopolitically at the centre of a very important society of Amerindian nations. Wendake (the Wendat country) was the heartland that was the origin and focus of the main trade networks linking this vast extended family of societies, whose spirit perfectly reflected the Amerindian's social ideal: interdependence and redistribution around the common circle.

We may assume that communications networks in the original Amerindian world, free of national boundaries, while they were far less rapid than today's, were functional and reliable, and that news about the Spanish military and epidemiological devastations reached the northern peoples after a few years at most.

In 1498, the Italian John Cabot reported having visited Nova Scotia and Labrador, while in 1501 the Portuguese Gaspar Corte-Real captured fifty-seven Amerindians, probably Beothuks. When Jacques Cartier arrived in 1534, the Amerindians had already suffered from epidemic diseases brought by Europeans.

Some recent opinions, even when well-supported, do not sufficiently recognize the terrifying consequences for Amerindians of the Europeans' arrival. In "European Contact and Indian Depopulation in the North-East: The Timing of the First Epidemics," Dean Snow and Kim M. Lanphear attempt to invalidate the hypothesis put forward by Henry F. Dobyns in *Their Number Become Thinned*, where he postulates on pandemics in the north-east during the sixteenth century. Moreover, they also appear to dismiss three fundamental considerations:

- First, while inland peoples such as the Mohawk—living in what is now the state of New York—could defend themselves against epidemics, coastal nations such as the St. Lawrence Wendat-Iroquois, the Mi'kmaq, and the Montagnais, who inevitably came into contact with European crews, could not. In fact, while no ship went up the St. Lawrence to Stadacona (now Quebec) before Jacques Cartier, a good number certainly did so during the rest of the sixteenth century.

- Secondly, the epidemic that ravaged Stadacona during the winter of 1535–36 (and that may well have had more than the fifty victims Cartier reports) was undoubtedly not the only one that occurred over the 115 years between the arrival of the first ships in the Gulf of St. Lawrence around 1500 and the first "official" epidemic of 1616.

• Thirdly, both the very nature of the culture and way of life of these Amerindian societies, that is, their close union and the uniformity of their cosmo-political conception, encouraged the spread of contagious diseases.

Once these elements are considered, it is likely that the St. Lawrence Wendat-Iroquois disappeared in the sixteenth century because of the epidemics that raged in the St. Lawrence valley before the beginning of the seventeenth century.

In other words, depopulation of the northern part of North America had already begun in the sixteenth century, probably spreading panic through Amerindian society at large. Taioagny and Domagaya, the two sons of Donnacona, the *"seigneur* of Canada," made a forced journey to France in 1534, returning in 1535. Cartier thought that he could use them to disorganize the Amerindian country, but as it turned out they bore him a barely concealed suspicion. Better than anyone, these chief's sons were aware of the danger. Cartier left after having defied the Amerindian order, spurned their advice (which cost the lives of twenty-five members of his crew who, unprepared for the Canadian climate, died of scurvy at the beginning of winter), and captured the father of the two young men along with nine other members of their family, including at least one young girl.

While it is certain that the bulk of pre-contact Amerindian society did not live in perfect, constant harmony, archaeology informs us that those Amerindians did not experience significant conflicts, likely because they had the ideological and social means to maintain relative peace among themselves. "In every case," writes archaeologist James A. Tuck, "village and tribal movements A.D. 1000–1500 are devoid of drastic population shifts, conquests and the annihilation of whole prehistoric populations."[4]

It is very likely that the Wendat-Iroquois migrated north from southern countries, taking root fairly recently at the heart of the Algonquian world. Their way of life—they were farmers and traders with a remarkable gift for political organization—had enabled them, long before the Europeans arrived, to establish particularly harmonious relations with other nations. History and even prehistory prove beyond a doubt that the vast majority of the Algonquian nations had long since assigned the Wendat confederation a key role in the political, commercial, cultural, and religious sectors of a vast and strategically located territory.

It appears that at the time of European contact, the confederacy of the Five Nations Iroquois was the only one not yet integrated into this extensive trading system. Ironically, the people who originally were probably the least numerous and geopolitically the most marginal were the only ones able to resist the invader and provide a refuge for the survivors of previously stronger nations. In that way, the ideology common to all aboriginal nations was able to survive.

There is every reason to believe that the decimated residents of Stadacona, led to Wendake by Donnacona's descendants, as revealed by archaeology[5]—tried once they were resettled there to persuade the Wendats to form a great league of nations. It is conceivable that the central idea was open resistance to the pale and dangerous visitors and that, frustrated at having been ignored, a certain "prophet" named Deganawidah, a member of that ideological clan, had taken his message to the Iroquois nations. The latter, located outside the great Wendat trading network and thus spared the task of facing the Europeans head-on, were more receptive to the message.

According to Iroquois tradition, it was a Wendat—one "whose people had not wanted to listen to him"—who disclosed the prophetic message about the need to form the Iroquois league.

Most of the speculations by Elizabeth Tooker as to when the Iroquois confederacy was founded place it around 1540 to 1590, a period that corresponds fairly closely to the Wendat-Iroquoian exodus to Huronia.

In any case, the Wendat were traditionally considered as standard-bearers for the Amerindian ideology which claims that, if the world is to be and to remain what it is, it must be founded on communication and exchange between humans of all origins. The vision of a prophet of the resistance, no matter how enlightened, can never take ascendancy over the ideology of a society of nations that groups together hundreds of thousands of individuals, one that has always been nurtured at the inspiring, appeasing sources of the great circle.

In 1894, the historian J.N.B. Hewitt pointed out that "no league or confederation of peoples was perhaps ever formed without a sufficient motive in the nature of outside pressure."[6] We may assume that the Wendat, because of the refugees they took in by virtue of a clear cultural kinship (for example, the Stadaconans), or adopted, apparently by force (as seems to have been the case for at least part of the Hochelagans[7]), felt the need to reform their confederacy before the Five Nations Iroquois did, and this led to the consolidation of the Iroquois confederacy. As the Wendat were chiefs of the great Amerindian society of the north-east, they inevitably devised a union that was centred on trade. Naturally there was a place in it for the French and other Europeans, despite the disastrous consequences of their coming: it lasted about half a century, if we bear in mind that a pandemic in 1520 to 1524 had "almost certainly reached the Seneca"[8] and other neighbours of the Wendat long before its European carriers arrived, and that yet another, between 1564 and 1570, had made them abandon some of their villages.

The Iroquois, realizing the extent of the disaster, opted for defence. By allying themselves against the French-Amerindian force, they now declared their dissidence from prehistoric political and trading organization. The Iroquois made the difficult but inevitable decision to embark upon a war they knew would be very long and destructive, and whose logic was utterly foreign to Amerindian thinking.

According to Amerindian cultural logic, the Iroquois were the north-eastern nations best situated to resist the invasion, although they had virtually no chance of succeeding. Consequently, the Iroquois nations were no longer "the worst of all savages" or "the Indians of Indians" as they have so often been called. Instead, they were an extremely valorous people who, to enable the Amerindian race to survive, had to fight against the European powers, forcibly adopting nations that were already gravely decimated. For the Iroquois, the goal of this war was to extinguish the power of strangers in the way one extinguishes a raging fire. With extraordinary strength of character, they had to eliminate part of their own race so as to save it.

To explain the Iroquois' political offensive in relation to the French, historian John A. Dickinson quotes ethnohistorian Bruce G. Trigger: "The majority of Huron were killed or captured as a result of the general warfare that was going on between the Mohawk and the French; however, the emphasis that the Mohawk placed on capturing Huron prisoners reflected their long-term ambition to incorporate all of the Huron who had come to Quebec into their own society or, failing this, to kill them." "Thus," Dickinson observes, "the French would be deprived of allies."[9] He concludes by stating that when the Iroquois attacked Long Sault, they did not intend to destroy the colony by massacring settlers, but to paralyze it by abducting most of the remaining Huron warriors—mercenaries in the service of New France. "If the [Iroquois] army went up the Ottawa River," Dickinson explains,

> it is because their goal was to take Annaotaha [the chief of the Hurons] and his companions; Dollard's band was completely outside the Iroquois' preoccupations. For seven years, the Iroquois had been trying by every means possible to destroy [that is, to take away from the French] the whole Huron colony and here, at long last, was the chance to do it. Marie de l'Incarnation was amazed that the enemy's army was content with "so few people," but the reason is that this small group was the quarry the Iroquois had been looking for. For the Iroquois, the meaning of Long Sault was not the defeat of the seventeen Frenchmen, but the annihilation of the remaining Huron warriors. For them, it was a great victory.[10]

In the final analysis, both the Wendat and the Iroquois realized that they could not unite, because of the age-old order of the country. The Wendat noted impassively that the end was rapidly approaching. They would never accept the numerous peace overtures by their Iroquois cousins, nor would they make the choice—which seemed to the Jesuits so logical—of eliminating those priests who "established themselves in the heart of the Country [Wendake] to better bring about its ruin."[11] The Wendat, like any people, were ineluctably caught in the logic of their civilization. They had to trade until the end, like beavers who will get caught in traps until they are extinct: they were victims of their own nature.

The historiographic concept of "the destruction of Huronia by the Iroquois" is an axiom in the traditional history of the north-east that justifies North American sociopolitical attitudes. In the light of Amerindian autohistory, this cliché becomes an example of the manipulation of history, absolving Europe (particularly France) of the destruction of the most politically significant aboriginal people north of Mexico, a people who best represented the Amerindian interethnic fabric in north-eastern North America. This is a spectacular historic fraud: responsibility for the sociodemographic calamity in the north-east is assigned not to microbes, but to the Iroquois.

Karl H. Schlesier refers us to the Jesuits' pitiful descriptions of the Wendat and other nations in 1640, after several successive epidemics:

> Disease, war and famine are the three scourges with which God has been pleased to smite our Neophytes since they have commenced to adore him, and to submit to his Laws …. All these events have so greatly thinned the number of our Savages that, where eight years ago one could see eighty or a hundred cabins, barely five or six now can be seen; a Captain, who then had 800 warriors under his command, now has not more than thirty or forty; instead of fleets of three or four hundred canoes, we see now but twenty or thirty. And the Pitiful part of it is, that these remnants of Nations consist almost entirely of Women.[12]

Later, Schlesier asks, "Where after these tremendous losses, are the men supposed to have come from to fight continuous wars during this period? … These wars sprung only from the imagination of scholars."[13]

Traditional Amerindian Values of the Wendat-Iroquois in Lafitau's Time

Our twofold aim here is an historical rehabilitation of the Iroquois, and a demonstration of their profound adherence to the Amerindian value system. Even if the defensive action of the Five Nations towards the Europeans—particularly the French—was basically a fight to the finish between two civilizations, the Iroquois continued to live according to essential Amerindian values. From what we know of the present vitality of Amerindian social consciousness, we can study a particularly revealing description of Iroquois (and, in secondary fashion, Wendat) cultural consciousness at the beginning of the eighteenth century, left by the Jesuit Joseph-François Lafitau.

This missionary, who lived among the Wendat and then among the Iroquois, knew these peoples intimately. His *Customs of the American Indians* is an unusually valuable account of their philosophy and spirituality.

Lafitau, whose church was facing a rise in religious skepticism, drew from the Amerindian peoples a series of arguments to support a thesis of many contemporary theologians concerning the innate existence of a religious sense in man. For thinkers of the time, the "*sauvages amériquains*" were "the humans who show themselves in the most simple form in which they can be conceived to exist."

To an informed modern reader, Lafitau's work may seem to go beyond his original objective. In reality, he contributed to alleviating the Amerindians' crushing historical burden and was one of the rare individuals who conceded them any right to survival. Moreover, Lafitau's work provides a solid mass of arguments and evidence that help restore dignity to the people descended from the "savage" nations Lafitau describes. Even more, he enables modern men and women to acquire or rediscover respect and a salutary admiration for human nature.

"Deganawidah [founder of the league of the Iroquois] brought a message of peace, say the contemporary Iroquois ... . He devised the means of lifting up men's minds with the condolence ritual [addressing the emotions in order to attain reason], which provided for paying presents to the aggrieved. The same ceremony on a broader scale took former enemies into a network of alliances."[14]

The contemporary Seneca historian John Mohawk helps us penetrate deeper inside Iroquois thinking about their confederacy. He stresses the importance in Iroquois society of the development of oratorical art, since for them as for all Amerindians, no one has arbitrary power over any other person. Hence the importance of the art of persuasion. For John Mohawk, the "greatness" of the confederacy of the Five Nations comes from its high development of this art. He adds:

> This greatness [of the oratorical art] is the very idea of the Hodenosaunee: all human beings possess the power of rational thought; all human beings can think; all human beings have the same kinds of needs; all human beings want what is good for society; all human beings want Peace .... Out of that idea will come the power ... that will make the people of the Five Nations among the most influential thinkers in the history of human thought .... The basic fundamental truth contained in that idea is that so long as we believe that everybody in the world has the power to think rationally, we can negotiate with them to a position of Peace.[15]

Almost three centuries ago, Lafitau, like all contemporary observers of Amerindian society, emphasized how the Wendat and the Iroquois kept order in their councils. He was impressed by their confidence (which they still possess today) in the human's capacity for rational thought, provided that society respected individuality. "In general, we may say that they are more patient than we in examining all the consequences and results of a matter. They listen to one another more quietly, show more deference and courtesy towards people who express opinions opposed to theirs, not knowing what it is to cut a speaker off short, still less to dispute heatedly: they have more coolness, less passion, at least to all appearances, and bear themselves with more zeal for the public welfare."[16]

Faced with the Amerindians' choice of gentle persuasion in their relations with their fellows, as opposed to the coercive modes of European societies, Lafitau experienced the same sense of wonder as European chroniclers of all times:

> While the petty chiefs of the monarchical states have themselves borne on their subjects' shoulders and have many duties paid them, they have neither distinctive mark, nor crown nor sceptre nor consular axes to differentiate them from the common people. Their power does not appear to have any trace of absolutism. It seems that they have no means of coercion to command obedience in case of resistance. They are obeyed, however, and command with authority;

their commands, given as requests, and the obedience paid them, appear entirely free .... Good order is kept by this means; and in the execution of things, there is found a mutual adaptation of chiefs and members of society and a hierarchy such as could be desired in the best regulated state.[17]

By observing some of the social traits noted by Lafitau, we can better understand how the integrity of the human person, as well as the quality of relations between humans, are at the heart of Amerindian social ideology. He frequently contrasts Amerindian solidarity with the European competitive spirit:

> They should ... be done this justice, that among themselves, they spare each other more than Europeans do. They regard, with reason, as something barbarous and ferocious, the brutality of duels and the ease of mutual destruction introduced by a point of honour badly misunderstood .... They are no less astonished by the indifference of the Europeans for their fellow countrymen, by the slight attention paid by them to the death of their compatriots killed by their enemies.[18]

Lafitau openly admires the strength of the Amerindian social fabric, source of the individual's keen respect for the private life of others. This helps explain the gift-giving mechanisms for preventing and settling conflicts.

The Amerindian Conflict

In Lafitau's day, Amerindian societies, especially the Iroquois and Wendat, were in profound political disarray because of the European presence. In this stormy climate, the missionary was much better able to portray the Amerindian character than if the time had been peaceful. Much has been said about Amerindian cruelty and torture. As the Iroquois of that period were the prototype of the "cruel American savage," they contributed, in spite of themselves, to the elaboration of that image, one that was later applied to all Amerindians. Using Lafitau's descriptions and observations, we will now present a brief analysis of this historiographical "knot."

In the Amerindian ideological universe, "war for the sake of war," to use Lafitau's expression, does not exist. War—if the term can even be used with reference to Amerindian societies—is always the result of disruption of the political order, provoked by an enemy agent. The Iroquois, like all Amerindians, resigned themselves to war while being fully aware of its gravity: "The Council," Lafitau reports, "decides on war only after considering the plan for a long time and weighing with mature consideration all the factors pro and con."[19]

Because Amerindians saw their compatriots as the ultimate wealth, war assumed a meaning for them that compels admiration. In the conflict between Amerindians and Euroamericans, the Iroquois, as the most engaged Native people, were the ones who most often went to war, and consequently they lost the largest number of members. It was logical, then, for these nations to try to capture replacements for those who had been killed or seized; thus they did not simply indulge in murderous expeditions, as we are often led to believe.

"The loss of *a single person*," Lafitau writes, "is a great one, but one which must necessarily be repaired by replacing the person missing with one or many others, according to the importance of him who is to be replaced."[20]

On this matter, Lafitau shows us how, in a natural and matriarchal society, the women recognized as sages (matriarchs) have supreme control over even the nation's military affairs. When there is a loss of one or many persons,

> it is not up to the members of the same household [the longhouse, which among the Wendat and Iroquois could contain as many as 200 people] to repair this loss, but to all those men who have marriage links with that house, or their *Athonni*, as they say; and in that fact, resides the advantage of having many men born in it. For these men, although isolated at home and limited to themselves, marry into different lodges. The children born of these different marriages become obligated to their fathers' lodge, to which they are strangers, and contract the obligation of replacing them; in this way the "matron" (matriarch) who has the principal authority in this household, can force these children to go to war if it seems best to her, or keep them at home if they have undertaken a war displeasing to her.
>
> When, then, this "matron" judges it time to raise up the tree again, or to lay again on the mat someone of her family whom death has taken away from her, she addresses herself to some one of those who have their Athonni at her home and who she believes is most capable of executing her commission. She speaks to him by a wampum belt, explaining her intention of engaging him to form a war party. This is soon done.[21]

When it is time to set out and capture replacements, the leader of the expedition (still according to Lafitau) makes a public prayer, accompanied by all his relatives, who have dressed and adorned themselves in their best attire, as is done at the farewell feast for one who is about to die—for going to war is going towards death. All those who remain in the village hasten to obtain a relic from those who are leaving, and to give them some present. "Together," Lafitau tells us, "they exchange robes, coverings, or whatever other goods they may have. A typical warrior, before leaving the village, is despoiled more than twenty or thirty times."[22]

For Amerindians, no success or victory is great enough to make them forget, even for a moment, the value of one lost human life. In their society, the cult of the human, or of being (as opposed to the cult of having), assumes its full force and meaning. Lafitau is astonished at their respect for the dead:

> They have such respect for each other that, however complete may be their victory, and whatever advantage they may have gained from it, the first sentiment which they show is that of grief for those of their people whom they have lost. All the village has to participate in it. The good news of the success is told only after the dead have been given the first regrets which are their due …. The women do the same thing in regard to the men who have gone hunting or to war. For, at the moment of their return, they go to wait for them on the shore. And in place of showing (them) the joy which they must feel at seeing them arrive in good health, they begin by weeping for those of their relatives who died in the village during their absence.[23]

The Treatment of Captives

Of all the Amerindians, the Iroquois are known for the intensity of their defence against the crushing European invasion. For two centuries, from 1500 to 1700, they had to concentrate their strength in order to maintain the existence of a union of Amerindian nations. In response to the formidable onslaught of the epidemics, to say nothing of the European ideological assault, they developed a policy of adoption: as stated earlier, their "wars against the Wendat and their allies aimed above all at restoring their own numbers."

In Native societies in general, war, "established by the need to protect oneself from injustice, to repulse force by force and to right the injuries which the tribes might have received from each other, [is] also sanctified by religion."[24] Yet for the Amerindians, war, as made known to them by the white man, never became the exercise of destruction and extermination it represents for other cultures. In 1609, Champlain was indignant at the behaviour of the Wendat and Montagnais, who cried victory when the Mohawk fled after a French musket-shot cost them three of their chiefs. Champlain did not comprehend why his Amerindian allies did not set out in pursuit of the Iroquois, to exterminate them to the last man; he claimed that the Wendat and Montagnais were "cowards" who "know nothing about making war."

But it is the Amerindians, not the Europeans, who have been given the title of champions of cruelty in the history books. This view is wrong. Amerindians never inflicted torture on anyone because of religious or political ideas. During the two hundred years of the crusades, millions of people were killed because they did not share the crusaders' beliefs. To establish a point of comparison with America, the Dominican bishop Bartolomé de Las Casas wrote in 1552: "We furnish as a very sure and true number, that during the said forty years (1492–1532), have died because of the said tyranny and infernal works of the Christians, unjustly and in tyrannical manner, more than 12 million persons, men, women, and children, and I believe, trusting that I do not err that it was, in reality, more than 15 million."[25]

As for the Amerindians, if one of their warriors took a human life he did so only to gain respect for his nation, following a process always marked by the same humanity that characterizes his social vision of the great circle. Lafitau, in fact, recognized the rationality of the Amerindians' behaviour: "If they did not return the same treatment to those who treat them inhumanly, they would become their dupes, and their moderation would only serve to harden their enemies. The gentlest people are forced to put aside their natural gentleness when they see that it becomes a pretext for barbarous neighbours to become prouder and more intractable."[26]

The Iroquois themselves—and Lafitau supports them—deny being crueler than any other nation, white or Amerindian. Lafitau wrote: "The Iroquois, so fearsome to the French on account of the great number[27] of those they caused to perish in these frightful tortures, have gained an even worse reputation with us than all the other tribes …. To hear the Iroquois speak, however, they claim to be less cruel than the others and treat the captives thus only by reprisal."[28]

Their treatment of captives shows the very humane nature of the Iroquois people, even in the midst of the catastrophe represented by European interference in Amerindian society.

Returning from a capture expedition, those who had captives to offer clans who needed them gave them away ceremonially. "The warriors who give a slave [more correctly, a captive]," Lafitau recounts, "award him with their belt which has served as a symbol of his engagement in their enterprise, or serves them as parole, to say that they have fulfilled their obligation."[29]

Among the Iroquois in particular, it was very unusual for prisoners—who had been captured with such difficulty, and whose lives were eminently precious to a nation so frequently decimated—to be condemned to torture by fire. Indeed, their fate would have stirred the envy of more than one hostage of a "civilized" country. Lafitau tells us that, after being handed over, "the captives are led to the lodges to which they have been given and introduced …. There, they are immediately given something to eat. The people of this household, however, their relatives and friends, are still weeping for the dead whom these captives replace, as if they were losing them entirely, and in this ceremony shed genuine tears to honour the memory of those persons, to whom the sight of these captives recalls a bitter recollection, renewing their grief in their loss."[30]

The adoption was then formally carried out, in a way that shows that the Amerindian social ideal is based and focused on maintaining and developing relations between humans, as well as on faith in the capacity for reasoning of all humans, so long as their dignity is recognized. Lafitau observes:

> Among the Iroquois and Huron, it [the condition of "slave"] is gentler in proportion as that of those thrown into the fire is more cruel. The moment that he enters the lodge to which he is given and where he is to be kept, his bonds are untied …. He is washed with warm water to erase the colours with which his face was painted and he is dressed properly. Then he receives visits from relatives and friends of the family into which he is entering. A short time afterwards a feast is made for all the village to give him the name of the person whom he is resurrecting. The friends and allies of the dead man also give a feast to do him honour: and from that moment, he enters upon all his rights. If the captive is a girl, given to a household where there is nobody of her sex in a position to sustain the lineage, it is good fortune for this household and for her. All the hope of the family is placed in this captive who becomes the mistress of this family and the branches dependent on it. If the captive is a man who requickens an Ancient, a man of consequence, he becomes important himself and has authority in the village if he can sustain by his own personal merit the name which he takes.[31]

Cruelty

The severity of Amerindian punishment should not be seen as cruelty, madness, or blindness. On the contrary, it was compassionate, logical, and rational, and was dictated by the Amerindian's unshakeable morality, modelled on nature herself.

If we avoid sentimentality, cruelty can be evoked only in the context of aggression and domination, and not self-defence. It is therefore absurd—and unfair—to talk about the cruelty of persons who are only defending themselves, for such cruelty is a legitimate and noble act of physical self-protection, as well as an equally noble effort to safeguard the honour which has been imperilled by the assailant's deed. Cruelty is therefore an argument to justify aggression, which is itself linked to a desire for domination or, in other words, destruction, partial or total.

Among Amerindians, human sacrifice did not have the character of social diversion it had for the Romans. Even less did it represent a punitive act that was religious or political in nature. Torture was, indeed, intended to be a way of killing the war itself; to achieve this, harshness was the best guarantee of success. By aiming violently at the actual enemy, it imposed respect and restraint, and so can be considered a more humane response to violence than are the conventional means used by so-called civilized societies.

In 1626, in view of the difficulties presented by the conversion of Natives, Father Joseph Le Caron warned the young priests whose ambition was to die as martyrs in Canada: "The general opinion [of Amerindians] is that one must not contradict any one, but leave each one have his own thinking. There is, here, no hope of suffering martyrdom: the Savages do not put Christians to death for matters of religion; they leave every one to his belief."[32]

The cruelty of the Amerindian was simply political. Once again, Lafitau helps us penetrate to the core of Amerindian philosophy through a description of the scene preceding the torture of an enemy by the Iroquois. "From the appearance of everyone assembled around a wretch who is going to end his days in the most horrible torment, we should guess that there is no question of such a bloody tragedy as is about to take place before their eyes. All exhibit the greatest calm in the world. They are seated or lying on mats as they are in the councils. Each one talks loudly with his neighbour, lights his pipe and smokes with the most marvellous tranquillity."[33]

Among Amerindians, the sacrifice for political reasons of a human being was devoid of hatred or sadism. It was a considered, rational, and necessary act. The person to be tortured was fully aware of this and did not try to elude his fate. "In the intervals in which they are left in repose," reports Lafitau, "they talk coldly of different matters, of news, of what is happening in their country, or they inform themselves calmly of the customs of those who are busy burning them."[34]

The Amerindians' well-known heroic steadfastness under torture results from an unshakeable faith in their moral and spiritual values. Lafitau, like all missionaries, admires them for that: "This heroism is real and the result of great and noble courage. What we have admired in the martyrs of the primitive church which was, in them, the result of grace and a miracle, is natural to these people and the result of the strength of their spirit. The Savages, as I have already shown, seem to prepare for this event from the tenderest age."[35]

Just as victims showed great dignity and courage, so did those who had to sacrifice them show their compassion, proving once more the centrality of the human being in the Amerindian social vision: "When a captive is burned among the Iroquois," Lafitau notes, "there are few who do not pity him and say that he is worthy of compassion. Many ... have not the courage to be present at his execution .... Some ... give him relief when he asks for something."[36]

Cannibalism

The French philosopher Michel de Montaigne claimed that "there is nothing barbarous or savage in that nation [Amerindians], from what I have been told, except that each man calls barbarism, whatever is not his own practice; for indeed it seems we have no other test of truth and reason than the example and pattern of opinions and customs of the country we live in."[37]

The notion of cannibalism as practised by "primitive" cultures is a product of the racist thinking of so-called civilized societies. In a society where the human being was at the centre, how did one dispose of the body of the individual who had to be tortured? How was the dignity of the human race to be preserved?

We know that evoking the Amerindians' bloody cruelty was a powerful means used by the colonial (mainly religious) authorities to attract the favour, sympathy, and financial support of their country's upper classes. Aside from this self-seeking attitude, some sources, particularly oral accounts, indicate that torture and its corollary, cannibalism, never had the importance attributed to them. Besides, our autohistorical study of Amerindian philosophy has provided ample evidence to destroy this fable.

One fact is certain, however, and it deserves the greatest respect: Amerindians did sometimes consume one or several parts (for example, the heart) of the body of a prisoner who died a particularly courageous death. The Amerindian gesture of consuming human flesh was as consistent with their conception of the great circle as was their proverbial generosity. When they had to defend themselves against their fellow humans, they did not like to kill instantaneously or massively as is done with mechanical weapons. They preferred to glorify their captive enemies in death by giving them the chance to die courageously. The remains of a life thus ennobled until death and in death could not be simply thrown away as garbage; they deserved to be eaten. Amerindians had to treat with honour the flesh of those whose lives they had to take. They consumed it because they thought they must: they had been required to destroy persons who, deep down, they admired and loved because they were brothers whose hearts were filled with love, trust, and veneration for their Creator, and thus for their fellow human beings.

Morality

In his *Customs of the American Indians*, Lafitau compares Amerindian morality favourably with European. He maintains that Amerindian moral force invariably diminished upon contact with whites. He talks about the northern nomads as being "more distant peoples, who are fortunate enough not to know us [Europeans]."[38]

Amerindians practised to a high degree those individual and social virtues known as Christian. According to Lafitau, they were charitable: "If a household of famished people meets another whose provisions are not entirely exhausted yet, the latter share with the newly-arrived the little food which they have left, without waiting to be asked, although in so doing, they are left exposed to the same danger of perishing as those whom they are helping at their expense, with such humanity and nobility of soul. In Europe under similar circumstances, we would find little disposition to such noble and magnanimous generosity."[39]

Similarly, their courtesy to visitors should be edifying to people of any culture: "Whoever enters their home is well-received," Lafitau observes. "The one who arrives or comes to visit has scarcely entered than food is put before him, without saying anything: and he himself eats without ceremony, before opening his mouth to declare the subject which brings him."[40]

Respect Between the Sexes

The Amerindians' modesty and their discretion in matters of sex are well-documented. Lafitau recounts customs that fell into disuse because of the example of the French. One such custom, according to Lafitau, was "to pass the first year after the marriage without consummating it. Any advance made before that time would be insulting to the wife and would make her think that the alliance was sought less because of esteem for her than out of brutality."[41]

Another Amerindian custom, still practised among the Iroquois and others, does not allow an individual to marry another member of the same clan. This is true even if the person has been adopted by the clan, "for," as Lafitau explains, "since by giving them life the name of a particular person of this family is revived in them, they are given all the rights of adoption and represent those being resurrected as if they were those people themselves."[42]

The Amerindian of Lafitau's time would break off his intimate life with his wife as soon as a pregnancy occurred; "the general rule for all Savages is to stop living with their wives from the moment they declare themselves pregnant."[43]

Being Faithful to One's Word

Lafitau cites an "old Huron" who told him that "it was a law from time immemorial in their country that a village had a right to put to death anyone who ... did not fulfil the obligations of his pledge."[44] Friendship is sacred among Amerindians. The ties that bind friends together are stronger than the ties of blood. An individual cannot marry a friend's relative, since the bonds of their friendship make them kin. Usually, Lafitau tells us, "friends follow each other to the stake."[45]

Respect for Ancestors' Souls

Finally, Amerindians were admired by the first Euroamericans, especially the priests, because of their remarkable devotion to the souls of their dead. To the missionaries and perhaps more particularly to Lafitau because of the thesis he was defending, this natural disposition of the Amerindian was proof of the immortality of the soul, and so of the existence of God. Echoing numerous European observers, Lafitau wrote:

> It could be said that all their work, all their sweating and all their trade comes back almost solely to doing honour to the dead. They have nothing precious enough for this. And so they sacrifice their beaver robes, maize, axes, and wampum, in such quantity that it could be believed they attach no importance to them, although they constitute all the wealth of the country. They can be seen almost naked in the winter cold, while they have, in their chests, good fur or woolen robes destined for the funeral duties. On these occasions, each person makes it a point of honour or religion to appear liberal to the point of magnificence or prodigality.[46]

Conclusion

Despite historians' tendency to produce an image of the Amerindian that serves the interests of colonialist societies, Amerindian ideology has lost nothing of its essence. To cite historian Robert E. Berkhofer, "The remarkable persistence of cultural and personality traits and ethnic identity in Indian societies in the face of white conquest and efforts at elimination or assimilation"[47] is proof that America has never had and will never have any lasting spiritual culture other than its Native one. White America has lost the cultural battle it waged against the Amerindian people. Most ironically, the Iroquois nation, which has most often served as a pretext for whites to denigrate the aboriginal population, is now recognized even internationally as one of the most vibrant Amerindian cultures in the Americas. According to Mohawk historian and journalist Doug George, the Iroquois possess "an innate gift for organization." "You can find innumerable references in the historical documents that demonstrate the ability of the Iroquois people to pull it out of the fire, when things look their darkest, to create something out of that."[48] He points out that the Iroquois periodical *Akwesasne Notes*, founded in 1968, is "a device created [by the Iroquois] that has given stimulus to Indian movements across the hemisphere."[49]

Historically, the Iroquois' vision of peace was not limited to the Native people of North America, but has always been universal. To cite George again: "In 1656, a Mohawk delegation ... went to Quebec City and asked the French [who had the technology to do it] to take this message of Peace throughout the world ... to bring all the Nations together at Onondaga, under the Great Tree of Peace .... These were people who were gifted with world vision 300 years before the Europeans finally, after two World Wars, stumbled across it."[50]

Today, the Iroquois still acknowledge "the duty of trying to reach the non-Native world as well." George adds that "even on the other side of the [Atlantic] Ocean ... we can see the influence of the Confederacy in movements like the Green Party that's taking hold among the young people of Europe, transcending national boundaries, an expression of the concern [in] those nations that they have 'a responsibility for their generations up until the seventh generation' [following the Amerindian maxim]."[51]

This triumph of Iroquois traditionalism, despite the fact that Amerindian culture has been severely undermined by the shock of contact, is proof enough in our opinion of the solid strength of America's original philosophy.

Notes

1. Karl H. Schlesier, "Epidemics and Indian Middlemen: Rethinking the Wars of the Iroquois," *Ethnohistory* 23, 2 (1976): 131.

2. *Ibid.*, 29.

3. Interview with Louis Hall Karaniaktajeh (aged sixty-eight), painter and writer of the Mohawk nation of Kahnawake, at Kahnawake, 5 July 1985, author's personal files.

4. James A. Tuck, "Northern Iroquoian Prehistory" in *Handbook of North American Indians*, vol. 15, *Northeast*, ed. Bruce G. Trigger (Washington, DC: Smithsonian Institution, 1978), 324.

5. Elizabeth Tooker, "The League of the Iroquois: Its History, Politics and Ritual" in *Handbook of North American Indians*, vol. 15, ed. Trigger, 419–22.

6. John Napoleon Brinton Hewitt, cited in ibid., 421–22.

7. William Douw Lightall, *Hochelagans and Mohawks* (Ottawa: J. Hope and Sons, 1899), 208–9.

8. Henry F. Dobyns, *Their Number Become Thinned: Native American Population Dynamics in Eastern North America* (Knoxville: University of Tennessee Press, 1983), 314–21.

9. Bruce G. Trigger, *The Children of Aataentsic: A History of the Huron People to 1660*, cited in "Annaotaha et Dollard vus de l'autre côté de la palisade," ed. John A. Dickinson, *Revue d'histoire de l'Amérique française* 35, 2 (1981): 171.

10. *Ibid.*, 177–78.

11. Reuben Gold Thwaites, ed., *The Jesuits' Relations and Allied Documents, 1610–1791*, vol. 15 (New York: Pageant Books, 1959), 171.

12. Schlesier, cited in *ibid.*, vol. 25, 105, 109.

13. *Ibid.*, 141.

14. William N. Fenton, "Northern Iroquoian Culture Patterns," in *Handbook of North American Indians*, vol. 15, ed. Trigger, 315.

15. Remarks by John Mohawk, Seneca historian and professor at the University of Buffalo, New York, during a conference on Iroquois communications, 11–12 April 1985, at the Native American Center for the Living Arts, Niagara Falls, New York, author's personal files.

16. Joseph-François Lafitau, *Moeurs des Sauvages américains comparées aux moeurs des premiers temps*, ed. Edna Hindie Lemay, vol. 2 (Paris: Maspéro, 1983), 88.

17. *Ibid.*, 83.

18. *Ibid.*, vol. 1, 99.

19. *Ibid.*, vol. 2, 12.

20. *Ibid.*, 6 (my emphasis).

21. *Ibid.*, 6–7.

22. *Ibid.*, 27.

23. *Ibid.*, vol. 1, 80.

24. *Ibid.*, vol. 2, 13.

25. Bartolomé de las Casas, *Brevisima Relacion de la Destruccion de las Indias*, trans. Georges Sioui (Santiago de Chili: Editorial Nascimiento, 1972), 30.

26. Lafitau, *Moeurs des Sauvages américains*, vol. 2.

27. Université de Montréal historian John A. Dickinson has carried out a critical study of the "great number" of French victims of the Iroquois during this period. See Dickinson, "La guerre iroquoise et la mortalité en Novelle-France, 1608–1666," *Revue d'histoire de l'Amérique française* 36, 1 (June 1982): 31–47.

28. Lafitau, *Moeurs des Sauvages américains*, vol. 2.

29. *Ibid.*

30. *Ibid.*

31. *Ibid.*, 111.

32. Joseph Le Caron, "Plainte de la Nouvelle-France dite Canada à la France sa germaine" (factum) (Paris, 1626).

33. Lafitau, *Moeurs des Sauvages américains*, vol. 2., 88.

34. *Ibid.*, 95.

35. *Ibid.*, 91.

36. *Ibid.*, 98.

37. Donald H. Frame, ed., *Montaigne's Essays and Selected Writings*, cited in *Friend and Foe*, ed. Cornelius J. Jaenen (Toronto: McClelland and Stewart, 1973), 122.

38. Lafitau, *Moeurs des Sauvages américains*, vol. 2., 31.

39. *Ibid.*, vol. 1, 234.

40. *Ibid.*, 232.

41. *Ibid.*, 157.

42. *Ibid.*, 145.

43. *Ibid.*, 146.

44. *Ibid.*, 23.

45. *Ibid.*, 182.

46. *Ibid.*, vol. 2, 151–52.

47. Robert E. Berkhofer, Jr., "The Political Context of a New Indian History," *Pacific Historical Review* 40, 3 (1971): 358.

48. Remarks by Doug George, historian and journalist of the Mohawk nation of Akwesasane (Quebec, Ontario, and New York), during a conference on Iroquois communications, 11–12 April 1985, at the Native American Center for the Living Arts, Niagara Falls, New York, author's personal files.

49. *Ibid.*

50. *Ibid.*

51. *Ibid.*

CHAPTER
2 SOCIETY IN NEW FRANCE

The structured society of New France, with the *habitant* toiling under the benign if firm hands of the seigneur, the *curé* and the royal officials, remains one of the strongest images in Canadian history. The feudal remnant drawn so vividly by Francis Parkman and George M. Wrong, among others, was transferred to the textbooks and repeated for generations, becoming true by repetition. This concept of a regimented colony became so entrenched in both historical studies and popular literature that forty years of revisionist scholarship failed to dislodge it. There was little sympathy for the paternalist French regime among the Whig historians who created the stereotype, and they found congenial readers. In the 1950s, historians rediscovered the history of New France. In the process, they reconstructed a significantly different *ancien régime*. The pastoral scenes and an official society of orders remained, but its personality was distinguished by its diversity and its irregularity. In the view of some, the typical *canadien* of the era was to be found in the bustling, urban communities rather than on the farm.

Among historians, the focus of the debate on the nature of society has ranged from the role of the state, to the role of the military, the church, the economy, the family and the environment. In the 1950s and 1960s no individual contributed more to the revision of the history of New France than W.J. Eccles, whose "The Society of New France, 1680's–1760" is included here. With the fervour of a possessed iconoclast, Eccles demolished cherished images about the colony, especially those of the imperious Parkman. Eccles was captivated by the *ancien régime* and its values. The advantages of that aristocratic state, when placed in juxtaposition with the English to the south, became self-evident in Eccles' prose. He did not reject the society of orders, but he did revise the picture, using the traditional sources and methodology of historians.

Jan Noël also toiled in those court records and travellers' accounts, but her interests were different from those of Eccles. Whereas Eccles envisioned a male, paternalistic society in which women were marginal but necessary, in "New France: Les femmes favorisées," Noël moved women out of the shadows and challenged several assumptions about women, family and, ultimately, society in New France. She began with the "pre-private" family of the non-industrial world, showing that in the "fluid situation" of New France, the demographic and economic circumstances permitted women to play many roles: *"Dévotes* and traders, warriors and landowners, smugglers and politicians, industrialists and financiers."

The third selection, "Individuals and Society," by Jacques Mathieu is from *La Nouvelle-France: Les Français en Amérique du Nord XVIe-XVIIIe siecle.* Mathieu has little tolerance for the impressionists who tell stories. Apparently, he considers Eccles to be just such an impressionist, since he ignores his work entirely. Mathieu turned instead to the sources and techniques of *l'Ecole des Annales* of France, examining demography, occupation, the economy, and mentality. The product is an alternative vision of the society of New France. Eccles was not impressed with this revision, and he wrote a very negative review of Mathieu's study in *Revue d'historique de l'Amerique francais* in the Autumn of 1992. In the next issue of that journal, Mathieu and Eccles squared off with competing and insulting missives. The student would be justified in questioning whether or not it was the nature of society in New France that was the real issue in such an exchange.

Suggestions for Further Reading

Bosher, John F., "The Family in New France," in *In Search of the Visible Past*, ed. Barry Gough. Waterloo: Wilfrid Laurier University Press, 1975.

Dechêne, Louise, *Habitants et Marchands de Montreal au XVIIe siecle*. Paris: Plon, 1974.

Desloges, Yvon and Marc Lafrance, "Dynamique de croissance et société urbaine: Québec au XVIIIe siècle, 1690–1759," *Histoire sociale/Social History*, XXI, no. 42 (novembre 1988), 251–68.

Eccles, W.J., *Canadian Society During the French Regime*. Montreal: Harvest House, 1968.

_____, *Essays on New France*. Toronto: Oxford, 1988.

_____, "The Social, Economic, and Political Significance of the Military Establishment in New France," *Canadian Historical Review*, LII, no. 1 (March 1971), 1–22.

Gadoury, Lorraine, Yves Landry and Hubert Charbonneau, "Démographie différentielle en Nouvelle-France: villes et campagnes," *Revue d'histoire de l'Amérique française*, 38, no. 3 (hiver 1985), 357–78.

Lachance, Andre, "Women and Crime in Canada in the Early Eighteenth Century, 1712–1759," in *Crime and Criminal Justice in Europe and Canada*, ed. L.A. Knafla. Waterloo: Wilfrid Laurier University Press, 1981, 157–97.

Miquelon, Dale, *New France 1701–1744: "A Supplement to Europe."* Toronto: McClelland and Stewart, 1987.

THE SOCIETY OF NEW FRANCE, 1680's–1760

W.J. Eccles

In the middle of the eighteenth century, a Swedish gentleman named Peter Kalm travelled through the English and French colonies in North America. He wrote an endearing description of the Canadian *habitants* whom he met in the farms, villages and towns along the St. Lawrence River in the year 1749:

> The common man in Canada is more civilized and clever than in any other place of the world that I have visited. On entering one of the peasant's houses, no matter where, and on beginning to talk with their men or women, one is quite amazed at the good breeding and courteous answers which are received, no matter what the question is. One can scarcely find in a city in other parts, people who treat one with such politeness both in word and deed as is true everywhere in the homes of the peasants in Canada.

These people had been living under the direct supervision of the French kings since the year 1663. That was when Louis XIV turned what had been a struggling colony into a comparatively thriving royal province. Under this French regime, which lasted until 1760, the social and political framework of Canada took on some resemblance to that of today's welfare states.

Although it is true that the people had little say in how they were governed, yet they accepted this as being perfectly natural. At the same time, the officials appointed over them by the king and his ministers were always closely checked to ensure that they did not abuse their authority. The whole structure of society and government was paternalistic, based on responsibilities and duties rather than on freedom and privileges. The people had to obey the royal officials in all things, but these same officials were held responsible for their security and well-being.

In 1686, when Jean Bochart de Champigny was appointed Intendant of New France, he was given very detailed instructions governing all aspects of his responsibilities:

> His Majesty wishes him to know that his entire conduct must lead to two principal ends; the one to ensure that the French inhabitants established in that country enjoy complete tranquility among themselves, and are maintained in the just possession of all that belongs to them, and the other to conserve the said inhabitants and to increase their numbers by all means possible ...
>
> His Majesty wishes him to visit once a year all the habitations that are situated between the ocean and the island of Montreal, to inform himself of all that goes on, pay heed to all the inhabitants' complaints and their needs, and attend to them as much as he possibly can, and so arrange it that they live together in peace, that they aid each other in their necessities and that they be not diverted from their work.

From *The Ordeal of New France* (Toronto: Canadian Broadcasting Corporation, 1967), 96–106. Reprinted by permission of the author.

In other words, the Intendant, as the King's representative, was to act as the father of the king's large family of loyal subjects living on the banks of the St. Lawrence River.

That the king would not tolerate the abuse of his subjects by the officials was made plain in 1679. Complaints had been received that the Governor of Montreal had imprisoned people arbitrarily. Louis XIV issued an edict forbidding this practice. The officials were ordered on pain of severe penalties not to imprison anyone unless they had been duly charged by a court of law. Oddly enough, that same year, in England, Parliament passed a similar act under rather similar circumstances; the act known as *Habeas Corpus*. In fact, the common people of New France had as much, and likely more, personal freedom than had the people of England at this time, where only some 10 per cent of the population had a vote and parliament ruled in the interests of the land-owning class with far less solicitude for the common people than was shown by the appointed officials of New France for the Canadian *habitants*.

Another essential difference between seventeenth-century society in Canada and in England was that in Canada it might be described as essentially aristocratic, whereas society in England was coming more and more to be bourgeois in outlook. This may become clearer if we try to see what the chief aims of the people were, what they regarded as constituting the good life.

To the Canadians, as to the French in France, the good life was that of the noble who could appreciate the better things, had the means to enjoy them and made the most of them, without condescending to inquire too closely into the sordid mechanics of their procurement. The main aim was to live well, to enjoy the best available without counting the cost. But in England, as elsewhere in Protestant Europe, bourgeois standards were coming more and more to the fore. In this society work was an end in itself, a sign of virtue; pleasure was suspect, poverty was a mark of sin, and the surplus product of labour was not to be consumed but reinvested to create new wealth.

Before the end of the seventeenth century Canadian society had assumed the pattern that it retained to the end of the French regime. At the top were the royal officials; the Governor, the Intendant and the senior officers of the military establishment, all men sent out from France and who expected to return to France one day. Beside them were the clergy, but the Crown officials had far more authority over them than the state has today. After 1663, when the colony was taken over by the Crown from a private company, there was never any real doubt that the state was supreme in New France. For the most part the clergy of New France were, in comparison with those in France, singularly well-educated and many of them were persons of exceptionally strong character. But they had their thoughts and aspirations fixed more on the next world than this; thus they always remained a class apart.

Of the purely Canadian social groups the *seigneurs* ranked highest; some, but not all, were nobles; some had begun active life in the colony as peasants or soldiers and had achieved the rank of *seigneur* by sheer ability and drive. Many of them got their wealth from the fur trade. In the towns of Quebec, Montreal and Trois Rivières there was a sizeable middle class and urban working class; in fact, between 25 and 40 per cent of the colony's population were town dwellers or lived within easy reach of one or other of the three towns compared to 15 per cent in France. In the country, on the *seigneuries*, lived the remainder of the population, the *habitants*, who tilled their lands, paid their modest dues to their *seigneurs* and their tithe of one twenty-sixth of their grain to the church, and were far better off than the peasants of France, or indeed of England, where a third of the people existed at a bare subsistence level. In 1691 the Intendant, Champigny, reported to the minister in France:

> Those who try to make something of their land are rich, or at least live very comfortably, having their fields and fishing close by their homes and a goodly number of cattle in pasture.

In 1749, Peter Kalm, professor of natural history and economy at the University of Abo, toured the English colonies and New France and commented on how civilized the Canadian *habitants* were:

> I travelled in various places during my stay in this country. I frequently happened to take up my abode for several days at the homes of peasants where I had never been seen before, and who had never heard of or seen me, and to whom I had no letters of introduction. Nevertheless they showed me wherever I came a devotion paid ordinarily to a native or a relative. Often when I offered them money they would not accept it. Frenchmen who were born in Paris said themselves that one never finds in France among country people the courtesy and good breeding which one observes everywhere in this land. I heard many native Frenchmen assert this.

Thus the Swedish traveller in 1749. And the Marquis de Denonville, writing earlier in 1686, observed this of the Canadians:

> They are all big, well-built and firmly planted on their feet, accustomed whenever necessary to live on little, robust and vigorous, very obstinate and inclined to be dissolute, but quick-witted and vivacious.

By the middle of the eighteenth century it appeared to some Frenchmen that the Canadian *habitant* was, in fact, too affluent. In 1753 a French officer named Franquet, after a trip from Quebec to Montreal, noted in his journal:

> Stopped at Madame Lamothe's at La Chenaye and was very well received, a good dinner, and everything well served. We passed a very comfortable night in clean beds fit for a duchess ... Judging by the furnishings of that house, one would have to say that the country folk are too well off.

This same officer was, however, rather reactionary in his views. He declared that the colony was in danger of being ruined by the excellent education which the girls received from the grey nuns of the Congregation of Notre Dame:

The bad that results is like a slow poison that tends to depopulate the countryside; once educated, the girls wish to be ladies, they become affected in their manners, they want to live in the town, they will marry no one but a merchant and look down on the condition in which they were born.

The daughters of the *seigneurs* and more affluent merchant families were educated by the Ursuline nuns whose main aim was to turn out well-bred and learned young ladies. They were given the usual religious instruction, Latin and French grammar and literature, good penmanship and mathematics. In addition they were taught something of botany and chemistry in order to be able to prepare simple herbs and drugs; and also such things as drawing and embroidery. But more significantly, they were taught to be good conversationalists, to have charming manners, and to know how to please. Peter Kalm in 1749 was quick to remark on the manners of the Canadian girls:

> The difference between the manner and customs of the French in Montreal and Canada, and those of the English in the American colonies, is as great as that between the manners of those two nations in Europe. The women in general are handsome here; they are well-bred and virtuous, with an innocent and becoming freedom. They dress up very fine on Sundays; about the same as our Swedish women, and though on the other days they do not take much pains with other parts of their dress, yet they are very fond of adorning their heads. The hair is always curled, powdered and ornamented with glittering bodkins and aigrettes. Every day but Sunday they wear a little neat jacket, and a short skirt which hardly reaches halfway down the leg, and sometimes not that far. And in this particular they seem to imitate the Indian women ...
>
> The ladies in Canada, and especially at Montreal, are very ready to laugh at any blunders strangers make in speaking, but they are very excusable. People laugh at what appears uncommon and ridiculous. In Canada nobody ever hears the French language spoken by any but Frenchmen, for strangers seldom come there, and the Indians are naturally too proud to learn French, and compel the French to learn their language. Therefore it naturally follows that the sensitive Canadian ladies cannot hear anything uncommon without laughing at it. One of the first questions they put to a stranger is whether he is married; the next, how he likes the ladies in the country, and whether he thinks them handsomer than those of his own country; and the third, whether he will take one home with him ... Nobody can say that they lack either charm or wit.

Although the facilities in the colony were inadequate to give the entire populace an education, in the towns at least the emphasis was always on quality. At the Petit Séminaire in Quebec, at the Jesuit College or the Sulpician's seminary in Montreal, the boys received as good an education as could have been had in any provincial city in France. In 1687 the Abbé Dudouyt in Paris instructed the masters at the Petit Séminaire:

> You must limit yourself to thirty students, select them well and weed out those who do not apply themselves. It is far better to have a few students of high calibre than many indifferent ones.

In addition to education, the clergy were responsible for the hospitals, for alms houses for the poor and aged and indigent. Although the hospital at Quebec, the Hôtel Dieu, had an excellent reputation, its doctors followed the established rules of seventeenth- and eighteenth-century medicine. One had to be very hale indeed to survive that treatment.

If herbal remedies and a few well-known drugs failed to effect a cure, bleeding and purging were invariably inflicted on the patients.

When the superior of the Sulpicians, for example, was stricken with a very severe pain in his side, accompanied by fever and violent headaches, he was bled six times but, it was reported, he only became weaker. He was then thoroughly purged but, to everyone's regret, died two days later.

But the main concern of the clergy was, however, the spiritual and moral well-being of the people. It was in this last connection that, in the seventeenth century, they sometimes came into conflict with the secular authorities. At this time the clergy were very puritanical and tended to regard as sins matters that were accepted as quite normal elsewhere. Ladies' fashions, for example, frequently caused Bishop Laval and his successor, St. Vallier, to thunder denunciations from the pulpit. The ladies of Quebec and Montreal always insisted on dressing according to the latest fashions at the court of Versailles, which dictated very low-cut gowns and elaborate hair styles.

In 1682 Bishop Laval declared in a pastoral letter that women were appearing at mass in very luxurious garments, as though dressed for a ball; and what was far worse, some came dressed in a scandalous manner:

> They come wearing indecent gowns, revealing scandalous views of their nude shoulders and bosoms, or contenting themselves by covering their bare flesh with transparent veils which serve only to heighten the effect of their shameful nakedness. They come with their heads uncovered or with their curled and beribboned coiffures covered only by a piece of lace in a fashion most undignified for a Christian and which detracts from the sanctity of the church.

Such apparel was, the Bishop declared, forbidden. But the ladies appear to have paid no attention, for the complaints continued, and Bishop St. Vallier ordered the priests to refuse absolution to those who so comported themselves, not merely outdoors but also in their homes. To this stricture the ladies protested, and the secular authorities supported them, declaring that the clergy were going too far. The minister at Versailles and the clerical authorities in France quickly ordered the Canadian clergy to cease annoying the people in this fashion, and they had to obey. As any married man could have predicted, in their battle against female vanity the clergy were certain to go down to defeat.

The civil authorities had other more dreary problems to cope with—some of which are still with us today. In Montreal traffic was a continual source of annoyance. Most of the streets were only eighteen feet wide, and pedestrians were frequently run down by wagons or sleighs. The Intendant Raudot complained that those on horseback or driving vehicles paid no heed to pedestrians and expected them always to get out of the way. Present-day pedestrians in Montreal might well be inclined to remark: *"Plus ça change, plus c'est la même chose."*

In the country districts the depredations of goblins—the "lutins"—appear to have been a serious problem. They were reputed to sneak into barns at night and get into all kinds of mischief with the livestock. The *habitants*, however, had a method of curbing their activities which was reputed to be very effective; it consisted of placing a pail of cinders behind the stable door so that any goblin entering could not fail to upset it. The goblin then had to pick up the cinders piece by piece in order to remove all traces of his passage.

This took quite a time, and when the task was completed he, or it, had neither time, energy nor inclination to start tying horses' tails together. Very rarely did a goblin return to a stable where he had had this experience.

A more tangible problem in Montreal, Quebec and Trois Rivières was the excessive number of taverns. Any house became a tavern merely by hanging an evergreen branch over the door. In 1726 the Intendant Dupuy limited the number of licenses and issued stringent regulations which are quite revealing:

> It is hereby forbidden for tavern keepers, hotel keepers, and inn keepers to sell soldiers anything to drink in the morning except a little brandy or wine, nor to sell any liquor to lackeys or domestic servants, in or out of livery, at any hour of the day, without the written permission of their masters, on pain of fifty *livres* fine, and the closing of the establishment for a second offence ...
>
> It is forbidden for tavern keepers, hotel keepers and inn keepers to accept from any youth, valet or soldier, in payment for wine or other drinks, any table ware, cutlery or other utensils, on pain of being named accepters of stolen goods and of being punished as such.

The staple food of the Canadians was white bread. Plenty of it was available, and along with it went quantities of meat and fish. Early in December animals were slaughtered and game was brought in, enough to last the entire winter. The meat and game was then packed in barrels between layers of straw and left in the barns to freeze. If a mid-winter thaw lasted too long everyone went on short rations.

The Swedish visitor Peter Kalm was favourably impressed with the diet of the Canadians:

> The meals here are in many respects different from those in the English provinces. They breakfast commonly between seven and eight and the Governor-General can be seen at seven o'clock, the time when he has his levée. Some of the men dip a piece of bread in brandy and eat it; others take a dram of brandy and eat a piece of bread after it. Chocolate is likewise very common for breakfast, and many of the ladies drink coffee. I have never seen tea used here.
>
> Dinner is exactly at noon. People of quality have a great many dishes and the rest follow their example, when they invite strangers. The loaves are oval and baked of wheat flour. For each person they put a plate, napkin, spoon and fork. (In the English colonies a napkin is seldom or never used.) Sometimes

they also provide knives, but they are generally omitted, all the ladies and gentlemen being provided with their own knives. The spoons and forks are of silver, and the plates of Delft ware. The meals begin with a soup with a good deal of bread in it. Then follow fresh meats of various kinds, boiled and roasted, poultry, or game, fricassees, ragouts, etc., of several sorts, together with different kinds of salads. They commonly drink red claret at dinner, either mixed with water or clear; and spruce beer is likewise much in use. Each one has his own glass and can drink as much as he wishes, for the bottles are put on the table. Butter is seldom served and if it is, it is chiefly for the guest present who likes it. But it is so fresh that one has to salt it at the table. After the main course is finished the table is always cleared. Finally the fruit and sweetmeats are served, which are of many different kinds; walnuts from France or Canada, either ripe or pickled; almonds, raisins, hazelnuts, several kinds of berries, and cranberries preserved in treacle. Cheese is likewise a part of the dessert. Immediately after dinner they drink coffee without cream. They say no grace before or after their meals, but only cross themselves, a custom which is likewise omitted by some.

Peter Kalm, of course, visited the colony in the middle of the eighteenth century, a few years before the British conquest, and at a time when the Canadian economy was flourishing. The fur trade was bringing rich returns to the Montreal merchants; such industries as ship-building, mining and smelting, lumbering and fishing were now well-established. The population was beginning to grow rapidly, and had the conquest not intervened, New France would have begun to expand in every way. It appears just to have reached what a latter-day American economist has called the "take-off point." In both the towns and the countryside the people were well-housed. The churches, and in the older-established *seigneuries*, both the manor houses and the humbler homes of the *habitants*, were mostly built of stone. Inside they were well-enough furnished. The more well-to-do imported their furnishings from France; the *habitants* made do with locally-made products. This furniture was generally made of white pine, and frequently of a high order of craftsmanship. The Canadian craftsmen developed great skill in wood carving and wrought iron work, and the pieces that have survived are highly prized today in both Canada and the United States. The churches were adorned with fine carved figures and wood panelling, painted in light blues, terra cotta, creamy white, accented with gilt, giving the interiors a light, spacious and very pleasing—almost gay—appearance. In recent years numerous oil paintings, mainly of religious subjects, have come to light. Although rather primitive, many of them have great charm and some have considerable artistry. All things considered, New France by the mid-eighteenth century was quite an affluent society. In 1752 the French officer Franquet remarked of Montreal:

The people there are generally very well off, they never travel on foot, in summer they ride in carriages and in winter use sleighs. They nearly all have horses. Usually they keep as many as there are boys in the family, who use them only for sport and to pay court to their lady friends.

And a few years later an Irish observer had this to say of the river empire's metropolis:

> On the fourteenth of this month I had an opportunity of viewing the interior parts of Montreal; and for delightfulness of situation, I think I never saw any town to equal it ... It stands on the side of a hill sloping down to the river with the south island of St. Helen, all in front; which forms a most agreeable landscape, the river here being about three miles across ... The streets are regular, the houses well-constructed ... and ... there are several pleasant gardens within the walls... Besides these, there are many other gardens and beautiful plantations without the gates ... at an agreeable distance, on the north side of the town... I saw no paintings, or anything remarkably curious, in their churches or other religious houses; everything carried an air of neatness, simplicity, and plainness.
>
> The inhabitants are gay and sprightly, much more attached to dress and finery than those of Quebec, between whom there seems to be an emulation in this respect; and, from the number of silk robes, laced coats, and powdered heads of both sexes, and almost of all ages, that are perambulating the streets from morning to night, a stranger would be induced to believe Montreal is entirely inhabited by people of independent and plentiful fortunes.

That was how Montreal appeared in September 1760 to Captain John Knox of the forty-third Regiment of Foot in General Amherst's invading army.

The calm and prosperity of New France could not last, could not survive untouched by the great struggle for domination between the European powers, chiefly France and Britain. In September of 1760, the Montreal described by Captain Knox had capitulated to victorious British armies. Fifteen years later, under British rule, the colony was to be invaded and partly occupied by a new breed of men from the south, calling themselves "Americans."

But these events, and many more to follow, would only attach the Canadians more firmly than ever to their great sources of strength: their families, their land, their language, their faith and their race.

NEW FRANCE: LES FEMMES FAVORISÉES

Jan Noël

> *You constantly behold, with renewed astonishment, women in the very depths of indigence and want, perfectly instructed in their religion, ignorant of nothing that they should know to employ themselves usefully in their families and who, by their manners, their manner of expressing themselves and their politeness, are not inferior to the most carefully educated among us.*[1]
>
> *Les femmes l'emportent sur les hommes par la beauté, la vivacité, la gaité [sic] et l'enjouement; elles sont coquettes et galantes, préfèrent les Européens aux gens du pays. Les manières douces et polies sont communes, même dans les campagnes.*[a][2]

From *Atlantis*, 6, no. 2 (Spring 1981), 80–98. Reprinted by permission of *Atlantis*.

... les femmes y sont fort aimables, mais extrêmement fières.[b][3]
*... elles sont spirituelles, ce qui leur donne de la supériorité sur les hommes
dans presque tous les états.*[c][4]

Many a man, observing the women of New France, was struck by the advantages they possessed in education, cultivation and that quality called *esprit* or wit. Even an unsympathetic observer of colonial society, such as the French military officer Franquet, who visited New France in 1752–53, admitted that its women *"l'emportent sur les hommes pour l'esprit, généralement elles en ont toutes beaucoup, parlant un français épuré, n'ont pas le moindre accent, aiment aussi la parure, sont jolies, généreuses et même maniérées."*[d][5] He notes, albeit with disapproval, that women very commonly aspired to stations above those to which they were born.[6] The Swedish naturalist Peter Kalm, who deplored the inadequate housekeeping of Canadian women, nevertheless admired their refinement.[7]

Those for whom history is an exercise in statistics have taught us caution in accepting the accounts of travellers, which are often highly subjective. However the consensus (particularly that of seasoned observers such as Charlevoix and Kalm) on the superior education and wit of women in New France suggests that their views are founded on something more than natural male proclivity towards *la différence*. Moreover, historians' accounts of society in New France offer ample evidence that women did indeed enjoy an exceptionally privileged position in that colony. The position was so privileged, in fact, that it contrasts favourably not only with that of their contemporaries in France and in New England, but probably also with twentieth-century Canadian women as far as entrepreneurial activity is concerned.

How did the women of New France acquire a superior education? How did they come to be involved in commerce? What gave rise to their vaunted *esprit*? There is no single answer to these questions. The truth is a compound of three separate factors. First, studies of Western Europe under the *ancien régime,*[e] indicate that ideas about women's roles were surprisingly flexible and varied. Secondly, the particular demographic configuration of New France gave female immigrants a number of advantages not available to their counterparts in Europe. Thirdly, the colonial economy, with its heavy emphasis on war and the fur trade presented women with a special set of opportunities. Thus, as we shall see, cultural, demographic and economic conditions combined to produce the remarkable women of New France.

---

[a] The women surpass the men in beauty, liveliness, mirth and cleverness; they are flirts and forward, prefer men from Europe to those around them. Pleasant and polite manners are common, even in the countryside.

[b] ...the women are very agreeable but extremely proud.

[c] ...they are witty, which makes them superior to the men in almost every way.

[d] possess greater intelligence than the men, are generally quite intelligent, speak a refined French without the least accent, also like personal adornments, are pretty, generous and even genteel.

[e] the European political and social system before the French Revolution.

Women and the Family Under the *Ancien Régime*

The notion of "woman's place" or "women's role," popular with nineteenth-century commentators, suggests a degree of homogeneity inappropriate to the seventeenth century. It is true that on a formal ideological level men enjoyed the dominant position. This can be seen in the marriage laws which everywhere made it a wife's duty to follow her husband to whatever dwelling place he chose.[8] In 1650, the men of Montreal were advised by Governor Maisonneuve that they were in fact responsible for the misdemeanours of their wives since *"la loi les établit seigneurs de leurs femmes."*[f][9] Under ordinary circumstances the father was captain of the family hierarchy.[10] Yet, it is clear that this formal male authority in both economic and domestic life was not always exercised. Of early seventeenth-century France we are told that:

> si la prééminence masculine n'a rien perdu de son prestige, si elle n'a eu à se défendre contre aucune revendication théorique ... elle a dû ... souvent se contenter des apparences et abandonner devant les convenances et les exigences du public l'intérêt positif qu'elle défendait.[g][11]

The idea of separate male and female spheres lacked the clear definition it later acquired. This is in part related to the lack of communication and standardization characteristic of the *ancien régime*—along sexual lines or any others. Generalizations about women are riddled with exceptions. Contradicting the idea of female inferiority, for example, were the semi-matriarchal system in the Basque country, and the linen workers guild, in which a 1645 statute prevented a worker's husband from engaging in occupations unrelated to his wife's business, for which he often served as salesman or partner. More important, because it affected a larger group, was the fact that noblewomen were frequently exempt from legal handicaps affecting other women.[12]

One generalization, however, applies to all women of the *ancien régime*. They were not relegated to the private, domestic sphere of human activity because that sphere did not exist. Western Europeans had not yet learned to separate public and private life. As Philippe Ariès points out in his study of childhood, the private home, in which parents and children constitute a distinct unit, is a relatively recent development. In early modern Europe most of domestic life was lived in the company of all sorts of outsiders. Manor houses, where all the rooms interconnect with one another, show the lack of emphasis placed on privacy. Here, as in peasant dwellings, there were often no specialized rooms for sleeping, eating, working or receiving visitors; all were more or less public activities performed with a throng of servants, children, relatives, clerics, apprentices and

---

[f] the law makes them lords over their wives.

[g] if the male predominance has lost nothing of its authority, if it has not had to struggle against any theoretical claim, it has still had to be satisfied with appearances and make sacrifices to keep up appearances and to fulfil the requirements of the public good that it supports.

clients in attendance. Molière's comedies illustrate the familiarity of servants with their masters. Masters, maids and valets slept in the same room and servants discussed their masters' lives quite openly.[13]

Though familiar with their servants, people were less so with their children. They did not dote on infants as parents do today. It may have been, as some writers have suggested, that there was little point in growing attached to a fragile being so very apt, in those centuries, to be borne away by accident or disease. These unsentimental families of all ranks sent their children out to apprentice or serve in other people's homes. This was considered important as a basic education.[14] It has been estimated that the majority of Western European children passed part of their childhood living in some household other than their natal one.[15] Mothers of these children—reaching down, in the town, as far as the artisan class—commonly sent their infants out to nursemaids and in fact had very little to do with their physical maintenance.[16]

This lack of a clearly defined "private" realm relates vitally to the history of women, since this was precisely the sphere which they later were to inhabit.[17] Therefore it is important to focus on their place in the pre-private world. To understand women in New France one first must pass through that antechamber which Peter Laslett appropriately calls "the world we have lost." Its notions of sexuality and of the family apply to France and New France alike.

In this public world people had not yet learned to be private about their bodily functions, especially about their sexuality. For aid with their toilette, noblewomen did not blush to employ *hommes de chambre* [h] rather than maids. The door of the bedchamber stood ajar, if not absolutely open. Its inhabitants, proud of their fecundity, grinned out from under the bedclothes at their visitors. Newlyweds customarily received bedside guests.[18] The mother of Louis XIV held court and chatted with visitors while labouring to bring *le Roi Soleil* [i] into light of day. Humbler village women kept lesser court among the little crowd of neighbours who attended the midwife's efforts.[19] On the other side of the ocean, Franquet, arriving at Trois-Rivières in 1753, enjoyed the hospitality of Madame Rigaud de Vaudreuil who, feeling poorly, apparently received her visitors at bedside; farther west, he shared a bedroom with a married couple at Fort St. Jean.[20] From the seventeenth century to the colony's last days, clerics thundered more or less futilely against the *décolletage* of the *élite*.[j][21] Lesser folk leaned towards short skirts[22] and boisterous public discussion of impotent husbands.[23] Rape cases also reveal a rather matter-of-fact attitude. Courts stressed monetary compensation for the victim (as if for trespass on private property) rather than wreaking vengeance on the lustful villain.[24] There was not the

---

[h] valets

[i] the Sun King

[j] necklines of the upper classes

same uneasiness in relations between the sexes which later, more puritanical, centuries saw, and which, judging by the withdrawal of women from public life in many of these societies, probably worked to their detriment.

Part of the reason these unsqueamish, rather public people were not possessive about their bodies was that they did not see themselves so much as individuals but as part of a larger more important unit—the family. In this world the family was the basic organization for most social and economic purposes.[25] As such it claimed the individual's first loyalty.[26] A much higher proportion of the population married than does today.[27] Studies of peasant societies suggest that, for most, marriage was an economic necessity:

> Le travail, particulièrement en milieu rural, était alors fondé sur une répartition des tâches entre les sexes: les marins et colporteurs sont absents plusieurs mois, leurs femmes font valoir les terres; les pêcheurs des marais vont au marché, les femmes à la pêche; le laboureur travaille aux champs, sa femme à la maison, c'est elle qui va au marché; dans le pays d'Auge, "les hommes s'occupent des bestiaux et les femmes aux fromages." Pour vivre il fallait donc être deux, un homme et une femme.[k][28]

The family was able to serve as the basic economic unit in pre-industrial societies because the business of earning a living generally occurred at home. Just as public and private life were undifferentiated, so too were home and workplace. Agricultural and commercial pursuits were all generally "domestic" industries. We see this both in France and in New France. Removal of the man from home for most of the working day, an event which Laslett describes as the single most important event in the history of the modern European family,[29] was only beginning. The idea of man as breadwinner and woman as home-maker was not clearly developed. Women's range of economic activity was still nearly as wide as that of their husbands. Seventeenth-century France saw women working as bonesetters, goldbeaters, bookbinders, doubletmakers, burnishers, laundresses, woolfullers and wigmakers. Aside from their familiar role in the textile and clothing industries, women also entered heavy trades such as stoneworking and bricklaying. A master plumber, Barbe Legueux, maintained the drainage system for the fountains of Paris. In the commercial world, women worked as fishmongers, pedlars, greengrocers, publicans, moneylenders and auctioneers.[30] In New France, wives of artisans took advantage of their urban situation to attract customers into the taverns they set up alongside the workshop.[31] It was in farm work, which occupied most of the population, that

---

[k] Especially in rural areas, work was then based on the division of labour between the sexes. Since sailors and carters were absent for several months, their wives had to cultivate the land. Freshwater fishermen go to market while their wives go fishing. The ploughman works in the field while his wife works in the house as well as going to market. In the Auge region, "the men tend the animals and the women produce cheese." In order to survive, there had to be two, a man and a woman.

male and female tasks differed the least of all. *Habitantes* in New France toiled in the fields alongside the men; and they almost certainly—being better-educated than their French sisters—took up the farmwife's customary role of keeping accounts and managing purchases and sales.[32] Studies of Bordeaux commercial families have revealed that women also took a large role in business operations.[33] Marie de l'Incarnation's background as manager of one of France's largest transport companies,[34] shows that the phenomenon existed in other parts of France as well.

Given the economic importance of both spouses, it is not surprising to see marriage taking on some aspects of a business deal, with numerous relatives affixing their signatures to the contract. We see this in the provisions of the law which protected the property rights of both parties contracting a match. The fact that wives often brought considerable family property to the marriage, and retained rights to it, placed them in a better position than their nineteenth-century descendants were to enjoy.[35]

In New France the family's importance was intensified even beyond its usual economic importance in *ancien régime* societies. In the colony's early days, "all roads led to matrimony. The scarcity of women, the economic difficulties of existence, the danger, all tended to produce the same result: all girls became wives, all widows remarried."[36] Throughout the colony's history there was an exceptionally high annual marriage rate of eighteen to twenty-four per thousand.[37] The buildup of the family as a social institution perhaps came about because other social institutions, such as guilds and villages, were underdeveloped.[38] This heightened importance of the family probably enhanced women's position. In the family women tended to serve as equal partners with their husbands, whereas women were gradually losing their position in European guilds and professions.[39] We see this heightened importance of the family in the government's great concern to regulate it. At that time, the state *did* have a place in Canadian bedrooms (whose inhabitants we have already seen to be rather unconcerned about their privacy). Public intervention in domestic life took two major forms: the operation of the legal system and governmental attempts at family planning.

The outstanding characteristic of the legal system in New France—the *Coutume de Paris*[1]—is its concern to protect the rights of all members of the family. The *Coutume de Paris* is considered to have been a particularly benevolent regional variation of French law.[40] It was more egalitarian and less patriarchal than the laws of southern France which were based on Roman tradition. The *Coutume* reinforced the family, for example, by the penalties it levied on those transferring family property to non-kin.[41] It took care to protect the property of children of a first marriage when a widow or widower remarried.[42] It protected a woman's rights by assuring that the husband did not have power to alienate the family property (in contrast to eighteenth-century British law).[43]

---

[1] the body of customary law in force in the region of Paris.

The Canadians not only adopted the Parisian *coutume* in preference to the Norman *coutume,* which was harsher;[44] they also implemented the law in a way which maximized protection of all family members. Louise Dechêne, after examining the operation of the marriage and inheritance system, concludes that the Canadian application of the law was generous and egalitarian:

> Ces concentions matrimoniales ne nous apparaissent pas comme un marché, un affrontement entre deux lignées, mais comme un accord désintéressé entre les familles, visant à créer une nouvelle communauté, à l'assister si possible, à dresser quelques barrières à l'entour pour la protéger....
>
> La même simplicité, la même générosité président au partage des successions....[m] 45

The criminal law, too, served to buttress family life with its harsh punishments for mistreatment of children.[46]

The royal administration, as well as the law, treated the family as a matter of vital public concern. The state often intervened in matters which later generations left to the individual or to the operations of private charity. Most famous, of course, is the policy of encouraging a high birth rate with financial incentives. There were also attempts to withdraw trading privileges from *voyageurs* who showed reluctance to take immigrant women to wife.[47] Particularly in the seventeenth century, we see the state regulating what modern societies would consider intimate matters. However, in a colony starved for manpower, reproduction was considered a matter of particularly vital public concern—a concern well demonstrated in the extremely harsh punishments meted out to women who concealed pregnancy.[48] We see a more positive side of this intervention in the care the Crown took of foundlings, employing nurses at a handsome salary to care for them, and making attempts to prevent children from bearing any stigma because of questionable origins.[49]

State regulation of the family was balanced by family regulation of the state. Families had an input into the political system, playing an important role in the running of the state. Indeed, it might be argued that the family was the basic political unit in New France. In an age when some members of the *noblesse* [n] prided themselves on their illiteracy, attending the right college was hardly the key to political success. Marrying into the right family was much more important. Nepotism, or rewarding one's kin with emoluments, seemed a most acceptable and natural form of patronage for those in power.[50] In this sense, a good marriage was considered a step upward for the whole family, which helps to explain why choice of spouse was so often a family decision.[51]

---

[m] These marriage agreements do not appear to us to be business arrangements or to turn the two families into adversaries. Rather, they are disinterested agreements between families and are intended to create a new household and, if possible, to help it erect a few defenses to provide protection.

The same simplicity and generosity apply when settling estates.

[n] nobility

These family lines were particularly tightly drawn among the military élite in New France. Franquet remarked that *"tous les gens d'un certain ordre sont liés de parenté et d'amitié dans ce pays."*[o] [52] In fact, with top military positions passing down from generation to generation, by the eighteenth century this élite became a caste.[53]

In this situation, where the *nom de famille* [p] was vastly more important than that of the individual, it was apparently almost as good for political (though not military) purposes to be an Agathe de Repentigny as a LeGardeur de Repentigny. Moreover, women's political participation was favoured by the large role of entertaining in political life. For the courtier's role, women were as well-trained as men, and there seems to have been no stigma attached to the woman who participated independently of her husband. Six women, Mesdames Daine, Pean, Lotbinière, de Repentigny, Marin, and St. Simon, along with six male officers, were chosen by the Intendant to accompany him to Montreal in 1753.[54] Of the twelve only the de Repentignys were a couple. It is surprising to see women from the colony's first families also getting down to what we would today consider the "business" end of politics. Madame de la Forest, a member of the Juchereau family, took an active role in the political cliques which Guy Frégault describes.[55] Mme. de la Forest's trip to France to plead the cause of Governor de Ramezay was inconsequential, though, in comparison with that of Mme. de Vaudreuil to further Governor Vaudreuil's cause in 1709. *"Douée d'un sens politique trés fin,"*[q] [56] she soon gained the ear of the Minister of Marine. Not only did she secure the Governor's victory in the long conflict with the Intendants Raudot (father and son) and win promotion for his patrons; she appears to have gone on to upstage her husband by becoming the virtual director of colonial policy at Versailles for a few years. Vaudreuil's biographer discusses the influence Madame de Vaudreuil exerted with the Minister Pontchartrain who so regularly sought her comment on colonial patronage that supplicants began to apply directly to her rather than to the minister.[57] Contemporaries agreed that her influence was vast:

> Pontchartrain, rapporte Ruette d'Auteuil, ne lui refuse rien, "elle dispose de tous les emplois du Canada, elle écrit de toutes parts dans les ports de mer des lettres magnifiques du bien et du mal qu'elle peut faire auprès de lui," et le ministre "fait tout ce qu'il faut pour l'autoriser et justifier ses discours." Riverin confirme que ... "ce n'est plus qu'une femme qui règne tant présente qu'absente."[r] [58]

---

[o] in this country, all the members of a certain class are connected by friendship and family relationships.

[p] family name

[q] Possessing a very subtle political sense

[r] Ruette d'Auteuil reports that Pontchartrain denies her nothing and that "she controls all the postings in Canada. She writes proud letters from every seaport that she can do anything with him," and that the minister "does everything necessary to give her authority and to support what she says." Riverin confirms that "this involves nothing more than a woman who rules whether she is present or not."

Governor Frontenac's wife (though not a *Canadienne*) also played an important role at court dispelling some of the thunderclouds which threatened her husband's stormy career.[59]

As for the common folk, we know even less about the political activity of women than that of men. That women participated in a form of popular assembly is hinted at in a report of a meeting held in 1713 (in present-day Boucherville), in which Catherine Guertin was sworn in as midwife after having been elected *"dans l'assemblée des femmes de cette paroisse, à la pluralité des suffrages, pour exercer l'office de sagefemme."*[s] [60] Were these women's assemblies a general practice? If so, what other matters did they decide? This aspect of *habitant* politics remains a mystery, but women, as historians of "crowds" have found, were certainly part of the "pre-industrial crowd."[61] Along with their menfolk, they were full-fledged members of the old "moral economy" whose members rioted, took what was traditionally their rightful share (and no more) when prices were too high or when speculators were hoarding grain.[62] The women of Quebec and Montreal, who rioted against the horsemeat rations and the general hunger of 1757–58, illustrate this aspect of the old polity.[63]

In sum, women's position during the *ancien régime* was open-ended. Although conditions varied, a wide range of roles were available to women, to be taken up or not. This was so because the separate spheres of men and women in *ancien régime* societies were not so clearly developed as they later became. There was as yet no sharp distinction between public and private life: families were for most purposes the basic social, economic and political unit. Owing to the underdevelopment of other institutions (the guild, the *seigneurie*, the village), this situation was intensified in New France. The activities of breadwinner and home-maker were not yet widely recognized as separate functions belonging to one sex or the other. All members of the family also often shared the same economic functions, or at least roles were interchangeable. Nor had the symbolic, the honorific, the stylistic aspects of government yet been separated from the business end of politics and administration. These conditions, typical of most of pre-industrial France, were also found in New France, where particular demographic and economic conditions would enable the colony's women to develop their freedoms and opportunities to the fullest.

Demographic Advantages

Demography favoured the women of New France in two ways. First, the women who went there were a highly select group of immigrants. Secondly, women were in short supply in the early years of the colony's development, a situation that worked in their favour.

---

[s] in this parish's women's committee, with the majority of the votes, in order to carry out the duties of midwife.

The bulk of the female immigrants to New France fall into one of two categories. The first was a group of extremely well-born, well-endowed and highly dedicated religious figures. They began to arrive in 1639, and a trickle of French nuns continued to cross the ocean over the course of the next century. The second distinct group was the *filles du roi*,[t] government-sponsored female migrants who arrived between 1663 and 1673. These immigrants, though not as outstanding as the *dévotes*,[u] were nevertheless privileged compared to the average immigrant to New France, who arrived more or less threadbare.[64] The vast majority of the women (and the men) came from the Ile-de-France and the northwestern parts of France. The women of northern France enjoyed fuller legal rights, were better-educated, and more involved in commerce than those of southern France.[65] When they set foot on colonial soil with all this auspicious baggage, the immigrants found that they had yet another advantage. Women constituted a small percentage of the population. As a scarce resource, they were highly prized and therefore in an excellent position to gain further advantages.

The first *religieuses*[v] to arrive in New France were the Ursulines and Hospitallers who landed at Quebec in 1639. These were soon followed by women who helped establish Montreal in 1642. Their emigration was inspired by a religious revival in France, which is thought to have arisen in response to the widespread pauperism following the French civil wars of the sixteenth century. The seventeenth-century revival distinguished itself by tapping the energies of women in an unprecedented way.[66] Among its leaders were Anne of Austria and a number of the leading ladies at court.[67] In other parts of France, women of the provincial élite implemented the charity work inspired by Saint Vincent de Paul.[68] Occurring between 1600 and 1660, this religious revival coincided almost exactly with the period when the fledgling Canadian colony, besieged by English privateers and by the Iroquois, was most desperately in need of an injection of immigrants, money and enthusiasm.[69] It was at this moment that the Jesuits in Quebec appealed to the French public for aid. Much to their surprise, they received not a donation but a half-dozen religious zealots, in person. Abandoning the centuries-old cloistered role of female religious figures these nuns undertook missionary work which gave them an active role in the life of the colony.[70] Thus the great religious revival of the seventeenth century endowed New France with several exceptionally capable, well-funded, determined leaders imbued with an activist approach to charity and with that particular mixture of spiritual ardour and worldly *savoir-faire*[w] which typified the mystics of that period.[71] The praises of Marie de

---

[t] daughters of the King

[u] religious-minded women

[v] nuns

[w] sophistication

l'Incarnation, Jeanne Mance and Marguerite Bourgeoys have been sung so
often as to be tiresome. Perhaps, though a useful vantage point is gained if one
assesses them neither as saints nor heroines, but simply as leaders. In this capacity, the nuns supplied money, publicity, skills, and settlers, all of which
were needed in the colony.

Marie de l'Incarnation, an extremely competent business woman from Tours,
founded the Ursuline Monastery at Quebec in 1639. Turning to the study of
Indian languages, she and her colleagues helped implement the policy of as-
similating the young Indians. Then, gradually abandoning that futile policy,
they turned to the education of the French colonists. Marie de l'Incarnation developed the farm on the Ursuline *seigneurie* and served as an unofficial adviser
to the colonial administrators. She also helped draw attention and money to the
colony by writing some 12,000 letters between 1639 and her death in 1672.[72]

An even more prodigious fund-raiser in those straitened times was Jeanne
Mance, who had a remarkable knack for making friends in high places.[73] They
enabled her to supply money and colonists for the original French settlement on
the island of Montreal, and to take a place beside Maisonneuve as co-founder of
the town.[74] The hospital she established there had the legendary wealth of the
de Bullion family—and the revenues of three Norman domains—behind it.
From this endowment she made the crucial grant to Governor Maisonneuve
in 1651 which secured vitally needed French troops—thus saving Montreal.[75]
Mance and her Montreal colleague Marguerite Bourgeoys both made several voyages to France to recruit settlers. They were particularly successful in securing
the female immigrants necessary to establish a permanent colony, recruiting sizeable groups in 1650, 1653 and 1659.[76]

Besides contributing to the colony's sheer physical survival, the nuns materially raised the living standards of the population. They conducted the schools
which were attended by girls of all classes, and from both of the colony's races.
Bourgeoys provided housing for newly arrived immigrants and served in a capacity perhaps best described as an early social worker.[77] Other nuns established
hospitals in each of the three towns. The colonists reaped fringe benefits in the
institutions established by this exceptionally dedicated personnel. The hospitals,
for example, provided high-quality care to both rich and poor; care which compared favourably with that of similar institutions in France.[78] Thus, the *dévotes*
played an important role in supplying leadership, funding, publicity, recruits and
social services. They may even have tipped the balance towards survival in the
1650s, when retention of the colony was still in doubt.

In the longer run, they endowed the colony with an educational heritage,
which survived and shaped social life long after the initial heroic piety had
grown cold. The schools that the *dévotes* founded created a situation very different from that in France, where education of women in the seventeenth
century lagged behind that of men.[79] The opinion-setters in France sought to justify this neglect in the eighteenth century and a controversy began over whether

girls should be educated outside the home at all.[80] Girls in Montreal escaped all
this. Indeed, in 1663 Montrealers had a school for their girls but none for their
boys. The result was that for a time Montreal women surpassed men in literacy,
a reversal of the usual *ancien régime* pattern.[81] The superior education of
women which Charlevoix extolled in 1744 continued until the fall of New France
(and beyond)—a tendency heightened by the large percentage of soldiers, generally illiterate, among the male population.[82] The Ursulines conducted schools
for the élite at Quebec and Trois-Rivières. This order was traditionally rather
weak in teaching housekeeping (which perhaps accounts for Kalm's famous
castigation of Canadian housewifery). Nevertheless they specialized in needle-
work, an important skill since articles of clothing were a major trade good
sought by the Indians. Moreover the Ursulines taught the daughters of the
élite the requisite skills for administering a house and a fortune—skills which,
as we shall see later, many were to exercise.[83]

More remarkable than the Ursuline education, however, was that of the
Soeurs de la Congrégation,[x] which reached the popular classes in the countryside.[84] Franquet was apparently shocked by the effect of this exceptional
education on the colonial girls. He recommended that the *Soeurs'* schools be
suppressed because they made it difficult to keep girls down on the farm:

> Ces Soeurs sont répandues le long des côtes, dans des seigneuries où elles ont
> été attirées pour l'éducation des jeunes filles; leur utilité semble être démontrée,
> mais le mal qu'en résulte est comme un poison lent qui tend à dépeupler les
> campagnes, d'autant qu'une fille instruite fait la demoiselle, qu'elle est maniérée,
> qu'elle veut prendre un établissement à la ville, qu'il lui faut un négociant et
> qu'elle regarde au dessous d'elle l'état dans lequel elle est née.[y] [85]

The second distinct group of female immigrants to New France was the famous *filles du roi*, women sent out by the French government as brides in order
to boost the colony's permanent settlement. Over 900 arrived between 1663
and 1673.[86] If less impressive than the *dévotes*, they too appear to have arrived
with more than the average immigrant's store of education and capital. Like the
nuns, they were the product of a particular historical moment which thrust
them across the sea. The relevant event here is that brief interlude in the 1660s
and 1670s when the King, his Minister Colbert and the Intendant Talon applied an active hand to colonial development.[87]

---

[x] Sisters of the Order of the Congregation

[y] These nuns can be found all along the river, in the *seigneuries* where they have been attracted in
order to educate the young girls. Their usefulness seems evident but the evil that results from their
presence works like a slow poison that tends to reduce the rural population because a girl who has
received an education begins to act above her station and to put on airs. She then wants to set herself up in town and to insist on marrying a merchant, eventually deciding that her social class at
birth is now beneath her.

There has been much historical controversy about whether the *filles du roi* were pure or not.[88] More relevant to our discussion than their morality are their money and their skills. On both these counts, this was a very selective immigration. First of all, the majority of the *filles du roi* (and for that matter, of seventeenth-century female immigrants generally) were urban dwellers, a group which enjoyed better access to education than the peasantry did.[89] Moreover, the *filles du roi* were particularly privileged urbanites. Over one third, some 340 of them, were educated at the Paris Hôpital Général. Students at this institution learned writing and such a wide variety of skills that in France they were much sought after for service in the homes of the wealthy. 6 per cent were of noble or bourgeois origin. All the *filles* brought with them a 50–100 *livres* ᶻ dowry provided by the King; most supplemented this with personal funds in the order of 200–300 *livres*.[90] According to Lanctôt, among lay immigrants, these women constituted the immigration *"la plus stricte, la plus saine et la plus recommandable de toute cette époque."*ᵃᵃ [91] The Parisian origins of many *filles du roi*, and of the nuns who taught their children, probably account for the pure French accent which a number of travellers attributed to the colony's women.[92]

These two major immigrant groups, then, the nuns and the *filles du roi*, largely account for the superior education and "cultivation" attributed to the colony's women. Another demographic consideration also favoured the women of New France. As a result of light female emigration, men heavily outnumbered women in the colony's early days; a balance was not attained until 1710.[93] It might be expected that, as a scarce commodity, women would receive favoured treatment. The facility of marriage and remarriage, the salaries women received, and the leniency of the courts and the administrators towards women, suggest that this hypothesis is correct.

Women had a wider choice in marriage than did men in the colony's early days. There were, for example, eight marriageable men for every marriageable woman in Montreal in 1663. Widows grieved, briefly, then remarried within an average of 8.8 months after their bereavement. In those early days the laws of supply and demand operated to women's economic advantage, as well. Rarely did these first Montreal women bother to match their husband's wedding present by offering a dowry.[94] The colony distinguished itself as "the country of the *douaire* not of the *dot*."ᵇᵇ [95]

Other economic indicators suggest that scarcity served women well. Observers of women's salaries in the nineteenth and twentieth centuries are used to finding them ranging from one-half to two-thirds those of men. This list of 1744 salaries of New France therefore comes as something of a surprise:

ᶻ pounds

ᵃᵃ the most demanding, the healthiest and the most to be recommended for the whole period.

ᵇᵇ "the country of the marriage settlement not of the marriage portion."

Un professeur de collège	400 *livres*
Une institutrice	500 *livres*
Une sage-femme attachée à	
l'Hôtel-Dieu de Québec	400 *livres*
le prévot des maréchaux	500 *livres*
le lieutenant général de Montréal	450 *livres*
le procureur du roi (Mtl.)	250 *livres*
un conseiller ordinaire au	
Conseil Supérieur	300 *livres*
un Missionnaire au Poste	
de la mer de l'Ouest	600 *livres*[cc] [96]

Perhaps the government, as in later centuries, led the way as an "equal opportunity" employer. At any rate, nursemaids hired by the government acquired not only the civil servant's dignity and job security but were paid, we are told, their salaries in cash, in advance, and at a rate "more than the towns-people were accustomed to pay for the nursing of their own children."[97]

In the social and legal realm we also find privileges which may have been attributable to the shortage of women. Perhaps it is due to the difficulties of replacing battered wives that jealous husbands in New France were willing to forego the luxury of uncontrolled rage. Some of the Intendants even charged that there were libertine wives in the colony who got away with taking a second husband while the first was away trading furs.[98] Recent indications that New France conformed rather closely to French traditions make it unlikely that this was common.[99] But the judgements of the Sovereign Council do offer evidence of peaceful reconciliations such as that of Marguerite Leboeuf, charged with adultery in 1667. The charge was dismissed when her husband pleaded before the Sovereign Council on her behalf. Also leaving vengeance largely to the Lord was Antoine Antorche, who withdrew his accusation against his wife even after the Council found her doubly guilty.[100] In this regard the men of New France differed from their Portuguese brothers in Brazil, who perpetrated a number of amorous murders each year; also from their English brethren in Massachusetts, who branded or otherwise mutilated their errant wives and daughters.[101] When such cases reached the courts in New France the judges, too, appear to have been lenient. Their punishments for adulterous women were considerably lighter

---

[cc] A male teacher in a college	400 pounds
A female teacher	500 pounds
A midwife working at the Hôtel-Dieu in Quebec City	400 pounds
The provost marshall	500 pounds
The lieutenant-general for Montreal	450 pounds
The royal procurator (Montreal)	250 pounds
An ordinary member on the Superior Council	300 pounds
A missionary stationed at Western Posts	600 pounds

than those imposed in New England. Other female offenders, such as the whiskey trader captured in 1661, received a much lighter punishment than men convicted of identical offences. A further peculiarity of the legal system in New France, which suggests that women were closer to being on an equal footing with men than in other times and places, was the unusual attempt to arrest not only prostitutes but their clients as well.[102]

Another indication of the lenient treatment Canadian women enjoyed is the level of insubordination the authorities were willing to accept from them. There was a distinct absence of timidity *vis-à-vis* the political authorities. In 1714, for example, the inhabitants of Côte St. Leonard violently objected to the Bishop's decision to cancel their membership in the familiar church and enrol them in the newly erected parish of Rivière-des-Prairies. A fracas ensued in which the consecrated altar breads were captured by the rebellious parishioners. An officer sent to restore order was assailed by angry women:

> L'huissier chargé d'aller assigner les séditieux, raconte que toutes les femmes l'attendaient "avec des roches et des perches dans leurs mains pour m'assassiner," qu'elles le poursuivirent en jurant: "arrête voleur, nous te voulons tuer et jeter dans le marais."[dd] [103]

Other women hurled insults at the Governor himself in the 1670s.[104] An even more outrageous case of insubordination was that of the two Desaulniers sisters, who by dint of various appeals, deceits and stalling tactics, continued to run an illegal trading post at Caughnawaga for some twenty-five years despite repeated orders from Governors, Intendants and the ministry itself, to close it down.[105]

A further indication of women's privileged position is the absence of witchcraft persecution in New France. The colony was founded in the seventeenth century when this persecution was at its peak in Western Europe. The New Englanders, too, were burning witches at Salem. Not a single Canadienne died for this offence.[106] It is not—as Marie de l'Incarnation's account of the 1663 earthquake makes clear[107]—that the Canadians were not a superstitious people. A scholar of crime in New France suggests that this surprising absence of witchcraft hysteria relates to the fact that *"depuis le début de la colonie une femme était une rareté trés estimée et de ce fait, protégée de la persécution en masse."*[ee] [108]

Thus, on the marriage market, and in their protection from physical violence, women seem to have achieved a favourable position because of their small numbers. Their relatively high wages and lighter court sentences may also have been related to the demographic imbalance. Moreover, the original female immigrants arrived in the colony with better-than-average education and capital, attributes which undoubtedly helped them to establish their privileged status.

[dd] The officer responsible for apprehending the troublemakers states that all the women were waiting for him "with rocks and sticks in their hands that they were going to kill me with," and that they chased him, swearing, "Stop, thief, we want to kill you and throw you in the pond."

[ee] "since the early days of the colony, women have not been numerous and have thus been greatly respected and, as a result, protected from mass persecution."

Economic Opportunities

Even more than demographic forces, the colonial economy served to enhance the position of women. In relation to the varied activities found in many regions of France, New France possessed a primitive economy. Other than subsistence farming, the *habitants* engaged in two major pursuits. The first was military activity, which included not only actual fighting but building and maintaining the imperial forts, and provisioning the troops. The second activity was the fur trade. Fighting and fur-trading channelled men's ambitions and at times removed them physically from the colony. This helped open up the full range of opportunities to women, whom we have already seen had the possibility of assuming a wide variety of economic roles in *ancien régime* society. Many adapted themselves to life in a military society. A few actually fought. Others made a good living by providing goods and services to the ever-present armies. Still others left military activity aside and concentrated on civilian economic pursuits—pursuits which were often neglected by men. For many this simply meant managing the family farm as best as one could during the trading season, when husbands were away. Other women assumed direction of commercial enterprises, a neglected area in this society which preferred military honours to commercial prizes. Others acted as a sort of home-office partner for fur-trading husbands working far afield. Still others, having lost husbands to raids, rapids or other hazards of forest life, assumed a widow's position at the helm of the family business.

> New France has been convincingly presented as a military society. The argument is based on the fact that a very large proportion of its population was under arms, its government had a semi-military character, its economy relied heavily on military expenditure and manpower, and a military ethos prevailed among the élite.[109] In some cases, women joined their menfolk in these martial pursuits. The seventeenth century sometimes saw them in direct combat. A number of Montrealers perished during an Iroquois raid in 1661 in which, Charlevoix tells us, "even the women fought to the death, and not one of them surrendered."[110] In Acadia, Madame de la Tour took command of the fort's forty-five soldiers and warded off her husband's arch-enemy, Menou D'Aulnay, for three days before finally capitulating.[111]

The most famous of these seventeenth-century *guerrières* [ff] was, of course, Madeleine de Verchères. At the age of fourteen she escaped from a band of Iroquois attackers, rushed back to the fort on her parents' *seigneurie* and fired a cannon shot in time to warn all the surrounding settlers of the danger.[112] Legend and history have portrayed Madeleine as a lamb who was able, under siege, to summon up a lion's heart. Powdered and demure in a pink dress, she smiles very sweetly out at the world in a charming vignette in Arthur Doughty's *A Daughter of New France, being a story of the life and times of Magdelaine de Verchères*, published in 1916. Perhaps the late twentieth century is ready for her as she was: a swashbuckling, musket-toting braggart who extended the

---

[ff] warrior women

magnitude of her deeds with each successive telling, who boasted that she never in her life shed a tear; a contentious thorn in the side of the local curé (whom she slandered), and of her *censitaires,*[gg] (whom she constantly battled in the courts).[113] She strutted through life for all the world like the boorish male officers of the *campagnard* [hh] nobility to which her family belonged.[114] One wonders how many more there were like her. Perhaps all trace of them has vanished into the waste-baskets of subsequent generations of historians who, with immovable ideas of female propriety, did not know what on earth to do with them—particularly after what must have been the exhausting effort of pinching Verchères' mus-cled frame into a corset and getting her to wear the pink dress.

By the eighteenth century, women had withdrawn from hand-to-hand com-bat, but many remained an integral part of the military élite as it closed in to become a caste. In this system, both sexes shared the responsibility of marry-ing properly and of maintaining those cohesive family ties which, Corvisier tells us, lay at the heart of military society. Both also appealed to the Ministry for their sons' promotions.[115]

What is more surprising is that a number of women accompanied their husbands to military posts in the wilderness. Wives of officers, particularly of corporals, traditionally helped manage the canteens in the French armies.[116] Almost all Canadian officers were involved in some sort of trading activity, and a wife at the post could mind the store when the husband had to mind the war. Some were overzealous. When Franquet rode into Fort Saint Frédéric in 1752 he discovered a terrific row among its inhabitants. The post was in a virtual state of mutiny because a Madame Lusignan was monopolizing all the trade, both wholesale and retail, at the fort; and her husband, the Commandant, was en-forcing the monopoly.[117] In fact, Franquet's inspection tour of the Canadian posts is remarkable for the number of women who greeted him at the military posts, which one might have expected to be a male preserve. Arriving at Fort Sault Saint Louis he was received very politely by M. de Merceau and his two daughters. He noted that Fort Saint Frédéric housed not only the redoubtable Madame Lusignan but also another officer's widow. At Fort Chambly he "spent the whole day with the ladies, and visited Madame de Beaulac, an officer's widow who has been given lodging in this fort."[118]

The nuns, too, marched in step with this military society. They were, quite literally, one of its lifelines, since they cared for its wounded. A majority of the invalids at the Montreal Hôtel Dieu were soldiers, and the Ursuline in-stitution at Trois-Rivières was referred to simply as a *hôpital militaire.*[ii] [119] Hospital service was so vital to the army that Frontenac personally inter-vened to speed construction of the Montreal Hôtel-Dieu in 1695, when he was

---

[gg] tenants

[hh] rural

[ii] military hospital

planning a campaign against the Iroquois.[120] In the colony's first days, the Ursulines also made great efforts to help the Governor seal Indian alliances by attempting to secure Iroquois students who would serve as hostages, and by giving receptions for Iroquois chiefs.[121]

Humbler folk also played a part in military society. In the towns female publicans conducted a booming business with the thirsty troops. Other women served as laundresses, adjuncts so vital that they accompanied armies even on the campaigns where wives and other camp followers were ordered to stay home.[122] Seemingly indispensable, too, wherever armies march, are prostitutes. At Quebec City they plied their trade as early as 1667. Indian women at the missions also served in this capacity.[123] All told, women had more connections with the military economy than is generally noted.

While warfare provided a number of women with a living, it was in commerce that the *Canadiennes* really flourished. Here a number of women moved beyond supporting roles to occupy centre stage. This happened for several reasons. The first was that the military ethos diverted men from commercial activity. Secondly, many men who entered the woods to fight or trade were gone for years. Others, drowned or killed in battle, obviously never returned.[124] This left many widows who had to earn a livelihood. This happened so often, in fact, that when in 1710 women finally overcame the population imbalance due to their weak immigration, the tables turned quickly; they soon outnumbered the men, and remained a majority through to the Conquest.[125] Generally speaking, life was more hazardous for men than for women[126]—so much so that the next revolution of the historiographic wheel may turn up the men of New France (at least in relation to its women) as an oppressed group.

At any rate, women often stepped in to take the place of their absent husbands or brothers. A surprising number of women traders emerge in the secondary literature on New France. In the colony's earliest days, the mere handful of women included two merchants at Trois-Rivières: Jeanne Enard (mother-in-law of Pierre Boucher) who "by her husband's own admission" was the head of the family as far as fur-trading was concerned; and, Mathurine Poisson, who sold imported goods to the colonists.[127] At Montreal there was the wife of Artus de Sully, whose unspecified (but presumably commercial) activities won her the distinction of being Montreal's biggest debtor.[128] In Quebec City, Eleonore de Grandmaison was a member of a company formed to trade in the Ottawa country. She added to her wealth by renting her lands on the Ile d'Orleans to Huron refugees after Huronia had been destroyed. Farther east, Madame de la Tour involved herself in shipping pelts to France. Another Acadian, Madame Joybert, traded furs on the Saint John River.[129]

With the onset of the less pious eighteenth century, we find several women at the centre of the illegal fur trade. Indian women, including "a cross-eyed squaw named Marie-Magdelaine" regularly carried contraband goods from the Caughnawaga Reserve to Albany.[130] A Madame Couagne received Albany contraband at the other end, in Montreal.[131] But at the heart of this illegal trade were the Desaulniers sisters, who used their trading post on the Caughnawaga reserve as an *entrepô*[jj] for the forbidden English strouds, fine textiles, pipes, boots, lace, gloves, silver tableware, chocolate, sugar and oysters which the Indians brought regularly from Albany.[132] Franquet remarked on the power of these *marchandes*,[kk] who were able to persuade the Indians to refuse the government's request to build fortifications around their village.[133] The Desaulniers did not want the comings and goings of their employees too closely scrutinized.

These *commerçantes*,[ll] honest and otherwise, continued to play their part until the Conquest. Marie-Anne Barbel (*Veuve* [mm] Fornel) farmed the Tadoussac fur trade and was involved in diverse enterprises including retail sales, brick-making and real estate.[134] On Franquet's tour in the 1750s he encountered other *marchandes* besides the controversial "Madame la Commandante" who had usurped the Fort Saint Frédéric trade. He enjoyed a more restful night closer to Montreal at the home of Madame de Lemothe, a *marchande* who had prospered so well that she was able to put up her guests in splendid beds which Franquet proclaimed "fit for a duchess."[135]

A number of writers have remarked on the shortage of entrepreneurial talent in New France.[136] This perhaps helps to account for the activities of Agathe de St. Père, who established the textile industry in Canada. She did so after the colonial administrators had repeatedly called for development of spinning and weaving, with no result.[137] Coming from the illustrious Le Moyne family, Agathe St. Père married the ensign Pierre Legardeur de Repentigny, a man who, we are told, had "an easygoing nature." St. Père, of another temperament, pursued the family business interests, investing in fur trade partnerships, real estate and lending operations. Then in 1705, when the vessel bringing the yearly supply of French cloth to the colony was shipwrecked, she saw an opportunity to develop the textile industry in Montreal. She ransomed nine English weavers who had been captured by the Indians, and arranged for apprentices to study the trade. Subsequently these apprentices taught the trade to other Montrealers on home looms which Madame de Repentigny built and distributed. Besides developing the manufacture of linen, drugget and serge, she discovered new chemicals which made use of the native plants to dye and process them.[138]

Upon this foundation Madame Benoist built. Around the time of the Conquest, she was directing an operation in Montreal in which women turned out, among other things, shirts and petticoats for the fur trade.[139] This is a case of woman doing business while man did battle, for Madame Benoist's husband was commanding officer at Lac des Deux Montagnes.

[jj] warehouse

[kk] women merchants

[ll] dealers

[mm] Widow

This absence of male entrepreneurs may also explain the operation of a large Richelieu lumbering operation by Louise de Ramezay, the daughter of the Governor of Montreal. Louise, who remained single, lost her father in 1724. Her mother continued to operate the sawmilling operation on the family's Chambly Seigneury, but suffered a disastrous reverse due to a combination of flooding, theft and shipwreck in 1725. The daughter, however, went into partnership with the Seigneuress de Rouville in 1745 and successfully developed the sawmill. She then opened a flour mill, a Montreal tannery and another sawmill. By the 1750s the trade was flourishing: Louise de Ramezay was shipping 20,000 *livres* loads, and one merchant alone owed her 60,000 *livres*. In 1753 she began to expand her leather business, associating with a group of Montreal tanners to open new workshops.[140]

Louise de Ramezay's case is very clearly related to the fact that she lived in a military society. As Louise was growing up, one by one her brothers perished. Claude, an ensign in the French navy, died during an attack on Rio de Janeiro in 1711, Louis died during the 1715 campaign against the Fox Indians, La Gesse died ten years later in a shipwreck off Ile Royale. That left only one son, Jean-Baptiste-Roch, and, almost inevitably, he chose a military career over management of the family business affairs.[141] It may be that similar situations accounted for the female entrepreneurs in ironforging, tilemaking, sturgeonfishing, sealing and contract building, all of whom operated in New France.[142]

If military society was the warp for this network of trading women, family connections were the woof. Madame Benoist belonged to the Baby family, whose male members were out cultivating the western fur trade. Her production of shirts made to the Indians' specifications was the perfect complement. The secret of the Desaulniers' successful trade network may well be that they were related to so many of Montreal's leading merchants.[143] The fur trade generally required two or more bases of operation. We saw earlier in our discussion that this society not only placed great value on family connections but also accepted female commercial activity. It was therefore quite natural that female relatives would be recruited into business to cover one of the bases. Men who were heading for the west would delegate their powers of attorney and various business responsibilities to their wives, who were remaining in the colony.[144]

We find these husband-wife fur trade partnerships not only among *"Les Grandes Familles"*[nn] but permeating all classes of society. At Trois-Rivières women and girls manufactured the canoes which carried the fur trade provisions westward each summer. This was a large-scale operation which profited from fat government contracts.[145] In Montreal, wives kept the account-books while their husbands traded. Other women spent the winters sewing shirts and petticoats which would be bartered the following summer.[146]

[nn] The Leading Families

The final reason for women's extensive business activity was the direct result of the hazards men faced in fighting and fur trading. A high proportion of
women were widowed; and as widows, they enjoyed special commercial privileges. In traditional French society, these privileges were so extensive that
craftsmen's widows sometimes inherited full guild-master's rights. More generally, widows acquired the right to manage the family assets until the children
reached the age of twenty-five (and sometimes beyond that time). In some instances they also received the right to choose which child would receive the
succession.[147] In New France these rights frequently came into operation; and
they had a major impact on the distribution of wealth and power in the society.
In 1663, for example, women held the majority of the colony's seigneurial land.
The *Veuve* Lemoyne numbered among the twelve Montreal merchants who,
between 1642 and 1725, controlled assets of 50,000 *livres*. The *Veuve* Fornel
acquired a similar importance later on in the regime. Some of the leading merchants at Louisbourg were also widows. The humbler commerce of tavernkeeping
was also frequently a widow's lot.[148]

Thus, in New France, both military and commercial activities which required a great deal of travelling over vast distances were usually carried out
by men. In their absence, their wives played a large role in the day-to-day economic direction of the colony. Even when the men remained in the colony,
military ambitions often absorbed their energies, particularly among the
upper class. In these situations, it was not uncommon for a wife to assume direction of the family interests.[149] Others waited to do so until their widowhood,
which—given the fact that the average wife was considerably younger than
her husband and that his activities were often more dangerous—frequently
came early.

Conclusion

New France had been founded at a time in Europe's history in which the roles
of women were neither clearly nor rigidly defined. In this fluid situation, the
colony received an exceptionally well-endowed group of female immigrants during its formative stage. There, where they long remained in short supply, they
secured a number of special privileges at home, at school, in the courts, and in
social and political life. They consolidated this favourable position by attain-
ing a major role in the colonial economy, at both the popular and the directive
levels. These circumstances enabled the women of New France to play many
parts. *Dévotes* and traders, warriors and landowners, smugglers and politicians, industrialists and financiers; they thronged the stage in such numbers that
they distinguish themselves as *femmes favorisées*.

Notes

1. F.-X. Charlevoix, *History and General Description of New France* (New York: Harper, 1900), Vol. 3: p. 28.

2. Cited in R.-L. Séguin, "La Canadienne aux XVIIe et XVIIIe siècles," *Revue d'historie de l'Amérique français,* XIII, (mars 1960), p. 492.

3. Séguin, "La Canadienne," p. 500.

4. *Ibid.*

5. L. Franquet, *Voyages et mémoires sur le Canada* (Montréal: Editions Elysee, 1974), p. 57, recording a tour in 1752–53.

6. *Ibid.,* p. 31.

7. Séguin, "La Canadienne," pp. 492, 505.

8. G. Fagniez, *La Femme et la société française dans la première moitié du XVIIe siècle* (Paris: J. Gambler, 1929), p. 154.

9. Marcel Trudel, *Montréal, la formation d'une société* (Montreal: Fides, 1976), p. 216–217.

10. John F. Bosher, "The Family in New France," in *In Search of the Visible Past,* Barry Gough, ed. (Waterloo, Ont.: W.L.U. Press, 1976), p. 7.

11. Fagniez, *Femme et société française,* p. 121.

12. *Ibid.,* pp. 149, 104, 193.

13. Philippe Ariès, *Centuries of Childhood* (New York: Vintage 1962), pp. 392–406.

14. *Ibid.,* pp. 365–66.

15. Peter Laslett, "Characteristics of the Western Family Considered over Time," *Journal of Family History,* 2 (Summer 1977), pp. 89–115.

16. Richard Vann, "Women in Preindustrial Capitalism," in *Becoming Visible: Women in European History,* R. Bridenthal, ed. (Boston: Houghton Mifflin, 1977), p. 206.

17. *Ibid.,* pp. 206–8; Ariès, *Centuries of Childhood,* pp. 397–406.

18. Fagniez, *Femme et société française,* pp. 122–23; 179.

19. Vann, "Women in Preindustrial Capitalism," p. 206.

20. Franquet, *Voyages,* pp. 135 and 61.

21. Séguin, "La Canadienne," p. 499 and R. Boyer, *Les Crimes et châtiments au Canada française du XVIIIe au XXe siècle* (Montreal: 1966), p. 391.

22. Séguin, "La Canadienne," p. 506.

23. Boyer, *Crimes et châtiments,* p. 351.

24. *Ibid.,* pp. 344–46.

25. Laslett, "Western Family," p. 95.

26. I. Foulché-Delbosc, "Women of Three Rivers, 1651–1663," in *The Neglected Majority,* A. Prentice and S. Trofimenkoff, eds. (Toronto: McClelland and Stewart, 1977), p. 26.

27. Bosher ("The Family," p. 3) found the marriage rate in New France to be about three times that of modern-day Quebec.

28. This information is taken from a study of Normandy, which was the birthplace of many of the Canadian colonists. J.M. Gouesse, "La Formation du couple en Basse-Normandie," *XVIIe Siècle,* Nos. 102–3 (1974), p. 56.

29. Laslett, "Western Family," p. 106.

30. Fagniez, *Femme et société française,* pp. 99–104, 108, 111, 114–16.

31. Louise Dechêne, *Habitants et marchands de Montréal au XVIIe siècle* (Paris: Plon, 1974), p. 393.

32. Fagniez, *Femme et société française,* pp. 101, 1913, Séguin, "La Canadienne," p. 503; also G. Lanctôt, *Filles de joie ou filles du roi* (Montréal, 1952), m pp. 210–13.

33. Cf. Paul Butel, "Comportements familiaux dans le négoce bordelais au XVIIIe siècle," *Annales du Midi,* Vol. 88 (1976): pp. 139–157.

34. M.E. Chabot, "Marie Guyart de L'Incarnation, 1599–1672," in *The Clear Spirit,* M. Innis, ed. (Toronto: University of Toronto Press, 1966), p. 28.

35. Bosher, "The Family," p. 7; H. Neatby, *Quebec, The Revolutionary Age* (Toronto: McClelland and Stewart, 1966), p. 46.

36. Foulché-Delbosc, "Women of Three Rivers," p. 15.

37. Bosher, "The Family," p. 3. I have rounded his figures.

38. Dechêne, *Habitants et marchands,* p. 434, and Bosher, "The Family," p. 5.

39. Vann, "Women in Preindustrial Capitalism," p. 205; cf. also Alice Clark, *Working Life of Women in the Seventeenth Century* (London: Cass, 1968), chs. V, VI; and Fagniez, *Femme et société française,* for the scarcity of women's guilds by the seventeenth century.

40. *Ibid.,* p. 168 ff.

41. Y. Zoltvany, "Esquisse de la Coutume de Paris," *RHAF* (decembre 1971).

42. Foulché-Delbosc, "Women of Three Rivers," p. 19.

43. Neatby, *Quebec,* p. 46.

44. Fagniez, *Femme et société française,* p. 147.

45. Dechêne, *Habitants et marchands,* pp. 423–24.

46. A. Morel, "Réflexions sur la justice criminelle canadienne au 18e siècle," *RHAF,* 29 (septembre 1975), pp. 241–253.

47. Lanctôt, *Filles de joie,* p. 219.

48. Boyer, *Crimes et châtiments,* pp. 128–29.

49. W.J. Eccles, "Social Welfare Measures and Policies in New France," *Congreso Internacional de Americanistas,* IV, (1966), Seville, pp. 9–19.

50. J. Bosher, "Government and Private Interests in New France," in *Canadian History Before Confederation,* J.M. Bumsted, ed. (Georgetown, Ontario: Irwin-Dorsey, 1972), p. 122.

51. Bosher, "The Family," pp. 5–7; Fagniez, *Femme et société française,* p. 182.

52. Franquet, *Voyages,* p. 148; cf., also Frégault, *Le XVIIIe siècle canadien* (Montréal: Collection Constantes, 1968), pp. 292–293.

53. W.J. Eccles, "The Social, Economic and Political Significance of the Military Establishment in New France," *Canadian Historical Review,* LII (March 1971), pp. 8–10.

54. Franquet, *Voyages,* pp. 129–30. For another, similar trip, *cf.* pp. 140–42.

55. Frégault, *Le XVIIIe Siècle,* pp. 208–9, 216–21.

56. *Ibid.,* pp. 229–30.

57. Y. Zoltvany, *Philippe de Rigaud de Vaudreuil* (Toronto: McClelland and Stewart, 1974), p. 110; also p. 217.

58. Frégault, *Le XVIIIe Siècle,* pp. 228–30.

59. W.J. Eccles, *Frontenac: The Courtier Governor* (Toronto: McClelland and Stewart, 1959), p. 29.

60. *Rapport de l'archiviste de la province de Québec,* 1922–23, p. 151.

61. For example, George Rudé, *The Crowd in the French Revolution* (New York: Oxford, 1959).

62. Superbly described in E.P. Thompson, *The Making of the English Working Class* (London; Penquin, 1976), Ch. Three.

63. Séguin, "La Canadienne," pp. 498–99.

64. Jean Hamelin, "What Middle Class?" *Society and Conquest,* Miquelon, ed. (Toronto, 1977), pp. 109–110; and Dechêne, *Habitants et marchands,* p. 44, who concludes that the largest contingents of male immigrants arriving in seventeenth-century Montreal were *engagés* and soldiers.

65. H. Charbonneau, *Vie et mort de nos ancêtres* (Montréal: Presses de l'université de Montréal, 1975), p. 38; A. Burguière, "Le Rituel du mariage en France: Pratiques ecclésiastiques et pratiques popularies, (XVIe–XVIIIe siècle)," *Annales E. S. C.,* 33e annee (mai-juin 1978), p. 640; R. Mousnier, *La famille, l'enfant et l'éducation en France et en Grande-Bretagne du XVIe au XVIIIe siècle* (Paris: Sorbonne C.D.U., 1975); Fagneiz, *Femme et société française,* p. 97. Commercial activities, however, also prevailed among the women of Bordeaux, an important port in the Canada trade. (*Ibid.,* p. 196).

66. Fagniez, *Femme et société française,* pp. 267, 273–74, 311–12, 360–61.

67. Claude Lessard, "L'Aide financière de l'Eglise de France à l'Eglise naissante du Canada," in *Mèlanges d'histoire du Canada français offerts au professeur Marcel Trudel.* Pierre Savard, ed. (Ottawa: Editions de l'Université d'Ottawa, 1978), p. 175.

68. Fagniez, *Femme et société française,* pp. 311–321.

69. Marcel Trudel, *The Beginnings of New France,* (Toronto: McClelland and Stewart, 1973). For a gloomy assessment of the neglected colony during this period.

70. G. Brown *et al.,* eds., *Dictionnary of Canadian Biography* (hereafter *DCB*), (Toronto: U. of Toronto Press, 1966–) Vol. 1, p. 118; and J. Marshall, ed., *Word from New France* (Toronto: Oxford, 1967), p. 2.

71. Fagniez, *Femme et société française,* pp. 320–33, 358. Of course, not all *religieuses* were competent as leaders. Madame de la Peltrie, for example, patron of the Urusline convent, appears to have been a rather unreliable benefactress. Despite her firsthand knowledge of the difficulties under which the Ursulines laboured, her "charity" was quixotic. In 1642, she suddenly withdrew her support from the Ursulines in order to join the colonists setting off to found Montreal. Later she again held back her funds in favour of a cherished chapel project, even though the Ursulines' lodgings had just burned to the ground.

72. Chabot, "Marie Guyart de l'Incarnation," pp. 27, 37; *DCB,* 1, p. 353; Lessard, "Aide financière," pp. 169–70.

73. *DCB,* Vol. 1; pp. 483–87; also Lessard, "Aide financière," p. 175.

74. This is the interpretation given by G. Lanctôt in *Montreal under Maisonneuve* (Toronto: Clarke Irwin, 1969), pp. 20–24, 170.

75. *Ibid.,* p. 188.

76. Lanctôt, *Filles de joie,* p. 81 and Trudel, *Montréal,* p. 21. The Hôtel-Dieu de Montréal also sponsored immigrants from 1655 to 1662 (Lanctôt, *Filles de joie,* p. 81.)

77. Trudel, *Montréal,* p. 84.

78. Eccles, "Social Welfare Measures," p. 19; F. Rousseau, "Hôpital et société en Nouvelle-France: l'Hôtel-Dieu de Québec à la fin du XVIIᵉ siècle," *RHAF,* Vol. 31 (juin 1977), p. 47.

79. Mousnier, *La famille l'enfant et l'éducation,* pp. 319–31.

80. Vann, "Women in Preindustrial Capitalism," p. 208.

81. Trudel, *Montréal,* p. 276, 87; P. Goubert, *The Ancien Régime* (New York: Harper, 1974), p. 262.

82. Neatby, *Quebec,* p. 237; French soldiers had a literacy rate of 3 to 4 per cent. A. Corvisier, *L'Armée française de la fin du XVIIᵉ siècle au ministère de Choiseul* (Paris: Presses universitaires de France, 1964), p. 862.

83. Fagniez, *Femme et société canadienne,* p. 191.

84. Séguin, "La Canadienne," p. 501, lists nine of these schools in addition to the original one in Montreal.

85. Franquet, *Voyages,* pp. 31–32.

86. According to Lanctôt, (*Filles de joie,* pp. 121–30) there were 961. Silvio Dumas counts only 774 (*Les Filles du roi en Nouvelle France,* Québec, 1972, p. 164). Other estimates have ranged between 713 and 857.

87. J.-N. Fauteux, *Essai sur l'industrie au Canada sous le Régime Francais* (Quebec: Proulx, 1927), "Introduction."

88. For the record, it now seems fairly well established that the females sent to New France, unlike those sent to the West Indies, were carefully screened, and any of questionable morality returned by the authorities to France. Lanctôt (*Filles de joie*) and Dumas, (*Filles du roi*) agree on this. See also Foulché-Delbosc, "Women of Three Rivers," pp. 22–23.

89. Dechêne finds a majority of *Parisiennes* among the Montréal *filles* (*Habitants et marchands,* p. 96). Lanctôt states that one-half of the 1634–63 emigrants were urbanites and that two-thirds of the *filles* were from Ile-de-France (*Filles de joie,* pp. 76–79 and p. 124). On education in France see Mousnier, *La famille, l'enfant et l'éducation,* pp. 319–25.

90. Lanctôt, *Filles de joie,* pp. 110–130, 207.

91. *Ibid.,* p. 226.

92. Séguin, "La Canadienne," p. 492; Franquet, *Voyages,* p. 57.

93. J. Henripin, *La Population canadienne au début du XVIIIᵉ Siècle* (Paris: Presses universitaires de France, 1954). The overall population was sixty-three percent male in 1663 (Trudel, *Beginnings,* p. 261), an imbalance which gradually declined.

94. Trudel, *Montréal,* pp. 45–47, 108, 113.

95. Foulché-Delbosc, "Women of Three Rivers," p. 19.

96. Frégault, *Le XVIIIᵉ Siècle,* p. 144.

97. Eccles, "Social Welfare Measures," p. 18.

98. Cole Harris, *The Seigneurial System in Early Canada* (Québec: P.U.L., 1968), p. 163.

99. The richest single source for evidence along these lines is Dechêne's *Habitants et marchands.*

100. Boyer, *Crimes et châtiments,* p. 326.

101. Toronto *Globe and Mail,* 29 October 1979, p. 1; Boyer, *Crimes et châtiments,* pp. 329, 340. Cf. also N. Hawthorne's novel, *The Scarlet Letter,* based on an actual occurrence.

102. Boyer, *Crimes et châtiments,* p. 329, 350, 361–62; also Morel, "Justice criminelle canadienne."

103. Dechêne, *Habitants et marchands,* p. 464.

104. Séguin, "La Canadienne," pp. 497–99.

105. Jean Lunn, "The Illegal Fur Trade Out of New France 1713–60," *Canadian Historical Association Report,* (1939), pp. 61–62.

106. Boyer, *Crimes et châtiments,* pp. 286–87.

107. Marshall, *Word from New France,* pp. 287–95.

108. Boyer, *Crimes et châtiments,* p. 306.

109. Eccles, "The Social, Economic and Political Significance of the Military Establishment," *op. cit.*

110. Charlevoix, *New France,* Vol. 3, p. 35.

111. Ethel Bennett, "Madame de La Tour, 1602–1645," in *The Clear Spirit,* M. Innis, ed. (Toronto: U. of Toronto Press, 1966), p. 21.

112. *DCB,* Vol. 3, pp. 308–13.

113. *Ibid.,* pp. 308–13; and Boyer, *Crimes et châtiments,* pp. 338–39.

114. For a splendid description of the attitudes and lifestyle of this class in France, see p. de Vaissière, *Gentilhommes campagnards de l'ancienne France* (Paris, Perin 1903).

115. G. Frégault, *Le Grand Marquis,* (Montréal: Les Etudes de l'Institut d'Histoire de l'Amerique française, 1952), pp. 74–75 and Corvisier, *L'Armée française,* p. 777.

116. *Ibid.,* pp. 762–63, 826.

117. Franquet, *Voyages,* pp. 56, 67–68, 200.

118. *Ibid.,* p. 35, 76, 88.

119. Dechêne, *Habitants et marchands,* p. 398; Franquet, *Voyages,* p. 16.

120. *DCB,* Vol. 2, p. 491.

121. Marshall, *Word from New France,* pp. 27, 213, 222–23, 233.

122. Dechêne, *Habitants et marchands,* p. 393; Franquet, *Voyages,* p. 199; Foulché-Delbosc, "Women of Three Rivers," p. 25; Corvisier, *L'Armée française,* p. 760.

123. Boyer, *Crimes et châtiments,* pp. 349–51; Dechêne, *Habitants et marchands.* p. 41. Dechêne concludes that, considering Montreal was a garrison town with a shortage of marriageable women, the degree of prostitution was normal or, to use her term, *conformiste* (pp. 437–38).

124. Eccles, "The Social, Economic and Political Significance of the Military ...," pp. 11–17; Dechêne, *Habitants et marchands,* p. 121.

125. Séguin, "La Canadienne," pp. 495, 503.

126. Trudel, *Montréal,* pp. 30–33; and Charbonneau, *Vie et mort,* p. 135.

127. Foulché-Delbosc, "Women of Three Rivers," p. 25.

128. Trudel, *Montréal,* p. 163.

129. Bennett, "Madame de la Tour," p. 16; Madame Joybert was the mother of the future Madame de Vaudreuil. *DCB,* Vol. 1, p. 399. For E. de Grandmaison, see *DCB,* Vol. 1, p. 345.

130. Lunn, "Illegal Fur Trade," p. 62.

131. Eccles, *Canadian Society ..., op. cit.,* p. 61.

132. Lunn, "Illegal Fur Trade," pp. 61–75.

133. Franquet, *Voyages,* pp. 120–21.

134. Lilianne Plamondon, "Une femme d'affaires en Nouvelle-France: Marie-Anne Barbel, Veuve Fornel," *RHAF,* 31 (septembre 1977).

135. Franquet, *Voyages,* pp. 156–58.

136. For example, Hamelin in "What Middle Class?" The absence of an indigenous bourgeoisie is also central to the interpretation of Dechêne in *Habitants et marchands.*

137. Séguin, "La Canadienne," p. 494.

138. For accounts of Agathe de Saint-Père, see *DCB,* Vol. III, pp. 580–81; Fauteux, *Industrie au Canada,* p. 464–69; and Massicote, *Bulletin des Recherches historiques* (hereafter BRH), 1944, p. 202–07.

139. Neatby refers to this activity in the early post-Conquest era (*Quebec*, pp. 72–73); Franquet encountered Madame Benoist in 1753 (*Voyages,* p. 150).

140. For a discussion of the de Ramezay's business affairs Cf. Massicote, *BRH,* 1931, p. 530; and Fauteux, *Industrie au Canada,* pp. 158–59, 204–15, 442.

141. *DCB,* Vol. II, p. 548.

142. Fauteux, *Industrie au Canada,* pp. 158; 297, 420–21, 522; and P. Moogk, *Building a House in New France* (Toronto: 1977), pp. 60–64.

143. Lunn, *Illegal Fur Trade,* p. 61.

144. See Moogk (*Building a House,* p. 8) for one case of a husband's transfer of these powers.

145. Franquet, *Voyages,* p. 17.

146. Dechêne, *Habitants et marchands,* pp. 151–53, 187, 391; and Séguin, "La Canadienne," p. 494.

147. Charbonneau, *Vie et mort,* p. 184; Fagniez, *Femme et société française,* pp. 111, 182–84. A recent study by Butel ("Comportements familiaux") has documented the phenomenon of widows taking over the family business in eighteenth-century Bordeaux.

148. Trudel, *Beginnings,* p. 250. This was largely due to the enormous holdings of Jean Lauzon's widow. Dechêne, *Habitants et marchands,* pp. 209 and 204–5, 393; Plamondon, "Femme d'affaires." W.S. MacNutt, *The Atlantic Provinces* (Toronto: McClelland and Stewart, 1965), p. 25.

149. This happened on *seigneuries* as well as in town, as in the case M. de Lanouguère, "a soldier by preference," whose wife, Marguerite-Renée Denys, directed their *seigneurie* (*DCB,* Vol. 1, p. 418).

NEW FRANCE
The French in North America, XVI–XVIIIth Century

Jacques Mathieu

Individuals and Society

The relations between individuals and society in New France were more complex than the division into three orders (clergy, nobility and third estate) or the socio-professional classifications might lead one to believe. In the first place, there was no society of orders in Canada in the 18th century even though different individual statuses existed. The *Coutume de Paris* defined the legal frameworks which laid down for each individual, according to age and sex, rights and responsibilities within a family community and with respect to others. Less clear-cut legal situations existed, such as the status of natives, slaves, foreigners and, up to a certain point, Protestants.

From *La Nouvelle-France: Les Français en Amérique du Nord XVIe–XVIIIe siècle,* © Éditions Belin, Paris, 1991. Translation by Édition Électronique Niche.

The French model, which persisted, had a profound effect on the social hierarchy. It influenced the nature of individuals' aspirations. On the other hand, *life in New France brought about changes*, notably in the distribution of wealth, which gave new dimensions to Canadian society. Between the characteristics of the society of orders and the equality of opportunity at the outset, there existed a considerable area of divergence where different social relationships were formed. Between the quarrels of precedence which marked the 17th century and the complaints which, in the 18th century, revealed the fact that domestics "spoke loudly," there appears to have been a significant development.

The junction of political and religious authority had resulted in the identification of those who belonged to society and those who were on its fringes. In this royal colony, only the King's subjects were entitled to his full protection. Only the children of God were admitted to society in this catholic, apostolic and Roman colony. *A number of individuals*, because of their membership in a different ethnic or religious group, were *just barely tolerated* in the hope that they would adapt and return to the ranks of society.

1. The Lower Statuses

a. Amerindians The Amerindians, and particularly those who were the allies of the French, remained for the most part grouped in nations legally independent from the French, which did not mean that they were not politically or economically subjugated. But integration into French colonial society could be achieved only through assimilation. Since the charter of the *Compagnie des Cent-Associés* in 1627, the native, in order to be recognized as a French subject with the same rights, privileges and honours, had merely to accept baptism. In theory, this was the sole condition for entry into French society. In actual fact, even the Indians who were baptized and settled on reserves or in missions created for them and who had learned agriculture or a trade kept their way of life and their original ethnic affiliation. Only a few women, integrated into a family through adoption or marriage, eventually belonged to this colonial society. *The low percentage of interbreeding prevented integration of the two societies.* Despite intermittent economic exchanges and a certain domination by the French authorities, they lived side by side. Relationships were maintained through diplomatic channels, on a nation-to-nation basis. The Amerindians were not directly affected by the French institutions and administration. They received, with more or less dispatch, the notices sent through an intermediary, most often the missionaries who lived among them. The services which they accepted, or sometimes solicited, were dispensed as acts of charity or gestures of friendliness. Lastly, these nations had been dramatically affected by the effects of the French presence. Wars, epidemics and devastation of the hunting grounds had led to a considerable decrease in the Amerindian population in the St. Lawrence Valley. Numbering at least 8000 at the time of the discovery, the Amerindian population was reduced to 3000 individuals by the middle of the 18th century.

b. Slaves   *Slaves* did not even have political status. They were in a state of absolute dependance on their masters, who sold or bought them as they pleased, often for purposes of prestige or for specific needs. Marcel Trudel estimates that there were 4000 of them in the St. Lawrence Valley between 1627 and 1760. To the 1200 black slaves who came from Africa via the Antilles or from the English colonies, were added about 2400 Amerindians from the Mississippi Valley. *Their living conditions*, free from ill-treatment, *were similar to those of domestics* or servants. However, their life expectancy was less than 20 years.

c. Foreigners   *Some foreigners suffered other forms of discrimination.* About 100 British colonials were taken prisoner as a result of the wars of the early 18th century. In 1702, then in 1710, the King gave letters of naturalization to those who agreed to convert to Catholicism. From then on, they could marry, practise any trade and be granted land. The situation of Protestants was rather similar. They had been specifically excluded from the colonization venture as early as 1627; but 400 of them settled in New France. They were subject to the denunciations and pressures of the clergy, which was extremely hostile to these heretics. Deprived of ministers of religion, unable to practise their faith, excluded from certain professions such as doctor, notary, officer of the law as well as from all administrative functions, they could not marry or receive a religious burial without abjuring. The overwhelming majority therefore resigned themselves to this, although a certain number left no official record of their abjuration. One only notes that after having their children baptized in the Protestant church before leaving France, some Protestant parents had their children baptized in the Catholic faith once they had arrived in Canada.

d. Itinerant Vendors   The *itinerant vendors*, merchants who came to the colony every year during the commercial season, also were considered to be somewhat like foreigners. *Opposition to the itinerant vendors* intensified progressively during the 18th century. The merchants and traders of the colony succeeded in having their commercial rights restricted on the pretext of unfair competition. In any case, on the eve of the Conquest, a few Protestant merchants dominated colonial commerce and played a major economic role.

e. The Disadvantaged   Particular social conditions also affected the status of certain groups of persons, and appears to have deprived them, partially or temporarily, of their rights.

Like every society, that of New France included physically or mentally *handicapped persons, criminals, poor people* and lonely *old people*. They were generally shut away in the general hospital as a preventive measure or through charity. The institution sought to put everyone to work, to make each person play a role in order that he not be a burden to the community. The office of the poor also sought to eliminate mendicity by obtaining tools and work for each. Likewise, abandoned children were taken in charge by the Crown which tried to place them in a family. In short, the Administration favoured a system of social aid in which the most disadvantaged were taken in charge by persons and institutions in return for various compensations. These social contracts, often signed in the presence of a notary, enabled an individual to alienate his assets—most frequently his labour—in return for food, shelter and sometimes small favours. Thus, some persons, especially old people, alone and unable to provide for their needs, gave themselves to religious communities which agreed to take care of them until their death. Children "taken in charge by the King" were put in the care of a nurse for two years, then placed in a family until the age of 20. Likewise, the apprenticing or placing in domestic service of children at three or four years of age was similar to adoption. A work contract subordinated them to a family-type authority, to which they owed obedience in all that was lawful.

We know little about the fate of these persons, just as we often do not know about the circumstances which may have led to such a situation. It sometimes happened that some apprentices became well-known masters who were respected and relatively wealthy. The disadvantage of the initial situation is less well known. Apart from the handicapped, young orphans and old people without kin, what circumstances could have forced these people to place themselves entirely in the service of others? An analysis of female domestic service, based on the Quebec census of 1744, provides a few clues. Its geographical and social origin did not differ from that of the society as a whole. The proportion of rural and urban dwellers, of identified poor and of daughters of married persons corresponds to the general distribution. But we find an over-representation of people in an unfavourable family situation: widows, female orphans and illegitimate children. Above all, we discover the weight of family responsibilities: two-thirds of female domestics had from 6 to 14 brothers and sisters.

All these persons who hovered around the fringes of the principal social unit constituted nevertheless rather small minorities.

2. *The Principal Social Statuses*

The *Coutume de Paris* imposed on the family the principle of community of property. Under the quasi-absolute authority of the husband, the economic and social capital and the honour of the family community was administered in accordance with this principle. Hence *the importance of marriage agreements* for the possible purposes of sharing and passing on of an inheritance that was as much economic and social as it was cultural.

a. The Family   In New France in the 18th century, the family was essentially conjugal. At the very most, some of the children took special care of parents who had become unable to provide for their own needs. It is also possible that the late marrying of young men (28.1 years on average) allowed for a phase of mutual aid. Living under the paternal roof, these young people were able to prepare for their future autonomy. But households consisting of two married couples remained the exception. When this situation occurred, it was always of a temporary nature. It did not constitute a way of life. *A family had 9 births on the average,* but only 5.1 children survived to adulthood. This average masks some considerable disparities. Families died out because all their children were cut down in their infancy or youth. Others lost few or no children. Above all, there was a great number of second and third marriages, constituting some 20% of marriages contracted. Deaths and remarriages brought dynamics into the family, particularly through marriage or the departure of the children.

b. Men   Law and folklore combined to indicate the *preponderant position reserved for men* in the community between spouses. Article CCXXV of the *Coutume de Paris* made the husband "Lord over movable and immovable property." To this lord went all honours and all rights. He could dispose of the property of the community as he willed, even without the consent of his spouse. He could also dispose of the income from the personal property (separate estate) that his spouse had brought to the community. The only reservation concerned the impossibility of relinquishing the separate estate of his spouse without her consent.

If the woman who "took a husband" also "took a country," reality was less clear-cut. Many husbands delegated powers to their spouses by means of general and special powers of attorney signed in the presence of a notary. It was thus not rare that they had their wives represent them in court. Wives also had powers because of her responsibilities towards her children. The presence of the wife in court was most often related to family matters and the transmission of property. Lastly, whether it had to do with farmers or artisans, the family's source of income often took the form of a family enterprise in which each partner performed some of the tasks. But men, who came of age at 25, appeared to be undisputed masters, having the responsibility of respecting and treating properly those who depended on them.

c. Women   Women came of age at 25; but at that age, most of the time, they had already replaced the guardianship of their fathers by the not less heavy-handed one of husbands. In this legal system, women enjoyed only certain protections specified in the law or marriage agreements. They had the power to renounce the community when their spouses died if they judged that they would get from it for themselves and their children more debts than property. They also could claim their separate estates, the dowers promised by their husbands or the share (rightful) falling to them, that is what they possessed prior to marriage and a sum (dower, rightful or preference legacy) equivalent to about a year's income depending on their station or that of their spouses. On the death of her husband, a woman could also continue the community of property until her children came of age or until she remarried. She then exercised the rights previously devolved upon her husband. We have thus seen a few widows who were very active in business make a name for themselves in major economic enterprises. But this was rather the exception than the rule.

In the social sphere, *the wives acquired their husbands' status*; hence complex and varied marriage and family strategies in the choice of spouses as in the creation of social networks. Social practices in this regard were defined according to material considerations, which were guarantees at that time of harmonious social functioning; after that, love and sensitivities could be taken into account. An example among others: the engineer in chief of the colony, in charge of fortifications, provided each of his daughters with 10,000 livres as an advancement of part of their inheritance (the average salary of a qualified craftsman at that time varied from 360 to 500 livres) and gave nothing to his sons. He thus settled matters of inheritance in advance. The sons, however, took advantage of the education they had received, of their fathers connections and of the opportunities that he provided them with to begin the practice of their chosen professions. The father's action was no doubt intended to attract husbands of quality. He would have succeeded in marrying his daughters to men of a high social status that they would inevitably share. We thus see, in urban areas, a kind of *general exchange between families of the same social standing*. Everywhere else, in each rural community, similar considerations appeared to be taken into account in the forming of marital unions. Children of seigneurs, militia officers and tradesmen married among themselves. Unions were formed among people of the "first rank" or families of the "top of the plateau" rather than with those of the hinterland or of the foot of the seigneurie. However, the situation was the same for men and women. A young man residing on good riverside land could marry a daughter of a family settled on the less attractive lands of the interior and thus raise her to his own social station. But the reverse was not true. A girl who married a young man of lower social status would be likely to go down in the social ladder.

d. Widows and Widowers

A brief survey should now be given of the fate of widows and widowers. In New France in the 18th century *widowhood or widowerhood was frequently followed by a second marriage*. This even appears to have been encouraged by the civil and religious authorities. Family-centered enterprises, the dispersal of the settlement and the quasi-absence of villages would not have made it possible to create those places of sociability where a lonely individual would be able to survive through the rendering of small services to the community. Remarriage offered the simplest and most effective solution. Widows and widowers found new spouses rather easily. These were either unmarried persons or persons who had also lost their spouses. Despite the favour of the authorities, remarriage retained a particular nature in the minds of people. Depending on custom, widows sometimes remarried in the

parishes of their spouses rather than in their own. In almost half of the marriages involving a widow and a widower, the future spouses requested and
obtained a dispensal of banns, thus decreasing the attention surrounding their
union. Lastly, woe betide widowers who took too young a wife: they exposed
themselves to an uproarious hullabaloo.

e. Children   On the average, there were nine children per family, who were
born every 28 months; but barely one out of two survived to adulthood. There
were two mortality peaks in infancy: at birth or at the time of weening.
Epidemics also killed a good number of young people in certain localities and age
brackets, but never sufficiently to affect the demographic structure.

Children were always subject to a family-type authority, as indicated by the
fate reserved for foundlings. If the father died, a guardian and a deputy guardian
were appointed to look after the material, but also spiritual, interests of the
child. Observers of the period agree that their education was less strict than in
France. *The number of children who received an elementary education was
somewhat limited.* There even appears to have been a decline in literacy from
the 17th to the 18th century. Children were called upon very early, from the age
of 5 or 6, to participate in the family work, whether on the farm or in a shop.
When they reached the age of 15, they were considered to be capable of doing
work comparable that of adults, without necessarily being responsible for it.
The way in which boys were prepared for the life which awaited them is known
to some extent. Some began to clear the land that they would occupy and that
they sometimes already owned. Others went to learn a trade. A significant
number, impossible to determine in the present state of research, would try,
as we have seen, to build up a little nest egg by fishing or trading in furs.

In law as in mentalities, *equality among children appears to have been of
prime importance*. Parents were even strictly forbidden to attempt to favour
one child over another in the sharing out of property bequeathed. This egalitarian
attitude appears to have been so well accepted that even the sharing of plots of
land would sometimes be done by a drawing of lots in order to prevent any injustice and quarreling; which did not preclude compromises from time to time,
while at the same time maintaining the values of fairness, if not of equality, at
the end of the day. It was in this context that we must place the advancements
of parts of an inheritance given to girls when they married.

The legal system that provided for a strictly egalitarian sharing of property and assets after the death of parents probably served as the basis for the
social perception according to which equality reigned among *individuals who received equal chances at the outset*. In the main, fortunes were passed on to each
generation and, in each family, assets were shared out just about equally among
the children. In the absence of concentrations of wealth, whether movable or immovable, each had, so to speak, to recommence anew with very few vested
interests and assets and on the same footing with his brothers and sisters. The

system contained numerous loopholes and did not prevent the expression of family strategies. In addition, the initial social position, defined by the situation or the father's favour, clearly influenced the rest of the children's lives. Of course, good fortune, associated with skill, work and reputation, may have made it possible for some to rise rapidly in the social ladder. The majority, however, were obliged to live with the inertia and dilatoriness of the French hierarchy. Between this egalitarianism and this social organization into a hierarchy the destiny of each individual in New France was forged.

3. Social Structuring

The organization and functioning of society in the 18th century differed notably from the previous century. A certain oldness of the settlement—and especially its extension—favoured *the creation of more populated centres and, consequently, a tightening of the rules of life in society.* In absolute figures, the number of rural inhabitants quadrupled between 1690 and 1720. From that time on, there was more land being exploited and less attractive land to be cleared. Management and devolution of property methods became clearer. The colony's two urban areas, Quebec and Montreal, became cities in the true sense of the word. The offering of services such as education, law and hospitalization increased, but, above all, the urban area created its own needs and its own market. In the liberal professions, as among trades people, a system of competition was introduced. In these dense population centres, where the holders of political and economic power resided, the social strata were more sharply defined especially since New France experienced a long period of peace between 1713 and 1744.

The social spectrum was less open than in France. We find in the colony neither a higher clergy (except the bishop of Quebec), a nobility or great fortunes; at the other end of the spectrum free men had greater opportunities. Free from taxes (except for the rent) and tallage, the land was free and the achieving of the mastery in a trade remained accessible to all after 6 years of practice. A daughter of the Old World, this society adapted its structures to the New World.

In the image of the society of Old France, socio-professional groups enjoyed privileges or rights whose forms were inspired by those of the Middle Ages. The army, civil administration and religious communities in particular included a fair proportion of nobles. Traditional organizations into a hierarchy were accentuated there by the importance of the role of the State and of its administrative organization. *The context of a new country gave rise to a system of promotion* based on its new realities.

a. The Privileged   Nobles, military officers, officers of the civil administration and upper middle-class persons grown rich through business and favoured by the political authorities shared an altogether similar way of life. They formed unions with each other through marriage, benefitted from the granting of seigneurial land and held simultaneously offices, titles and functions.

Since the end of the 17th century, the colonial authorities of the colony no longer gave out patents of nobility to colonials who performed acts or exploits worthy of reward. The *nobility* was replenished only through immigration or renewed itself through its descendants, especially as venality of offices did not exist in the colony. It tended to decrease relatively as it mingled increasingly with the other groups. Moreover, since 1689, it could, without losing rank and title, engage in commerce and various non-manual activities. A stage was reached where it was no longer possible to differentiate it clearly from the other elements of the society's élite.

The army, in which the majority of the nobles were to be found, constituted *one of the most powerful levers of social advancement*. Even during the long period of peace, New France resembled an entrenched camp. Forts were built on the threatened frontiers, fortifications were erected at Quebec and Montreal, and an imposing fortress stood at Louisbourg. A chain of fortified posts, also serving as fur trading posts, was placed under the responsibility of military officers. These post commanders, installed on the borders of the French possessions, enjoyed many advantages. Their promotion depended no more on their rank or seniority than on their titles. The favour of the colonial authorities, and in particular that of the Governor, appeared to be of prime importance. As a consequence, their membership in the dominant class, the excellence of their relations with the Amerindian nations and therefore their ability to conduct commerce and share the income therefrom favoured their social elevation. From the 17th to the 18th century, the positions occupied by native-born Canadians in this sector increased considerably. Officers were increasingly recruited in the colony. Their numbers went from a third of the strength at the beginning of the 18th century to the quasi-totality of the colony's regular troops at the end of the French regime. In the absence of war, career-advancement was rather slow. A cadet took 10 years to become an ensign, 15 years to be promoted to the rank of lieutenant, while promotion to the rank of captain—5 years later— occurred a few years prior to discharge from the army. A certain number were afterwards decorated with the Croix de Saint-Louis, an honour which assured its holders a pensioner's pay.

The officers of the civil administration experienced a system rather similar to that of military officers. Those who held the highest positions came from France. Their sojourn in the colony often constituted only a stage in their career.

The clergy of the colony *had the very great respect* of the authorities as well as of the population. Quite uniformly educated, it exerted a profound influence on the faithful, even though *its temporal power appears to have been somewhat reduced*. Religious devotion seems to have been constant and deviant practices rare. In the 18th century, there was an insufficient number of priests to celebrate all the masses paid for by the population. On the one hand, the Bishop did not succeed in having the tithe increased from one twenty-sixth to one thirteenth, the collection rate fixed in France. There subsisted notable differences in conduct, value and prestige among the communities who recruited their members exclusively in France and those who admitted Canadians to their ranks. Canadians, although increasingly numerous, succeeded seldom and with difficulty in obtaining positions of trust and responsibility. On the other hand, the power of the Bishop over the religious communities and the regular clergy was strengthened. The successor of François de Laval, Mgr. de Saint-Vallier, took away from the *Séminaire des Missions Étrangères* the appointment of parish priests and the management of cures. In the 18th century, parish organization developed.

A final group succeeded in carving out an enviable place for itself at the head of the colonial hierarchy. It was composed of the merchants who had benefitted from the favours of the authorities, obtained a seigneurie and sometimes a position in the administrative hierarchy. The support of the authorities, and of the Intendant in particular, often contributed to ensuring financial success and encouraged the creation of a network of relationships. *Power, money and relationships combined to glorify with a certain prestige persons who had come to belong to the best society.* The historian Cameron Nish has defined them as *bourgeois gentilhommes* because of their degree of wealth, the positions they held concurrently, their relationships and their way of life. To their children, they sought less to bequeath assets than positions or titles in the military or civil administration: this was the means of making membership in a dominant group permanent.

b. Notables Notables emerged as the colony's population increased: the local communities which came into being provided themselves with institutions which brought their incumbents a certain social superiority.

In the 18th century, *parish priests* became irremovable. They generally enjoyed the support of their congregations. Churches and presbyteries were quickly built despite occasional opposition concerning their cost and location. Parish priests had supreme control of temporal power, since the fabric and the churchwardens were completed devoted to them. Nevertheless, the Bishop sometimes had to intervene in order to improve the ordinary and have sacred vases of quality bought. The *churchwardens* were chosen by and from among the notables. They belonged to the leading families and the majority of them, born in the parish, had lived there for at least ten years and had a family of at least 5 children and more at the time of their election. Their education was not very different from that of the common people since only 20% of them could sign their name. However, but there was no doubt about their material wealth. They offered a dower or left property higher than one-third of the average. *Geographical stability, family network, relative wealth and irreproachable morality earned them the respect of the community of the faithful.*

The parish priest/churchwarden couple had its counterpart on the civil sphere in the *seigneur*, or his representative, and the *miller*. Even though three-quarters of the seigneurs did not reside in their seigneuries, they built a manor house on them, often of imposing dimensions, where their tenants had to go and pay feudal dues. In the 17th century, the unstable miller lived poorly from the service that the seigneur offered to his tenants. In the 18th century, the practice of the trade improved. The miller established greater permanence in the trade as well as in localization. Often more competent, he owned more property. Defined at the outset as a service to rural dwellers, his professional activity came more to resemble an urban-type commercial enterprise. The best millers, in the manner of business people, leased the construction and operation of the mill. Most of them knew how to write, and a number of them formed marriage unions with business people, thus forming a small local notability.

In a country like Canada, the *militia* played an important role. During periods of armed conflict, and particularly in the 18th century, it provided the colony with protection. Often led by former officers of the regular troops, it grouped, in theory, all able-bodied men from 16 to 60. They were subjected to periodic drills and participated, fifteen days a year, in fortification work. The militia officer who led them belonged to the rural community and maintained few relationships with urban dwellers. In the 18th century, the Intendants increasingly made them local agents of their authority, charging them with circulating their ordinances and having them complied with and managing the building of roads and bridges. The militia officer had the same education as the mass of the habitants. He stood apart from them through his seniority in the community, his family relationships and an enviable economic position. In the 18th century, the militia officer was less characterized by his military qualities than by his characteristics of notable. He could flaunt a certain social success and his average age, 55, offered guarantees of experience, maturity and credibility which made of him a natural intermediary between the population and the administrators of the colony.

c. *Range of Small Trades*

As a result of their level of wealth, way of life and limited social aspirations, *the farmers and craftsmen had comparable social status. Opportunities for social promotion were few*. A bad harvest or a year of famine, as occurred on about twenty occasions between 1700 and 1750, dampened hopes and slowed progress. A little luck, a lot of work on the land or in the shop made it possible for them to bequeath a little property to their children. In the towns, almost half of the craftsmen owned their homes, which included a shop. The other half lived from day labour. In the country, although the habitants were the owners of their land and a few of them could build up a modest surplus, almost half lived in debt and in an almost complete state of destitution. One out of every other child had to start out where his father or grandfather had begun, by clearing the forest.

At the bottom of the social ladder, the soldiers, enlisted men and the young men on apprenticeship divided their time between the hope of better days and acceptance of fate. The Indians, for their part, were subjected to the pressures of French policy. Living on reservations or urged to hunt, more or less subjected to the quest for French material goods, destroyed by epidemics and alcohol, subjected to the policy of alliances of the Europeans, they ceased seeing the Europeans as brothers and defined themselves as their children.

4. Social Reproduction In this nascent society and expanding territory, *hopes of social promotion were still permitted* and they remained deeply rooted. The myth of the New World and of its wealth lived on. Observers of this period, the civil or religious authorities and visitors, did not fail to mention as a common mental characteristic *the tendency to "raise oneself up."* Everywhere was observed this affection of dressing up or believing oneself to be of a title or rank higher than was actually the case. Ordinary priests did not consider themselves to be inferior to canons when it was not the bishop. A number of bourgeois appropriated the title of master. In the industrial sectors of shipbuilding or the forges of Saint-Maurice, workers aspired to the mastery, shop foremen considered themselves to be as competent as the builder in chief. The day labourer declared himself to be an artisan, the artisan described himself as a specialized worker, the latter saw himself as a foreman, the carpenter claimed to be a builder, the stoker thought himself to be a caster and the mason defined himself as an architect. As for the farmer, we know that he would accept no other title than that of habitant. Even domestics, wrote an observer, reacted "indignantly" to the requests of their masters. The honorific epithet or the rank that was exhibited symbolized social aspirations.

These pretensions exemplified a certain perception of social reality. Only a very small number would win at this lottery in the 18th century, but it would not be for want of having tried. One of the most prominent characteristics of the society of New France was *mobility*: geographical, professional—indeed social.

The reasons for this mobility do not always appear to be positive. Some production sectors soon became saturated and many people such as leather workers, for example, sacrificed years of apprenticeship and acquired skills to turn to other more promising areas of activity. Thus the workers of the Saint-Maurice forges often came from outside the Government of Trois-Rivières and their former trade had no connection with the forge.

Mobility was not less great in rural areas. Of course, the historiography of New France emphasized the image of the farmer permanently attached to the soil and passing on his land to his children. *Every other child was one too many: to prevent the splitting up of the land, he had to leave the paternal property* and frequently the locality of his birth in order to find enough to live on elsewhere and start a family. Likewise, farmer families consisting of several adult children abandoned a cleared plot in order to acquire more extensive lands in *new areas of colonization*. Forty percent of the habitants who made up these new communities were composed of these large families; as for the rest, they were mostly young men, either recently married, or attracted by the opportunity of contracting a marriage in the area.

This social dynamic is observed at all levels of society. The senior officials of the colony's administration did not remain long in their posts. The authorities were appointed by the King or his Minister. In the colony, the positions giving access to wealth depended on the favour of the Intendant or the Governor.

Dependence on the authorities in place did not encourage tenure of status and function. Great fortunes generally appear to be of short duration. They were rarely transmitted from generation to generation.

The society of New France in the 18th century appeared to partake of two movements, two value systems, two social models. On the one hand, the legal bases of the social functioning, reinforced by the importance of the political, military, economic and administrative role of the State, favoured *an almost total transplantation of the French model* defining the station of persons. Adaptation to the new demographic and geographical context led to the introduction of new rules of social interplay: *the society was "canadianized"* and became aware of its differences.

The social élite, which obtained positions of trust and responsibility, still came mainly from France. Its presence was frequently of short duration. The sojourn in the colony constituted only a stage in a career plan which was resolutely France-oriented. But in order to meet the new challenges that adapting to the New World posed, nobles worked hard, commoners obtained seigneuries, merchants were given administrative responsibilities. The members of this apparently disparate élite formed close ties through marriage. They formed a group that was not hermetically closed, to be sure, but which was marked by a specific social identity. The mass of the population, from the apprentice to the master or from the enlisted man to the habitant, participated in the same collective destiny. The chances of rising considerably in the social hierarchy were rather slender. People did not, so to speak, leave their stations. This did not prevent claims from being asserted or living conditions from changing.

CHAPTER

3 BUSINESS AND PRIVATE ENTERPRISE IN NEW FRANCE

For a variety of reasons, the history of business and private enterprise in New France has, until quite recently, been largely ignored. In part this was because, up to about twenty-five years ago, the field of Canadian business history itself was still in its infancy. Historians of New France therefore tended to focus primarily on more traditional issues, such as imperial relations, government policy, institutional structures, the European-Amerindian interaction, the Church and the military.

For many years, too, the study of private enterprise in New France was looked upon almost as a contradiction in terms. From the perspective of Francis Parkman, the nineteenth-century American historian whose works on New France dominated the field well into the twentieth century, colonial enterprise was not at all free. In his view, the authoritarian, mercantilistic policies of absolutist France stifled individual business initiative in the colony to the point of suffocation. What barely existed could hardly be analysed.

The reinterpretation of the place of business in New France began in a major way during the 1930s and 1940s, with the emergence of the University of Montreal "nationalist" school of historians led by Maurice Séguin, Guy Frégault, and Michel Brunet. Indebted to their mentor, Abbé Lionel Groulx, the greatest concern of these men was to affirm the existence of a dynamic, locally-based *"bourgeoisie"* in New France, and that entailed demonstrating the economic vitality, real and potential, of the colony. Far from damning successive French administrations, *à la* Parkman, for heavy-handed interference in the business affairs of New France, the Montreal school attributed much of the colony's growth to initiatives by the state, and criticized it for not doing more to promote colonial enterprise.

The counter-school of historians from Laval University, headed by Jean Hamelin and Fernand Ouellet, disagreed fundamentally with the idea that the economy of New France was sufficiently strong and diversified to support an indigenous bourgeoisie. Only the fur trade, Hamelin argued, was capable of generating sustained profits, and for most of New France's existence those profits were drained out of the colony to France. On the matter of the impact of the state on business in New France, the Laval historians were closer to their Montreal rivals, agreeing that government initiatives were often responsible for what economic development did take place, although, less sanguine about the economic possibilities of the day, they were also less inclined to blame the state for failing to do more.

The debate over the nature of society and the economy of New France goes on, energized in the last decade by the Marxist analyses of a younger generation of historians and political scientists. For individuals like Gérald Bernier and Vinh Ta Van, the question at issue is the extent to which pre-capitalist and/or capitalist modes of production had penetrated the colony's essentially feudal society by the time of the Conquest.

Contributing to the debate, too, were other historians who examined in detail the business system itself. Two such studies are presented here. Together they demonstrate the complexity of the private-enterprise world of New France. The first, by Dale Miquelon, provides an overview of New France's role in the French imperial, mercantilistic economy in the eighteenth century. The second reading is a chapter from Michael Bliss's history of Canadian business, *Northern Enterprise*. Both of these articles address the three central questions posed about business and private enterprise in New France: what were the strengths and weaknesses of the business system? What impact did the state have on private enterprise, and *vice versa*? To what extent was the business system a creature of France rather than of New France?

Suggestions for Further Reading

Bernier, G., "Sur quelques effets de la rupture structurelle engendrée par la Conquête au Québec: 1760–1854," *Revue d'histoire de l'Amérique française*, 35, no. 1 (juin 1981), 69–95.

Bosher, J., "A Quebec Merchant's Trading Circles in France and Canada: Jean-André Lamaletie before 1763," *Histoire sociale / Social History*, IX, no. 19 (May 1977), 24–44.

————, "Government and Private Interests in New France," *Canadian Public Administration*, X, no. 2 (1967), 244–257.

Brunet, Michel, *La présence anglaise et les Canadiens*. Montréal: Beauchemin, 1964.

Frégault, Guy, *La société canadienne sous le régime français*. Ottawa: Société historique du Canada, 1954.

Hamelin, Jean, *Economie et Société en Nouvelle-France*. Québec: Les Presses de l'Université Laval, 1960.

Miquelon, Dale, *Dugard of Rouen: French Trade to Canada and the West Indies, 1729–1770*. Montreal: McGill-Queen's University Press, 1978.

————, "Havy and Lefebvre of Quebec: A Case Study of Metropolitan Participation in Canadian Trade, 1730–60," *Canadian Historical Review*, LVI, no. 1 (March 1975), 1–24.

Nish, Cameron, *Les Bourgeois-gentilshommes de la Nouvelle-France, 1729–1748.* Montréal: Fides, 1968.

Ouellet, Fernand, *Histoire économique et sociale du Québec, 1760–1850.* Montréal: Fides, 1966.

Parkman, Francis, *The Old Regime in Canada.* London: Macmillan, 1899.

Pritchard, J., "Commerce in New France," in *Canadian Business History*, ed. D. Macmillan. Toronto: McClelland & Stewart, 1972.

————, "The Vogage of the *Fier*: An Analysis of a Shipping and Trading Venture to New France, 1724–1728," *Histoire sociale / Social History*, IV, no. 11 (April 1973), 75–97.

Reid, A.G., "General Trade Between Quebec and France During the French Regime," *Canadian Historical Review*, XXXIV, no. 1 (March 1953), 18–32.

Séguin, Maurice, "La Conquête et la vie économique des Canadiens," *L'Action Nationale*, XXVIII, no. 4 (1946).

Ta Van, Vinh, "La Nouvelle France et la Conquête: Passage du Féodalisme au Capitalisme," *Cahiers d'histoire de l'Université de Montréal*, II, no. 2 (1982), 3–25.

CANADA'S PLACE IN THE FRENCH IMPERIAL ECONOMY: AN EIGHTEENTH-CENTURY OVERVIEW

Dale Miquelon

In 1702 the French geographer, Guillaume Delisle, wrote of "The utility that the different nations of Europe established in America have drawn from that land." This usefulness made America important and it had become "as it were, a supplement to Europe." This designation, "A Supplement to Europe," seems to me to encapsulate in a true and striking manner the eighteenth-century French response to Canada, or for that matter to Africa or Asia.[1]

Canada was a part of the French Empire from the early seventeenth century until 1763. This imperial connection was the result of the spontaneous and unorchestrated activities of fishermen and merchants and of the directive activity of the French state. Statesmen and businessmen, theoreticians and men of action, all assumed that Canada existed for the benefit of France and not for its own self-realization. The relevant economic theory was mercantilism. The economy was one of primary production, and the engine that drove that economy was imperial trade. The royal manna of expenditures for provisioning, garrison pay, and the building of fortifications was from time to time scattered upon the grateful colony and late in the day came to rival and even surpass the short-run

From *French Historical Studies*, XV, no. 3 (Spring 1988), 432–443. Reprinted by permission of *French Historical Studies*.

importance of trade. From the voluminous evidence, the following paragraphs tease out three strands that give some idea of "Canada's Place." These are, first, mercantilist thinking within the Ministry of Marine; second, the developing economy of trade and military spending within the Empire; and third, the impact upon Canada of changes in the nature of trade and in levels of military spending.

Jérôme de Pontchartrain, the Minister of Marine who presided over Canada's destiny from 1699 to 1715, took office as a young man. His youthful openness and desire to do his work well disarm us at the same time as his penchant for solving all questions with mercantilist axioms warns us of his unpromising pedantry. This is especially clear in the letters exchanged between Pontchartrain and his old teacher, Vauban. Upon one of the marshal's letters on Canada, Pontchartrain pencilled what would become the refrain of his administration: "Would cost a lot," "great expense," "expense."[2] To Vauban's lyrical description of "the colonies of Canada" the young minister rejoindered with ill grace: "The worst of all. One gets nothing from them; they cost a lot, etc."[3]

In common with Colbertists before and after him, Pontchartrain encouraged the production of naval stores in Canada and even the building of ships, because these helped to lessen French dependence on the Baltic countries. Nor was he exceptional in worrying about Canada's overdependence upon the failing fur staple and in his desire for Canadian economic diversification. When he writes to Canadian administrators of the "idleness and sloth of the inhabitants that prevent this colony from being peopled," or directs an Intendant to encourage trade, "which enriches the people and draws them from an idleness that is often the cause of many misfortunes," we easily recognize the mercantilist faith in the nostrum of trade and the view of the peasantry espoused by mercantilist administrators, confronting and offended by the nonchalance of a pre-industrial workforce.[4]

Pontchartrain differed from Colbert and many others by his opposition to the notion of colonial self-sufficiency, which seemed to him contrary to the economic *raison d'être* of empire. But we do find development in Pontchartrain's thought and deviations from theory that are arresting, given the definitive character of his dicta, which sketch out a most doctrinaire mercantilism. During the War of the Spanish Succession, when there was little money to spare in Marine coffers, he sent two potters and a spinner to Canada and authorized an annual gratuity for a Montreal woman who had established a weaving manufacture. Two years running, he warned the Canadian Intendant against permitting colonial manufactures, only to add, "This ought to be the general view; however, their establishment in Canada ought not to be absolutely prevented, especially among the poor."[5]

The minister also gave a very limited acceptance to the idea of the multilateral benefits of empire. For him the most important model of empire remained that of a series of bilateral trade relations between the mother country and each colony. His restrictive views on intercolonial trade were challenged by the altered circumstances imposed by the war. Although Pontchartrain had long feared that the colonies if left to their own devices would exchange sugar and flour, cutting into the trade of the French Atlantic ports, he nevertheless, in 1708, in the midst of war, recommended the abolition of duties levied in Martinique on Canadian produce. He had come to see that, as in the case of shipbuilding, colonial supply of flour could prevent dependence upon foreigners. Indeed, in the following year he was even willing to permit foreign ships to carry foreign flour to the West Indies. French merchants, he wrote, would starve the colonists rather than renounce their monopoly or starve the kingdom to make scarcity profits in the West Indies. But a minister had to guarantee the subsistence of both Frenchmen and colonials. Here is the mercantilist dilemma. The colonists, Pontchartrain pointed out, "are not of a more lowly condition than others that they should be so roughly treated."[6] As far as Canada was concerned, he drew attention to the weakness of its agricultural economy, but hoped that the colony could be a point of supply in years of emergency.

The supply problems of the war years (1702–13) had made Canada appear the natural provisioner of the Newfoundland colony of Plaisance (now Placentia, Newfoundland), although Pontchartrain had also called Acadia to that role in 1707. At that time he had fretted that the self-sufficiency and surplus production necessary to make his own plan work were "entirely contrary to the general principle of colonies, which is to draw all their needs from the state."[7] Impressed by Canada's ability to feed Plaisance, Pontchartrain, after the war, specifically assigned Canada the task of provisioning the new colony of Ile Royale. The Governor and Intendant were instructed "to leave navigation between Québec and Ile Royale entirely free."[8] Under the stress of war, Pontchartrain had learned that economic theory was useful only to the extent that it served the needs of the state.

Pontchartrain's son, Frédéric de Maurepas, who was Minister of Marine from 1723–1749, was no less a mercantilist than his father or Colbert. Of the essential continuity of policy, there is no better evidence than the Letters Patent of 1727 that reiterated legislation of 1670, 1698, and 1720 prohibiting foreigners from trading within the Empire. Maurepas' attention was particularly drawn to Canada because in order to enforce the Letters Patent of 1727 some substitute for the illegal trade of the French West Indies with the English colonies had to be found. The department's outward correspondence during the Maurepas years abounds with exhortations that intercolonial trade be stepped up. In particular, Maurepas hoped that the shipment of Canadian wood, flour, peas, and horses to Martinique in return for molasses and rum would replace the illegal trade of the island with New England. Tariff exemptions were provided to encourage the desired traffic. The *pacte coloniale* had become unabashedly multilateral.

Maurepas expressed sympathy with deregulation provided that it was in the framework of the imperial system, as is evident from two of his directives: "Regulation should be occasional, temporary, and only when absolutely needed";

and "Encouragement is the only method that can be used, and success waits upon time and the industry of men."[9] Of course, the Canadian fur trade remained tightly regulated, and antipathy to regulation did not imply any liberal *angst* concerning intervention in general. Canadian shipbuilding and even iron mining and smelting were subsidized. Sealing and fur trading concessions remained the gift of the Crown.

Between 1699 and the early 1720s Canada's place had evolved in official thinking from that of a supplier of furs and a few incidental staples to the mother country to being also an emergency supplier of provisions and wood to Plaisance and the West Indies. Subsequently it was the designated provisioner of Louisbourg and was also much encouraged to maintain a brisk and regular trade to Martinique and St. Domingue, even in peacetime. Certain Canadian manufactures were at first tolerated to sustain the poor, then encouraged to diversify the economy, and (in the case of ships and bar iron) to make up for metropolitan deficiencies. Both Pontchartrain and Maurepas came to understand that the Canadian economy had to be diversified, and Maurepas (by accepting the advice of the Canadian Intendant, Gilles Hocquart) thought it also had to be capitalized and given some degree of autonomous direction by the development of colonial entrepreneurs.[10]

In 1701 Louis XIV determined that Canada, with its fur trade, could be useful to the Empire in a political rather than an economic sense by binding the interior tribes to itself and thereby keeping the English out of the North American interior. It was only after the Peace of Utrecht (1713) that the garrisoning of posts in the Great Lakes hinterland and an improving fur trade gave substance to this imperial plan. On Lake Ontario a deficitary trade with strategically important Indians was maintained for *raison d'état*, and after 1744 much money and effort were expended to use Canada as a bulwark against British expansionism—witness Governor de La Galissonière's famous question, "We ask if a country can be abandoned ... when by its position it affords a great advantage over its neighbours?"[11] Yet it is remarkable that the Ministry of Marine persisted in thinking of Canada in mercantilist fashion as a colony that, with the regrettable exception of wartime, ought to pay its way. There are indubitable touches of liberalism in administrative documents (as for example when the Bureau de Commerce in supporting iron mining and smelting suggested that the competition would be good for the French iron industry[12]); nevertheless, in general one can say that the conception of Canada's place in the imperial economy remained always mercantilistic, although this mercantilism became increasingly practical, supple, and even generous.

The link between colonial production and the Empire was shipping, and we can learn much from contractions, expansions, and changes in the general pattern of ship movements. From a plateau in the 1680s and 1690s, Québec-France trade declined sharply in the first two decades of the eighteenth century, recovered to its old level in the 1720s and 1730s, and experienced an abrupt increase in the 1740s. Traffic bottomed out in 1709–13 and peaked in 1729–36 and after 1740. In the 1690s La Rochelle, although sharing the Québec trade with Bordeaux, nevertheless enjoyed an ascendency that it never recovered thereafter. It met stiff competition from other French ports with little previous experience in Canadian trade (notably Rouen) in the 1720s and 1730s and in the 1740s was supplanted by Bordeaux.[13] Québec-France traffic was only part of the story, but it does provide us with a base upon which a total picture can be built. So what is the total picture?

Quite clearly, we are observing a reflection of the fur trade—the staple production that linked colony and metropolis. These statistics mirror the collapse of the beaver market beginning in the later 1690s, compounded by French failure to control the sea in the War of the Spanish Succession, the slow growth after 1710 of a restructured European market absorbing greater quantities of furs other than beaver, and the stabilization of the trade from a point in the 1720s.[14] But there is more to this than a simple return to business as it had been in the "good old days," something which is indicated by the participation of so many new competitors among the French ports after 1720. Canada traditionally suffered from a trade deficit, its growing population demanding a greater value in imports than the fur staple could buy. The result was a chronic pool of debt and the large place among Canadian exports of much capital in the form of bills of exchange founded primarily in the French government's expenditures in Canada. A large part of this fiduciary paper represented the cost of maintaining garrisons and building fortifications. This "invisible export" explains why the imbalance of trade was not invariably disastrous. But in the 1730s and 1740s the trade deficit declined dramatically—1739 and 1741 were in fact years of trade surplus—and bills of exchange constituted an ever smaller part of exports.[15] Behind this was economic diversification and, in fact, a new role in imperial trade.

Canada's new role had its roots in the Empire's wartime difficulties. While traditional trades stagnated and the price of wheat fell steadily, the Empire was unable to supply Plaisance and Martinique with provisions.[16] Canadians were first attracted to the sea by the lure of these two markets and by the promise of even greater profits from privateering. Of the latter, Governor Vaudreuil remarked that there was not "a more glorious nor a more suitable way to occupy youth."[17] In 1704 Canadian private enterprise built its first ship, the *Joybert*. During the war, Canadian ships made several voyages to Martinique, but Plaisance was the ideal market for Canadian entrepreneurs with small ships and little capital. When Plaisance was lost to Great Britain (1713) and replaced by Ile Royale, with its capital of Louisbourg, Canadians continued to play their new role at the new port.[18] At first this trade in provisions and lumber grew slowly, but it abruptly doubled in 1727. In that same year, the trade to Martinique, carried on by both French and Canadian shippers, also burst into life. The triangular trade, idealized by many mercantilists, had become a reality.

Without Louisbourg (for which Plaisance was the model and the miniature), triangular trade would not have been possible. Louisbourg helped by providing *entrepôt* facilities, enabling some Canadian shippers to specialize in bringing cargo to Louisbourg, while other West Indian or French shippers carried it to the Caribbean. But much more important was the new opportunity to sell Canadian cargoes of biscuit and rough flour to the soldier-fisherman population centred at Louisbourg and with the proceeds to buy dried cod. This was added to cargoes of Canadian wood and grain destined for the West Indies, making them more valuable and more saleable than they would otherwise have been. The return for Canadians was not West Indian produce—there was a limit to the amount of rum and molasses Canadians could consume—but rather credits to shore up the deficitary trade with France.[19] The last and most considerable increase of all in Québec-France traffic—the increase after 1740—is possibly a deceptive statistic. To a great extent it reflects a massive import of flour and war *matériel* into Canada and, far from being a healthy sign of an expanding commerce, is an indication of the final submergence of New France's economic role within the Empire by its military and strategic role. The place of fiduciary paper in Canada's exports expanded once again as military spending increased to unprecedented levels and as the new trades suffered from war on the high seas as well as from difficulties of production and marketing.

So far, we have not got much closer to the colony than to observe from an Olympian distance the arrival and departure of vessels from its shores. We have yet to see from the inside how the colony was responding to the exigencies of empire. Fur remained the pre-eminent export and earner of purchasing power. The fur trade, which dovetailed with the military and strategic needs to support far-flung alliances with Indians and to keep Anglo-Americans out of the Great Lakes and Mississippi basins, maintained Canada's link with the forest and the Indian and their imponderable influence.[20] The garrisoning of the western posts and the emoluments of the officer corps that directed them were paid for by the fur trade, which thus was charged with providing economic rents in addition to businessmen's profits. In this instance, then, the military establishment, which is usually seen as making an economic contribution to Canada, absorbed Canadian resources at least commensurate with the protection it afforded the trade. In the final analysis, the Empire failed the fur trade. It either could not absorb all the beaver produced or it could not absorb it at an appropriate price. As a result, countless bundles of beaver made the journey from Montréal to Albany, even after the revival of French demand, and hence to absorption in another imperial market.

As we have seen, in the eighteenth century, Canada was able to profit from the demand for agricultural exports in other parts of the Empire. Census figures for 1723 show a large increase in the area of land under cultivation.[21] One should not squeeze an Old Regime statistic too hard, but we can take this as a symbolic date. More and more land was put to the plough, especially in the 1730s. Prices were better and price swings were more contained. Increasing numbers of sawmills (ten in 1710, seventy in 1739) produced more and more lumber, the invariable companion to provisions in the new trades. New sealing posts along the coast of Labrador, over half of them established in the 1730s, added seal oil to Canada's outbound cargoes. Shipbuilding experienced a "take-off" in 1724, and ships became important items of export to balance imports. In 1738 the blast furnace at the St. Maurice Forges was lighted for the first time. Thus, responding to the needs of empire, Canada was moving beyond its fur-trade base and frontier beginnings. More spending power, more European goods, a more sedentary and Europeanized lifestyle were the results.

Yet the brave new world of the 1720s and 1730s came apart. In 1736 and 1737 there were disastrous crop failures, and the poor crop of 1741 was followed by failures in 1742 and 1743. The new trades collapsed. Indeed, Canada was already being muscled out of the Louisbourg and West Indian markets by Anglo-American shippers with a much more reliable hinterland and shorter ocean crossings. Canadian industries without markets and without food for workers came to a standstill. The Canadian agricultural sector was simply too small, in too tricky a climate, and too distant from its markets to be counted on year after year. As François Havy and Jean Lefebvre, two French merchants resident in Canada, observed, "If provisions are abundant for two or three years running, they become rare and dear for two or three years too."[22] And Canadian farmers were not really cash crop producers; rather, as most farmers in the eighteenth century, they were peasants disposing of modest surpluses. To link them to an export market really placed them on an economic frontier quite out of phase with their traditional outlook and technology. The Empire failed Canada by being unable to protect Canada's markets, whereas Canada failed the Empire by being unequal to the new role it had been called upon to play.

After 1744 Canada became preoccupied with and swallowed up in war. The plethora of military works brought considerable money into the country. Workshops buzzed with activity, and military contractors chalked up fat profits. But war was only profitable if its destruction could be kept at a distance and if trade continued in spite of it. Canada had experienced this good fortune from 1713 to 1744, but would not know it again until after 1815. Knowledgeable merchants were not deceived by glittering wartime profits. As Havy and Lefebvre wrote in the midst of war, "We need a good peace in order to be able to work solidly at increasing the trade of the country."[23]

The impetus for Canadian economic development in the first half of the eighteenth century was external—imperial, but also more than imperial. It finds its origin in what many French historians, following François Simiand, call a "phase A" movement of rising prices and plentiful money. This is the context of prosperity that affected Canada through the revival of French trade in Europe and on many seas and also through the French state's capacity to invest heavily in North America by establishing garrisons and small military works in Canada, and most particularly, by building the fortress of Louisbourg. This phase of Canada's experience is consistent with Canada's history throughout as a primary producer, sensitive—sometimes painfully so—to the vagaries of world markets from which mercantilist devices can provide only modest protection.

Notes

1. This quotation from Guillaume Delisle, "Des descouvertes qui ont été faites dans l'Amérique [1702]" in AN, Archives de la Marine (hereafter AM), Hydrographie, 2 JJ 57 (ex. 115[xi]) 12 E, has provided me with a title for a new general history, *New France, 1701–1744: "A Supplement to Europe"* (Toronto, McClelland and Stewart, "The Canadian Centenary Series," 1987). The series attempts to do for Canadian history what W. L. Langer's "The Rise of Modern Europe" series did for European history, consolidating the extant historiography and enriching it with new documentary research. This essay, read at the Society for French Historical Studies meeting in Minneapolis in March, 1987, presents a theme from the book that the author hopes is of interest to the non-Canadianist. As is evident from the notes, this branch of the history of New France remains indebted to the great strides made in the field in the 1970s. Current work, which still resists generalization, is concentrated to a considerable extent in agricultural history, historical demography, and the social aspects of economic development.

2. Louise Dechêne, ed., *La Correspondance de Vauban relative au Canada* (Québec, 1968), 26–27, marginalia to Vauban à Pontchartrain, Lille, 7 jan. 1699.

3. Ibid.

4. AN, Archives des Colonies (hereafter AC), B, vol. 34 pt. 1, fol. 15, mémoire du roi aux Vaudreuil et Bégon, Marly, 15 juin 1712; ibid. vol. 78, ministre à Bégon, Marly, 27 juin 1712.

5. AN, AC, B, vol 27, pt. 3, fol. 231, ministre à Raudot, Versailles, 9 juin 1706 at fol. 235. On Pontchartrain's ideas on self-sufficiency and interdependence, see ibid., vol. 24, fol. 20. "Mémoire pour servir d'instruction au Comte Denos choisis par le roy pour commander dans les Isles Françoises," Marly, 9 fév. 1701; ibid., fol. 236, Pontchartrain à Galiffet, Versailles, 7 déc. 1701; ibid., AC, B, vol. 20, fol. 22, Pontchartrain à Villebon, Versailles, 26 mars 1698.

6. AN, AC, B, vol. 31, fol. 515, ministre à D'Aguesseau, 27 sept. 1709, the last of a number of letters from Pontchartrain to Vaucresson, Bégon, d'Aguesseau, and others that illuminate this question. For his original, doctrinaire position, see ibid., vol. 18, fol. 147, "Instruction que le Roy a ordonné estre ez mains du Sr. Robert," Fontainebleau, 12 oct. 1695 and ibid., vol. 23, fol. 62, mémoire du roi à Beauharnois, Versailles, 6 mai 1702.

7. Ibid., vol. 29, pt. 3, fol. 198, ministre à Goutins, Versailles, 30 juin 1707.

8. Ibid., vol. 35, pt. 3, fol. 274v, mémoire du roi aux Vaudreuil et Beauharnois, Versailles, 27 jan. 1713.

9. Ibid., vol. 50, fol. 160, ministre à Beauharnois, Versailles, 5 août 1727; Maurepas à Dupuy, 24 mai 1728. Marine policy during the Maurepas years can be grasped very nicely from the minister's correspondence with the Canadian Intendant Gilles Hocquart in AN, AC, B, vols. 53–88 and CIIA, vols. 51–89 (1729–1748). Whereas Jérôme de Pontchartrain's role in policy-making is abundantly clear from holograph letters and marginalia, Maurepas' is less certain. It is in the formal sense implying the minister's ultimate responsibility that we state such-and-such a policy to have been Maurepas'. The Letters Patent of 1727 and the earlier legislation they embody are in AN, AD vii 2a.

10. Capitalization is manifest in government grants to develop the Saint-Maurice forges and the government take-over of that industry and in the Crown's considerable investment in shipbuilding and the development of naval stores. A policy of developing a strong Canadian merchant class by government concessions and financial support is attributed to Intendant Hocquart in Donald J. Horton, "Gilles Hocquart, Intendant of New France, 1729–1748" (Ph.D. diss., McGill University, Montréal, 1974).

11. "Memoir on the French Colonies in North America, December, 1750," in *Documents Relative to the Colonial History of the State of New York,* ed. John R. Brodhead and Edward B. O'Callaghan (Albany, N.Y., 1858), X:220–32.

12. Quoted in Cameron Nish, *François-Etienne Cugnet: Entrepreneur et entreprises en Nouvelle-France* (Montréal, 1975), 59.

13. See James Pritchard, "The Pattern of French Colonial Shipping to Canada before 1760," *Revue française d'histoire d'outre-mer* 63 (1976): 189–210. See also Pritchard, "Ships, Men, and Commerce: A Study of Maritime Activity in New France" (Ph.D. diss., University of Toronto, 1971), 488–96.

14. Little work has been done on beaver marketing. It is not clear whether demand for smaller hats in the 1690s reduced the market or whether smaller unit size was compensated for by greater volume. It is also not clear whether improvement in the general market in the 1720s resulted from a radical restructuring of demand, with non-beaver supplanting beaver, or from a more moderate restructuring, with non-beaver adding to a reviving sale of beaver. It is possible that the sale of a good proportion of beaver may have been masked by its being redirected from Paris to London by smuggling through New York.

15. The dramatic reduction in drafts is evident in the accounts of Havy and Lefebvre, merchants of Québec. See my *Dugard of Rouen: French Trade to Canada and the West Indies, 1729–1770* (Montréal, 1978), 81. This microscopic examination of a single firm is complimented by John Bosher's numerous studies in French merchant history, most recently, *The Canada Merchants, 1713–1763* (Oxford, 1987). A table of best estimates of the balance of trade drawn from the correspondence between Hocquart (AC, C11A) and Maurepas (AC, B) has long been conveniently available in A. Jean E. Lunn, "Economic Development in New France, 1713–1760" (Ph.D. diss., McGill University, Montréal, 1942), now published in French as *Développement économique de la Nouvelle-France, 1713–1760* (Montréal, 1986).

16. See the graph of Québec City wheat prices in Jean Hamelin, *Economie et société en Nouvelle-France* (Québec, 1960), 61.

17. AN, AC, C11A, vol. 21, fol. 54V, Vaudreuil à Pontchartrain, 4 nov. 1703.

18. The role of Placentia, easily overlooked, is considered in F. J. Thorpe, "Fish, Forts, and Finance," Canadian Historical Association *Historical Papers* (1971), 52–64, and Pritchard, "Ships, Men, and Commerce."

19. On the importance of the Louisbourg market to Canada, see AN, AC, C11A, vol. 62, fol. 77, Hocquart au ministre, Québec, 11 oct. 1734; ibid., vol. 63, fol. 73, "Réponse au mémoire du roy, Québec, 13 Oct. 1735"; ibid., vol. 65, fol. 28, "Réponse au mémoire du roy, 1736." On the geographical, climatological, and attitudinal difficulties of Canada-West Indies trade, see AN, AC, C8A, vol. 39, fol. 337–372, "Mémoire sur le service des Isles du vent de l'Amérique, 6 xbre 1728," Versailles; ibid., vol. 56, fol. 110, "Eclaircisments données [*sic*] à M. De Ranches par M. de la Croix"; AN, AC, C8B, vol. 3, "Mémoire de Vaucresson, 25 jan. 1713." On the advantages offered by Louisbourg, see AN, AC, C8A, vol. 42, fol. 245, d'Orgeville au ministre, Fort-Royal, 2 sept. 1731; AN, AC, C11A, vol. 69, fol. 243, Hocquart au ministre, Québec, 2 oct. 1738; ibid., vol. 79, fol. 319, idem à idem, Québec, 8 oct. 1743. On purchase of French goods with trade credits, see AN, AC, C11A, vol. 61, fol. 65, "Réponse au mémoire du roy, Québec, 7 oct. 1734"; ibid., vol. 76, fol. 187, "Mémoire sur le commerce de Canada, 1741"; AN, AC, C8A, vol. 53, fol. 411, De La Croix au ministre, 28 déc. 1741.

20. The signal importance of strategic considerations and not just economic ones in explaining the French presence in the North American interior has become a commonplace among New France historians. The thesis is most particularly associated with the works of W. J. Eccles, *The Canadian Frontier, 1534–1760* (New York, 1969; Albequerque, 1974) and *France in America* (New York, 1972). The story of smuggling is told in T. E. Norton, *The Fur Trade in Colonial New York, 1686–1776* (Madison, 1974). The fortunes of the French fur trade can be glimpsed in the problematical records of fur traders going west (see Gratien Allaire, "Les Engagements pour la traite des fourrures—évaluation de la documentation," *Revue d'histoire de l'Amérique française* 34 (1980): 3–26 or of the movement of furs from Canada to France (see Tom Wien, "Castor, peaux, et pelleteries dans le commerce canadien des fourrures, 1720–1790," in *"Le Castor fait tout": Papers of the Fifth North American Fur Trade Conference,* ed. B. Trigger, L. Dechéne, and T. Morantz (Montréal, 1987).

21. AN, AC G[1,] Recensements, vols. 460–61. Mercantilist administrators understood the value of statistics, including censuses. Estimates of harvests and of exports, tables of prices, and numerous economic ordinances are to be found in AN, AC C11A-C11G as well as AC G[1] and other series. Canadian historians continue to cite the copious tables in Lunn, *Développement économique,* drawn from this material, which have not been superseded.

22. AN, AC, C8A, vol. 55, fol. 340, Havy et Lefebvre à de La Croix, Québec, 30 mai 1743 (copy).

23. Public Archives of Canada, Collection Baby, fols. 829–833, à Pierre Guy, 19 mai 1746.

DOING BUSINESS IN NEW FRANCE

Michael Bliss

It is sometimes still believed that French colonial policy deliberately retarded the economic development of New France. Suppose that the point of having colonies was to accumulate wealth in the mother country through importing cheap raw materials and exporting expensive manufactured products. Surely, then, colonies existed to export raw resources and import finished products? In such a framework colonial production should remain primitive, lest it compete effectively with the metropolis. In the 1730s Barthélemy Cotton, an enterprising employee of the fur-exporting company in New France (the Compagnie des Indes), began making and selling beaver hats locally. He and a former apprentice, Joseph Huppé, became the principal hatters in Quebec and Montreal respectively, supplying the local market and even exporting semi-finished hats to France. Although the colonials were only making a few hundred hats a year, the Minister of Marine ordered their business closed. At Huppé's Montreal shop, "Au Chapeau Royale," the royal officials smashed his basins and his dyeing and fulling vats and carried off the rest of his equipment to the king's storehouse. The infant hat-making industry of New France, perhaps one of the most "natural" directions in which fur trading could have evolved, was literally destroyed by French fiat. It seems a clear case of French mercantilism stifling the entrepreneurial energies and opportunities of the Canadians.

The crushed hatters were a notorious, but isolated case, in which the real issue was probably the way they diverted furs rightfully belonging to the Compagnie des Indes. The real and constant French policy toward New France, implemented to the point of absurdity, was almost the reverse of doctrinaire specialization on primary products. Practical French officials believed the colony had to have a diversified economic base before it could build any kind of export capacity, that without greater exports it would continue to be a drain on the French treasury, and that almost anything it tried to export, other than furs, would obviously compete with the produce of France. They felt they had to try to stimulate growth anyway, and far from suppressing the entrepreneurial instincts of the Canadians, the king's officials in France and Canada did all they could to encourage colonial development. They supported and subsidized all kinds of wealth-creating schemes and complained bitterly when the Canadians failed to develop opportunities which seemed so alluring.

Jean Talon, the first Intendant of New France after the royal takeover of the colony in 1663, tried to implement Jean-Baptiste Colbert's aim of diversifying the economy. The officials founded and funded a host of enterprises. Talon tried

From *Northern Enterprise* by Michael Bliss (Toronto: McClelland and Stewart, 1987), 55–77. Reprinted by permission of the Canadian Publishers, McClelland and Stewart, Toronto.

to stimulate agriculture, shipbuilding, mining, fishing, local manufacturing of leather, beer, shoes, and other consumer goods, and the export of almost everything, both to France and to the French sugar islands in the Caribbean. Talon's intendancy saw a whirlwind of innovation, as the king's money seeded his pet enterprises and the king's storehouses accumulated their products. Talon usually had a direct interest in the projects, functioning as a combined Intendant-entrepreneur. After two years of work he reported enthusiastically to Colbert that the colony was rapidly becoming self-sufficient in a variety of its needs and would soon export substantial surpluses. He sent trial shipments of timber and planks, cod, eels, and seal oil to France and the West Indies, and predicted huge volumes of future exports.

The exporting might be done in Canadian-made ships, for Talon dreamed of exploiting the limitless forest to build ocean-going vessels. He sent inspectors to survey the woods and in 1670–71 began regulating the northern forest with ordinances giving the king's carpenters first claim on oak and other wood used in shipbuilding. In a shipyard on the St. Charles River near Quebec, Talon organized the construction of several sizeable hulls. Some were sold to the Crown, some to a private syndicate of which Talon was a member. Supported at first by Colbert's enthusiasm and the Department of Marine's largesse, Talon planned to build huge warships on the St. Lawrence: a 450-ton, 42-gun hull was laid down, and wood was cut for a 600 to 800 ton monster. One of the attractions of shipbuilding as an industry was the belief that it could stimulate subsidiary enterprises, such as tar works, hemp production, and forges to make fittings.

Even before Talon left New France in 1672 it was becoming clear that his dreams were wildly impractical. The only resource the colony could contribute to shipbuilding, for example, was wood—and not even a lot of that, for good-quality oak was scarce along the lower St. Lawrence. Most of the carpenters and other artisans who put together the crude Canadian hulls had to be imported from France. So were all their tools and all the fittings and rigging that went into the ships. Huge construction costs led officials to realize that perhaps it would be more economic to export the wood to France and build the ships there. But timber for shipbuilding from Canada could not compete in France with either local supplies or imports from the Baltic countries.

All of Talon's other enterprises were uneconomic and did not survive their sponsor's departure from the colony. The brewery, for example, which had adequate supplies of local grain (as well as hops grown on Talon's *seigneurie*) and for whose product there would seem to have been an obvious demand in the fur-trading colony, had actually only existed because Talon insisted on a quota limiting the import of wine and spirits from France. As soon as Talon left the regulations were eased; the brewery closed, and finally its owner—Talon—sold the building to the Ministry, which converted it into a residence for future Intendants. Brewing never became more than a household industry in a colony that imported huge volumes of French wine and brandy.

Colbert and Talon had failed to understand the immense handicaps in New France to almost anything other than the fur business. This was a tiny colony one thousand kilometres up a treacherous river in a harsh northern land whose soil was thin and the climate bitterly cold. The St. Lawrence River is often seen as the bountiful artery of the north in Canadian economic history. In fact, sailing ships had a devil of a time ascending the artery in summer, and in winter the river was frozen for five months and impassable for a sixth. It was much less costly and time-consuming to do business with the West Indian islands or any of the ports on the Atlantic seaboard than it was to get ships up to Quebec. Not that there was much business to be done at Quebec anyway. The colony's total export of furs in most years would fill only one ship, unless the cargo was broken up for security or other purposes. Other than furs there was hardly anything else at Quebec that could not be bought more cheaply elsewhere.

Canadian wood was uneconomic to export, if only because of transportation costs. All Canadian products were uneconomic in open competition with the British colonies to the south. But since imperial policy usually forbade the French to trade with the English, there did seem to be a potential market for Canadian foodstuffs and other products in the French West Indies. The prospect of creating a triangular trade between Canada, the Antilles, and Europe appealed to generations of merchants and officials. It worked well for the British with their England-New England-Caribbean triangle. Aside from the extra length of the sailing voyages, however, the French triangle was hampered by the fact that the *habitants* who tilled small farms along the St. Lawrence only rarely produced significant surpluses of wheat, oats, peas, or other products. The land was not very good; the farming techniques were primitive; whatever profits there might be in the export trade were too small or irregular to stimulate concerted efforts to improve the situation.

The real breadbasket of the northeastern part of the continent was not a few acres of usually snow-covered soil producing a few thousand bushels of this or that grain; it was the fishing grounds downriver, in the Gulf of St. Lawrence, and out on the Banks in the Atlantic. A major geographical gulf between furs and fish had been created when the fur trade moved up the river to Quebec and beyond. Quebec-based entrepreneurs did try to look back eastward and exploit the fishing possibilities of the north shore and Labrador, but it proved almost impossible for the upriver fur-trading colony to harvest the bounty of the sea. Without a second staple product to export, New France was bound to remain a fur-trading backwater, a couple of towns and a few thousand small farmers up a very long creek.

Talon and Colbert had sensed the limits of the St. Lawrence in the 1670s and had considered trying to create some kind of *entrepôt* or trading centre somewhere in Acadia, a slumbering, much-neglected land, mostly wilderness, only nominally connected to New France. An eastern port would facilitate Atlantic trading on the one hand and the movement of goods in and out of the St. Lawrence on the other. Most planning of this kind was suspended during the long period of bitter warfare first with the Iroquois and then with the British that ended with the Treaty of Utrecht in 1713—which gave much of Acadia to the British (who renamed it Nova Scotia). Then a French military decision to create a great fortress on Ile Royale (Cape Breton Island) had exactly the economic effect that optimists could have hoped for. Within a few years of its foundation, Louisbourg, which included a thriving town on an excellent year-round harbour, was exporting more fish than Canada was exporting furs. Soon Louisbourg had a total maritime trade absolutely greater than Canada's and on a *per capita* basis many times larger. In the 1720s and 1730s Ile Royale was France's busy Atlantic base for legitimate trade with the West Indies, substantial illicit trading with New England and Newfoundland, and, because Louisbourg needed food other than fish, very useful trading with Canada. This later trade declined after the late 1730s, however, because of major crop failures in Canada. From then until the Conquest Canada often had difficulty feeding itself, let alone supplying Louisbourg's needs. New England traders happily filled the gap.[1]

There was always a certain amount of Canadian trade, and New France did became host to a few enterprising Frenchmen hoping to make their fortunes in the New World. In certain periods there were considerable fortunes to be made in the fur trade. The greatest fortune was probably the several hundred thousand *livres* accumulated by Charles Aubert de la Chesnaye, who came to the colony as a young agent for Rouen merchants in 1655. His early transactions are lost in obscurity, but La Chesnaye soon emerged as a grand merchant trader (*négociant* in the French distinction between general shipping wholesalers and the smaller *marchands* who handled goods in later stages of distribution), importing products for his storehouse in Quebec, maintaining a presence in the fur trade, and, typical of his breed, taking an interest in any other venture that looked reasonably profitable. He became involved in the lumbering activities Talon promoted, tried to develop fishing concessions downriver from Quebec, and was interested in a local brickworks. La Chesnaye also became Canada's first important moneylender, advancing cash to both *habitants* and *seigneurs*, including such notables as Bishop Laval, who borrowed 10,600 *livres* from him to help pay for the *seigneurie* of Beaupré. (La Chesnaye made those investments in return for *contrats du rente*, a kind of bond that paid him 5 to 5é per cent interest, had no maturity date, but was probably negotiable among the handful of other fur traders and merchants making up Quebec's circle of *hommes d' affaires*).

La Chesnaye's enterprises flourished so well and widely that he was able to go home and live for several years in the 1670s in La Rochelle, which had replaced Rouen and St. Malo as the principal source of ships and investors for the Canada trade. Only the death of his Canadian partner obliged La Chesnaye to return to the colony to handle the difficult job of untangling all the estate questions affecting the partnership. He then decided to stay on the spot where so many of his assets were tied up.

La Chesnaye's most frequent investments were in land. He purchased or was granted interests in more of the tracts of land denominated as *seigneuries* than anyone else in the history of New France. Under the semi-feudal seigneurial system a *seigneurie* theoretically generated wealth to its proprietor from the *cens et rentes* and other dues paid by its inhabitants. These *censitaires* benefited reciprocally from some of the obligations incumbent on the *seigneur,* notably a requirement to help the settlers develop the land by providing such local facilities as a mill for grinding their grain. Historians of New France have concluded that the seigneurial system was close to nonfunctional, generating little revenue for the *seigneurs* and having an almost imperceptible effect on the development of farms and settlements. With so much land available for the taking, who would bother with landlords? Canadian *seigneurs* could not hope to emulate French ancestors whose flourishing estates and letters of nobility meant that they and their children were aloof from the sordid scramble for money. Seigneurial status did not signify much real wealth in the New World.

Upwardly-mobile Canadians kept trying. Virtually every successful merchant in New France's history repeated La Chesnaye's progress in becoming *seigneur*, part *seigneur*, or multiple *seigneur*. A few were even able to match his triumph in being granted letters of nobility in 1693, thus becoming a true *gentilhomme.* De Chesnaye seems to have aspired to the title, calling himself *noble homme* for years previously. Merchants who chose a path to *seigneuries* and the aristocracy have sometimes been criticized as following a course of waning entrepreneurial zeal. Perhaps, but the transition was not peculiar to French-Canadian or even French merchants. The passion for landholding and titles affected businessmen from Prussia to New England, and seems to be, as the great French social historian, Fernand Braudel, has argued, a phenomenon of all places and periods.

It was rooted in vague but powerful desires for rest and respectability, and also at many times and places—including even New France—a shrewd sense that land was not a bad investment. Even if the income from a *seigneurie* on the St. Lawrence was slight, it might be a profitable short- or long-term speculation. Trafficking in *seigneuries* contradicted the feudal notion of grants in perpetuity, but it took place constantly in both New and old France—in other words, a market had developed for real estate. *Seigneuries* were also a relatively secure investment, in the sense that the land could not easily founder in a storm, be captured by privateers, or be carried off by an invading army. Nor could its value be deliberately debased in the way that gold and silver coinage had been through the centuries and would be many times in the future. Finally, as landed proprietors throughout Europe were beginning to realize in the eighteenth century, improved agricultural and other resource development techniques could produce huge increases in income. Merchants everywhere understood that land was a fundamental source of most wealth.

Aubert de la Chesnaye might have left a greater legacy in Canada if he had limited himself to his *seigneuries* or a genteel semi-retirement as a noble. At its peak his fortune was estimated at 800,000 *livres*, about $1.6 million in modern purchasing power, making him easily the richest Canadian businessman of the seventeenth century, perhaps the richest in the history of New France. He appears to have been ruthlessly single-minded in his acquisition of wealth. In 1665 he was fined for having sold shoes from his Quebec store at prices higher than those allowed by the Conseil Souverain in one of its attempts at price-fixing. A trading permit issued to La Chesnaye by the Governor of New York in 1684 indicates involvement in the illegal trade with the British. Some of his enemies even accused him, probably falsely, of provoking war with the Iroquois to advance his trading interests.

La Chesnaye's risk-taking was disastrous enough as it was. In the 1680s he was one of the leading spirits in a French challenge to the British fur-trading presence in Hudson Bay. As we see later, the French and Canadian Compagnie du Nord was a strikingly bold and dashing venture—and it failed. The merchants of Quebec had no more success a few years later when they formed the Compagnie du Colonie to take over the European marketing of their furs from French *concessionaires* who seemed to be garnering poor returns. The venture was a fiasco because of an extreme glut of furs in France, and the Canadians accumulated heavy debts.

Aubert de la Chesnaye died in 1702. The little we know of the personality of the man who was New France's original *brasseur d'affaires* suggests a man of deep contradictions. He owned one of the larger houses in Quebec, but had some of his curtains made from old tablecloths. He owned a wig and shirts trimmed with lace, but commonly dressed in flannel trousers, a serge jacket, and an old beaver hat. In his will he apologized to those he had wronged, though he could not recall any specific offences, stated that his main interest had been in developing the colony rather than acquiring material goods, and asked to be buried in the paupers' cemetery of the Hôtel-Dieu in Quebec. Perhaps this last request was simple realism, for La Chesnaye's liquid assets at his death were only 125,000 *livres*. His debts totalled 480,000 *livres*. The sale of his properties did not bring in enough further revenue to cover the obligations. This premier Canadian fortune had been lost by the time of its accumulator's death.

Many of La Chesnaye's generation of Canadian merchants and fur traders lost their wealth more easily than they had accumulated it. François Hazeur, for example, participated in many of the same business endeavours as La Chesnaye, losing money in lumbering, fishing, and the Tadoussac fur-trading concession. When Hazeur died in 1708, Quebec's Governor wrote that he was "missed by everyone because of his merit, his virtues, and his uprightness." He was also insolvent. Dennis Riverin, said by contemporaries to possess "an extraordinary spirit of gain," managed to cling to power and influence only through official favouritism after most of his ventures had failed. Charles Guillimin, another of Quebec's richest merchants, tried to entrench himself with a good marriage and a number of acts of military prowess and good citizenship, including loaning 40,000 *livres* to the government at Quebec during a financial crisis. Unfortunately Guillimin made the loan in Canada's distinctive playing-card money during a period of inflation and took a severe loss when France decided to redeem the card notes at far less than face value. His biographer concludes: "Guillimin's career had followed a pattern that was not untypical of many of New France's merchants: apparent prosperity and increasing social prestige dissipated almost at an instant by administrative decisions taken in France and by the normal vicissitudes of the Canadian economy." By the early 1700s these vicissitudes had included extreme fluctuations in returns from the fur trade, the collapse of the compagnies *du Nord* and *du Colonie*, the erratic development policies of the Department of Marine, the fortunes of war, and, as in Guillimin's case, the problem of the currency.

The currency is always a problem. In the eighteenth-century world the basic medium of exchange was *specie*, that is, gold and silver coins. There never seemed to be enough *specie* in circulation and it did not circulate easily enough to meet the needs of commerce. The mercantile world had long since developed various sorts of paper—evidences of debt and orders to pay at some future date—which merchants, shippers, buyers and sellers could and did freely create, circulate, and pass from hand to hand. One form of circulating paper was the simple promise to pay (*bon* from "*bon pour*"), the ancestor of the notes that Canada's banks would issue during the nineteenth century. Another was the bill of exchange, an order to pay somewhat resembling today's cheque.

Specie was particularly scarce in New France because chronic trade deficits caused it to move back to France (in payment of debts) and because the French government was often reluctant, sometimes unable, to meet its obligations in hard coin. In 1685, one of the years when the Department of Marine had not shipped out money, and with his unpaid soldiers having to hire themselves out to colonists, the Intendant Jacques de Meulles issued distinctive notes by cutting up playing cards, assigning denominations, and signing them. Printed paper currency had already been invented in England and Sweden but had yet to appear in France. The first cards were soon redeemed, but the situation repeated itself and the "*monnaie de carte*" became a useful local circulating medium. Confidence in the card money was probably increased when an enterprising counterfeiter was fined, ordered to make restitution, publicly flogged, and banished.

The value of the paper debt instruments circulating in New France—bills of exchange, notes, card money, and other variants—depended on the likelihood of their being duly redeemed for the promised amount of *specie*. Merchants lived or died according to their skill and/or luck at not being caught with paper that had lost its value—such as a bill of exchange drawn on a French merchant who had just failed and could not pay. Uncertainties about redemption tainted almost all notes, including those issued by the government. The greater the uncertainty the greater the impediment to trade. Then, as now, trade flourished best in an atmosphere of confidence in the paper currency.

The greatest impediment to confidence was the French government's reluctance to pay its bills. The practice of issuing playing cards or other government notes became an habitual way of meeting local obligations. But the discovery that *specie* was not immediately needed meant that a fundamental check on government thrift in the colony had been removed. Local administrators developed a tendency to "spend" more than anyone in the Department of Marine had authorized and afterwards urge the case for the mother country redeeming the debt paper they had issued. The mother country was not always willing to oblige. During the War of the Spanish Succession at the beginning of the eighteenth century, for example, the sheer quantity of paper issued by the king's agents in New France led to significant inflation. Then the realization that France might not, probably could not, redeem the notes at face value led to still more deterioration in the currency's value, causing immense hardship for merchants such as Charles Guillimin. The colonials managed to transfer some of the loss to ignorant French exporters who thought they could safely take payment in bills of exchange drawn upon the Department of Marine. When the treasury of France simply did not produce the coin to redeem these bills, the paper-rich merchants of La Rochelle in 1715 sued the Treasurer General of Marine, who was declared personally responsible for the debt. The Crown coolly suspended recourse to the courts and promised to pay the bills *"le plus promptement qu'il sera possible."* After more delays and uncertainties the Canadian card money and other paper was redeemed at about one-half its face value. Soon there were more issues of card money.

By about 1720 economic conditions in New France had stabilized after several decades of war, inflation, fur gluts, and other problems. The second quarter of the eighteenth century saw considerable population growth, substantial expansion of land under cultivation, and the stimulus to trade and production created by the building of the fortress of Louisbourg. During the peaceful 1720s and 1730s it seemed as though the colony might fulfill some of the aspirations of enthusiastic officials by producing a more diversified range of goods and improving its balance of trade. Elaborate and wildly optimistic plans were drawn up to increase agricultural production in the colony, and there was a renewal of official interest in schemes to produce every imaginable vegetable and mineral product—ranging from domesticated buffalo through developing a trade to the West Indies in Amerindian slaves. Some of the ideas were absurdly far-fetched; others, such as attempts to mine copper near Lake Superior or the coal deposits on Ile Royale, were several centuries premature. A few, such as the program to foster hemp-growing and the founding of a local iron industry, seemed as though they almost worked.

Hemp was the fibre used to make rope. The Department of Marine thought it could easily become an export crop for the colony. Surely if the habitants could be encouraged to grow hemp the merchants would develop a good trade in it. In 1720 Intendant Michel Bégon began applying the stimulus by offering to buy hemp for 60 *livres* a quintal. Barrels of seed were imported from France and distributed to interested growers. The hemp plan could hardly fail, in a sense, for the government's price was so high (in France hemp sold at 22 to 24 *livres* per quintal), that *habitants* filled the king's storehouses with hemp. Local merchants had too much good sense, though, to take over a trade that required paying more than twice the French price for hemp while ignoring normal quality standards. With 234,000 pounds of hemp in storage in 1730, the government finally eliminated the price subsidy, but had no idea what to do with its unexportable fibre.

Why not make the hemp into rope in the colony, thus adding more value on the spot and creating a new industry? But there were no Canadian ropemakers. Intendant Gilles Hocquart, a particularly enthusiastic promoter of diversification, decided to encourage French ropemakers to emigrate, then help set them up in business so they could train Canadian apprentices while creating a new Canadian industry. Several ropemakers came out in the 1730s. The industry failed. Canadian hemp was of poor quality. So was Canadian rope. Local shipowners and shipbuilders met their needs from France whenever possible. As soon as the Department stopped paying exorbitant prices for poor-quality hemp, the *habitants* stopped growing hemp. Nothing came of proposals to import expert hemp-growers from France. No one is known to have tried to smoke the hemp. Considerable amounts of tobacco were grown for smoking in the colony, but elaborate official attempts to stimulate tobacco production for export also bogged down in problems of quality and price.

The most practical of many proposals for mineral development centred on deposits of soft iron in bogs near the St. Maurice River above Trois-Rivières. Why not take advantage of the ore to build a smelter and forge and make iron products for the colony—stoves, kettles, tools, and so on? Local officials who had been promoting state development of the resource for years were delighted when the fur trader and seigneur of St. Maurice, François Poulin de Francheville, came forward with his own scheme in 1729. The founding of Canada's first manufacturing facility included sending a blacksmith to study methods of iron-making in New England and the obtaining of a loan from the government. Several merchants joined the company Francheville formed, work began, and in the early 1730s a few thousand pounds of Canadian bar iron were produced at the St. Maurice forge.

The sudden death of the founder, Francheville, in 1733 led to suspension of operations, reorganization of the company, and a plea for technical help from France. A French expert, Olivier de Vézin, who was lured out at a high salary, declared that Francheville's installations were absurdly primitive and recommended scrapping them. Vézin drew up a plan for iron works capable of producing 600,000 pounds of bar iron a year, two-thirds of which would be exported to France. An investment of about 100,000 *livres*, Vézin estimated, would yield a profit of about 60,000 *livres* annually. "This is an enterprise whose success is assured," Intendant Hocquart wrote to the Minister of Marine after receiving Vézin's report. "As, however, it will be necessary to advance much money before drawing a profit, I have every reason to fear that this project will fail if you, My Lord, are not pleased to support and favour it...."

With substantial state aid and participation, a new Compagnie des Forges du St. Maurice was formed in 1737 to undertake the work. Jean Lunn described the venture in a splendid Ph.D. thesis on New France's economy written long before the parallels to modern Canada were apparent:

> Indications of the disaster which was to overtake the enterprise were evident from the beginning.... By October 1737, when the establishment was announced to be complete, the total expenditure was 146,588 *livres* instead of the 100,000 *livres* estimated.... In 1737 Hocquart had made over to the company the remainder of the loan of 100,000 *livres* agreed upon, but the partners declared that they must have an additional 82,642 *livres*. Their need was so pressing the Hocquart took it upon himself to advance them 25,233 *livres* to be deducted from the 82,642 *livres* which he begged the Minister to lend....
>
> The Minister replied in accents of horror and indignation. The king was being gradually more and more deeply involved. First it was only 10,000 *livres*, then it was 100,000 *livres*, then delays were proposed in repaying the loan and now it was another 82,000 *livres* of which 25,000 *livres* had already been advanced. It seemed clear to the Minister that there had been much waste and extravagance. Nevertheless he did consent to the new loan....
>
> Further shocks were in store for the minister. In 1738 the company foresaw that it would not be able to meet its first payment due in 1739 and the king had to agree to another year's delay.... De Vézin's estimate had proved completely unreliable, for expenses far exceeded and production fell far short of what had been anticipated.... Constant breakdowns of the furnace interfered seriously with production.... The Forges were operated by a staff of costly, dilatory, insubordinate and discontented workmen.
>
> According to De Vézin's original estimate the Forges should have manufactured 2.4 million pounds of iron during the four years from 1737–41. Instead total production for the period was about 1 million pounds.... Up to the end of September 1741 returns from the sale of iron amounted to 114,473 *livres*. The sale of stock on hand and some other assets later produced 39,184 *livres*. Total expenditure however was 505,356 *livres*, leaving the Forges with a deficit of 351,699 *livres*, less the value of the property at St. Maurice. In October 1741 the partners handed in their resignations and declare the company bankrupt. This was the end of the private exploitation of the mines of St. Maurice.
>
> The enterprise collapsed under a burden of technical, administrative and financial incompetence.

The major private entrepreneur who lost his fortune in the St. Maurice fiasco was François-Etienne Cugnet, the only member of the company with access to funds to advance to the firm. It was not clear that all the funds advanced were rightfully his. The Crown took over the forges, which continued to make iron goods for local consumption to the end of the French regime and long afterward. The operations were not profitable.

Intendants like Hocquart often complained that the merchants of the colony lacked the resources to invest in such attractive prospects as the St. Maurice forges. Ten years' residence in the sugar islands would be enough to make a man rich, Hocquart wrote in the prosperous year of 1735, "whereas in this colony the greatest individual fortunes, with a single exception, are of 50 to 60 thousand *livres*. Of these there may be four or five. Common fortunes are not greater than 20 to 30 thousand *livres*, and are moreover few in number." Historians have echoed his and other complaints in concluding that a lack of investment capital was a major factor retarding the economic development of New France. And just as capital was in short supply, so was labour, leading to endless complaints about shortages of cheap, skilled labour limiting growth.

These judgements confuse cause and effect. If real opportunities for profitable industrial diversification had existed in New France, both labour and capital would have been attracted from Europe, as they were to all the areas in the Americas, South, Central, and North, where greater opportunities existed than could be found in *cap de nada*. The endless and mostly futile attempts to stimulate the development of every conceivable industry in New France—Joseph-Noël Fauteux's 1927 account of them in his *Essai sur L'Industrie du Canada sous le Régime Français* runs to 555 pages—show that there was no shortage of public and private entrepreneurs trying to exploit opportunities. But there was a shortage of opportunities, a lack of products that could be made in Canada and sold profitably in or outside the colony.

Even the fur trade had settled down by the 1720s into a business with little prospect of great rewards. We see later how the French were extending and rationalizing their trade in constant competition with the English to their north and south. As W. J. Eccles has written, they were also "militarizing" it, subordinating economic considerations to their strategic needs *vis-à-vis* Englishmen and Indians. The men in the trade were beginning to specialize as operators of inland posts, or as Montreal-based outfitters bringing in goods from Quebec and hiring *engagés* for the trip to the interior. Not many of them accumulated fortunes.

The largest individual investments were made by the import-export merchants moving goods in and out of Quebec, the *négociants* of the Lower Town who were the biggest fish in the small colonial pond. Most were the agents or factors or partners of French *négociants*, big shipping merchants of Rouen, Bordeaux, and particularly La Rochelle, who had dominated business from Canada since taking over from Dutch traders in the 1660s.

A single trading voyage was often an enterprise in itself, with a special partnership having been formed in France to finance it and the profits (or losses) being divided at the end. An eighteenth-century merchant "company" was usually a fixed-term partnership, often of members of a family, with unlimited liability and no provision for share transfers. (In Europe the limited liability partnership had gradually developed out of this situation as a way to mobilize capital and conduct business over longer distances and among members of different families. Allowing a partner to transfer his shares in a firm, with or without his partners' consent, increased flexibility still further. It was one more short step, taken as early as the sixteenth century, to the creation of a joint-stock company in which all shares were fully and publicly transferable. The Hudson's Bay Company was the only such organization to operate in Canada before the nineteenth century.) Most of the Canadian trade was done by merchant partners; some tried a voyage or two and sailed on to a more profitable trade; others found success and increased the length, size, and capital base of their partnership agreements to underwrite more ventures.

The best-known French merchant in the Canada trade was Robert Dugard of Rouen, whose investment in a single ship that traded to Quebec in 1730 led to the formation of the Société du Canada, a long-term partnership under Dugard's management. The Société owned and outfitted a fleet of up to eight ships, maintained a warehouse and very active agents in Quebec, and in handling 10 to 20 per cent of the colony's trade was deeply interested in expansion, particularly to the West Indies.

Dugard and company's ships brought a myriad of consumer goods into Quebec. A single cargo included a wide variety of woollen, linen, and cotton cloth, blankets and garments, shoes, hats, gloves, knives, flat-irons, Dutch stoves, weights, locks, bridal mounts, roasting spits, shoe scrapers, combs, mirrors, window panes, plates, mugs, teapots, spoons, salad bowls, garden vases, foot warmers, paper, writing plumes, penknives, pipes, playing cards, pepper, nutmeg, cloves, cheese, salt, vinegar, dried prunes, almonds, and forty-two barrels of red wine, seven of white, ten of anisette, and ninety half-barrels of brandy. The supplies were for the colonists, for trade with the natives, and for the illicit trade with the English. All trade goods were sold at the firm's warehouses to other merchants or middlemen who shipped them up to Montreal, the centre of both the fur trade and the smuggling trade. Retailers and fur traders often purchased on credit extended by the *négociants*, settling their accounts after the goods had been resold or traded.

The Société's ships left Quebec with cargoes of furs and the occasional surpluses of flour, barrel staves, planks, and fish products that the colony was able to export in the good years. Sometimes the ships came north from or sailed south to the West Indies; Louisbourg was often used as an *entrepôt* to pick up or exchange cargoes. Even at the best of times trade between Canada and the Indies did not flourish. Canada was not much of a market for rum or molasses or slaves. Worse, as specific studies of individual voyages indicate, it was almost impossible to pick up a cargo in Quebec as valuable as the one brought in: thus the voyage out brought far lower returns than the voyage in. Canadian historians visiting La Rochelle, France, used to be shown streets whose cobblestones were said to have come across the Atlantic as ballast from a country with nothing else to export. Robert Dugard's Société du Canada earned trading profits of about 10 per cent on its investment, not the fabulously high figures of popular and some scholarly belief, but between two and three times as much as could be earned in interest on less risky ventures.

Dugard and his associates, including the young cousins François Havy and Jean Lefebvre who were sent out to be the firm's factors in Quebec, were interested in any kind of enterprise, French or Canadian, that looked particularly profitable. In the late 1730s, for example, they took advantage of a system of royal bounties on ships built in Canada (another department program to stimulate Canadian industry) to launch the first of a total of six major ships they built in the colony. The last three of these were built after the bounties were ended, and were instanced by Hocquart as evidence that significant private shipbuilding really was feasible in Canada after all. In fact Havy and Lefebvre reported to France that the ships were very expensive to build, and the program seems to have been a kind of loss-leader to support the Société's Quebec trade. New France's card money and some of its other paper was not negotiable outside the colony. An importer accepting payment in the local currency needed to convert it into an exportable product. Shipbuilding was one way of turning Canadian card money into a product that could be sold in France.

Shipbuilding continued in New France, on a small scale for local needs, and as a crown venture after the opening of a royal shipyard, largely at Hocquart's urging, in 1739. The private industry disappeared in the war years of the 1740s and 1750s, but there was fairly constant production of naval vessels at the king's shipyard in Quebec. As in Talon's era, all the skilled shipbuilders, including the director of the works, were brought from France. One Canadian-born blacksmith at the shipyards determined to quit the job, causing the Intendant to comment that *"comme il est Canadien il préfère sa liberté a estre assujeti à une cloche."* In addition to high labour costs, it turned out that the contractors did not deliver properly selected and seasoned wood for the hulls. Neither cost nor quality justified the operation of the royal shipyard. Significant subsidiary industries, such as tar-making, did not develop. The shipyard's demand for labour and material is thought to have contributed to the demise of the more limited but perhaps more economic private sector of the industry.

Both Havy and Lefebvre had an eye for other opportunities in the colony, and soon came to play an important role as both lenders and investors in attempts to develop fishing and sealing operations downstream from Quebec. Like Havy and Lefebvre, most of the men active in Robert Dugard's Société du Canada were Huguenots, French Protestants whose religion was banned in their homeland and its colonies. A fairly large proportion of the merchants trading to Canada in the eighteenth century had overt or covert Huguenot connections. There is no clear evidence, in this or any other period, that such an incidental correspondence can sustain a view of Protestant businessmen as being more "capitalist" or enterprising in their values than Catholics. The old Weber-Tawney hypothesis of a correlation between the Reformation and the rise of capitalism has led to too many simplistic generalizations implying that a Protestant was bound to be a better businessman than a Catholic or that Protestant countries like England were bound to be more enterprising than Catholic ones like France. There is little hard, statistically sound evidence of significant differences in business behaviour between Huguenots and Catholics, in either France or Canada.

A merchant was a merchant, a man trained by experience to assess opportunities, weighing risk against the possibility of gain. Well before Benjamin Franklin's *Poor Richard's Almanack*, austere European merchants were instilling their sons, clerks, and apprentices with a code of hard work, thrift, and the avoidance of personal indulgence. Success in business was never guaranteed to come easily. The eighteenth-century commercial world was fraught with everyday risks, hazards, and insecurities that would horrify a later age, and there were hardly any institutions (such as commercial intelligence services, effective courts, credit-rating agencies, or corporate structures) to help merchants cope with threats to their livelihood.

They tried to minimize risks by creating or becoming part of information, credit, and agency networks—business systems—making possible long-distance and long-term transactions. A man had to have connections he could trust. No wonder that most pre-modern firms—and a good many even in modern times—began as family affairs, and expanded through the recruitment of a web of offspring, nephews, cousins, and in-laws. The next step was from kin to kind, as trusted fellow-townsmen or churchmen became part of a merchant's network of "correspondents," associates, or agents.

Quebec's trade, then, was handled by groups of merchants with family, regional, and religious ties: men whose contacts had alerted them to opportunities and whose networks made it possible to exploit these opportunities with a minimum of defalcation, dishonesty, or other commercial disaster. Historians have recently concentrated on piecing together the links among what J.R. Bosher calls these "clans" or "swarms" of businessmen, tracing the growth, shifts, and declines in the webs of colonial commerce.

Not many purely Canadian-based merchants were prominent in the transatlantic trade. Men operating from the mother country had too many advantages in access to insurers, credit, ships and outfitters, and profitable cargoes to be easily challenged by enterprising colonials. Nor, as the Intendants had pointed out, were there many colonial merchants whose local enterprises had profited enough to finance expansion into more costly and more risky ventures. French merchants and their Quebec agents handled about two-thirds of the colony's external trade. Sometimes the representatives of French firms, or French traders who sailed into Quebec and bought and sold goods on the spot, were criticized as *"marchands forains."* Locals complained that the outsiders had unfair cost advantages, dumped goods at low prices, competed directly with retailers, and did not have a stake in the colony's well-being. Would the Crown please protect them from such unfair competition, they sometimes petitioned.

There were several dozen *négociants* and *marchands* in the towns of Quebec and Montreal, and a larger number of small shopkeepers, traders, tavern-keepers, and artisans, engaged in buying and selling, providing services, and producing domestically crafted goods. Trade was often sleepy and apparently non-competitive, but there could be a fierce struggle for livelihoods, particularly on the margin where farming or labouring shaded into commerce. Carting in Quebec, for example, was so vulnerable to unrestrained competition and rate-cutting that Intendants fixed the number of carters at ninety (in a town of about five thousand residents), issuing numbered tin tags to be affixed to their horses' collars. Merchants complained about the carters' fixed high rates. Town shopkeepers complained about competition from countryfolk who persistently refused to limit their selling to designated markets. Country shopkeepers had to compete with pedlars, wandering *marchands forains*, and town merchants who came out to buy directly from *habitants*, perhaps in hope of cornering the local supply of a product. In a small colony ravaged by periodic crop failures and containing so few producers, markets could so readily produce unattractive prices that Intendants issued a host of regulations fixing prices, trying to ensure fair dealing, and otherwise controlling the market.

Accusations of price-gouging, monopoly, and greed were the usual accompaniment of commerce in the eighteenth century and afterwards. Contrapuntally, merchants complained about taxes, customs duties, and all other vexatious regulations. The bourgeoisie of Quebec and Montreal were self-conscious enough to occasionally consider creating a *bourse* or exchange—a meeting place for trading—and they sometimes appointed one of their number to present a petition to the authorities. The most common subject of petitions was the need for the government to maintain merchant confidence and a sound currency by honouring the cards, bills, and notes issued in its name.

Most merchants in the colony were not specialized, and would dabble in any promising venture. As with La Chesnaye and his like, there were no rigid lines between occupations or classes, nobility and bourgeoisie. Merchants became *seigneurs, seigneurs* engaged in all kinds of trade, all of the élite intermingled in government positions and councils, and marital bonds linked men and families with common tastes in wealth, power, and prestige. Cameron Nish's designation of the successful merchant of New France as a *bourgeois gentilhomme* seems fundamentally sound—so long as it is understood (following Molière) that most eighteenth-century merchants were *bourgeois gentilhommes*. The Canadians differed from type only in being somewhat less prosperous.

Limited opportunities in the colonial economy made it difficult for little men to ascend into the ranks of the merchant bourgeoisie. Of course a few made it: Jean Brunet, a Montreal butcher who was able to retire comfortably after many years in the trade; Jacques Campot, who started as a blacksmith at Detroit and became a substantial general merchant; Ignace-François Delezenne, the most successful of several reasonably prosperous silversmiths in New France, who became a *seigneur* and in the last years of the colony ran a small industry manufacturing trade silver. Growth at Louisbourg after 1725 probably created more opportunities for mobility there than in Quebec or Montreal. Michel Daccarrette, who began as a small fisherman and sometimes privateer out of Plaisance, Newfoundland, moved to Louisbourg and developed fishing stations on Ile Royale that employed as many as 170 men bringing in more than 100,000 *livres* worth of cod in a season. As the Daccarrette family expanded into shipping, both to France and the West Indies, and to general merchandising, a once-poor fisherman now owned a comfortable Louisbourg house tended by servants and slaves. The *Dictionary of Canadian Biography* memorializes a handful of other men and families who prospered similarly from their skill in capturing the bounty of the New World. Many more tried and fell short, disappearing from history in the mean obscurity of their birth.

Merchants' wives and daughters were sometimes surprisingly active in commerce. With the family unit as the most common basis for a business, in an age of hazardous voyages, long absences, and early death, wives and widows often took an active hand in managing affairs and property. When Francheville of the St. Maurice ironworks died in 1733, for example, his thirty-six-year-old widow, Thérèse, herself the daughter of a prominent Montreal merchant, carried on with his affairs, gradually withdrawing from the forges and investing her inheritance in loans to other merchants. (Her one disastrous mistake was a proposal to sell the family's black slave, Marie-Joseph-Angélique; Marie set fire to the Francheville house in Montreal and fled with her white lover. Forty-six houses and the Hôtel-Dieu were destroyed by the flames; the slave was tortured, hanged, and burned.) Marie-Ann Barbel, mother of fourteen children to Louis Fornel, also managed his businesses during his visits to Labrador sealing stations. After his death Marie-Ann took over the sealing concession, working with his former partners, Havy and Lefebvre, and adding the fur-trading concession at Tadoussac. "*Veuve Fornel et compagnie*," as she signed her business documents, tried other ventures, such as founding a small pottery when imports from France were interrupted by war. "The country has a resource in Mademoiselle Fornel," Havy and Lefebvre wrote. "She has a very good craftsman and her earth proves good."

Agathe de Saint-Père, Mme. de Repentigny, organized a "factory" to make cloth for the colony during a wartime blockade in 1705. Her workers were nine English weavers whom she had ransomed from Indian captors. They taught Canadian apprentices the trade, other Montrealers picked it up, and the little industry came to involve twenty looms on Montreal island producing 120 ells of cloth a day. It survived the departure of the English weavers and operated under Mme. de Repentigny's control until 1713. This energetic businesswoman, mother of the Canadian textile industry (the one "manufacturer" listed in the early volumes of the *Dictionary of Canadian Biography*), experimented with new materials ranging from bark fibres to buffalo hair and discovered several new dyes. It seems that neither she nor the widow Fornel, however, could compete with French imports in peacetime.

The grand dame of Canadian lumbering was the "very noble young lady" Louise de Ramezy, unmarried daughter of a Governor of Montreal, who took over management of a sawmill on one of her family's properties, ran it for three decades—sometimes through a foreman—and became involved in at least two other sawmills and a tannery in addition to her own *seigneurie*. Another female *seigneur*, owner of the Ile d'Orléans, mother of sixteen, was Charlotte-Françoise Juchereau, who styled herself the Comtesse de Saint-Laurent. "People might perhaps have forgiven her vanity and her usurping the title of countess," an Intendant wrote, "if she had at least paid her bills." The three Demoiselles Desaunier kept a notorious trading shop on the Caughnawaga Indian lands outside Montreal. Everyone knew it was the centre for the illegal fur trade with Albany, but the sisters fought off repeated state attempts to dislodge them, and stayed in business for a quarter-century. Of course wives and daughters did not normally engage in either licit or illicit commerce in New France, and when women married, their husbands normally controlled their property. Historians have tended to pay more attention to the strong-minded heroines of the religious communities, Jeanne Mance, Marguerite Bourgeoys, or Marie de l'Incarnation, than to the equally tough *femmes d'affaires* who occasionally seized opportunities created by the precariousness of life in the little colony.

"We need a good peace," Havy and Lefebvre wrote to a correspondent in France in 1746, "in order to be able to work solidly at increasing the trade of the country. It must be hoped that God will give us the grace soon to see the end of the war." Their hopes were not realized. For most of its history New France was literally embattled, functioning primarily as a military outpost of empire rather than a fur-trading or agricultural colony. The only period of peace and reasonable security in the colony's history ended in the early 1740s; there followed years of war, preparations for war, undeclared war, and war again, culminating in the British conquest of 1759–60.

For many merchants the wars were disastrous. Robert Dugard's Société du Canada had six ships wrecked or captured during the War of the Austrian Succession in the 1740s. Even through the firm's insurers paid promptly (particularly those based in the enemy capital of London; the Londoners sometimes charged lower rates, some said because they could warn a client of the movements of British fleets), the losses forced the Société to withdraw from Canadian trade. At Louisbourg Michel Daccarrette lost his property and his life during the

British siege and capture of Louisbourg in 1745. François Havy's personal fortune and many other merchants' modest accumulations of wealth disappeared in the rubble of Quebec and the destruction of the colony's currency during the Seven Years' War. War destroyed normal trade and many normally conservative traders.

But war also threw up a new breed of risk-takers. It created a huge growth industry servicing the state, supplying troops, provisioning the colony, transporting equipment. The public officials who profited from this opportunity brought the confusion of public and private interests in New France to a climax that finally played itself out in wild inflation, profiteering, scandal, trials and imprisonment, along with military defeat.

Remember that eighteenth-century governments did not expect public officials to set their private interests aside. In an age before the bureaucratization and professionalization of government, part of the compensation for taking the trouble to serve the state was the prospect of using office for private profit. Everyone in Bourbon France did it; every major official in New France was involved in fur trading or other enterprises. Collectors and administrators of the king's revenues kept the accounts in their own name, often investing the money in their own ventures. Consider François Foucault, the king's storekeeper at Quebec from 1715 to 1740. "It was not always clear whether the large credits Foucault extended were from his own or from the king's revenues," his biographer writes. "Consequently, when a creditor proved insolvent, he could shift the loss from his own to the king's ledger." Foucault ran his private store at Quebec in the same location as the king's store, and had a habit of trading with himself, hiding rake-offs through the use of agents or aliases. This was not particularly unusual in the colony. What was the point of holding an office if you didn't make something out of it?

As military business ballooned during the wars of the 1740s and 1750s so did the opportunities available to the holders of strategic offices. Led by François Bigot, the last Intendant of New France, the officials seized their chance. A native of Bordeaux, Bigot had served as financial commissary of Louisbourg, engaging in several commercial ventures and investing in privateering on the side, before being posted to Quebec in 1748. During his twelve years as Intendant, Bigot was the centre of an elaborate private operation, in which many military officers and senior officials of the colony participated, to supply profitably the colony's wartime needs. One important partnership included Bigot, Jacques Bréard (the financial controller at Quebec), and the Bordeaux shipping firm of David Gradis et fils. It operated as La Société du Canada, but was very different from Dugard's group of peacetime traders. Gradis, a major outfitter to the King of France, sent ships to Quebec where Bigot and Bréard purchased their cargoes on behalf of the government at prices they set; they then collected half the profits from the voyages. The Bigot group's interests included a small fleet of ships in the Louisbourg-West Indies trade and a company formed secretly to buy furs at interior posts which were supposed to be sold at auction in Quebec.

Bigot routinely awarded contracts and concessions to such friends and associates as Michel Péan (adjutant at Quebec), Louis Pennisseaut, Marie-Ann Barbel, Guillaume Estèbe, and others, taking a personal stake in their ventures. His most enterprising crony was Joseph-Michel Cadet, a Canadian-born merchant butcher, who began to prosper selling meat to the Crown and expanded into supplying other foods. Bigot made him purveyor general, responsible for provisioning all the garrisons and eventually the civilian population during the desperate war of the late 1750s. Cadet then organized the Grande Société, a partnership in which all of them had an interest, from which he bought most of the provisions. The gang of purveyors and profiteers was knit together by ties of kin, friendship, avarice, and, at the top, the sexual favours of Angélique "Lélie" Péan, Canada's equivalent of Madame Pompadour.

As the noose of British power tightened around the St. Lawrence in the late 1750s, Quebec and Montreal reeked with defeatism, cynicism, and a scramble for booty. Everyone knew the accounts were crooked; the worst swindles were in Indian presents—goods the officials just redirected into private trade. Citizens had nicknamed the Bigot crowd's stores at Quebec and Montreal "La Friponne"—the rogue or rip-off. With the spectre of famine haunting the colony, prices having risen 800 per cent in four years, and paper "money" everywhere, the élite revelled in gambling and balls. The commander of the French troops in North America, Louis-Joseph de Montcalm, saw venality everywhere:

> Everybody appears to be in a hurry to make his fortune before the Colony is lost, which even, many, perhaps, may desire as an impenetrable veil over their conduct. The craving after wealth has an influence on the war, ... Instead of reducing the expenditures of Canada people wish to profit by everything; why abandon positions which serve as a pretext to make private fortunes? Transport is distributed to favourites. The agreement with the contractor is as unknown to me as it is to the public. 'Tis reported that those who have crowded into trade, participate in it. Has the King need of purchasing goods for the Indians? Instead of buying them directly, a favourite is notified who purchases at any price whatever; then M. Bigot has them removed to the King's stores, allowing a profit of one hundred and even one hundred and fifty per cent, to those whom it is desired to favour. Is artillery to be transported, gun-carriages, carts, implements to be made? M. Mercier, commandant of the artillery, is the contractor under other people's names. Every thing is done badly and at a high price. This officer, who came out twenty years ago as a simple soldier, will soon be worth about six or seven hundred thousand *livres*, perhaps a million....

Montcalm's own defeatism and incompetence contributed to the British victory on the Plains of Abraham on September 13, 1759. When the colony finally capitulated in September 1760, most of those who had done well in New France's last years sailed back to France, taking whatever wealth they could salvage.

For Bigot and Cadet the scavenge was well into the millions of *livres*. But defeat did not veil misconduct. The French government developed an intense interest in finding someone to blame for the fall of Canada. Bigot, Cadet, and fifty associates were flung into the Bastille, and, in the notorious *"Affaire du Canada,"* were convicted of defrauding the Crown and plundering the colony. Their penalties included fines, restitution payments, banishment, and the destruction of their reputations. Another penalty paid by everyone with money from New France's last phase was the loss of more than half its value, for France repudiated most of the notes and cards that had been issued in its name.

The supreme irony of the *Affaire du Canada* was that most of the profiteers and criminals had contributed more to the preservation of the colony than their accusers. Montcalm's opinion notwithstanding, Bigot and Cadet were both brilliant administrators, two of the smartest, most efficient men ever to hold high office in New France. Their private schemes succeeded so well largely because they were so effective in carrying out their public duty to supply the colony. Gradis *et fils* slipped supply ships into Quebec, for example, more regularly than the French navy got vessels through British blockades. Cadet risked his fortune to get his own ships through in 1758 and 1759 at a time when no one else had the vigour and daring to attempt the feat. He fed the besieged colony to the end, doing well by doing his duty. If the censorious Montcalm had done his job of generalship equally well, the French regime in America might have had a different fate.

The high prices that plagued the colony in its last years were partly due to the Bigot gang's skimmings, but they were mostly caused by inflation. Government spending had soared, war impeded production, and holders of paper shrewdly lost confidence in the French government's promises to redeem it. But everyone needs scapegoats for inflation and defeat. Bigot and company were not unusually villainous by the standards of eighteenth-century France or New France; if anything they were unusually competent products of that century's office-holding system. They did a spectacular job of making the system work. But while they won the battles to keep the civil side of the colony going, the soldiers and the government lost the war.

New France had always been an economically precarious colony, highly dependent on the vagaries of the fur trade, unable to develop other staple products for export. After the boom years of the fur trade, a few Canadian merchants had emerged to trade with the handful of French-based merchants who controlled colonial shipping. The greatest opportunities the colony offered were not to profit from the natural development of a community and its resources, but to get inside the king's purse when it was wide open to finance wars. The risk of exploiting the state and its needs might have been manageable if only the war had been won. When it was lost, the state turned on the risk-takers in its need to find excuses for the loss of Canada.

Notes

1. For several centuries smuggling was the principal activity in what we now call the "underground" or "black" economy, the network of transactions that take place beyond the ken of the state and therefore never show up in statistics. All of the subjective evidence from the French regime in Canadian history—as well as some hard evidence about the movement of French furs to Albany—suggests a very high volume of illicit trade. It may have been so high as to pose a challenge, some historians feel, to the whole idea of a comparatively poor colony with little to export. The difficulty with this view, aside from the problem of evidence, is that it would have to be applied to all other settlements, whose inhabitants were not likely to be less adept smugglers than Canadians. The comparative disadvantage of New France in the Atlantic trade, licit and illicit, would remain.

CHAPTER

4 THE EXPULSION OF THE ACADIANS

Although Champlain's decision in 1608 to establish a settlement at Quebec meant that henceforth French colonizing activity in North America would be centred on the St. Lawrence, a French presence stubbornly persisted in what became known as Acadia. Never very large in terms of population, and frequently handed back and forth between the French and British in the ongoing imperial rivalries of the age, Acadia gradually acquired a distinct character of its own. Its location meant both isolation from the main centre of French power at Quebec, and considerable contact with the colonies to the south. Although the fur trade was of some importance to Acadia, its economy was much more agriculturally based than that of New France.

Acadia changed hands for the last time during the War of the Spanish Succession. The Treaty of Utrecht, which formally ended that war in 1713, left Acadia in British hands. The British thus were confronted with the problem which would arise in a much greater way later in the century: the position of a French and Catholic colony in an Empire which was English and Protestant. This first experiment ended in 1755 with the forcible deportation of virtually the entire Acadian population, estimated at about 10,000 people.

The readings in this section place significantly different emphasis on that expulsion, though neither questions the immensity of the tragedy. The first was written in 1955 on the two-hundredth anniversary of the deportation by C. Bruce Fergusson, and may be considered a justification for the British action. Fergusson placed great emphasis on the question of the oath of allegiance. He argues that when the Acadians refused to choose between the only two options open to them—to remain French nationals and to leave Nova Scotia, or to become full and unqualified British subjects—the Acadians themselves were ultimately the authors of their own fate.

The second reading, "1748–1755: Community Devastated," is a chapter from *The Contexts of Acadian History, 1686–1784* by Naomi Griffiths. Griffiths has spent her career since her arrival from Britain in the 1950s studying the Acadians. This study is a synthesis of her work. If Fergusson looked at the Acadians through the eyes of the British, Griffiths has multiple vision, though her sympathies are solidly with the victims. She emphasized the complexity of not only the immediate issues, but also the nature of Acadian society itself. The Acadians were certainly helpless pawns in a struggle for imperial supremacy between Britain and France, but to Griffiths there "was no need for extraordinary measures of brutality to ensure a submissive population."

Suggestions for Further Reading

Brebner, J.B., *New England's Outpost: Acadia before the Conquest of Canada*. New York: Columbia University Press, 1927.

Daigle, Jean, "Acadia, 1604–1763: An Historical Synthesis," in *The Acadians of the Maritimes: Thematic Studies*, ed. Jean Daigle. Moncton: Centre d'études acadiennes, 1982.

Grant, Helen, "The Deportation of the Acadians," *Nova Scotia Historical Quarterly*, Special Supplement (1975), 101–19.

Griffiths, Naomi, *The Acadian Deportation: Deliberate Perfidy or Cruel Necessity?* Toronto: Copp Clark, 1969.

Griffiths, Naomi, *The Acadians: Creation of a People*. Toronto: McGraw-Hill Ryerson, 1973.

Reid, John G., "Acadia and the Acadians: In the Shadow of Quebec," *Beaver*, LXVII, no. 5 (October-November 1987), 26–31.

Reid, John G., *Six Crucial Decades: Times of Change in the History of the Maritimes*. Halifax: Nimbus, 1987.

THE EXPULSION OF THE ACADIANS

C. Bruce Fergusson

Some observers have said that Germany's annexation of Alsace-Lorraine was worse than a crime—it was a blunder; others have seemed to say that the expulsion of the Acadians was not a blunder but rather a crime. However that may be, history caught up with the Acadians in 1755, when 6,000 or more of them were uprooted from their beloved lands in Nova Scotia, placed on board ships and deported to British colonies to the south. Ninety-two years later, moreover, in a blend of fact and fancy, Longfellow caught them up in the unforgettable lines of the poem *Evangeline*. Since that time, it seems, the warp of

From *Dalhousie Review*, XXV, no. 2 (1955), 127–135. Reprinted by permission of *Dalhousie Review* and Mrs. Evelyn Fergusson.

fact and the woof of imagination have been so interwoven by poetic licence in a memorable mosaic of sentimentality and suffering, that it is difficult to separate fact from fancy and to get at the sober truth of the matter. Yet even the most aloof observer must feel sympathy for any group of people who experience the testing of exile from their accustomed place, no matter whose the responsibility for the exile, and no matter whether that forced expatriation was deserved or undeserved. That being the case, the heart goes out to the Acadians of 1755, without any need for the head to appreciate anything of the circumstances, or for any question to be asked of the why or the wherefore. But the two-hundredth anniversary of that event should provide the occasion for real attempts to understand what actually happened in 1755, and why and how it took place.

Was the expulsion of the Acadians a misfortune or was it a disaster? Were they the undeserved victims of misfortune, or did they reap disaster from their own folly? These are the salient questions which should be borne in mind whenever consideration is given to the fate of the Acadians in the year 1755. Their story, it is clear, is an admirable illustration of the relative strength of the ties that bind, and of the forces that influence, a people, as well as a supreme example of how a dramatic and colourful episode in the history of any people may be readily translated into the misty realm of romance, so that careful attention is needed for an adequate realization and a proper understanding. The story of the Acadians may be regarded as a tale that is told. But its versions differ, some of them are marred or distorted by emotion or bias, by artificial colouring or by unfounded judgements, and new appraisals are sometimes needed.

Centre or core of the Acadian problem was the oath of allegiance. One important factor was the fact that between the final capture of Port Royal by the British in 1710 and the fateful year 1755 most of the Acadians were unwilling to take the unconditional oath of allegiance. They refused to take the unqualified oath, insisted that they should not be required to take up arms in the event of war, and advanced the rather fantastic claim that they should be regarded as "French Neutrals."

Clearly the Acadian demand was an extraordinary one. It was the accepted conception then as now that the obligations incumbent upon those living within the bounds of the authority of a state included the taking of the oath of allegiance to that state. That was the case when New Sweden was obliged to submit to the New Netherlands in 1655, with those Swedes who desired to remain on the Delaware being expected to give an oath of unqualified allegiance to the new authority. That was also the case when the New Netherlands was obliged to submit to the English in 1664, and the Dutch about the Hudson and elsewhere were expected to do the same, if they remained beyond the period of a year. It was likewise the case, so far as France was concerned, when Frontenac received instructions respecting the expedition against New York, in the event of its capture, in 1689; and when the Duke d'Anville received instructions relating to his formidable but ill-fated expedition of 1746. Furthermore, this rule of broad international application was applied not only to the French in Canada after 1763, but also to those of Louisiana after 1803 when that territory became part of the United States, and to the Mexicans of northern Mexico after its cession to the United States in 1847.

Until the war was officially brought to a close by the Treaty of Utrecht in 1713 the situation was rather unsettled, with the articles of capitulation agreed upon at the surrender of Port Royal applying only to those within three miles of the fort and with the other Acadians anxious and uncertain about what the future held in store for them. One of the articles of capitulation provided that the inhabitants within the *banlieue*, an area having a radius of a cannon shot or three miles from the fort, should remain upon their estates, with their corn, cattle and furniture, for two years, if they were not desirous of leaving before the expiration of that time, they taking the oaths of allegiance to Her Britannic Majesty. In accordance with the terms of this article, the inhabitants within the *banlieue*—fifty-seven heads of families—did take such oaths by the end of the third week of January 1711, and that, in itself, seemed to portend auspiciously. But the war had not yet ended, French agents were active and the Acadians outside the *banlieue*, not being included in the articles of capitulation, were in a state of uneasiness and uncertainty. These Acadians applied to the British Governor for protection and offered to take the oath of allegiance. But the Governor who told them that by the arbitrament of war they had become prisoners, and who had collected a tribute from them, could give them no terms until Her Majesty's more particular orders were received. As a result of uncertainty over their situation the Acadians outside the *banlieue* became uneasy, tried to keep the Indians hostile to the English and attempted to stir up the Acadians within the *banlieue* who had already taken the oath of allegiance. Further apprehension was also caused by the hostile designs of the Indians and the French from Canada, as well as by the influence of the French missionary priests. That this apprehension was justified is clear from the fact that a party of sixty-five Englishmen which was sent in two flat boats and a whaleboat in June 1711 for the purpose of encouraging friendly Acadians in supplying wood and timber for the garrison was ambushed by a war party of French and Indians and all but one of them were killed or captured. Soon even those Acadians within the *banlieue* who had taken the oath of allegiance joined their compatriots in blockading the fort at Annapolis Royal, and the English were not only threatened with assault but with being one and all put to the sword.

The Treaty of Utrecht brought the war to an end. By it such of the Acadians as might choose to leave Acadia or Nova Scotia were free to do so within the space of a year,[1] taking with them their personal effects; while a letter of Queen Anne permitted such emigrants to sell their lands and houses. Those who remained in Nova Scotia were guaranteed freedom of worship under certain conditions. These were that they should accept the sovereignty of the British Crown, and that they and their pastors should keep within the limits of British law.

Now two roads lay before the Acadians, and it was a momentous question for themselves and for the local British authorities which one of them they would choose: whether they would remove themselves to French territory within the year stipulated in the Treaty of Utrecht, or remain in Nova Scotia and become British subjects. The one course meant their continuance as French nationals but their abandonment of their lands in Nova Scotia; the other meant the retention of their lands, the taking the oath of allegiance to the British monarch and the relinquishment of their French citizenship. Neither of these alternatives was their choice. Instead they tried for many years to combine what they wished of the two alternatives and eventually found themselves in an untenable position.

The best time to have settled the question of the oath was immediately after the Treaty of Utrecht. Then the Acadians numbered fewer than 2,000 and, if the interests of security, as well as international propriety, demanded that they take the oath or leave Nova Scotia and they persisted in refusing to do the one or the other, their deportation then would neither have been as formidable nor regarded with so much disfavour as forty-two years later when they had increased to five or six times that number. The reason why the question was not then settled was that the Acadians themselves were loath to leave their fertile meadowlands in Nova Scotia, whence they drew subsistence by means of cattle raising and farming, for uncleared and unknown or less fertile lands elsewhere, where much hard work would be needed, and the British authorities in Nova Scotia had neither the forces nor the resources to press the question to an issue. Other factors also supported the tendency to let matters drift; including the anxiety of the French authorities to maintain good relations with the British at a time when they were involved in difficulties with Spain.

Time and again the Acadians were given the opportunity to take the oath of allegiance. But the French authorities, who found that the Acadians were in the main reluctant to remove to Cape Breton Island, soon saw and seized advantages in the situation and employed French agents and French missionaries for the purpose of keeping the Acadians faithful to King Louis. This was indeed an anomalous state of affairs: the "year" of the Treaty of Utrecht soon passed; most of the Acadians remained in Nova Scotia; French missionaries, who were French agents as well as Roman Catholic priests, strove to keep the Acadians attached to both their religion and the French interest, and, on occasion, openly avowed that their object was to keep the Acadians faithful to the French monarch; none of these missionaries was ever molested by the British authorities, except when detected in practices alien to his proper functions and injurious to the government; freedom of worship continued to be accorded to the Acadians, notwithstanding the fact that most of them persisted in refusing to take the oath of allegiance, the condition on which they had acquired that privilege; and the British government, in spite of the concern of the British authorities in Nova Scotia, did nothing effective either to have the

French missionaries in that colony give a pledge that they would do nothing contrary to the interests of Great Britain or to have them replaced by other priests to be named by the Pope at the request of the British government.

The chief reasons for this anomalous state of affairs were the feebleness of British authority in Nova Scotia, the neglect and the apathy of the British ministers and the fact that the Acadians leaned so heavily on their French spiritual and temporal advisers. For a while, it is true, the *imperium in imperio* which existed was such that the inner power seemed to wax and strengthen every day while the outer relatively pined and dwindled. But the time was to come when the British ministers would waken from their lethargy, bestir themselves and, warned by the signs of the times, send troops and settlers into the Province at the eleventh hour. Then it was that the Acadians were to find how deplorable their position really was. Perhaps the only thing that could have averted the danger of Acadian hostilities or revolt and have made unnecessary the harsh measures to which such conduct afterwards gave rise was for the British ministry to have sent out a force sufficient both to protect the inhabitants against French terrorism and to leave no doubt that the King of England was master of Nova Scotia in fact as well as in name. But such did not take place until after long delay and until the problem had attained greater proportions. In the meantime, although those Acadians who remained in Nova Scotia had been transferred by France to the British Crown by the Treaty of Utrecht, French officers on occasion denounced them as rebels and threatened them with death if they did not fight at their bidding against Great Britain, and British officers threatened them with expulsion if they did not remain loyal to King George. These were the horns of the dilemma for the Acadians; and while for a time they avoided both they were ultimately confronted with the necessity for a decision they had tried to avoid.

French policy after 1713 reveals that France was unwilling to reconcile herself to the loss of Acadia, although it had with its ancient limits been ceded to Great Britain by the Treaty of Utrecht. Nor was France to neglect Nova Scotia or Acadia, even if for years Great Britain was to do so. On Ile Royale the French not only built up a mighty base at Louisbourg, as the watchdog and protector of the Gulf and the approaches to Quebec, and as the base and the guardian for the fishery, but also established there a Governor who was charged with the management of Acadian affairs, and who had zealous and efficient agents among the Acadians in the missionary priests, who were sent into Nova Scotia by the Bishop of Quebec, or in a few cases by their immediate ecclesiastical superiors in Ile Royale, and whose services in keeping the Acadians in the French interest were recognized and acknowledged by French political leaders and officials. At first the French authorities endeavoured to induce the Acadians to migrate to Ile Royale, where the growing power of the fortress at Louisbourg was a symbol that France was preparing to contest the supremacy of the continent with Great Britain, and sent envoys into Nova Scotia, with the permission of the local British officials, to visit the Acadian settlements and to tell the Acadians what inducements they were prepared to give them to remove. A few of the Acadians did go to Ile Royale, and nearly all of them in the emotion of the moment signed declarations of their willingness to migrate to French territory, but it was soon seen that this mood quickly changed and that the Acadians in the main had no inclination to leave their homes. At the same time the British authorities, realizing the value of settlers in Nova Scotia, hopeful of having the Acadians become loyal British subjects, and having no desire to see them migrate to Ile Royale where they would greatly add to the numbers and the strength of a potential enemy near at hand, were almost as anxious to keep the Acadians in Nova Scotia as they were forty years later to get them out of it. Soon, moreover, the French authorities realized that the Acadians were of greater benefit to France by remaining in Nova Scotia, whence they could furnish Ile Royale with much-needed supplies, where religion and patriotism might be combined or confused in keeping them in the French interest, and where in time of war they might be a source of strength for French invaders aiming at the re-capture of old Acadia or a fifth column which would be a decisive factor in any test of strength. If the Acadians had really wished to emigrate, the British Governor could have done little to stop them for his authority hardly extended beyond gunshot of his fort at Annapolis Royal and all the Acadians except those of Annapolis and its immediate neighbourhood were free to go or stay at will.

While most of the Acadians maintained a careful neutrality in times of trouble, and Mascarene himself declared that their refusal to fight for the French besiegers was one reason for the success of his defence of Annapolis on one occasion, French designs involved the Acadians and some of them were implicated in hostile acts against the British in Nova Scotia. During the 1720s French authorities not only strove to foment trouble between the Indians and the English but they joined the Indians in a raid on Canso. On the outbreak of the War of the Austrian Succession, the French from Ile Royale seized Canso before the British on this side of the Atlantic were aware of the outbreak of hostilities. They then attacked Annapolis. In this attack Duvivier, the French commander, expected help from the Acadians who were French in blood, faith and inclination; and the latter, who would not join him openly lest the attack should fail, did what they could without committing themselves and made a hundred and fifty scaling ladders for the besiegers. To this seizure of Canso and this attack on Annapolis a contemporary French writer attributes the dire calamity which soon befell the French. When the capture of Louisbourg in 1745 by New Englanders with the aid of a British naval squadron was followed by French plans to retake it, reconquer old Acadia, burn Boston and lay waste to the other seaboard towns, French officials counted on aid from the Acadians for their designs. The result was the assembling of a vast armada, comprising nearly half the French navy, and carrying 3,150 veteran troops, under the Duc d'Anville, in 1746. This formidable expedition set out from France, and Ramesay, with a large body of Canadians, was sent to Acadia to cooperate with d'Anville's force. News of this design and the appearance at Chebucto of part of d'Anville's ill-fated fleet caused great excitement among the Acadians, who undoubtedly expected that they would soon again come under the Crown of France. Fifty of them went on board the French ships at Chebucto to pilot them to the attack on Annapolis. To their dismay, however, they found that no such attack would then be made. Early in the next year, when Coulon de Villiers and his men in the depth of the winter led his men from Beaubassin to Grand Pré, where in the dead of night they attacked Colonel Arthur Noble and his force, who were quartered in Acadian houses, and killed many of them in their beds, a number of Acadians acted as guides for Coulon's band and assisted them in other ways. With the restoration of Louisbourg to France, the British Government founded Halifax as a counterpoise to it and commenced their first real attempt at settling Nova Scotia. By the time of the eve of the Seven Years' War it was clear that a showdown would soon be reached with respect to North America. In 1755 Braddock was defeated on the Monongahela and Beauséjour was captured by New England troops. At the siege of Beauséjour about 300 Acadians aided the French.

The developments of the 1740s, with French attacks on Canso and Annapolis, the d'Anville expedition, the massacre at Grand Pré, and other French designs, as well as the capture of Louisbourg and its restoration and the founding of Halifax, meant a heightened interest and an increased activity in Nova Scotia. New efforts to have the Acadians take the oath of allegiance to the British monarch had no better result than previous ones. British activity at the Isthmus of Chignecto, with a view to protecting the peninsula from French encroachments, were followed by two matters of very special significance. One, in 1750, was the first forcible removal of the Acadians: resolved that the Acadians at Beaubassin should be preserved from the contaminating influence of the British, Le Loutre, who had been unable to prevent the British from reaching that village, went forward with his Indians and set fire to it, in order to force its inhabitants to go to territory claimed by the French near Beauséjour, a short distance away. This was the beginning of the dispersal of the Acadians. Besides these, through great pressure from the French they migrated in such numbers that by 1752 2,000 of them were to be found in Ile St. Jean (Prince Edward Island), and about seven hundred in Ile Royale (Cape Breton Island). The other, in 1751, was an interesting commentary on the attitude of the French authorities towards the Acadian claim to neutrality which those authorities had encouraged while the Acadians remained under British sovereignty: this was the order of Governor La Jonquière that all Acadian refugees near Beauséjour who did not take the oath of allegiance to the French monarch and enlist in the militia companies would be branded as rebels and chased from the lands which they occupied.

Subsequently, just after the capture of Beauséjour in 1755, while the New England troops, who had achieved that victory, were still in Nova Scotia, and British ships of the line still lay in Halifax harbour, Governor Lawrence of Nova Scotia and his council at Halifax decided that the safety of the colony required

that the Acadians should take the oath of allegiance, which they had so often refused to do, or be deported from the province. They again refused, and they were
thereupon deported to British colonies. In the circumstances, and particularly
after the attacks on Annapolis Royal in 1744 and 1745 and the deeds done at
Grand Pré in 1747, it seems both unfair and inappropriate to attempt to pin
the chief responsibility for this decision on either Lawrence of Nova Scotia or
Shirley of Massachusetts.

Lack of space prevents an account of the hardships experienced by those
Acadians who were expelled or a description of the efforts made by the British
authorities to keep families and people from the same community together.
Suffice it to say that it might appear that the expulsion was unnecessary, for if
the old situation had persisted for but another few years until the French menace on the continent had been eradicated the problem would no longer have
existed, or if the Acadians could have taken the oath of allegiance prior to 1755,
as those who remained in the Province and those who returned to it afterwards
did, those harsh deeds would not have been done. Not many years after 1755,
at any rate, probably about 2,000 of the exiled Acadians returned to Nova
Scotia, where, along with a like number who escaped the expulsion, they received grants of land, took the oath of allegiance and assumed their full place
in the life of the Province. On the two hundredth anniversary of that catastrophe which emerged from the vicissitudes of war and threats of war, all Nova
Scotians of every racial origin rejoice with those of Acadian descent in marking
the great achievements of the last two centuries.

Notes

1. There have been different views as to the beginning and the end of the "year" of
   this Treaty, and some have held the untenable one that it was still in effect at the
   time of the founding of Halifax.

1748–1755: COMMUNITY DEVASTATED

Naomi E.S. Griffiths

The main theme of this monograph is that the building and development of
Acadian society was a much more complex process than has usually been
thought, and that a great deal more investigation is needed about a wide variety of questions of Acadian history. This theme was developed in [my] first two
chapters by the description of the two powerful and contrasting polarities in
Acadian life: that of the wider world and that of the Acadian community itself.
Much about Acadian society not only links that society to experiences of other

From *The Contexts of Acadian History, 1686–1784* (Montreal and Kingston: McGill-Queen's
University Press, 1992), 62–94.

societies made up of newcomers to the North American continent but is also a consequence of the very existence of these other societies. Further, the emergence of Acadia is obviously related to the broader story of the European migration to North America, and a good part of Acadian developments can be best understood in the context of North American and European history. At the same time, however, Acadia is neither Quebec nor New England, and Acadian life is not just a transposition of European customs. There is a unique Acadian experience, developed partly because of the particular combination of European migrants who came to the colony, partly because of the very environment of the lands settled, and partly because of the peoples already on the territory claimed, the Micmac and Malecite. Acadian life in the late seventeenth and early eighteenth centuries produced a distinct society. Local conditions produced particular problems which were solved by distinctively Acadian methods.

In many ways, it is inevitable that the impact of the forces outside the small settlements of early Acadia should be seen as being more powerful in the early decades of Acadian history, and the internal strengths of this growing community visibly gain power with its very development. In the period that is the subject of this chapter, 1748–56, however, Acadian history is determined by an almost equal balance of internal and external forces. This most traumatic period of Acadian history, the era of exile and proscription, is an era dominated by a major world war. That the Acadians survived the death and destruction that the world war brought them is due, above all, to the nature of the Acadian community itself. Bitter imperial rivalry between England and France brought the suffering. It was the strength of the Acadians that allowed them to endure the years of deportation, to preserve a measure of social coherence and identity in exile, and to re-root their community, after a generation of turmoil, once again in the Maritimes.

The theme of the complexity of Acadian history—the contention that the Acadians are no simpler than the rest of humankind—is crucial for an understanding of the period 1748–84, the period of this chapter and the following. Much of what is considered general knowledge about the Acadian deportation is more myth than history. Had the Acadians been a society of simple and devout peasantry, who were ignorant victims of imperial policies they were too naive to understand, their community would never have survived the attempt to destroy it between 1755 and 1764.[1] It is important to be clear at the outset that these years really did see a policy, not for the physical extermination of those who were Acadian, but for the eradication of the idea of an Acadian community. Charles Lawrence, Lieutenant-Governor of Nova Scotia in 1755 and the person who must bear the major responsibility for the policy of the exile and proscription of the Acadians, was quite clear as to what he wanted.[2] He wrote a circular which was dispatched from Halifax on 11 August 1755[3] to inform the other governors of British colonies in North America that the deportation of Acadians was under way. After listing the reasons why he considered the deportation necessary, he stated that, "it was judged a necessary and the only practicable measure to divide them [the Acadians] among the Colonies where they may be of some use, as most of them are healthy strong people; and as they cannot easily collect themselves together again it will be out of their power to do any mischief and they may become profitable and it is possible, in time faithful subjects."

The Acadians were to be exiled from the lands they thought their own, and divided among other British colonial societies in North America where it would be impossible for them to organize themselves as a distinct and separate community. They were to be assimilated within the context of each separate colony, from Massachusetts to Georgia, and become undifferentiated from the majority within each colony, unique as individuals but not as a distinct group. Lawrence had an unsophisticated perception of the unity of the other colonial societies in British North America, and certainly no conception of the individuality of, for example, German settlement groups in Pennsylvania or the Scots-Irish in Connecticut.[4] But his main purpose was clear and his judgement unequivocal: the Acadians must cease to exist as a coherent and separate society and become, in terms of political and civic standing, absorbed into the mass of the other culture.

Surprisingly, Lawrence's ambition failed. While many an individual Acadian perished and many indeed did find themselves assimilated into some other society, an Acadian group identity continued to exist. While there were circumstances in the nature of the exile and proscription which contributed, the continuation of an Acadian identity was largely due to the characteristics that had become the hallmark of Acadian identity before 1755. Any assessment of why exile did not triumph has to start from an appreciation of the nature of the Acadian community before 1755.

The size of Acadian population in 1755 has still not been established, even after the splendid work by Jean Daigle and Robert Leblanc published in the first volume of *The Historical Atlas of Canada*.[5] But disagreement about how many people should be numbered as part of the community that year—15,000, 18,000, or even 20,000—is less important than what we do know: the whereabouts of the major concentrations of this population and the main thrust of their expansion.

The older settlements of the Acadian population, those in the neighbourhood of Annapolis Royal, Cape Sable, and La Heve, whose roots are in the 1630s, while significant, are by 1755 much less so than those of the Minas Basin and Chignecto Isthmus, which were established in the 1670s and 1680s. The Acadian population of Annapolis Royal in 1755 was probably 2,000 and the other settlements—Cape Sable and La Heve—would number at most 400 people.[6] The most populous centres of Acadian life at that time were to found through the stretch of country from the Minas Basin to the valleys of the Memramcook, the Petitcodiac, and the Shepody. Settlements along the Minas Basin, communities which ran from the base of Blomindon to the gentle hills of what was then called Cobequid (Truro), traced their beginnings back to the 1680s. In 1755 their combined population was in the region of 5,000.[7]

Similarly, the families of Beaubassin, whose houses looked out on the Chignecto Basin from the higher terraces near present-day Amherst and Sackville, lived on land settled at around the same time as the Minas Basin. Bishop St. Vallier had visited the area in 1686, finding it a charming region and estimated that 150 people lived on the edges of what he described as *"un des plus beaux havres du monds."*[8] In 1755 the population there was probably 3,000.[9]

The most recently established settlements of the Acadians in 1755 were those of the area known to them as "Trois-Rivières": the valleys of Shepody, Petitcodiac, and Memramcook.[10] Small hamlets grew of there from 1731 onwards, when Blanchards, Legers, Dubois, and other families moved out from the Minas Basin, just as earlier members of their families had once moved from the Port Royal settlements to the Minas Basin. The "Trois-Rivières" settlement was the most considerable new expansion of Acadian settlement after 1730. By 1755, the population of these river valleys probably totalled between 200 and 300.

While the settlements just enumerated are the most populous of the Acadian community, they represent just that. They are not the totality of the Acadian people in 1755. There were also Acadians settled along the coast from the Baie des Chaleurs to Baie Verte on sites first explored in the 1630s and 1640s, the time of Nicholas Denys and his imaginative enterprises. The most important of these were around the mouth of the Miramichi and at Cocagne and Shediac, also tidewater sites. Further, while there is some dispute as to whether there was year-round settlement by Acadians on the Madeleine Islands at this time, there is ample evidence that these were known and exploited as rich fishing grounds by both Acadian and Micmac.[11] The Acadian interest in Canso should not be overlooked, nor that there were also Acadians along the Saint John River Valley, as far inland as Jemseg. Acadians had settled, along with more recent French migrants, on Ile St. Jean and in parts of Ile Royale. Linked by direct kinship ties to people living within the major centres of Acadian population, as well as by ties of trade and custom, language, religion and common experience, these people numbered close to 3,000.

The Acadian demographic experience was not that different from the pattern of demographic development elsewhere in colonial North America. The growth of the Acadian population, from roughly 3,000 in 1713 to at least 15,000 in 1755, may have been slightly more rapid than that experienced generally in colonial America, but not overwhelmingly so. Jim Potter has pointed out that "different colonies experienced very different growth rates at different periods."[12] For example, in the eighteenth century the average decennial growth rate in New England was 27 per cent. The comparable demographic studies of Acadians have not yet been completed, but it is unlikely that their population growth would be much greater than this.[13] Similarly, the way in which the settlements of the Acadians moved from the Annapolis Basin, along the river valleys and through the marshlands of the Bay of Fundy, as well as to the river mouths along the Atlantic coast, has a striking similarity to patterns of expansion found elsewhere—in Maine and other New England colonies, as well as in Quebec.

The variation of settlement patterns to be found within the colony was much the same as that of New France. Mid eighteenth-century Kamouraska, Quebec City, and Montreal, for example, had as much distinctiveness from each other as they had features in common. Similarly, as has been outlined in the previous chapter, Acadian life in different parts of the territory revealed subtle distinctions between settlements, as well as clear similarities of experience. The Annapolis Valley Acadians had lived dominated by farming, hunting, and fishing, but a fair number of them were connected to the comings and goings of the officials of the small colony. Acadians were pilots for the incoming ships from Europe and, occasionally, part of the tiny bureaucracy.[14] Some pursued commerce and trade, or small-scale home industries in woodwork or textiles.

The settlers of the Minas Basin had lives which were shaped by dyke-building and an agriculture rich enough to allow for exports, not only to other communities within the colony, but also to Louisbourg and to Boston.[15] There is some evidence that trade was also carried on with the West Indies.[16] This meant a very different daily round than that of those settled along the Atlantic shore north of Cape Tormentine, or newly arrived on Ile St. Jean. The inhabitants of one such outpost, Mirliguesch, were referred by Le Loutre as a mixed collection of "Acadians and … Savage."[17] Lives in these settlements would be dominated by hunting and fishing, with subsistence agriculture producing no surplus for trade.

The Acadian society was strengthened, as were the other European colonies in North America, by a wide variance of lifestyles.[18] However, there were a number of significant features which helped to give those who lived in the different settlements of particular colonies a strong sense of common purpose. One of the most important of such unifying factors for the Acadians was external pressure arising from the fact that Acadians were considered colonials, and their lands, a colony. While this is true for all European settlements in North America at this time, the Acadians had a particularly complex colonial status. A large part of Acadian distinctiveness arose from the impact upon the Acadian polity of the imperial policies of both France and England. The alternating administration of their society by French and English officials, each for considerable periods, helped to produce that mindset among the Acadians which led them to develop a distinctive policy of neutrality. French and English attempts to control the lands the Acadians settled were accompanied by international boundary commissions and the development of military installations. The founding of Louisbourg and the establishment of Beauséjour by the French were matched by the establishment of Halifax and the organization of Fort Lawrence and Fort Edward by the English. The living space of the Acadians was one of the centres in North America for the conflicting territorial ambitions of two great empires, England and France.

I have suggested elsewhere that one of the keys to understanding the development of Acadian identity is recognizing the reality of their experience as a border people.[19] It is important to realize that the political status of this border varied. In the seventeenth century and until the 1740s, "Acadia or Nova Scotia" was at one of the most important junctions of Anglo-French claims in North America. The colony was a border that made part of the frontier between empires and saw frequent skirmishes which greatly hindered development of the settlements. But, until 1744, "Acadia or Nova Scotia" as a whole was not a battlefield. After 1744, however, the Acadians saw an episode of the war between the Empires involve the heartlands and peripheries of their communities simultaneously. Military historians have noted that by the early 1740s the Missaquash river was the effective boundary between French and English control.[20] It was a boundary that, in the expansion of their communities, the Acadians had ignored when their colony was the meeting place of empires. They continued to ignore it when the colony became an actual battleground of imperial forces.

In the eyes not only of London and Paris but also of officials in New England and New France, Acadia and the Acadians were a disputed resource. Their lands were seen as a legitimate area for control both by London and by Paris. France and England both considered the Acadians' male population as a possible source of military strength.[21] In sum, Acadia was perceived as a colony and the Acadians as colonials. This is not surprising, for it was partly true. For the Acadians, however, their colonial status was less a central and deciding factor of their political being than it was just another aspect of life, something with which one coped, not something by which one was controlled. Even the system of deputies, a system first structured by the English solely for the purpose of communicating their commands to the scattered settlements,[22] served to reinforce the Acadian sense of their own independence. Over the decades since 1710, the delegates, originally chosen to act as representatives of official direction from Annapolis Royal, became officials themselves. They, not the clergy, became the indispensable arbiters of community life. Occasionally constables and officers of the court at Annapolis, they were more often, as Brebner has summarized it, "registrars-general for their district, [those who] recorded titles, sales, and other transfers, marriage settlements and inheritances, and were regarded by a commission of 15 per cent on the seigneurial fees they collected and small fees for executing deeds."[23] This organization of local government gave the Acadian population considerable experience in self-leadership. We do not know precisely how the delegates were elected by the community, but we do know that they were elected. Thus, before exile, the Acadian people were accustomed to select spokesmen to present their views to others who considered themselves more powerful. This situation could not help but encourage the Acadians to think of themselves having very considerable political rights, even if they were not entirely self-governed.

Further, the Acadian sense of control over their daily lives was enhanced by the fact that, as in most North American colonial settlements, the family was the most important social institution.[24] For the majority of Acadians the family and the household not only formed the basis of their daily experience but also structured their relationships to the wider community and their working world.[25] Throughout the length and breadth of the Acadian settlements the family and household shaped life for most individuals, whether one looks at the traditional patterns of life on farms in the Annapolis Valley, the mixed trading and farming economies of the Minas basin, or the new ways of life being tried in the Trois-Rivières area; or whether one analyses the Beaubassin settlements and considers the outposts of Acadian life at the mouth of the Miramichi or in Merliguesch. In the two most fundamental aspects of the community, landholding and religion, family and kin connections played the most significant roles.

To deal with kinship ties first: family relationships within and among the Acadian communities made a close net of interconnections. It was a net, not a solid piece of cloth. Before exile, as afterwards, the Acadians showed a considerable ability to absorb newcomers into their community .... Even in the older settled Acadian parishes of Annapolis, Minas, and Beaubassin, newcomers accounted for a significant percentage of marriage partners.[26] Within a particular Acadian hamlet or village one can find an intricate series of intermarriages, brothers in one family marrying sisters from another, marriages within the then-forbidden relationship of second-cousin. However, such a pattern of relationships existed alongside families who had no ties to their neighbours, not even by marriage of distant relatives. There has been little comparison of the kin structure of Acadian villages with contemporary villages elsewhere, either in North America or in Europe, and it is not yet possible to say whether the kin lines of Acadian parishes were closer than those to be found in south-western France, in New England, or along the St. Lawrence. One can assert, however, that in 1755 Acadian family life was flourishing and as vital to the Acadian sense of community as was family life elsewhere in British North America.

The Acadian family and household were the economic arbiters of the community, made more powerful because of very lax official control of the Acadians' exploration and settlement of new lands. After 1713 landholdings were granted to individuals directly and Acadians in many settlements paid quit-rents for their property.[27] But the officials at Annapolis Royal and later at Halifax were in no hurry to grant any obviously unchallengeable titles to property since the tenure of land was, as Clark wrote, inextricably linked in the official mind with an unqualified oath of allegiance which the Acadians showed no sign of accepting.[28] The result was predictably chaotic. But land claims by

Acadians were registered and suits between Acadians about land were judged by the officials at Annapolis Royal.[29] At the same time, especially in the Trois-Rivières region, Acadians, in the words of their own deputies, "[took] possession of and improved large portions of lands"[30] claimed as timberland reserves by the Crown, and ignored any and all demands made by officials to cease and desist. The first settlers in the present-day Dieppe-Moncton region were, as Paul Surette has discovered, two kin groups of families linked by marriage among siblings and cousins.[31] The organization of the plans of these hamlets along the Petitcodiac was not by official survey and land grant: it was by agreement between the pioneers themselves. The Acadian family was the arbiter of plans for new settlements, and it was between kin groups and households that boundaries were claimed and agreed.

As well as being the real authority behind land clearance and distribution, the family was crucial in the maintenance of religious belief. Catholic life gained its daily reality in the practices of the home. Few of the Acadian settlements had resident priests. In 1748, there were five priests reported in action, excluding Le Loutre whose activities were mostly peripatetic and centred upon the Micmac. There was de Miniac, "half blind," de la Goudalie, "quite old and a little deaf," and Desenclaves, who suffered "from a weak chest." This left Chauvreulx and Girard, who were apparently hale and hearty.[32] Basically, each Acadian settlement could count on a visit from a priest annually, and those in the three main regions of Acadian life—the Annapolis Valley, the Minas Basin, and Beaubassin—could also count on a priest residing in the region most years. Weekly Mass was the privilege only of those living within an hour or so's journey of the major parish churches, and priestly blessing or weddings and baptisms took place only when a priest came to a particular neighbourhood. This was a common practice for eighteenth-century Catholicism. A great deal more must be written about Acadian religious practices, based on archival records, including those of the Archdiocese of Quebec, rather than the wishful thinking of nineteenth- and twentieth-century myth makers.[33] It is no slur on the devotion of the Acadians to point out that the rites of the Church were less easily available to them before 1755 than they were after 1830, nor that Acadian interpretation of Catholicism before 1755 was based as much upon individual faith as upon clerically imposed discipline. During the years of exile among mostly Protestant communities of the British colonies in North America, the family framework of Catholic belief proved to be a major factor in Acadian survival.

This crucial importance of family within Acadian society has been unaccountably neglected, given the immense interest in genealogy that has characterized Acadian studies.[34] The archival resources have rarely been examined in detail to discover whether members of particular families played consistently dominant roles in the Acadian settlements.[35] Were the Leblancs unusual in being linked to British interests, given the number of men of that name who acted as notaries and delegates throughout the settlements? What would an analysis of landholding size and numbers of herds and flocks tell us about the economic stratification among the Acadians? The work to answer such questions remains to be done,[36] as does the work to tell what place trading, hunting, and fishing held in each of the Acadian communities at this time.[37] At the moment, one has merely the major outlines of Acadian life on the eve of the deportation. Much of the process of Acadian life has yet to be uncovered.

But even with such a host of questions yet unanswered, it is clear that in 1755 the Acadians were seen as a distinctive society by those who considered themselves their rulers. Sent out by London to govern "Acadia or Nova Scotia" in 1749, Edward Cornwallis informed the delegates who had been brought to meet him that "It appears to me that you think yourselves independent of any government; and you wish to treat with the king as if you were so."[38]

The new Governor was right. By the mid eighteenth-century the Acadians did indeed consider themselves a people. Further, they considered that this meant they had definite political rights in society. Acadian policy throughout the years leading up to the deportation was largely based on this conviction that they had, at the very minimum, a negotiating strength in any confrontation with officials, whether military, civil, or clerical, English or French. As late as 10 June 1755, the people of Minas offered to promise "our unshaken fidelity to his Majesty, provided that His Majesty shall allow us the same liberty that he has granted us."[39] This sense of political existence is not without parallel in colonial societies: it is similar to one of the motivating forces behind the American revolution.

It is unlikely that the Acadians ever envisaged exile as a likely fate, even during the tumultuous decade that preceded their deportation. Their tactics were strongly influenced by a belief that the worst that could occur would be a temporary dislocation into French-controlled territory. Ever since 1713 the possibility of Acadian emigration had been part of the rhetoric political discussion between the English and the Acadians. Such movement had almost always been envisaged in terms of Acadian wish and English opposition. But towards the end of the war of the Austrian succession (usually known in North America as King George's War), the then Lieutenant-Governor of Nova Scotia, Paul Mascarene, reported that there were rumours among the Acadian settlements that "a great force was coming from New England to transport or destroy them."[40] He also reported that every effort was immediately taken to scotch the report. Governor Shirley of Massachusetts[41] issued a proclamation in the fall of 1746 in which he declared

> in His Majesty's name, that there is not the least foundation for any Apprehensions of His Majesty's intending to remove the said Inhabitants of Nova Scotia from their settlements and Habitations: but that on the contrary it is His Majesty's Resolution to protect and maintain all such of 'em as have adhered to, and shall continue in their Duty and Allegiance to him in the quiet and peaceable Possession of their respective Habitations and Settlements and in the Employment of all their rights and Privileges as his Subjects.[42]

Given the Acadian belief that they had demonstrated their loyalty very adequately in recent years, it would not be surprising for their delegates to consider that their policy of independent neutrality needed no particular adjustment after 1749.

In fact, once open warfare between England and France had been brought to a halt by the treaty of Aix-la-Chapelle in 1748, the relationship between the majority of the Acadian settlements and English officials became much as it had been before fighting gave red snow to Grand-Pré.[43] In 1749, both England and France immediately set about reorganizing their forces and England, in particular, looked to the strengthening of her position in North America. Louisbourg had been returned to France, causing thunderous criticism from Boston.[44] Plans were now made in London to strengthen the British hold on Nova Scotia. A new regime was inaugurated to oversee the foundation of Halifax as well as the establishment of Lunenburg with Protestant migrants.[45] Acadia was to become Nova Scotia, a colony that would be a reliable outpost of the British Empire instead of a region of doubtful security inhabited by people with questionable loyalty to His Britannic Majesty.

Edward Cornwallis arrived, as has been noted, to take over as Governor of the colony on 21 June 1749.[46] While he managed to fulfil a fair number of the aspirations of those who had appointed him, his attempt to make the Acadians take an unqualified oath of loyalty—without any provision for their remaining neutral during an Anglo-French confrontation—was met with a replay of past Acadian responses.[47] On 31 July 1749 the assembled delegates from the Acadian settlements heard Cornwallis proclaim that their position within the colony must be regularized by the swearing of an unqualified oath. On 6 September 1749 the Acadians presented the Governor and his council with a petition that requested a renewal of the oath administered to them twenty years earlier by Governor Phillips, an oath which in Acadian eyes had never been repudiated by them nor annulled by the British. Should this petition be denied, the Acadians stated, they would then quit the colony. Cornwallis and his administration made the same response to this reply that their predecessors had done to previous similar rejoinders: inaction. This could be fairly taken as tacit acceptance of the Acadian terms. As Brebner wrote, "the relations between Governor and *habitants* had fallen into the old ruts and were wearing them deeper."[48] In these circumstances, it is unlikely that many Acadians envisaged being sent into exile as a distinct possibility even as late as spring 1755. At any rate no alteration can be discerned in Acadian attitudes about the oath during the years 1749–55.

However, if the general outlines of Acadian politics towards the English did not change, the converse is not true. Despite the similarity of official policy on the question of the oath itself, there were fundamental differences between the regimes of Mascarene and his predecessors and of Edward Cornwallis and his successors. John Bartlett Brebner opened his chapter on these years, which he called "Caught between the duellists," with a striking description of the meeting of Mascarene and five of his councillors with Cornwallis, on the deck of the HMS *Beaufort* in Chebucto Bay, 12 July 1749.[49] For Brebner this meeting represented the start of a radically new policy for the colony, which was "to be prosecuted vigorously and with generous financial support."[50]

This new policy was a direct consequence of the Treaty of Aix-la-Chapelle which had been signed in 1748. During negotiations, the British diplomats had given back Ile Royale and its "great fortress" of Louisbourg to the French, in return for concessions elsewhere. Now came London's attempt to redress the balance in British North America. The policy decided upon had three major features: the establishment of an English stronghold on the Atlantic coast of the colony to offset Louisbourg, the general enhancement of the military presence of the English within centres of Acadian population, and a scheme for the assisted emigration of Protestants to the colony. The establishment of Halifax was the most dramatic sign of the new order. Clark called its building "the greatest public porkbarrel yet opened in North America" and cited the parliamentary votes for the construction of the city between 1749 and 1753 as a measure of the opportunities created. They were "1749, £40,000; 1750, £57,583; 1751, £53,928; 1752, £61,493; 1753, £94,616; and 1755, £49,418."[51] While construction proceeded neither as smoothly nor as swiftly as its planners had hoped, proceed it did.[52] Despite its reputation as a place where one-half of the city lived by selling rum to the other, by 1750 it was asserted that there were 750 brick houses in Halifax.[53] Its population fluctuated wildly, because it was a port of entry for new migrants to the colony. Clark estimates that at one point in 1750 there were as many as 6,000 people living about its streets.[54] Its core population during the period 1749–55 was somewhere in the region of 3,000.[55] During the early years, many migrants moved on to other British colonies. From the outset, however, Halifax attracted a small but steady flow of immigrants from New England. Many opportunists came for the government contract, to sell rum, or to further the smuggling trade between Boston and Louisbourg. Just as many came because they saw a chance for their long-term betterment in the changing circumstances of Nova Scotia. As traders, fishermen, merchants, craftsmen, and even lawyers, they brought a great deal of experience and ability to the new society. At the very least, Halifax gave Cornwallis a strength that no previous English administration in the colony had possessed.

The establishment of Halifax was crucial for the success of the new policy for Nova Scotia, but it was only part of the scheme evolved by London and Boston.[56] The general strengthening of English military presence throughout the colony that took place at the same time was equally important. The Annapolis garrison was reorganized, and Fort Edward was built at Pisiquid, with a road connecting it to Halifax. In September of 1750, Major Charles Lawrence built a fort, which he named after himself, on the south side of the Misseguash. All these actions brought the reality of the English possession of the colony to the heart of the Acadian settlements in a new and vivid manner.

The third feature of the policy that Cornwallis and his successors pursued was the foundation of Lunenburg and the settlement by 1754 of upwards of 2,000 "Foreign Protestants" there and in the immediately surrounding area. This neighbourhood was that known to the Acadians as Merligash and La Heve. Winthrop Pickard Bell wrote the classic study of this project.[57] He disentangled the mixture of motives that lay behind London's willingness to assist foreign Protestant migration to Nova Scotia at that time and illuminated the complex history of their establishment there. Bell made it clear that after 1749 the officials concerned with these migrants envisaged them as being established in townships of their own. Whatever might have been the dream of Governor Shirley of Massachusetts—that mingling English settlements among the Acadian villages "as contiguous to theirs as maybe" would enhance their loyalty to Great Britain—this vision was no more than advice and advice not followed.[58] Again, as in the case of Halifax, the settling of new migrants proved much more difficult in practice than had been anticipated. But, like Halifax, by 1754 something considerable had been achieved: the foundations of the new community had been laid. The new town of Lunenburg had been laid out, with no concessions made to the steep hillside on which it was built. The grid-iron plan had been used, yielding roughly horizontal streets running parallel to a narrow waterfront and cross streets running at right angles straight up the hill.[59] While the years 1755 to 1763 were hard for these new migrants, in 1754 a settlement was in place, with sawmills in operation, some houses built, some farms laid out, and a number of craftsmen plying their trades.

All this action meant a major change in the political situation of the Acadians. Before 1749, while their lands were the border between two empires, it seemed clear, from an Acadian point of view, that one of these empires, France, was more concerned with the territory than the other. "Acadia or Nova Scotia" could be considered as a distant outpost of the British empire. But it could also be seen as the moving frontier of the French. France had the most impressive military establishment at Louisbourg. Small English trading vessels might ply the waters off the coasts of the colony, but French shipping was more visible. French military action brought war directly into the Acadian settlements in the 1740s. Until the conclusion of hostilities and the fall of Louisbourg, from the Acadian perspective French military force could be considered the more daring and often the more successful. With the foundation of Halifax and the establishment of new forts, this situation was radically altered.

Further, until 1749, it had also seemed clear that Acadian development would set the pattern for the future of the colony. The Acadians had been the clear majority of the population within "Acadia or Nova Scotia" since sometime in the 1720s, when their numbers surpassed the Micmac population. Acadians were the settlers of the colony. Their lifestyle was its economy. With the arrival of migrants for Halifax and Lunenburg, this no longer seemed obvious. Whilst the English military presence could be dismissed as a temporary phenomenon, the establishment of new villages and towns presaged a more enduring transformation.

If the Acadians seemed to react slowly to these new elements in the life of the colony, the French and the Micmac responded rapidly. As John Reid has pointed out, the French had few grounds on which to object to this outburst of energetic action by the English.[60] But this did not stop an attempt by France to lay *de facto* claim to as much territory in the area as possible. While peace supposedly reigned between the two empires throughout the world as a result of the treaty of 1748, and while an international commission was working to establish the boundaries of "Acadia or Nova Scotia,"[61] the day-to-day life on the frontiers of that colony was punctuated by raid and counter-raid, ambush and seige.[62] Fort Lawrence would soon be faced by Fort Beausejour, whose construction was begun in April 1751 scarcely more than a kilometre from the earlier fortification. In the Anglo-French struggle for dominance in North America, 1748 marked a truce rather than a peace.

The Micmac aided the French by exerting their own pressure on both the English and the Acadians during these years. Throughout the years of the European exploration and settlement of "Acadia or Nova Scotia," the Micmac had never stopped considering themselves the rightful tenants of the land. In 1720 they had affirmed their rights of possession by saying: "This land here that God has given us which we can be accounted a part as much as the trees are born here.... We are masters independent of everyone and wish to have our country free."[63] The Micmac were not so much allies of the French in the 1750s as they were a people convinced of their autonomy and taking all means to ensure their continued independence. England seemed a greater threat than France to this goal. So the Micmac not only mounted raiding parties against Halifax and Lunenburg, they also helped the French make the Acadian communities of Beaubassin a war zone. In 1750 the Micmac, accompanied and abetted by the French missionary priest, Jean-Louis Le Loutre, helped to force some Acadian migration from the Beaubassin villages by setting fire to both houses and church.[64]

The extent to which the Acadians remained strictly neutral in these years has been hotly debated. In my view, there is no doubt that the bulk of the Acadians adhered to the policy. There is no evidence of a major rejection of British rule throughout the Acadian settlements. But there is also no doubt in my mind that some Acadians not only traded with Louisbourg and neglected to supply local English garrisons but also supported French activities against the English. There is documentary evidence about the participation of young Acadian men, in particular, in French and Micmac raiding parties.[65] Once more, the key to understanding Acadian action is to consider them as a normal human society, hence as a polity that would contain a variety of views even though a majority would finally unite in support of a common policy. Cornwallis concluded his term of office in August 1752, handing over to Colonel Peregrine Hopson. This latter gentleman only remained in the colony until October 1753, but retained the governorship of the colony until 1755. When he sailed for England, Colonel Charles Lawrence was appointed as Lieutenant-Governor.

Lawrence had had a long career in the military, in the colonial service, and in the colony. He was thirty-eight when he was gazetted major and had joined his regiment in the 1747 occupation of Louisbourg.[66] Whatever one may think of his political abilities, his career shows considerable military perspicacity. There is no doubt that he framed his policies as Lieutenant-Governor in the light of his military experiences, as will become clear below.

International events are of paramount importance for understanding what happened to Acadian society as Lawrence entered upon his term of office. The new policy introduced by Cornwallis, a policy of increased English interest and presence within the colony, was largely the result of international concerns. It was a policy that prepared for war. It had been framed in the context of a bitter struggle between the English and French colonies in North America. This flamed into open warfare in the spring of 1754 with the clash of the French and American militia in the Ohio Valley. The French were quite as much concerned for boundaries of their empire as were the English and appointed Roland-Michel Barrin de la Galissonière as "commander in chief" of New France. His mission was the "restructuring" of the French empire in North America, a "restructuring" that would necessitate stopping "the undertakings of the English."[67] 1755 was the last year of prologue, the final year of preparatory clash and skirmish the outbreak of worldwide war, a war which would involve battles between France and England not only in North America and Europe but also in Asia. This war became known as the Seven Years' War and the peace treaties that brought it to a close in 1763 effectively ended the power of the French empire in North America. In the declaration of war issued from Kensington on 18 May 1756, England put in pride of place the "usurpations and encroachments made by the French upon the English territories and settlements ... in the West Indies and North America ... particularly in the province of Nova Scotia."[68] France issued her declaration from Versailles on 9 June 1756. The events of exile and proscription, which would so profoundly shape the identity of the Acadian community for the next centuries had their immediate cause in the tensions of the New World. Although European men and money were deeply involved in the strategy and tactics of the war effort in North America before 1756, the deportation of the Acadians was, fundamentally, rooted in North American realities and perceptions.

The most obvious of these realities is a matter of political geography: the tactical and strategic possibilities to both sides of the land settled by the Acadians. Moreover, by 1755 "Acadia or Nova Scotia" was not only the border between two rival empires but also in itself a region with considerable tactical importance for both powers.

We have a great deal of information on how Lawrence saw his own policy. There is no doubt that for him military matters were an understood priority. He shaped his policy for the colony accordingly. He wrote, at length, to Governor Shirley of Massachusetts, to other Governors of British colonies in North America, and to the authorities in London.[69] Lawrence's policy resulted from the wish to make Nova Scotia a secure and flourishing outpost of the British Empire in North America. He was convinced by 1753, when he was made lieutenant-governor of the colony, that the refusal of the Acadians to take an unqualified oath of loyalty to the British crown made them a major obstacle to the fulfilment of this ambition.[70] He held two completely different, but in his view interdependent, objectives: first, the preservation of British possessions in North America, and, second, the strengthening of Nova Scotia as a crucial and significant part of those possessions.

By the spring of 1755, Lawrence had become thoroughly convinced that his colony could not become a reliable outpost of the British Empire while the Acadians were among its people. Thus the best possible solution was to send them to be assimilated among the populations of the other British North American colonies. In the circular to the governors of these colonies quoted from earlier, this was made plain.[71] Lawrence informed his fellow governors of the unique opportunity now available: "The success that has attended his Majesty's arms in driving the French from the Encroachments they had made in this province," he wrote, "furnished me with a favourable opportunity of reducing the French inhabitants of this Colony to a proper obedience to His Majesty's Government or forcing them to quit the country." He went on to state that "I offered such of them as had not been openly in arms against us, a continuance of the Possession of their lands, if they would take the Oath of Allegiance, unqualified with any Reservation whatsoever." "But this," he also stated, "they have most audaciously as well as unanimously refused." Lawrence therefore turned to the council of the colony "to consider by what means we could with the greatest security and effect rid ourselves of a set of people who would forever have been an obstruction to the intention of settling this Colony and that it was now from their refusal to the Oath absolutely incumbent upon us to remove." The circular continued: "As their numbers amount to near 7000 persons the driving them off with leave to go whither they pleased would have doubtless strengthened Canada with so considerable a number of inhabitants; and as they have no cleared land to give them at present, such as able to bear arms must have been immediately employed in annoying this and neighbouring Colonies. To prevent such an inconvenience it was judged a necessary and the only practicable measure to divide them among the Colonies."

Lawrence may have known what he was about and why, but the debate that has raged over the deportation of the Acadians ever since has been bitter and wide-ranging.[72] Whose influence ensured that the proposal of deportation became reality? Governor Shirley of Massachusetts?[73] What part did London play?[74] Was the determining factor the opinions of the British admirals Boscawen and Mostyn who arrived that spring? Can the whole episode really be summed up, as Guy Fregault believed, as an act of war, and be accepted in that context?[75]

For the Acadians in 1755 such questions must have been of considerably less importance than the events of the dispersion itself. Perhaps the only such matter that would have been argued among them would have concerned their own tactics. The crucial meetings between Acadian and English officials took place in early July, but these meetings were the culmination of an eventful spring. The incident that provided Nova Scotia with the opportunity to deport the Acadians, and to which Lawrence referred in his circular, was the fall of Beausejour, which had capitulated on 16 June 1755. While the campaign to capture the fort had been in progress, efforts had also been made to ensure that the Acadian population, as a whole, would remain quiet. In April and May orders were sent out to the Minas Acadians to surrender not only any weapons they might possess but also their boats.[76] A petition from the Acadians for the return of their possessions was written on 10 June and received in Halifax at the time when Lawrence received the news that Beausejour had fallen and that about 300 Acadians had been found in arms within the fort.[77]

A meeting of the Council, presided over by Lawrence, took place at the Governor's House on 3 July 1755.[78] The petition sent from Minas was discussed with a number of the signatories. The Council took the Acadians point by point through the petition and concluded by asking the Acadians to take an unqualified oath of loyalty to the King. It is obvious from the Minutes of this meeting that the Councillors found the petition "an Insult upon His Majesty's Authority." In it the Acadians had insisted that they had not only not violated their oaths but had kept faithful "in spite of the solicitations and dreadful threats of another power." They had affirmed their intentions of so keeping faith "provided that His Majesty shall allow us the same liberty that we have enjoyed formerly." In sum, the attitude of the Acadians was that they had proved their political neutrality to the government by their past actions and should now be rewarded. The Council was completely unpersuaded by the proofs offered and demanded further assurances. The Acadians, by such phrases as "Permit us, if you please, Sir, to make known the annoying circumstances in which we are placed, to the prejudice of the tranquillity we ought to enjoy," showed that, in their own eyes, they had the right to argue with English officials. The Acadians had held this attitude from the time of Françoise Perrot in 1688. It was a point of view consistently repudiated by those sent from Europe to govern them. It was the attitude that was maintained by all of the Acadian delegates throughout the July meetings of 1755. Polite, unafraid, and obdurate the Acadians offered a qualified oath. The council minutes for 28 July conclude as follows:

> As it had been before determined to send all the French Inhabitants out of the Province if they refused to Take the Oaths, nothing now remained to be considered but what Measures should be Taken to send them away, and where they should be sent to.[79]

There is one indication that other tactics might have been considered among the Acadians. When finally convinced that exile was imminent, some of the delegates from the Minas Basin did offer an unqualified oath of allegiance. The offer was made on 4 July 1755 only to be rejected by Lawrence and the Council on the grounds that "there was no reason to hope their proposed compliance proceeded from an honest Mind and could be esteemed only the Effect of Compulsion and Force."[80]

But such discussions among the Acadians in 1755 would have been over-shadowed completely by the events of the deportation itself. The vast majority of the population was shipped away, either in the last six months of 1755 or at some point over the next six years. The last attempt at completing the deportation came in 1763.[81] Those who remained mostly took refuge along the river banks of the Saint John and the Miramichi, or survived more or less as prisoners of war within Nova Scotia. In 1764 Acadians were once more permitted to own land in Nova Scotia.[82] Some 165 families are noted as being in the colony at the time, a population of perhaps a thousand.[83] The size of the pre-deportation population of the Acadians is a matter of considerable debate, with estimates ranging from around 13,000 to more than 18,000. I now consider the second figure to be the more likely. In their work for *The Historical Atlas of Canada*, Jean Daigle and Robert Leblanc present a lower figure, 13,000. They have published the following table of the distribution of the Acadian population at the time of the Peace of Paris in 1763: Massachusetts, 1,000; Connecticut, 650; New York, 250; Maryland, 810; Pennsylvania, 400; South Carolina, 300; Georgia, 200; Nova Scotia, 1,250; St. John river, 100; Louisiana, 300; England, 850; France, 3,500; Quebec, 2,000; Prince Edward Island, 300; Baie des Chaleurs, 700. The total is 12,660.[84]

Again, as with the estimation of the total population of the Acadians in 1755, the numbers can only be taken as approximate, as their authors themselves remark. Questions remain not only about the actual figures, but also about possible groupings of Acadians that have been overlooked: what about the Acadians who had arrived in Santo Domingo?[85] What about the Acadians in the Channel Islands? The more important question, however, is the reconciliation of these statistics with the pre-deportation figures and with the available figures for death tolls among the exiles between 1755 and 1763. Whatever the precise figures may be, there is no doubt that the Acadian community was devastated. The breaking of a people from lands where they had been established for more than three generations was a matter of force and coercion. The Acadians were now officially regarded by the English as a hostile population, whose only rights were to be deported. Lawrence, basing his instructions on work done sometime earlier by surveyor Morris,[86] on 31 July 1755 sent out his explicit directions for the officers who would carry out the operation.[87] There has been considerable debate about whether these instructions show a criminal mind or merely a painstaking administrator at work.[88] The immediate consequence of the instructions being sent was that the military set about their implementation. For the officers who received them, their duty was plain. As John Winslow, the army officer in charge of the removal of the Acadians from the Grand-Pré area, wrote to Lawrence, "altho this is a Disagreeable Part of Duty we are Put Upon I am Sensible it is a Necessary one."[89]

This judgement was the common opinion shared by most of those engaged in carrying out the task. In the words of Major Handfield, the officer in charge of the Annapolis Royal area, it was a "most disagreeable and troublesome part of the Service."[90] But it was policy; the work was to be done. Though Winslow would write to Captain Murray, the officer engaged in the deportation from Fort Edward, that "Things are very heavy on my Harte and hands," he would conclude the sentence, "But as it is shall I question not be able to Skuffell Throh."[91] Once the decision had been taken, the deportation was set in motion and the military carried it out with the inevitable infliction of considerable suffering. But there is no evidence that the cruelty of circumstances was generally augmented by a planned policy of terror.

There was no need for extraordinary measures of brutality to ensure a submissive population. The Acadians were stunned by events. Winslow considered that even when gathered together on the shores, waiting to embark on the transports, the Acadians were not even then fully persuaded that they were "actually to be removed."[92] The reality, even if it had been fully expected, would have been psychologically stunning. Settlements burned, cattle driven off, lives now entirely at the command of soldiery: within days the Acadians were turned from a free and flourishing people into a crowd of refugees. Winslow has left us an account of the first embarkation from the Minas Basin: his journal reads, "October 8th: began to Embarke the Inhabitants who went of very Solentarily and unwillingly, the women in Great Distress Carrying off Their Children in their Arms, Others Carrying their Decrepit Parents in their Carts and all their Goods moving in Great Confusion and appeared a scene of Woe and Distress."[93] This "Woe and Distress" was only the beginning.

The Acadians suffered appalling losses in consequence of the deportation, first on board ship and second on arrival at their various destinations. Shipboard conditions in the eighteenth century were dreadful.[94] Those who sailed with the naval squadron under the command of Admirals Boscawen and Mostyn, which had arrived in Halifax on 28 June 1755, were so severely battered by scurvy, typhus, and yellow fever that they could scarcely manoeuvre the ships into Halifax harbour. The condition of soldiers and sailors arriving at Quebec City in the 1750s was much the same.[95] Conditions for civilians were no better. One traveller of 1734 recorded that passengers were lumped together regardless of sex. He continued, "We were crammed into [this] dark foul place like so many sardines; it was impossible to get into bed without banging our heads and our knees twenty times.... The motion of the vessel would dismantle the apparatus, slinging people into each others' cots."[96]

The circumstances which the exiles experienced were equally as bad, though probably not worse. The condition of the ships putting into Boston, but bound for colonies further south, was reported as bad, the Port authorities remarking that, "The vessels in general are much too crowded; their allowance of Provisions short being 1lb of Beef 5lb of Flour & 2lb of Bread prt men [sic] per week and too small a quantity to that allowance to the Ports they are Bound to especially at this season of the year; and their water very bad."[97]

Half of the 415 people shipped on the *Edward Cornwallis*, destination South Carolina, died en route.[98] While this is the largest number of known deaths for one ship, tolls of 20 and 30 per cent were not uncommon. At least two of the ships, the *Violet* and *Duke William*, carrying Acadians to Europe, sank with the loss of all on board.[99] Ocean-going travel was hazardous in the eighteenth century, and the Acadians were not spared any of its dangers.

The impact of disease on the Acadians, once they had arrived at their destination, was almost equally devastating. The Acadian communities had relatively little acquaintance with epidemics of smallpox, typhoid, yellow fever, and other such infectious diseases before exile, and thus no real community immunity to these illnesses. Further, the resistance to infection of those exiled, after the physical conditions of their journeyings, was very weak. The ravages of smallpox, for example, were severe among those who arrived in Pennsylvania.[100] The disease was even more brutal to those who arrived in England by way of Virginia. The death toll was so great, about 25 per cent of their number, as to lead to a charge of genocide by France against England.[101]

Causing up to 50 per cent death-rates on shipboard, with diseases cutting a further swathe through those who landed among strangers, the actual physical consequences of the deportation of the Acadians sent into exile were ruinous. It must also be remembered that the policy of deportation and exile, begun in 1755, continued until the Peace of Paris. As late as 1762, Jonathon Belcher, who had been the Attorney-General of the colony under Lawrence and who succeeded him as Lieutenant-Governor,[102] was still attempting to deport those Acadians who had somehow escaped earlier efforts. Belcher was convinced that "it will by no means be safe to suffer the Acadians to remain in this Province as settlers,"[103] and so more shiploads of Acadians were sent to Boston in the spring of 1762. That jurisdiction promptly sent them back to Halifax.[104]

Between 1755 and 1762, the majority of the Acadian community that had been built up throughout the present-day Nova Scotia, New Brunswick, and Prince Edward Island over a course of some 150 years was uprooted. In spite of what became a policy of eradication during these years, some Acadians remained in Nova Scotia at the close of the war in 1763. The Acadian people still existed, they still considered themselves distinct as a community, and they still sought to control their own destiny. As soon as their proscription was ended, in 1764, exiles began to return and rebuild the Acadian community.

Notes

1. The historiographical debate has produced countless volumes, but much of the argument can be found summarized in N.E.S. Griffiths, *The Acadian Deportation: Deliberate Perfidy or Cruel Necessity?* (Toronto, 1969).

2. I should note here that in making this judgement, I am not trying to answer the vexed question of who was responsible for the Acadian deportation. I merely assert that it was Lawrence who accepted the policy as viable though he did not invent it, and who, from 1755 until his death in 1760, initiated and followed through its implementation.

3. "Circular letter from Governor Lawrence to the Governors on the Continent," *Report Concerning Canadian Archives for the Year 1905*, 3 vols. (Ottawa: Public Archives of Canada, 1906), 2: App. B, 15–16.

4. The literature on colonial British America is both extensive and excellent. However, on this issue see in particular Walter Allen Knittle, *Early Eighteenth Century Palatine Emigration: A British Government Redemptioner Project to Manufacture Naval Stores* (Baltimore, 1970); and N.D. Landsman, *Scotland and Its First American Colony, 1683–1675* (Princeton, 1985) especially chapter 6, "A Scots' Settlement or an English Settlement: Cultural Conflict and the Establishment of Ethnic Identity," 163 ff.

5. Jean Daigle and Robert Leblanc, in R. Cole Harris, ed., *Historical Atlas of Canada: From the Beginning to 1800* (Toronto, 1987), 1: Plate 30.

6. The French government called for a report on the Acadian settlements in 1748. This is printed in *Le Canada Français* (1889), 1: 44. It estimates that Port Royal had 2,000 communicants. The original document is in the Archives de la Marine, Paris. I put these figures forward very tentatively. The document of the Archives de la Marine gives ninety families for these settlements, roughly 450 people. My estimate is derived from deportation figures rather than from earlier parish records, and it needs verification. It is interesting to note the extent to which the obvious predominance of the Minas Basin and Chignecto Isthmus has left the Acadian population of these older areas (e.g., Port Royal) relatively unexamined by scholars.

7. *Le Canada Français* gives 4,850, which I would accept as a minimum.

8. H. Têtu and C.O. Gagnon, eds., *Mandements, lettres pastorales et circu laires des évèques de Quebec* (1887), "Voyage de St. Vallier," 216.

9. *Le Canada Français* cites 2,500, but the population of the settlements of the Memramcook, the Petitcodiac, and the Shepody areas may be included in that figure.

10. I am much indebted to the recent work on this development by Paul Surette, *Petitcoudiac: Colonisation et destruction, 1731–1755* (Moncton, 1988).

11. Aliette Geistdoerfer, *Pêcheurs Acadiens, Pêcheurs Madelinots: Ethnologie d'une communauté de pêcheurs* (Quebec, 1987); Frederic Landry, *Pêcheurs de métier* (Iles de la Madeleine, 1987); and Charles A. Martin, ed., Les Micmacs et la mer (Montreal, 1986).

12. Jim Potter, "Demographic Development and Family Structure," in Jack P. Greene and J.R. Pole, eds., *Colonial British America: Essays in the New History of the Modern Early Era* (Baltimore, 1984), 139.

13. On population rates and their methodology during this period see F. Ouelett, "L'accroissement naturel de la population catholique québecois avant 1850: aperçus historiques et quantitatifs," *L'Actualité économique. Revue d'analyses économique*, 59 no. 3 (1983).

14. One was even a clerk to the Justices of the Peace. J.B. Brebner, *New England's Outpost* (New York, 1927), 150.

15. Clark, *Acadia: The Geography of Nova Scotia* (Madison, 1968), 230 ff.

16. Captain Charles Morris, "A Brief Survey of Nova Scotia," NA, MG18, D10, cap. 5, p. 4.

17. "Biographie de Jean-Louis Le Loutre," Archives Departementales de la Vendée, Papiers Lanco, vol. 371, 2.

18. The archaeological work is know being done on Upper Belle Isle marsh, as well as the imaginative work by Azor Vienneau for the film "Premières Terres Acadiennes," will help us to visualize the richness of Acadian life. It will complement work already completed for the Acadian Village on the outskirts of Caraquet. The work of Jean Claude Dupont, *Histoire d'Acadie* (Moncton, 1977) and Dupont, *Histoire Populaire de l'Acadie* (Moncton, 1979) needs to be read with an eye to the author's own caution as to the applicability of his information. Time and place are not constant throughout these volumes, and the works need to be read carefully bearing this in mind.

19. N.E.S. Griffiths, *Creation of a People* (Toronto, 1973); and Griffiths, "The Acadians," *DCB*, 4: xxvii–xxxi.

20. George F. Stanley, *New France: The Last Phase, 1744–1760* (Toronto, 1968), 74–75.

21. Their assumptions do not answer our question about Acadian attitudes. Duvivier certainly considered that the neutrality of the Acadians had been responsible for his defeat and lack of success in the expeditions of 1744. See Griffiths, "The Acadians." As far as both British and French policy-makers were concerned, however, the Acadian men were seen as a possible military force.

22. Brebner, *New England's Outpost*, 62 and 149 ff.

23. *Ibid.*, 152.

24. "It is hardly an exaggeration to say that until the late eighteenth century the major social and economic organization in Massachusetts was the family ... Lacking a state bureaucracy, standing army and police force, implementation of state policy depended on the family ... The family was also the centre of economic activity, for there were no banks, insurance companies, corporations or other formal economic organizations." P.D. Hall, "Family Structure and Economic Organization: Massachusetts Merchants, 1700–1850," in T. Hareven, ed., *Family and Kin in Urban Communities, 1700–1930* (New York, 1977), 39.

25. The relationship between family and household is one of the most interesting questions being discussed by those working in the field of family history. The work of Michael Mitterauer and Reinhard Sieder—*The European Family Patriarchy to Partnership* (Chicago, 1983)—in disentangling the change from "whole house" to family household leads to a demand for detailed analysis of Acadian kin relationships within a household, as well as for description of ties between households within settlements and from settlement to settlement.

26. Clark, *Acadia*, 203–4.

27. Lists of quit-rents paid in Grand-Pré and elsewhere in the 1750s can be found in the Brown Manuscripts, "Papers relating to Nova Scotia, 1720–1791," additional Mss. 19071, f. 138–48, British Museum. One of the best analyses of Acadian land-ownership claims is Winthrop Pickard Bell's *The "Foreign Protestants" and the Settlement of Nova Scotia* (Toronto, 1961), 79 and the footnotes for same, 80–3.

28. Clark, *Acadia*, 197.

29. See, for example, "Petition of Reny and Francois Leblancs Against Antoin Landry" Council Minutes, Garrison of Annapolis Royal, 7th January, 1731/2, PANS *Original Minutes of His Majesty's Council at Annapolis Royal, 1720–1739* (Halifax, 1908), 207.

30. PANS, *Nova Scotia Archives II: A Calendar of Two Letter-books and One Commission Book in the Possession of the Government of Nova Scotia* (Halifax, 1900), 221.

31. Paul Surette, *Petcoudiac*, 17. The author defines marriage through male participation, and by so doing overlooks the more complex reality of interrelationship
between households.

32. "Description de l'Acadie avec le nombre des paroisses et le nombre des habitants—1748," *Le Canada français*, 1: 44.

33. Micheline Dumont Johnson: *Apôtres ou agitateurs: la France missionaire en Acadie*
(Quebec, 1970) makes a good beginning in attempting to assess the influence of the
priests on the Acadians during the eighteenth century.

34. This includes the work in progress by Stephen White (see above, chapter 1, n. 33);
Placide Gaudet, "Acadian Genealogy and Notes," *Report for 1905*; and Bona
Arsenault, *Histoire et genealogie des Acadiens* (Moncton, 1965).

35. Maurice Bosc is undertaking, for an MA at the University of Moncton, a study of marriage alliances which should tell us something about the pattern of social hierarchy
among the settlements at this time.

36. While the work demands a painstaking trek through a wide variety of archival
holdings, material that suggests patterns of economic holdings is available. The
theoretical advances in family studies made by scholars such as John Demos, *Past,
Present and Personal: The Family and Life Course in American History* (Oxford,
1986); and Tamara Hareven and Andrejs Plakens, eds., *Family History at the
Crossroads: A Journal of Family History Reader* (Princeton, 1987) should be used to
provide a clearer understanding of questions concerning Acadian social stratification, the economic activity within households, and the ways in which education,
and social welfare are reinforced by political attitudes.

37. We have, for example, documents giving trade at Louisbourg from Acadie in livestock,
wood and flour: in 1740 such exports were valued at 26,940 *livres*, inclusive of some
5,423 *livres* of furs and skins. New England exports to Louisbourg for the same
year were valued at 48,447 *livres*, including some 4,448 *livres* of axes and hatch-
ets. J.S. McLennan, *Louisbourg From Its Foundation To Its Fall, 1713–1758* (1918)
contains relevant colonial documents outlining this trade.

38. "Minutes of the Council, Wednesday the 6th of October, 1749," T.B. Akins, *Selections
from the Public Documents of the Province of Nova Scotia* (Halifax, 1869), 174.

39. *Ibid.*, "Minutes of the Council," 247.

40. "Mascarene to Newcastle, Annapolis Royal, 23rd January 1746–47," *Report for
1905*, 2: App. C, 46.

41. The role of Massachusetts in Nova Scotia history is both important and complex.
Brebner in *New England's Outpost* presents a masterly analysis of the relationship from the point of view of imperial policy. George Rawlyk's *Nova Scotia's
Massachusetts: A study of Massachusetts-Nova Scotia Relations, 1630 to 1784*
(Montreal, 1978) is a complex monograph, centring upon the intricacies of colonial
interaction. For present purposes, it is necessary to understand only that, without any hierarchy being stated, the relationship between the colonial
administrators of Massachusetts and Nova Scotia was frequently one of senior and
junior officials.

42. "Enclosure in letter of 20th October, 1747, Mascarene to Newcastle," *Report for
1905*, 2: App. C, 47.

43. Accounts of the impact of the hostilities during the 1740s upon the Acadians abound. One of the best is in R. Rumilly, *Histoire des Acadiens* (Montreal, 1955), 1: 286–344, but see also G.F. Stanley, *New France.*

44. The most politic expression of these views is contained in "Governor Shirley to the Duke of Bedford, February 18, 1748/9," PRO, NSA, 148–49. For interpretations see Brebner, *New England's Outpost*, 118 ff.; and L.H. Gipson, *The British Empire Before the American Revolution, Zones of International Friction: The Great Lakes Frontier, Canada, The West Indies, India, 1748–1754* (New York, 1942), 5: 180.

45. The work of Winthrop Pickard Bell, *The "Foreign Protestants" and the Settlement of Nova Scotia*, already cited, is a seminal work of meticulous scholarship on this subject.

46. Murray Beck, "Edward Cornwallis," *DCB*, 4: 168–71.

47. The papers to this exchange are in, *Report for 1905*, 2: App. C, 49 ff. A full analysis of the interchange is given by Brebner, *New England's Outpost*, 181 ff. Brebner's opinion of the Acadians, however, is that they had little sophisticated appreciation of the probable consequences of their actions.

48. Brebner, *New England's Outpost*, 183.

49. *Ibid.*, 166.

50. *Ibid.*

51. Clark, *Acadia*, 338 and 339 n. 24.

52. There is an account of the first year of Halifax in *Northcliffe Collection, Reports* (Ottawa: Public Archives of Canada, 1926), 68–76. See also Winthrop Pickard Bell, *The "Foreign Protestants,"* 347 ff.

53. Hugh Davidson, "Description of Conditions [1750] in Nova Scotia," in Adam Shortt, V.K., Johnston and Gustave Lanctot, eds., *Documents relating to Currency, Exchange and Finance in Nova Scotia with Prefatory Documents, 1675–1758* (Ottawa, 1933), 319.

54. Clark, *Acadia*, 338.

55. Thomas B. Akins, "History of Halifax City," *Collections of the Nova Scotia Historical Society 8* (1895): 3–272.

56. Rawlyk, *Nova Scotia's Massachusetts*, 190 ff.

57. Winthrop Pickard Bell, *The "Foreign Protestants."*

58. *Ibid.*, 318.

59. *Ibid.*, 426.

60. For one of the most perceptive discussions of events in "Acadia or Nova Scotia" at this time see John G. Reid, *Six Crucial Decades: Times of Change in the History of the Maritimes* (Halifax, 1987), 29–60.

61. This commission provoked a great many pamphlets, arguing for one viewpoint or another, and a massive collection of documents; but it achieved nothing. However, see *Memoires des Commissaires du Roi et du Ceux de Sa Majeste Britannique* (Paris, 1755); and *Memorials of the English and French Commissaries Concerning the Limits of Nova Scotia* (London, 1755).

62. Stanley, *New France*, gives the most detailed account of this period but A.G. Doughty, *The Acadian Exiles: A Chronicle of the Land of Evangeline* (Toronto, 1916), 72–82 is very clear about the sequence of incidents.

63. "Antoine and Pierre Couaret to Governor Philipps, 2 October 1720," PRO, CO 217/3, f 155–56, cited in L.F.S. Upton, *Micmacs and Colonists: Indian—White Relations in the Maritimes, 1713–1867* (Vancouver, 1972), 199, n. 41.

64. One of the best accounts of this action is in D.C. Harvey, *The French Regime in Prince Edward Island* (New York, 1970), 137 ff.

65. N.E.S. Griffiths, *The Acadian Deportation*.

66. Dominick Graham, "Charles Lawrence," *DCB*, 3: 361–66.

67. La Galissoniere to the Minister, 25 July 1749. NA C-11-A: 93, 138; on this gentleman's career see Lionel Groulx: *Ronald-Michel Barrin de La Galissoniere 1693–1756* (Toronto, 1970).

68. Cited in B. Murdoch, *A History of Nova Scotia or Acadia*, 2: (Halifax, 1865), 310.

69. Almost all of this correspondence has been printed in Akins, *Nova Scotia Documents*, and *Report for 1905*.

70. "Tho I would be very far from attempting such a step [imposing the unqualified oath] without Yourships approbation, yet I cannot help being of the opinion that it would be much better, if they refuse the oaths, that they were away," in "Lawrence to the Lords of Trade, August 1st, 1754," 55, p. 187 ff., and partially printed *Nova Scotia Archives* 1, 212–14.

71. "Circular letter from Governor Lawrence to the Governors on the continent," *Report for 1905*, 2: App. B., 15–16.

72. See the comments of the Abbé Raynal in his *Histoire philosophique et politique de l'etablissement dans les deux Indes* (La Have, 1760), 360. A generation ago there were more than two hundred books and articles in print about the deportation of the Acadians. See the bibliographic guides published by the Centre d'études Acadiennes particularly Helene Harbec and Paulette Leversque eds., *Guide bibliographique de l'Acadie, 1976–1987* (Moncton, 1988).

73. While this has been a favourite conclusion of historians such as Brebner, George Rawlyk hotly contested this judgement in *Nova Scotia's Massachusetts*, 199 ff.

74. On this question see Placide Gaudet, *Le Grand Dérangement* (Ottawa, 1922).

75. "Nova Scotia is at war and is engaged in a movement of intense colonization. The dispersion of the Acadians constitutes an act of war and is a factor in this movement" [translation], *La Guerre de la Conquête* (Montreal, 1955), 272.

76. *Le Canada francais*, 1: 138–39.

77. On this episode and its impact on Lawrence see Brebner, *New England's Outpost*, 199–202 and 212–213.

78. Akins, *Nova Scotia Documents*, 247 ff.

79. "Council Minutes," PANS, RG 5, vol. 187.

80. The issue is discussed extensively by Brebner, *New England's Outpost*, 216 ff.

81. Murdoch, *History of Nova Scotia*, 2: 426.

82. The Lords of Trade were very hesitant about admitting the Acadians as subjects after the Peace of Paris, 1763. However, as of 5 November 1764, Governor Wilmot offered those remaining in Nova Scotia the opportunity to take an oath of allegiance

to the British Crown and to be granted land. The correspondence between Wilmot and the Lords Commissioners for Trade and Plantations on this issue is partially published in *Report for 1905*, App. J., 210–16.

83. A report of 1767 estimates the Acadian population of Nova Scotia as 1,265. *Ibid.*, App. L, 255–56.

84. Jean Daigle and Robert Leblanc, in R. Cole Harris, ed., *Historical Atlas of Canada*, Plate 30. A report to the French government of 1763 estimates the total Acadian population in 1763 as 12,866: some 866 divided among the British sea-ports, some 2,000 in France and 10,000 among the British colonies in North America, *Report for 1905*, 2: App. G, 156.

85. G. Debien, "Les Acadiens à Saint Dominique," in Glenn Conrad, ed., *The Cajuns: Essays on Their History and Culture* (Louisiana, 1978), 255–330.

86. Brown Mss., Add. Mss. 19071–19073, British Museum. There is considerable debate about whether these instructions had been prepared as early as 1751.

87. Printed in toto in the *Northcliffe Collection*, 80–83.

88. For the first view see E. Lauvrière, *La Tragédie D'une Peuple* (Paris, 1922), 1: 465, for the latter, Brebner, *New England Outpost*, 225. It has been demonstrated for the late twentieth century that these characteristics are not necessarily mutually exclusive.

89. Printed in *Report for 1905*, 2: App. B, 17. John Winslow had been born in Massachusetts in 1703 and at the time of the deportation he was a captain in the British army, stationed in Nova Scotia. He has left a journal of the summer and autumn of 1755 which has been fully printed in *Collections*, Nova Scotia Historical Society, 3: 71 ff. See biography of him by Barry Moody in *DCB*, 4: 774.

90. Major John Handfield to Winslow, 3 September 1755: Boston, MA, Municipal Library.

91. Winslow to Murray, 5 September 1755: *Report for 1905*, 2: App. B., 29.

92. Winslow to Lawrence, 17 September 1755: *Report for 1905*, 2: App. B., 12.

93. Winslow's Journal in *Collections* (Nova Scotia Historical Society, 1888), 3: 166.

94. "The number of seamen in time of war who died by shipwreck, capture, famine, fire or sword are but inconsiderable in respect to such as are destroyed by the ship diseases and the usual maladies of intemperate climates," wrote Dr. James Lind at the beginning of the Seven Years' War. The figures for that war bear him out: 133,708 men were lost by disease or desertion, compared with 1,512 killed in Action," N.R.S. Lloyd, *The Health of Seamen* (1965), cited in Christopher Lloyd, *The British Seaman, 1200–1860: A Social Survey* (Paladin, 1968), 234.

95. Gilles Proulx, *Between France and New France: Life Aboard the Tall Sailing Ships* (Toronto, 1984), in particular the tables for sickness of sailors arriving in Quebec, 1755–59, 114.

96. "Rev. Father Nau to Rev. Father Richard, Québec City, 20 October, 1734," *Rapports des Archives de l'Archévêque du Québec, 1926–1927* (Quebec, 1927), 267.

97. *Report for 1905*, 2: App. E, 81.

98. "Report of the Edward Cornwallis," Andrew Sinclair, Master, 17 November 1755; "210 dead, 207 in health," in Council Records (Columbia, S.C.), 480.

99. Brown Manuscripts, Add. Mss. 19071, British Museum.

100. "Commissioners of the Poor, Report October 1756," in J. MacKinney, ed., *Votes and Proceedings, Pennsylvania* (Harrisburg, 1931), 6: 4408.

101. Much of this story is covered in N.E.S. Griffiths, "The Acadians of the British Sea-Ports" *Acadiensis* 4 (1976): 67–84.

102. "March 20th 1760, Order-in-Council," PANS, RG 5, vol. A, 70.

103. "Jonathon Belcher to His Excellency Governor Murray, Halifax March 25th, 1762," *Report for 1905*, 2: App. L, 263.

104. The correspondence on this issue from Belcher to the Board of Trade and also to Lord Egremont, Secretary of State, has been partially printed in Akins, *Nova Scotia Documents* 329 ff.

CHAPTER
5
THE FRENCH MILITARY IN NEW FRANCE DURING THE SEVEN YEARS' WAR

The Battle of the Plains of Abraham on 13 September 1759 is one of the few world-class events in Canadian history. Usually included in lists such as the One Hundred Most Important Battles in History, it marked the zenith of the first British Empire. In Britain to this day, General James Wolfe remains a magical name to school children. In Canada there is an ambivalence about the siege, the soldiers, the generals and the outcome. Francis Parkman created icons for Canadians with his two-volume *Montcalm and Wolfe* (1884), the story of a battle between valiant heroes on both sides. The tragic Shakespearean ending provided the necessary grief and the glimmer of a better world. Regardless of any reality, that image of brave French and British soldiers fighting for survival and supremacy suited Canadian needs for over half a century.

Since the Second World War, the picture of the battle and the participants has been renovated. Guy Frégault's *La Guerre de la conquête* (1955) was a major reappraisal from a Canadian perspective. The Marquis de Montcalm and the Europeans emerged as inferior, if not incompetent, soldiers, while the *canadiens*, as epitomized by Pierre de Rigaud, Marquis de Vaudreuil, were pictured as inspired worthies obstructed by Montcalm, François Bigot and other Europeans. Wolfe, a bully and a terrorist who won by default, was vilified. C.P. Stacey took a less ideological position in his military analysis, *Quebec, 1759:*

The Siege and the Battle (1959). His study of generalship, however, found Montcalm and Wolfe both wanting. A competent strategist, Montcalm made disastrous tactical errors, while Wolfe, a dismal strategist, saved himself from disgrace by successful tactics on the field of battle. W.J. Eccles rejected even that praise for Wolfe. He delighted in telling his students that anybody except the British could have taken Quebec in half the time. Like Frégault, he depicted the *canadiens* as soldiers *par excellence*. In "The French Forces in North America During the Seven Years' War," the first selection, Eccles provided an overview of French military activity over much of the life of the colony.

Neither old soldiers nor wars are ever laid to rest, however, and it was not long before the battle was joined. Peter E. Russell in 1978 rescued the British regulars in a study of warfare in both Europe and America during the 1740s and 1750s (see *Suggestions for Further Reading*). Recently, Martin L. Nicolai examined the French military in both its European and North American theatres, and arrived at similar conclusions in "A Different Kind of Courage: The French Military and the Canadian Irregular Soldier During the Seven Years' War." He rejected the criticisms of the European military as unwarranted, and offered a less sanguine but perhaps more realistic view of the *canadien* soldier.

Suggestions for Further Reading

Frégault, Guy, *Canada: The War of the Conquest*. Toronto: Oxford University Press, 1969.

Russell, Peter E., "Redcoats in the Wilderness: British Officers and Irregular Warfare in Europe and America, 1740-1760," *William and Mary Quarterly*, XXXV, no. 4 (October 1978), 629-152.

Stacey, C.P., *Quebec, 1759: The Siege and the Battle*. Toronto: Macmillan of Canada, 1959.

————, "The British Forces in North America during the Seven Years' War," *Dictionary of Canadian Biography*, Volume III. Toronto: University of Toronto Press, 1974, xxiv-xxx.

Stanley, George F.G., *New France: the Last Phase, 1744-1760*. Toronto: McClelland & Stewart, 1968.

Steele, I.K., *Guerillas and Grenadiers: The Struggle for Canada, 1689-1760*. Toronto: Ryerson, 1969.

THE FRENCH FORCES IN NORTH AMERICA DURING THE SEVEN YEARS' WAR

W.J. Eccles

From 1713 to 1744 France and England were at peace, the span of one generation. During those years French overseas trade steadily increased. Trade with the French colonies rose from 25 million *livres* a year in 1710 to 140 million by

1741. In the latter year the total of French overseas trade was valued at 300 million *livres,* that is £12.5 million sterling. Much of this trade was with the Spanish empire, one half to seven-ninths of the goods shipped from Cadiz being French in origin. France now supplied all continental Europe with sugar and coffee, and in addition French fishermen were garnering the lion's share of the fisheries on the Grand Banks and in the Gulf of St Lawrence. But while French trade had expanded during the 1730s, that of England had remained stationary. Moreover, a sizable proportion of England's overseas commerce consisted of contraband trade with the Spanish colonies. Thus, when Spain began taking effective measures to curb this illicit traffic the English commercial community became alarmed; half of the world's maritime commerce might still be under the British flag but were its trade to continue to stagnate while French industry and commerce kept on expanding, then England, its population less than half that of France, might well go the same way as the Netherlands, and eventually be reduced to the status of a fourth-rate power. It was to forfend this possibility that England went to war with Spain in 1739, and with France in 1744.

The British government did not pursue that war, the War of the Austrian Succession, known to the English colonies as King George's War, effectively. It chose to engage France on the continent where the poorly officered British army proved no match for the Maréchal de Saxe, the foremost soldier of his age. In North America a combined Anglo-American and British naval force captured Louisbourg in 1745 (*see* William Pepperrell and Peter Warren), but it was not until 1747 that the Royal Navy gained the upper hand and succeeded in severing temporarily France's communications with her colonies. By 1748 the belligerents were exhausted and in October of that year the treaty of Aix-la-Chapelle was signed, which merely restored the *status quo ante bellum.* France recuperated rapidly and her overseas trade quickly recovered. The English commercial community now became convinced that a better-conducted spoiling war was essential to prevent the French overtaking them in the struggle for supremacy. The French, on the other hand, had no desire for a maritime war—they had too much to lose; nevertheless, they still had to prepare for it.

Although the West Indies were the great prize—by 1740 the exports of the French islands were valued at 100 million *livres* a year and their imports, mainly slaves, at 75 million—the north Atlantic fisheries were also extremely valuable, particularly since they were regarded as vital by both Britain and France for the training of seamen needed to man their fleets. In 1754, 444 ships from France fished in these waters, employing some 14,000 sailors. In addition the resident maritime population of Île Royale (Cape Breton Island), Îles de la Madeleine, and Gaspé provided a large number of mariners. It was estimated that the loss of these fisheries would cost France 15,000 experienced seamen, nearly a third of her total supply. Canada, on the other hand, produced little except furs, in good years some wheat for export to Louisbourg, and a few ships built at Quebec by the crown at great expense (*see* Pierre Lupien, *dit* Baron, and Louis-Pierre Poulin de Courval Cressé). This colony was, in fact, an economic liability much of the time. Politically and militarily, however, Canada was regarded as valuable to curb the expansion of the English colonies, hence of England's commercial strength, and to protect Louisiana for whose resources great hopes were entertained. Moreover, it was calculated that in time of war the Canadians, with the aid of a few reinforcements from France, would be able to tie down a much larger British army and a sizable part of the Royal Navy, thus preventing their deployment elsewhere. The success enjoyed by the Canadians against the Anglo-Americans in the previous wars gave every reason for confidence in this policy.

The fortress of Louisbourg was therefore strengthened to serve as a naval base for a fleet to protect the fisheries, guard the entrance to the St. Lawrence, and prey on British shipping. When an influential group of Anglo-American land speculators began to implement their scheme to seize the Ohio valley, thereby threatening the French hold on the west, a Canadian force was dispatched, on orders of the minister of Marine, to drive the Americans out (*see* Paul Marin de La Malgue). Forts were then built in the region. In 1754 came the first clash of arms near Fort Duquesne (Pittsburgh, Pennsylvania). Although war between England and France was not declared until 1756, this skirmish in the wilderness marked the beginning of the Seven Years' War (*see* Joseph Coulon de Villiers de Jumonville).

Unfortunately for France the government, its personnel, and methods, were to prove inadequate to meet the challenge offered by Great Britain and her new-found ally, Prussia. Louis XV could rarely bring himself to make decisions and when he attended council meetings he concerned himself with trivia. Moreover, until 1761 when the Duc de Choiseul was given charge of the ministries of War, Marine, and Foreign Affairs, the ministers, all of them mediocrities or worse, did not remain long in office. During the course of the war there were four Ministers of Foreign Affairs, four Controllers-General of Finance, four Ministers of War, and five Ministers of Marine. Their ministries were grossly understaffed and overworked, which resulted in interminable delays and too often in non-decisions. To cap it all, the entire decision-making process was beset by intrigue of Byzantine proportions, the king being to the fore in this activity.

Nor were the instruments of government policy, the armed forces, in better condition. Under Louis XIV, and later under Napoleon, the French army was the best in Europe. Under Louis XV it sank to a low level of efficiency. After the demise of the Maréchal de Saxe its commanders were incompetent. Defence predominated over offence in their thinking. Here too intrigue was rife. Every general in the field knew that many about him, and at the court, were scheming to have him removed. At the regimental level also officers were not distinguished by competence, the military capacity of most of the colonels being virtually nil. Commissions were purchased; money and family connections, not merit, governed advancement.

As is always the case, military tactics were dominated by the principal weapon employed, in this instance the smooth-bore, flint-lock, muzzle-loading musket, mounted with a bayonet, making it both a fire and a shock weapon. Even well-trained soldiers could fire no more than two or three rounds a minute; loading and firing required some twelve movements executed to command and drum beat. At close range, under eighty paces, a musket volley could be murderous, but at that distance there was barely time to reload before the enemy's charge, if it were not checked, reached the line. In battle two basic formations were employed, the line and the column. The line, three ranks deep, depended on the fire power of the musket followed by a bayonet charge against the shattered foe. Attack by column depended on the shock effect of an attack on a narrow front to pierce and shatter the enemy's line. Deployment in line demanded the most rigorous discipline to make the men stand fast and deliver measured volleys against the charging foe. Attack by column also required discipline to have the men press on into the hail of fire. The swifter their advance, the fewer volleys they had to endure. The British army relied on the line; the French at this time still had a predilection for the column, believing that the charge with the *arme blanche* was better suited to their poorly trained troops with their impetuous temperament.

To manoeuvre the troops on the battlefield, and have them attack either in line or in column, required that they receive at least eighteen months of basic training on the drill ground until they became virtually automatons. After that, five years' experience was deemed necessary to produce a good, dependable soldier. Iron discipline was the essence of it all, instilled by fear and by *esprit de corps*. The men had to be rendered more afraid of their own officers than of the enemy, and to be willing to stand and die rather than turn and run. Everything depended on the ability of the officers to manoeuvre their troops, and on the discipline and training of the men once battle was joined. Compared to other European armies the French army was deficient on both counts. Its officers lacked spirit and professional training, its men were badly instructed, poorly drilled, and wretchedly disciplined; its equipment, with the exception of the Charleville musket, was inferior. The supply system and the cannon were both antiquated, essentially the same as in the time of Louis XIV. All attempts at reform had been blocked by reactionary elements or vested interests.

The French navy was in a better state than the army. Its ships were superior to those of the Royal Navy. They could outsail and outgun the British ships. A French ship of fifty-two guns was a match for a British seventy-two. The reverse was true of the officers of the two navies. The British officers were better trained and more aggressive. Although the Royal Navy was in poor shape at the onset of the war it had twice as many ships as the French and its reserve of seamen was much greater. To make matters worse for the French, before war was declared the Royal Navy seized 800 French merchant ships and 3,000 seamen. This was a crippling blow. Moreover, during the course of the war epidemics in the French ports took a heavy toll. At Brest alone, in 1757-58, 2,171 sailors died in a four-month period. Many others fled the ports to avoid the contagion. The navy was reduced to impressing landsmen who had never been afloat to work their ships. Yet despite the superiority of the Royal Navy supply ships reached Quebec every year until 1760 (*see* Jacques Kanon), after the city had been taken by Wolfe's army.

When hostilities began the French had three distinct military forces at their disposal in North America: the colonial regular troops (*troupes de la Marine*), the militia, and the Indian allies. The colonial regulars were infantry units raised for guard duty in the naval ports of France and for service in the colonies. They were the creation of Louis XIV's great minister Jean-Baptiste Colbert and were under the control of the Ministry of Marine, not of the Ministry of War, hence were known as the *troupes franches de la Marine*. To obviate the abuses rampant in the regimental organization of the army Colbert had incorporated these marines in independent companies rather than in regiments. Commissions were not purchased but were obtained on merit and, of course, influence. A good reference was essential. Each company consisted of a captain, a lieutenant, a brevet ensign, a second ensign, two cadets, two sergeants, three corporals, two drummers and forty-one soldiers. By 1758, twenty companies of these marines were stationed at Louisbourg and twenty-one in Louisiana. In Canada there were thirty companies in 1756. In that year their strength was increased to 65 non-commissioned ranks per company, and the following year their number was raised to forty companies with a nominal strength of 2,760 officers and men.

During the half-century following the establishment of the colonial regulars, the officer corps became Canadian although the other ranks were nearly all recruited in France. By the 1740s commissions were reserved for the sons of serving officers, who were invariably *seigneurs*. Unlike the regiments of the French army the colonial regulars gave no direct entry into the commissioned ranks, except for such privileged persons as the son of a governor general (*see* Joseph-Hyacinthe and Louis-Philippe de Rigaud de Vaudreuil). With that notable exception, every would-be officer had to serve in the ranks for several years as a cadet. Despite this arduous training, so eager were the Canadians for commissions that in 1728 the age for entry as cadets was lowered to fifteen, and the waiting list became ever longer. Promotion could not be accelerated by purchase, only by a display of exceptional valour in action, and even then, *only* when a vacancy occurred through death or retirement. This condition served to inculcate a very aggressive spirit in the corps.

When the Seven Years' War began most of the officers of the colonial regulars had had years of military experience at the western posts, in the Fox and Chickasaw campaigns, and in savage raids on the frontier settlements of the English colonies (*see* Louis Coulon de Villiers, Jacques Legardeur de Saint-Pierre, François-Marie LeMarchand de Lignery, Nicolas-Joseph Noyelles de Fleurimont). In addition to their training in the drill manoeuvres demanded in European style warfare these troops had had to master the art of guerilla fighting both against and alongside the Indian nations. They could travel long distances, winter or summer, living off the land if need be, strike swiftly, then disappear before the enemy could muster a force to counter attack. Against them the American provincial troops and militia were no match. Great mobility, deadly marksmanship, skilful use of surprise and forest cover, high morale and, like the Royal Navy, a tradition of victory, gave the colonial regulars their superiority. Just how effective they could be was demonstrated when, in 1755, 250 Canadians with some 600 Indian allies destroyed Edward Braddock's army of 1,500 (*see* Jean-Daniel Dumas).

Supporting, and frequently serving alongside, the colonial regulars were the militia units. In 1669 Louis XIV had ordered the establishment of militia companies for colonial defence. Each company comprised all the able-bodied men between fifteen and sixty in a parish and was commanded by a captain of militia (who also had important civil functions), with a lieutenant, one or two ensigns, and sergeants. They all served without pay. During the wars against the English colonies and hostile Indian nations the militia was called out for war parties, to repel invading forces, for *corvées* to supply the frontier fortresses, or for the building of military roads.

When properly utilized this Canadian militia was a formidable fighting force, but its men were of little use in European-style warfare. Faced with regular army units in the open, firing massed volleys, they took cover or fled. They would not stand and be shot at while waiting for an order to fire back. There were other limits to the use that could be made of these *habitant* soldiers; many of them had to be released for work on the land in the spring and in late summer for the harvest; others had to serve in the canoe brigades to the western posts. A muster roll of 1750 lists 165 companies varying in number from 31 to 176, comprising 724 officers, 498 sergeants, 11,687 men; in all, 12,909. This total may well be too low, by as much as 25 per cent; it gives for one company a total strength of fifty-five whereas a separate muster roll of that particular company lists seventy-six names, half of whom are noted as fit to go on detachment. An important factor with these militiamen was their high morale. When they were ordered to Quebec in 1759 to help defend the city against Wolfe's army, Montcalm and his staff were astounded by the number that appeared, boys of twelve, old men of eighty-five, all demanding muskets and the right to serve. The contrast with the militia of the English colonies could not be more marked.

In addition to the colonial regulars and the militia the French had the aid of a horde of Indian allies, Micmacs, Abenakis, Ottawas, Algonkins, Delawares, Shawnees, to mention a few. The British, significantly, had virtually none. The operative word here is "allies," for these nations would take orders from no one—indeed their own chiefs had no authority over the warriors. They did not regard themselves as an auxiliary force of the French, but as allies in a joint effort against a common foe. Another inducement was the liberal supplies of food, clothing, arms, and munitions provided by the French, as well as the bounties paid for scalps and prisoners. Although they proved to be highly effective in guerilla warfare, the Indians could never be relied on. They were subject to whims that appeared strange to Europeans. After being well supplied a war party would set out but, *en route*, suffer a change of heart and quietly disperse. Yet mixed war parties of Canadians and Indians did wreak havoc on the Anglo-American settlements and tied down enemy forces vastly superior in numbers. The enemy's supply lines were constantly threatened, his advanced bases frequently destroyed. The mere knowledge that a French force had Indians with it was sometimes enough to cause a large Anglo-American force to flee or surrender. As scouts and intelligence agents the Indians were particularly useful. Although their verbatim reports were, on occasion, imaginary tales of things not seen, they could take prisoners far behind the enemy's lines who revealed much when questioned by the French. By such means the French were usually better informed than were the British of the opponent's dispositions and intentions.

When, in 1754, the British government decided to launch an all-out assault on New France without the formality of a declaration of war, it detached two battalions of regular troops for service in America. France had to counter this threat by reinforcing its units at Louisbourg and in Canada. A serious military and administrative problem immediately emerged. The colonies were in the charge of the Ministry of Marine but its colonial regular troops could not be expanded rapidly enough to meet the emergency. Recourse had to be had to the regiments of the French regular troops (*troupes de terre*, so called because most of them took their titles from the provinces of France where they were raised) under the Ministry of War, and the Mutual hostility of these two ministries was extreme. Moreover, the Governor-General of New France, always an officer in the Marine, was commander-in-chief of all the French forces in North America whether stationed at Louisbourg, in Canada, or Louisiana. The council of ministers, however, agreed that divided responsibility would be fatal, and that unity of command, at such a remove from the centre of authority, was essential. It was therefore concluded that the reinforcement of six army battalions from the regiments of La Reine, Artois, Bourgogne, Languedoc, Guyenne, and Béarn, 3,600 officers and men all told, would be placed under the orders of the Ministry of Marine, which would be responsible for their pay and maintenance.

Two of the battalions, Artois and Bourgogne, went to Louisbourg. The other four went to Canada. In 1756 a battalion each from the La Sarre and Royal Roussillon regiments were shipped to Quebec, and in 1757 two more battalions from the Régiment de Berry were sent to Canada. Each battalion had an officer corps made up of a lieutenant-colonel in command, an adjutant (*aide-major*), and a surgeon major; a captain, a lieutenant, and a sub-lieutenant (*sous-lieutenant*) of grenadiers; twelve fusilier captains, twelve lieutenants, and two ensigns. The other ranks consisted of the grenadier company comprising two sergeants, two corporals, two lance-corporals, one drummer, thirty-eight grenadiers; twenty-four fusilier sergeants, twenty-four corporals, twenty-four lance-corporals, twelve drummers, and 396 fusiliers; a total strength of 557. The grenadier company in each battalion was an élite group of shock troops, men chosen for their superior physique, martial appearance, and training. One of their functions was to stand directly behind the line in battle to prevent, with their bayonets, the fusiliers from turning tail—as occurred at Carillon in 1758 when some of the de Berry regiment made to bolt. If a section of the line reeled under an assault, the grenadiers stepped into the breach.

Separate from both the French regular troops and the colonial regulars were the engineers, represented by two French officers, Nicolas Sarrebource de Pontleroy and Jean-Nicolas Desandrouins, and a company of artillery. At this time the artillery was the weakest branch in the French army. The unit in Canada, commanded by François Le Mercier, comprised eight officers, three of them Canadians, four sergeants, ten cadets, and eighty-six gunners. The engineers were mainly concerned with fortifications. Pontleroy agreed with Montcalm that all the fortifications in the colony, including Quebec, were worthless and could not resist an assault let alone bombardment. On some points, however, Pontleroy's testimony is palpably false, for example his statement that there was no dry moat beneath the walls of Quebec. After Quebec fell to the British the French officers, including Desandrouins, deemed its defences virtually impregnable. As for the frontier fortresses, in their criticisms the French officers ignored the fact that they had been built to fend off the feeble Anglo-American forces and hostile Indians, not a British army which, although its engineers were poor, had in the Royal Regiment of Artillery one of the finest artillery corps in the world.

At Louisbourg the four battalions from the regiments of Artois, Bourgogne, Cambis, and Volontaires Etrangers, along with 1,000 colonial regulars and 120 gunners, all came under the orders of the commandant, Augustin de Boschenry de Drucour. For the battalions serving in Canada, however, a general staff had to be appointed. Baron Jean-Armand de Dieskau accepted the appointment as commanding officer with the rank of major-general (*maréchal de camp*)—making him one of 170 holding that rank in the French army. He was given a staff consisting of a second in command, an adjutant (*major*), an aide-de-camp, a war commissary (*commissaire des guerres*) in charge of supplies, and two partisan officers for detached duties.

Great care was taken in the drafting of Dieskau's instructions to prevent any conflict or misunderstanding between him and the newly appointed Canadian-born Governor-General, Pierre de Rigaud, Marquis de Vaudreuil. They carefully spelled out that the Governor-General was in full command of all the military forces. Dieskau was to take his orders from Vaudreuil, and whether he liked them or not he had no alternative but to obey them to the letter. The governor general was required to leave the details of the command of the army battalions to Dieskau but the latter had to keep the commander-in-chief informed of their strength, deployment, and everything else needed to enable him to make the most effective use of them in any operations he chose to undertake. When, in

1756, the Marquis de Montcalm replaced Dieskau he received the same instructions and the same restricted authority. He and his officers were also subordinate to the governments at Montreal and Trois-Rivières, which consisted of a local governor, a king's lieutenant (*lieutenant du roy*), a town major, and an adjutant (*aide-major*). The army battalions were there for one main purpose, to defend the colony, and they had to take their orders from the colonial authorities.

The council of ministers also decreed, not only that the French regular troops would, contrary to custom, be paid during the Atlantic voyage but that they would be paid over double the normal rate while serving in America. It was anticipated that the colonial regulars would protest, since the increase was not accorded them, but it was pointed out that they were defending their homeland. Their officers, and some of the men who had married in the colony, could enjoy the pleasures of their own homes and attend to their personal and business affairs when not campaigning. The French officers, on the other hand, had to face the prospect of years of exile from their families and friends in a colony where life was harder, and more expensive, than in France. Unfortunately, there was friction between the army and marine officers at the outset, and the pay differential aggravated the problem. More specifically it caused trouble when replacements for both corps were sent from France. The men all wanted to be incorporated into the higher paid French battalions.

Many of the French officers found campaigning in the North American wilderness not at all to their liking. The tedium of garrison duty at the remote frontier forts sapped their morale. Some of them were physically incapacitated and nearly driven out of their minds by the clouds of mosquitoes and stinging flies. Receiving news from home only once a year, and being unable to cope at such a remove with trouble that might arise, was hard to bear. Some of them were repelled by the seeming barbarism of the Indians and wanted nothing to do with them. The guerilla tactics of the Canadians, both regulars and militia, were remote from their concepts of how war should be waged. Even by European standards the French army was seriously deficient in reconnaissance and light infantry units trained for skirmishing and scouting duties. When army companies were detached to serve with the Canadians on their frontier raids their officers were disconcerted to discover that no mobile field hospitals or baggage trains went with them. Were they to be wounded they would have to make their way back to a French base as best they could before receiving medical attention. Their food supplies and equipment they had to carry on their backs like common soldiers. When rivers were encountered they had to wade or swim across. Resentful Canadians who were ordered to carry them across on their backs had an unfortunate habit of tripping in mid-stream. Some of the French officers declared that this was not warfare at all, and they refused to have any part in it. For them military operations required a secure, comfortable base, with servants, camp followers, clean linen, well-prepared food, and wine, close by the chosen field of battle or fortified place, where all the paraphernalia of siege warfare could be brought into play.

The Canadians formed a low opinion of the French officers, and the latter thought that the Canadians had far too high an opinion of themselves. The Canadians thought the French troops displayed too great a reluctance to seek out the enemy, preferring to remain on the defensive and let the enemy come to them. The defeatist attitude of Montcalm and several of his officers did nothing to ease the situation. While the French troops were employed in garrison duty, taking part in a campaign each summer, then remaining in their dispersed quarters all winter, many of the Canadians were fighting on the enemy's frontiers all year round. Vaudreuil felt constrained to complain to the Minister of Marine that the French officers were too loath to abandon their comforts for active campaigning. He also complained that some of these officers, including Montcalm, abused the Canadians shamefully, and that unless a stop were put to it there could be serious trouble. He stated bluntly that the moment hostilities ended he wanted the French troops shipped back to France. One cause of this problem, attested to in considerable detail by an official of the Marine recently arrived from France, may well have been that the French army in Europe, since the days of Louis XIV, had fought its wars on foreign soil and was accustomed to live largely off the land, treating the hostile population of the occupied territory with scant regard.

In this controversy one thing stands out clearly: the calibre of the French officers was much lower than that of the Canadians. Among the senior regimental officers physical and mental competence was not always in evidence. In 1758 Montcalm informed the Minister of War that the commandants of the Béarn and Royal Roussillon battalions were *hors de combat* and ought to be retired. In fact, only one lieutenant-colonel, Étienne-Guillaume de Senezergues de La Rodde of the La Sarre regiment was fit for active campaigning. After the battle of Carillon Montcalm had to ship nine officers back to France as quietly as possible. One, a knight of Malta and scion of an illustrious family, had been insane for some time and it had become impossible to conceal his condition; five others were sent back for displaying a want of courage—or as Montcalm put it, *"pour avoir manqué à la première qualité nécessaire à un soldat et à un officier"*—two for stealing from their fellow officers and one for having displayed considerable talent as a forger. Two other officers were allowed to resign their commissions, for good cause. Montcalm pleaded with the minister to see to it that replacements not be sent merely because their regiments, or their families, wanted to be rid of them. Meanwhile, he was obliged to fill the vacancies by granting the sons of Canadian officers lieutenants' commissions. Vaudreuil, although he sanctioned this solution, pointed out that it had established a bad precedent since these young officers entered the service with a higher rank than the Canadians in the colonial regular troops who had had several years of active campaigning. He added that too many of them could never have hoped to obtain commissions in the Canadian regulars.

Because the population of New France was only a fraction of that of the English colonies, some 75,000 compared to over 1.5 million it is frequently assumed that the outcome of the war was a foregone conclusion. If numbers alone were what counted then Britain's ally, Prussia, also could not have escaped destruction. Such comparisons can be misleading since the size of the forces that either side could bring to bear was governed by the nature of the terrain, communications, and supply routes. The British had 23,000 regulars in America by 1758, but they were not able to make very effective use of their provincial levies. The largest force they could deploy in a campaign against Canada was 6,300 regulars and 9,000 provincials at Lake Champlain in 1758. That army was routed by Montcalm's 3,500 regulars. Similarly, at Quebec in 1759 Wolfe arrived with 8,500 troops, mostly British regulars. By September his force was reduced to 4,500 effectives. To oppose them the French had over 15,000 men—regulars, militia, and Indians. It was not numerical superiority that conquered Canada but poor generalship on the part of Montcalm that lost Quebec in one battle.

During the course of the war, however, the effectiveness of the British army improved, that of the French declined. On the British side the introduction of short-term enlistments and the popularity of the war brought forth higher-quality recruits for the regulars. Officers who proved to be too incompetent were weeded out; in some instances they were replaced by highly competent Swiss professional soldiers who, ironically, introduced the Canadian methods and tactics in the wilderness campaigns that the French officers sneered at. On the French side the quality of the reinforcements sent from France was low. They were mostly raw recruits, the sweepings of the streets. Some of them were even cripples who had to be shipped back. To make matters worse they brought disease with them that spread through the ranks and among the civilian population in epidemic proportions. In 1757, 500 troops were hospitalized and more than half of them died. Thus as the number of veteran trained soldiers dwindled through the wastage of war the quality of the regulars declined badly. By 1759 both the French battalions and the colonial regulars were not of the calibre they had been three years earlier. Among the French regulars discipline was not maintained; there were mutinies; morale sank to a low ebb. Thieving, looting, and other crimes became rampant. The war commissary was kept busy sending men before the council of war. He complained, "We spend our life having the rogues punished." The effectiveness of the French battalions was further reduced by Montcalm's decision to bring them up to strength by drafting Canadian militiamen into their ranks. It required more than the grey-white uniform of the French army to make regular soldiers out of them, capable of fighting in line. They did not receive the harsh, intensive, parade-ground training that that type of warfare demanded. The lack was to prove fatal on the Plains of Abraham.

Another frequently-stated reason for the conquest of New France is inadequate supplies. The question requires more critical scrutiny than it has received to date. Far too much tainted subjective evidence has been accepted at face value. Owing to crop failures and the greatly increased number of mouths to feed, estimated to be 17 per cent, the colony could not produce enough food to supply its needs. It was dependent on supplies shipped from France, but the supply ships reached Quebec every year up to 1759. In 1757 Montcalm reported that a three years' supply of clothing for the troops had arrived and there was nothing to worry about on that score. Moreover, sizable quantities of food and other military supplies were captured by the French; enough to maintain the army for months were captured at Oswego (Chouaguen) and Fort William Henry (Lake George, New York). There is no viable evidence that military operations were curtailed by a shortage of supplies. Poor distribution and the *habitants'* distrust of inflated paper money obliged the urban population to tighten its belt and eat unpalatable food at times, such as horse meat, but no one starved.

Account also has to be taken of the fact that the British had supply problems. The chicanery of their colonial supply contractors and the provincial assemblies was notorious. At Quebec in 1759 over a quarter of Wolfe's army was on the non-effective list, suffering from the dietary diseases, dysentery and scurvy. Moreover, owing to the military ineptitude of the Anglo-Americans, the British had to import in far larger numbers than the French the most essential military commodity of all, fighting men. Had no regular troops been imported by either side, the Canadians would certainly not have been conquered.

In 1758 Vaudreuil had contrasted the attitude of the colonial regular troops towards the war with that of the French regulars. For the Canadians, he wrote, the colony was their homeland; it was there that they had their families, lands, resources, and aspirations for the future. The French troops on the other hand, being expatriates, wanted only to return home with their honour intact, without having suffered a defeat, caring little what wounds the enemy inflicted on the colony, not even about its total loss.

The events of 1759 and 1760 made all too plain that there was more than a little truth in these charges. After the *débâcle* on the Plains of Abraham the French officers refused to give battle again, despite the fact that they outnumbered the British three to one and still held Quebec. The following year their failure to recapture the city they had abandoned and to block the British drive up Lake Champlain, the arrival of three British armies at the portals of the colony, the failure of reinforcements to arrive from France, all meant that further resistance was completely hopeless. James Murray, advancing up the river from Quebec, ravaged and burned the homes of the Canadians who had not laid down their arms. At one point his men got out of hand and some Canadian women were violated. Yet Lévis and his staff still demanded that the British be resisted for the honour of the army, which meant their personal honour and future careers. When many of the Canadians deserted to protect their homes and families the French officers wanted them apprehended and shot. French troops were sent to seize at gunpoint the last remaining cattle of the *habitants*, who resisted vigorously since this was all that was left them to feed their families during the coming winter. Even when the British stood at the gates of Montreal in overwhelming strength, and although the sacking of the town might ensue, Lévis demanded that the capitulation terms be rejected because Jeffery Amherst had churlishly refused to grant the French the honours of war. Vaudreuil would not heed him and capitulated to spare the colony further devastation. The king subsequently declared, in a savagely worded letter from the Minister of Marine, that Vaudreuil should not have accepted the terms; that he should have heeded Lévis and continued to resist, come what may, for the honour of French arms. The missive made plain that the loss of the colony and the plight of the Canadians were of no consequence compared to the army's having surrendered without receiving the right to march out of Montreal bearing its arms, flags unfurled, and drums beating.

After the surrender arrangements had to be made for the transport of the regular troops, the civil officials, and the Canadians who chose to quit the colony rather than remain under the British, some 4,000 in all. Of the 2,200 French regular troops who remained on strength, 500 to 600 opted to stay in the colony; upwards of 800 had previously deserted to that end. Among them were 150 British deserters who had enlisted in the French forces. Vaudreuil and Lévis allowed these deserters to make themselves scarce before the capitulation, but most of them were subsequently rounded up by the British. Some French soldiers were persuaded to enlist in the British army, but one of their officers remarked that now they had discovered they were to be transported to serve elsewhere few would be tempted to follow their example.

The officer corps of the colonial regular troops, with the exception of those too severely wounded to make the voyage, crossed to France where they were retired from the service on half pay. With the conclusion of peace in 1763 twenty-one officers returned to Canada to settle their affairs, then went back again to France hoping to receive appointments on the active list. Others quietly gave up and returned to Canada to eke out a living on their seigneurial lands. Those who held the cross of the order of Saint-Louis were in a difficult position as the oath of the order prevented them becoming subjects of His Britannic Majesty without the consent of the king of France. Several of those who chose to remain in France eventually received active appointments in the service, in Gorée, the West Indies, or Guiana. Louis-Thomas Jacau de Fiedmont, for example, the brave gunner captain who, at Jean-Baptiste-Nicolas-Roch de Ramezay's council of war that opted to surrender Quebec, declared that they should hold out until the ammunition was exhausted, eventually became Governor of Guiana. Another, Gaspard-Joseph Chaussegros de Léry, returned to Canada and became a member of the Legislative Council of Quebec but sent his young sons to France. One of them, François-Joseph, gained entry into the reformed and prestigious corps of engineers. He ultimately rose to be commander-in-chief of the engineers in Napoleon's Grande Armée. His name is engraved on the Arc de Triomphe along with those of Napoleon's other great generals. For some of these Canadian officers the career was all important; for others, it was their homeland that mattered. Some, at least, who chose the latter did so because, owing to age or lack of means and influential connections, they saw no future for themselves in the service of their king. Their cause was truly lost.

As for the soldiers of the colonial regular troops who returned to France, when an attempt was made to have them enlist in French regiments not one of them would do so. Their almost unanimous response was that they knew the route to Halifax and they could easily find their way back to Canada from there. The Maréchal de Senneterre commented: "All those who have returned from Quebec and Montreal appear to have a great love for that country."

A DIFFERENT KIND OF COURAGE: THE FRENCH MILITARY AND THE CANADIAN IRREGULAR SOLDIER DURING THE SEVEN YEARS' WAR

Martin L. Nicolai

In recent decades two historians of Canada during the Seven Years' War, Guy Frégault and William J. Eccles, have attacked their predecessors' adulation of Louis-Joseph, Marquis de Montcalm, by portraying him as a poor strategist, a mediocre tactician, and a defeatist. However true this might be, they also portray the French officer corps, including their commander, as contemptuous of Canadians and irregular warfare.[1] During the course of the Canadian campaign, Montcalm and his officers did demonstrate a general lack of respect for the petty raiding of *la petite guerre* and an ambiguous attitude towards the Canadian soldier. This, however, was less a rejection of irregular warfare than an expression of their belief that a more structured and sophisticated use of irregular tactics was necessary when the enemy was no longer simply a colonial militia but a large, well-organized army complete with highly trained regiments of heavy and light infantry. As Ian Steele makes clear, the Seven Years' War in North America marks the end of the days of small-scale raiding and the advent of professional armies on the continent. The war, he states, was won by conventional, European-style battles and sieges, not by skirmishes in the woods.[2]

At first complacent in their use of Canadian irregulars, relying on local practice and their knowledge of the use of light troops in Europe during the War of the Austrian Succession, the French eventually attempted to bring Canadian soldiers onto the conventional battlefield not simply as sharpshooters roaming on the flanks but as actual light infantry operating on the central line of battle in close cooperation with the heavy infantry of the French *troupes de terre*. There is every sign that the Frenchmen finished the campaign convinced by the success of Canadian light troops that units of properly led and disciplined light infantry were a valuable part of a European army.

From *Canadian Historical Review*, LXX, no. 1 (March 1989), 53-75. Copyright 1989 by University of Toronto Press. Reprinted by permission of University of Toronto Press.

The War of the Austrian Succession (1740–48) was the training ground of most of the French officers who came to Canada with the Baron von Dieskau and the Marquis de Montcalm, and it was during this war that irregular troops were first employed on a large scale by modern armies. In 1740–41 the young Austrian empress Maria Theresa mobilized her Croatian and Hungarian military borders on the Ottoman frontier and moved them for the first time to the central European front in an attempt to eject Frederick the Great's troops from Silesia. They performed invaluable service in every campaign, and in 1744 Field Marshal Traun successfully forced the Prussians out of Bohemia by threatening Frederick's supply lines and harassing his foraging parties. Over 40,000 Serbo-Croatian "Grenzer" would serve in the Habsburg armies during the War of the Austrian Succession and about 88,000 during the Seven Years' War.[3] These fierce soldiers were usually dispatched on independent operations against enemy outposts and communications, but sometimes they played a small part on the battlefield as sharpshooters posted on the flanks. Faced by these irregulars, the French, Prussians, and British responded by recruiting some light troops of their own. In the Seven Years' War all of the major European armies raised units of irregulars and light infantry and cavalry, and their use gradually became more sophisticated.[4]

The French army began very early to adapt to this new aspect of warfare. Although the use of skirmishers had disappeared in France at the end of the seventeenth century because of the widespread obsession with the firepower of the line, interest in these troops slowly revived during the following decades. There were experiments with skirmishers in military exercises as early as 1727, but only necessity during the 1740s forced the French to raise light troops in any numbers. During the winter of 1744, the Maréchal de Saxe, who had extensive previous experience with light troops in eastern Europe and had written the first modern treatise to deal with the subject, raised a number of *compagnies franches* or free companies for the French army, and would have formed more if the minister of war had approved. He eventually commanded five regiments of light troops, usually combining infantry and cavalry in these units, and by 1748 there were 5,000 of them in the French army. At Fontenoy in 1745 Saxe used his irregulars on the battlefield itself, sending a screen of skirmishers against the British centre while he deployed his army. He also stationed Monsieur de Grassin's new 1,200-strong Régiment des Arquebusiers in the Bois de Berry on his left flank, where their deadly independent fire or *feu de chasseur* made a British attempt to secure their flank exceedingly difficult. Saxe also used skirmishers at Laufeld in 1747. The tactics of this general, who was one of the greatest commanders of the eighteenth century, were studied with great care by other French officers. Although the French did not make extensive use of skirmishers during the War of the Austrian Succession itself, their presence was customary during the peacetime military exercises of 1748 to 1755 and no French military writer of this period neglected to discuss them.[5]

Montcalm and François-Gaston, Chevalier de Lévis, both served in Bohemia and Piedmont during the War of the Austrian Succession, and had more than enough experience with irregulars on both campaigns.[6] During the operations around Prague in late 1742 and during the subsequent retreat to Germany, Hungarian hussars and other light cavalry constantly harassed French foraging parties and other units, greatly hampering the ability of the Maréchal de Belle-Isle to supply his troops, obtain information about the main Austrian army, or easily manoeuvre his forces.[7] In Piedmont, Charles Emmanuel III organized his Piedmontese mountaineers or *barbets* in militia units, and these men fought beside the king's regular troops in the endless mountain battles of this campaign, also overrunning the French communications outposts in the mountain valleys, taking few prisoners in the process. Throughout most of 1745 and 1746 Montcalm protected sections of the French communications in the Ligurian Alps against repeated attacks by the *barbets*, and in one daring night operation the French colonel led his troops, some of whom were mountain fusiliers, over "impracticable paths" to surprise and capture 150 *barbets* in a village. To counter the Piedmontese militia, the Franco-Spanish recruited two battalions of Catalonian mountaineers from the Pyrenees called *Miquelets*—many of whom were former bandits—and equipped them with carbines.[8]

The exposure of many members of the officer corps to irregular warfare in Europe made them appreciate the effectiveness of this type of military activity. Irregulars could severely hamper reconaissance, slow an army's advance, and harry an enemy's communications so severely that large numbers of fighting men had to be withdrawn from the main body simply to guard the army's baggage and lines of supply and communication. There was, as a result, a general recognition among military men by the end of the 1740s that irregular troops, fortunately or unfortunately, had a role to play in wartime, if only to defend one's own force against enemy irregulars.

What impressions did French officers have of Canadian soldiers during the first few years of the Seven Years' War? One prominent characteristic of the Canadian *habitants*, noted by all of the officers, was their willingness to perform military service, an attitude which was in striking contrast to that of the average French peasant. The long wars against the Iroquois in the seventeenth century, which forced all Canadian males to take up arms and learn Indian methods of irregular warfare, engendered a military ethos among Canadians which was fostered by intermittent campaigns against the English in company with Canada's Indian allies.[9] The reputation of Canadians as a "race of soldiers" was confirmed by the French officers, whose constant refrain in their writings was to contrast the Canadians' skill and courage with their indiscipline.[10] Colonel François-Charles de Bourlamaque, for instance, believed that Canada possessed far more "naturally courageous men" than any other country, and although Canadian militiamen were not accustomed to obedience, when they found firmness and justice in their officers they were quite "docile."[11] They possessed a different "kind of courage," wrote Louis-Antoine de Bougainville, for like the Indians, Canadians exposed themselves little, organized ambushes, and fought in the woods behind a screen of trees, defeating in this way an entire British army under General Braddock.[12] Despite his criticisms of Canadian indiscipline, Bougainville was careful to qualify his remarks: "God knows we do not wish to disparage the value of the Canadians ... In the woods, behind trees, no troops are comparable to the natives of this country."[13] Some of the least charitable comments on Canadians came from the Baron von Dieskau's second-in-command, Pierre-André de Gohin, Chevalier de Montreuil, who, blaming the irregulars for his commander's humiliating defeat at Lake George in 1755, declared sarcastically that the "braggart" Canadians were well adapted for skirmishing, being "very brave behind a tree and very timid when not covered."[14]

Despite a tendency among many officers to make generalizations about Canadian soldiers, most realized that not all Canadian males were experienced irregulars. Stereotypes may have been reinforced, however, by the presence of several hundred *coureurs de bois* and other experienced woodsmen among the militia companies and transport troops, especially before 1785. Captain Jean-Guillaume-Charles de Plantavit de La Pause de Margon, Chevalier de La Pause, found that there was no proper system of drafting soldiers in the parishes, with the result that the same men were chosen each year to fill the parish militia quota. These, according to La Pause, were the poorest *habitants*, presumably men with little land and a greater inclination towards hunting, long-term work as *coureurs de bois*, or related activities which provided the military skills useful for irregular warfare.[15] Bougainville differentiated between the men of the districts of Montreal and Trois-Rivières, who were considered more warlike and accustomed to voyages in the west, and those of the Quebec area, who tended towards proficiency in fishing and other nautical pursuits.[16] Similarly, Lieutenant Jean-Baptiste d'Aleyrac and Montcalm's junior aide-de-camp, Captain Pierre Marcel, made fun of the militia of the cities of Montreal and Quebec, "composed of all kinds of workers, wholesale merchants, who never go to war."[17] Despite these views, however, the officers felt that their generalizations about Canadians were justified.

Constant contact with Indian allies in wartime and the success of their tactics resulted in Canadians adopting not only Indian methods of fighting but also their attitudes towards war, such as the idea that victory involved inflicting losses on the enemy without incurring any and that the campaigning season was over when a victory, however insubstantial, had been achieved and honour gratified. In addition, native ritual boasting of prowess in war may have encouraged some Canadian soldiers to advertise their military talents in a flagrant manner. French officers noticed these characteristics, and generally realized that they were cultural borrowings from the Indians, but they were too ethnocentric and accustomed to professional military conduct to sympathize very much with this type of behaviour.

The Canadian penchant for boasting was of minor concern. Boasts "after the Canadian fashion, that one of their number could drive ten Englishmen" only boosted morale, and this behaviour was considered no more than a minor annoyance.[18] The Canadian and Indian custom of returning home *en masse* every time a "coup" was made, however, was subjected to considerably more criticism. La Pause recounted how the comical race of Canadians departed after the Battle of Carillon, rushing off in their boats within hours, moving "day and night, forgetting, losing and often leaving people behind if they did not embark fast enough." After visiting their families, he noted, they would return at an exceedingly leisurely pace to resume the campaign.[19] At other times, as when muskets had to be fired in an attempt to stem the exodus of Canadian officers and men after the fall of Fort William Henry—a factor which may have influenced Montcalm's decision to discontinue the offensive—the French were even less amused.[20] This behaviour at Oswego and on other occasions decidedly undermined the French officers' respect for Canadian soldiers. Even though they recognized the special nature of the Canadian "race," they expected them, as Frenchmen, to be more amenable to discipline than the Indians.

During the early years of the war the French officer corps simply accepted the traditional role of their Canadian militia and Indian allies. The recent battle on the banks of the Monongahela proved that the Canadians already had considerable potential, and there did not seem to be any immediate need to do more than instil Canadians with obedience and a basic orderliness. Captain Pierre Pouchot regarded Braddock's defeat on the Monongahela as an "impressive lesson" for regular troops who could not fire steadily and were unacquainted with the style of fighting of their opponents, although he did not believe that properly organized and trained regular soldiers should be defeated by irregulars.[21] Training Canadians as heavy infantry was pointless because they already performed satisfactorily as scouts, raiders, and sharpshooters, duties which admirably suited the "natural spirit" of the local people.[22] French officers, accustomed to the mosaic of provinces which made up their country, each with its own distinct culture and identity, saw Canadians as a very peculiar set of fellow Frenchmen. It was easiest to adapt to their particular nature and use their skills rather than try to make them more like other Frenchmen and amenable to European-style heavy infantry training. As Pouchot's companion-in-arms Captain Nicolas Sarrebource de Pontleroy of the Royal Corps of Engineers pointed out, Canadians were brave, but without discipline they could not be expected to fight in open fields against regular troops; they were not even equipped for such an eventuality.[23] The war was not yet desperate enough to require a complete rethinking of the role of irregular troops.

Baron Johann Hermann von Dieskau, who was one of Saxe's aides-de-camp and had experience with light troops in eastern Europe, undoubtedly derived much of his confidence in irregulars from his former commander.[24] However, he learned the limitations of irregular infantry during his campaign against

William Johnson in 1755. Leaving behind most of his French troops, he forged ahead with a mixed force of regulars, Canadian militia, and Indians to mount a surprise attack on Fort Edward. He properly posted flank guards of Canadians and Indians to prevent his small column from being ambushed, but was obliged to give up his plans to attack Fort Edward when the Iroquois refused their assistance. He was soundly beaten in an assault on Johnson's entrenchments at the foot of Lake George. Dieskau had not foreseen that Johnson's force would be both entrenched and alerted, for under these conditions he required more regular troops and a few cannon. His Canadians and Indians were simply unable to participate in a conventional assault. While irregulars were occasionally capable of capturing forts and other fortifications if they had the advantage of surprise, they could do little if the garrison was prepared for their attack.[25]

The Marquis de Montcalm, who arrived in New France in 1756 to take command of the French forces, was by a combination of experience, necessity, and advice persuaded to employ the regulars and irregulars in the separate roles to which they were most accustomed. The Chevalier de Montreuil, who condemned the "blind confidence" of Dieskau in his Canadian advisers, made certain to instruct Montcalm to rely upon his regulars and to employ his Canadians and Indians only in harassing the enemy.[26] Montcalm viewed raiding expeditions, especially those directed against military targets, as useful in harassing enemy troops and lowering their morale. He also believed that successful raids maintained the offensive spirit in his troops and encouraged the Canadian civilian population, although he abhorred the atrocities committed by his aboriginal allies just as he had hated the tortures inflicted on prisoners by the Slavic Pandours and Italian *barbets*.[27]

Irregulars were perceived to have a particular role: they tied down large numbers of enemy militia on the frontiers and lines of communication, carried out reconaissance, ambushed detachments of enemy troops, and provided some firepower during sieges and other engagements. Both Captain Jean-Nicolas Desandroüins and Lévis wrote approvingly concerning the contributions of the militia during the sieges of Oswego in 1756 and Fort William Henry the following year. Desandroüins found that the Canadians and Indians showed great enthusiasm at Oswego, and while they wasted a great deal of ammunition firing all day, they did succeed in lowering the garrison's morale. It obviously did not occur to him, however, that they might have captured the fort by themselves, or that the irregulars were anything more than auxiliaries.[28]

The year 1758 was a turning point in the war and in French tactics. For this campaign the British massed an army of 6,000 regulars and 9,000 provincials at Fort William Henry and advanced on Fort Carillon. Among these regulars were several new specially trained light infantry regiments and Robert Rogers' Corps of Rangers.[29] Few Canadians arrived in time for the Battle of Carillon, and the shortage of irregulars obliged the French to station two companies of *volontaires* in front of the abattis while it was under construction—*volontaires* being the contemporary French term for light infantry. These regular soldiers, probably the pickets from each of the battalions, skirmished all day with the enemy's abundant light troops, and successfully held them at bay while the abattis was hastily completed. Just as the battle opened, the French *volontaires* withdrew to the protection of the abattis or to the army's left flank.[30] A group of 300 Canadians who were present were ordered to leave the protection of the abattis and open independent fire on the flank of one of the attacking British columns, but refused to do so. A few had to have shots fired over their heads to prevent their fleeing the field, although in the latter case Bougainville admitted that "It is true that these were not Canadians of the good sort."[31] Canadians were not accustomed to fighting on the open battlefield and, having only *habitant* militia officers and occasionally a Canadian colonial regular officer of the *troupes de la Marine* to lead them, could not easily be coerced into exposing themselves to enemy fire. Even worse than the refusal of the Canadians at Carillon to follow orders was the rout of Canadian troops during a forest encounter in August 1758 with Roger's Rangers.[32]

Montcalm resolved at the end of this campaign that a higher level of discipline and cooperation was needed from his Canadian soldiers. His aide-de-camp and close friend Bougainville concluded, correctly, that "Now war is established here on a European basis of campaign plans, armies, artillery, sieges, battles. It is not a matter of making *coup*, but of conquering or being conquered. What a revolution! What a change!"[33] Indeed, the arrival of large regular armies in America had changed the nature of war on the continent. Montcalm believed that a concentration of his forces was necessary to confront the English along the major invasion routes, and he advocated a release of as many of the troops in the garrisons in the west as possible without undermining the Indian war effort. He saw that the Indians tied down large numbers of enemy militia on the frontiers, but doubted that a major French presence in the west had much effect in diverting British regular troops—the chief danger to New France, in his opinion—away from the central front.[34] The British were better able to respond to attacks by irregulars, and raids against military targets in the Lake George area were becoming more and more costly. Irregulars now found it more difficult to defeat regulars without the support of French or French colonial heavy infantry, and these troops had to be conserved for the principal engagements. Montcalm felt that large-scale raids no longer paid off in terms of the manpower, supplies, and effort invested, and he hoped that the Indians and small numbers of Canadians could maintain sufficient pressure on the English to keep them more or less on the defensive. By the fall of 1758 Montcalm knew that no ambush or raid was going to stem the advance of massive English armies against Montreal or Quebec; what he needed were large numbers of regular soldiers and disciplined light infantry who could be depended on to fight in a series of conventional battles.[35]

Montcalm believed that masses of poorly equipped and undisciplined Canadian militiamen who consumed his extremely limited food supplies were of minimal assistance to his army; rather, he needed regulars to reinforce his depleted battalions, which even at full strength were outnumbered approximately four to one by the British.[36] He therefore obtained Vaudreuil's consent to select 4,000 of the best militiamen and divide them into three groups. The first group was to be incorporated into the regular battalions of the line, the second into the *troupes de la Marine,* and the third was to be organized separately in the customary militia brigades. A total of approximately 3,000 Canadians were intended for the incorporations.[37]

This reorganization was intended to serve several purposes. First, each company of the *troupes de terre* and *troupes de la Marine* would be augmented by fifteen men, and would therefore add good shots, canoeists, and workers to the existing body of regulars, improving the ability of these troops to fight, travel, and build fortifications. Montcalm hoped to have the French and Canadian soldiers teach each other what they knew, making the regulars better woodsmen and the Canadians more dependable infantrymen. The Canadians, who customarily fell sick in large numbers on campaign because they lacked clothing, proper shelter, and enforced camp sanitation, would now live with the regulars in tents and receive uniforms, food, and other supplies. In addition, there had always been a serious lack of officers among the militia—sometimes only one for every 200 men—which resulted in a lack of supervision, discipline, and leadership in battle. Incorporated troops would receive abundant attention from the numerous officers and sergeants of the French line troops and *troupes de la Marine,* thereby, it was hoped, improving discipline and reducing desertion. Montcalm and his fellow officers claimed to have no worries that Canadians would be mistreated in their new companies, for "They live very well with our soldiers whom they love," and their complaints would be addressed by the general himself.[38] The militia and the French-recruited *troupes de la Marine* already camped together, so it was not expected that there would be any serious difficulty in uniting Canadians and the *troupes de terre.*[39]

The 1,000 remaining militiamen would be organized in their customary "brigades" of approximately 150 men, each theoretically comprising five companies of thirty men. Three soldiers of the *troupes de la Marine* were usually attached to each company as sergeants, and they gave the Canadians a modicum of discipline and military training.[40] According to Montcalm's plans for 1759, his picked militiamen would be placed under the best militia officers, subjected by special ordinance to the same rules of discipline as the regulars, and since there were fewer militiamen on continuous service, they could be better fed, clothed, armed, and even possibly paid for their longer period on campaign. As a further incentive, Montcalm proposed that distinguished Canadian soldiers receive marks of honour, including gratuities, and that small pensions be granted to those crippled by their wounds. The rest of the militia would remain at home prepared at a moment's notice to assemble and join the troops in the field.[41] All of these ideas centred around an attempt to organize and obtain the most efficient performance possible from irregular troops, either as raiders or as sharpshooters on the edges of the battlefield.

The decision to organize this special militia force to act independently of or in concert with regular troops had the full support of Montcalm's regular officers. Parscau du Plessis and Pouchot both noted the potential of Canadians to form "light companies," and in 1757 La Pause had the idea of establishing four companies of *partisans* composed of French and Canadian troops and guided by Indians; at any one time one or two of these companies could be in the field harassing the enemy. Bourlamaque made a similar proposal that a troop of 150 volunteer *chasseurs* adept at *la petite guerre* be maintained in the colony in peacetime, usefully employing the *coureurs de bois* whom he believed usually resided in unproductive debauchery among the Indians.[42]

Montcalm's intention to create a new army for the campaign of 1759, however, was only partially fulfilled. The *levée en masse* of the Canadian militia and the need to arm, feed, and supply thousands of these soldiers resulted in an abandonment of the plan to organize a set of elite militia brigades. The only special Canadian units to be formed were a small cavalry detachment led by French officers and the *réserve de Repentigny,* which was attached to Bougainville's command to patrol the riverbank upstream from Quebec during the siege. Neither unit took part in the Battle of the Plains of Abraham.[43] The planned militia incorporations, however, did take place in the late spring, just before the arrival off Quebec of the first ships of a fleet bearing a large British and American colonial army under Major-General James Wolfe. The number of Canadians actually incorporated is unknown, but it is doubtful whether more than 500 or 600 men joined the 3,000 or more regulars at Quebec.[44] Montcalm had only three months to train his Canadian regulars, simply an insufficient amount of time to produce the kind of soldier he wanted. Judging by the behaviour of the incorporated Canadians on the Plains of Abraham, it seems that very little effort had been made to drill them at all, and the abysmal performance of the regulars suggests that drill was not a high priority in the French army in Canada. After the battle, one of Montcalm's aides wrote in Montcalm's journal that "The French soldier no longer knew any discipline, and instead of molding the Canadian, he assumed all of his faults."[45]

The French officers were extremely pleased by the behaviour of the Canadian militia in the Battle of Montmorency on 31 July, for the militiamen were chiefly responsible for repelling a landing by 500 British grenadiers and Royal Americans. Lining the top of the slope overlooking the river, the militia opened a vigorous fire on the climbing troops, inflicting heavy casualties and forcing them to retreat to their boats. The French regulars, held in reserve immediately behind the Canadians, did not have to be committed to the action.[46] According to Captain Pierre Cassagniau de St. Félix of the Régiment de Berry, the French generals lacked "any great dependence on the prowess of the Canadians" until this action, "for they intermixed them with their regulars, and gave the latter public orders to shoot any of them that should betray the least timidity: however, they behaved with so much steadiness throughout the whole cannonading, and, upon the approach of [the enemy] troops up the precipice, fired with such great regularity, that they merited the highest applause and confidence from their Superiors."[47] This experience may have encouraged the officers to believe that the incorporated Canadians and militia would show more steadiness in any upcoming engagements.

On the morning of 13 September 1759, as Wolfe's army assembled on the Plains of Abraham and the French brought up their main force, platoons from the districts of Quebec, Montreal, and Trois-Rivières were detached from their militia brigades and sent forward with the pickets of the Régiment de Guyenne to harass the British troops from behind rocks and bushes all along the front of their line. After pushing back some British advance posts, these soldiers kept up a galling fire on the British regulars. Canadian militia and some Indians scattered in the woods on the two edges of the battlefield also kept up a steady fire from the cover of trees and underbrush.[48] Then, at about ten in the morning, Montcalm ordered the advance. In the centre, the battalions of Béarn and Guyenne formed a single deep column. On their right and left, at some distance, two other bodies of regulars formed shallower columns with a much wider frontage than the central formation. In the columns the incorporated Canadians were sandwiched in the second rank, no doubt to keep them in order. There were almost certainly more of them in the ranks further back in the columns.[49] Montcalm was clearly following the military ordinance of 1755, which recommended that attacks be made by a series of two-battalion columns.[50]

The officers lost control of their men almost immediately. The enthusiastic soldiers surged forward at an excessively fast pace, and as they marched over the rough terrain without pausing to dress ranks, they quickly lost cohesion.[51] As they approached the British line they began to collide with the advanced platoons of Canadian militia, which because of the rapidity of the advance had no time to retire in the intervals between the columns, two of which had very wide frontages. This caused further havoc in the French formations.[52] The columns began to move obliquely towards the British flanks, and at a distance of about 130 metres, extreme musket range, the French troops came to a sudden halt and fired several ineffectual volleys. The incorporated Canadians dropped to the ground to reload, as was their custom in an exposed position, and as the French officers urged the troops to advance, many if not all of the Canadians suddenly deserted their units and retired to the right where the platoons of skirmishers were joining the Canadians and Indians who lined the woods on the British flank.[53] This unorthodox behaviour—which left the regular officers somewhat nonplused—demonstrates just how little instruction the Canadian troops had received or accepted.

Pouchot commended the resistance of the militiamen on the right flank, but he also explained that the main attack "confused the [incorporated] Canadians who were little accustomed to find themselves out of cover." This was, however, the kindest assessment of the incorporated Canadians to be made by the French officers whose records are extant. Malartic accused them of cowardice, and others blamed them for setting the French regulars in disarray and abandoning their proper place in the line. The Canadians were shielded from further criticism by the fact that almost immediately after the Canadians left the ranks, the French regulars, who advanced in places to within approximately forty metres of the enemy line, broke under the impact of devastating British volleys and fled madly to the walls of Quebec and across the St. Charles River.[54]

At the conclusion of the Battle of the Plains of Abraham, as the French regulars abandoned the battlefield in complete disorder, the Canadians went far in redeeming themselves for their somewhat weak performance during the main encounter, this time in their traditional role as irregular soldiers. A quarter of Fraser's Highlanders were shot down as they attempted in vain to drive the Canadian rearguard from the woods, and they were obliged to retreat and regroup. A further attack by 500 British regulars from three regiments finally drove the Canadians back to the St. Charles.[55] The Chevalier de Johnstone, who observed this half-hour-long rearguard action, had nothing but lavish praise for their performance.[56] Pouchot and several other officers mentioned this resistance with approval, although they deplored the indiscipline among the Canadians in the columns.[57]

The French officers had underestimated the extent to which Canadians were attached to the tactics which they had practised for over four generations. Like the Indians, Canadians firmly believed that they should fight in their traditional manner, even if they recognized that conventional heavy infantry tactics might be appropriate for Europeans. Pre-industrial societies are extremely resistant to change because survival is so closely linked to practices—passed on by an oral tradition—which have been proven effective by generations of experience. Also, unlike the American colonists to the south, Canadians had no tradition of training in conventional tactics to make them open to such ideas. As usual, Canadians did their best in their traditional role fighting as skirmishers, and this would be taken into account when the tactical role of Canadians was reassessed for the next campaign, that of 1760.

The Chevalier de Lévis was not present at the Battle of the Plains of Abraham, but the news of the Canadian rearguard action confirmed his already high opinion of the effectiveness of Canadian militiamen when they fought under conditions for which they were trained. Ever since his arrival in Canada he had shown great interest in the use of irregular troops, and this goes far to explain why he was so popular with Vaudreuil and the Canadian officers. As early as 1756, Lévis had outlined the role he expected his light troops to play. In a directive he specified, first, that the *"troupes de la Marine* and those of the colony will fight in their manner on the flanks of the *troupes de terre*."[58] This role of light troops in guarding the flanks was relatively orthodox in the French army, and was practised from Fontenoy to the middle of the Seven Years' War in both Europe and Canada. Second, Lévis attempted to work out a system whereby regulars and irregulars could support each other in battle and compensate for their respective weaknesses. Of particular significance is the fact that he designated some regular troops to serve as light infantry: "M. de Montreuil will also detach all the good shots of his regiment, who will fight *à la canadienne*, and will keep together only a part of his detachment to receive those who fight *à la canadienne*, so that, in case they were obliged to withdraw, they could do so with security behind the detachment, which, being in order, would face the enemy and give the troops who had fought as skirmishers [*à la légère*] time to rally and recommence the fight.[59] Light infantry depended on line troops for protection on the open battlefield because they lacked the density to deliver the concentrated firepower of a large body of men. In the days when one musket meant one bullet, a few men could do little harm to an advancing infantry unit unless they continually retreated to a new position and renewed their fire.

Meanwhile, parallel tactical developments were taking place in Germany, where light troops were employed by the French army at Sundershausen and Lutternberg in 1758 and at Bergen, Lippstadt, and Minden the following year. Until 1759 grenadiers, pickets, and entire line battalions detached as *volontaires* were used as light infantry, but during the winter of 1758–59 several regiments decided of their own accord to form detachments of fifty men to serve as light infantry, and these soldiers proved so useful at Bergen, in the retreat from Minden, and in other engagements that at the end of the 1759 campaigning season a number of officers successfully urged the Maréchal de Broglie to institute light infantry companies throughout his army. This allowed a battalion to be a self-contained unit which could depend on itself and not on special light infantry battalions elsewhere in the army when it met the enemy during or between major battles. Despite opposition from the Duc de Choiseul, battalion light infantry companies were confirmed by Broglie's French army drill instructions of 1764 and 1769 and officially instituted in 1776, just in time for the Comte de Rochambeau's campaign in America.[60]

It seems unlikely that Lévis knew of Broglie's reforms of the autumn of 1759, since the British blockade of the St Lawrence began in May and communications with France via Acadia were tenuous in the extreme. This makes it especially interesting that he should organize battalion light infantry companies at exactly the same time as Broglie. Both generals, however, were carrying the primarily post-1748 practice of detaching battalion grenadiers and pickets as skirmishers to its logical conclusion.

During the winter of 1759–60 Lévis decided to continue the incorporation of Canadian troops into the regular battalions, but on a significantly different basis than that envisioned by his later commander. Lévis's instructions for the organization of his army in 1760 specified that three companies of militia would be attached to each regular battalion, and to command these companies he designated "a captain who would be the best for this assignment and to manage the *habitants* with gentleness, and three lieutenants to command the said companies."[61] It is especially important to note that these Canadian troops were to be attached to the battalion in independent companies and not merely assimilated into the ranks of the regulars. Their role on the battlefield was explained in detail: "When it is necessary to march in column, they will march by companies or by half-company at the head of the brigade, and when it is necessary to place themselves in order of battle to fight, they will go forward forming a first line, leaving from one division to the next an equal distance to occupy the entire front of the line."[62] In other words, the light infantry would spread out to form a skirmishing line in front of the regular troops. "Once they are thus formed, they will march forward and seek to make use of the most advantageous situations to approach as closely as possible and fire on the enemy, and follow him closely if he withdraws."[63] Lévis further explained that if the skirmishers were pushed back, they would rally and form line in the intervals between the two-company divisions and then march forward with the whole army, firing volleys and then charging with the bayonet.[64]

We see here the final development of the light infantryman, no longer an irregular sharpshooter roaming on the edges of the battlefield but a regular soldier trained to prepare the way for the decisive attack. This not only required a high degree of training and flexibility, but also called for an intelligent, motivated soldier quite different from the automatons advocated by most of the leading generals of the day.[65] Each regular battalion was equipped with light infantry and could employ them offensively or defensively whenever the need arose.

In the spring of 1760 the Chevalier de Lévis incorporated 2,264 Canadian militiamen into his eight battalions of *troupes de terre* and two battalions of *troupes de la Marine*.[66] A full 38 per cent of the rank and file of the average battalion was Canadian, with 226 Canadians and 361 regulars in this "average" unit combining to raise its strength to 587 men. There were, however, significant variations from unit to unit, especially in terms of the proportion of Canadians to Frenchmen. In the case of the Régiment de Languedoc, the incorporated Canadians slightly outnumbered the regulars.[67] At the Battle of the Plains of Abraham, the incorporated Canadians had constituted only about 10 per cent of the regulars present. Lévis's militiamen, who wore their traditional costumes and were accompanied by their Canadian *habitant* militia officers and French regular NCOS under the command of French regular officers, were organized in units separate from the French troops in the battalions and, of course, were not officially enlisted in the regular army. While it was usual for three strong companies to be attached to each battalion, in a number of cases more were involved; this is probably due to the fact that Canadian militia companies varied widely in size, and Lévis was reluctant to amalgamate companies from different localities.[68]

The French met the British at Sainte-Foy, on the edge of the Plains of Abraham, and a fierce, desperate battle ensued which left four times as many men dead and wounded as the more celebrated engagement of the previous September.[69] The Canadian militia companies, stationed in front and in the intervals between their battalions, kept up a relentless, accurate fire on the British regulars who, despite repeated attacks, failed to make any impression on their French opponents. The effectiveness of the Canadian troops greatly impressed Malartic: "The Canadians of the four brigades of the right, those who were in the intervals or in front of the brigades, fired a long time and most opportunely. They did a lot of harm to the English."[70] A reserve battalion composed of the townsmen of Montreal and Trois-Rivières under Repentigny of the colonial regulars advanced to fill a gap in the line accidentally created by the withdrawal of a battalion of the Régiment de La Reine, and fighting in a semblance of close order kept a battalion of Germans of the Royal American Regiment and other British regulars at bay.[71] The Canadians showed great steadiness and bravery in this battle, and took part in the set-piece attacks which drove in the British flanks and forced General Murray to order a hasty retreat with the loss of all of his guns.[72] Lévis singled out Dominique Nicolas de Laas de Gustede, a captain in the Régiment de La Reine and commander of the 223 Canadians of his battalion, for distinguished conduct. Although Laas never received orders to advance, when he saw Royal Rousillon and Guyenne marching against Fraser's brigade on the British left flank, he led his Canadian soldiers forward to join in the successful attack.[73] Canadian militiamen had already cleared this flank of Murray's light troops by nearly annihilating the force of American and Highland Rangers sent into the woods to operate against the French right.[74] The fact that nearly one-fifth of the French casualties at Sainte-Foy were Canadians suggests just how heavily engaged they were.[75]

Companies of Canadian skirmishers under French officers had formed a long line in front of their battalions, covering both the French heavy infantry and the gaps between the battalions and remaining in position despite British artillery and musket fire at close range. Joined to their respective battalions by French regular officers, they were able to offer valuable assistance to the heavy infantry and were supported by their fire. A Canadian militia battalion under a Canadian colonial regular officer had actually replaced a battalion of regulars in the line of battle, and other Canadian light troops covered the flanks and defeated trained enemy light infantry. Canadian troops had therefore performed in several roles: as skirmishers in front of the heavy infantry preparing and taking part in the decisive attack, as skirmishers acting offensively and defensively on the flanks, and as heavy infantry in the line of battle.

French officers, including Lévis, Malartic, and artillery lieutenant Joseph Fournerie de Vezon, were unanimous in praising the steadiness, effectiveness, and dash of the Canadian soldiers, and there is little doubt that the officers considered the military reforms of 1760 a great success.[76]

On both sides of the Atlantic, French military men faced the problem of how to increase the efficiency of irregular soldiers while retaining their special attributes of initiative and independence and their unique fighting skills. On each continent they met the problem in a similar way by giving their irregulars more discipline and better leadership, while at the same time cultivating their special *esprit de corps*. Conventional discipline and irregular tactics were combined to produce a new soldier with the ability to deal with a variety of opponents and battlefield situations. They also increased the cooperation between conventional and light troops until the latter, instead of being employed in a completely auxiliary role as scouts and raiders, became an effective tool on the classic, eighteenth-century battlefield.

The French officers who served in Canada during the Seven Years' War were obliged to fight under conditions which were very different from those which they had known in Europe, but their past experience and awareness of important trends in military tactics helped to prepare them for this new campaign. The growing ability of the enemy to deal with irregulars on their line of march and the likelihood of major encounters between the British and French armies meant that Canadians had to expand their skills by learning to fight on the conventional battlefield against enemy light and heavy infantry. Montcalm displayed a lack of judgment in filling the ranks of his regulars with undrilled Canadians, and was not sufficiently imaginative or ambitious enough to develop a closer cooperation between his regulars and irregulars. This job was left to Lévis to accomplish by placing militia units under regular officers and carefully linking these new light infantry units to his regular battalions so as to ensure close mutual support between these two corps—a change which paralleled reforms taking place simultaneously in the French army in Germany. The result was a decisive victory at Sainte-Foy, and this accomplishment justified the faith French officers had in the potential of Canadian militiamen to become what even they might have considered professional soldiers.

Notes

1. For historians who favour Montcalm see Francis Parkman, *France and England in North America,* part 7: *Montcalm and Wolfe,* 2 vols. (Boston 1884); Henri-Raymond Casgrain, *Guerre du Canada, 1756–1760: Montcalm et Lévis,* 2 vols. (Quebec 1891); and Lionel-Adolphe Groulx, *Histoire du Canada depuis la découverte,* 2 vols. (Montreal 1950). For highly critical perceptions of the French general see Guy Frégault, *La Guerre de la conquête* (Montreal 1955); William J. Eccles, "The French Forces in North America during the Seven Years' War," *Dictionary of Canadian Biography* (DCB), III, xv–xxiii; W.J. Eccles, "Montcalm, Louis-Joseph de, Marquis de Montcalm," DCB, III: 458–69; and W.J. Eccles, "Rigaud de Vaudreuil de Cavagnial, Pierre de, Marquis de Vaudreuil," DCB, IV: 662–74. Charles P. Stacey, *Quebec, 1759: The Siege and the Battle* (Toronto 1959), and George G.F.G. Stanley, *New France: The Last Phase, 1744–1760* (Toronto 1968), maintain a more neutral attitude.

2. Ian K. Steele, *Guerrillas and Grenadiers: The Struggle for Canada, 1689–1760* (Toronto 1969). I use the term "irregular" to denote light troops without extensive formal military training. "Light infantry" I define as formally trained light troops, who were often regulars rather than militia or auxiliaries.

3. With the addition of the Hungarian hussars, these light troops formed a very substantial proportion of the Habsburg forces. John F.C. Fuller, *British Light Infantry in the Eighteenth Century* (London 1925), 46–9; Gunther E. Rothenberg, *The Military Border in Croatia, 1740–1881* (Chicago 1966), 18–20; John Childs, *Armies and Warfare in Europe, 1648–1789* (New York 1982), 116–17; and Hew Strachan, *European Armies and the Conduct of War* (London 1983), 30.

4. For further discussion of Austrian, Prussian, and British light troops in the European theatre during the Seven Years' War see Fuller, *British Light Infantry,* 59–75; Strachan, *European Armies,* 30–5; Childs, *Armies and Warfare in Europe,* 118–20; Rothenberg, *Military Border in Croatia,* 40–52; and Christopher Duffy, *Frederick the Great: A Military Life* (London 1985), 314, 319–20.

5. Maurice de Saxe, *Reveries on the Art of War,* trans. Thomas R. Phillips (Harrisburg, Penn. 1944), 1–11. The *Reveries* were written in 1732 and circulated in manuscript long before they were published in 1757. Saxe deals extensively with irregular infantry and cavalry on pages 40–1, 48, and 50. See also Jean Colin, *L'Infanterie au XVIIIe siècle: La Tactique* (Paris 1907), 47–51, 71; Robert S. Quimby, *The Background of Napoleonic Warfare: The Theory of Military Tactics in Eighteenth-Century France* (New York 1957), 84–5; Jon M. White, *Marshal of France: The Life and Times of Maurice, Comte de Saxe* (London 1962), 129, 147, 157–8; Fuller, *British Light Infantry,* 49–54; Strachan, *European Armies,* 31; and Childs, *Armies and Warfare in Europe,* 118.

6. Thomas Chapais, *Le Marquis de Montcalm (1721–1759)* (Quebec 1911), 16–22, and Lévis, *Journal, Collection des manuscrits du maréchal de Lévis (Lévis MSS),* I, 24. Montcalm was aide-de-camp to the Marquis de La Fare in Bohemia, and was colonel of an infantry regiment in Piedmont. Lévis served as a captain in Bohemia and as an adjutant (*aide-major*) with the army in Piedmont; in 1748 he was promoted colonel. Both men displayed extraordinary bravery, and Montcalm suffered wounds on a regular basis.

7. Rohan Butler, *Choiseul,* I: *Father and Son* (Oxford 1980), 304–5, 343, 363.

8. Spenser Wilkinson, *The Defence of Piedmont 1742–1748: A Prelude to the Study of Napoleon* (Oxford 1927), 163–4, 208, 309–17; Butler, *Choiseul,* I, 500–52; White, *Marshal of France,* 222; Fuller, *British Light Infantry,* 54; and Strachan, *European Armies,* 31.

9. See William J. Eccles, "The Social, Economic, and Political Significance of the Military Establishment in New France," *Canadian Historical Review 52* (1971): 1–22, for an examination of the impact of war and the military establishment on Canada's inhabitants.

10. Georges-Marie Butel-Dumont, *Histoire et commerce des colonies angloises dans l'Amérique septentrionale, où l'on trouve l'état actuel de leur population, & des détails curieux sur la constitution de leur gouvernement, principalement sur celui de la Nouvelle-Angleterre, de la Pensilvanie, de la Caroline & de la Géorgie* (Paris 1755), 40.

11. François-Charles de Bourlamaque, "Memoire sur le Canada," *Lévis* MSS, V, 102. See also James Johnstone, "The Campaign of Canada, 1760," *Collection de manuscrits contenant lettres, mémoires, et autres documents historiques relatifs à la Nouvelle-France, recueillis aux archives de la Province de Québec ou copies à l'étranger* (MRNF), IV, 254, 262; Pierre Pouchot, *Memoir Upon the Late War in North America between the French and English, 1755–60,* 2 vols., ed. and trans. Franklin B. Hough (Roxbury, Mass. 1866), II, 45; Louis-Guillaume de Parscau du Plessis, "Journal de la campagne de *la Sauvage* frégate du Roy, armée au port de Brest, au mois de mars 1756 (écrit pour ma dame)," *Rapport de l'archiviste du Province de Québec* (RAPQ) (1928–9), 221; and Peter Kalm, *Travels into North America,* trans. John R. Foster (Barre, Mass. 1972), 492, for further comments on the warlike spirit of Canadians.

12. Louis-Antoine de Bougainville, "Mémoire sur l'etat de la Nouvelle-France," RAPQ (1923–4), 58.

13. Bougainville to Mme Hérault, 20 Feb. 1758, Louis-Antoine de Bougainville. *Adventure in the Wilderness: The American Journals of Louis Antoine de Bougainville, 1756–1760,* ed. and trans. Edward P. Hamilton (Norman, OK 1964), 333.

14. Montreuil to d'Argenson, Montreal, 12 June 1756, *Documents Relative to the Colonial History of the State of New York* (NYCD), ed. E.B. O'Callaghan (Albany 1859), x, 4 9. See also anonymous, "Situation du Canada en hommes, moyens, positions," RAPQ (1923–4), 9, a memoir probably by Bougainville, and the account by La Pause, who uses almost the same words as this anonymous officer in describing the inability of Canadians to "defend themselves with countenance." Jean-Guillaume-Charles; Plantavit de La Pause, chevalier de La Pause, "Mémoire et observations sur mon voyage en Canada," RAPQ (1931–2), 66.

15. La Pause, "Mémoire et observations sur mon voyage en Canada," 10.

16. Bougainville, "Mémoire sur l'état de la Nouvelle-France," 58.

17. Jean-Baptiste d'Aleyrac, *Aventures militaires au IXVIIIe siècle d'après les mémoires de Jean-Baptiste d'Aleyrac,* ed. Charles Coste (Paris 1935), 131; Pierre Marcel, "Journal abrégé de la campagnes de 1759 en Canada par M. M[arcel] ayde de camp de M. le Mis. de Montcalm," in Arthur C. Doughty and G. W. Parmelee, *The Siege of Quebec and the Battle of the Plains of Abraham* (Quebec 1901), V, 299.

18. Pouchot, *Memoir,* I, 35, 37, and II, 45

19. La Pause, "Mémoire et observations sur mon voyage en Canada," 66.

20. Bougainville, *Journals,* 174; Stanley, *New France,* 162; Steele, *Guerillas and Grenadiers,* 108; La Pause, "Journal de l'entrée de la campagne 1760," RAPQ (1932–3), 384; and Lévis, *Journal,* 1, 12.

21. Pouchot, *Memoir,* I, 41–3.

22. This common philosophy of the time was best illustrated by Montesquieu, who in *De l'esprit des lois* explained the idea that people in a particular environment develop a special character which the laws had to be made to fit rather than making people fit the laws.

23. Nicolas Sarrebource de Pontleroy, "Mémoire et observations sur le project d'attaquer les postes ennemis en avant de Québec, et sur celui de surprendre la place ou de l'enlever de vive force," 18 Jan. 1760, *Lévis* MSS, IV, 199.

24. J.R. Turnbull, "Dieskau, Jean-Armand (Johan Herman?), Baron de Dieskau," DCB, III, 185–6. Dieskau's first name is sometimes erroneously given as Ludwig August.

25. Steele, *Guerillas and Grenadiers,* 91; Stanley, *New France,* 102–3; and Guy Frégault, *Canada: The War of the Conquest,* trans. Margaret M. Cameron (Toronto 1969), 103–6. This latter book is a translation of *La Guerre de la conquête* (Montreal 1955).

26. Chevalier de Montreuil, "Detail de la marche de Monsieur de Dieskau par Monsieur de Montreuil," MRNF, IV, 1–4; Montreuil to d'Adabie, St Frédéric, 10 Oct. 1755, MRNF, IV, 9; Montreuil to d'Argenson, Montreal, 2 Nov. 1755, MRNF, IV, 13; and Montreuil to d'Argenson, Montreal, 12 June 1756, NYCD, X, 419. Montcalm, La Pause, and Pouchot shared similar ideas regarding the cause of Dieskau's defeat. See Montcalm to d'Argenson, 28 Aug. 1756, National Archives of Canada (NA), MG 4, A1, vol. 34 7, no 208; La Pause, "Mémoire et observations sur mon voyage en Canada," 20; and Pierre Pouchot, *Memoir,* I, 46–7.

27. Montcalm to Moras, Quebec, 19 Feb. 1758, NYCD, X, 686–7. See also Bougainville, *Journals,* 42.

28. Charles Nicolas Gabriel, *Le Maréchal de camp Desandroüins, 1729–1792: Guerre du Canada, 1756–1760, Guerre de l'indépendence américaine, 1780–1782* (Verdun 1887), 50–64, and W. J. Eccles, "Lévis," DCB, IV, 477–82

29. The French officers had a consistently high opinion of British regulars and a consistently low opinion of American provincials. They referred to the provincials only in order to point out their numbers and incompetence. They did, however, have respect for the Royal American Regiment and Rogers' Rangers—both regular units—even though they enjoyed recounting the numerous abortive or disastrous operations mounted by the Rangers. For the development of light infantry tactics in the British army in North America during the Seven Years' War see Peter Russel, "Redcoats in the Wilderness: British Officers and Irregular Warfare in Europe and America, 1740 to 1760," *William and Mary Quarterly* 3rd ser. 35 (1978): 629–52; Fuller, *British Light Infantry,* 76–110; Hugh C.B. Rogers, *The British Army in the Eighteenth Century* (London 1977), 73; Strachan, *European Armies,* 28; and for a long-term view, Peter Paret, "Colonial Experience and European Military Reform at the End of the Eighteenth Century," *Bulletin of the Institute of Historical Research* 37 (1964): 47–59.

30. Bougainville, *Journals,* 230. In the French army, pickets were not selected on a rotational basis; instead, they formed permanent units which were often detached for special duties.

31. Bougainville, *Journals,* 238. See also Gabriel, *Desandrouins,* 182, and Doreil to Belle-Isle, Quebec, 28 and 31 July 1758, RAPQ (1944–5), 138 and 150–2. In these last two letters, war commissary André Doreil passed on to the minister of war confidential information which he had obtained from Montcalm.

32. For French reactions to this incident see Gabriel, *Desandrouins,* 203–6; Bougainville, *Journals,* 261–2, and Montcalm to Moras, Montreal, 11 July 1757, MRNF, IV, 105–6. In 1756 1900 Canadian militiamen served in the ranks, but another 1100 were needed for transport work and for building fortifications. By 1758 1500 Canadians were employed on the western supply routes alone. George F.G. Stanley, *Canada's Soldiers: The Military History of an Unmilitary People,* rev. ed. (Toronto 1960), 23.

33. Bougainville, *Journals,* 252. Henderson believes that Bougainville may have copied passages from Montcalm's journal into his own, rather than the contrary, since duplicated passages often have a later date in Bougainville's journal. In my opinion, however, Bougainville authored parts of the general's official journal, then copied his handiwork into his own a few hours or days later. The style of the common passages seems more characteristic of Bougainville than of Montcalm. I have therefore ascribed the quoted passage to Bougainville and not to Montcalm, who also records it: Montcalm, *Journal, Lévis* MSS, VII, 419. Susan W. Henderson. "The French Regular Officer Corps in Canada, 1755–1760: A Group Portrait" (PhD thesis, University of Maine, Orono, 1975), 115–16.

34. Stanley, *New France,* 220–1; Steele, *Guerillas and Grenadiers,* 109; Henderson, "The French Regular Officer Corps in Canada," 102; Montcalm to Vaudreuil, Carillon, 26 July 1758, NYCD, X, 760–1; Montcalm to Cremille, Montreal, 12 April 1759, MRNF, IV, 224–5; and Montcalm to Le Normand, Montreal, 12 April 1759, NYCD, X, 966.

35. Montcalm, "Réflexions générales sur les mesures à prendre pour la défense de cette colonie," 10 Sept. 1758. *Lévis* MSS, IV, 45–6, and Stanley, *New France,* 220–1. Eccles claims, incorrectly, that Montcalm believed that "the guerrilla warfare on the English colony's frontiers had to cease." Eccles, "Montcalm," 463.

36. Bougainville, *Journals,* 199.

37. Montcalm, "Réflexions générales sur les mesures à prendre pour la défense de cette colonie," 45–8.

38. Ibid.; anonymous, "Milices du Canada: inconvenients dans la constitution de ces milices qui empêchent leur utilité; moyens d'en tirer partie, la campagne prochaine," Jan. 1759, RAPQ (1923–4), 29–31; and anonymous, "The Siege of Quebec in 1759," *The Siege of Quebec in 1759: Three Eye-Witness Accounts,* ed. Jean-Claude Hébert (Quebec 1974), 52. Canadian officers of the *troupes de la Marine* were especially plentiful, for at the beginning of the war sixty of them commanded 900 soldiers. Stanley, *Canada's Soldiers,* 27.

39. D'Aleyrac, *Adventures militaires,* 33, 58.

40. Montcalm, "Réflexions générales sur les mesures à prendre pour la défense de cette colonie," 45–8, and d'Aleyrac, *Aventures militaires,* 58.

41. Montcalm, "Réflexions générales sur les mesures à prendre pour la défense de cette colonie." 45–8, and anonymous, "Milices du Canada," 29–31.

42. Parscau du Plessis, "Journal de la campagne de *la Sauvage,*" RAPQ (1928–9), 221. Pouchot, *Memoir,* I, 37; La Pause, "Mémoire sur la campagne à faire en Canada l'année 1757," RAPQ (1932–3), 338; and François-Charles de Bourlamaque, "Memoir on Canada," NYCD, X, 1149.

43. Stacey, *Quebec, 1759,* 117

44. See Lévis, *Journal,* I, 209, and H.-R. Casgrain, *Montcalm et Lévis,* II, 97, for an indication of the numbers incorporated; Casgrain suggests several hundred. See Doughty and Parmelee, *Siege of Quebec,* III, 154, and John Knox, *An Historical Journal of the Campaigns in North America For the Years 1757, 1758, 1759, and 1760,* ed. Arthur G. Doughty (Toronto 1914), II, 105–6, for estimates of the size of the French army on the Plains of Abraham.

45. Montcalm, *Journal,* VII, 613.

46. For the Battle of Montmorency see Casgrain, *Montcalm et Lévis,* II, 133–4; Lévis, *Journal,* I, 187–8; anonymous, "Memoirs of the Siege of Quebec, from the Journal of a French Officer on Board the Chezine Frigate," Doughty and Parmelee, *Siege of Quebec,* IV, 249–50; Gordon Donaldson, *Battle for a Continent: Quebec 1759* (Toronto 1973), 138–40; Stanley, *New France,* 226–7, and Chapais, *Montcalm,* 610–11.

47. Pierre Cassagniau de St Félix, cited in Knox, *Historical Journal,* II, 6.

48. Armand Joannès (Hermann Johannes), "Mémoire sur la campagne de 1759 depuis le mois de mai jusqu'en septembre," Doughty and Parmelee, *Siege of Quebec,* IV, 226, and Marcel, "Journal abrégé de la campagne de 1759 en Canada," ibid., V, 296.

49. Doughty and Parmelee, *Siege of Quebec,* III, 160; Foligné, "Journal de Foligné," ibid., IV, 205; and La Pause, "Mémoire et observations sur mon voyage en Canada," 97. For scholarly accounts of the battle see Stacey, *Quebec, 1759,* 145–8; Donaldson, *Battle for a Continent,* 175–83; William J. Eccles, "The Battle of Quebec: A Reappraisal," *Proceedings of the Third Annual Meeting of the French Colonial Historical Society* (1977), 70–81. Also, Stanley, *New France,* 299–32; Doughty and Parmelee, *Siege of Quebec,* III, 131–72; and Philippe-Baby Casgrain, *Les Batailles des Plaines d'Abraham et de Sainte-Foye* (Quebec 1908), 1–68.

50. Quimby, *The Background of Napoleonic Warfare,* 86. The Ordinance of 1755 was influenced by both Folard and Saxe.

51. H.-R. Casgrain, *Montcalm et Lévis,* II, 249; Lévis, *Journal,* I, 209; and Marcel, "Journal abrégé de la campagne de 1759 en Canada," Doughty and Parmelee, *Siege of Quebec,* V, 296.

52. Joannès, "Mémoire sur la campagne de 1759," 226, and Marcel, "Journal abrégé de la campagne de 1759 en Canada," 296.

53. Joannès, "Mémoire sur la campagne de 1759," 226, and Anne-Joseph-Hippolyte de Maurès de Malartic, Comte de Malartic, *Journal des campagnes au Canada de 1755 à 1760 par le comte de Maurès de Malartic,* ed. Gabriel de Maurès de Malartic and Paul Gaffarel (Paris 1890), 285.

54. Pouchot, *Memoir,* I, 217; Malartic, *Journal,* 285; Joannès, "Mémoire sur la campagne de 1759," 226; and Marcel, "Journal abrégé de la campagne de 1759 en Canada," 296.

55. Stacey, *Quebec, 1759,* 152; P.-B. Casgrain, *Plaines d'Abraham et Sainte-Foye,* 53–6; Donaldson, *Battle for a Continent,* 187–9; Stanley, *New France,* 232; Chapais, *Montcalm,* 662; and Doughty and Parmelee, *Siege of Quebec,* III, 151, 171–2.

56. Doughty and Parmelee, *Siege of Quebec,* III, 164, 172.

57. Pouchot, *Memoir,* I, 217.

58. Lévis, *Journal,* I, 51.

59. Ibid.

60. Colin, *L'Infanterie au IXVIIIe siècle,* 75–80, 106–13, 126; Quimby, *The Background of Napoleonic Warfare,* 92, 98–9; Fuller, *British Light Infantry,* 69–70, 118–23; and Eugène Carrias, *La Pensée militaire française* (Paris 1960), 170.

61. Lévis, "Instructions concernant l'ordre dans lequel les milices attachées à chaque bataillon seront formées pour camper et servir pendant la campagne," *Journal,* I, 248.

62. Ibid., 250. The divisions Lévis mentions here include two companies, each about thirty men strong.

63. Ibid., 250–1.

64. Ibid., 251. See also Lévis, "Instruction concernant les dispositions et ordre de bataille qui doivent suivre toutes les troupes," and "Instructions concernant l'ordre dans lequel les milices attachées à chaque bataillon seront formées pour camper et servir pendant la campagne," ibid., 243–54, as well as Lee Kennett, *The French Armies in the Seven Years' War: A Study in Military Organization and Administration* (Durham, NC 1967), 29–30.

65. Strachan, *European Armies,* 23–5.

66. Data derived from table in Lévis, *Journal,* I, 257. Lévis lists 6,910 troops, including 2,264 incorporated militia and militia officers (who were *habitants,* not professionals) 3,610 regulars, and 266 regular officers. There was also a battalion of Montreal militia, 180 Canadian cavalry, and 270 Indians.

67. Ibid., 257.

68. Ibid., 253, and La Pause, "Mémoire et observations sur mon voyage en Canada," 107.

69. For scholarly accounts of the battle see Jean-Claude Lizotte, Jacques Gervais, and Carl Lavoie, "La Bataille de Sainte-Foy," *Mémoire: Magazine d'histoire et patrimoine,* nos 2–3 (1985): 4–21; P.-B. Casgrain, *Plaines d'Abraham et Sainte Foye,* 69–90; George M. Wrong, *The Fall of Canada: A Chapter in the History of the Seven Years' War* (Oxford 1914), 143–54; Stanley, *New France,* 244–8; Parkman, *Montcalm and Wolfe,* II, 348–51; and H.-R. Casgrain, *Montcalm et Lévis,* II, 350–6.

70. Malartic, *Journal,* 319.

71. P.-B. Casgrain, *Plaines d'Abraham et Sainte-Foye,* 69, 87.

72. H.-R. Casgrain, *Montcalm et Lévis,* II, 351, 355; Malartic, *Journal,* 319 note: and anonymous, "Narrative of the Expedition against Quebec, under the orders of Chevalier de Lévis, *Maréchal des Camps et Armées* of the King," NYCD, X, 1083. This last account is Canadian, and is attached to one of Vaudreuil's letters to Berryer, dated Montreal, 3 May 1760.

73. Lévis, *Journal,* I, 267; H.-R. Casgrain, *Montcalm et Lévis,* II, 355–6; Vaudreuil to Berryer, Montreal, 3 May 1760, NYCD, X, 1076; and Stanley, *New France,* 248.

74. Stanley, *New France,* 247–8.

75. Casgrain's casualty figures are not completely reliable, but they indicate that about 17 per cent of the French casualties were Canadian, or 150 men. Casgrain, *Montcalm et Lévis,* II, 356.

76. Lévis, *Journal,* I, 267; Malartic, *Journal,* 319; and Fournerie de Vezon, "Evénements de la guerre en Canada depuis le 13 7bre 1759 jusqu'au 14 juillet 1760," RAPQ (1938–9), 6–7.

CHAPTER
6 THE MEANING OF THE CONQUEST

No subject has generated more controversy, particularly among French-Canadian historians, than the impact of the Conquest on *la société canadienne*. In the modern, post-1945 era, that controversy centred on two conflicting interpretative approaches. One was the neo-nationalist Montreal school, heir to the Abbé Lionel Groulx tradition, composed of men such as Maurice Séguin, Guy Frégault, Michel Brunet and Cameron Nish. A proponent of the "decapitation thesis," this school viewed the Conquest as catastrophic, eliminating by 1800 the middle-class élites so vital to the economic and national development of the colony. Challenging this interpretation was the Laval "liberal" school of historians consisting of individuals such as Jean Hamelin, Fernand Ouellet and Marcel Trudel. While agreeing that by 1800 Quebec lacked a dynamic bourgeoisie, these historians found the explanation not in the Conquest but in the flawed nature of the society of New France itself. What had never existed, they argued, could not be decapitated.

More recently, this debate has taken a somewhat different turn. Applying modified Marxist analyses to the issue, a younger generation of Québecois political scientists has concluded that the traditional historical interpretations, nationalist and liberal alike, have missed the mark. What was really important about the Conquest, argue individuals such as Gerald Bernier and Vinh Ta Van, is that it caused a "structural rupture" in the economy of New France. The sudden, rapid and external imposition of capitalism onto an essentially feudal society, they believe, was both cataclysmic and far-reaching in its consequences.

Because of its nationalistic overtones, the debate between the Montreal and Laval schools of historians is as much about the future of Quebec as about the history of New France, and no final "winner" can ever be declared. Keeping this in mind, the readings in this unit move beyond theory to fact, evaluating the traditional interpretations of the Conquest by reference to specific historical circumstances. In "A Change in Climate: The Conquest and the *Marchands* of Montreal," José Igartua tests the decapitation thesis by examining the impact of the new socio-economic order of the post-Conquest world on the merchants of Montreal. Generally his findings substantiate the thesis, although Igartua acknowledges that if Canada had remained in French hands "there is no guarantee that other changes would not have affected the Montreal merchants."

French historian John Bosher also examines the impact of the Conquest on the merchant class, but from a much broader cosmopolitan perspective. Indeed, Bosher has long argued that both the Montreal and Laval schools interpret the Conquest within a too-narrow North American framework; New France, in his view, was first and foremost a colony whose fate very much depended upon the fortunes of the mother country. In *The Canada Merchants, 1713–1763*, from which the second reading has been excerpted, he places the Conquest and its legacy for the Canada merchants in the context of the critical eighteenth-century commercial and religious policies of the French government. "France," he concludes, "lost Canada in the course of financial, military and religious crises that simultaneously undermined Bourbon official society by revealing its weaknesses."

Suggestions for Further Reading

Bernier, Gerald, "Sur quelques effets de la rupture structurelle engendrée par la Conquête au Québec: 1760–1854," *Revue d'histoire de l'amérique-française*, 35, no. 1 (juin 1981), 69–95.

Blain, Jean, "Economie et société en Nouvelle-France—L'Historiographie au tournant des années 1960: La réaction à Guy Frégault et à l'école de Montréal—La voie des sociologues," *Revue d'histoire de l'amérique-française*, 30, no. 3 (décembre 1979), 323–62.

Bosher, John F., *Business and Religion in the Age of New France*. Toronto: Canadian Scholars' Press, 1994

Bosher, John F., *The Canada Merchants, 1713–1763*. Oxford: Clarendon Press, 1987.

Brunet, Michel, *French Canada and the Early Decades of British Rule*. Ottawa: Canadian Historical Association, 1971.

Igartua, José, "A Change in Climate: The Conquest and the *Marchands* of Montreal," *CHA Historical Papers* (1974), 115–35.

_____, "Le comportement démographique des marchands de Montréal vers 1760," *Revue de l'histoire de l'amérique-française*, 33, no. 3 (décembre 1979), 427–45.

_____, "The Merchants of Montreal at the Conquest: Socio-Economic Profile," *Histoire Sociale/Social History*, VIII, no. 16 (November 1975), 275–93.

Miquelon, Dale, ed., *The Debate on the Bourgeoisie and Social Change in French Canada, 1700–1850*. Toronto: Copp Clark Publishing, 1977.

Ouellet, Fernand, "Michel Brunet et le problème de la conquête," *Bulletin des Recherches historiques*, 62 (avril-mai-juin 1956), 92–101.

Sanfilippo, Matteo, "Du féodalisme au capitalisme? Essai d'interprétation des analyses marxistes de la Nouvelle-France," *Histoire Sociale/Social History*, XVIII, no. 35 (mai 1985), 85–98.

Seguin, Maurice, "La conquéte et la vie économique des Canadiens," *Action nationale*, XXVIII, no. 4 (1946–1947), 308–26.

Standen, S. Dale, "The Debate on the Social and Economic Consequences of the Conquest: A Summary," in Phillip P. Boucher, ed., *Proceedings of the Tenth Meeting of the French Colonial Historical Society*, University Press of America, 1985.

Ta Van, Vinh, "La Nouvelle France et la Conquête: Passage du Féodalisme au Capitalisme," *Cahiers d'histoire de l'Université de Montréal*, II, no. 2 (printemps 1982), 3–25.

A CHANGE IN CLIMATE: THE CONQUEST AND THE *MARCHANDS* OF MONTREAL

José Igartua

When the British government issued the Royal Proclamation of 1763, it assumed that the promised establishment of "British institutions" in the "Province of Quebec" would be sufficient to entice American settlers to move north and overwhelm the indigenous French-speaking and Papist population. These were naive hopes. Until the outbreak of the American Revolution, British newcomers merely trickled into Quebec, leading Governor Carleton to prophesy in 1767 that "barring a catastrophe shocking to think of, this Country must, to the end of Time, be peopled by the Canadian Race ..."[1] But the British newcomers, few though they were, had to be reckoned with. By 1765 they were powerful enough to have Governor Murray recalled and by 1777 they would be strong enough to command the majority of investments in the fur trade.[2] Did their success stem from superior abilities? Did the British take advantage of the situation of submission and dependence into which the Canadians had been driven by the Conquest? Did the newcomers gain their predominance from previous experience with the sort of political and economic conditions created in post-Conquest Quebec?

Historians of Quebec have chosen various ways to answer these questions. Francis Parkman was fond of exhibiting the superiority of the Anglo-Saxon race over the "French Celt."[3] More recently the studies of W.S. Wallace, E.E. Rich, and D.G. Creighton took similar, if less overt, positions.[4] One of the best students of the North West fur trade, Wayne E. Stevens, concluded: "The British merchants ... were men of great enterprise and ability and they began gradually to crowd out the French traders who had been their predecessors in the field."[5]

The French-Canadian historian, Fernand Ouellet, attributed the rise of the British merchants to the weaknesses of the Canadian trading bourgeoisie: "*Son attachement à la petite entreprise individuelle, sa répugnance à la concentration,*

From *Historical Papers* (The Canadian Historical Association, 1974), 115–34.

*son goût du luxe de même que son attrait irrésistible pour les placements assurés
étaint des principaux handicaps.*" ["Its attachment to small personal businesses,
its aversion to amalgamation, its taste for luxury, along with its irresistible attraction to safe investments were major handicaps."] No evidence is given for
this characterization and the author hastens to concede that before 1775 "*le
problème de la concentration ne se pose pas avec acuité,*" [amalgamation did not
come into focus as an issue,"] but for him it is clear that the economic displace-
ment of the Canadians resulted from their conservative, "*ancien Régime*" frame
of mind, bred into them by the clergy and the nobility.[6] Ouellet painted British
merchants in a more flattering light as the agents of economic progress.[7]

Michel Brunet has depicted the commercial competition between the British
newcomers and the Canadian merchants as an uneven contest between two
national groups, one of which had been deprived of the nourishing blood of its
metropolis while the other was being assiduously nurtured. For Brunet the
normal and natural outcome of that inequality was the domination of the conqueror, a situation which he sees as prevailing to the present day.[8]

Dale B. Miquelon's study of one merchant family, the Babys, shed new light
on the question of British penetration of Canadian trade. It outlined the growth
of British investments in the fur trade and the increasing concentration of
British capital. The author concluded:

> The French Canadians dominated the Canadian fur trade until the upheaval of
> the American Revolution. At that time they were overwhelmed by an influx of
> capital and trading personnel. English investment in the top ranks of investors
> jumped by 679 per cent and was never significantly to decline. Even without ex-
> planations involving the difference between the French and English commercial
> mentalities, it is difficult to believe that any body of merchants could recover from
> an inundation of such size and swiftness.[9]

This conclusion had the obvious merit of staying out of the murky waters of
psychological interpretations. But Miquelon's own evidence suggests that the
"flood theory" is not sufficient to account for the Canadians' effacement; even before the inundation of 1775–83, British investment in the fur trade was growing
more rapidly than Canadian. By 1772, to quote Miquelon, the "English [had]
made more impressive increases in the size of their investments than [had] the
French, and for the first time [had] larger average investments in all categories."[10]

It is difficult not to note the ascendancy of the British in the fur trade of
Canada even before the American Revolution. The success of the British merchants, therefore, was rooted in something more than mere numbers. It was
not simply the outcome of an ethnic struggle between two nationalities of a
similar nature; it was not only the natural consequence of the Canadians' conservative frame of mind. It arose out of a more complex series of causes, some
of them a product of the animosities between Canadians and British, others
inherent to the differences in the socio-economic structures of the French and
British Empires; together, they amounted to a radical transformation of the
societal climate of the colony.

The aim of this paper is to gauge the impact of the Conquest upon a well-defined segment of that elusive group called the "bourgeoisie" of New France. It focuses on Montreal and its Canadian merchants. Montreal was the centre of the fur trade and its merchants managed it. Historians of New France have traditionally seen the fur trade as the most dynamic sector of the colony's economy; by implication it is generally believed that the fur trade provided the likeliest opportunities for getting rich quickly and maintaining a "bourgeois" standard of living.[11] It is not yet possible to evaluate the validity of this notion with any precision, for too little is known about other sectors of the economy which, in the eighteenth century at least, may have generated as much or more profit. Research on the merchants of Quebec should provide new information on the wealth to be made from the fisheries, from wholesale merchandising, and from trade with Louisbourg and the West Indies. But if one is concerned with the fate of Canadian merchants after the Conquest, one should examine the fate of men involved in the sector of the economy of Quebec which was the most dynamic *after* the Conquest, the fur trade. The paper examines the impact of the arrival of (relatively) large numbers of merchants on the Montreal mercantile community, the attitude of British officials towards the Canadians, and the changing political climate of the colony. It is suggested that it was the simultaneous conjunction of these changes to the "world" of the Montreal merchants, rather than the effect of any one of them, which doomed the Canadian merchants of Montreal.[12]

The Montreal Merchants at the End of the French Regime

In 1752 a French Royal engineer passing through Montreal remarked that "*la plupart des habitants y sont adonnés au commerce principalement à celui connu sous le nom des pays d'en haut*" ["most of the inhabitants are involved in trade, chiefly in what is known as the 'upcountry' trade"].[13] It was only a slight exaggeration. By the last year of the French regime one could count over 100 *négociants*, merchants, outfitters, traders, and shopkeepers in Montreal. The overwhelming majority of them had been in business for some years and would remain in business after the Conquest. Over half were outfitters for the fur trade at some time or other between 1750 and 1775; these men comprised the body of the merchant community of Montreal. Above them in wealth and stature stood a handful of import merchants who did a comfortable business of importing merchandise from France and selling it in Montreal to other merchants or directly to customers in their retail stores. Below the outfitters a motley group of independent fur traders, shopkeepers, and artisans managed to subsist without leaving more than a trace of their existence for posterity.[14]

The fur trade, as it was conducted by the merchants of Montreal before 1760, had little to do with the glamorous picture it sometimes calls to mind. For the outfitter who remained in Montreal, it was not physically a risky occupation; its management was fairly simple and the profits which it produced quite meager. For the last years of the French regime the fur trade followed a three-tier system. For Frontenac (present-day Kingston) and Fort Niagara were king's posts; they were not lucrative and had to be subsidized to meet English competition. The trade of Detroit and Michilimackinac, as well as that of the posts to the south-west, was open to licencees whose numbers were limited. Some *coureurs de bois* (traders without a licence) also roamed in the area. The richest posts, Green Bay and the posts to the north-west past Sault Sainte Marie, were monopolies leased by the Crown to merchants or military officers.[15] The export of beaver was undertaken by the French *Compagnie des Indes*, which had the monopoly of beaver sales on the home market. Other furs were on the open market.

The system worked tolerably well in peacetime: there was a stable supply of furs, prices paid to the Indians had been set by custom, the prices paid by the *Compagnie des Indes* were regulated by the Crown, and the prices of trade goods imported from France were fairly steady. There was competition from the Americans at Albany and from the English on the Hudson Bay, to be sure, but it appeared to be a competition heavily influenced by military considerations and compliance with Indian customs.[16]

The system faltered in wartime. Beaver shipments to France and the importation of trade goods became risky because of British naval power. Shipping and insurance costs raised the Canadian traders' overhead, but the Indians refused to have the increase passed on to them. This was the most obvious effect of war, but it also produced general economic and administrative dislocations which led H.A. Innis to conclude that it " ... seriously weakened the position of the French in the fur trade and contributed to the downfall of the French *régime* in Canada.[17]

Nevertheless, outside of wartime crises, the fur trade of New France was conducted with a fair dose of traditionalism. This traditionalism resulted from two concurrent impulses: Indian attitudes towards trade, which were untouched by the mechanism of supply and demand and by distinctions between commercial, military, political or religious activities; and the mercantilist policies of France, which tried to control the supply of furs by limiting the number of traders and regulating beaver prices on the French market. While the fur trade structure of New France had an inherent tendency towards geographic expansion, as Innis argued, it also had to be oligopolistic in nature, if investments in Indian alliances, explorations, and military support were to be maximized. Open competition could not be allowed because it would lead to the collapse of the structure.[18]

It is not surprising, therefore, that most outfitters dabbled in the fur trade only occasionally. On the average, between 1750 and 1775, the Canadian merchants of Montreal invested in the trade only four times and signed up about eleven *engagés* each time, not quite enough to man two canoes. Few merchants outfitted fur trade ventures with any regularity and only six men hired an average of twelve or more *engagés*, more than twice before 1761 (see Table 1).

TABLE 1   Largest Canadian Fur Trade Outfitters in
Montreal, 1750–1760

Name	Total No. of Years	of hirings	Yearly Average
CHARLY, Louis Saint-Ange	6	85	14.1
GODET, Dominique	5	85	17.0
LECHELLE, Jean	4	130	32.5
LEMOINE MONIERE, Alexis	7	300	42.8
L'HUILLIER CHEVALIER, François	7	90	12.6
TROTIER DESAUNIERS, Thomas-Ignace "Dufy"	5	129	25.8

Source: "Répertoire des engagements pour l'ouest conservés dans les Archives judiciaires de Montréal," *Rapport de l'Archiviste de la province de Québec*, 1930–31, pp. 353–453; 1931–32, pp. 242–365; 1932–33, pp. 245–304.

Three of these were unquestionably wealthy: Louis Saint-Ange Charly, an import merchant who, unlike his colleagues, had a large stake in the fur trade, realized 100,000 *livres* on his landholdings alone when he left the colony for France in 1764; Thomas-Ignace Trotier Desauniers "Dufy," who in a will drawn up in 1760 bequeathed 28,000 *livres* to the Sulpicians; the illiterate Dominique Godet, who in a similar document of 1768, mentioned 5,000 *livres* in cash in hand, land in three parishes in the vicinity of Montreal, *"Batiment & Bateaux qui en dependent,"* around 5,000 *livres* in active debts, and two black slaves.[19] Two other large outfitters left relatively few belongings at the time of their death: Alexis Lemoine Monière left less than 1,000 *livres*, all of it in household goods, and François L'Huillier Chevalier just slightly more.[20] Little is known about the sixth man, Jean Léchelle.

If the fur trade made few wealthy men among those who invested heavily in it, it would be hard to argue that less considerable investors were more successful. It is not unreasonable to conclude that the fur trade was not very profitable for the overwhelming majority of outfitters and that it only sustained a very limited number of them each year. Yet the French had reduced costly competition to a minimum and had few worries about price fluctuations. How would Canadian outfitters fare under a different system?

The Advent of the British Merchants

With the arrival in Montreal of British traders, the workings of the fur trade were disputed. At first, the licensing system was maintained and some areas were left to the exclusive trade of particular traders.[21] But from the very beginning the trade was said to be open to all who wanted to secure a licence, and the result could only be price competition. With individual traders going into the fur trade, the organization of the trade regressed. The previous division of labour between the *Compagnie des Indes*, the import merchants and outfitters, the traders, the *voyageurs*, and the *engagés* was abandoned and during the first years of British rule the individual trader filled all of the functions previously spread among many "specialists."

The story of Alexander Henry, one of the first British merchants to venture into the upper country, illustrates the new pattern of trade. A young man from New Jersey, Alexander Henry came to Canada in 1760 with General Amherst's troops.[22] With the fall of Montreal Henry saw the opening of a "new market" and became acquainted with the prospects of the fur trade. The following year, he set out for Michilimackinac with a Montreal outfitter, Etienne Campion, whom he called his "assistant," and who took charge of the routine aspects of the trip.[23] Henry wintered at Michilimackinac. There he was urged by the local inhabitants to go back to Detroit as soon as possible for they claimed to fear for his safety. Their fears were not without foundation, but Henry stayed on. His partner Campion reassured him: " ... the Canadian inhabitants of the fort were more hostile than the Indians, as being jealous of British traders, who ... were penetrating into the country."[24] At least some of the Canadians resented the British traders from the outset and a few tried to use the Indians to frighten them away.[25]

Henry proceeded to Sault Sainte Marie the following year. In the spring of 1763, he returned to Michilimackinac and witnessed the massacre of the British garrison during Pontiac's revolt.[26] He was eventually captured by the Indians and adopted into an Indian family with whom he lived, in the Indian style, until late June 1764. Undaunted, Henry set out for the fur trade again, exploring the Lake Superior area. He was on the Saskatchewan River in 1776, tapping fur resources which the French had seldom reached.[27] Finally he settled down in Montreal in 1781 and while he did join the North West Company after its formation, he seldom returned to the upper country himself.[28]

Henry was not the first British merchant to reach the upper country. Henry Bostwick had obtained a licence from General Gage before him in 1761,[29] and the traders Goddard and Solomons had followed Henry into Michilimackinac in 1761. By early 1763 there were at least two more British merchants in the area.[30] In Montreal alone there were close to fifty new merchants by 1765. Governor Murray's list of the Protestants in the district of Montreal gives the names, the origins, and the "former callings" of forty-five.[31] Over half of them came from England and Scotland and 20 per cent were from Ireland. Only 13 per cent came from the American colonies and an equal number came from various countries (Switzerland, Germany, France, Guernesey). In the proportion of more than three to one, the newcomers had been merchants in their "former calling." The others had been soldiers and clerks. Many of the newcomers were men of experience and enterprise. Among them were Isaac Todd, Thomas Walker, Lawrence Ermatinger, Richard

Dobie, Edward Chinn, John Porteous, William Grant, Benjamin Frobisher, James Finlay, Alexander Paterson, Forrest Oakes, and the Jewish merchants Ezekiel and Levy Solomons, all of whom became substantial traders.[32]

The arrival of so many merchants could only mean one thing: strenuous competition in the fur trade. Competition ruthlessly drove out those with less secure financial resources or with no taste for sharp practices. Among the British as among the French, few resisted the pressures. The story of the trader Hamback is not untypical. Out on the Miami River in 1766 and 1767, he found that competition left him with few returns to make to his creditor William Edgar of Detroit. "I live the life of a downright exile," he complained, "no company but a Barrel of drunken infamous fugitives, and no other Comfort of Life."[33]

The Canadian merchants of Montreal had competition not only from British merchants in their town, but also from American merchants moving into Detroit and Michilimackinac. William Edgar, a New York merchant, was at Niagara in late 1761.[34] In 1763 he was established at Detroit, where he conducted a brisk trade supplying individual traders at Michilimackinac and in the South-West District.[35] From Schenectady, the partnership of Phyn and Ellice also carried on a profitable supply trade for the fur traders of the interior.[36]

Competition also came from the French on the Mississippi, who were trading in the Illinois country and the Lake Superior region. These French traders could all too easily link up with French-speaking traders from Canada, whose help, it was feared, they could enlist in subverting the Indians against British rule.[37] This always troubled Sir William Johnson, the Superintendent for Indian Affairs, who refused to abandon his suspicions of the French-speaking traders from Canada.

This many-sided competition produced a climate to which the Canadian merchants were not accustomed. The increased number of fur traders led to frictions with the Indians, smaller returns for some of the traders, and unsavory trade practices.[38] Even the retail trade was affected. Merchants from England flooded the market at Quebec "with their manufactures, so much so that they are daily sold here at Vendue Twenty per Cent below prime Cost."[39] In 1760 alone, the first year of British occupation, £60,000 worth of trade goods had been brought into Canada.[40] From 1765 to 1768 the pages of the *Quebec Gazette* were filled with notices of auctions by merchants returning to England and disposing of their wares after unsuccessful attempts to establish themselves in the trade of the colony.[41]

By 1768 some thought the Canadians still had the advantage in the fur trade, even though there was "Competition" and a "strong Jealousy" between Canadian and English. The Canadians' "long Connections with those Indians," wrote General Gage, "and their better Knowledge of their Language and Customs, must naturaly for a long time give the Canadians an Advantage over the English ... "[42] Sir William Johnson had expressed a similar opinion the previous year and had deplored the British merchants' tactics: "The English were compelled to make use of Low, Selfish Agents, French, or English as Factors, who at the Expence of honesty and sound policy, took care of themselves whatever became of their employers."[43]

Another observer, the Hudson's Bay Company trader at Moose Factory, complained of "Interlopers who will be more Destructive to our trade than the French was." The French had conducted a less aggressive trade: they "were in a manner Settled, their Trade fixed, their Standards moderate and Themselves under particular regulations and restrictions, which I doubt is not the Case now."[44] Competition was forcing the British merchants in Montreal into ruthless tactics, a development which upset the Hudson's Bay Company man and which would unsettle the Canadians.

The pattern of British domination of the fur trade began to emerge as early as 1767. Trading ventures out of Michilimackinac into the North-west were conducted by Canadians, but British merchants supplied the financial backing. The North-west expeditions demanded the lengthiest periods of capital outlay, lasting two or three years. British merchants, it seems, had better resources. Of the fifteen outfitters at Michilimackinac who sent canoes to the North-west in 1767, nine were British and six were Canadian; the total value of canoes outfitted by the British came to £10,812.17, while the Canadians' canoes were worth only £3,061.10. The British outfitters—most notably Alexander Henry, Isaac Todd, James McGill, Benjamin Frobisher, Forrest Oakes—invested on the average £1,351.12 and the Canadians only £510.5. The average value of goods invested in each canoe stood at £415.17 for the British and £278.6 for the Canadians.[45] The Canadians' investment per canoe was only two-thirds that of the British and the Canadians were already outnumbered as outfitters in what would become the most important region of the fur trade.[46]

Open competition was not conducive to the expansion of the fur trade and an oligopolistic structure reminiscent of the French system soon reappeared as the only solution.[47] This led to the formation of the North West Company in the 1780s but already in 1775, those Montreal merchants who had extended their operations as far as the Saskatchewan felt the need for collaboration rather than competition. Again developments in the more remote frontiers of the fur trade foretold of events to occur later in the whole of the trade: the traders on the Saskatchewan were almost all of British origin.[48] The fur trade was returning to the structures developed by the French, but during the period of competition which followed the Conquest the Canadians were gradually crowded out. There was some irony in that. Why had the Canadians fared so badly?

The Attitude of Government Officials

Much has been made of the natural sympathies of Murray and Carleton towards the Canadians and their antipathies towards the traders of their own nation. Yet for all their ideological inclinations there is no evidence that the governors turned their sentiments into policies of benevolence for Canadians in trade matters. Rather, it is easier to discover, among the lesser officials and some of the more important ones as well, an understandable patronizing of British rather than Canadian merchants. Colonial administrators may not have set a deliberate pattern of preference in favour of British merchants. But the Canadian merchants of Montreal, who put great store by official patronage, cared not whether the policy was deliberate or accidental; the result was the same.

Official preferences played against the Canadian traders in many ways. First, the lucrative trade of supplying the military posts was given to British and American merchants as a matter of course, and this occasion for profit was lost to the Canadians. Under the French regime some of the Montreal merchants, notably the Monières and the Gamelins, had profited from that trade.[49] Now it fell out of Canadian hands. This advantage did not shift to the sole favour of the British merchants of Quebec. New York and Pennsylvania traders were also awarded their share of the trade. The firms of Phyn, Ellice of Schenectady and Baynton, Wharton, and Morgan of Philadelphia received the lion's share of that business while the upper country was under the jurisdiction of Sir William Johnson.[50] But this was of little comfort to the Canadians.

Less tangible by-products of the British occupation of the former fur trading areas of New France are more difficult to assess than the loss of the supply trade; they were, however, quite real. One was the British military's attitude towards Canadians. The military were wary of French-speaking traders in Illinois and on the Mississippi. Although the French from Canada had been vanquished, French traders in the interior could still deal with France through New Orleans. No regulations, no boundaries could restrain French traders operating out of Louisiana from dealing with the Indians, and the Canadians who were confined to the posts protested against the advantage held by the French traders.[51] But who were these French traders? Did they not include Canadian *coureurs de bois* and wintering merchants? How could one really tell a French-speaking trader from Canada from a French-speaking trader out of New Orleans? Were not all of them suspect of exciting the Indians against the British, promising and perhaps hoping for France's return to America?[52] As late as 1768, when Indian discontent in the West threatened another uprising, General Gage failed to see any difference between French-speaking Canadians and the French from New Orleans.

> There is the greatest reason to suspect that the French are Endeavouring to engross the Trade, and that the Indians have acted thro' their Instigation, in the Murders they have committed, and the Resolutions we are told they have taken, to suffer no Englishman to trade with them. And in this they have rather been Assisted by the English Traders, who having no Consideration but that of a present gain, have thro' fear of exposing their own Persons, or hopes of obtaining greater influence with the Indians, continualy employed French Commissarys or Agents, whom they have trusted with Goods for them to Sell at an Advanced price in the Indian Villages.[53]

Gage's suspicions of the French traders were nurtured by Sir William Johnson, who had to keep the Indians on peaceful terms with one another and with the British. It was part of Johnson's function, of course, to worry about possible uprisings and about subversive individuals. His job would be made easier if he could confine all traders to military posts where they could be kept under surveillance. But the traders had little concern for Sir William's preoccupations. If British traders were irresponsible in their desires of "present gain," the Canadian traders' vices were compounded by the uncertainty of their allegiance to the British Crown:

> Since the Reduction of that Country [Canada], we have seen so many Instances of their [the Canadian traders'] Perfidy false Stories & Cª. Interested Views in Trade that prudence forbids us to suffer them or any others to range at Will without being under the Inspection of the proper Officers agreeable to His Majesty's Appointment ...[54]

Johnson's attitude spread to the officers under him, even though Carleton had found nothing reprehensible in the Canadians' behaviour.[55] Johnson's deputy, George Croghan, believed there was collusion between the French from Canada and the French from Louisiana.[56] In 1763 the commandant at Michilimackinac, Major Etherington, had displayed a similar mistrust of the Canadians.[57] Major Robert Rogers, a later commandant at Michilimackinac, checked the Canadians by trading on his own account.[58]

The British military's mistrust of the French traders from Canada was understandable. Before 1760, one of the major reasons for the American colonials' antagonism towards New France had been the French ability to press the Indians into their service to terrorize the western fringes of American settlement. Thus there was an historical as well as a tactical basis for the military's attitude towards the Canadians. But British officers failed to recognize that not all Canadian traders were potential troublemakers and that there was indeed very little tangible evidence, as Carleton had reminded Johnson, of any mischief on their part. The military's attitude was directed as much by ethnic prejudice as by military necessity.

The Canadian traders could not fail to perceive this prejudice, and it dampened their spirits. Perhaps the military's attitude, as much as competition, forced the Canadians into partnerships with British merchants. (The express purpose of the bonds required for the fur trade was to ensure loyal conduct; what better token of loyalty could there be for a Canadian trader than a bond taken out in his name by a British partner?) The military's mistrust of the Canadian traders did not lessen with time. The advantage which this prejudice gave British traders would continue for some twenty years after the Conquest, as the American Revolution rekindled the military's fears of treasonable conduct by the Canadians.

Other patronage relationships between British military officials and British traders also deprived the Canadians of an equal chance in the competition for furs. It is hard to evaluate precisely the effect of such patronage; only glimpses of it may be caught. Later in 1763 a Philadelphia merchant who had lost heavily because of Pontiac's uprising wrote to William Edgar in Detroit that Croghan was in England where he was to "represent the Case of the Traders to his Majesty" and that General Amherst had "given us his faithful promise that he will do everything in his power in our behalf."[59] In 1765 Alexander Henry was granted the exclusive trade of Lake Superior by Major Howard, the military commandant at Michilimackinac. Nine years later Henry received the support of such patrons as the Duke of Gloucester, the consul of the Empress of Russia in England, and of Sir William Johnson in an ill-fated attempt to mine the iron ore of the Lake Superior area.[60]

These were obvious examples of patronage; other forms of cooperation were less visible. Another correspondent of William Edgar, Thomas Shipboy, asked Edgar to represent him in settling the affairs of a correspondent at Detroit and at Michilimackinac where, he added, "if you find any Difficulty in procuring his effects I dare say the Commanding officer will be of Service to you if you inform him in whose [sic] behalf you are acting ... "[61] Benjamin Frobisher also asked Edgar to "use your Interest with Capt. Robinson" to put a shipment of corn aboard the government vessel which sailed from Detroit to Michilimackinac.[62] Such shipping space was scarce and was only available through the courtesy of military officers or the ships' captains. Here again British traders put their social connections to good use. A last resort was sheer military force. Out on the Miami River, the trader Hamback saw "little hope of getting any thing from [Fort] St. Joseph at all, if I don't get protected, by the Commanding Officer, who might easily get those [Canadian] rascals fetch'd down to Detroit if He would ... "[63]

None of this patronage appears to have been available to Canadians. It is impossible to ascertain the degree to which military suspicions and patronage lessened the Canadians' chances in the fur trade. But more important, perhaps, than the actual loss of opportunities was the psychological handicap imposed upon the Canadians. What heart could they put in the game when the dice were so obviously loaded?

The Merchants' Political Activities

The enmity between British merchants and the military, the merchants' growing agitation in favour of "British liberties" and their sentiments of political self-importance have been ably told by others and need not be retold here.[64] What needs to be underlined is that political agitation was unfamiliar to the Canadians. They had had no experience in these matters under French rule. Only on rare occasions during the pre-Conquest years had the Canadian merchants engaged in collective political representations; such representations were elicited by the Governor or the Intendant to obtain the merchants' advice on specific issues.[65] As French subjects, the Canadian merchants of Montreal had lacked the power to foster their economic interests through collective political action.

After 1760, the Canadian merchants would gradually lose their political innocence under the influence of the British merchants. During the thirty years which followed the Conquest they would make *"l'apprentissage des libertés anglaises"* and in 1792 they would take their place in the newly-created legislative assembly more cognizant of the workings of the British constitution than the British had expected.[66] But that is beyond the concern here. In the years preceding the American Revolution the Montreal merchants were still looking for bearings. They showed their growing political awareness by following in the *Quebec Gazette* the political and constitutional debates which were rocking the British Empire. The merchants also began to voice their concerns in petitions and memorials to the authorities in the colony and in London.

The *Quebec Gazette* was the province's official gazette and its only newspaper before 1778. The paper published public notices for the Montreal district and occasional advertisements sent in by Montrealers as well as matters of concern to Quebec residents. It also made an effort to publish Canadian news of a general character. It closely followed the debates raging across the Atlantic over the Stamp Act and the general issues of colonial taxation. It reported on changes in the Imperial government and on contemporary political issues in England, notably the Wilkes affair.[67]

The pages of the *Gazette* also served on occasion as a forum for political discussion. In September 1765 a "Civis Canadiensis" declared his puzzlement at all the talk of "British liberties" and asked for enlightenment. The following year, a Quebec resident wrote a series of letters arguing that the colony should not be taxed.[68] In 1767, a debate arose on the British laws relating to bankruptcy and their applicability in Quebec.[69] Because of the pressures of Governor Carleton the *Gazette* stifled its reporting of controversial issues after 1770 and thereafter had little to print about American affairs.[70] In 1775 the *Gazette*'s political outpourings were directed against the American rebels and towards securing the loyalty of those Canadians who might be seduced by revolutionary propaganda.[71] The paper had become more conservative in its selection of the news but those Canadians who read the *Gazette* had been made familiar with the concepts of personal liberty, of "no taxation without representation," of the limited powers of the sovereign, and of the rights of the people. The *Gazette*'s readers most probably included the leading merchants of Montreal.

The *Gazette* was not the only instrument for the learning of British liberties. Anxious to give the appearance of a unanimous disposition among all merchants in Montreal, the British merchants often called on their Canadian *confreres* to add their names to various memorials and petitions dealing with the political and the economic state of the colony. The Canadian merchants who signed these petitions and memorials represented the top layer of the Canadian mercantile group in Montreal. Those who signed most often were the import merchants and the busy outfitters.

These Canadian merchants followed the political leadership of the British merchants. From 1763 to 1772 their petitions were either literal translations or paraphrased equivalents of petitions drafted by British merchants. It was only in December 1773 that they asserted views different from those of their British counterparts.[72] They petitioned the king that their "ancient laws, privileges, and customs" be restored, that the province be extended to its "former boundaries," that some Canadians be taken into the king's service, and that "the rights and privileges of citizens of England" be granted to all.[73]

The Canadians were becoming aware of their own position and were seeking to consolidate it against the attacks of the British element. The demand for the maintenance of the "ancient laws" was designed to counter British demands for British laws and representative institutions. The Canadians opposed the latter since, in their view, the colony was "not as yet in a condition to defray the expences of its own civil government, and consequently not in a condition to admit of a general assembly."[74] The demand for "a share of the civil and military employments under his majesty's government" came naturally to those who had lived under the French system of patronage. The Canadians had been accustomed to seek official patronage as the main avenue of upward mobility. The prospect of being denied such patronage was "frightful" to them, since they had little familiarity with alternate patterns of social promotion.[75]

In style as well as in content the Canadian merchants' petitions and memorials revealed differences in attitudes between Canadians and British. British memorials and petitions were rarely prefaced by more than the customary "Humbly showeth" and went directly to the point. In their own memorials and petitions, the Canadians first took "the liberty to prostrate themselves at the foot" of the royal throne and surrendered themselves to the "paternal care" of their sovereign. They often appealed to the wisdom, justice, and magnanimity of the king.[76] Their formal posture of meekness contrasted sharply with the self-assertion of the British. The Canadians' "Habits of Respect and Submission," as one British official put it,[77] may well have endeared them to Murray and Carleton, but those habits constituted a psychological obstacle against their making full use of their new-found "British liberties" to foster their own economic interest.

Conclusion

With the fall of Montreal to British arms in September 1760 something was irrevocably lost to the Canadian merchants of that city. More than the evil effects of the war, the tribulations over the fate of the Canada paper, or the post-war commercial readjustments, the most unsettling consequence of the Conquest was the disappearance of a familiar business climate. As New France passed into the British Empire, the Montreal outfitters were thrown into a new system of business competition, brought about by the very numbers of newly-arrived merchants, unloading goods in the conquered French colony and going after its enticing fur trade. In opening up the trade of the colony to competition, the British presence transformed Canadian commercial practices. The change negated the Canadian merchants' initial advantage of experience in the fur trade and created a novel business climate around them.

Competition in trade, the new political regime, the Canadian merchants' inability to obtain the favours of the military, all these created a mood of uncertainty and pessimism among the Montreal merchants. The merchants could only conclude from what was happening around them that the new business climate of the post-Conquest period favoured British traders at their expense. They can be understood if they were not eager to adapt their ways to the new situation.

It may be argued, of course, that the changes which produced the new situation are subsumed under the notion of "Conquest" and that the previous pages only make more explicit the "decapitation" interpretation advanced by the historians of the "Montreal school."[78] It is true enough that the new business climate described here may not have been created after the Seven Years' War had Canada remained a French possession. But there is no guarantee that other changes would not have affected the Montreal merchants. During the last years of the French regime they had reaped few profits from the fur trade. After the Conquest they continued in the fur trade much on the same scale as before. The Montreal merchants were not "decapitated" by the Conquest; rather, they were faced in very short succession with a series of transformations in the socio-economic structure of the colony to which they might have been able to adapt had these transformations been spread over a longer period of time.

This paper has attempted to show that the fate of the Canadian merchants of Montreal after the Conquest followed from the nature of trade before the Conquest and from the rate at which new circumstances required the merchants to alter their business behaviour. But it should be remembered that the decapitation hypothesis still remains to be tested in the area of the colony's economy which was most heavily dependent upon the control of the metropolis, the import-export trade of the Quebec merchants. Only a detailed examination of the role and the activities of the Quebec merchants, both before and after the Conquest, will fully put the decapitation hypothesis to the test.

Notes

1. Public Archives of Canada [hereafter PAC], C.O. 42, vol. 27, f. 66, Carleton to Shelburne, Quebec, 25 November 1767; quoted in A.L. Burt, *The Old Province of Quebec* (2 vols. Toronto, 1968), 1, p. 142.

2. See Burt, *Old Province*, I, Chapter VI; Dale B. Miquelon, "The Baby Family in the Trade of Canada, 1750–1820" (Unpublished Master's thesis, Carleton University, 1966), pp. 145–46.

3. Francis Parkman, *The Old Regime in Canada* (27th ed. Boston, 1892), Chapter XXI, especially pp. 397–98.

4. W. Stewart Wallace, ed., *Documents Relating to the North West Company* (Toronto, 1934); Wallace, *The Pedlars From Quebec and Other Papers on the Nor'Westers* (Toronto, 1954); E.E. Rich, *The Fur Trade and the Northwest to 1857* (Toronto, 1967); Rich, *The History of the Hudson's Bay Company*, II (London, 1959); D.G. Creighton, *The Empire of the St. Lawrence* (Toronto, 1956).

5. Wayne F. Stevens, *The Northwest Fur Trade 1763–1800* (Urbana, Ill., 1928), p. 25.

6. Fernand Ouellet, *Histoire économique et sociale du Québec 1760–1850* (Montreal, 1966), p. 77.

7. *Ibid.*, pp. 104–6.

8. Michel Brunet, *Les Canadiens après la Conquête, 1759–1775* (Montreal, 1969), pp. 173–74, pp. 177–80.

9. Miquelon, "The Baby Family," p. 158.

10. *Ibid.*, p. 142.

11. The implication is unwarranted. A given economic sector can be dynamic and even produce the largest share of marketable commodities and still provide individual entrepreneurs with meager profits. The macro-economic level of analysis should not be confused with the micro-economic level. Jean Hamelin showed that only around 28 per cent of the profits from the beaver trade remained in Canada. Since the Canadians had an assured market for beaver, one can wonder how much more profitable it was for them to deal in other peltries. See Hamelin, *Economie et Société en Nouvelle-France* (Quebec, 1960), pp. 54–56.

12. The obvious economic explanation for the downfall of the Canadian merchants after the Conquest has to be dismissed. The liquidation of Canadian paper money by France hurt most of all those British merchants who bought it from Canadians for speculation. Canadian merchants had already compensated in part for the anticipated liquidation by raising prices during the last years of the Seven Years' War. Those Montreal merchants who had the greatest quantity of French paper were not driven out of business; on the contrary the most prominent merchants were able to open accounts with British suppliers soon after the Conquest without too much difficulty. See José E. Igartua, "The Merchants and *Négociants* of Montreal, 1750–1775: A Study in Socio-Economic History" (Unpublished Ph.D. thesis, Michigan State University, 1974), Chapter VI.

13. Franquet, *Voyages et mémoires sur le Canada en 1752–1753* (Toronto, 1968), p. 56.

14. For a more elaborate description of the size and the socio-economic characteristics of the Montreal merchant community at this time, see Igartua, "The Merchants and *Négociants* of Montreal," Chapter II.

15. See H.A. Innis, *The Fur Trade in Canada* (Rev. ed. Toronto, 1956), pp. 107–13.

16. See Abraham Rotstein, "Fur Trade and Empire: An Institutional Analysis" (Unpublished Ph.D. thesis, University of Toronto, 1967), p. 72.

17. Innis, *Fur Trade*, p. 117. For his discussion of the impact of war on the fur trade and on New France, see pp. 114–18.

18. In theory, the French licensing system set up to restrict the trade remained in operation from its re-establishment in 1728 to the end of the French regime; only twenty-five *congés* were to be sold each year. In practice, military officers in the upper country could also acquire for a modest fee exclusive trade privileges for their

particular area. With some care, concluded one author, they could make an easy fortune. See Emile Salone, *La Colonisation de la Nouvelle-France* (Trois-Rivières, 1970), p. 390, pp. 392–93. No clear official description of the licensing system was found for the period from 1750 to 1760, but the precise way in which the fur trade was restricted matters less than the fact of restriction.

19. On Charly see PAC, RG 4 B58, vol. 15, 19 September 1764, pass by Governor Murray to "Monsr. Louis Saint-Ange Charly [and his family] to London, in their way to France agreeable to the Treaty of Peace ... "; Archives Nationales du Québec à Montréal [formerly Archives judiciaires de Montréal; hereafter ANQ-M], Greffe de Pierre Panet, 16 août 1764, no. 2190. Trotier Desauniers "Dufy's" will is in *ibid.*, 29 juillet 1760, no. 1168, and Godet's will is in *ibid.*, 28 décembre 1768, no. 3140.

20. The inventory of Monière's estate is in *ibid.*, 28 décembre 1768, no. 3141; that of L'Huillier Chevalier's in *ibid.*, 15 [?] juin 1772, no. 3867.

21. See Alexander Henry, *Travels and Adventures in Canada* (Ann Arbor University Microfilms, 1966), pp. 191–92.

22. W.S. Wallace, *Documents Relating to the North West Company*, Appendix A ("A Biographical Dictionary of the Nor'Westers"), p. 456.

23. See Henry, *Travels*, pp. 1–11, p. 34.

24. *Ibid.*, p. 39.

25. *Ibid.*, p. 50. Cf. the rosier picture painted by Creighton, *The Empire of the St. Lawrence*, p. 33.

26. Henry, *Travels*, pp. 77–84. The Indians killed the British soldiers but ransomed the British traders, giving to each according to his profession.

27. Henry, *Travels*, pp. 264–92.

28. See Wallace, *Documents*, p. 456; Milo M. Quaife, ed., *Alexander Henry's Travels and Adventures in the Years 1760–1776* (Chicago, 1921), pp. xvi–xvii.

29. Henry, *Travels*, p. 11; *Henry's Travels*, p. 12 n. 6.

30. Rich, *History of the Hudson's Bay Company*, II, p. 9.

31. See PAC, C.O. 42, vol. 5, ff. 30–31, Murray's "List of Protestants in the District of Montreal," dated Quebec, 7 November 1765.

32. See Miquelon, "The Baby Family," pp. 181–87.

33. PAC, MG 19 A1, 1, William Edgar Papers, vol. 1, p. 97, F. Hamback to W. Edgar, 2 November 1766. See also *ibid.*, p. 95, Hamback to D. Edgar, 29 October 1766, and pp. 104–6, same to Edgar, 23 March 1767.

34. *Ibid.*, vol. 1, p. 12.

35. See *Ibid.*, vols. 1 and 2.

36. R.H. Fleming, "Phyn, Ellice and Company of Schenectady," *Contributions to Canadian Economics*, IV (1932), pp. 7–41.

37. See Marjorie G. Jackson, "The Beginnings of British Trade at Michilimackinac," *Minnesota History*, XI (September, 1930), 252; C.W. Alvord and C.E. Carter, eds., *The New Regime 1765–1767* (Collections of the Illinois State Historical Library, XI), pp. 300–1; Alvord and Carter, eds., *Trade and Politics 1767–1769* (Collections of the Illinois State Historical Library, XVI), pp. 382–453.

38. See "Extract of a Letter from Michilimackinac, to a Gentleman in this City, dated 30th June," in *Quebec Gazette*, 18 August 1768; see also Rich, *History of the Hudson's Bay Company*, II, p. 26: "The suspicions between the Pedlars [from Quebec], and their encouragements of the Indians to trick and defraud their trade rivals, especially by defaulting on payments of debt, were widespread and continuous."

39. *Quebec Gazette*, 7 January 1768.

40. Burt, *Old Province*, I, p. 92.

41. The flooding of the Quebec market by British merchants was part of a larger invasion of the colonial trade in North America. See Marc Egnal and Joseph A. Ernst, "An Economic Interpretation of the American Revolution," *William and Mary Quarterly*, Third Series, XXIX (1972), pp. 3–32.

42. Quoted in Alvord and Carter, eds., *Trade and Politics*, p. 288.

43. *Ibid.*, p. 38.

44. Quoted in E.E. Rich, *Montreal and the Fur Trade* (Montreal, 1966), p. 44.

45. These figures are somewhat distorted by the inclusion of a single large British investor, Alexander Henry, who outfitted seven canoes worth £3,400 in all. See Charles E. Lart, ed., "Fur Trade Returns, 1767," *Canadian Historical Review*, III (December, 1922), pp. 351–358. The definition of the North West as including Lake Huron, Lake Superior, and "the northwest by way of Lake Superior" given in Rich, *Montreal and the Fur Trade*, pp. 36–37, was used in making these compilations. The French traders were "Deriviere," "Chenville," St. Clair, Laselle, "Guillaid [Guillet]," and "Outlass [Houtelas]."

46. See Rich, *Montreal and the Fur Trade*, pp. 36–37.

47. Jackson, *Minnesota History*, XI, pp. 268–69.

48. Rich, *History of the Hudson's Bay Company*, II, p. 68.

49. On the Monières, see Igartua, "The Merchants and *Négociants* of Montreal," Chapter II. On the Gamelins, see Antoine Champagne, *Les La Vérendrye et les postes du l'ouest (Quebec, 1968), passim*.

50. See R.H. Fleming, *Contributions to Canadian Economics*, IV, 13; on Baynton, Wharton and Morgan, see *The Papers of Sir William Johnson* [hereafter *Johnson Papers*], 14 vols. (Albany, 1921–1965), V, VI, XII, *passim*.

51. PAC, C.O. 42, vol. 2, ff. 277–80, petition of the "Merchants and Traders of Montreal" to Murray and the Council, Montreal, 20 February 1765; *Johnson Papers*, V, pp. 807–15, memorial and petition of Detroit traders to Johnson, 22 November 1767; XII, pp. 409–14, 1768 trade regulations with the merchants' objections.

52. See Alvord and Carter, eds., *The New Regime*, pp. 118–19, and *Trade and Politics*, p. 39, p. 287; see also Stevens, *The Northwest Fur Trade*, p. 44.

53. *Johnson Papers*, XII, p. 517, Thomas Gage to Guy Johnson, New York, 29 May 1768.

54. *Ibid.*, V, p. 481. See also Alvord and Carter, eds., *The New Regime*, pp. 118–19; *Johnson Papers*, V, p. 362; Alvord and Carter, eds., *Trade and Politics*, p. 39; *Johnson Papers*, V, pp. 762–64; XII, pp. 486–87; Stevens, *The Northwest Fur Trade*, p. 28.

55. PAC, C.O. 42, vol. 27, ff. 81–85, Carleton to Johnson, Quebec, 27 March 1767.

56. *Johnson Papers*, XII, pp. 372–75, Croghan to Johnson, 18 October 1767.

57. Henry, *Travels*, pp. 71–72.

58. See PAC, C.O. 42, vol. 26, f. 13, Court of St. James, Conway [Secretary of State] to the Commandants of Detroit and Michilimackinac, 27 March 1766. See also Alvord and Carter, eds., *Trade and Politics*, pp. 207–8, Gage to Shelburne, 12 March 1768; p. 239, Johnson to Gage, 8 April 1768; p. 375, Gage to Johnson, 14 August 1768; p. 378, Gage to Hillsborough, 17 August 1768; p. 384, Johnson to Gage, 24 August 1768; p. 599, Gage to Hillsborough, 9 September 1769. More than trading on his own account, Rogers was suspected of setting up an independent Illinois territory. He was eventually cleared. See "Robert Rogers," *Dictionary of American Biography*, XVI (New York, 1935), pp. 108–9, and *Johnson Papers*, V, VI, XII, XIII, *passim*.

59. PAC, William Edgar Papers, vol. 1, pp. 43–44, Callender to Edgar, n.p., 31 December 1763.

60. Henry, *Travels*, pp. 191–92, p. 235.

61. PAC, William Edgar Papers, vol. 1, p. 90, Thos. Shipboy to Rankin and Edgar, Albany, 21 August 1766.

62. *Ibid.*, p. 201, Benjamin Frobisher to Rankin and Edgar, Michilimackinac, 23 June 1769.

63. *Ibid.*, pp. 104–6, F. Hamback to Edgar, 23 March 1767.

64. The most detailed account is given in Burt, *Old Province*, I, Chapters VI and VII. See also Creighton, *Empire of the St. Lawrence*, pp. 40–48.

65. See for instance E.Z. Massicotte, "La Bourse de Montréal sous le régime français," *The Canadian Antiquarian and Numismatic Journal*, Third Series, XII (1915), pp. 26–32.

66. See Pierre Tousignant, "La Genèse et l'avènement de la Constitution de 1791" (Unpublished Ph.D. thesis, Université de Montréal, 1971).

67. See the *Quebec Gazette* of 15 September 1766 and the issues from June to September 1768.

68. See *Quebec Gazette*, 26 September 1765. Tousignant, "La Genèse," pp. 21–39, points out the political significance of this letter.

69. See texts by "A MERCHANT" in the 10 and 17 December 1767 issues, and rebuttals in the 24 and 31 December 1767 and 7 and 21 January 1768 issues.

70. Tousignant, "La Genèse," p. 39.

71. See issues of 13 and 27 July, and 5 October 1775.

72. Canadian notables of Quebec broke with the "Old Subjects" earlier: a petition, thought to date from 1770 and signed by leading Canadians of that city, asked for the restoration of Canadian institutions. See Adam Shortt and Arthur G. Doughty, *Documents Relating to the Constitutional History of Canada* (2nd ed. Ottawa, 1918) [hereafter *Docs. Const. Hist. Can.*], I, pp. 419–21.

73. The petition and the memorial are reproduced in *Docs. Const. Hist. Can.*, I, pp. 504–6, pp. 508–10.

74. *Ibid.*, I, p. 511. The British merchants of Montreal signed a counter-petition in January 1774, requesting the introduction of an assembly and of the laws of England. See *ibid.*, I, pp. 501–2.

75. Recent historians have highlighted the influence of the military and civil administrations as sources of economic and social betterment in New France. See Guy Frégault, *Le XVIIIe siècle canadien* (Montreal, 1968), pp. 382–84; W.J. Eccles, "The Social, Economic, and Political Significance of the military Establishment in New France," *Canadian Historical Review*, LII (March, 1971), pp. 17–19; and Cameron Nish, *Les Bourgeois-Gentilhommes de la Nouvelle-France* (Montreal 1968), *passim*.

76. See PAC, C.O. 42, vol. 24, ff. 72–73v.; *ibid.*, ff. 95–95v; *ibid.*, vol. 3, f. 262; *Docs. Const. Hist. Can.*, I, pp. 504–8.

77. See *Docs. Const. Hist. Can.*, I, p. 504.

78. Maurice Séguin, of the History Department of the Université de Montréal, was the first to present a systematic interpretation of the Conquest as societal decapitation. His book, *L'Idée d'indépendance au Québec: genèse et historique* (Trois-Rivières, 1968), which contains a summary of his thought, was published twenty years after its author first sketched out his thesis. Guy Frégault's *Histoire de la Nouvelle-France, IX. La guerre de la Conquête, 1754–1760* (Montreal, 1955) is a masterful rendition of that conflict, cast as the *affrontement* of two civilizations. Michel Brunet, the most voluble of the "Montreal school" historians, has assumed the task of popularizing Séguin's thought. See Brunet, "La Conquête anglaise et la déchéance de la bourgeoisie canadienne (1760–1793)," in his *La Présence anglaise et les Canadiens* (Montreal, 1964), pp. 48–112. Brunet developed the point further in *Les Canadiens après la Conquête, I: 1759–1775* (Montreal, 1969). An abridged version of Brunet's position is provided in his *French Canada and the Early Decades of British Rule, 1760–1791* (Ottawa, 1963). For a review of French-Canadian historiography on the Conquest up to 1966, see Ramsay Cook, "Some French-Canadian Interpretations of the British Conquest: Une quatrième dominante de la pensée canadienne-française," *Canadian Historical Association* *Historical Papers*, 1966, pp. 70–83.

MERCHANTS AT THE CONQUEST

John F. Bosher

For most merchants in the Canada trade, the conquest of Canada by Great Britain in 1759–60 was a catastrophe. But this platitude does not do justice to the complexity of the crisis brought on by the War of the Austrian Succession (1743–48) and the Seven Years' War (1756–63). The naval and military defeats were partly the result of weaknesses in a financial system dependent on the credit of government financiers. Unable to pay its debts and defeated in battle, the government suspended the Canada bills on 15 October 1759 and soon went bankrupt altogether.

These catastrophic events led to three more crises. First, the Crown blamed the events in Canada, financial and military, on its own officials, and put about fifty of them on trial in the noisy *affaire du Canada*, which gave the Crown an excuse to reduce its Canadian debts, but publicized the essential corruption of

From *The Canada Merchants, 1713–1763* (Oxford: Clarendon Press, 1987), ch. 10, 191–216.

Bourbon official society. Secondly, most Canada merchants who had not gone bankrupt earlier, notably the big Huguenot merchants, now collapsed one after the other. Thirdly, the Society of Jesus, one of the pillars of the Counter-Reformation, was dragged into the bankruptcy of its Martinique trading firm and assaulted by the Jansenist Parlements. Having abandoned the cause of the Counter-Reformation in the 1750s, the Crown was persuaded to outlaw the Society in 1762–64 at the same time that it was turning its back on that other pillar of the Counter-Reformation, the colony of New France. These events marked a profound change in religious policy that matched the changes wrought by the British government in New France. The Crown began to set itself against the persecution of Huguenots, and to give way to the Atlantic trading society that had grown so powerful in the eighty-five years since the revocation of the Edict of Nantes. Bourbon official society was doomed in old France as well as in New France. So brief a summary of such startling events leaves much to be explained.

Louis XV's government, dogged throughout the mid-century wars by a shortage of funds, was soon unable to pay sailors and their families, or merchants for goods and services, and went bankrupt in October and November 1759.[1] This bankruptcy was not merely a result of momentary weakness owing to unfortunate circumstances or to mistakes in judgement. Nor was it a result, as so many historians have thought, of fighting on too many fronts at once. The French financial system was fundamentally and inherently weaker than those of Great Britain, the Dutch Republic, and even perhaps of Brandenburg-Prussia. Its weaknesses, as I have explained elsewhere, were to bring it before long to the brink of the French Revolution.[2] Already in the 1750s and 1760s the Crown was hampered in its war effort and discredited among its own people, especially its merchants, because it could not pay its way as well as its British, Dutch, and Prussian enemies could.

Merchants in the Canada trade suffered directly from their government's inability to pay. As early as March 1748, a partner in Dugard's *Société du Canada* reported from Paris that Maurepas, the Secretary of State, and Mouffle de Géorville, the naval Treasurer General, kept putting him off with promises. "It seems that we have to have ourselves listed on the *État de distribution*" he wrote. "Furthermore, *chez* Monsieur de Maurepas I saw a list of more than twenty merchants in the same case as we are in ... *C'est le diable pour tirer de l'argent du Roy.*"[3] Ten years later, on 18 October 1758, the Crown appointed five magistrates, the famous "Fontanieu Commission," to examine and settle the debts of the Ministry of Marine and Colonies totalling some 42 million *livres* of which 12 million were for the War of the Austrian Succession (1743–48), 3 million for the inter-war years (1748–55), and 27 million for the years 1755 to 1758. Some officials put the debt much higher than that.[4]

Among the ministry's creditors were most of the shipping merchants in the Canada and Louisbourg trades. These had engaged their ships at one time or another to transport soldiers, munitions, supplies, or food to Canada. When the Crown had engaged certain vessels, such as *La Complaisante, Le Pacquet de*

Londres, Le Cytoen, La Maréchale de Broglie, and *La Badine*, for transport to Canada in 1758, and then delayed and sent the ships to the West Indies, the merchant owners naturally claimed compensation. Not only had the Crown deferred its debt to them, but the Commission set up to deal with these debts now proceeded to reduce many of them on the grounds that the Crown had been a victim of wartime profiteering when it had signed the original contracts. By the end of 1759, the Commission had received creditors' claims to a total of 4,338,734 *livres*, and had cut them down to 3,368,137 *livres*.[5]

This was excessively arbitrary considering that there were two sides to the question of wartime contracts. We know from much scattered evidence that wartime freight rates to Quebec and other transatlantic destinations rose steeply as a result of British naval supremacy. *Paillet et Meynardie* wrote to François Chevalier of Montreal on 26 April 1758, "our enemies are ready to come out with immense forces, with which they threaten to blockade our ports of France, which is very easy for them ... our warships think only of saving themselves ...," etc.[6] Marine insurance premiums rose from about 5 per cent in peacetime to 40 per cent in the early years of both mid-century wars, and by the later years insurance was practically unobtainable in France. "Insurance is eating up profits," Pierre Guy wrote from Montreal as early as 1747.[7] French losses in shipping were extremely heavy, especially in the Seven Years' War. Crews and ships became scarce. Return cargoes could seldom be found, as merchants often complained. As any merchant could see, the wartime shipping market had naturally imposed high freight rates: 240 *livres* and then 400 *livres* per ton soon became normal for Canadian cargoes, this without any profiteering. "Freight rates at Bordeaux amount to 400 *livres* a ton, and it is impossible to buy insurance," Meynardie *jeune* wrote on 19 May 1758.[8] Early the next year, *Paillet et Meynardie* reported from La Rochelle, "We wanted to freight an entire ship for 550 *livres* a ton, but we were refused."[9] Even while the Fontanieu Commission was at work in spring 1760, the Minister approved freight rates to Canada of 400 *livres* per ton.[10]

On receiving objections, argued along these lines, to the Crown's refusal to honour its contracts, the Commission showed a typical eighteenth-century misunderstanding of the inflationary process. Fontanieu himself remarked that merchants who complained were merely piqued at losing their ill-gotten profits. "It seems that the avarice of a considerable number of the merchants at our ports led them to form a sort of conspiracy among themselves to profit from the urgent needs of the Kingdom, and to make immense gains by extorting exorbitant prices for ships which the *ordonnateur* and the Ministers of Marine had to hire (*affréter*) to take defenders and munitions of all kinds to the colonies, and goods which these same merchants supplied for prices just as exorbitant."[11] In this belief the Fontanieu Commission cut down many of the Crown's debts.

Among the debts to merchants were wartime loans to the naval establishments at certain ports. For instance, in 1757 four merchants of Le Havre had lent 124,000 *livres* to the Marine Intendant, Ranché, at 6 per cent annual interest. Two years later, the Fontanieu Commission was examining the five credit notes with suspicion, inquiring whether the loans had been authorized by the minister, and so on. When they decided that 6 per cent interest was "against the general laws of the State," and that Ranché had no business borrowing on his own personal signature but should have arranged for the naval treasurer's agent to borrow, they were putting the merchant lenders in an awkward position.[12] Furthermore, they were ignoring the desperate circumstances that must have driven Ranché, even in 1757, to borrow as he did. We have no records concerning the treasurer's agent at Le Havre, but the agents at Lorient and Rochefort were already in difficulties.[13] At the end of the previous war, to take another example, the Intendant at Rochefort had borrowed 126,000 *livres* from various merchants of La Rochelle, the Treasurer General being some 176,000 *livres* behind in the payments authorized for that port, and had been begging for permission to borrow a great deal more.[14]

More damaging for the Canada merchants was the government's suspension and reduction of the Canadian bills; that is, the bills of exchange and promissory notes that had been common currency in Canada. These had long been issued in all French colonies by the governing authorities in payment for goods and services. According to the Bourbon financial system, an Intendant or other responsible official authorized payments in the form of signed *ordonnances* but did not make payments. To be cashed, an *ordonnance* had to be taken to the agent of a Treasurer General for Marine and Colonies who was one of those venal financiers or *comptables* entrusted with the management of all government funds from the collection of taxes to the payment for goods and services. The Treasurer General's agent at Quebec might cash *ordonnances* with silver coin if he had it, as in 1755 and 1756 when coin had been shipped out from France, but he usually issued his own promissory notes (*billets de caisse*) or the famous playing-card money which he later took back in exchange for the bills of exchange he would draw once a year on his employer in Paris, the Treasurer General. These payments in paper need careful study because much nonsense has been written about them, chiefly in the antiquated belief that the only sound currency is gold or silver coin.

The Crown paid merchants at Quebec in somewhat the same way that one merchant paid another. For most debts of more than a few *livres*, merchants everywhere used some form of paper payment because coin was awkward and costly to transport, scarce and consequently hoarded, and kept in reserve for a few special purposes: dowries for daughters marrying or entering convents; advances to the crews of departing ships; occasional household spending to maintain the family's local credit; and paying certain local debts, such as bills of exchange presented when due, also in order to maintain personal credit. The credit thus maintained was the basis for business transactions. Merchants usually opened current accounts with one another, as with their suppliers far and near, and their local tradesmen. Accounts were reckoned up and settled periodically.

Otherwise, a payment might be made with a promissory note or a bill of exchange, and these were endorsed from one person to another until they fell due. Most notes and bills—millions of them—were thrown away when they had served their purposes, but in notarial minutes we find copies of those few that were rejected, protested, or not honoured for one reason or another, and these show that this type of payment was scarcely any different from bills drawn by the treasurer's Quebec agent on the Treasurer General in Paris.[15] The only real difference was that the Treasurer General, like a dead, dishonest, or bankrupt merchant, failed to honour the bills drawn on him at Québec. He failed, first, because the Crown could not supply him with the funds he needed and, secondly, because on 15 October 1759 the Crown ordered him to accept no more of them, and publicly suspended all Canadian bills.

This was the first step in a general financial disaster that amounted to the bankruptcy of the French government. On 26 October, the Crown was obliged to suspend the *rescriptions* of the Receivers General of Finance and the notes of the General Farm of Taxes, and on 14 November the notes of the consortium of *Beaujon, Goossens et Compagnie* that had been financing the Marine and Colonies since the beginning of the year. But these were the principal paper currencies with which the Crown had been paying merchants and others in France, the metropolitan equivalent of the Canadian bills. Its paper notes discredited, the government was now bankrupt; that is, unable to pay its debts or to meet its commitments. Had it been a private firm, its creditors would now have assembled to press its debtors, sell its property, cash its other assets, and generally recover whatever they could from the wreckage. That is, in fact, what the revolutionary National Assembly began to do in 1789. In 1759, however, the Crown was still determined to defend itself with its own absolute authority. It dismissed the Controller General of Finances, Étienne Silhouette, on 21 November. By royal decree it defended *Beaujon, Goossens et Compagnie* and the other paying services from prosecution in the courts, took stock of its own debts, decided which to honour and which to repudiate, marshalled the funds accumulating meanwhile from tax revenues, slowly resumed payments with some of the suspended notes, and by such authoritarian means gradually restored its normal financial procedures and the public confidence that depended on normalcy. On 2 February 1760, Berryer told the naval Intendant at Bordeaux to be ready to send to Canada three boxes containing 30,000 printed bills of exchange and 18,000 *billets de caisse* that were to arrive shortly from the director of royal printing, Anisson Duperron.[16] Normal payments were never resumed, however, on the Canadian bills in which so much of the profit from the Canada trade was still held.

For at least three reasons, the Crown made a special case of the Canadian bills. First, Canada being now in British hands, the holders of bills that were still there were likely to become British subjects, and their payment was a contentious diplomatic issue. Secondly, the Crown, unfamiliar with the phenomenon or even the concept of inflation, was convinced that the enormous sums paid out at Quebec during the war had been fraudulent, and acted on that conviction by arresting its officials in the *affaire du Canada*. The third reason was to cut down government debt. The Crown was able to use the *affaire* as a moral justification for deferring and reducing its payments on the Canadian bills. Of the original 90-odd million *livres*, only 37,607,000 *livres* were eventually recognized, and this sum was converted into *reconnaissances* bearing interest at 4 per cent per annum, a rate at which the French government could not borrow on the money markets at the time. This policy had a devastating effect on many of the Canada merchants, and its consequences were also felt throughout Europe. "Nothing has been paid since 18 October 1759," *Paillet et Meynardie* wrote to their Montreal agent on 1 February 1761, "and so long as the war lasts nothing will be paid. At the peace, arrangements will be made but not sooner, from which you see how distressing this is for those who counted on being paid."[17] From the merchants' point of view, this was the most discreditable of the crises that racked France in the years 1759–63, and it was remembered years later on the eve of the French Revolution.[18]

The bankruptcies that ensued among some of the biggest Canada merchants are attributable partly to the suspension of the Canada bills, partly to wartime losses of ships and cargoes, partly to the loss of Canada and Louisbourg, and partly to unpaid accounts of bankrupt debtors. *Bérard et Canonge* of Bordeaux, in whose firm Testas of Armsterdam held a one-third interest, collapsed on 22 November 1759, listing among their bad debts some 3,841 *livres* due from Bossinot, Denel, Giron and Quenel (*sic*), all of Quebec.[19] When Jacques Garesché of La Rochelle went bankrupt on 28 July 1760 he claimed among his assets 12,000 *livres* owing by the Crown for ships rented, 40,000 *livres* owing at St. Domingue, and 23,000 *livres* owing by insurers on *Gracieuse*, seized on 7 February 1758 returning from Canada and St. Domingue. He also claimed a staggering loss of 38,000 *livres* owing by the bankrupt Canada merchant Pierre Blavoust.[20] At Montauban, Étienne Mariette soon went bankrupt, pulling down other merchants with him, and turned over all his assets to his creditors on 18 April 1760.[21] At Bordeaux, Étienne Caussade failed on 2 August 1762.[22] Pierre Boudet was immediately in difficulties in the autumn of 1759, but managed to stave off bankruptcy until 31 December 1764 when his creditors forced him to retire on an allowance of 600 *livres* a year, and his sons went off to seek their fortunes, one to Louisiana, the other to Pondicherry.[23] Simon Lapointe's widow at La Rochelle failed on 9 March 1764, unable to recover from the loss of her well-established trade with friends and relatives in Canada.[24] When the Bordeaux firm of *Fesquet et Guiraut* failed in 1765, they claimed losses of 40,800 *livres* on three vessels sailing to Quebec, *La Fortune*, *Le Rostan*, and the schooner, *Les Bons Amis*.[25]

On 3 March 1766, *Paillet et Meynardie* of La Rochelle reported to their creditors that they were forced to stop making payments owing to "the misfortunes that have affected their trade since the seizure of Canada by the English, either by losses suffered, by the delay of funds in royal paper, of funds in America, or by the scarcity of money which prevents the recovery of what is owing to them."[26] Seven years later, Jean-Mathieu Mounier, who had returned from Canada with a fortune of 300,000 *livres*, intending to continue his trade at La Rochelle, ascribed his bankruptcy of 8 November 1773 to many causes, but prominent among them were the loss of Canada and the Crown's failure to honour the Canadian bills.[27]

The financial collapse of the French government had led directly to the collapse of many Canada merchants, but it had also led indirectly to that end. That is, the war was lost in 1759–60, and Canada was not relieved, partly because the Crown could no longer make payments. By 1758, the war in all its theatres was being fought on credit, not only the organized credit of the Estates of Languedoc, Brittany, and other provinces, but the short-term, haphazard, private credit of the government's own financiers, including the Treasurers General for the Navy and Colonies. As early as 1750, indeed, they had raised a loan of 4 million *livres* that was still outstanding in 1758, by which time the accumulated interest totalled nearly 2 million *livres*.[28] In 1758, the Treasurers General and their agents in the ports were being pressed for more and more payments at a time when they could not recover their money by the usual method of negotiating rescriptions drawn by the Receivers General of Finance on their own agents in provincial towns. The correspondence of Laurent Bourgeois, naval treasurer's agent at the small ports of Lorient and Port Louis, shows him advancing more and more of his own and his friends' money to settle naval debts with such merchants as Robert Dugard of Rouen, whose sailors, he reported, "have been in the most frightful misery for a long time."[29] By October 1758 he was desperately begging for funds and quoting his own advances in thousands of *livres*.

His personal predicament reflected a general situation. A naval official wrote to the Intendant of finance charged with assigning tax revenues to the spending departments, "Our poor navy is already in disorder by its inability to cope with an infinity of essential payments.... "[30] The ministers were particularly alarmed at the enormous sums the colonial Intendants were drawing in bills of exchange. If these bills were ever to be suspended, the Secretary of State for Marine and Colonies wrote to the Controller General of Finance as early as February 1758, the navy would be discredited and unable to carry on.[31] Some of the bigger Canada merchants in France were aware of the danger. "Paper on the treasury is being scorned," Admyrault *fils* wrote to a correspondent at Quebec on 28 January 1759, "No one wants to take it, though it is being paid punctually at maturity. People fear a distressing emergency (*un évènement fâcheux*); may this serve you as a warning."[32]

It was in these difficult circumstances, and to avoid discredit, that the firm of *Beaujon, Goossens et Compagnie* were called in to assist in financing the navy and colonies. At the same time, a merchant banker of Bayonne, Jean-Joseph Laborde (1724–94), was called in to furnish a million *livres* a month to the army by a contract of 3 December 1757; then, by another contract of 13 October 1758, to take charge of military financing in general up to 50 million livres or more a year; and finally, as Court Banker, to pay French diplomats abroad, subsidies to foreign allies, and other such obligations, this beginning on 4 February 1759 with the retirement of the previous Court Banker, Jean Paris de Montmartel.[33] When the crisis came the next autumn, *Beaujon, Goossens et Compagnie* went bankrupt, on 14 November 1759, and Laborde nearly did. The French government, now unable to pay for goods and services, called upon old friends and anyone it could think of in a desperate effort to send out ships and men.

Early in December, the Minister, Berryer, composed a letter proposing to that old friend of the ministry, Abraham Gradis at Bordeaux, that he send a military expedition to Canada disguised as a trading expedition because "at the moment the navy has not enough vessels to detach a force sufficient for that expedition."[34] He soon thought better of this idea, and decided on 10 December not to send the letter. But in January 1760, Berryer hatched another scheme for a privateering expedition to Canada to consist of three ships of the line, a frigate, and two fly-boats to be financed by selling 400 shares worth 4,000 *livres* each and so producing 1,600,000 *livres*. The Crown was to take 150 shares, Gradis 50, and the banking firm of *Banquet & Mallet* were to sell the remaining 200 shares in Paris.[35] This scheme, too, was dropped. The tiny merchant fleet that sailed for Canada from Bordeaux in April 1760 accompanied by *Le Machault*, a royal naval vessel, was a subject of hard bargaining between the minister and some merchants of Bordeaux, notably Lamalétie recently returned from Quebec, to make them pay for as much as possible.[36] In this "violent crisis in French finances," as Berryer afterwards called it, funds were so desperately scarce that he refused all unnecessary expenses, such as a subsidy the Abbé Reignière requested for his new invention of "an inflammable and inextinguishable firework suitable for being thrown by arrows, cannon or mortar on the enemy vessels."[37]

The crisis was compounded by the reluctance of investors to place money in French government funds. Foreign investors tended to avoid French loans. "The last loan in England in December [1759]," Bertin, the new Controller General of Finance, wrote to Miromesnil on 23 June 1760, "was subscribed by capitalists whose funds had been intended for our loans; this is established by details I have from Holland, from Switzerland and from Germany that would make you tremble.... "[38] In a humbler way, French loans were being abandoned in Canada also. When Guy *fils* stopped for a month in London on his way home to Montreal in May 1763, he decided to have Goguet send the family's funds from France so that he could invest them "in the public funds or annuities on the company for which the State is responsible, and therefore nothing is more secure," as he wrote to his mother. "This money will yield at least 3 per cent in the worst circumstances. It would have yielded up to 5 per cent, 10 per cent or even

15 per cent if I had been here two months ago. I might have bought into some of those funds that would have yielded up to 15 per cent and better. There is another advantage. This is that the exchange rate is at thirty-two and one-eighth *deniers sterling* for a crown (*écue*) ... etc."[39]

Canada was lost in battle and in bankruptcy. But it was also abandoned, as historians have pointed out. Choiseul foresaw the possibility of a rupture between Great Britain and its North American colonies once the threat of attack from New France was removed.[40] However, a policy of abandoning Canada, for whatever reason, could only have been adopted by abandoning the religious policy that had sustained the colony since Cardinal Richelieu's time in the early seventeenth century. To Church and State, Canada was a Roman Catholic imperial outpost. The French Church supported the Canadian Church as a mission; most of the Canadian clergy came from France; and the Crown paid them.[41] Supporting Canada and persecuting Huguenots were parts of the same religious policy, much weakened in the eighteenth century, but still established. In the 1750s, however, the Crown gave up its old religious policy. This was a profound change.

The change was first visible when the enlightened Chancellor, Lamoignon, and other royal officials began to urge the bishops to adopt a more lenient policy towards Protestants.[42] The bishops remained firmly opposed to recognizing Protestant marriages and baptisms, but in the middle 1750s—in 1757, according to Dale Van Kley—the Crown washed its hands of the *dévot* clergy's repressive cause and ceased to enforce the declaration of 1724 against Protestants and the edict of 1695 against Jansenists.[43] In the 1750s, Protestants at La Rochelle and Bordeaux were unofficially allowed to worship in private and to keep parish registers for the first time since the seventeenth century. The humiliating brass plaque that a royal Intendant had fixed on the door of the Minimes church at La Rochelle, to celebrate the king's defeat of the town in 1628, was ceremonially removed by royal orders on 1 November 1757.[44] At Versailles during the 1750s, Lamoignon de Malesherbes, the Chancellor's son, directed the government censorship service in a new liberal spirit.[45] In the 1760s, certain ministers and officials of the Crown responded sympathetically to Voltaire's appeal on behalf of the abused Huguenot merchant, poor Jean Calas, and his English Huguenot wife. Here and there during these years, some authorities began to remove the dangers and anxieties that had beset Protestants for more than a century. In the 1770s, the tolerant Turgot and the Protestant Swiss banker, Necker, were destined to become ministers of the Crown, and in 1787, a royal decree was at last to take the first step towards offering Protestants legal recognition as citizens.

Already, thirty years earlier, Huguenot merchants from Canada found Bordeaux and La Rochelle less oppressive than before the War of the Austrian Succession (1743–48). A certain relaxing of the old anti-Protestant laws made life less insecure and less disagreeable. When Jean-Mathieu Mounier returned from Quebec at the Conquest, he lived for a few years like a minor *philosophe*, accumulating a library of some 1,500 works, many of them in several volumes, and a collection of scientific instruments with which he made experiments in the manner of the age. In 1760 and again in 1764–65, he visited several French towns, and he also spent two years in Paris. By 1774 and doubtless earlier, he had learned to use the deists' expression, *"l'être suprême."*[46] For him and other Huguenots, France was becoming less oppressive and less dangerous. In a famous study, Daniel Mornet saw a major change after 1748 when Montesquieu of Bordeaux published his influential *De l'esprit des lois* based on a comparative study of different civilizations.[47] One of Montesquieu's friends, Mathieu Risteau, was a Huguenot merchant at Bordeaux who sometimes sent ships and goods to Canada. Risteau and his wife, Marie Renac, were in close touch with other Huguenot merchants, such as the Goudal, Rauly, and Dumas families. These and their friends cannot have been ignorant of the changing climate of opinion which Montesquieu expressed and which this later phase of Mounier's life illustrates.

One of the forces that helped to create that climate was the famous movement of Jansenists and Richerists among the clergy and magistrates. This movement triumphed just as the Seven Years' War was coming to an end, when the Society of Jesus, so powerful in France and Canada alike, was brought to trial and soon afterwards suppressed.[48] The triumphant followers of Edmond Richer (1560–1631) and Cornelius Jansen (1585–1638) had not forgotten how Louis XIV and the Jesuits had crushed them in obedience to papal orders expressed in bulls like *Unigenitus* (8 September 1713). *Unigenitus* had condemned 101 Jansenist propositions which read like the theology of a Protestant group in favour of simplicity of worship, Bible-reading in the vernacular, the voice of the laity, the power of divine grace, and much else.[49] When Louis XIV died in September 1715, many opponents of *Unigenitus* were recalled from exile or pardoned and began their teaching again, especially in the Faculty of Theology in Paris. In the 1720s and 1730s some tried to bring about a union with the Anglican and Russian Churches.[50] Meanwhile, radical Richerists still in exile, a sort of French presbyterian movement, secretly circulated Jansenist books printed in Holland, and a weekly journal, *Nouvelles ecclésiastiques*, and drew the support of many *parlementaires*.[51]

They eventually succeeded in discrediting their worst enemies, the Jesuits, in a celebrated affair that began in 1755 when British ships seized several French ones that happened to be carrying goods to France for the Jesuit West Indian mission on the island of Martinique. As a result of these losses at sea, the Jesuits' correspondents at Marseille, *Jean Lioncy et Gouffre*, went bankrupt in February 1756. Their assembled creditors tried to make their debtors pay, according to the usual procedures of the times, and soon discovered that the biggest debtor was Antoine de La Valette, the head of the Jesuit mission at St. Pierre, Martinique, who managed large plantations and a considerable transatlantic trade. As the many legal cases arising from this bankruptcy proceeded, de La Valette's superiors and the entire Society of Jesus were dragged in. The Paris Parliament held them responsible for de La Valette's unredeemed bills of exchange and so declared in a decision of 8 May 1761. By then the struggle had blossomed into a noisy political affair in which Jansenist magistrates succeeded in having the Paris Parlement condemn the Society, on 6 April 1761, as illegal and dangerous because of its "vicious nature" and "anarchical, murderous and parricidal doctrines."[52] Other Parlements rallied to this view, and after much deliberation and negotiation, Louis XV and his council issued an Edict in November 1764 which finally suppressed the Society of Jesus throughout the kingdom. Their many houses, colleges, and estates were confiscated, and this once-great Catholic agency disappeared from France, and, after Clement XIV's encyclical, *Dominus ac Redemptor Noster* (21 July 1773), from the world. One of the greatest pillars of the Counter-Reformation, and of clerical power in New France, had been laid low.

This great revolution—for such it was—fascinated all observers at the time. A clerk in the offices of the Treasurer General of the Marine reported on it to the Treasurer's agent at La Rochelle, while also reporting news of the *affaire du Canada*. "Monsieur de Vaudreuil, Governor-General of Canada, was put in the Bastille a few days ago," he wrote on 3 April 1762, "and they say he was arrested with fifteen other people who are not named. That is all the news I can tell you except about the Jesuits who are at last *f[outus]*. They shut up shop on the first of this month and they are all in their house on the rue Saint Antoine."[53] The suppression of the Jesuits was a step towards the destruction of the Church's power that was accomplished in Canada at this time by the British conquest, and in France thirty years later by the French Revolution.[54]

While the affair of the Jesuits was in full swing, another affair held the French administration of Canada up to public scrutiny in a general arrest and investigation of some fifty colonial officials. This, the famous *affaire du Canada*, exposed the greedy machinations of the Intendant, the naval controller, the purveyor, a long list of king's storekeepers and military and naval officers.[55] The Minister of Marine and Colonies, a former Lieutenant-General of Police, was already talking in 1759 of giving orders "to stop the calamities that bad administration has brought upon that colony, or at least to have those who have taken part in them punished."[56] For the observing public, this affair began on 17 November 1761 when the Purveyor General, Cadet, and the Intendant, Bigot, were arrested with many other officials from New France, high and low, about the same time. On 12 December, a commission or tribunal of the Châtelet criminal court was named to investigate and to judge the various crimes of which the arrested men were to be accused.

During the next two years, a very black picture of the colonial administration was gradually revealed and summed up at last in the final judgement of 10 December 1763, printed and published in many copies. Bigot was banished from the realm forever, Bréard for nine years, and immense fines were imposed on most of the principal accused in order to extract their ill-gotten gains from them. Meanwhile, other colonial officials were under scrutiny, and several were arrested, denounced, and sentenced to various punishments. For instance, the treasurer's agent in Louisiana, Destrehan, was dismissed in 1759, and their former agent at Louisbourg, Jean Laborde (1710–81), for many years a busy transatlantic shipping merchant on the side, was imprisoned in the Bastille on 16 March 1763 and held until 25 August 1764 after he had signed over all his assets to the Crown in a detailed notarial document.[57] The Intendant at Martinique and such scriveners in his service as Lachenez were suspected of trading and cheating like their colleagues in Canada.[58]

The *affaire du Canada* was intended to persuade the French public that the defeat of the French forces in Canada was owing to corrupt, self-seeking officials. The *affaire* was timed, furthermore, to coincide with the negotiations that ended with the ignominious Peace of Paris signed on 10 February 1763. If much public opinion easily blamed the condemned officials, some observers saw them as mere scapegoats for the failures and misdeeds of higher officials and financiers in Paris. "You know that the Sieur Cadet, Purveyor General in Canada, has been put in the Bastille," wrote François Havy to Robert Dugard on 14 February 1761. "There are at present a great many in Paris who would deserve it much more than he because they were the cause of the trouble."[59] In the words of Mouffle d'Angerville, nephew of a Treasurer General for the Marine and Colonies, the government made scapegoats of the Canadian officials because it was "too weak to attack the abuses at their source and to punish the big culprits."[60] The biggest "culprit" of all, as the revelations of these *affaires* suggested, was Bourbon society itself, anchored as it was to the absolute authority of Church and State.

When the trade and graft of royal officials and financiers was shown together with the official and financial connections of Catholic merchants, the fabric of Bourbon society appeared as tainted with corruption as Guy Frégault, Cameron Nish, and others have presented it.[61] But most Huguenot or New Convert merchants had only the most superficial connection with it, and were scarcely part of it all, being social outcasts. The principal exceptions to this general statement were a few New Converts like François Maurin, Pierre Glemet, and Abraham Gradis. Maurin's name appears in connection with the depredations of the officer, Péan, the Purveyor General, Cadet, the Intendant, Bigot, and several king's storekeepers. A relative of the Mouniers, Maurin had served as Cadet's Montreal manager under Péan's direction from 1756 to 1760, married a Dagneau Douville de Quindre in 1758, generally blended with Bourbon society, and returned to France in 1760 with a fortune of nearly 2 million *livres*. He was sentenced with the rest, banished from Paris for nine years and heavily fined. So well did he mix with Bourbon society that his twentieth-century biographer apparently did not know he was a Huguenot.[62]

Glemet had a somewhat similar connection with the condemned officials, though he made less profit and accordingly suffered less. Abraham Gradis had been deeply involved with Bigot, Bréard, and the rest, and was saved from incrimination only by Choiseul's repeated intervention on his behalf. On 12 October 1762, for instance, Choiseul wrote to Sartine to stop any further investigation of Gradis' affairs: "I desire that the last documents Sieur Gradis sent me, and which I gave you yesterday, should suffice for Messieurs the Commissioners."[63] Gradis had served the Crown during the war, as well as the colonial officials, and was to go on being useful to Choiseul in the future. But such cases as these were exceptions. The few Jews and Huguenots who had been in business with the condemned officials from Canada had not been related to them in the way that Catholic merchants had. Merchants such as those whom Cadet had used as his correspondents at Bordeaux and La Rochelle had not intermarried with officials and financiers.

Choiseul and Sartine thought well enough of several New Converts during the *affaire* to consult them in establishing standard prices for the decade 1749–59. By an order of 6 September 1762, the Châtelet court in Paris and the *Présidial* court at La Rochelle ordered the police to consult *Meynardie frères*, Thouron the younger, François Havy, Admyrault, and Jean-Mathieu Mounier.[64] The Catholic, Soumbrun, was mentioned, but not consulted. At Montauban, the Huguenot merchants Pierre de Lannes, Jean-Jaques Gauthier, and Joseph Rouffio were also trusted in establishing standard prices.[65] One Catholic merchant, but only one, Lamalétie of Bordeaux, was asked for his account books.[66] Thus, in seeking honest merchants seriously engaged in the Canada trade, but not too deeply involved with the criminal officials of the colony, the Crown eventually consulted seven Huguenots and only one Catholic. We can easily see why as we follow the French authorities in their investigation of the Canadian officials and their business partners, merchants such as Guillaume Estèbe, Jean-Patrice Dupuy, Denis Goguet, Louis Pennisseault, Lemoine Despins, and the many who had become king's storekeepers.

Much of their shady business is revealed in the biographies of Estèbe, Pennisseault, Bréard, Cadet, Bigot, and others in the *Dictionary of Canadian Biography*, volume iv (Toronto, 1979). By way of example, let us here sketch the business dealings of one who does not appear therein, Jean-Patrice Dupuy (1732–86) of Bordeaux. He served his cousin, Lamalétie, and Lamalétie's partner, Admyrault, as a commission agent at Montreal from 1754 to 1756; and in 1757, back in Bordeaux, he sent consignments of merchandise out to Lamalétie and Estèbe, still in Quebec.[67] Meanwhile, on 20 October 1756 he formed a company with Péan, the notorious adjutant at Quebec, and Jean-Baptiste Martel, the royal storekeeper at Montreal. It was a transatlantic trading company founded for seven years beginning on 1 January 1757 under the name of *Dupuy fils et compagnie*, and Dupuy directed it and had a one-third interest in it representing 133,333 *livres* of the total capital fund of 400,000 *livres*, whereas

Péan had a one-quarter interest, or 100,000 *livres* investment. It seems that Martel was to put up five-twelfths of the capital fund and hold the largest interest, but in any event the company dissolved on 14 May 1760 and re-formed without Martel on the basis of an equal sharing of profits and losses. This new partnership was to continue without term until either Péan or Dupuy decided to withdraw, and when at last they wound up their affairs on 30 May 1768, Dupuy in effect bought out Péan with payments totalling just over 51,000 *livres* and a promise to take over all the company's debts as well as its assets.[68]

Long before this, in 1759, even before the Crown had begun to prosecute the Canadian officials and others of the *grande société*, Dupuy had begun to serve as a business agent for two of those officials who were later arrested, prosecuted, and sentenced to heavy fines. For one of them, the aforementioned Martel, Dupuy purchased for 100,000 *livres* a furnished house "with six statues in the garden, each on its pedestal, a little mutilated and blackened by time," in the expensive Chartrons district of Bordeaux, this in his own name to conceal the identity of Martel for whom he acted as *prête-nom*.[69] And three years later, after Martel's arrest, Dupuy rented the house for him to another Bordeaux merchant for seven years at a rent every six months of "3,800 *livres* while the present war lasts and 4,500 *livres* in peacetime." Meanwhile, by a formal agreement of 9 February 1760, Martel paid another 100,000 *livres* for a one-third interest in Dupuy's share in the *Régie ou ferme générale des droits réunis*, a tax-collecting agency founded in September 1759 by the Controller General of Finance to help in meeting the financial crisis of the time. Already, on 20 October 1759, Dupuy had sold another third interest, also for 100,000 *livres*, to Jean-Victor Varin de la Mare, the notorious former *commissaire de la Marine* at Montreal. A royal commission set up to deal with the property of Bigot, Varin, and the other major criminals of the *affaire du Canada* traced this transaction in 1764 and soon recovered from Dupuy what he still held of Varin's 100,000 *livres*, but I have no evidence that they knew of Martel's share.[70]

As if this were not enough, on 31 December 1760 Dupuy went to one of the business agents (*prête-nom*) of Péan and Bigot, and others from Canada, a certain Nicolas-Félix Vaudive, who was an *avocat au Parlement et greffier de l'audience du grand conseil du Roi*, and the son of a merchant jeweller and goldsmith of Paris, and borrowed 50,000 *livres* to invest in the tax farm of the *Devoirs de Bretagne*. The Crown confiscated this sum in 1764 as being part of Bigot's estate and Dupuy handed it over.[71] Another of Dupuy's unsavoury business arrangements showing how widely he cast his net in the field of maritime and colonial business was made in 1762 with a well-known financier, the *régisseur des économats*, Marchal de Sainscy, who managed the Crown's funds from vacant benefices and other ecclesiastical property. De Sainscy took a one-quarter interest in a project of Dupuy's for buying large quantities of the sort of merchandise that would sell in the colonies, and two ships, *Le Casque* and *Le Cheval Marin*, but by 1771 this project had proved to be a failure.[72]

Notwithstanding Dupuy's shady dealings with officials arrested in the *affaire du Canada*, he was not himself arrested. But he was denounced to the investigating commission, evidently by someone who knew much about his affairs. The denunciation illustrates the hostile public feelings the *affaire du Canada* aroused against what I have called, for convenience, Bourbon official society. It runs,

> The most important man to arrest in the *affaire du Canada* is a certain Dupuy, merchant, living at Bordeaux in the Chartron quarter, formerly a clerk in Canada. He is the secret confidential agent of Messieurs Bigot, Péan, Varin, and Martel. It is he who has cashed for them, in France and here the Treasury bills of exchange they have entrusted to him.
>
> He used to return to France almost every year with these gentlemen's papers. He would collect the sums from the Treasurer General and with that money would buy a prodigious quantity of notes of the royal lottery. He has bought thirteen millions worth of thousand-*livre* shares in the general farms [of taxes] from the late Monsieur du Vergier, cashier to Monsieur de Montmartel. He has bought all the good bearer notes (*papier au porteur*). He has bought land for these gentlemen. He has bought Martel's house in Bordeaux which is rented in his name. In a word, that man is informed of all the money they have invested. The Commission would learn more from that man alone in a week than they could learn in six months by a lot of research.[73]

Dupuy was one of those Canada merchants from a family that was a part of Bourbon official society, related to the Lee, O'Quin, and Bennet families who had come to Bordeaux from Ireland in the seventeenth century, and related also to the Lamalétie family which had married into the Foucault family of officials in Canada. He was typical, then, of the merchants linked in business and marriage with officials and financiers.[74]

To sum up, France lost Canada in the course of financial, military, and religious crises that simultaneously undermined Bourbon official society by revealing its weaknesses. The Crown went bankrupt, owing to faults in the financial system from which the English and Dutch systems did not suffer. The ministry blamed the huge Canadian debts and the loss of the colony on the rapacity of its own officials, and tried them in a noisy affair that revealed widespread corruption in Bourbon official society. The odium this trial brought upon the colonial administration helped the Crown to abandon New France without losing face altogether. When the Crown gave up Canada it was turning its back on a Roman Catholic imperial mission, and it could do this in the 1750s because it had at last given up leading the Counter-Reformation. As another result of the same change, the Crown also abandoned the Society of Jesus to its enemies and eventually banished it. As the Age of the Enlightenment dawned, Bourbon official society, always founded on royal policy, began to crumble. The old differences between Catholic and Protestant merchants were ceasing to matter in old France as well as in what had been New France.

***

Conclusion

France gave up Newfoundland and Acadia in 1713 and the rest of New France half a century later. This was the same half-century in which the aggressive Roman Catholic empire of Louis XIV was transformed into the crumbling, tolerant monarchy of the pre-revolutionary Enlightenment. At the beginning of it, Catholic families with branches on both sides of the Atlantic had a monopoly of trade and shipping to New France; at the end, Huguenot families had a large share, perhaps most of it. At the beginning, the typical Canada merchant was a man with relatives in the magistracy, in the priesthood, in the ranks of the government financiers, and so was part of the society that had formed around the ruling families at court, part of the hierarchy of patronage created by the Bourbon kings. At the end, the typical Canada merchant was related to other merchants in Amsterdam, London, Hamburg, Geneva, even Boston, and some belonged to the cosmopolitan world of maritime business that had grown up in the Protestant seaports. In the early eighteenth century Church and State kept Protestant merchants out of the Canada trade unless they disguised themselves as Roman Catholics; in mid-century the State abandoned the Church's cause, even abandoned the Society of Jesus, and tolerated Protestants who conformed to Catholic practices.

A social study of merchants in that half-century, those in the Canada trade at any rate, shows basic religious differences. Most Huguenots and Catholics, like most Jews, married within their own religious communities. A marriage in that age was a family treaty based on a negotiated contract, just as a business partnership was. Contracts in marriage or in business were usually founded on the trust that grew out of a common religious tradition. For merchants, the two religious traditions were, moreover, profoundly different in that French Catholics were part of the approved, legal society of Bourbon France in which the clergy were extremely powerful. French Protestants, on the other hand, were outcasts and outlaws who survived by submitting themselves and their children to Catholic baptism, marriage, and other sacraments.

The two traditions were politically different also: a Catholic merchant belonged to the authoritarian hierarchy of Church and State; whereas a Huguenot merchant was part of the Calvinist or reformed Church that had no priestly hierarchy and had not submitted to secular authority. In addition, the Huguenot merchant had strong ties with the communities of Huguenot refugees in Protestant cities. Merchants had a strong voice in the governments of those cities, and also in the central governments of Holland and Great Britain. The cosmopolitan business world of those countries, which for convenience we may call Atlantic trading society, was much freer than society in France, where Church and State censored the press, interfered in municipal government, and even controlled people's movements between France and the colonies. Religious differences were thus linked with different political traditions.

The Huguenot merchants who stayed in France did so for a variety of reasons. Some were from families too poor and numerous to emigrate. Lands and houses, kith and kin, kept others in those Huguenot communities which survived collectively at La Rochelle, Bordeaux, Rouen, Nîmes, Montauban, Paris, and other towns. The *abjuration* or "conversion" that was rewarded with official posts or advantageous marriages kept some in France, apparently "New Converts" but often merely trimming to the political winds and hoping for better times later. Historians have been too quick to think that any Huguenot who abjured had truly converted. Then, in the eighteenth century many Huguenots found profit in their position as French "agents" of Atlantic trading society. With relatives in the ports of the Protestant Baltic and North Sea, and the Protestant Atlantic, they were well-placed to export wine and brandy, woollens, furs, and colonial sugar, and to import American tobacco, Baltic naval stores, and Irish foodstuffs. These trading families found life easier in France as persecution died down gradually here and there after Louis XIV's death.

The Canada trade was opened to them, it is clear, in the 1730s. In the 1740s the Crown began to call on them, and on Jews also, to transport men, munitions, and foodstuffs to the colonies. Long wars at sea against heavy odds drove the French ministers to rely more and more on New Converts with their foreign trading networks and their ample resources. Religious scruples began to be set aside, and the Canada trade became increasingly cosmopolitan, less and less in the hands of the old Catholic trading families. German, Swiss, and Austrian fur buyers began trading with New France. The established Catholic families were hard-pressed. Those who could—Pascaud, Goguet, Lamalétie, Trottier Désauniers—bought offices and married their children to noble or office-holding families, which had always been their inclination in any case. Others failed and went bankrupt: Bourgine, Blavoust, Soumbrun, Jung, Guillaume Pascaud, and more. Still others carried on in partnership with government officials in Canada, as indeed did a few New Converts, Jewish and Protestant.

Army officers, naval officers and storekeepers, and government financial agents had always traded in the colonies, adding to their meagre and uncertain emoluments by using their power for profit. They have to be counted as part-time merchants in any serious study of the Canada trade. After all, officials and financiers dominated the business life of Paris and the great monopoly companies, and had much authority in Bourbon official society. The mid-century wars offered them unprecedented opportunities in New France, where the Crown was spending more and more in the imperial cause. In old France, too, agents of the Treasurers General of Finance went into maritime trade. Government financiers invested in privateering ventures or speculated, like Prévost, in marine insurance.

The French government depended on its financiers for loans as well as for services, and in the Seven Years' War strained their resources beyond the limit. Efforts to supplement the financiers' resources with the funds of merchant bankers could not save the rickety Bourbon credit system, and its collapse in autumn

1759 began on 15 October when it suspended the Canadian bills. As a result, the Crown could no longer send out ships and men, or command the services of merchants in the Canada trade. Nor could it pay its debts to them. Added to the cruel blow of the colony's loss to Great Britain, the government's bankruptcy set off a series of failures among the Canada merchants. To save money and to save face, the government blamed its own officials in Canada for the Canadian debts and defeats. The trial of these scapegoats revealed much corruption in Bourbon official society, and some of the big merchants were implicated.

The revelations of the notorious *affaire du Canada*, beginning in 1761, helped the government to turn its back on New France, an expensive white elephant it then seemed, and no efforts were made to recover the colony thereafter. The Huguenots who stayed in Canada suddenly found themselves free and respectable, eligible for offices from which Catholics were now excluded. But the trade between New France and old France was just as suddenly stopped. Many a cargo intended for Canada, in a warehouse at La Rochelle or Bordeaux, had to be disposed of elsewhere. "There is still no news concerning the shipping of the merchandise in storage here belonging to Canadians," Goguet wrote from La Rochelle to Madame Guy at Montreal on 1 May 1763, and went on to explain that the British government would allow no such shipments.[75]

Suddenly passengers between Canada and France had to go by way of British ships and British ports, like young Guy who spent some weeks in London in May 1763 on his way home to Montreal from La Rochelle, "which will give me the time," he wrote to his mother, "to make acquaintances here, which is very easy to do."[76] Suddenly the ships in the Canada trade were British or British-American ships, such as the *Nettleton* which reached Dartmouth from Quebec on 1 January 1760, the *Experiment* which landed on the same day in Virginia, having come from Quebec, and the *Peter Beckford* which landed at New York on 11 January; and the sixteen vessels at the Downs, not far from London, announced by *Lloyd's List* on 11 April 1760 as "remains for Quebec." The ports in the Canada trade were soon established as London, Bristol, Cowes, Falmouth, Plymouth, Cork, Greenock, and a dozen colonial ports. The Canada merchants now had names like William and Robert Hunter, William and John Grant, John Schoolbred, Robert Ellice, James Phyn & Co., Muir & Co., Buchanan, and John Cochrane.[77] But theirs is another story.

Notes

1. These financial difficulties of the French government I have discussed in various articles such as "Les Trésoiriers de la Marine et des Colonies sous Louis XV: Rochefort et La Rochelle," *Revue de la Saintonge et de l'Aunis*, tome v (1979), pp. 95–108, "The French Government's Motives in the *affaire du Canada*, 1761–63," *English Historical Review*, vol. xvci (1981), pp. 59–78; and "Financing the French navy in the Seven Years' War: *Beaujon, Goossens et Compagnie*," *Business History* (London), vol. 28 (July 1986), pp. 115–33.

2. J.F. Bosher, *French Finances 1770–1795: From Business to Bureaucracy* (Cambridge, 1970), 370 pp.

3. AN, 62 AQ 35, France (Paris) to Dugard (Rouen), 14 Mar. 1748 and 28 Apr. 1748.

4. Henri Legohérel, "Une Commission extraordinaire du Conseil d'État du Roi: La Commission de Liquidation des Dettes de la Marine et Colonies (1758–68)," *Faculté de Droit et Sciences économiques de Dakar* (Paris, 1968), 32 pp., and AN, Colonies E 45, "Précis concernant la dette du Roy pour le Canada (29 June 1764)"; BN, ms. fr. 11340, Le Normand de Mézy.

5. BN, ms. fr. 11337, Berryer to Fontanieu, 18 May 1759; BN, ms. fr. 11338, Fontanieu to Berryer, 31 Dec. 1759.

6. Bibl. mun. de La Rochelle, ms. 1954.

7. Université de Montréal, Collection Baby, U 5113.

8. *Ibid.* U 8503; AN, Colonies, B 108, Minister to the Marseille Chamber of Commerce, 18 Feb. 1758.

9. Collection Baby, U 9256 (1 Feb. 1759).

10. J.F. Bosher, *Business and Religion in the Age of New France, 1600–1700: Twenty-two Studies* (Toronto, Canadian Scholars' Press, 1994), Chapter 21, "Shipping to Canada in Wartime," pp. 464–486.

11. BN, ms. fr. 11336, fols. 14 ff.

12. BN, ms. fr. 11337, Fontanieu to Berryer, 27 Apr. 1759.

13. Arch. de la Marine, Lorient, 1E5 I, Laurent Bourgeois (Lorient) to de Selle (Paris), 14 June 1758.

14. Arch. de la Marine, Rochefort, 1E 145, Maurepas to de Givry, 14 July 1748 and 17 Nov. 1748.

15. I have found copies of about forty such bills of exchange from Quebec in the minutes of half a dozen Bordeaux notaries between 1716 and 1756: Bernard, Lagénie, Lamestrie, Parran, Rauzan, and Séjournée *l'ainé*.

16. AN, Colonies B 112, fol. 35, Min. to Rostan, 2 Feb. 1760.

17. Bibl. mun. de La Rochelle, ms. 1954, *Paillet et Meynardie* (La Rochelle) to François Chevalier (Montréal), 1 Feb. 1761.

18. Simon-Joseph-Louis Bonvallet des Brosses, *Moyens de simplifier la perception et la compatibilité des deniers royaux*, 1789 (Bibliotheque nationale Lb^{39} 7248), p. 89 note.

19. ADG, 7 B 428; Butel, "La Croissance commerciale," vol. i, pp. 176, 687–88.

20. A.D. Ch. Mar., Fredureaux-Dumas (LR), 28 July 1760, *Traité du sieur Jacques Garesché ..., [sic]*.

21. A.D. Tarn-et-Garonne, David Delmas (Montauban), 22 Dec. 1762, *Accord*, 13 pp.

22. ADG, 7 B 528.

23. A.D. Char. Mar., 4J 5, notes Garnault, and Tardy (LR), 31 Dec. 1764 to 16 June 1765, *abandon de biens*.

24. A.D. Ch. Mar., Tardy (LR), 9 Mar. 1764, *abandon de biens*.

25. ADG, 7 B 429. For details of these and other voyages, see J.F. Bosher, *Men and*

Ships in the Canada Trade: A Biographical Dictionary (Ottawa: Environment Canada, 1992), *passim*.

26. A.D. Ch. Mar., Tardy (LR), 3 and 10 Mar. 1766, *Réunion des créanciers*, 7 pp.

27. A.D. Ch. Mar., B 1757, *État à peu près ....*

28. AN, f⁴ 1008, *Mémoire: situation du Sieur de Géorville*, 3 Feb. 1762; Armand Rébillon, *Le États de Bretagne de 1661–1789* (Paris, 1932), p. 730, shows six million *livres* lent to the Crown in 1758 and another six million in 1760, all at 5 per cent interest.

29. Arch. de la Marine (Lorient), 1 E⁵ 1, Bourgeois to Mouffle de Géorville, 23 Jan. 1758 etc.

30. AN, Colonies B 108, Le Normand de Mézy to Boullogne, Intendant of Finance.

31. AN, Colonies B 108, fols. 64–67. By April 1758, the Treasurers General for the Colonies were unable to find a million *livres* to pay Simon Darragory, a French merchant in Spain, for shiploads of food sent to Canada on Spanish ships with false neutral passports.

32. Université de Montréal, Collection Baby, U 21.

33. On *Beaujon, Goossens et Cie* see Bosher, "Financing the French navy"; Laborde's career is explained in his memoirs, edited by Yves-René Durand, in *Annuaire-Bulletin de la Société de l'Histoire de France, année 1968–1969* (Paris, 1971), pp. 75–162.

34. AN, Colonies B 110, Berryer to Gradis, a letter dated only December 1759 with a note added, "Le 10 Dec. 1759 monseigneur a suspendu l'expédition de cette lettre et de l'état dont il y est question."

35. Jean de Maupassant, "Abraham Gradis et l'approvisionnement des colonies (1756–63)," *Revue historique de Bordeaux*, 2e année (1909), pp. 250 ff.

36. AN, Colonies B 112, *passim* from Jan. to Apr.

37. AN, Marine B² 362, Berryer to Regnières, 23 Nov. 1759.

38. Marcel Marion, *Histoire financière de la France* (Paris, 1914), vol. i, p. 209.

39. Université de Montréal, Collection Baby, U 5065, Guy (London) to Mme Guy (Mtl.), 20 May 1763.

40. For example, Marcel Trudel, *Louis XVI, Le Congrès américain et le Canada, 1774–1789* (Quebec, 1949).

41. Guy Frégault, *Le XVIIIᵉ siècle canadien* (Montreal, 1968), ch. 3, "L'Église et la société canadienne"; Cornelius J. Jaenen, *The Role of the Church in New France* (Toronto, 1976), ch. 3.

42. Grosclaude, *Malesherbes*, ch. 15, "Les Affaires des Protestants."

43. Dale Van Kley, *The Damiens Affair and the Unravelling of the ancien régime, 1750–1770* (Princeton, 1984), pp. 269, 351 note 17; and see above, pp. 116–18.

44. Père B. Coutant, *Les Minimes* (La Rochelle, 1968), ch. 4, "L'Affaire des plaques."

45. Grosclaude, *Malesherbes*, ch. 3.

46. A.D. Ch. Mar., B 1757, *État à peu près de mes malheureuses affaires*, 28 Jan. 1774.

47. Daniel Mornet, *Les Origines intellectuelles de la Révolution française, 1715–1787* (1933), 4th ed. (Paris, 1947), part ii, ch. 1, p. 71; ADG, Rauzan (Bx.), 27 Oct. 1753; Bernard (Bx.), 7 Aug. 1718, marriage contract of Risteau and Renac.

48. Jean Egret, "Le Procès des Jésuites devant les Parlements de France 1761–1770," *Revue historique*, vol. cciv (1950), pp. 1–27; D.G. Thompson, "The Fate of the French Jesuits' Creditors under the ancien régime," *English Historical Review*, vol. 91 (1976), pp. 255–77.

49. Anne Fremantle, *The Papal Encyclicals in their Historical Context* (NY, 1956), p. 99.

50. Edmond Préclin, *Les Jansenistes du XVIIIe siècle et la Constitution Civile du Clergé* (Paris, 1929), p. 545.

51. *Ibid.*, p. 132.

52. Van Kley, *The Jansenists and the Expulsion of the Jesuits from France*, pp. 92, 134.

53. A.D. Ch. Mar., B 4055, Couteau (Paris) to Brunet de Béranger (LR), 3 Apr. 1762.

54. Hilda Neatby, *Quebec, The Revolutionary Age, 1760–1791* (Toronto, 1961), 300 p. p.19; Marcel Trudel, *L'Église canadienne sous le régime militaire, 1759–1764*, 2 vols. (Quebec, 1956–57).

55. Bosher, "The French Government's Motives in the *affaire du Canada, 1761–63*."

56. AN, Colonies B 110, fol. 220, Berryer (Paris) to Péan (Que.), 22 July 1759.

57. AN, MC, Étude XXXIII 553, 12 July 1764, *Compte de transport de créance au Roy le Sieur La Borde*.

58. AN, Colonies B 111, fol. 65, Minister to Le Mercier de la Rivière, 13 Oct. 1761 and 31 Oct. 1761.

59. AN, 62 AQ 36, Havy to Dugard, 14 Feb. 1761.

60. Moufle d'Angerville, *Vie privée de Louis XV*, vol. iv, p. 71.

61. Frégault, *François Bigot, Administrateur francais*; Nish, *Les Bourgeois-gentilshommes de la Nouvelle-France, 1719–1748*.

62. *DCB* vol. iii, pp. 441–42.

63. Bibl. de l'Arsenal (Paris), Bastille ms. 12, 145, fols. 83–84, 323, 374; Bibl. nat., ms. fr. 11338, Berryer to Fontanieu, 25 Jan. 1760.

64. A.D. Ch. Mar., B 1796, *Procès-verbal destinés des négotiants faisant le commerce du Canada*, 14 Sept. 1762, 35 pp.

65. Bibl. de l'Arsenal, Bastille ms. 12, 144, fol. 162, Choiseul to Sartine, 28 June 1762.

66. ADG, 3 B 248, Sénéchaussée-présidial, *Procès-verbal transport*, 14 Sept. 1762, 5 pp.

67. Dupuy's story is told in another context in J.F. Bosher, "A Quebec merchant's Trading Circles in France and Canada: Jean-André Lamalétie before 1763," *Histoire sociale* (Ottawa), vol. ix (1977), pp. 24–44.

68. ADG, Faugas (Bx.), 30 May 1768, *Cession et dissolution de Sossiété (sic) Péan et Dupuy*, 8 pp.

69. ADG, Guy (Bx.), 16, 17 Feb. 1769, and 8 oct. 1762.

70. AN, MC, Étude XXX, 9 Feb. 1760, *société*, and 20 Oct. 1759, *société* with attached notes; V⁷ 353, entry for 3 Apr. 1764.

71. AN, MC, étude LVII, 8 May, 31 Dec. 1760, and 20 Feb. 1761.

72. AN, MC, Cordier (Paris), 18 Mar. 1771, *procuration* of which a copy in ADG, Faugas (Bx.), 6 Apr. 1771.

73. Bibl. de l'Arsenal, Bastille ms. 12, 145, fol. 6; 12, 143, fol. 313.

74. Bosher, "A Quebec Merchant's Trading Circles," genealogical chart.

75. Université de Montréal, Collection Baby, U 4663.

76. *Ibid.* U 5065, Guy (London) to Mme Guy (Mtl.), 20 May 1763.

77. R.H. Fleming, "Phyn, Ellice and Company of Schenectady," *University of Toronto Studies in History and Economics*, vol. iv (1932), pp. 7–41; Jacob M. Price, "Buchanan & Simson, 1759–1763: A Different Kind of Glasgow Firm Trading to the Chesapeake," *William and Mary Quarterly*, 3rd series, vol. xl (1983), pp. 3–41; David Geddes, "How Habeas Corpus Came to Canada: the Bills on Credit Scandal in Quebec, 1783," *Three Banks Review* (London), no. 112 (Dec. 1976), pp. 50–65; and "John Cochrane's Troubles," *ibid.*, no. 111 (Sept. 1976), pp. 56–60.

CHAPTER

7 THE LOYALIST EXPERIENCE

The American Revolution was among the most important wars in Canadian history. While the Seven Years' War gave unquestioned supremacy to the British in North America, Canada was marginalized in the aftermath. The American Revolution, on the other hand, rescued Canada from that vast Anglo-American empire and created not just one new nation but two. It also defined the nature of what became known as British North America. The Catholic, French Canada of the *ancien régime* became a bilingual, bicultural, multidenominational colony with the arrival of thousands of United Empire Loyalists, the losers in that American War of Independence. The Loyalists spread across the old French empire, from the eastern tip of Cape Breton Island to western outposts like Detroit. They became the dominant population in the newly created colonies of Upper Canada, New Brunswick and Prince Edward Island. Even in Lower Canada, they occupied whole regions and challenged French dominance.

Since they were the first to reject the American Dream, the Loyalists fascinate historians in the United States, who have analysed those untypical ancestors in an attempt to understand who they were and why they pursued their un-American activities. This has also attracted Canadians, since the Loyalist mentality was transported north during and after the Revolution. Wallace Brown, author of the first article, has written widely on what he calls *The King's Friends: The Composition and Motives of the American Loyalist Claimants* (1965). In "'Victorious in Defeat': The American Loyalists in Canada," he offers the traditional, sympathetic overview of the Canadian experience. Others have been less kind, and there is a significant body of "Loyalist Myth" literature that describes in both positive and negative terms the convolutions of the Loyalist image in Canada over time. The ups and downs are usually tied to attitudes about monarchy, empire, imperialism, anti-Americanism, and the increasing obscurity of the Loyalists with the passage of time.

In most of this Loyalist literature the role of women, both during and after the Revolution, has rarely been considered. With the rethinking of Canada's past from several perspectives over the past quarter-century, Loyalist women have finally been rediscovered. Janice Potter examines several in "Patriarchy and Paternalism: The Case of Eastern Ontario Loyalist Women." Their courageous activities in the Revolutionary War went unrecognized later in British North America, because of "a well-defined power structure in which there were clearly prescribed social roles." This is the position of modern feminist historians, who expose the concept of natural order implicit in the oppressive patriarchal systems.

Suggestions for Further Reading

Bell, David, "The Loyalist Tradition in Canada," *Journal of Canadian Studies*, V, no. 2 (May 1970), 22–33.

Brown, Wallace and Hereward Senior, *Victorious in Defeat: The Loyalists in Canada*. Toronto: Methuen, 1984.

Condon, Ann Gorman, *The Envy of the American States: The Loyalist Dream for New Brunswick*. Fredericton: New Ireland Press, 1984.

Errington, Jane, "Loyalists in Upper Canada: A British American Community," in *"None was ever better ..." The Loyalist Settlements of Ontario*, ed. S.F. Wise, D. Carter-Edwards and J. Witham. Stormont, Dundas and Glengarry Historical Society, 1984.

MacKinnon, Neil, *The Unfriendly Soil: The Loyalist Experience in Nova Scotia, 1783–1791*. Kingston and Montreal: McGill-Queen's University Press, 1986.

MacNutt, W.S., "The Loyalists: A Sympathetic View," *Acadiensis*, VI, no. 1 (Autumn 1976), 3–20.

McCalla, Douglas, "The 'Loyalist' Economy of Upper Canada, 1784–1806," *Histoire sociale / Social History*, XVI, no. 32 (November 1983), 279–304.

Mills, David, *The Idea of Loyalty in Upper Canada, 1784–1850*. Kingston and Montreal: McGill-Queen's University Press, 1988.

Moore, Christopher, *The Loyalists: Revolution, Exile, Settlement*. Toronto: Macmillan of Canada, 1984.

Rawlyk, George, "The Federalist-Loyalist Alliance in New Brunswick, 1784–1815," *Humanities Association Review*, XXVII, no. 1 (Spring 1976), 142–160.

Upton, L.S.F. (ed.), *The United Empire Loyalists: Men and Myths*. Toronto: Copp Clark, 1967.

Wise, S.F., "The Place of the Loyalists in Ontario and Canadian History," *"None was ever better ..." The Loyalist Settlements of Ontario*, ed. S.F. Wise, D. Carter-Edwards and J. Witham. Stormont, Dundas and Glengarry Historical Society, 1984.

VICTORIOUS IN DEFEAT: THE AMERICAN LOYALISTS IN CANADA

Wallace Brown

> *"They [the Loyalists] would rather go to Japan than go among the Americans where they could never live in peace."*
>
> Col. John Butler, a New York Loyalist who emigrated to Canada.

As the War for Independence drew to a close, thousands of American Loyalists were looking for new homes.[1] The most attractive location because of proximity, availability of land and continuing royal rule, was what was left of British North America, constituting in 1783 three colonies: Nova Scotia, which included the future New Brunswick; the Island of St. John, renamed Prince Edward Island in 1799; and the ancient province of Quebec, which since 1774 stretched west to include the Great Lakes region. The term Canada, except as a synonym for Quebec, is an anachronism before 1867 (the date of Confederation); but it will be used in this essay to designate the entire area. The Maritimes refers to Nova Scotia, New Brunswick and Prince Edward Island.

Most Loyalists arrived in Nova Scotia by ship, at government expense, from New York City, the last great British stronghold in the "lost thirteen" colonies. The invasion began in October, 1782, with the descent of 300 Americans on the Annapolis Valley. Thousands more soon followed into the peninsula where the greatest concentration, perhaps 10,000, was at Port Roseway, renamed Shelburne, after the man who was the patron of Governor John Parr, but by no means a hero to the Loyalists on account of the generous peace terms he had negotiated with the rebels. A Spring and a Fall fleet in 1783 brought a host of refugees to the St. John valley, some of whom founded the city of Saint John at the river's mouth and Fredericton, seventy miles upstream. Other settlements were made at Passamaquoddy Bay (notably St. Andrews), Sackville, Bay Chaleur and the Miramichi River. Other Loyalists were lured to the Island of St. John, mainly the Malpeque-Bedeque isthmus, where Summerside, the island's second largest town, was founded.

The results of the influx into the Maritimes were dramatic. A new province, New Brunswick, was split off from Nova Scotia, the 15,000 Loyalists swamping the pre-Loyalist population of about 4,000 New Englanders and Acadians. Nova Scotia was further partitioned—temporarily, in this case—when hitherto little-developed Cape Breton Island, acquired from France in 1763, became a separate colony as a result of the arrival of 400 Loyalists who more than doubled the

From *History Today*, 27, no. 2 (1977), 92–100. Reprinted by permission of *History Today*.

existing population. The Americans could not take over the rump of Nova Scotia; but, numbering at least 15,000, they slightly outweighed the old inhabitants. On the Island of St. John the up to 1,000 immigrants, almost equalling the existing population, were a force to be reckoned with.

Arrival in Quebec was much more sporadic than in the Maritimes as the Loyalists, often pushing hand-carts, trickled in by various water-assisted routes, including the St. Lawrence and Hudson-Mohawk rivers, and Lakes Oneida and Champlain. Some sailed across Lake Ontario, frequently to the Bay of Quinte; others followed the southern shore to the Niagara peninsula; others pushed on to the Thames River and the northern shore of Lake Erie; a few even ascended the Mississippi and settled at Detroit. Again the results were the founding of new towns including New Johnstown (now Cornwall) and Cataraqui (now Kingston), and partition when the western area became Upper Canada (the future Ontario) in 1791. In Upper Canada, as in New Brunswick, the Loyalists, numbering perhaps 7,000, took over a wilderness area from a small pre-Loyalist population of only a few hundred; but in the original colony of Quebec 70,000 French Canadians were not directly threatened by the 1,000 Loyalist immigrants, half of whom settled in the outlying Gaspé peninsula, and half in the old inhabited area, mainly at Sorel and Machiche. Later, the Eastern Townships received some Loyalists.

Government was ill-prepared for the arrival of the Tories, though Governor Frederick Haldimand in Quebec proved much more capable and sympathetic than Governor Parr in Nova Scotia. Halifax and Saint John were severely overcrowded. In the former, churches and warehouses served as temporary quarters, and in both tent-cities sprang up. Congestion, but not always hardship, was relieved when many refugees moved to take up government land grants. Contemporary accounts are few, but some evidence about life in early Fredericton survives. All too soon the Loyalists faced the hard Canadian winter in tents covered with boughs or in half-finished log cabins. Some unfortunates froze to death; others only escaped by organizing shifts through the night to keep the fires going. The want of bedding might be supplied by heated boards. Even in 1787 the Reverend Jacob Bailey, a talented Loyalist from Massachusetts, reported from Annapolis County, Nova Scotia, that: "Many families are confined to a single apartment built with sods, where men, women, children, pigs, fleas, bugs, mosquitoes and other domestic insects mingle in society."

In western Quebec there was also much hardship. In July 1784, it was stated that "the settlers at Cataraqui are in great disorder, not having yet got upon their land, many of them unprovided with a Blanket to cover Them, scarce any Turnip seed and neither Axes nor Hoes for Half of Them." Brighter reports soon followed; but 1789 was known as the "hungry year" when "dreadful circumstances" were noted: "one spoonful of meal per day, for one person" was the ration; wild leaves, such as beech, were eaten; famished domestic animals were bled Masai-style; one family "leaped for joy at one robin being caught, out of which a whole pot of broth was made."

The Canadian land was quite capable of supplying a living at a simple farming level, but first came the back-breaking work of clearing the forest. Even Beverly Robinson Jr., scion of one of the richest New York families, recounted in 1784 that: "He is now settling a new farm in Nova Scotia by beginning to cut down the first tree and erect a loghouse for the shelter of his wife and two small children, and to accomplish that is obliged to labour with *his own* hands" (my italics). We see here the influence of the frontier at work in a Turnerian way.

Under the strain of the new environment, grown men wept like children and some cracked up completely. Filer Diblee and his family came from a prosperous middle class background in Connecticut. Their Loyalism resulted in an odyssey of flight, imprisonment and persecution which ended with their arrival at the Kingston peninsula, New Brunswick, where they survived the winter of 1783–84 in a log cabin. But Diblee's "fortitude gave way" at the prospect of imprisonment for debt; he "grew Melancholy, which soon deprived him of his Reason"; and one day in March, 1784, "he took a Razor from the Closet, threw himself on the bed, drew the Curtains, and cut his own throat." Though she lost her house twice by fire, his widow struggled on in what she called "this frozen Climate and barren Wilderness."

Groups as well as individuals were unfortunate. The Loyalist boomtown, Shelburne, had a magnificent harbour, but otherwise was so badly located that it rapidly declined to a hamlet. Port Mouton, Nova Scotia, was settled by over 2,000 refugees, mainly disbanded soldiers, in 1783 and quickly the town of Guysborough was built, and a road hacked through the woods to Liverpool. But in 1784 the town was destroyed by fire, a fate that struck several Loyalist settlements. Most of the inhabitants left and founded the present Guysborough on Chedabucto Bay, Nova Scotia, while some others founded St. Stephen in New Brunswick. Typically, most Loyalist set-backs were temporary. Most Shelburners found new homes. Even the Diblee family endured.

The arrival of the Loyalists in Canada marks the beginning of a great epic tale insufficiently appreciated by historians or the public. It ranks with the history of the Jesuit missionaries and the *coureurs de bois*, but has never found its Parkman.

Although plagued with difficulties, the Loyalists had many advantages. The environment was not completely hostile. Trees that had to be removed also supplied fuel and material for houses, tools and furniture; winters that inflicted frostbite also provided a free "deep-freeze" for the abundant game and fish; governments that were cursed for incompetence and ingratitude granted tax exemptions, issued provisions, medicines, clothes, tools, seeds, boards, and, most important of all, surveyed and granted, free of charge, land—the basis of survival for most people in those days. For a fortunate minority government largesse went further. Ex-officers received half pay for life; some Loyalists got pensions and lump-sum grants in compensation for losses sustained by the Revolution; all of this injected much-needed capital into Canada and ultimately benefited all the inhabitants. A very small minority got government offices, especially in the new provinces of New Brunswick and Upper Canada, but there were never enough to satisfy the vociferous Loyalists' demands. The scorned pre-Loyalist inhabitants were helpful as suppliers and informants. For example, in New Brunswick the Acadians sold cleared land and provisions to the Loyalists, while the Indians introduced them to fiddlehead greens (the edible shoots of a wild fern that are still a local delicacy). Though some observers noted the "vice of every kind, incident of the camp," that prevailed among the many Loyalists who settled as groups of disbanded regiments, particularly at Niagara, on the St. John River and the upper St. Lawrence, others stressed the advantages that military discipline and cohesiveness gave.

It has nurtured the self-esteem of some Canadians, especially New Brunswickers, to consider the Loyalists as mainly colonial aristocrats and Harvard graduates, in the same way it has flattered Virginians to consider themselves the progeny of Cavaliers. In fact, the vast majority of Loyalists were modest farmers (plus some artisans) who were well-suited to pioneering. But the Loyalist myth of gentility has a grain of truth; there *was* a significant minority of the "better sort," again especially in New Brunswick. Sergeant-Major William Cobbett, on duty in New Brunswick in the 1790s, was amazed to find "thousands of captains ..., without soldiers, and of squires without stockings or shoes," some of whom were happy to serve him a glass of grog. There were few fee-paying clients for doctors or lawyers. Not surprisingly a number of gentlemen Loyalists left Canada. For example, no less than six members of New Brunswick's first assembly, which met in 1785, had returned to the United States before the session was completed!

Nevertheless the contribution of the élite Loyalists to Canada, especially to government, politics, the law, religion and culture, must be acknowledged and can be suggested by listing a few names. Edmund Fanning (North Carolina) and Sir John Wentworth (New Hampshire) became the lieutenant-governors of the Island of St. John and Nova Scotia respectively; John Saunders (Virginia) and William Smith (New York) became chief-justices of New Brunswick and Quebec; Philip Marchington and Richard Cartwright (both from New York) were leading merchants in Nova Scotia and Upper Canada respectively; Sir John Johnson and Gabriel Ludlow (both from New York) became prominent office-holders in Quebec and New Brunswick; the Reverend Jonathan Odell (a poet of distinction from New Jersey) became the long-serving provincial secretary of New Brunswick; and so it went even to succeeding generations—Simon Fraser, the great explorer, was the son of a Loyalist; Sir Leonard Tilley, a father of Confederation, was a grandson.

Most Loyalists were subsistence farmers; but there were other areas of economic endeavour. Canada was slated by the British government to replace the former thirteen colonies as the purveyor of fish, timber and other supplies to the British West Indies. Indeed, some so-called Loyalists only migrated when they learned that the Navigation Acts would be applied against the United States. The West Indian market encouraged Canadian agriculture, fishing and lumbering; but supply never equalled demand, and the British frequently had to open the West Indian trade to the United States. Even much of the early Nova Scotia and New Brunswick timber exports were American, frequently illegally obtained. The French Revolutionary and Napoleonic wars stimulated the Maritime mast trade; but much of it was not in Loyalist hands, and people tended to be diverted from agriculture, which partly explains why the Maritimes were chronically short of food.

The Loyalists dreamed of making the new provinces "a showcase for the continent," "the envy" of the United States; but sometimes the dream fell short. The Maritimes were poor by American standards. In 1790 William Pitt, influenced by *laissez-faire* principles and the United States policy of selling public lands, ended free land grants in British North America. Lord Dorchester, the Governor of Quebec, ignored the order; little land worth having remained in Nova Scotia; but the ban, which lasted seventeen years in New Brunswick, stunted development. On the Island of St. John most Loyalists could not get clear title to their land because of a complicated matter of absentee ownership. Some refugees bought new land; many simply squatted; others moved away. The issue, which was not resolved until 1875, cast a pall over the island, but stimulated reform politics during the first half of the nineteenth century. Upper Canada suffered from isolation and the barrier of the rapids of the St. Lawrence; but the rich soil presaged a prosperous future in what became the wealthiest part of Canada.

There is a chorus of contemporary testimony that most Loyalists, apart from a few who had "contracted ... rum and idle habits ... during the war," made good settlers. For example, Patrick Campbell visiting Upper Canada in the early 1790s, was impressed with the "immense industry" of the Loyalists, who, he claimed, had cleared more land in eight years than the French had in one hundred; James MacGregor visiting Prince Edward Island in the early nineteenth century found the Loyalists "industrious and independent," very well-suited to coping with "a country in a state of nature." In 1802 Edward Winslow, a descendant of the Pilgrim Father of the same name, looked back at the history of his fellow New Brunswick Loyalists with modest satisfaction. "Immense labour" had transformed a wilderness into a prosperous farming community. "Enquire among 'em. Are you oppressed with taxes? No. Does anybody interrupt you in matters of conscience? No. Do the laws afford you sufficient protection. Why yes." After a few years the Loyalists were strung out along a line of permanent, mainly agricultural, settlements from Cape Breton to Detroit,[2] and they had created two new provinces and several important towns. This is their prime contribution to Canada. They are the English founding fathers, analagous to the Virginians and Puritans of the early seventeenth century.

There remain two questions to be answered: what kind of society did the Loyalists create; and what was their legacy to Canada? The Loyalists were essentially good Americans, rarely docile Tories. As early as May, 1783, the royal surveyor, Benjamin Marston, a Loyalist himself, was complaining about the "curs'd Republican Town meeting Spirit" that made his life in Shelburne a trial. Bishop Charles Inglis was appalled by the democratic implications of "free pews" (i.e., not assigned according to rank) at Trinity Church, Kingston, New Brunswick. The Maritimes were (and are) susceptible to United States frontier-style revivalism; and from the start the hopes of the élite for a strong, established, Anglican Church were disappointed, despite the appointment in 1787 of Inglis as Bishop of Nova Scotia with jurisdiction over New Brunswick and Quebec, and the setting aside of "clergy reserves" of land in the Maritimes and Upper Canada. Too many Loyalists were Erastian. Élite hopes for an hereditary aristocracy were frustrated, and it was even difficult to live in gentlemanly style. Thus, the very wealthy John Saunders sat on his great estate, the Barony, near Fredericton, unable to attract tenants—men naturally preferred to work their own land.

The single characteristic common to the Loyalists was quarrelsomeness. The old inhabitants could not be expected to relish the intrusion, even if the refugees had been exceptionally reticent. Generally the Loyalists disliked the old inhabitants of Canada whom they considered had been too friendly to the American Revolution. "Languid wretches," said Edward Winslow in New Brunswick; "exulting in their beloved Ignorance," said Jacob Bailey in Nova Scotia; "idle" and "indolent," said Benjamin Marston in the Island of St. John; "the Darkest Corner of the Dominion," said William Smith in Quebec.

But the most bitter quarrels were between Loyalists, usually between the élite and the rest. The tone was set even before the evacuation of New York when a group known as the Fifty-Five, on account of their high social standing, petitioned for special large land grants of 5,000 acres each in Nova Scotia. A howl of protest resulted and the scheme was thwarted. The first New Brunswick election in November 1785 led to rioting in St. John which crystallized two parties: the minority, aristocratic Upper Covers, versus the majority, plebeian Lower Covers. In 1787 Lord Dorchester had to send a committee to investigate Loyalist unrest in the future Upper Canada. The committee reported "a very dangerous Jealousy and want of Confidence ... between the Majority of the settlers and their late officers." In New Brunswick the political dispute culminated in "the Glenie affair," in which James Glenie, a Scottish timber merchant, not a Loyalist, led the opposition to Governor Thomas Carleton and the official clique in Fredericton which in 1792 lost its majority in the assembly. The affair finally turned on whether the council had the constitutional right to interfere with the initiate money bills. From 1795 to 1798 an impasse meant no revenue was collected at all until a compromise allowed both houses to initiate.

In Nova Scotia the situation was complicated by a powerful segment of "old comers," and no real Loyalist party developed. But the Loyalists were in the thick of politics and led a thrust against the council. A Halifax by-election of 1788 was marked by rioting and murder; and, a year later, the Loyalists were charged with rebellion. Order was restored in 1791 when Governor Parr, who had long complained about the Americans—they "almost wish to take over the government"—died and was replaced by a Loyalist, Sir John Wentworth.

W. S. MacNutt, the best historian of the Maritimes, comments on the early political history of Nova Scotia and New Brunswick that it was firmly in the tradition of the former American colonies, that "replicas of the constitutional struggles ... of New York and Massachusetts were ... the common lot of the two provinces."

Now to consider the Loyalist legacy. It must be stressed that only in New Brunswick did the Loyalists remain a majority for very long, and even there they were engulfed by other immigrants after the War of 1812. They and their descendants retained political power almost until Confederation; but from the early years the economy was dominated by Scots. Direct Loyalist influence was much more ephemeral elsewhere in Canada. In Upper Canada by 1812 only one-fifth of the population of 100,000 were Loyalists or their children, although most of the remainder were American-born; these were the so-called "late Loyalists," American frontiersmen who were simply attracted by Governor John G. Simcoe's offer of free land in an area where the land was very good. Many Canadians with no Loyalist background, however, have acquired Loyalist attitudes. For example, John Strachan arrived in Upper Canada from Scotland in 1799 with pro-American convictions, but by 1809 was convinced that "true liberty" did not exist in the United States; later in the nineteenth century in New Brunswick, Protestant Irish immigrants became "Loyalized," a process aided by intermarriage.

The Loyalists helped establish Canada's tradition of a "cultural mosaic," which is held to contrast with America's alleged, homogenizing melting pot. From the start most Loyalists preferred to leave the French alone, and their own settlements were frequently fragmented; for example, in the Upper Canadian Townships Roman Catholic Scots and Presbyterian Scots kept apart. The Loyalist influx also brought many loyal Iroquois, who settled along the Grand River, and a number of black Loyalists who founded settlements in the Maritimes that persist to this day.

The Loyalists and the British government set the political structure of English Canada which was only in embryo in Nova Scotia before 1783. The aim was to avoid the "mistakes" that had caused revolution to the south. New Brunswick may serve as a model that was generally copied. The lower houses were believed to have become too powerful; so the powers of the appointed council and the Governor, who was made financially independent, were strengthened. The élite were encouraged by appointment to the council and government office, and as JPs in the counties—the New England township was scrupulously avoided. The colonial government of New Brunswick was made less dependent on the home-country; more internal self-government was allowed than had been the case in America. Conservative social institutions, like the Church of England, were supported; and with sad memories of Revolutionary agitation in the American cities still vivid, the capital was moved from Saint John to the inland village of Fredericton. (Many Loyalists had a Jeffersonian dislike of commerce and cities.) But the tone in New Brunswick was far from entirely conservative; the British never attempted to tax the North American colonies directly; thus the essential early goal of the Revolution was secured. In the words of W. S. MacNutt, "democracy ran riot in the Loyalist citadel"; the suffrage was for all men, and the city government of Saint John, with its annual elections, was one of the most democratic bodies of its kind in North America. The Revolution not only made Americans free, but also Canadians, who found that "subjects" could be just as happy as "citizens."

French-Canadians owe much to the Loyalists. The Constitutional Act of 1791, partly because of Loyalist agitation, began representative government in Quebec and introduced freehold land tenure. At the same time, the French way of life, including legal and religious systems, was maintained. The Loyalist numbers doomed the French to become a minority; but the Loyalist strength enabled Canada to withstand the onslaught of American imperialism. It is doubtful if French culture could have survived within the American union.

The Loyalist tradition is often decried in Canada because it has been held responsible for the development of aristocratic governing cliques, known as the Family Compacts. In fact, the Family Compacts were not a Loyalist phenomenon. True, in Upper Canada about half of the leading members of the compact were second-generation Loyalists, men like Sir John Beverley Robinson; but Loyalists' descendants were an important component of the opposition, and the rebellion of 1837 similarly found them on both sides. In New Brunswick the Loyalists were also on both sides of the compact question. Lemuel Allen Wilmot, a grandson of a Poughkeepsie Loyalist, led the struggle, successful in 1836, for New Brunswick to gain control of Crown lands, an important landmark on the road to full self-government. During the same period Joseph Howe, whose father was a loyal Massachusetts newspaper editor, played a similar role in leading the forces of Nova Scotia democracy. Nevertheless, the aristocratic British proclivity of some Loyalists and their descendants has frequently gone against the Canadian grain. The tone was set in 1789 when the Quebec Council resolved to have the Loyalists and their posterity discriminated, from future settlers, "giving them a Marke of Honor," the right to put UE (Unity of Empire) after their names, hence the expression United Empire Loyalists.

New Brunswick is *par excellence* the Loyalist province; and a brief account of some influences there may be appropriate. On the positive side, there is a cultural tradition. In 1784 the Loyalists laid the foundations of the University of New Brunswick at Fredericton, where the residence of the poet, Jonathan Odell, began a literary tradition that leads directly to Bliss Carman and others. On the negative side, we find an over-dependence on government, a scramble for office and patronage, a morbid absorption in politics that sapped more wholesome initiative, particularly economic. Writing in this vein in 1904, John Davidson, a Scottish professor, now perhaps understandably forgotten, at the University of New Brunswick, found the Loyalist tradition baleful. He quoted a local: "in this country men think five dollars of government money is worth ten dollars from anybody else," and added that New Brunswick was the only country he knew where professional and business men had to do their legitimate work at night because politics took up the day.

Discussion of the efforts of the Loyalists often centres on explanations of why Canada is so different from the United States. Such items as law, Parliamentary government and the monarchy are obvious; but Canada's relatively peaceful western expansion, and a general lack of lynching, are also listed. It is even argued that several Canadian provinces have elected mild socialist governments during the last few decades because of the Loyalists. More of a class structure was maintained in Canada, and Canadians, far from starting with a distrust of government authority, positively embrace it.

The Loyalists offered a valid critique of the Revolutionary ideals and moral absolutism. The Nova Scotian writer, Thomas C. Haliburton, the grandson of a Loyalist and a popular satirist, had Sam Slick say simply "there is no tyranny on airth equal to the tyranny of a majority." Similar sentiments were expressed by the Reverend Mather Byles, who, watching the hysteria surrounding the funeral of a victim of the Boston "massacre" in 1771, opined: "They call me a brainless Tory; but tell me ... which is better to be ruled by one tyrant three thousand miles away, or by three thousand tyrants one mile away?"

The Loyalists have profoundly influenced Canadian nationalism. They began an abiding love-hate attitude toward the Great Republic. During the War of 1812, by opting out, the Maritimes demonstrated the love; but there was a bitter struggle in Upper Canada. The Loyalists took pride in victory of sort; but more important were the myths and symbols established: the Loyalist militia had beaten the Yankees; Laura Secord had led her cow through the American lines. Fear of the United States has remained, and Unity of Empire has frequently been invoked as a shield, as in the 1880s which witnessed one of several Loyalist revivals.

It is true that there is a certain Canadian dourness resulting from three losing traditions: French, Scottish and Loyalist. But a Canadian poet's description of the latter is also apt:

> Not drooping like poor fugitives they came
> In exodus to our Canadian wilds
> But full of heart and hope, with heads erect
> And fearless eyes victorious in defeat.

Notes

1. For a general account see my article "Escape from the Republic: The Dispersal of the American Loyalists," *History Today,* February, 1972.

2. Detroit, although legally in the United States by the peace treaty of 1783, was not evacuated until after the signing of Jay's Treaty in 1794, when the Loyalists moved across the border into Canada.

PATRIARCHY AND PATERNALISM: THE CASE OF THE EASTERN ONTARIO LOYALIST WOMEN

Janice Potter

Although the American Revolution did not alter the legal or political rights of women, it changed their lives dramatically in other ways.[1] With the men away fighting, women were forced to shoulder the burden of running the farm, the estate, or the business, and as a result there was less rigidity in the sexual division of labour, women gained confidence in their abilities, and men had more respect for women and their contributions to society. Those experiences were reinforced by public recognition of women's contribution to the Revolution and by the ideology of the Revolution. For example, boycotts of British cloth meant that wearing homespun became a sign of patriotism and that spinning, one of the most time-consuming and clearly feminine domestic chores, was raised in status. Moreover, there was an antipatriarchal aspect of the Revolution that fostered less authoritarian and more reciprocal relationships between men and women. Republican ideology, with its emphasis on voluntary consent, also allowed more scope for women. There was "greater mutuality and reciprocity" in marriages and in some cases "more egalitarian marital relationships."[2] The belief in the need to raise a moral and upright citizenry also enhanced the status of motherhood and made it easier for women to obtain an education, since it was they who would be raising the children. The result was more confident, self-reliant women, some of whom decided not to marry, and a society that valued more highly the domestic sphere generally and women specifically.

But what was the situation of Loyalist women, whose actions did not receive the same recognition and for whom there was no equivalent to republican ideology? The existing material on Loyalist women includes books about individuals, papers about specific groups, such as Loyalist women who filed claims for compensation, and an interesting thesis discussing Loyalist women in general terms.[3] This paper, however, considers in a preliminary way the effect of the Revolution on one specific group of Loyalist women—those who lived on the frontiers of New York, New England, and Pennsylvania and eventually settled in the townships created along the St. Lawrence River and Lake Ontario between Longueuil and the Bay of Quinte in what is now eastern Ontario.

Despite the diversity of their ethnic origins, the eastern Ontario Loyalist women shared a common background characterized by paternalism and patriarchy, and their experiences during the Revolution were similar. Virtually all went through several stages in the course of becoming refugees: they were

From *Ontario History*, LXXXI, no. 1 (March 1989), 3–24. Reprinted by permission of the author, the Ontario Historical Society and *Ontario History*.

harassed or persecuted, they were forced to flee to British bases for protection, they lived under British military rule in what might be called refugee camps, and with aid from the British they were eventually resettled.

Information about these women can be found in the few personal letters and diaries that have survived, in the claims Loyalists made for compensation from the British government, and in the records of the Patriot committees that interrogated Loyalists and of the British authorities who had to supervise and provision them. And, from records such as military registers, provisioning lists, returns of Loyalists, and land grants, it is possible to compile a reasonably precise statistical profile of the eastern Ontario Loyalists.

The 1786 census reveals that the 1,800 families, or 4,661 individuals, living along the St. Lawrence River and the eastern end of Lake Ontario were an ethnically diverse group that included many recent immigrants. Of the eastern Ontario Loyalists whose birthplace is known, about 45 per cent were foreign and about 45 per cent American-born.[4] Many of the American-born belonged to ethnic groups that had retained their native language, group cohesiveness, and other aspects of their culture. The largest of the ethnic minorities were the Germans, who accounted for about 30 per cent of the total and of whom one-quarter were immigrants and the rest Americans of German ancestry. About 5 per cent were Dutch, mostly more traditional members of the Dutch Reformed Church who had kept their culture and language.[5] Another group of American-born Loyalists who had retained their distinctive culture were the Mohawk Indians, who had played an important military role in the Revolution.

The largest of the immigrant groups, constituting 24 per cent of the total, were the Scots. Many were Highlanders and Jacobites who had emigrated because of poverty and the enclosure of their lands. In the colonies they retained their Gaelic language, Catholic religion, and other aspects of their culture.[6]

Whether American- or foreign-born, the vast majority of eastern Ontario Loyalists had lived on the frontiers of colonial society and were farmers. Over 70 per cent came from the northern New York counties of Tryon, Charlotte, and Albany. About 2 per cent came from each of New Jersey, Connecticut, and Pennsylvania, and many of the Pennsylvanians were from the frontier settlements along the Susquehanna River.[7] They had all been part of the mass movement to the frontiers after the Seven Years' War.

A common theme in the social relationships of many eastern Ontario Loyalists was paternalism. Paternalism has been variously defined as interference with people's liberty for their own good and as the determination by one person what is in the best interests of another. A paternalistic relationship need not be harsh, however, and can even be cooperative in that it is a close and affectionate relationship in which the dependent party feels the need for guidance and is willing to exchange some independence or security.[8] But in such a relationship there is a hierarchy or at least inequality—there are superiors and subordinates, leaders and followers—and the dominant party feels an obligation to protect the interests of the subordinate in return for loyalty and deference.

Eighteenth-century paternalism was exemplified in the relationship between some New York landlords and their tenants. In spite of the rush to the frontiers for land, not all colonial Americans managed to acquire land of their own. In the case of the eastern Ontario Loyalists, only 20 per cent had held their land in freehold, and some had shared land or squatted on disputed land, but the vast majority had been tenants on the northern New York manorial estates owned by families like the Johnsons; indeed, at least 20 per cent of the Loyalist claimants who settled in what is now eastern Ontario had been tenants of the Johnsons.

The Johnsons ran their 20,000-acre estate like quasi-feudal lords. They helped their tenants financially, burned the debtor bonds of over-extended tenants, and helped artisans like Richard Mandevell, a "Breeches Maker" who later settled in eastern Ontario, establish themselves in the local village. They also built roads, schools, and mills; introduced sheep and new crops; and at Johnstown, the county seat, established a county fair and built the local jail, courthouse, and Anglican church.[9] In return for looking after the interests of their tenants, the Johnsons expected loyalty and deference—letters to them from tenants and others, for example, often began, "May it Please your Lordship." When the Revolution came, the Johnsons' tenants formed an armed guard to protect their landlord, and when he fled to Canada, they followed.[10]

There were also other paternalistic relationships between eastern Ontario Loyalists and various authorities. Many of the colonists, of German Palatinate or French Huguenot ancestry, were Protestants who had fled to England in search of religious freedom and who revered George III as a defender of Protestantism. The Highlanders were accustomed to an authoritarian society, and their family and clan structure was patriarchal. And the Mohawk, although they considered themselves an independent people, spoke of the king as a father and looked to the British government to protect them from the rapaciousness of the powerful New York landlords who spent much of the eighteenth century defrauding the Indians of their land. As they fled the frontiers of the colonies for Canada, the Loyalists who later settled in eastern Ontario did so in groups and as families. This can be seen by comparing them to the immigrants who had come to the colonies in the mid-eighteenth century. As the table below illustrates, 74.3 per cent of the immigrants were male and 25.7 per cent female, whereas 70.6 per cent of the adult eastern Ontario Loyalists were male and 29.4 per cent female.

	Percentage of Males	Percentage of Females
Immigrants	74.3	25.7
Eastern Ontario Loyalists	70.6	29.4

Even these statistics underestimate the female Loyalists in that boys as young as ten belonged to the Loyalist regiments and could be listed as adult male settlers rather than as children, whereas girls of the same age were considered children. Moreover, whereas the number of children per adult female in early eighteenth-century New York had been only 1.88, among eastern Ontario Loyalists there were about 2.4 children per adult woman.[11]

The social and family structure in which these Loyalists and other colonial Americans lived was also patriarchal if we take patriarchy to mean "the manifestation and institutionalization of male dominance over women and children in the family and the extension of male dominance over women in society in general. ... [It] implies that men hold power in all the important institutions of society and that women are deprived of access to such power."[12] Colonial American society was patriarchal in several senses. Women could not participate in the political process, they could not get a higher education, and men controlled the most basic commodity in the society—land. Not only was the title to the family's property in the man's name, but a widow who remarried lost ownership of her property to her new husband. A married woman's identity was subsumed in that of her husband's. "A married couple," in the words of one historian, "became like a legal fiction: like a corporation, the pair was a single person with a single will"—the husband's. Even within the household it was common for the man to make all of the major decisions about finances and even about raising the children, and in any marital separation the man retained custody of the children.[13]

Patriarchal relationships, like paternalistic ones, did not mean that there could not be affection between husband and wife. To cite one example, a 1776 letter from Alexander McDonald, a captain in the Royal Highland Emigrants stationed in Halifax, to his wife in the colonies began, "My dear Susannah" and ended tenderly, "I have no time to write more. ... Kiss the children for me and believe the one forever to be yours." Yet the patriarchal nature of the relationship was revealed in the instructions he gave her about all aspects of her life: "Keep the Child always clean and well dress'd and you must appear in yr best Colours yourself." Of a fellow soldier, he wrote, "Keep the old gentleman always at a distance from you and never let him again appear in the House."[14]

The subordination of women in the colonial American family was revealed in the diary of Dothe Stone, sister of the eastern Ontario Loyalist, Joel Stone. As Dothe's list of births illustrates, marriage and childbirth were central to women's lives. The average woman was married in her early twenties to a man from one to five years older; she could expect to be pregnant within twelve months, and her childbearing years became a cycle of pregnancy, birth, and lactation.[15]

The birth and care of children, combined with women's other tasks, meant that their life centred on the home. The family farm was the basic economic and social unit on the frontier, and although some women did have to help with clearing and farming the land, women's jobs were more often milking the cows, taking care of the chickens, planting and tending the garden, and harvesting the orchard. As well, they cared for the house, salted beef and pork, preserved fruit and stored vegetables, made cider and cheese, and dried apples. A major chore was making clothing: Dothe writes of spending days with her sisters at spinning wheels. Whereas her husband might get away from home by going fishing or hunting or by travelling to town for supplies or to do business, the woman, especially if she had small children (which was almost always), was tied to the home.[16]

Colonial women found security in what was familiar to them—their homes, their families, and their circle of community friends and relatives. Dothe wrote fondly of her favourite room, her "once loved chamber," and her diary is full of excitement when describing social events, such as weddings, or gatherings at which a fiddler led the party in singing and dancing. Dothe also relied heavily on female companionship. Tasks like spinning were done in the company of other women; women helped each other in childbirth and child rearing, and most of them lived in the same house as, or close to, other female relatives. Some of Dothe Stone's sweetest memories were of times spent with her sisters: "Sunday afternoon Sister Hannah and I have been walking to the far part of Davis' South lots, being very tyred, I lyed down under a pretty bush, I tied my long pocket handkerchief about my head, and took a stone for a pillow and never did I rest more sweetly, while Sister Hannah set by me making some excellent verses about the gracefullness of my appearance."[17] Home, family, and female companionship were what mattered most to colonial women.

Patriarchy was also evident in the Stone family. Whether unmarried and living in her father's or brother's house, or married and in her husband's, Dothe Stone's life was run by men. Her brother, whom she lived with for nine years, "supported and directed" her and made all the decisions, including the one to move, without consulting her. The image of the father as patriarch was captured by Dothe when she described "my Dad an old gentleman ... in the other room with a large family of likely children gathering round and looking to him for support."[18]

Relationships within the colonial family were patriarchal, and even women themselves spoke of their own inferiority and dependence. Widows, like the strong-minded Patriot, Mary Fish, for example, described themselves as "a poor weak and helpless creature, [who] could do nothing but lie at the foot of mercy and look for direction." "What," she asked rhetorically, "Could a feble [*sic*] woman do."[19] Statements like these do not necessarily mean that women inwardly accepted the notion of their helplessness and inferiority. What they do mean, however, is that the social norms were such that women felt the need to express their feminine dependence and weakness.

But the notions of female helplessness and dependence were brought into question by the Revolution, which posed new challenges for Patriot *and* Loyalist women and forced many to adopt new roles. To Loyalist women, attached to their homes and local surroundings, accustomed to the security of friends, relatives and neighbours, and used to relying on men to direct their lives and make important decisions for them, the Revolution was a shattering experience. Patriot women, it is true, were left to manage the family and farm or business in their husbands' absence; but at least most remained in their homes and communities. Many Loyalist women, however, lost everything they valued most. Their families were scattered and the men who had directed their lives, gone. Many were also wrenched from all that was familiar—their homes, their relatives, and their communities. What all Loyalist women shared was their experiences as refugees, which were far more challenging than those of most Patriot women.

The pattern was set in May 1776, when Sir John Johnson fled from his northern New York estate with 170 tenants to escape arrest by the Patriots and to seek refuge in Canada, leaving behind his wife, Lady Mary Watts Johnson, who was pregnant and already the mother of two children under two. Mary, or Polly, who was from a prosperous New York city merchant and banking family, had married Sir John in 1773 at the age of nineteen and moved north to live in Tryon County. When her husband fled, Polly could not accompany him because of her condition, the hastiness of his departure, and the extraordinary rigours of the trip. Disappointed at the escape of Sir John, the Patriots forced her to turn over the keys to "every place"; her husband's private papers were seized, his "books distributed about the country," and their home, Johnson Hall, plundered and "made a Barrack." Lady Johnson was held hostage in Albany, although she was in touch regularly with her husband through "Indian and white men ... sent through the Woods." After some twenty months in captivity, Lady Johnson escaped, travelling through enemy territory in the cold winter. Although she finally reached the British base in New York City, her youngest child died as a result of its traumatic experiences.[20]

Within months of Lady Johnson's escape the war that was to rage on the frontier for more than four years began, and the hostages in this vicious conflict were the women and the children. As the Patriots attempted to assert their control over the region by forcing suspected Loyalists to take oaths of allegiance or join the militia, many able-bodied Loyalist men were either arrested or followed Sir John Johnson's lead by escaping to British lines, reluctantly leaving their families behind. Once in Canada, most had to join the various Loyalist regiments that collaborated with the Indians to launch retaliatory raids on the American frontier. For the British, the raids had a military purpose: to harass the enemy and destroy food supplies for Patriot forces. For many Loyalist soldiers, the raids were an opportunity to seek revenge on their foes in the colonies, find new recruits, make contact with their families, and occasionally bring the families back to Canada. For the families, the raids complicated their already troubled lives by intensifying Patriot hatred of the Loyalists and compromising them even further, since the families often harboured or helped the raiding parties. As the raiding parties retreated to the safety of Canada, they left their families behind.[21]

With the men in their lives gone, Loyalist women were forced to assume new responsibilities, and some even actively engaged in the war effort. For example, three women were implicated in a plot to kidnap the mayor of Albany, and one, an Indian woman, confessed to having lured the mayor to the woods by reporting that she had found a dead body there.[22] Another woman was arrested and jailed along with twenty men for "having assisted in the destruction of Currey Town."[23] Women were arrested and some imprisoned for taking part in robberies, which were especially common at the manor of Rensselaerwyck in the late 1770s.[24] Loyalist women also provided intelligence and passed messages between the British in New York City and Canada.[25]

Two eastern Ontario Loyalist women who were unusually active in the war effort were associated with the Mohawk Indians. This is not surprising in light of the status of women in the matrilineal Mohawk society, where children belonged to the mother's rather than the father's clan and women chose and deposed the chiefs. The local economy of the predominantly agrarian Mohawk was controlled by the women, who were responsible for planting, harvesting, and distributing the crops. Mohawk matrons were also influential in war councils and in determining the fate of captives.[26]

One very influential Mohawk woman was Molly Brant, or Konwatsi'tsianienni. A member of a high-ranking Mohawk family, sister of the famous Mohawk chief, Joseph Brant, and a matron who had a great influence in the matrilineal Iroquois society, Molly Brant "was a person of great prestige in her nation and throughout the Confederacy." Her power and influence were heightened after 1759, when she became the wife in all but name of Sir William Johnson, superintendent of Indian affairs, with whom she had eight children. Equally at home in the Indian village, in the war council, as the charming and gracious hostess at Johnson Hall, or in running Johnson's huge estate during his frequent absences, Molly Brant was a remarkable woman.[27]

She helped many Loyalists escape to Canada, provided intelligence to the British, and played a decisive part in fostering the ties of loyalty, self-interest, and history that underpinned the Mohawk support for the British during the Revolution. After her home was plundered by the Patriots and she was forced to flee with her family to the safety of the Iroquois villages, Brant came to Canada in 1778 and moved from one British base to another, cementing the Mohawks' loyalty to the British. Daniel Claus, Indian agent and son-in-law of the late Sir William Johnson, said of Molly Brant, "One word from her is more taken notice of by the five nations than a thousand from any white man without Exception." The commanding officer at Carleton Island attributed the good behaviour of the Indians there to Brant's influence: "The Chiefs were careful to keep their people sober and satisfy'd, but their uncommon good behaviour is in a great Measure to be ascribed to Miss Molly Brant's influence over them, which is far superior to that of all their Chiefs put together, and she has in the course of this Winter done every thing in Her power to maintain them strongly in the King's interest." Brant's stature was recognized by the British government, which awarded her one of the largest pensions ever given to any Indian and built her a house at present-day Kingston, where she spent her last years.[28]

Another woman influential among the Mohawk was Sarah Kast McGinnis, an American-born Palatinate German, who as a child in northern New York lived with the Mohawks, was adopted by them, and learned their language. In the 1740s Sarah married an Irishman, Timothy McGinnis, who became involved with Sir William Johnson in the fur trade and as a captain in the Indian Department. After her husband was killed in the Seven Years' War, the widow McGinnis carried on his trading business.[29]

When the Revolution broke out, both sides courted Sarah because of her close association with the Iroquois, the Patriots offering her twelve shillings York currency a day and a guard of fifteen men. But Sarah and her family sided with the British and worked to cement the Iroquois' loyalty, actions that caused them to be persecuted by the Patriots. In 1777, as news spread of Burgoyne's expedition from Canada through northern New York, the Patriots considered it necessary to neutralize Loyalists like Sarah and her family. In Sarah's case, this involved arresting her son-in-law and then confiscating all her property. Sarah, her daughters, and grandchildren watched helplessly as their belongings were sold at public auction; they were then arrested and "so harshly used" that one granddaughter died. When the Patriots mistakenly concluded that the British had the upper hand in the region, Sarah and her family were released. Before they could be recaptured, they "escaped at night with only what they could carry on their backs" and left for Canada with British troops, although Sarah had to leave behind a son "who was out of his senses and bound in chains ... and who some time afterward was burnt alive."[30]

After arriving in Canada, Sarah agreed to a British request to return to northern New York, winter with the Iroquois, and try to counter the harmful effects of Burgoyne's defeat. On her arrival at "the most central village of the Six nations," the Indians "flocked to her from the remotest villages and thanked her for coming ... to direct and advise them in that critical time." Soon after her arrival, the Patriots sent messages to the Iroquois, "with a most exaggerated account of General Burgoyne's disaster" and "belts," inviting them to join the Patriots along with "threats" in case the Indians refused. In response to the Patriot overtures, the Indians "consulted with" Sarah and sought her "opinion and advice": "Then after that with an Authority and privilege allowed to women of Consequence only among Indians, [she] seized upon and cancelled the [Patriot] Belts, telling them such bad news came from an evil Spirit and must endanger their peace and union as long as it was in their sight and therefore must be buried underground."[31] When Sarah spent this long and difficult winter in the Indian villages, she was sixty-four years old.

Although Sarah Kast McGinnis's relationship with the Indians and her active participation in the Revolution were extraordinary, her other experiences were typical of those of other Loyalist women. As able-bodied Loyalist men on the frontiers either were arrested or fled, leaving their families behind, the sins of the fathers and husbands were visited on the wives and children. Patriot committees and mobs assumed, unless there was evidence to the contrary, that families were accomplices in the guilt of one member. If one member of a family fled or was arrested, the rest were vulnerable either to official interrogation by committees or to unofficial harassment by mobs or Patriot neighbours.

The case of the Cartwright family was not unusual. The father, Richard, Sr., a prosperous innkeeper landowner, and deputy postmaster of Albany, had shown his support for the Patriots in 1775 when he gave money to the Patriot expedition against Ticonderoga. But his daughter, Elizabeth, who was married to a British soldier and lived in Niagara, was in touch with his son, Richard, Jr., and when the local committee of correspondence discovered this in February 1777, it forced Richard, Jr., to give security for his future good behaviour. By October 1777 he could no longer give this guarantee, and with his young niece, Hannah, he left on a difficult journey through the northern New York wilderness to Canada. The parents, tainted by the Loyalism of their children, were mistreated, their property was confiscated, and within a year of their son's departure they were taken under guard to the border.[32]

The Cartwrights' experiences were shared by many Loyalist women who had to live with the consequences of their husbands' actions. With the men in their lives gone, the women not only had to assume responsibility for running the farm and taking care of their families, but also had to deal with Patriot harassment or persecution and in many cases they were forced to leave their homes to seek refuge behind the British lines. When Garnet Dingman, who was a squatter on land on the Susquehanna River, joined the British in 1781, he left his cattle, utensils, and furniture to his wife and friends; however, shortly after his departure, the "rebels," in the words of an observer, "stript [his wife] of every thing." Another Susquehanna River squatter was Jane Glasford, whose "husband was to [sic] old to serve, but he sent his Sons to serve" with Joseph Brant, whose troops took some of their stock and grain. Jane described what happened to her and her husband because of their son's military service: "The Rebels came in '79 & plundered them, & stript them of everything. She was almost starvd in her own house. They were all obliged to come away. ... Their house was burnt as soon as they left it." A similar fate was meted out to Mary Waldec, wife of a tenant in Tryon country who fled to Canada with Sir John Johnson in 1776. In 1777 the "rebels ... took most" of her "things ... and sold them at Vendue," and later Mary fled to Canada.[33] The wife of Philip Empy, who had refused to sign a Patriot oath and whose sons had joined the British, was jailed along with her children and then "beat," "abused" by four men, and left on the road. Friends rescued her, but she died soon after.[34]

The severity of the treatment meted out to Loyalist women depended on their husbands' connections and reputation among the dominant faction in the community. The case of two Vermont Loyalist women illustrates this point. Sarah Bottum was the wife of Justus Sherwood, a Vermont landowner, speculator, and entrepreneur in the timber business. Originally from Connecticut,

Justus had received his land in Vermont from the New Hampshire government, and he supported Ethan Allen and his brothers, the dominant faction in
the disputed territory. When Justus fell afoul of the local Patriots for refusing
to take an oath of allegiance and allegedly corresponding with the British, he was
threatened with execution and imprisoned, although he escaped and fled to
Canada. The Patriots ransacked the Sherwoods' cabin and destroyed some of
their belongings, but Sarah could look to her parents for help, and she was allowed to remain in Vermont until she decided to seek permission from the
Patriots to join her husband in Canada.[35]

The treatment of another Vermont Loyalist, Mary Munro, was much harsher
because her husband belonged to an unpopular faction in Vermont. John Munro,
originally from Scotland, had been granted large tracts of land by New York, and
this put him at odds with the dominant faction in Vermont, whose land grants
came from New Hampshire. Munro became even more unpopular when he was appointed justice of the peace and given the unenviable task of imposing law and
order on Ethan Allen and the Green Mountain Boys, who harassed New Yorkers
in Vermont. When the Revolution came and Munro supported the British, the
Council of Safety drove him from his home and seized all his property, except "a few
personal articles left for the support of his wife." Unlike Sarah Sherwood, who
had the support of her family, Mary Munro was treated very harshly by her neighbours and shunned by her own family. She wrote to her husband of her plight:

> I am in a poor state of health and very much distresst. I must leave my house
> in a very short time and God knows where I shall get a place to put my head in,
> for my own relations are my greatest enemies. ... They have distrest me be-
> yond expression. I have scarcely a mouthful of bread for myself or children. ...
> Is there no possibility of your sending for us? If there is no method fallen upon
> we shall all perish, for you can have no idea of our sufferings here ... my heart
> is so full it is ready to break.

Luckily, Mary Munro and her eight children did make their way to Canada
within a few months of this letter.[36]

Flight may have represented an end to persecution for many Loyalist
women; yet, it was also difficult for them to leave their homes and cut their
ties with their families, friends, and communities. Simon Schwartz, the son of
tenants of the Johnson family, who described his father's flight to Canada with
Sir John in 1776 and the harassment of other family members, stressed that his
mother had left only when she had to; she "would not come in [to Canada] before the House & builds [*sic*] were burnt." Women like Mrs. Schwartz usually had
no choice but to leave. If they left voluntarily, it was usually because their property had been confiscated or their homes destroyed and there were no relatives
or neighbours to protect them.

Some Loyalist women simply fled, but many others sought permission to
leave from Patriot committees. Either permission was granted and the women
escorted to the frontiers, or they were exchanged for Patriot prisoners being

held in Canada. Mary Cruger Meyers had been alone with seven children under thirteen since the summer of 1777, when her husband, John Walden Meyers, left to join Burgoyne. In October 1778 she and another Loyalist woman requested permission to go to New York.[37] After being dispossessed of their property, the wives of Loyalists in Tryon County petitioned the local Patriot committee to be either taken care of or allowed to join their husbands. Their latter request was eventually granted.[38] When women left, they could only take children under twelve with them; boys twelve and over were considered capable of bearing arms and had to be left behind.[39] Those going to British lines also had to pay all the costs of being escorted there and take fourteen days' provisions with them.[40]

By the late 1770s, however, many Loyalist women were forced to leave. Some were sent to Canada because they were destitute and "subsisted at public Expense." A more common reason for removing the women was that they had assisted the enemy. When their husbands, relatives, or friends returned to the frontiers from Canada to gather intelligence, to recruit, or to raid, the women provided food, shelter, and other forms of assistance, which only further incriminated them in the eyes of the Patriots. Rachel Ferguson and her daughters, for example, were brought before the local Patriot committee in 1779 "for harbouring and entertaining a Number of Tories who came down from Canada with an inte[n]tion of Murdering the Defenceless Inhabitants on the Western Frontiers."[41] For their efforts the Ferguson women were jailed and later forced to leave.

By July 1780 it was official policy in New York to "remove families of persons who [had] joined the Enemy." The families were given twenty days to prepare for their departure, their goods and chattels were to be sold to pay the costs, and any who ignored the edict were to "be liable to be proceeded against as Enemies of this and the United States."[42] Some women asked for and received a reprieve; but this required that "sundry well affected inhabitants" had to testify that the woman had "behaved herself in a becoming manner."[43] In other words, it was up to the woman to prove innocence by having well-known Patriots testify on her behalf. In the absence of such testimony, the woman was assumed to share the guilt of her husband.

Exile was the last stage in a process that profoundly altered the role and responsibilities of many Loyalist women. Like their Patriot counterparts, Loyalist women assumed the responsibility for running the household and farm in the absence of their husbands. But Loyalist women also had to endure harassment, persecution, and often poverty because of the actions of their husbands. Most difficult of all, perhaps, was the necessity of abandoning their homes, relatives, and communities.

In facing these adversities, women were often forced to assert themselves and assume what were generally considered to be male responsibilities. The more public and assertive role of women was illustrated by Polly Watts Johnson, who had the audacity, after being captured by the Patriots, to write directly to General George Washington to complain of being treated "with severity."[44] When an exchange had to be arranged for the prominent New York Loyalist Alexander White, it was his wife who undertook the negotiations with the British. Isabel Parker, who had "aided and succoured his Majesty's Scouts on secret service by procuring them provisions and intelligence and encouraging Sundry persons to join his Majesty's service at her great expense, peril and risk," interceded with the governor of Quebec on behalf of her son, who had been in the British secret service and had been arrested by the Patriots. Mrs. Jeremiah French, whose husband had joined the British and had all his property confiscated and his "cattle driven away and sold," was brought to the attention of the Vermont governor and council because she was "very turbulent and troublesome and refused to obey orders." Known for her "bitter tongue," Mrs. French proved so troublesome that the Patriots dispatched her to the British lines.[45]

Women were also forced to take more responsibility for looking after themselves and families. A group of New York Loyalist women who had established themselves near Saratoga petitioned the Patriots in 1780 for permission to go to Canada; in 1781 they were still on the frontier and regarded as a serious enough threat that they were ordered to move to the interior. The sixteen-year-old daughter of John McDonell, a Scots Loyalist from Tryon county, "was obliged to hire herself to an old Dutch woman to spin in order to prevent starving." And there was the case of Elizabeth Bowman, who, after her house on the Susquehanna River had been sacked by the Patriots and her husband and eldest son carried off, was left to care for eight children. The Indians helped them through the winter, and in the spring she moved to the Mohawk River and joined other Loyalist women to grow corn and potatoes. When the British rescued them in the fall and took them to Canada, there were five women, thirty-one children, and one pair of shoes.[46]

Exile marked the end of one stage of Loyalist women's refugee experience and the beginning of another. The women had left the American colonies as disaffected citizens considered a threat to the security of the new nation. In British territory they were burdens, mouths to be fed and bodies to be clothed and housed. When they reached Canada, they were usually destitute and the British unprepared for their arrival. In 1777 an officer in Niagara described the refugees flocking to that base: "They are almost naked and have been so long hiding in the woods, and almost famished that it is distressing to behold them.... I am informed that 50 are on their way, but so weak they can scarcely crawl. I wish your excellency's direction on how to dispose of them."[47] From Crown Point, a base at the other end of the outer perimeter of British defences, came similar accounts of the arrival of Loyalists who "had fled from persecution," especially in the winter when the lakes and rivers could be crossed by sleigh. Often British officials were uncertain what to do with the refugees, and families arriving in Niagara were often sent on to Montreal.[48]

When the women arrived at the bases, they were in need of food, clothing, and shelter. Most had been stripped of their property and many of their possessions before their flight. The journey itself across the wilderness of northern New York was gruelling. Reaching Canada involved either crossing one of the many lakes in an open boat or perhaps a sleigh in winter, or travelling along rugged trails since "there [was] no road by land to go with a carriage." Sir John Johnson and his tenants who fled from northern New York in 1776 travelled for nineteen days, during which they almost starved, going nine days without provisions, except "wild onions, Roots and the leaves of beech trees." When they reached Canada, their shoes were worn through and their clothes ragged.[49]

Sarah Bottum Sherwood's greatest ordeal during the Revolution was her trip to Canada, which began with a wagon ride over trails to the shores of Lake Champlain. Next was a boat trip across the lake and a thirty-mile trek through the bush to the closest British outpost. When Sarah undertook the trek, it was November; she had with her a slave, a child of three, and a baby; and she was seven months pregnant. But she succeeded and was reunited with her husband.[50]

When Loyalists arrived at British bases, penniless and exhausted by the rigours of their journey, they were at the mercy of paternalistic and patriarchal British military regimes. Even Sarah McGinnis, the tough sixty-four- year-old who had wintered with the Iroquois in 1777, was "in dire need" in Montreal the following year. Her daughter was "so scantily lodged" that her mother could not stay with her. She was also refused firewood by the officer in charge, who said that only the Governor could make such a decision. Sarah and her family were left "without any money or income except what they could earn by the needle."[51] Thus, Loyalists had to look to the British government to provide shelter, clothing, and rations and at the end of the war to chart their future.

The British government took care of its charges but expected deference and service in return. The British regimes were military ones that dealt quickly and harshly with dissenters. In return for their keep, men had to fight in the Loyalist regiments and women had to do washing and other domestic chores for the army. Questioning of the regime was neither common nor tolerated. When a group of Loyalists in Quebec petitioned the governor for more aid, for example, they were informed that if the governor's plans for them were not acceptable, they could go to Nova Scotia.[52]

Patriarchy and paternalism were also apparent in the last phase of the Loyalists' experience—their resettlement in what is now eastern Ontario. Under the direction of British officials, the Loyalists were transported into the interior and provided with food, clothing, agricultural equipment, and seeds. They were settled on land surveyed by British officials, and British army officers were there to preserve order and ensure that the governor's instructions were obeyed. Although the new communities were on the frontier, from the beginning there was a structure and hierarchy. In a society where land ownership was central to status, the size of one's land grant varied according to one's military rank, the British government compensated Loyalists for their losses on the basis of the value of their former assets in the American colonies, and Loyalist officers received half pay after their regiments were disbanded.[53]

Thus, when Loyalist women reached British lines, they were reintegrated into a paternalistic and patriarchal power structure. Within this paternalistic order there was a hierarchy. There were those who needed to be cared for and those responsible for administering the care, those in leadership roles and those who were clearly subordinates. Deference to authority was built into the military regimes, and deference was accorded to those dispensing benevolent care and expected of those receiving it. Even more so than the civil regimes in the American colonies, the military regimes in Quebec and New York City had no place for women and even shunned them as extra mouths to be fed and families to be housed. Women could only fit into such paternalistic and patriarchal power structures as subordinates needing care and protection.

This subordination was reflected in the Loyalist women's petitions for rations, subsistence, or compensation for losses. The very act of petitioning those in authority for aid cast all Loyalists in the role of supplicant; "the formulation of a petition," in the words of Linda Kerber, "begins in the acknowledgement of subordination."[54] Moreover, many Loyalist petitions were stylized litanies of loyalty, service, and sacrifice. But there was a difference in the substance of women's petitions: women based their claim to British assistance on their feminine frailty and on the service of their husbands. In fact, some did not even petition on their own behalf but had men request aid for them. When Catherine Peck, wife of one of Sir John's tenants who had fled to Canada in 1776, arrived in New York City "in hope of getting a Passage to Canada" and found herself and her child "destitute of any Sort of Support," it was an official from Indian Affairs who appealed to British officials to assist her.[55] Even Molly Brant, who had been so active in maintaining the loyalty of the Mohawk, had to seek male help when it came to approaching the British for support. She sought advice from her brother in 1779, and in 1780 two members of the Johnson clan and another associate discussed helping Molly and her daughters to get a pension from the British.[56] Of the twenty-six eastern Ontario Loyalist women who sought compensation from the British for their losses, four had men file their claims.[57]

Whether Loyalist women petitioned themselves or had others do it for them, what was stressed was their weakness, helplessness, and dependence. Citing a "numerous, small and helpless family" as his main burden, one Loyalist appealed to the governor of Quebec for subsistence, while another asked for aid for his "chargeable family." The Loyalist Jean McConell summed up perfectly the notion of female incapacity when she described herself as "feeble" and added that she also had "a family of daughters."[58] Feeble and helpless were the adjectives used most often by Loyalist women to describe themselves.[59]

These professions of feebleness were very much at odds with Loyalist women's recent experiences. The case of Phoebe Grant, or Grout, illustrates this point nicely. When her husband and son joined Burgoyne in 1777, the "rebels" seized his property and "effects" and turned her "and three helpless Female children Out of Doors destitute." She then had to "fly" to Quebec "for protection." Within days of her arrival in Quebec, her husband drowned and she was "obliged to provide for herself and her three children without an allowance from government which ceased on the death of her husband." After her husband's death she did "everything in her power to support herself," even though she was "in a country far from a single Friend and a stranger to the language." When Phoebe finally had to throw "herself and poor family at your Excellency's feet praying" for subsistence, she could not revel in her accomplishments and seek praise for even surviving such ordeals; all she could do was tell her story as a tale of suffering and depict herself, in her own words, as "a Feeble Woman."[60]

Why did Loyalist women describe themselves as feeble or helpless when their recent experiences suggested just the opposite? One reason was a practical reality. What the British needed from the Loyalists were able-bodied males to raid the frontiers, spy on the Patriots, bring in new recruits, supply British troops, or build fortifications. What they did not need or want was women and children, who, it was assumed, could perform none of these services and would be a burden to the British because they had to be fed, clothed, and housed. Thus, the only way for women to appeal to the British was to cite their husband's valued services, rather than their own undervalued ones, and to invoke the paternalism of the military regimes by stressing their vulnerability and need for protection.

Another reason, however, was that when they reached British lines, Loyalist women confronted a well-defined power structure in which there were clearly prescribed social roles. In the colonies during the Revolution, traditional relationships were disrupted and lines of authority far from clear. Women could and did do things they might have never dreamed of doing in peacetime, and their actions were of necessity considered socially acceptable, if only because the boundaries of socially acceptable behaviour are more flexible in wartime. However, at British bases lines of authority were not only clear, but were better defined than they had been in the colonies. Though there had been elements of paternalism and patriarchy in the pre-Revolutionary experiences of many Ontario Loyalists, the British regimes were much more patriarchal and paternal. And women could fit into such a power structure only as frail subordinates.

But the fact that women used the language of enfeeblement does not mean that they themselves accepted their own weakness. They were supplicants who had to petition for assistance and "the rhetoric of humility is a necessary part of the petition as a genre, whether or not humility is felt in fact."[61] Women had no choice but to stress their dependence and helplessness; whether they actually believed it is another matter.

Yet, whether or not women accepted their own weakness is beside the point. The language they used expressed accurately their position in the power structure. Whether or not they were weak and dependent, they were assumed to be so for all public purposes and were outwardly treated as such. On the other hand, the consistent use of certain words cannot be divorced from one's attitudes about oneself: if women were forced by circumstances to reiterate their helplessness again and again, how long was it before they came either to accept that helplessness was basic to their femininity or to allow their actions to be limited by their supposed weakness? The fact that the eastern Ontario Loyalist women were never allowed to speak of their achievements with pride meant that they never received in any measure the recognition accorded to Patriot women.

It is ironic that many eastern Ontario Loyalist women, though they overcame greater obstacles and met more devastating challenges during the Revolution than their Patriot counterparts, received less recognition. As well as having to take charge of their families and farms in the absence of their husbands, Loyalist women were dispossessed of their property, thrown out of their houses, and even jailed by the Patriots. They had to leave what was most dear to them—their homes, their relatives, and their friends—and travel through the wilderness to the British lines.

Yet these remarkable and heroic accomplishments were never recognized. When they reached British lines, they had to fit once again into a patriarchal power structure in which their inferiority and dependence were assumed. Needing British support, they had to stress their dependence and weakness to appeal to the paternalism of the British regime. Only their suffering and their husband's service counted with the British. Whereas republicanism at least potentially offered more scope to women, paternalism assumed inequality and deference. There were the weak and the strong, the leaders and the followers. Within such a framework, women could only be the weak followers.

Not only were the accomplishments of eastern Ontario Loyalist women not recognized by the British; they were also ignored by later generations. After the Revolution, myths grew up about the Loyalists' undying devotion to the British Empire or their upper class backgrounds, and tales were told of the men's heroism. Virtually ignored, however, were the heroic feats of the Loyalist women. Whereas the contributions of Patriot women, such as their spinning of homespun cloth, became part of the American folklore, the memories of the *travails* and victories of the eastern Ontario Loyalist women died with them.

These women were also ignored by Canadian historians, who, by focusing on the Revolutionary war on the frontier as it was run by the British and fought by the Loyalist regiments, have overlooked the essential fact that the war was a civil war in which women and children were of necessity participants. The experiences of the eastern Ontario Loyalist women and their part in the civil war that raged on the frontiers are an important part of Canadian history. Recognition of their accomplishments is long overdue.

Notes

1. Mary Beth Norton, *Liberty's Daughters: The Revolutionary Experience of American Women, 1760–1800* (Boston: Little, Brown, 1980); Linda Kerber, *Women of the Republic: Intellect and Ideology in Revolutionary America* (Chapel Hill, N.C.: Univ. of North Carolina Press, 1980). For another view, see Joan Hoff Wilson, "The Illusion of Change: Women and the American Revolution," In Alfred F. Young, ed., *The American Revolution: Explorations in the History of American Radicalism* (DeKalb: Northern Illinois Univ. Press, 1976), pp. 383–446.

2. Jay Fliegelman, *Prodigals and Pilgrims: The American Revolution against Patriarchal Authority, 1750–1800* (Cambridge: Cambridge Univ. Press, 1982); Norton, *Liberty's Daughters*, pp. 235, 229; Jacqueline S. Reinier, "Rearing the Republican Child: Attitudes and Practices in Post-Revolutionary Philadelphia," *William and Mary Quarterly*, 3rd ser., 39 (1982), 150–63.

3. See, for example, Mary Beacock Fryer, "Sarah Sherwood: Wife and Mother, an 'Invisible Loyalist'," in *Eleven Exiles: Accounts of Loyalists of the American Revolution*, Phyllis R. Blakely and John N. Grant, eds. (Toronto: Dundurn, 1982), pp. 245–64; Mary Beth Norton, "Eighteenth-Century American Women in Peace and War: The Case of the Loyalists," *William and Mary Quarterly*, 3rd ser., 33 (1976), 386–409; Katherine M.J. McKenna, " 'Treading the Hard Road': Some Loyalist Women and the American Revolution" (M.A. thesis, Queen's Univ., 1979).

4. M.S. Waltman, "From Soldier to Settler: Patterns of Loyalist Settlement in 'Upper Canada,' 1783–1785" (M.A. thesis, Queen's Univ., 1981), p. 58.

5. Waltman, "From Soldier to Settler," p. 60; Walter Allen Knittle, *Early Eighteenth Century Palatinate Emigration: A British Government Redemptioner Project to Manufacture Naval Stores* (Baltimore: Dorrance, 1937): Eula C. Lapp, *To Their Heirs Forever* (Picton: Picton Publishing Co., 1970); Alice P. Kenney, *Stubborn for Liberty: The Dutch in New York* (Syracuse: Syracuse Univ. Press, 1975); "The Albany Dutch: Loyalists and Patriots," *New York History*, 42 (1961).

6. Waltman, "From Soldier to Settler," p. 62; I.C.C. Graham, *Colonists from Scotland: Emigration to North America, 1707–1783* (Ithaca: Cornell Univ. Press, 1956); Hazel C. Mathews, *The Mark of Honour* (Toronto: Univ. of Toronto Press, 1965).

7. Waltman, "From Soldier to Settler." pp. 39–42.

8. Gerald Dworkin, "Paternalism," in Rolf Sartorious, ed., *Paternalism* (Minneapolis: Univ. of Minnesota Press. 1983), pp. 19–34; Donald Van De Veer, *Paternalistic Intervention: The Moral Bounds of Benevolence* (Princeton: Princeton Univ. Press, 1986), pp. 16–23; John Kleinig, *Paternalism* (Totow, N.J.: Rowman and Allaneld, 1984). pp. 4–5; Jack D. Douglas, "Cooperative Paternalism versus Conflictual Paternalism," in Sartorius, *Paternalism*, pp. 171–200; David Roberts. *Paternalism in Early Victorian England* (New Brunswick, N.J.: Rutgers Univ. Press, 1979), pp. 4–6.

9. Abbott Collection, Ms. 420, Letter and Reference for Richard Mandevell, Sir William Johnson, June 11, 1771. Quoted in Robert William Venables, "Tryon County, 1775–1783: A Frontier in Revolution" (Ph.D. thesis, Vanderbilt Univ., 1967), pp. 72, 64; Edward Countryman, *A People in Revolution: The American Revolution and Political Society* (Baltimore: Johns Hopkins Univ. Press, 1981), pp. 21, 33.

10. Countryman, *A People in Revolution,* p. 33.

11. Bernard Bailyn, *Voyagers to the West: A Passage in the Peopling of America on the Eve of the Revolution* (New York: Knopf, 1986), pp. 192–234; National Archives of Canada [hereafter NAC], *Haldimand Papers,* [hereafter HP], MG 21, B 168, p. 100, "Return of Loyalists, October, 1784"; Robert V. Wells, *The Population of the British Colonies in America before 1776* (Princeton: Princeton Univ. Press, 1975), p. 315.

12. Gerda Lerner, *The Creation of Patriarchy* (New York: Oxford Univ. Press, 1986), p. 239.

13. Kerber, *Women of the Republic,* p. 120; Joan R. Gundersen and Gwen Victor Gampel, "Married Women's Legal Status in Eighteenth-Century New York and Virginia," *William and Mary Quarterly,* 3rd ser., 39 (1982), 114–34.

14. NAC, Fraser Papers, MG 23, B 33, Alexander McDonald to his wife, in "Letters Extracted from the Letter Book of Capt. Alexander McDonald of the Royal Highland Emigrants written from Halifax, Windsor and Cornwallis between 1775 and 1779."

15. Archives of Ontario [hereafter AO], Joel Stone Papers, Dothe Stone Diary, 1777–1792 [hereafter Stone Diary]; Joy Day Buel and Richard Buel, Jr., *The Way of Duty: A Woman and her Family in Revolutionary America* (New York: Norton, 1984); Robert V. Wells, "Quaker Marriage Patterns in a Colonial Perspective," in Nancy F. Cott and Elizabeth Peck, eds., *A Heritage of Her Own: Toward a New Social History of American Women* (New York: Simon and Shuster, 1979), pp. 81–106; Norton, *Liberty's Daughters,* pp. 71–72; Laurel Thatcher Ulrich, *Good Wives: Image and Reality in the Lives of Women in Northern New England, 1650–1750* (New York: Knopf, 1982).

16. See, for example, Stone Diary; Norton, *Liberty's Daughters,* pp. 3–14.

17. Stone Diary, Oct. 22, 1783, p. 5; May 30, 1784, p. 11.

18. Stone Diary, Oct. 22, 1783, p. 5; Dec. 3, 1783, p. 8.

19. New Canaan Historical Society, Noyes Family Papers, pp. 39–47, Mary to Joseph and Rachel Fish, Aug. 6, 1769, May 30, 1772, privately owned, quoted in Buel, *The Way of Duty,* pp. 62–63, p. 67.

20. NAC, Claus Papers, C-1478, vol. 1, Sir John Johnson to Daniel Claus, Jan. 20, 1777.

21. Jack M. Sosin, *The Revolutionary Frontier, 1763–1783* (New York: Holt, Rinehart and Winston, 1967).

22. Victor Hugo Palsits, ed., *Minutes of the Commissioners for Detecting and Defeating Conspiracies in the State of New York: Albany County Sessions, 1778–1781,* 3 vols. (New York: J.B. Lyon, 1909), Aug. 13, 1781, vol. 2, 762–63.

23. *Ibid.,* July 25, 1781, vol. 2, 751–52.

24. *Ibid.,* Sept. 4, 1778, vol. 1, 224; May 20, 1778, vol. 1, 122; June 17, 1778, vol. 1, 146; Aug. 3, 1779, vol. 1, 398; Oct. 3, 1778, vol. 1, 252.

25. *Ibid.,* Nov. 8, 1780, vol. 2, 563; Jan. 29, 1781, vol. 2, 624; June 9, 1781, vol. 2, 733.

26. Barbara Graymont, *The Iroquois in the American Revolution* (Syracuse: Syracuse Univ. Press, 1972), pp. 17, 21–23.

27. Graymont, *The Iroquois in the American Revolution,* p. 47; *Dictionary of Canadian Biography,* vol. 4, 416–19; H. Pearson Gundy, "Molly Brant, Loyalist," *Ontario Historical Society Papers and Records,* 45 (1953), 97–108.

28. NAC, HP, vol. 21, p. 774, Daniel Claus to Governor Haldimand, Aug. 30, 1779; NAC, HP, vol. 21, p. 787, Captain Frazer to Haldimand, Mar. 21, 1780.

29. NAC, HP, vol. 21, p. 774, Daniel Claus to Governor Haldimand, Nov. 5, 1778.

30. NAC, HP, vol. 27, p. 302, Petition of Sarah McGinn, Audit Office 14.

31. *Ibid.*

32. Janice Potter and George Rawlyk, "Richard Cartwright, Jr.," *Dictionary of Canadian Biography,* vol. 5, 167–72.

33. *Report of the Public Archives of Ontario* [hereafter *PAO Report*], (Toronto: 1904), Claim of Garnet Dingman, p. 1038; claim of John Glasford, p. 1112; claim of Martin Waldec, p. 1121.

34. Petition by Philip Empy, Mar. 1, 1780, HP, vol. 21, p. 874.

35. *PAO Report,* Claim of Justus Sherwood; Ian Cleghorn Pemberton, "Justus Sherwood, Vermont Loyalist, 1747–1798," (Ph.D. thesis. Univ. of Western Ontario, 1973); Mary Beacock Fryer, *Buckskin Pimpernel: The Exploits of Justus Sherwood, Loyalist Spy* (Toronto: Dundurn, 1981), "Sarah Sherwood: ...," " *Eleven Exiles,* pp. 245–64; Queen's University Archives, H.M. Jackson, *Justus Sherwood: Soldier, Loyalist and Negotiator* (Kingston: n.p., 1958).

36. AO, John Munro Papers, Undated document; NAC, HP series B, vol. 214, p. 35.

37. Palsits, *Minutes of the Commissioners,* Oct. 1, 1778, vol. 1, 248.

38. "Petition of sundry women wives of tories for relief," n.d. Tryon County Committee of Safety Papers, in Kerber, *Women of the Republic,* p. 50.

39. Palsits, *Minutes of the Commissioners,* Aug. 1, 1778, vol. 1, 190.

40. *Ibid.,* Introduction, vol. 1, 57.

41. *Ibid., Minutes of the Commissioners,* Sept. 21, 1778, vol. 1, 237–38; Sept. 8, 1779, vol. 1, 441.

42. *Ibid.,* vol. 3, 795.

43. See, for example, the case of Elizabeth Hogel, in Palsits, *Minutes of the Commissioners,* vol 2, 540.

44. Mrs. Johnson to General Washington, June 16, 1776, Peter Force, *American Archives,* 9 vols. (Washington, D.C., 1837–53), 4th series, vol. 6, 930.

45. Palsits, *Minutes of the Commissioners,* Aug. 15, 1778, vol. 1, 206; NAC, HP, vol. 21, p. 875, Petition of Isabel Parker, AO, French Papers, Loveland Munson, "The Early History of Manchester."

46. Palsits, *Minutes of the Commissioners.* Oct. 29, 1780, vol. 3, 558; Apr. 30, 1781. vol. 3, 696; NAC, HP, vol. 73, p. 54, John McDonell to Mathews, Mar. 20, 1780; "A Letter from Mrs. Elizabeth Bowman Spohn," in J.J. Talman, *Loyalist Narratives from Upper Canada* (Toronto: Champlain Society, 1946). 315–22.

47. NAC, Colonial Office 42 [hereafter CO 42], vol. 36, B 33, pp. 2–3, R.B. Lernoult to Haldimand, Apr. 28, 1777.

48. CO 42, Q13, vol. 36, B 33, Sir Guy Carleton to Lord G. Germaine, May 27, 1777; NAC, Claus Papers, vol. 25, C 1485, Taylor and Diffin to Daniel Claus, Nov. 11, 1778, Claus Papers.

49. Claus Papers, C 1478, vol. 1, Johnson to Claus, Jan. 20, 1777.

50. Fryer, "Sarah Sherwood: ...," *Eleven Exiles,* pp. 245–64.

51. NAC, HP, vol. 21, p. 774, Claus to Haldimand, Nov. 19, 1778.

52. NAC, HP, vol. B 211, pp. 133–34, Memorial: Michael Grass and Loyalists from New York, Sorel, Jan., 1784. NAC, HP, vol. B 63, pp. 109–10, Mathews to Stephen DeLancey. Mar. 2, 1784.

53. H.V. Temperley, "Frontierism, Capital and the American Loyalists in Canada," *Journal of American Studies,* 13 (1979), 5–27.

54. Kerber, *Women of the Republic,* p. 85.

55. NAC, British Headquarters Papers, vol. 16, microfilm, reel M-348, [Name illegible] to Lt. Col. Roger Morris, Apr. 22, 1779.

56. NAC, Claus Papers, C 1478, Mary Brant to Joseph Brant, Oct. 5, 1779; C 1485, Captain Frazer to Daniel Claus, June 26, 1780.

57. Lydia Van Alstine, Flora Livingston, widow Obenholt, Margaret Hare.

58. NAC, HP, vol. 21, p. 875, Petition to Haldimand, Jan. 3, 1783; HP, vol. 21, p. 874, Petition of George Christie, Dec. 16, 1778; HP, vol. 21, p. 874, Petition of Jean McDonell, Nov. 30, 1782.

59. Mary Beth Norton, "Eighteenth-Century American Women in Peace and War: The Case of the Loyalists," *William and Mary Quarterly,* 3rd ser., 33 (1976), 386–409.

60. NAC, HP, A 776, Phoebe Grout, Petition.

61. Kerber, *Women of the Republic,* p. 85.

CHAPTER

8 INVENTED TRADITION: LAURA SECORD AND THE WAR OF 1812

"Laura Secord," Cecilia Morgan writes in the final selection in this chapter, "is best-known as the figurehead of a candy company." Just as one is confronted by a multiplicity of choices over flavour, content, shape, colour or wrapping in one of those stores, Laura Secord herself can be regarded as a "variety pack." While some have considered her a heroine extraordinaire, others have dismissed her claim as "too absurd for further discussion."[1] As recently as 1986, on the other hand, she was called "*la plus celebre des espionnes canadiennes,*"[2] yet a textbook with a strong feminist bias, published in 1993, does not even mention her.[3] Over the almost two centuries since the battle of Beaver Dams, for which she became famous, controversy has swirled about Laura Secord as each generation embellished the legend, fabricated a new Laura, rejected a previous Laura, or attacked those who wrote about her. In the process she has gone from profound obscurity, to mythological heroine, to questionable woman, to symbol for a movement.

It is unlikely that the Laura Secord conundrum will ever be resolved, for people will continue to make choices about her just as they make choices in the candy stores. The readings offered here represent three of those choices. The details of her life are quite straightforward, as presented by Ruth McKenzie in the first selection from the *Dictionary of Canadian Biography*. McKenzie had previously written the very sympathetic *Laura Secord: The Legend and the Lady*.

The second reading, by George C. Ingram, on "The Story of Laura Secord Revisited," is typical of the revisionist perspective that dominated historical writing into the 1960s. Ingram examined the previous literature critically, and offered new details as evidence to provide a modified analysis of the subject. The third selection is by contemporary feminist Cecilia Morgan on " 'Of Slender Frame and Delicate Appearance': The Placing of Laura Secord in the Narratives of Canadian Loyalist History." Morgan is concerned not about the actual historical events or even about Secord herself, but about the use of the Secord image over time. She begins with "the deeply gendered notions and assumptions" of world view that are dominant with males then follows the Secord legacy by "linking gender, race, nation, and empire in both past and present." It is the use of history, rather than history itself, that concerns Morgan.

Notes

1. W.S. Wallace, *The Story of Laura Secord: A Study in Historical Evidence* (Toronto, 1932), p. 25.

2. Hugh Halliday, "Secret Professionnel," *Holiday Canada*, no. 50, Vol. 5, 1986, p. 1697.

3. Margaret Conrad, Alvin Finkel and Cornelius Jaenan, *History of the Canadian Peoples: Beginnings to 1867* (Toronto: Copp Clark Pitman Ltd., 1993).

Suggestions for Further Reading

Errington, Jane, *The Lion, the Eagle and Upper Canada: A Developing Colonial Ideology*. Kingston and Montreal: McGill-Queen's University Press, 1987.

McKenzie, Ruth, *Laura Secord: The Legend and the Lady*. Toronto: McClelland and Stewart, 1971.

Mills, David, *The Idea of Loyalty in Upper Canada, 1784–1850*. Kingston and Montreal: McGill-Queen's University Press, 1988.

Robinson, Helen Caister, *Laura: A Portrait of Laura Secord*. Toronto: Dundurn, 1981.

Sheppard, George, "'Deeds Speak': Militiamen, Medals, and the Invented Traditions of 1812," *Ontario History*, LXXXIII, no. 3 (September 1990), 207–32.

Sheppard, George, *Plunder, Profit, and Paroles: A Social History of the War of 1812 in Upper Canada*. Kingston and Montreal: McGill-Queen's University Press, 1994.

Stanley, G.F.G., *The War of 1812: Land Operations*. Toronto: Macmillan of Canada in collaboration with the National Museum of Man, 1983.

Turner, Wesley, *The War of 1812: The War that Both Sides Won*. Toronto: Dundurn, 1990.

Wise, S.F., "Colonial Attitudes from the Era of the War of 1812 to the Rebellion of 1837," in S. Wise and R.C. Brown, *Canada Views the United States*. Toronto: Macmillan of Canada, 1967.

Zaslow, Morris, (ed.), *The Defended Border: Upper Canada and the War of 1812*. Toronto: Macmillan, 1964.

INGERSOLL, LAURA (SECORD)

Ruth McKenzie

INGERSOLL, LAURA (Secord), heroine; b. 13 Sept. 1775 in Great Barrington, Mass., eldest daughter of Thomas Ingersoll and Elizabeth Dewey; d. 17 Oct. 1868, at Chippawa (Niagara Falls, Ont.).

When Laura Ingersoll was eight, her mother died, leaving four little girls. Her father remarried twice and had a large family by his third wife. In the American War of Independence, Ingersoll fought on the rebel side, but in 1795 he immigrated to Upper Canada where he had obtained a township grant for settlement. His farm became the site of the modern town of Ingersoll. He ran a tavern at Queenston until his township (Oxford-upon-the-Thames) was surveyed. Within two years, about 1797, Laura married James Secord, a young merchant of Queenston. He was the youngest son of a loyalist officer of Butler's Rangers, who had brought his family to Niagara in 1778. James and Laura Secord were to have six daughters and one son.

They lived first at St. Davids but soon settled in Queenston. Early in the War of 1812, James, a sergeant in the 1st Lincoln militia, was wounded in the battle of Queenston Heights and was rescued from the battlefield by his wife. The following summer, when neither side had a firm hold of the Niagara peninsula, Laura heard on 21 June 1813, probably by listening to the conversation of some American officers dining at her house, that the Americans intended to surprise the British outpost at Beaver Dams and capture the officer in charge, Lieutenant James Fitzgibbon. It was urgent that someone warn Fitzgibbon and, since James was disabled, Laura resolved to take the message herself early the next morning.

The distance to the outpost by direct road was twelve miles but Laura feared she would encounter American guards that way and chose a roundabout route. She went first to St. Davids where she was joined by her niece, Elizabeth Secord, and then to Shipman's Corners (St. Catharines). Elizabeth became exhausted and Laura continued alone, uncertain of the way but following the general direction of Twelve Mile Creek through fields and woods. That evening, after crossing the creek on a fallen tree, Laura came unexpectedly on an Indian encampment. She was frightened, but after she explained her mission to the chief he took her to Fitzgibbon. Two days later, on 24 June 1813, an American force under Colonel Charles Boerstler was ambushed near Beaver Dams by some 400 Indians led by Dominique Ducharme and William Johnson Kerr. Fitzgibbon then persuaded Boerstler to surrender with 462 men to his own fifty men. In the official reports of the victory no mention was made of Laura Secord.

From *Dictionary of Canadian Biography*, Vol. IX (Toronto: University of Toronto Press, 1976), 405–7.

The Secords lived in poverty in the postwar years until 1828 when James, who had received a small pension because of his war wound, was appointed registrar, then judge (in 1833), of the Niagara Surrogate Court. In 1835 he became collector of customs at Chippawa. He died in 1841 leaving Laura without financial resources. She ran a school for children in her Chippawa cottage for a brief period. Petitions to the government for a pension and other favours were unsuccessful.

Laura Secord was eighty-five before she achieved wide public recognition for her heroic deed. While visiting Canada in 1860, the Prince of Wales (the future Edward VII) learned of Laura's twenty-mile walk. She had prepared a memorial for the prince describing her wartime service, and she also had placed her signature among those War of 1812 veterans who presented an address to him. After Albert Edward returned to England, he sent Mrs. Secord a reward of £100. She died in 1868, at the age of ninety-three, and was buried beside her husband in Drummond Hill Cemetery, Niagara Falls.

Laura Secord became celebrated as a heroine in history, poetry, and drama, after 1860. Legends grew; the favourite was that she had taken a cow with her on her walk, for camouflage, and that she had milked it in the presence of American sentries before leaving it behind in the woods. In fact, Mrs. Secord never mentioned a cow and it is unlikely that she encountered an American sentry. William F. Coffin apparently invented the episode for his book *1812, The War And Its Moral* (1864). According to another story, Laura had walked through the woods at night, on her bare feet. But she herself said, "I left early in the morning," and though she may have lost a slipper in the woods or fields, she was far too sensible to have started out barefoot. Her popular fame was such that two monuments were erected in her honour, one at Lundy's Lane in 1901, the other on Queenston Heights in 1910. Her portrait was hung in the parliament buildings in Toronto, and a memorial hall was established in the Laura Secord School at Queenston.

Some twentieth-century historians, however, have questioned her place in history. For example, W. Stewart Wallace in *The Story Of Laura Secord: A Study In Historical Evidence* (1932) concluded from the available documents that Mrs. Secord had undoubtedly taken a message to Fitzgibbon, probably on 23 June, but that she had arrived too late for her information to be of value. Lieutenant Fitzgibbon had said in his report on the battle of Beaver Dams: "At [John] De Cou's this morning, about seven o'clock, I received information that...the Enemy...was advancing towards me..." It was argued that this information, brought by Indian scouts, was Fitzgibbon's first warning. Wallace also cited a certificate written by Fitzgibbon in 1837 testifying that Mrs. Secord had brought warning of an American attack; unfortunately Fitzgibbon gave no specific date, and he wrote, he said, "in a moment of much hurry and from memory."

The puzzle of the chronology and of Laura's role in the events was solved when two earlier testimonials came to light, both written by Fitzgibbon, in 1820 and 1827, to support petitions the Secords had made to the government.

In the 1827 certificate, Fitzgibbon said that Mrs. Secord had come "on the 22nd day of June 1813," and that "in consequence of this information" he had placed the Indians in a position to intercept the Americans. Thus he made it clear that Laura's warning had indeed made the victory possible at Beaver Dams. It was a significant victory, and for her part in it Laura Secord became justly known as the heroine of the War of 1812.

Laura Secord typified pioneer women in her courage, endurance, and resolution in the face of adversity. Fitzgibbon remembered her as a person of "slender frame and delicate appearance," but underneath was a strong and persistent will.

THE STORY OF LAURA SECORD REVISITED

George C. Ingram

Scorned by her own generation, Laura Secord was enthroned as the queen of Upper Canadian pioneer womanhood in the last half of the nineteenth century and the first part of the twentieth century. Her claim to renown was her perilous journey to warn James Fitzgibbon of an impending American attack on Beaver Dams, an attack that came on 24 June 1813. Before Laura herself died in 1868, she had modestly asserted that her contribution had enabled Fitzgibbon to save the country. Her case was then taken up by poetic nationalists, ardent feminists, and uncritical historians who revelled in the romantic qualities of Laura's sylvan ramble and unhesitatingly added a few flourishes of their own. By 1913, a century after the fact, an impressive edifice had been constructed around Laura's walk.

By this time, the folklore surrounding Laura contained so many undocumented details that it became an easy target for the critical historian. Accordingly, in the next few decades Laura was stripped of all her achievements and left a shivering "myth"[1] who "played no part in determining the issue of the Battle at the Beaver Dams."[2]

Newly-discovered evidence shows that the "debunking" has gone too far. Laura Secord did give an early warning. She likely encountered an American sentry, and did undertake a perilous and lengthy walk, although the specific length of this walk cannot be known. With the debunkers, however, it must be agreed that Laura played only a limited role in the battle, not because she arrived too late, as her foremost critic W.S. Wallace has maintained,[3] but because Fitzgibbon and the Indian leaders chose to ignore her warning after it failed to come true exactly as expected. This circumstance becomes evident from an examination of the battle and an analysis of Laura's role in it.

From *Ontario History*, Vol. LVII, no. 2 (1965), 85–96.

Even those recent historians who are taking a long critical second look at the War of 1812 agree that the Battle of Beaver Dams fought on 24 June 1813, was an "important victory for the British."[4] It followed a number of significant events. On 27 May, the Americans had launched an amphibious attack against Fort George, forcing the hopelessly outnumbered British troops and militia under General John Vincent to retreat first to Beaver Dams and then to the British keep on Burlington Heights. The Americans had pursued rapidly, reaching Stoney Creek on 5 June. That night, an ingenious attack by the British forces completely routed the Americans and forced them to retreat first to the Forty, and then to Fort George. By 9 June, the Americans had abandoned all their newly-won positions on the peninsula and had concentrated their troops in Fort George. The British immediately cordoned the fort with centre-positions at De Cou's and St. Catharines.

At De Cou's there was a detachment of forty-six men of the 49th Regiment under Lieutenant James Fitzgibbon and a considerable body of Indians under Captains Ducharme, Kerr, and Norton. The latter harassed and molested the enemy's pickets and even fired on American troops at Queenston. Their activities probably led the American commander to decide to despatch a troop of 550 men under Lieutenant-Colonel Boerstler to eliminate this thorn in the side of the American position.

Boerstler set out from Fort George on the twenty-third of June and arrived in Queenston "about eleven o'clock p.m."[5] The next morning, "after daybreak,"[6] the detachment advanced, making contact with the British Indians "between eight and nine o'clock in the morning of the twenty-fourth."[7] The three-hour engagement that followed was fought solely between the Americans and the Indians. The latter surrounded, harassed and terrified the American troops. By the time that Fitzgibbon with his regulars came "to our aid,"[8] he was able to demand and obtain a surrender from Boerstler, who feared that his troops might face the bloody reprisals of the "tomahawk and the scalping knife"[9] if the Indians were allowed to continue. The entire American force capitulated and, with the exception of the militia men who were paroled, fell into the hands of the British. Captain De Haren, the senior officer for the area, arrived with reinforcements from his position at St. Catharines only after the American army had capitulated.

The victory was significant. This was the last time that the Americans ventured outside of Fort George with a force of any size. The Indians, who now had a free hand around the fort, effectively contained the American troops. "This army," wrote Porter of the American militia a month later, "lies panic-struck, shut up and whipped in by a few hundred miserable savages...."[10] In December, after months of virtual inaction, McLure, the American commander, fired Newark and abandoned Fort George.

What part did Laura Secord play in the actual events of the Battle of Beaver Dams? There can be no doubt that Laura did walk to De Cou's and did talk to James Fitzgibbon. Three certificates issued in 1820, 1827, and 1837 by Fitzgibbon attest to this fact.[11] It also appears quite certain that Laura arrived "on the twenty-second day of June 1813...after sun set"[12] and "on the morning of the second day after the information was given...[the] detachment was captured."[13]

If Laura walked on 22 June she either obtained her information that morning, which is highly unlikely because she set out very early, or the night before, that is, the twenty-first. In 1827, Fitzgibbon explained that "her husband had learned from an American officer the preceding night...that a detachment from the American army then in Fort George would be sent out the following morning [the twenty-third]...."[14] This testimony would immediately rule out Boerstler as the source of information as he did not arrive in Queenston with his troops until around 11:00 p.m. on the twenty-third.[15]

At least two possibilities arise as alternative sources. A detachment of the 13th Regiment under Colonel Chrystie had been stationed at Queenston "for a few days" and "was ordered back two days previous to the marching of the detachment [Boerstler's]."[16] This fact means that it left Queenston on the twenty-first or twenty-second depending on how one dates the "two days." Here was a possible source of information. And, if the detachment did not leave until the twenty-second, here is an explanation of the American picket which played such a prominent role in subsequent accounts of Laura's trials. Another source could have been the renegade Captain Chapin, whose raiders were circulating in the neighbourhood at this time and might have stopped for a meal in Queenston (a meal also crops up in most of the accounts). Certainly Chapin seems to have been prominent in recommending the attack of Beaver Dams.[17]

Both of these sources would have been mere speculation at this time because the American plan was not officially revealed until the twenty-third.[18] Professor Moir has suggested that "it is quite conceivable that the American plan for a surprise attack was common knowledge to the officers at Fort George."[19] The detachment at De Cou's was a thorn in the side of the American position, and if there was talk of moving against it, quite naturally officers close to the area of trouble would be discussing the matter as a form of wishful thinking, or perhaps armchair generalship. This talk would have been vague and uncertain on the twenty-first. Certainly it would not have been definite regarding times and numbers. This is probably the type of information that Laura carried to De Cou's.

Fitzgibbon himself was guarded in his assessment of the information. In 1820, he described it as "substantially correct,"[20] implying a general validity. But in 1827 he was more definite when he explained that "Colonel Boerstler, their commander, in a conversation with me confirmed fully the information communicated to me by Laura Secord."[21] At the very least, Laura Secord told Fitzgibbon of "an intended attack to be made by the Enemy upon the detachment"[22] and might have been more specific and reported that "a detachment from the American army then in Fort George would be sent out on the following morning (the twenty-third)...."[23]

What effect did Laura's information have on the outcome of the battle? It definitely gave an early warning. Fitzgibbon apparently took it very seriously at first and acted upon it:

> In consequence of this information, I placed the Indians under Norton together with my own Detachment in a situation to intercept the American Detachment and we occupied it during the night of the twenty-second.[24]

But he made no attempt that night to tell De Haren, his superior officer at St. Catharines, of the impending attack. The latter does not seem to have heard of the Americans' approach until the morning of the actual battle.[25] Certainly no attempt was made to rush in reinforcements until that time. Perhaps due to ambition or through suspicion of Laura's account, Fitzgibbon decided not to relay the news.

After maintaining the position during the night of the twenty-second, the troops disbanded again. On the morning of the twenty-fourth Fitzgibbon's men were not with the Indians.[26] One can imagine the ill-temper of the British troops after staying up all night chasing "paper tigers"! Fitzgibbon must have been an unpopular man around camp on the twenty-third. The Indians in Queenston on the twenty-third[27] might have been sent to discover if the enemy was approaching. They were there in the afternoon, well before Boerstler arrived, and their report probably heaped more suspicion on Laura's warning. The expectation of an attack quite likely then dwindled, bringing in turn a relaxation in vigilance.

Certainly neither the Indians nor Fitzgibbon's detachment was well-prepared on the morning of the twenty-fourth. Ducharme discovered the enemy's approach only at about 8:00 that morning when an Indian scout brought back word, while Fitzgibbon heard shortly after.[28] Only then was a messenger despatched to De Haren.[29] The engagement had already begun and had almost finished by the time that Fitzgibbon was able to move his men into position. In other words, in spite of, or because of Laura's early warning the installation was caught off guard. The failure of her prognostication to develop a forecast might have led Fitzgibbon "to doubt the veracity of Mrs. Secord's information";[30] furthermore, it could have lulled the detachment into false confidence. On the other hand, the installation could still have been kept on a sharper guard than usual; that is, the scouts which gave the crucial warning might not have been circulating under normal conditions.

Caught off guard as they were, neither Ducharme nor Fitzgibbon could very well stress in the official reports that they received information of an impending American attack a full two days before.[31] Instead, both mentioned the much more dramatic day-of-the-battle report brought in by the Indian scout. However, why did other accounts of the battle, even the informal ones, fail to mention advance information? Perhaps Fitzgibbon wished to keep Mrs. Secord in the background for fear of her life. She had come from behind the enemy lines and returned the next day. If her name was revealed, it would circulate, become known to the Americans, and the Secords in Queenston would suffer.

Mrs. Secord did come to Fitzgibbon on the twenty-second with information that an American attack would come on the twenty-third. Her information might have aided somewhat in bringing about the subsequent British victory, but it did not have the effect that it might have had simply because "the enemy did not come until the morning of the twenty-fourth."[32] In each of the certificates Fitzgibbon stressed this time lag as though he were attempting to explain some doubt which existed at the time. Only once did Fitzgibbon concede that "I am personally indebted to her for her conduct upon that occasion."[33] But never did he attribute the victory directly to her information.

* * *

Based on this shaky information, Laura Secord's story eventually achieved a tremendous popularity. The *fons et origio*, as Wallace maintained, rested with the Secord family and especially Laura in her later years. The explanation for the story's continued popularity and expansion after her death must be looked for elsewhere. Laura Secord was a woman and this in itself accounts for the avid interest shown by those of her own sex whose whimsical approach to historical study added details of decidedly doubtful validity. But Laura's walk must also be viewed within the larger context of the War of 1812 which has itself been surrounded by an aura of folklore. Central to this has been the myth of the militia, the tenacious idea, only recently attacked, that Upper Canada ensured her own survival.

In 1813, Bishop Strachan gave what was probably the earliest statement of the belief:

> It will be told by the future historians that the province of Upper Canada without the assistance of man or arms except a handful of regular troops repelled its invaders, slew or took them all prisoners, and captured from its enemies the greater part of the arms by which it was defended....And never, surely was greater activity shown in any country than our militia have exhibited, never greater valour, cooler resolution, and more resolved conduct; they have emulated the choicest veterans and they have twice saved the country.[34]

Strachan accurately predicted the viewpoint that historians would take. For almost a century and a half Upper Canadians and later Ontarians gloried in the fact that they alone had repulsed the neighbour to the South. The myth lived on through the nineteenth century, receiving strength and vigour with periodic appearances of histories of war and a barrage of shorter articles published in the journals of local historical societies.

When she conveyed her message to Fitzgibbon at Beaver Dams, Laura Secord became the only Upper Canadian involved in what was a significant battle of the campaign of 1813 on the Niagara peninsula. James Fitzgibbon, in charge of the small detachment of regulars, had fought in the 19th and 61st Regiments of Great Britain and only after the war became a resident of Upper Canada, although the fact that he did become a resident might have undermined Laura's earlier claims. The company under him was of the 49th Regiment, a troop of British regulars. The Indians, natives though they were, actually fought and won the battle, but could scarcely be considered for a position in the Canadian War of 1812 folklore. Of course, there was Captain Chapin. But he was a turncoat Upper Canadian who was fighting for the Americans, and the myth conveniently attempts to play down or reject such exceptional characters. Laura then, was the only true-blue Canadian eligible for veneration. The fact that she was a woman placed her in a category in which few dramatic examples could be found. She became the symbol of the pioneer Upper Canadian women sturdily defying the American invader—a symbol which at least made the Canadian resistance heterosexual.

Not until the middle of the twentieth century was the "myth of the militia" really challenged; and then, it was heartlessly swept aside by a military historian, C.P. Stacey, who maintained that the war had been won mainly by the British regulars. The new interpretation clashed vigorously with the already shaken "Whiggery" of Canadian historiography. No longer could the "victory" in 1814 be viewed as the first assertion, albeit weak, of a Canadian nation, which had almost single-handed and certainly without significant help from the mother country, repulsed an aggressive United States. Laura Secord, a significant part of the general myth of the War of 1812, has also fallen prey to the onslaught against the war.

* * *

The Secords were not very reticent about Laura's feat. In the course of the next three decades, it was used at least four times in attempts by the Secords to obtain concessions from the provincial government. In 1820, James Secord petitioned Lieutenant Governor Maitland for a grant of the military reserve at Queenston listing among his family's contributions the fact that

> [the petitioner's] wife embraced an opportunity of rendering some service at the risk of her life, in going through the Enemies' lines to communicate information to a detachment of His Majesty's troops at the Beaver Dams in the month of June 1813.[35]

Accompanying the petition was a certificate of proof from James Fitzgibbon.[36] The very fact that Secord felt obliged to include a certificate documenting the trip shows that the journey was not yet common knowledge. Fitzgibbon had received all of the credit for the victory in the battle, because of his official report and the fact that he had negotiated the surrender. Only two years earlier on 30 March 1818, Fitzgibbon had issued a similar document for W.J. Kerr, explaining that "with respect to the affair with Captain Boerstler, not a shot was fired on our side by any but the Indians."[37] But James Secord did not make any extravagant claims here, concerning the outcome of the battle. He merely noted, as did all of Fitzgibbon's certificates, that Laura communicated information to the detachment at De Cou's.

When the second certificate appeared in 1827,[38] James Secord was again "an applicant for some situation."[39] Maitland apparently turned down his request but did have "a favourable opinion of the character claims of Mr. Secord and his wife...and suggested to her that when the Brock's monument was completed she might have charge of it...."[40] The Secords seem to have refused this position.

By 1839, the June day walk had become the only card which the Secords played. Mrs. Secord petitioned for the grant of the

> Ferry at Queenston with Rent free. That your Excellency will be pleased to affix a small Rent upon the same as you in your judgement may seem just and right, say 50 per year, leaving therefore all herein stated and considering her great claim, and your memorialist indifferent circumstances, your Excellency will give her case Just and equitable consideration.[41]

By this time Laura's claim was much stronger. She gave, she argued:

> important enteligence of a meditated attack of the Americans upon our troops, and by which means 550 of the enemy were captured...and for which performance your Excellency's memorialist has never received the smallest compensation....[42]

The memorial was not even answered. This was harsh testimony of the shock that "officialdom" in Upper Canada placed in Laura's feat.

Undaunted as ever, Laura applied in 1841 for pensions for herself and her husband, who died in that year. This time the plea was more desperate and the claim much stronger:

> But for such information your Excellency's Petitioner is fully convinced the British troops must have been captured and by that means would have lost an important station.[43]

Again a certificate was appended to the petition, presumably the certificate of 1837. The Governor, Sir George Arthur, did not think the plea even warranted the placing of the petition before the Legislature. "In reply," wrote the Civil Secretary, "I am commanded to inform you, that His Excellency regrets that he does not feel himself warranted under all the circumstances of your case, in bringing it under the notice of the Legislature."[44] Again official disdain was shown for the contribution of Mrs. Secord.

A few years later, in 1845, the story of Laura Secord first appeared in print in the form of a letter written by Laura's son, Charles B. Secord, to the *Church*. The occasion was a debate in the House of Assembly "relative to the propriety of granting Col. Fitzgibbon £1,000 for his services in lieu of a grant of land."[45] A member of the Legislature, Mr. Aylwin, had protested that a Major Delormier, and not Fitzgibbon, deserved the credit for the British victory. Secord now set out to settle the record. His mother had been instrumental in the battle. She had overheard enemy officers plotting, had carried the message to Fitzgibbon, and the latter "in consequence of this information prepared himself to meet the enemy; and soon after, the attack being made, the American troops were captured.... Col. Fitzgibbon was the only officer who appeared to be in command, to whom my mother gave the information, and who acted the part he so nobly did on that occasion."[46] Fitzgibbon was returned to the spotlight and Mrs. Secord now added.

Laura's role now became public property and from this point can be dated the unrestrained elaboration of the Secord story. At first Laura herself, with her memory romanticized by the fancies of old age, provided the innovations. Gilbert Auchinleck's *History of the War Between Great Britain and United States of America During the Years 1812, 1813, 1814*, appeared in the *Anglo-American Magazine* of 1853. Laura's venture was not included in the actual text; but in a footnote the author quoted a long narrative by Laura herself, including, as had the account of 1845, the American sentries and the awesome Indians. When it came to an evaluation of her contribution, she was relatively subdued: "Benefiting from this information, Capt. Fitzgibbon, formed his plans accordingly and captured about 500 American infantry."[47]

Eight years later, in February 1861, Laura wrote her account for another history of the war, this time for Benson J. Lossing's anecdotal and highly personal *Pictorial Field Book of the War of 1812*. The strongest claim to date, both for the Battle of Beaver Dams and Laura's role, was advanced: "With the intelligence I gave him [Fitzgibbon] he formed his plans and saved his country...."[48] More interesting was the account of Lossing of the visit of the Prince of Wales in 1860. A list of signatures of veterans of the War of 1812 was being prepared to present to him and "Mrs. Secord applied for permission to place her name on the list."[49] The strange part was that she had to explain why her name should be on such a list. "Wherefore? was the natural question. She told her story...."[50] In other words, the story of Laura's contribution was not yet common currency, even in her own district. It was in the next half-century that Laura's feat received popularization.

Laura herself, in claiming in 1861 that Fitzgibbon had "saved his country" and that she had been the power behind the scene, went as far on the basic issue as any account that followed. But the attendant circumstances, the events surrounding Laura's walk, received an elaboration and romanticization that went far beyond even the imaginative mind of Laura's later life. Furthermore, Laura's exploit, like so many heroic deeds of the past, was called in to serve a variety of causes.

W.F. Coffin's *1812, The War and its Moral* was one of the first works to appear. In what seems to be in the main an inferential account, he gave many flourishes to the story. A cow is added to give Laura some protection in her walk, and Laura herself is described in far more detail than previously. The bovine extension, now an essential part of the folklore surrounding Laura, was solely a product of Coffin's imagination.[51]

Later Charles Mair—poet, author, and Canadian nationalist—saw in Laura Secord's exploit a way of whipping up nationalist fervour sadly lacking in the new dominion. His "Ballad for Brave Women," based mainly on information found in William Coffin, provided a moral example for all Canadian women:

> For a moment her Reason forsook her; she raved,
> She laughed, and she cried— "They are saved! they are saved!"
> Then her senses returned, and with thanks, loud and deep
> Sounding sweetly around her, she sank into sleep
> And Boerstler came up; but his movements were known.
> His force was surrounded, his scheme overthrown,
> By a woman's devotion—on stone be't engraved!
> The foeman was beaten, and Burlington saved.
>
> Ah! faithful to death were our women of Yore,
> Have they fled with the past, to be heard of no more?
> No, No! though his laurelled one sleeps on the grave;
> We have maidens as true, we have matrons as brave;
> And should Canada ever be forced to the test—
> To spend for our country the blood of her best—
> When her sons lift the linstock and brandish the sword
> Her daughters will think of brave Laura Secord.[52]

What better way could one find for kindling a spirit of unity than by reference to Canada's only war for survival and to the frail and yet heroic Laura?

Others who followed did not have such a grand aim, or, at least, the aim was considerably more parochial. Laura was taken up with enthusiasm by the members of the movement for equality of women. Mrs. Sarah A. Curzon, for instance, was a "Champion in Canada of woman's rights."[53] Her play, *Laura Secord*, ends with Fitzgibbon attributing his victory to "a brave woman's glorious deed,"[54] and in her preface Mrs. Curzon made her feelings even more explicit:

> But surely we who enjoy the happiness she [Laura] so largely secured for us, we who have known how to honour Brock and Brant, will also know how to honour Tecumseh and LAURA SECORD; *the heroine as well as the heroes of our Province—of our common Dominion*—and will no longer delay to do it, lest Time should snatch this happy opportunity from us.[55]

Mrs. E.A. Currie, authoress of *Laura Secord and Canadian Reminiscences*, was a member of the Women's Club of St. Catharines, the Daughters of the Empire, and the W.C.T.U.[56] "Always a Reformer," states her biographical note, [she] "has ever believed that the women of Canada are entitled to the same political privileges as the men; they have earned them by industry and self-sacrifice; was instrumental in securing a grant from Parlt. Towards erecting a memorial to Laura Secord on Queenston Heights."[57]

Miss Machar, a poetess, was "officially connected with the National Council of Women."[58] Her final stanza in *Laura Secord* waxes strongly:

> How British gallantry and skill
>> There played their noblest part,
> Yet scarce had won if there had failed
>> One woman's dauntless heart.[59]

Finally, Mrs. E.J. Thompson, important in establishing a memorial to Laura Secord at Queenston, was a member of the Daughters of the Empire, and the Woman's Canadian Club.[60]

All of these women were active in Women's associations—natural enough for women of their calibre, all were interested in the study of history, and some were descendants of United Empire Loyalists. Almost all of them were active in the movement for women's rights which were just gathering momentum in the 1890s and early 1900s. What better subject for such strong feminists than Laura Secord; one of their own sex whose contribution gave women a role in the War of 1812 and called history to their side? Their flair for dramatization and poetic licence added many new features to the story, while their feminine instincts introduced detailed, although poorly documented, appreciations of Laura's attire. Who but a woman could write that:

> She wore a cottage bonnet tied under her chin. She had balbriggin stockings with red silk clocks on the side, and low shoes with buckles.[61]

Miss Thompson added another movement, that of negro rights. Laura was able to overhear the American officers discussing plans of the campaign because she was forced to serve the Americans a meal herself. They had been abusive to her two coloured servants, Pete and Floss, and this simple Upper Canadian housewife who spent the next thirty years attempting to obtain a sinecure with a plea of poverty, had to don an apron herself. At the turn of the century as now, Canadians could not resist an opportunity of informing the Americans that they had "solved" their peculiar problem.

Since World War I, and since the formal achievement of women's rights, Laura has been ridiculed or neglected. Colonel William Wood, editor of *Select Documents of the Canadian War of 1812* declared of the Battle of Beaver Dams that "the result would have been the same without her."[62] In his *The War of 1812 on the Niagara Frontier*, L.L. Babcock concluded "it seems fairly clear that her good intentions were fruitless."[63] Finally Dr. Milo M. Quaife heartlessly indexed Laura as "SECORD, Mrs. Laura, myth."[64]

W.S. Wallace in his scholarly work, *The Story of Laura Secord: A Study in Historical Evidence*, presented what seemed to be the capping stone of debunking. Basing his conclusion mainly on the certificate of 1837, he found that

> Mrs. Secord did in the month of June 1813, make an attempt to convey information to the British troops at Beaver Dams; and it must be confessed that her picture of her encounter with the Indians has about it a strong air of verisimilitude. Of her courage and patriotism there is no question. But truth compels one to say that the story she told from memory in later years (and no doubt

sincerely believed) was seriously at variance with the facts, and that she played no part in determining the issue of the battle at the Beaver Dams.[65]

The Laura-ites reeled only temporarily from the attack, and the defence of Laura's virtues was soon taken up. It was helped by the discovery of further historical evidence. The certificate of 1820, published in 1934, and rediscovered by Dr. J.S. Moir in 1962,[66] and the certificate of 1827 published by Dr. Moir in 1959,[67] clear up a problem which had been central for Wallace.

From the vague 1837 certificate alone, Wallace could not see how Laura could have arrived in time to give Fitzgibbon valuable information. She came, but she came too late to have any effect on the outcome of the battle. The certificates of 1820 and 1827 are quite explicit on the matter. Laura took her walk on 22 June, leaving plenty of time to reach and to warn Fitzgibbon.

Wallace's charge that "Mrs. Secord's claim that she enabled Fitzgibbon to 'save the country' is too absurd for further discussion,"[68] is more serious. The Indians, not Fitzgibbon, won the Battle of Beaver Dams...by Fitzgibbon's own admission; they received their information and acted independently of Fitzgibbon's detachment. Therefore, Wallace would conclude, Laura's warning to Fitzgibbon, even if it came before the battle, had no impact on the battle's outcome.

However, Fitzgibbon's certificate of 1827, not available to Wallace, claimed that "the Indians under Norton together with my own detachment [occupied] a situation to intercept the American Detachment... during the night of the twenty-second."[69] This evidence would indicate that the Indians as well as Fitzgibbon had knowledge of the intentions of the Americans supplied by Laura Secord. They too were not well-prepared on the day of the battle, but it was in spite of Laura's warning. Again the possibility looms up that the scouts who gave the 7:00 warning of attack on the twenty-fourth were sent out because an attack was expected. But it is difficult to believe that such scouts or pickets would have been out as a normal procedure.

Up to this point, the argument seems to support the main contention of the debunkers: namely that Laura's mission had no influence on the eventual outcome of the battle. But it seems that the debunking of Laura has gone too far. Certainly the fictitious accoutrements of her walk—the cow, the milkstool, the servants, the various forms of dress—must be abandoned. There is simply no concrete evidence to support them. But the assessment of Laura's actual contribution to the Battle of Beaver Dams must be restated. She did arrive a full two days before the battle and did warn that the Americans were coming. Unfortunately her speed was not matched by the Americans whose tardiness brought them to Beaver Dams on 24 June, a day later than expected. By this time Fitzgibbon had already stayed up all night in ambush formation and, probably quite annoyed, rejected as false the information of that interfering woman. When the Americans finally arrived, the British troops and Indians had to organize themselves hastily. Only the fighting of the Indians and the Americans' great fear of the Indians won the day.

Laura Secord's information should have played a greater part in the outcome of the battle. As events turned out, it brought at most only a slightly increased precaution. But it was not Laura's fault that the British were not prepared. She arrived in plenty of time to warn Fitzgibbon and gave him information which was "substantially correct." Ironically, a defeat of the British force at De Cou's would have made the potential of her visit evident. Her testimony at a subsequent court-martial, revealing her early warning, would have brought out the sloppiness of Ducharme and Fitzgibbon. However, the British victory, left unnecessarily to chance, clouded over the British leaders' neglect of Laura Secord's message. For this reason, Laura was destined to struggle first with "officialdom" and now historians for a place in history which her walk well deserved.

Notes

1. See, for instance, Milo M. Quaife, *The John Askin Papers* (Detroit, 1931) as quoted in W.S. Wallace, *The Story of Laura Secord: A Study in Historical Evidence* (Toronto, 1932), p. 4.

2. Wallace, *op. cit.*, p. 26.

3. *Ibid.*, p. 23.

4. G.F.G. Stanley, "The Indians in the War of 1812," *Canadian Historical Review*, XXXI (1950), p. 158.

5. Boerstler's narrative, in General E. A. Cruikshank, *A Documentary History of the Campaign upon the Niagara Frontier in 1813*, pt. II (Welland, n.d.) p. 131.

6. *Ibid.*, p. 131.

7. *Ibid*, p. 151.

8. John Askin, *ibid.*, p. 203.

9. Captain W.J. Kerr's memorial, *ibid.*, 120–21.

10. Porter to Tompkins, July 27, 1813, *ibid.*, p. 283.

11. See *Appendices I, II*, and *III*.

12. Certificate of 1827.

13. Certificate of 1820.

14. Certificate of 1827.

15. Boerstler's narrative, *Cruikshank*, p. 131.

16. *Ibid.*, p. 135.

17. *Ibid.*, p. 130.

18. *Ibid.*, pp. 130–31.

19. J.S. Moir, "An Early Record of Laura Secord's Walk," *Ontario History*, LI (1959), 106.

20. Certificate of 1820.

21. Certificate of 1827.

22. Certificate of 1820.

23. Certificate of 1827.

24. Certificate of 1827.

25. Ducharme's Report in Cruickshank, *op. cit.*, p. 126.

26. W.J. Kerr's memorial, *ibid.*, p. 120.

27. *Ibid.*, p. 126 and p. 165. The Indians fired on some American troops in a boat on the Niagara River and killed two men.

28. *Ibid.*, p. 126. He mentions 7:00 but it is highly unlikely that he heard before Ducharme. They probably shared their source of information.

29. *Ibid.*, p. 126.

30. J.S. Moir, *op. cit.*, p. 107.

31. For Ducharme's Report see in Cruickshank, *op. cit.*, p. 126, and for Fitzgibbon's see *ibid.*, p. 111.

32. Certificate of 1827.

33. *Ibid.*

34. From the *Report of the Loyal and Patriotic Society*, quoted in C.P. Stacey, "The War of 1812 in Canadian History," *Ontario History*, L (1958), 156.

35. Petition of James Secord, 1820.

36. See *Appendix I.*

37. Fitzgibbon to Kerr in Cruickshank, *op. cit.*, pp. 120–21.

38. See *Appendix.*

39. Memorandum of J.B. Robinson quoted from J.S. Moir "An Early Record of Laura Secord's Walk," *Ontario History*, LI (1959), 108.

40. *Ibid.*, p. 108.

41. From Laura Secord's memorial of 1839, as quoted in Wallace, *op. cit.*, p. 10.

42. *Ibid.*, p. 9.

43. As quoted in *ibid.*, pp. 10–11.

44. *Ibid.*, p. 12.

45. Letter to the editor, *Church*, April 18, 1845.

46. *Ibid.*, April 18, 1845.

47. *The Anglo-American Magazine*, No. 5. III (November, 1853), p. 467. Also printed in *op. cit.*, pp. 127–28.

48. Benson J. Lossing, *Pictorial Field Book of the War of 1812* (New York, 1868) n., p. 621.

49. *Ibid.*, p. 621.

50. *Ibid.*, p. 621.

51. The story of the cow has apparently been "indignantly contradicted by a grand-daughter." See Wallace, *op. cit.*, p. 17.

52. Charles Mair, "A Ballad for Brave Women," *Tecumseh: A Drama and Canadian Poems* (Toronto, 1901), p. 147.

53. W.S. Wallace, *The Macmillan Dictionary of Canadian Biography*, 3rd ed. (Macmillan, 1963), pp. 167–68. Also entry in H.J. Morgan, *Canadian Men and Women of the Time* (Toronto, 1898), p. 235–36.

54. Sarah A. Cruzon, *Laura Secord, the Heroine of 1812: A Drama and other Poems* (Toronto, 1887), p. 66.

55. *Ibid.*, p. vi (Italics mine).

56. Entry in H.J. Morgan, ed., *Canadian Men and Women of the Time: A Hand-book of Canadian Biography of Living Characters*, 2nd ed. (Toronto, 1912), p. 289.

57. *Ibid.*, p. 289.

58. Entry in H.J. Morgan, *Types of Canadian Women* (Toronto, 1903), p. 226.

59. A.M. Machar, *Lays of the True North and Other Poems* (Toronto, 1887), p. 35.

60. Morgan, *Canadian Men and Women*, p. 1095.

61. E.J. Thompson, "Laura Ingersoll Secord," *Niagara Historical Society*, No. 25 (Niagara, 1913), p. 3.

62. As quoted in Wallace, *op. cit.*, p. 4.

63. *Ibid.*, p. 4.

64. *Ibid.*, p. 4.

65. *Ibid.*, pp. 25–26.

66. The certificate was published in the *Mail and Empire*, June 23, 1934. J.S. Moir makes a note of it in "Laura Secord Again," *Ontario History*, LIV (1962), p. 190.

67. Published in J.S. Moir. "An Early Record of Laura Secord's Walk," *Ontario History*, LI (1959), pp. 105–9.

68. Wallace, *op. cit.*, p. 25.

69. Certificate of 1827.

"OF SLENDER FRAME AND DELICATE APPEARANCE": THE PLACING OF LAURA SECORD IN THE NARRATIVES OF CANADIAN LOYALIST HISTORY

Cecilia Morgan

To most present-day Canadians, Laura Secord is best-known as the figurehead of a candy company, her image that of a young, attractive woman wearing a low-cut ruffled white gown.[1] Some may even harbour a vague memory from their high-school courses in Canadian history of her walk in 1813 from Queenston to Beaver Dams, to warn British troops of an impending American attack. From the mid-nineteenth century, the story of that walk has been told by a number of Canadian historians of the War of 1812 in Upper Canada. Its military implications in assisting the British during the War of 1812 have been the subject of some rather heated debate. Did Laura Secord actually make a valuable contribution to the war? Did her news arrive in time and was it acted

From *Journal of the Canadian Historical Association*, no. 5 (1994), 195–212.

upon? However, another and as yet little-discussed issue is the way in which late nineteenth- and early twentieth-century historians attempted to transform Secord into a heroine, a symbol of female loyalty and patriotism in this period's narratives of Loyalist history.

As historian Benedict Anderson argues, the formation of modern national identities has involved more than the delineation of geographically-defined boundaries and narrow political definitions of citizenship. Nations, Anderson tells us, are "imagined political communities," created by their citizens through a number of political and cultural institutions and practices: shared languages, newspapers, museums, and the census. Furthermore, as Anderson (and others) have emphasized, it is also within narratives of "the nation's" history that these imagined communities are formed and national identities are created.[2] To the promoters of late nineteenth-century Canadian nationalism and imperialism, such narratives were of critical importance in understanding Canada's link to Britain and British political, social, and cultural traditions. As Carl Berger argues in *The Sense of Power*, "history in its broadest cultural sense was the medium in which [these traditions were] expressed and history was the final and ultimate argument for imperial unity."[3] Those who wrote these historical narratives also worked diligently to create national heroes who symbolized loyalty and the preservation of the imperial link. Historians interested in early nineteenth-century Ontario history found that a cast of such figures lay conveniently close to hand: Major-General Sir Isaac Brock and the Upper Canadian militia, the colony's saviours during the American invasion of 1812.

But Brock and the militia were not the only significant figures to be commemorated and celebrated, for it was during this period that Laura Secord became one of the most significant female symbols of Canadian nationalism. As feminist historians have pointed out, the formation of imagined national communities has been frequently, if not inevitably, differentiated by gender. While Anderson's work has been extremely influential on historians' understanding of national identities, he fails to recognize "that women and men may imagine such communities, identify with nationalist movements, and participate in state formations in very different ways."[4] And, in their use of iconography, monuments, or written narratives of the nation's history, proponents of nationalism have frequently relied upon gender-specific symbols and imagery.[5] Yet in these textual and visual representations of nationalities, gender as an analytic category has also varied according to its context and has been influenced by other categories and relationships, particularly those of race, class, religion, and sexuality. By looking at the process whereby Secord became a national heroine and at the narratives that were written about Secord's walk, we can further our understanding of the links between gender, race, and imperialism in late nineteenth-century Canadian nationalism and feminism.[6]

Secord became part of the narratives of Loyalist self-sacrifice and duty to country and Crown primarily—although not solely—because of the attempts of women historians and writers who, from the 1880s on, strove to incorporate women into Canadian history and to dislodge the masculine emphasis of the nineteenth-century Loyalist myths of suffering and sacrifice. Women such as Sarah Curzon, the feminist writer, historian, and temperance advocate, insisted that white Canadian women, past and present, had something of value to offer the nation and empire and that their contribution as women to the record of Canadian history be acknowledged and valued. Secord, she (and others like her) argued, was not outside the narrative of Canadian history and she (and other women) therefore had a place in shaping the "imagined communities" of Canadian nationalist and imperialist discourse. Unlike that of other, potentially unruly and disruptive women in Canadian history, Laura Secord's image could be more easily domesticated to accord with late Victorian notions of white, middle class femininity.[7] It could also be moulded by feminists to argue for a greater recognition of the importance of such femininity to Canadian society. Moreover, Laura Secord was not an isolated figure. Ranged behind and about her was a whole gallery of women in Canadian history, from Madeleine de Verchères of New France to the anonymous, archetypal pioneer woman of the backwoods of Upper Canada; women, these "amateur" historians insisted, who were historical figures as worthy of study as their male contemporaries.[8]

Before discussing the writing of Laura Secord into Loyalist history, however, it is crucial to outline the gendered nature of the nineteenth-century narratives of the War of 1812. Historians who have studied Upper Canadian politics have duly noted that assertions of loyalty and sacrifice during the war became the basis for many claims on the Upper Canadian state, in the competition for land and patronage appointments and for compensation for war losses.[9] Donald Akenson, for example, has pointed to the way in which claims to loyal duty during the war were used in attempts to justify the access of some residents to certain material benefits. Such claims were also made to legitimate the exclusion of others from such rewards.[10] Yet what has not been included in these historians' analysis of sacrifice in the war as a bargaining chip in the struggle for material gains in Upper Canada, is the gendered nature of the narratives that were used. In Upper Canadians' commemorations of the War of 1812, the important sacrifices for Country and monarch were made by Upper Canadian men, frequently in their capacity as members of the militia who risked life and limb to protect women and children, homes and hearths, from the brutal rampages of hordes of bloodthirsty Americans. During the war, and in its aftermath, women's contributions to the defence of the colony were either downplayed or ignored, in favour of the image of the helpless Upper Canadian wife and mother who entrusted her own and her children's safety to the gallant militia and British troops.[11]

Personifying the whole, of course, was the masculine figure of Isaac Brock, the British commander who made the ultimate sacrifice for the colony when he died at the Battle of Queenston Heights in 1812. Brock provided those who shaped the history of the war with a dualistic image of nationalism, one that managed to celebrate both Upper Canadian identity and colonial loyalty to Britain. He was also a Christ-like figure, a man who had given both his troops and the colony beneficent paternal guidance and wisdom but who had not spared himself from the physical dangers of war—physical dangers that really only threatened men in the military. Those who contributed to the glorification of Brock claimed that he had provided an invaluable means whereby the colonists might resist the enemy's encroachments. Brock had inspired Upper Canadian men, who might emulate his deed or manly patriotism, and he had reassured Upper Canadian women that, come what may, they could look to their husbands, fathers, sons, and brothers for protection.[12]

This kind of narrative, which emphasized masculine suffering, sacrifice, and achievements, was not unique to that of the War of 1812. As Janice Potter-MacKinnon argues, the history of Upper Canadian Loyalism focused on male military service and the political identification of male Loyalists with the British Crown and constitution:

> Well into the twentieth century, loyalty was a male concept in that it was associated with political decision-making—a sphere from which women were excluded. The same can be said of the idea that the Loyalists bequeathed conservative values and British institutions to later generations of Canadians: women have had no role in fashioning political values and institutions. The notion that the Loyalists were the founders of a nation had obvious and unequivocal gender implications, the amateur historian William Caniff was right when he equated the "founders" with the "fathers."[13]

Admittedly there was no automatic and essential connection between military activities and masculinity in Canadian history for, as Colin Coates has pointed out, the woman warrior tradition was not unknown to nineteenth-century Canada.[14] But specific female images (or images of femininity in general) as symbols of loyalty and patriotism in Upper Canada are almost completely lacking in the discourses of the period, and they display a general reluctance to admit that women could have contributed to the war effort as civilians.[15] This silence about women, and the feminine—except as helpless victims to which the masculine bravery of Upper Canadian men was inextricably linked—was quite the opposite of the discourses of the French Revolution, with their glorification of Marianne; the American Patriot's figure of the republican mother; or even the more conservative use of the British figure of Britannia.[16]

The earliest efforts to call attention to Secord's contribution to the war were made by her husband James, by her son, and by Laura herself. In a petition written 25 February 1820 and addressed to Lieutenant-Governor Sir Peregrine Maitland, James Secord requested a licence to quarry stone in the Queenston military reserve. After mentioning his own wartime service—he had served as a captain in the militia—his wounds, and the plundering of his home by American troops, Secord claimed that "his wife embraced an opportunity of rendering some service, at the risk of her own life, in going thru the Enemies' Lines to communicate information to a Detachment of His Majesty's Troops at the Beaver Dam in the month of June 1813."[17] A second, similar petition was turned down in

1827 but Maitland did propose that Laura apply for the job of looking after Brock's monument. It is not clear whether Maitland was aware of the gendered and nationalist symbolism of a Canadian woman caretaking the memory of a British General; he did, however, have "a favourable opinion of the character and claims of Mr. Secord and his wife."[18] However, Maitland's successor, Sir John Colborne, was apparently not as well-disposed toward the family and the job went to Theresa Nichol, the widow of militia Colonel Robert Nichol.[19]

When James died in 1841, Laura submitted two petitions to Governor Sydenham: one that asked that her son be given his father's post as customs' collector and another that asked for a pension. Both cited her poverty, her lack of support since her husband's death, and her need to support her daughters and grandchildren. While her petitions used the language of female dependency noted by Potter-MacKinnon in Loyalist women's submissions, they also featured her service to her country in 1813 and her new position as the head of a household.[20] Her son Charles' article, published in an 1845 edition of the Anglican paper, *The Church*, publicized her walk, calling attention to his mother's service to her country and the British Crown.[21] Eight years later Laura Secord wrote her own account of her trek to warn the British Lieutenant James Fitzgibbon, in a piece that appeared in the *Anglo American Magazine* as part of a larger narrative of the war. While this article would be used and cited by others from the 1880s on, it was written in a straightforward manner, with few of the rhetorical flourishes or personal details that would characterize later accounts. And, while Secord concluded her story with the observation that she now wondered "how I could have gone through so much fatigue, with the fortitude to accomplish it," she did not stress her need to overcome physical frailty in reaching Fitzgibbon.[22]

Secord achieved some success in her campaign for some financial recognition on the part of the state in 1860, when she presented her story to the Prince of Wales during his tour of British North America. She was also the only woman whose name appeared on an address presented by the surviving veterans of the Battle of Queenston Heights to the Prince, in a ceremony attended by 500 visitors and at which a memorial stone was laid on the site where Brock fell. Her "patriotic services," claimed the *Niagara Mail* in 1861, were "handsomely rewarded" by the Prince with an award of £100.[23] One of her more recent biographies argues that the Prince "provided the magic touch that transformed the 'widow of the late James Secord' into the heroine, Laura Secord."[24]

However, Secord did not become a heroine overnight. Her own efforts to draw attention to the service she had rendered to her country should not be seen as attempts to create a cult for herself, but rather as part of the Upper Canadian patronage game, in which loyal service to Crown and country was the way to obtain material rewards.[25] Furthermore, she died in 1868, almost twenty years before her popularity began to spread. Still, references to Secord had begun to appear in a few mid nineteenth-century accounts of the War of

1812. For example, the American historian Benson J. Lossing's *The Pictorial Field-Book of the War of 1812* devoted a page to Secord and the Battle of Beaver Dams. The page's caption read "British Troops saved by a Heroine," and Laura's own written account was the voice that supplied Lossing with his information.[26] The Canadian historian and government official, William F. Coffin, elaborated on her story by adding the cow—which, he claimed, she had milked in order to convince the American sentry to let her pass. While some regard Coffin's account as yet another example of a romantically-inclined nineteenth-century historian playing fast and loose with the facts, his placing of Secord in a context of pioneer domesticity foreshadowed subsequent stories appearing two decades later.[27] Secord thus was not rescued from complete obscurity by Curzon and others in the 1880s and '90s; she was, however, given a much more prominent place in their narratives of the war and Upper Canadian loyalty.

Sarah A. Curzon has become known in Canadian women's history as a British-born suffrage activist and a founding member of the Toronto Women's Literary Society (which would later become the Canadian Woman's Suffrage Association) and the editor of a women's page in the prohibition paper, the *Canada Citizen*. But she was also an avid promoter of Canadian history and was one of the co-founders of the Women's Canadian Historical Society of Toronto (WCHS) in 1885, along with Mary Agnes Fitzgibbon, a granddaughter of Lieutenant James Fitzgibbon. Furthermore, Curzon and Fitzgibbon were supporters of Canada's "imperial connection" to Britain, a link which they believed would benefit Canada both economically and culturally.[28] Emma Currie was another major contributor to the campaign to memorialize Secord. Indeed, her book, *The Story of Laura Secord and Canadian Reminiscences*, was published in 1900 as a fund-raiser for a monument to the "heroine" of Upper Canada. Currie lived in St. Catharines, helped found the Women's Literary Club in that city in 1892, and would later join the Imperial Order of the Daughters of the Empire (IODE). She too was a supporter of the Women's Christian Temperance Union and women's suffrage.[29]

But these women were not alone in their crusade to win recognition for Secord. Other Canadian nationalist writers like Charles Mair, Agnes Maule Machar, and William Kirby praised Secord's bravery in their poetry and prose,[30] while local historical societies and those who purported to be "national" historians, such as Ernest Cruikshank, also published papers that focused on the Battle of Beaver Dams and acknowledged Secord's role in it.[31] Much of their work, as well as that of Curzon and Currie, was part of late Victorian Canadian imperialist discourse, which perceived the past as the repository of those principles (loyalty to Britain, respect for law and order, and the capacity for democratic government) that would guide the nation into the twentieth century.[32] As Berger has argued, the local history societies that spread in the 1880s and 1890s were part of this "conservative frame of mind" in which loyalism, nationalism, and history were inextricably linked.[33]

Tributes in ink comprised the bulk of this material but they were not the only efforts to memorialize Secord. As Currie's book indicates, printed material might be used to raise funds and spread awareness in order to create more long-lasting, substantive reminders, such as monuments and statues. On June 6, 1887, W. Fenwick, a grammar school principal in Drummondville, wrote to the *Toronto World and Mail* asking for better care for the Lundy's Lane grave-yard, a national monument to be erected to honour those who had died there, and a separate monument to Laura Secord. Curzon joined in a letter-writing campaign, calling for the women of Canada to take up the matter, and peti-tions were presented to the Ontario Legislature. When these were unsuccessful, the Lundy's Lane and Ontario Historical Societies mounted fund-raising drives for the monument, sending out circulars asking Canadian women and children to contribute ten cents and one cent respectively to the cause.[34] A competition for the sculpture was held and won by a Miss Mildred Peel, an artist and sculp-tor who also would paint the portrait of Secord hung in 1905 in the Ontario Legislature.[35] After fourteen years of campaigning, the monument was un-veiled 22 June 1901 at Lundy's Lane. In 1911, the Women's Institute of Queenston and St. David's felt that the village of Queenston (site of the Secord home during the War of 1812) had not done enough to honour Secord's memory and built a Memorial Hall as part of Laura Secord school. The gesture that en-sconced her name in popular culture came in 1913, when Frank O'Connor chose Secord as the emblem for his new chain of candy stores.[36]

While it was not suggested that celebrating Secord's contribution was the sole responsibility of Canadian womanhood, many aspects of this campaign were shaped by deeply gendered notions and assumptions about both past and present. The idea that women might have a special interest in support-ing the subscription drive, for example, or petitioning the Legislature, linked perceptions of both womanhood and nationalism, drawing upon the under-lying assumptions of self-sacrifice and unselfishness that lay at the heart of both identities.[37] Groups such as the WCHS, with their "unselfish patrio-tism," were exactly what the country needed, Kirby told Mary Agnes Fitzgibbon upon being made an honorary member of the society, adding "let the women be right and the country will be might!"[38] Moreover, while male writers and historians certainly expressed an interest in Secord, it is important not to overlook the significance of the participation of Anglo Celtic, middle and upper-middle class women in the writing of Canadian history, a task they frequently undertook as members of local historical societies. Such women scrutinized historical records in order to find their foremothers (in both the lit-eral and metaphorical sense).[39] However, they also were fascinated with the entire "pioneer" period of Canadian history, both French and English, and with both male and female figures in this context. For the most part, women members of historical societies researched and presented papers on as many Generals and male explorers as they did "heroines."[40]

There was, however, a difference in their treatment of the latter. They insisted that Canadian women's contributions to nation-building be valued, even though they had not achieved the fame and recognition of their male counterparts. To be sure, they did not offer alternative narratives of early Canadian history and tended to place political and military developments at its centre. Nevertheless, they sought to widen the parameters of male historians' definitions of these events in order to demonstrate their far-reaching effects on all Canadian society. In the meetings of organizations such as Canadian Women's Historical Societies of Toronto and Ottawa, papers were given on topics such as "Early British Canadian Heroines" or "Reminiscences" of pioneer women.[41] Women such as Harriet Prudis, who was active in the London and Middlesex Historical Society during this period, believed that while the history of the pioneer women of the London area

> records no daring deed ... nor historic tramp, like that of Laura Secord, yet every life is a record of such patient endurance of privations, such brave battling with danger, such a wonderful gift for resourceful adaptability, that the simplest story of the old days must bear, within itself, the sterling elements of romance. While they took no part in the national or political happenings of the day, it may be interesting to us, and to those who come after us, to hear from their own lips how these public events affected their simple lives.[42]

Their efforts were shared by male novelists and historians who not only glorified Secord but also wished to rescue other Canadian women of her era and ilk from obscurity.[43] However, as more than one honorary member of the WCHS told Fitzgibbon, Canadian women should have a special desire to preserve records of their past. According to Mair, "the sacred domestic instincts of Canadian womanhood will not suffer in the least degree, but will rather be refreshed and strengthened" by the Society's "rescuing from destruction the scattered and perishable records of Ontario's old, and, in many respects, romantic home life."[44] The collection of material concerning this latter area, Mair and others felt, should be the special work of Canadian women.[45]

The extent to which this relegation of the "social" realm to women historians set a precedent for future developments, whereby "romantic home life" was perceived as both the preserve of women and the realm of the trivial and anecdotal, is not entirely clear.[46] Certainly it does not appear to have been Mair's intention that these areas be perceived as trivial or unworthy of male historians' attention, while women such as Mary Agnes Fitzgibbon were as eager to research battles and collect military memorabilia as they were concerned with "primitive clothing, food cookery, amusements, and observances of festivals attending births and wedlock or the *charivari*."[47] Yet it was probably no coincidence that the first historian to seriously challenge the military value of Secord's walk was the male academic W.S. Wallace, who in 1930 raised a furor amongst public supporters of Secord with questions concerning the use of historical evidence in documenting her walk.[48]

This, then, was the context in which Laura Secord became an increasingly popular symbol of Canadian patriotism: one of feminism, history, patriotism, and imperialism. While many of these histories were, as Berger has pointed out, local and might seem incredibly parochial in their scope, their authors saw locally-based stories as having a much wider emotional and moral significance in the narratives of the nation.[49] Hence, narratives of Secord's contribution to the War of 1812 and to the colonial link with the British Empire were marked by the interplay of locality, nationality, and gender. First, Laura and James Secord's backgrounds were explored and their genealogies traced, in order to place them within the Loyalist tradition of suffering and sacrifice. For those writers who were concerned with strict historical accuracy, such a task was considerably easier for the Secords than for Laura's family, the Ingersolls. James' male ancestors had fought in the Revolutionary war for the British Crown and the many military ranks occupied by the Secord men were duly listed and acclaimed. Moreover, the Secords could claim a history of both allegiance to the British Crown and a desire for the protection of the British constitution; they were descended from Huguenots who arrived in New York from La Rochelle in the late seventeenth century.[50]

But it was not only the Secord men that had served their country and suffered hardships. The loyalist legacy inherited by both Laura and James had, it was pointed out, been marked by gender differences. As Curzon told her audiences, James Secord's arrival in Canada had been as a three-year-old refugee, part of his mother's "flight through the wilderness, with four other homeless women and many children, to escape the fury of a band of ruffians who called themselves the 'sons of Liberty.' After enduring frightful hardships for nearly a month, they finally arrived at Fort Niagara almost naked and starving." Curzon went on to comment that these were by no means "uncommon experiences." Frequently, she pointed out, Loyalist men had to flee "for their lives" and leave their women and children behind (as well as their "goods, chattels, estates, and money"). Their loved ones were then left to endure the terrors of the wilderness:

> unprotected and unsupported, save by that deep faith in God and love to king and country which, with their personal devotion to their husbands, made of them heroines whose story of unparalleled devotion, hardships patiently borne, motherhood honourably sustained, industry and thrift perseveringly followed, enterprise successfully prosecuted, principle unwaveringly upheld, and tenderness never surpassed, has yet to be written, and whose share in the making of this nation remains to be equally honoured with that of the men who bled and fought for its liberties.[51]

Unfortunately for Laura's popularizers, the Ingersoll family did not fit as neatly into the Loyalist tradition. Her father, Thomas, had fought against the British in 1776 and had seen his 1793 land grant cancelled as a result of British efforts to curb large-scale immigration of American settlers into Upper Canada.[52]

As J.H. Ingersoll observed in 1926, Laura's inability to claim the United Empire Loyalist pedigree "has been commented upon." However, some historians argued that Thomas Ingersoll came to Upper Canada at Lieutenant-Governor Simcoe's request.[53] For those poets and novelists who felt free to create Laura's loyalism in a more imaginative manner, her patriotism was traced to a long-standing childhood attachment to Britain. They insisted that she chose Canada freely and was not forced to come to the country as a refugee.[54] Moreover, despite these historians' fascination with lines of blood and birth, they were equally determined to demonstrate that the former could be transcended by environment and force of personality. The loyal society of Upper Canada and the strength of Laura's own commitment to Britain were important reminders to the Canadian public that a sense of imperial duty could overcome other relationships and flourish in the colonial context.[55]

Accordingly, these historians argued, it should come as no surprise that both Laura and her husband felt obliged to perform their patriotic duty when American officers were overheard planning an attack on the British forces of Lieutenant Fitzgibbon.[56] However, James was still suffering from wounds sustained at the Battle of Queenston Heights and it therefore fell to Laura—over her husband's objections and concern for her safety—to walk the twenty miles from Queenston to warn the British troops at Beaver Dams. (Here the linear chronology of the narratives was frequently interrupted to explain out that Laura had come to his aid after the battle when, finding him badly wounded and in danger of being beaten to death by "common" American soldiers, she had attempted to shield him with her own body from their rifle butts—further evidence that Laura was no stranger to wifely and patriotic duty.[57])

Laura's journey took on wider dimensions and greater significance in the hands of her commemorators. It was no longer just a walk to warn the British but, with its elements of venturing into the unknown, physical sacrifice, and devotion to the British values of order and democracy, came to symbolize the entire "pioneer womanish experience in Canadian history."[58] Leaving the cozy domesticity and safety of her home, the company of her wounded husband and children, Secord had ventured out into the Upper Canadian wilderness with its swamps and underbrush in which threatening creatures, such as rattlesnakes, bears, and wolves, might lurk.[59] And even when Sarah Curzon's 1887 play permitted Laura to deliver several monologues on the loveliness of the June woodland, the tranquillity of the forest was disrupted by the howling of wolves.[60]

But most serious of all, in the majority of accounts, was the threat of the "Indians" she might meet on the way. If Secord's commitment to Canada and Britain had previously been presented in cultural terms, ones that could be encouraged by the colonial tie and that might transcend race, it was at this point that her significance as a symbol of white Canadian womanhood was clearest. While her feminine fragility had been the subject of comment throughout the stories, and while her racial background might have been the underlying sub-text for this fragility, it was in the discussions of the threat of native warriors that her gender became most clearly racialized.[61] Unlike the contemporary racist and cultural stereotypes of threatening black male sexuality used in American lynching campaigns, however, her fears were not of sexual violence by native men—at least not explicitly—but of the tactics supposedly used by native men in warfare, scalping being the most obvious.[62]

To be sure, some stories mentioned that Secord had had to stay clear of open roads and paths "for fear of Indians *and* white marauders" (emphasis mine).[63] But even those who downplayed her fear of a chance encounter with an "Indian" during her journey were scrupulous in their description of her fright upon encountering Mohawks outside the British camp. Secord herself had stated that she had stumbled across the Mohawks' camp and that they had shouted "woman" at her, making her "tremble" and giving her an "awful feeling." It was only with difficulty, she said, that she convinced them to take her to Fitzgibbon.[64] As this meeting with the natives was retold, they became more menacing and inspired even greater fear in Secord. In these accounts, at this penultimate stage in her journey she stepped on a twig that snapped and startled an Indian encampment. Quite suddenly Secord was surrounded by them, "the chief throws up his tomahawk to strike, regarding the intruder as a spy."[65] In some narratives, he shouted at her "woman! what does woman want!" Only her courage in springing to his arm is the woman saved, and an opportunity snatched to assure him of her loyalty.[66]

Moved by pity and admiration, the chief gave her a guide, and at length she reached Fitzgibbon, delivered and verified her message—"and *faints*."[67] Fitzgibbon then went off to fight the Battle of Beaver Dams, armed with the knowledge that Secord had brought him and managed to successfully rout the American forces. In a number of narratives, this victory was frequently achieved by using the threat of unleashed Indian savagery when the Americans were reluctant to surrender.[68] While the battle was being fought, Secord was moved to a nearby house, where she slept off her walk, and then returned to the safety of her home and family. She told her family about her achievement but, motivated by fear for their security (as American troops continued to occupy the Niagara area) as well as by her own modesty and self-denial, she did not look for any recognition or reward. Such honours came first to Fitzgibbon.[69]

Women such as Curzon and Currie might see Secord's contribution as natural and unsurprising (given her devotion to her country) but they also were keenly aware that their mission of commemoration necessitated that their work appeal to a popular audience. These narratives were imbued with their authors' concerns with the relations of gender, class, and race and the way in which they perceived these identities to structure both Canadian society and history. For one, Secord's "natural" feminine fragility was a major theme of their writings. As a white woman of good birth and descent she was not physically suited to undertake the hardships involved in her walk (although, paradoxically, as a typical "pioneer woman" she was able to undertake the hardships of raising a family and looking after a household in a recently-settled area). Her delicacy and slight build, first mentioned by Fitzgibbon in his own testimony of her walk, was frequently stressed by those who commemorated her.[70] Her physical frailty could be contrasted with the manly size and strength of soldiers such as Fitzgibbon and Brock.[71] Nevertheless, the seeming physical immutability of gender was not an insurmountable barrier to her patriotic duty to country and empire. The claims of the latter transcended corporeal limitations. Even her maternal duties, understood by both conservatives and many feminists in late nineteenth-century Canada to be the core of womanly identity, could be put aside or even reformulated in order to answer her country's needs.[72] While her supporters did not make explicit their motives in stressing her frailty, it is possible to see it as a subtext to counter medical and scientific arguments about female physical deficiencies that made women, particularly white, middle class women, unfit for political participation and higher education.[73]

Furthermore, there were other ways to make Secord both appealing and a reflection of their own conceptions of "Canadian womanhood," and many historians treated her as an icon of respectable white heterosexual femininity. Anecdotes supposedly told by her family were often added to the end of the narratives of her walk—especially those written by women—and these emphasized her love of children, her kindness and charity towards the elderly, and her very feminine love of finery and gaiety (making her daughters' satin slippers, for example, and her participation as a young woman in balls given by the Secords at Newark). Indeed, they went so far as to discuss the clothing that she wore on her walk. Her daughter Harriet told Currie that she and her sisters saw their mother leave that morning wearing "a flowered print gown, I think it was brown with orange flowers, at least a yellow tint .... "[74] Elizabeth Thompson, who was active within the Ontario Historical Society and was also a member of the IODE, also wrote that Secord wore a print dress, adding a "cottage bonnet tied under her chin ... balbriggan stockings, with red silk clocks on the sides, and low shoes with buckles"—both of which were lost during the walk.[75]

For her most active supporters, the walk of Laura Secord meant that certain women could be written into the record of loyalty and patriotic duty in Canadian history, and female heroines cold gain recognition for the deeds they had committed. In the eyes of these historians, such recognition had heretofore been withheld simply because of these figures' gender, for in every other significant feature—their racial and ethnic identities, for example—they were no different than their male counterparts. But such additions to the narrative were intended to be just that: additions, not serious disruptions of the story's focus on the ultimate triumph of British institutions and the imperial tie in Canada. Like her walk, Secord herself was constructed in many ways as the archetypical "British" pioneer woman of Loyalist history, remembered for her willingness to struggle, sacrifice, and thus contribute to "nation-building." These historians also suggested that patriotic duties and loyalty to the state did not automatically constitute a major threat to late nineteenth-century concepts of masculinity and femininity. Secord could undertake such duties, but still had to be defined by her relations to husband and children, home and family. She did not, it was clear, take up arms herself, nor did she use her contribution to win recognition for her own gain.

In the context of late nineteenth- and early twentieth-century debates about gender relations in Canadian society, Secord was a persuasive symbol of how certain women might breach the division between "private" and "public," the family and the state, and do so for entirely unselfish and patriotic reasons. The narratives of Laura Secord's walk helped shape an image of Canadian womanhood in the past that provided additional justification and inspiration for turn-of-the-century Canadian feminists. These women could invoke memory and tradition when calling for their own inclusion in the "imagined community" of the Canadian nation of the late nineteenth century.[76] Furthermore, for those such as Curzon who were eager to widen their frame of national reference, Secord's legacy could be part of an imperialist discourse, linking gender, race, nation, and empire in both the past and the present.

Acknowledgement

Much of the research and writing of this paper was conducted with the financial assistance of Canada Employment. I would also like to thank Colin Coates, Mariana Valverde, and the *Journal's* anonymous readers for their much-appreciated suggestions and encouragement. The members of the gender, history, and national identities study group have provided invaluable comments and support: Lykke de la Cour, Paul Deslandes, Stephen Heathorn, Maureen McCarthy, and Tori Smith.

Notes

1. A Dorion Gray-like image that, as the company has enjoyed pointing out, becomes younger with the passage of time. See the advertisement, "There must be something in the chocolate," *Globe and Mail*, 25 November 1992, A14.

2. This term has been an invaluable methodological tool in thinking about the narratives of Secord. See Benedict Anderson, *Imagined Communities: Reflections on the Origin and Spread of Nationalism*, Revised Edition (London and New York, 1991). See also Eric Hobsbawm and Terence Ranger, (eds.) *The Invention of Tradition* (New York, 1983). Like Anderson's work, however, this collection does not address the complex relationships of gender, nationalism, and the "invented traditions" it analyses.

3. Carl Berger, *The Sense of Power: Studies in the Ideas of Canadian Imperialism 1867–1914* (Toronto, 1970), 78.

4. Catherine Hall, Jane Lewis, Keith McClelland, and Jane Rendall, "Introduction," *Gender and History: Special Issue on Gender, Nationalisms, and National Identities* 5:2 (Summer 1993): 159–64, 159.

5. Recent work by historians of Indian nationalism explores the use of female images, particularly that of the nation as mother. See, for example, Samita Sen, "Motherhood and Mother craft: Gender and Nationalism in Bengal," *Gender and History: Special Issue on Gender, Nationalisms and National Identities*, 231–43. See also the essays in *History Workshop Journal, Special Issue: Colonial and Post-Colonial History* 36 (Autumn 1993) and Mrinalini Sinha, "Reading *Mother India*: Empire, Nation, and the Female Voice," *Journal of Women's History* 6:2 (Summer 1994): 6–44.

6. One of the few Canadian historians to point to these connections has been George Ingram, in "The Story of Laura Secord Revisited," *Ontario History* LVII: 2 (June 1965): 85–97. Other works tackling these questions have looked at such areas as social reform. See Angus McLaren, *Our Own Master Race: Eugenics in Canada, 1885–1945* (Toronto, 1990) and Mariana Valverde, *The Age of Light, Soap, and Water: Moral Reform in English Canada 1885–1925* (Toronto, 1991).

7. For a heroine who was not so easily domesticated, see Colin M. Coates, "Commemorating the Woman Warrior of New France: Madeleine de Verchères, 1696–1930," paper presented to the 72nd Annual Conference of the Canadian Historical Association, Ottawa, June 1993; also Marina Warner, *Joan of Arc: The Image of Female Heroism* (London, 1981).

8. See, for example, the *Transactions* of both the Women's Canadian Historical Society of Ottawa and those of the Women's Canadian Historical Society of Toronto, from the 1890s to the 1920s.

9. David Mills, *The Idea of Loyalty in Upper Canada, 1784–1850* (Montreal and Kingston, 1988).

10. Donald H. Akenson, *The Irish in Ontario: A Study in Rural History* (Montreal and Kingston, 1984), 134.

11. See Cecilia Morgan, "Languages of Gender in Upper Canadian Politics and Religion, 1791–1850" (Ph.D. Thesis, University of Toronto, 1993), Chapter 11. It is interesting that, while the militia myth has been challenged by many historians, its gendered nature has received very little attention. See, for example, the most recent study of the War of 1812., George Sheppard's *Plunder, Profit, and Paroles: A Social History of the War of 1812 in Upper Canada* (Montreal and Kingston, 1994).

12. Morgan, 56–60; see also Keith Walden, "Isaac Brock: Man and Myth: A Study of the militia myth of the War of 1812 in Upper Canada 1812–1912" (M.A. Thesis, Queen's University, 1971).

13. Janice Potter-MacKinnon, *While the Women Only Wept: Loyalist Refugee Women in Eastern Ontario* (Montreal and Kingston, 1993), 158.

14. Coates, "Commemorating the Heroine of New France."

15. Morgan, chap II.

16. On the French Revolution, see Maurice Agulhon, *Marianne into Battle: Republican Imagery and Symbolism in France, 1789–1880* (Trans. by Janet Lloyd. Cambridge, 1981). For republican motherhood, see Linda Kerber, "The Republican Mother: Female Political Imagination in the Early Republic," in *Women of the Republic: Intellect and Ideology in Revolutionary America* (Chapel Hill, 1980); for Britannia, see Madge Dresser, "Britannia," in Raphael Samuel (ed.), *Patriotism, the Making and Unmaking of British National Identity*, Volume III: *National Fictions* (London, 1989), 26–49.

17. The petition is reprinted in Ruth McKenzie's *Laura Secord: The Legend and the Lady* (Toronto, 1971), 74–75. To date, McKenzie's book is the most thorough and best-researched popular account of the development of the Secord legend.

18. *Ibid.*, 76.

19. *Ibid.*, 76–77; also Sheppard, 221.

20. McKenzie, 84–85.

21. *Ibid.*, 49ff.

22. *Ibid.*, 91–92; also in Benson J. Lossing, *The Pictorial Field Book of the War of 1812* (New York, 1869), 621.

23. McKenzie, 102.

24. *Ibid.*, 103–4.

25. For an analysis of patronage in nineteenth-century Ontario, see S.J.R. Noel, *Patrons, Clients, Brokers: Ontario Society and Politics 1791–1896* (Toronto, 1990).

26. Lossing, 621.

27. William F. Coffin, *1812: The War, and Its Moral: A Canadian Chronicle* (Montreal, 1864), 148.

28. See Sarah A. Curzon, *Laura Secord, the Heroine of 1812: A Drama and Other Poems* (Toronto, 1887). For biographical sketches of Curzon and Fitzgibbon, see Henry James Morgan, *The Canadian Men and Women of the Time: A Hand-Book of Canadian Biography* (Toronto, 1898 and 1912), 235–36 and 400. Curzon's work is briefly discussed in Carol Bacchi's *Liberation Deferred? The Ideas of the English Canadian Suffragists, 1877–1918* (Toronto, 1981), 26–27 and 44, but Bacchi's frame of reference does not take in Curzon's (or other suffragists') interest in history as an important cultural aspect of their maternal feminism and imperialism.

29. Morgan, 1912, 288–89; see also Mrs. G.M. Armstrong, *The First Eighty Years of the Women's Literary Club of St. Catharines, 1892–1972* (n.p., 1972); Emma A. Currie, *The Story of Laura Secord and Canadian Reminiscences* (St. Catharines, 1913).

30. Charles Mair, "A Ballad for Brave Women," in *Tecumseh: A Drama and Canadian Poems* (Toronto, 1901), 147; William Kirby, *Annals of Niagara*, ed. and intro. by Lorne Pierce (Toronto, 1927, first ed. 1896), 209–10. Kirby had been Currie's childhood tutor in Niagara and both she and Curzon continued to look to him for advice, support, and recognition (Archives of Ontario [AO], MS 542, William Kirby Correspondence, Reel 1, Curzon and Currie to Kirby, 1887–1906). Kirby and Mair were made honorary members of the WCHS (AO, MU 7837–7838, Series A, WCHS papers, Correspondence File 1, William Kirby to Mary Agnes Fitzgibbon, April 11, 1896, Charles Mair to Fitzgibbon, May 8, 1896). For Machar, see "Laura Secord," in her *Lays of the True North and Other Poems* (Toronto, 1887), 35. See also Ruth Compton Brouwer, "Moral Nationalism in Victorian Canada: The Case of Agnes Machar," *Journal of Canadian Studies*, 20: 1 (Spring 1985): 90–108.

31. See, for example, "The Heroine of the Beaver Dams," *Canadian Antiquarian and Numismatic Journal* VIII (Montreal, 1879): 135–36. Many thanks to Colin Coates for this reference. See also Ernest Cruikshank, *The Fight in the Beechwoods* (Lundy's Lane Historical Society: Drummondville, 1889), 1, 13, 14, 19.

32. Berger, 89–90.

33. *Ibid.*, 95–96.

34. Janet Carnochan, "Laura Secord Monument at Lundy's Lane," *Transactions of the Niagara Historical Society* (Niagara, 1913), 11–18.

35. Carnochan, 13.

36. McKenzie, 118–19.

37. Marilyn Lake has made a similar argument about Australian nationalist discourse during World War I. See her, "Mission Impossible: How Men Gave Birth to the Australian Nation—Nationalism, Gender and Other Seminal Acts," *Gender and History: Special Issue on Motherhood, Race and the State in the Twentieth Century* 4:3 (Autumn 1992): 305–22, particularly 307. For the theme of self-sacrifice in Canadian nationalism, see Berger, 217. The links between the discourses of late-Victorian, white, bourgeois femininity and that of Canadian racial policy have been explored by Valverde in *The Age of Light, Soap, and Water*, in the contexts of moral reform, the white slavery panic, and immigration policies. See also Bacchi, *Liberation Deferred?*, ch. 7. For gender and imperialism in the British and American contexts, see Vron Ware, *Beyond the Pale: White Women, Racism and History* (London and New York, 1992). The seminal article on imperialism and British womanhood is Anna Davin, "Imperialism and Motherhood," *History Workshop Journal* 5 (Spring 1978): 9–65.

38. WCHS papers, MU 7837–7838, Series A, Correspondence File 1, Kirby to Fitzgibbon, April 14, 1896.

39. See, for example, Mrs. J.R. Hill, "Early British Canadian Heroines," *Women's Canadian Historical Society of Ottawa Transactions*, 10 (1928): 93–98; Harriet Prudis, "Reminiscences of Mrs. Gilbert Ponte," *London and Middlesex Historical Society Transactions* (1902, pub. 1907): 62–64.

40. Harriet Prudis, "The 100th Regiment," *L & M H S Transactions*, V (1912–1913), n.p.; Agnes Dunbar Chamberlin, "The Colored Citizens of Toronto," *WCHS of Toronto Transactions*, 8 (1908): 9–15; also the biography of Brock by Lady Edgar, one of the first presidents of the WCHS [*Life of General Brock* (Toronto, 1904)].

41. See note 37 above.

42. Prudis, 62.

43. See Ernest Green, "Some Canadian Women of 1812–14," *WCHS of Ottawa Transactions* 9 (1925): 98–109.

44. WCHS papers, MU 7837–7838, Series A, Correspondence File 1, Mair to Fitzgibbon, May 8, 1896.

45. *Ibid.*; see also WCHS papers, MU 7837–7838, Series A, Correspondence File 1, John H. to Fitzgibbon, May 6, 1896.

46. As Linda Kerber argues, it was precisely this relegation that women's historians of the 1960s and '70s had to confront in their attempts to lift women's lives from the "realm of the trivial and anecdotal." See her "Separate Spheres, Female Worlds, Woman's Place: The Rhetoric of Women's History," *The Journal of American History* 75: 1 (June 1988): 9–39, especially 37.

47. Mair to Fitzgibbon, May 8,1896.

48. W.S. Wallace, *The Story of Laura Secord* (Toronto, 1932). For a response to Wallace, see "What Laura Secord Did," *Dunnville Weekly Chronicle*, 35 (1932), reprinted from Toronto *Saturday Night*, June 22, 1932.

49. Berger, 96. As M. Brook Taylor has pointed out about the work of nineteenth-century writers such as John Charles Dent, Francis Hincks, and Charles Lindsey, "National historians were essentially Upper Canadian historians in Masquerade." See his *Promoters Patriots, and Partisans: Historiography in Nineteenth-Century Canada* (Toronto, 1989), 231.

50. Currie, 21–33.

51. Curzon, *The Story of Laura Secord, 1813* (Lundy's Lane Historical Society, July 25, 1891) 6–7.

52. See Gerald M. Craig, *Upper Canada: The Formative Years 1784–1841* (Toronto, 1963), 49, for a discussion of this shift in policy. McKenzie also argues that Ingersoll did not fulfill his settlement obligations (29). See also Currie, 38–39.

53. J.H. Ingersoll, "The Ancestry of Laura Secord," *Ontario Historical Society* (1926): 361–63. See also Elizabeth Thompson, "Laura Ingersoll Secord," 1. Others argued that Ingersoll was urged by Joseph Brant to come to Upper Canada (Ingersoll, 363). The Brant connection was developed most fully and romantically by John Price-Brown in *Laura the Undaunted: A Canadian Historical Romance* (Toronto, 1930). It has also been pointed out that Price-Brown picked up the story, "invented out of whole cloth" by Curzon, that Tecumseh had fallen in love with one of Secord's daughters. See Dennis Duffy, *Gardens, Covenants, Exiles: Loyalism in the Literature of Upper Canada / Ontario* (Toronto, 1982), 61. In Price-Brown's account, Tecumseh proposes just before he is killed; Laura, however, disapproves of the match (259–69).

54. Price-Brown, 16–17, 180–82.

55. Just as French-Canadians could overcome other ties (see Berger, 138–39).

56. Thompson, 2; Currie, 48; Ingersoll, 362.

57. Price-Brown's "fictional" account is the most colourful, since one of the American officers who did not intervene to save the Secords was a former suitor of Laura's, whom she had rejected in favour of James and Canada (252–5). See also Currie, 53–54.

58. Norman Knowles, in his study of late nineteenth-century Ontario commemorations of Loyalism, argues that pioneer and rural myths subsumed those of Loyalism ("Inventing the Loyalists: The Ontario Loyalist Tradition and the Creation of a Usable Past, 1784–1924," Ph.D. thesis, York University 1990). To date, my research on women commemorators indicates that, for them, both Loyalism (particularly people, places, and artifacts having to do with 1812) and the "pioneer past" were closely intertwined; both were of great significance and inspirational power in their interpretations of the past. See Elizabeth Thompson, *The Pioneer Woman: A Canadian Character Type* (Montreal and Kingston, 1991) for a study of this archetype in the fiction of Canadian authors Catherine Parr Trail, Sara Jeanette Duncan, Ralph Connor, and Margaret Laurence.

59. The most extensive description is in Curzon's *The Story of Laura Secord*, 11–12.

60. Curzon, *Laura Secord: The Heroine of the War of 1812*, 39–47.

61. While examining a very different period and genre of writing, I have found Carroll Smith-Rosenberg's "Captured Subjects/Savage others; Violently Engendering the new American" to be extremely helpful in understanding the construction of white womanhood in the North American context. See *Gender and History* 5: 2 (Summer 1993), 177–95. See also Vron Ware, "Moments of Danger: Race, Gender, and Memories of Empire," *History and Theory* Beiheft (1992); 116–37.

62. See Ware, "To Make the Facts Known," in *Beyond the Pale* for a discussion of lynching and the feminist campaign against it. Smith-Rosenberg points to a similar treatment of native men in Mary Rowlandson's seventeenth-century captivity narrative (183–84). While the two examples should not be conflated, this issue does call for further analysis.

63. Cruikshank, 13.

64. Secord in Thompson, 4–5.

65. See, for example, Blanche Hume, *Laura Secord* (Toronto, 1928), 1. This book was part of a Ryerson Canadian History Readers series, endorsed by the IODE and the Provincial Department of Education.

66. *Ibid.*, 15.

67. Curzon, *The Story of Laura Secord*, 13.

68. See, for example, Cruikshank, 18.

69. Currie, 52–53. Fitzgibbon supposedly took full credit for the victory, ignoring both Secord's and the Caughnawaga Mohawks' roles (McKenzie, 66–67). He later became a Colonel in the York militia and was rewarded for his role in putting down the 1837 rebellion with a £1,000 grant (89–90).

70. Fitzgibbon in Thompson, 6.

71. Hume, 4.

72. For example, in Curzon's play Secord is asked by her sister-in-law, the Widow Secord, if her children will not "blame" her should she come to harm. She replies that "children can see the right at one quick glance," suggesting that their mother's maternal care and authority is bound to her patriotism and loyalty (34).

73. See Wendy Mitchinson, *The Nature of their Bodies: Women and Their Doctors in Victorian Canada* (Toronto, 1991), especially "The Frailty of Women."

74. Currie, 71.

75. Thompson, 3. Balbriggan was a type of fine, unbleached, knitted cotton hosiery material.

76. See Hobsbawm and Ranger, "Introduction: Inventing Tradition," particularly their argument that invented traditions are often shaped and deployed by those who wish to either legitimate particular institutions or relations of authority or to inculcate certain beliefs of values (9). In this case I would argue that the Secord tradition served very similar purposes, although it was used to both legitimate and, for certain groups of women, to subvert.

CHAPTER

9 THE FUR TRADE AND THE NORTHWEST

The fur trade and Canadian history are indivisible. One might even speak of the tyranny of the fur trade as every trading post, canoe route, and fur battle was pursued by the antiquarians to the point of saturation. At the academic level, Harold Innis established an international reputation with his *The Fur Trade in Canada: An Introduction to Canadian Economic History* (1930), and he provided both an economic and a geographic explanation for Canada's existence. The fur trade was also the glue for A.S. Morton's *History of the Canadian West to 1870–71* (1939), a sympathetic examination of the Hudson's Bay Company as a western institution and eventual Canadian benefactor. To Morton, the Company was an enlightened paternalist with the best interests of its employees, its clients and native suppliers at heart. The fur trade certainly drew the Europeans into the west, and it is the interaction between the natives and the whites that dominates W.L. Morton's "The North West Company: Pedlars Extraordinary," reproduced here. Written in 1966, the article offers what Morton calls a "rather quaint" analysis of the labour market of the "happily primitive" natives. He then turns to the North West Company, the "greatest of all" Canadian fur trading companies and "the first successful combination of European capital and business enterprise with Indian skills."

In recent years, the studies of the fur trade, the native peoples and the companies have assumed a different character. Susan Giannettino, an anthropologist, examines "The Middleman Role in the Fur Trade: Its Influence on Interethnic Relations in the Saskatchewan-Missouri Plains." In a sense, Giannettino extends the middleman concept of the Hunt Thesis (*see* Chapter 1) to the prairies, though her concern is with the interior of the native society and the interaction among native groups. An even more significant departure in the study of the fur trade is obvious in Glen Makahonuk's "Wage-Labour in the Northwest Fur Trade Economy, 1760–1849." The relationship between the employees and the companies is placed squarely within the emerging capitalistic-labour system, and the notions of the benign parental companies are challenged at many levels. He points to the exploitive-adversarial encounters as a "clear expression of the disharmony and class tensions in the fur trade economy."

Suggestions for Further Reading

Brown, Jennifer S.H., *Strangers in Blood: Fur Trade Families in Indian Country*. Vancouver: University of British Columbia Press, 1980.

Carlos, A., "The Birth and Death of Predatory Competition in the North American Fur Trade: 1810–1821," *Explorations in Economic History*, 19, no. 2 (1982) 156–183.

Coates, K., "Furs along the Yukon: Hudson's Bay Company—Native Trade in the Yukon River Basin, 1830–1893," *B C Studies*, no. 55 (Autumn 1982), 50–78.

Friesen, Gerald, *The Canadian Prairies: A History*. Toronto: Oxford University Press, 1984.

Judd, Carol M. and Arthur J. Ray, *Old Trails and New Directions: Papers of the Third North American Fur Trade Conference*. Toronto: University of Toronto Press, 1980.

Judd, Carol M. "Native labour and social stratification in the Hudson's Bay Company's Northern department (1770–1870),"
Canadian Review of Sociology and Anthropology, 17, no. 4 (November 1980), 305–314.

Moodie, D. Wayne, "The Trading Post Settlement of the Canadian Northwest, 1774–1821," *Journal of Historical Geography*, 13, no. 2 (October 1987), 360–374.

Ray, Arthur, *Indians in the Fur Trade*. Toronto: University of Toronto Press, 1974.

Rich, E.E., *The Fur Trade and the North West to 1857*. Toronto: McClelland & Stewart, 1967.

THE NORTH WEST COMPANY: PEDLARS EXTRAORDINARY

W.L. Morton

That the North American fur trade was essentially a commercial marriage of primitive ways and needs to the more advanced techniques and demands of European and Chinese markets is one of those truths so evident and general that they could scarcely be proved if there were need. Similarly, the North West Company before 1821 was an extraordinarily successful union of the primitive culture of the forest Indian tribes with the sophisticated civilization of Western Europe. This paper tries to point the way toward a study of the company's effective merger of commerce and culture; it attempts to be a critical essay rather than a piece of research.[1]

Originally published in the Winter 1966 issue of *Minnesota History,* copyright 1967 by the Minnesota Historical Society.

Let us begin by noting that the North American Indian with whom the fur trade was conducted was an inland forest dweller. Unlike the Eskimo and the European, he neither lived by nor used the sea. Trade between him and the transoceanic European, accordingly, turned upon either the Indian going to the shore or the European going inland.

The earliest barter was of course entirely coastal, even when separated from fishing voyages and pursued as a distinct undertaking. The scattered references we possess to the fur trade of the sixteenth century all allude to trade on the coast, whether casual or at a seaside rendezvous. The first historically known rendezvous was Tadoussac on the Gulf of St. Lawrence; Quebec, Trois Rivières, and Montreal were each in turn meant to be the same, but the trade was carried steadily inland by the happy accident of the great sea entry of the St. Lawrence River. A similar entry was Hudson Bay, and a far more successful example of the coastal trade was that pursued by the Hudson's Bay Company from 1669 to 1774, until the competition of the trade from Canada forced the English company also to begin trading inland.

The obvious commercial advantage to Europeans of the coastal trade was that it placed on the Indians the cost of transporting furs to the seaside and goods inland. More significant to the theme of this paper is that for the Europeans it avoided the necessity of mastering the techniques and manners of Indian travel and life. Coastal trade provided a meeting place for commercial barter with a minimum of cultural exchange, whereas the inland trade could be carried on only by Indian means. The Europeans had to become "Indianized," and cultural exchange was greatly increased. The French traders led in this process, and the North West Company, as the heir of the Frenchmen, became the principal representative of European commerce and culture in the inland fur trade.

Before the rise and character of the company are discussed, it is necessary to examine the part played by one of the two partners in the fur trade—the primitive or Indian. The Indians of the northern forest zone were a semi-nomadic people who lived by food gathering: hunting, fishing, and picking fruits in season. Tribes like the Montagnais and the Cree, who depended purely on hunting and fishing, were more strictly speaking nomadic. Many tribes, however—notably the Iroquoian—had acquired the culture of Indian corn; some were harvesters of wild rice; and some tapped the hard maple for sugar.[2] The need to return to or remain by the cornfields, the rice lakes, and the sugar bushes explains why they are termed semi-nomadic, and even this is perhaps not to be applied to tribes like the Hurons or the Onondaga, whose lands were rich in corn. But these people had a "shifting" agriculture, and almost no Indian tribe was fully and finally committed to one spot—"settled" in the European sense of the word.

Even with supplements like corn, wild rice, and maple sugar, most Indians relied in the main on hunting and fishing for their food. Both meant considerable movement, dispersal in the winter to the hunting grounds, and congregation at the fishing runs and the fields and berry patches in summer.[3] On the hunt the Indian relied almost wholly on deer hide and beaver robes for his clothing. Thus his culture possessed two necessities of the fur trade: the means to live on the country as it was, and furs themselves.

Commerce with the whites might improve the means of hunting and of fishing. Such items as the gun, the iron hatchet, and the steel trap increased the Indian's efficiency, but his own culture had long provided the essential tools, such as the bow and arrow, the stone axe, and the deadfall—plus a forest craft not easily learned, let alone improved upon. To live in the forest it was imperative to be able to move, both as a lone hunter and in bands. This the Indian could do with a skill which the European was to surpass only by the aid of the mechanical inventions of the nineteenth century. The Indian possessed the canoe in its most exquisite form—the birchbark. This product of the northern forest and the remarkable craft of canoe-building was in fact to be the prime mover of the Canadian fur trade. It was used from the first by the Indian to bring furs to the coastal rendezvous, and by the European to penetrate inland. Fragile it was, but it possessed the inestimable advantage that it could be repaired on the spot, given a readily available supply of birch bark, spruce root, and spruce gum.

The canoe gave to the Indian a summer range of hundreds—even thousands—of miles. No such travel was possible in winter, but the Indian culture did provide means for the movement of men and goods necessary to hunting and following trap lines. Snowshoes and moccasins made walking possible over the deep, soft snow of the northern woods, and the toboggan enabled the hunter to transport his game and furs. These two means of movement were as indispensable to the fur trapping of the winter as the canoe was to the fur trade of the summer.

Thus there were in the primitive economy all but two of the elements needed to sustain the fur trade. These two—market demand and capital to finance a year's operation of fur collection, transport, and sale—Europeans were to supply, along with the management that was to bring all together in a functioning system. But it was not only tools and techniques that the Indian culture supplied to the trade. Most important of all was manpower.[4] The aboriginal Indian was the first hunter and trapper, the first canoeman and snowshoer, and the white trapper and voyageur were his pupils. In the lands that became the United States the latter largely supplanted him as trappers and boatmen, but in the Canadian forests the local Indian has remained the principal fur-taker down to the present. The fur trader relied not only on local hunters; he sometimes persuaded whole bands to move with him or used Indians like the eastern Iroquois, who found regular employment in following the trade.[5]

The work of the Indian hunter and trapper was augmented by that of the Indian woman, preparer of food, carrier of burdens, curer of furs, and sewer of shirts, leggings, and moccasins. These tasks, of course, were exclusively the squaw's work, such being the rigid division of labour between the sexes in the Indian culture. It was therefore practically impossible to live off the country and carry on the fur trade without the assistance of Indian women. It is not necessary to mention their additional role as mothers of new manpower, but it is perhaps fitting to recall the remarkable economy with which they performed all these necessary functions. As the Chipewyan chief, Matonabbee, pointed out in man-to-man fashion to Samuel Hearne, "Women were made for labour; one of them can carry, or haul, as much as two men can do.... the very licking of their fingers in scarce times, is sufficient for their subsistence.... [and they] keep us warm at night."[6]

Even this does not quite exhaust the services of the Indian woman to the fur trade. As in all commerce, there was a considerable element of diplomacy, which was necessary to soothe tribal rivalries and prevent tribal wars, and as in all diplomacy, women had a part to play. From the day of Pocahontas on, there are indications that women sometimes eased diplomatic relations between Indian and European. Certainly, as astute traders noted from time to time, marriage to a chief's daughter might well be good for business, and the kinship marriage conferred greatly eased the difficulty of persuading Indians to remain loyal to those who financed their hunt.

Children born of such unions came to be a significant and useful group in the fur trade. Not European, not Indian, although closer as children of the wilderness to the Indian way of life, the *métis*, or mixed-bloods, came to make up a large part of the work force and were a striking example of the Indianization of the European in the fur trade. They were in their own persons—not always happily—the very realization of that union of the primitive and the sophisticated that was the fur trade as practised by the North West Company.

In the Canadian fur trade, therefore, the only good Indian was not a dead one; he was, on the contrary, a live one who would follow his trap line. From this need for the Indian as a fur-gatherer arose the traders' interest in Indian population and the attempts to estimate it, as in the census of the Northwest recorded by Alexander Henry the Younger.[7] The Indian band had its own hunting grounds, a territory on the wildlife of which it could live by hunting, aided with such other food as could be grown or gathered. Hunting grounds were vague areas, changed by war or epidemic disease, or by deliberate migration, such as that of the Chippewa from north of Lake Huron westward to the Lake of the Woods and the Red River country. In exploring for new fur country it was therefore necessary to know not only the wildlife, food resources, and waterways; equally important were the number, disposition, and needs of the people. It was never enough that there should be beavers and martens; there must also be Indians from whom to buy food and purchase furs.

Solemnly to discuss the historic Indian in the language of a modern labour gazette is, of course, rather quaint. The Indian was a happily primitive person. He had not been made a labourer, a hand, or a businessman of punctual habits and tense drive by centuries of disciplined civilization. He suffered many miseries, but unemployment and gastric ulcers were not among them. He did only what was necessary to keep himself alive. It was exceedingly difficult to add to his wants, except by replacing a known article by a superior one of a like kind: a bow by a gun, a birch-bark vessel by a brass one, or a moose hide by a woolen blanket. Only liquor—and for the Plains Indian, the horse—created a want hitherto unknown and a means of inducing him to trap beyond the need to obtain the essentials of his simple life. Liquor, however, could not be used merely as a commodity, because drunken Indians were likely to become murderous and reduce their scant numbers at an alarming rate. Accordingly, the skilled trader used it as a treat, a loss leader, an inducement given freely to win the Indian to work.

To what degree the Indian ever understood or adopted European commercial and economic concepts of exchange is open to question. He was of course quite as intelligent a being as the European trader and had a very keen sense of how the primary producer benefited from the rivalry of competing buyers and of how he suffered from monopoly. But this arose from practical observation, not from economic reasoning. His culture gave exchange another meaning than the commercial one. His nomad's sense of hospitality to the stranger, his tribal sense of obligation to kindred, led him to give freely what others needed and to expect to receive freely in return. To him trade was reciprocity in giving, not mutual benefit in exchange.[8]

The Indian and even the *métis* lacked the commercial sense. He did not precisely understand credit or price changes, and he felt little obligation to pay debts. He did, however, acknowledge the obligation to give to those who had given to him, a sense that had to be kept alive by constant care lest the image of the trader who had given credit should fade in the presence of a rival who would offer new presents for the furs that should have gone to settle the accounts of his competitor.

Similarly, the Indian quite lacked any sense of the need to work for the morrow or to grow in riches. He met each day's needs if he could; if not, he starved, enduring privation with singular equanimity. Except for some individuals, he was as unsatisfactory a workman as he was a producer. How unsatisfactory he could be to a well-brought-up young Scot or Yankee can be seen on page after page in the journals of the younger Alexander Henry or of Daniel Harmon.[9] In this the Indian was the product of his total environment. His being so only increases the significance of the skills, endurance, and courage of the fur trader who had to be everything from doctor to policeman, while filling his canoes as well. The greatest accomplishment of such men was the North West Company, a mighty business organization that existed by the capacity of its wintering partners to induce the Indian to trap regularly.

It was this ability of the North West Company to use the manpower and the skills of primitive culture that made it at its height the greatest of all Canadian—perhaps of all—fur trading companies. Its ultimate failure was as a business concern, not as a fur-gathering organization. Probably the most significant commentary on its efficiency is the fact that between 1774 and the union of 1821 the Hudson's Bay Company adopted all of its field techniques except the use of the canoe.

The success of the North West Company stemmed in large part from adopting and developing the modes and personnel of the French fur trade as it existed before and in the years just after 1760. Personifying French skill in the trade were the *voyageurs*, or canoemen. Under the system of "engagement" young men from the Quebec parishes (usually bound for three-year terms) were employed and trained as *voyageurs*, then returned to the land and later re-engaged, or left as "freemen" in the Northwest. Some of the latter were employed at the wilderness posts in such capacities as smiths, carpenters, canoe builders, or axe men. Others were used as traders *en derouine*—that is, were sent to drum up business with the Indians and to collect debts in the form of furs. Still others, if literate, might rise from clerks to be "bourgeois." The bourgeois was the trader who had invested his skill, his courage, and (if he had any) his money. He was responsible for the returns from the district to which he had been assigned.[10]

The *voyageurs* remained both the symbol and mainstay of the Canadian fur trade, but as traders the French generally proved too individualistic, too much devoted to small and limited enterprises, and too poor at business to compete with their Yankee or Scottish rivals.[11] It may well have been this, rather than lack of access to capital, which explains the gradual replacement of the French-Canadian bourgeois by Scottish, English, and American traders after 1760.

The Nor'Westers also adopted the canoe, as developed by the French in the *cânot de maitre* and the *cânot du nord*, and the custom of provisioning the brigades with dried corn and grease to Grand Portage. Also taken over was the use of the fur post in all its variations from a log shack for a winter's occupation to the stockaded fort with its component dwelling houses, stores, and shops. (The Hudson's Bay Company used forts also, but those on the shores of the bay were English structures built by naval carpenters, not wilderness stockades.) Incorporated, too, as the name indicates, was the *regale* or treat—liquor given the Indian in the spirit of nomadic good fellowship to establish cordial relations and encourage the hunter to trap for his friends.

The *regale* was only a symbol of the French genius for accepting the Indian with all his casualness, his moodiness, his sensitivity, his insistence that the door always be open to him, his expectation that if in need he would be given what he required. In these respects the Nor'Westers, especially the Scots, were apt pupils of the French, and often succeeded where the Englishmen and the Orkney men in the service of the Hudson's Bay Company failed, through private reserve or restraints imposed by the organization. (It is of course to be noted also that the detachment of the Bay men usually preserved them from involvement in the passions, feuds, and trickery of Indian life and often was rewarded in the long run by a reputation for honesty and fair dealing.)

Another North West inheritance from the French were the *métis*, with all that their existence implied. The rough judgement that on balance the *métis* added to the strength and success of the North West Company is probably defensible. They were an important part of the labour force of the Canadian fur trade, particularly in their role as buffalo hunters during the company's last years. By 1816, the year of the affair at Seven Oaks, they probably held the fate of the Northwest in their hands. One of the first needs of the united company was to conciliate them and to employ them as dependents of the fur trade and as defenders against the Sioux.[12]

All these inherited and borrowed techniques for dealing with the wilderness were combined by the shrewd Nor'Westers with a superior business organization. Connections with English business houses gave the Canadians access to higher quality trade goods and better credit than their French counterparts had secured. When the *entrepôt* for much of the American fur trade, formerly centred at Albany and New York, was shifted to Montreal, the size and vigour of the business was increased proportionately. The result was a great strengthening of the trade in capital and managerial ability and also an extraordinary concentration of resources. Thus for nearly three decades the North American fur trade, both that of the southwest (the American Northwest) and that of the Canadian Northwest, was centred in Montreal.

The growth of the company from partnership to partnership has been explained in terms of the need to combine and to marshal the resources and bear the costs of deeper penetration into the Northwest.[13] This was indeed an important reason for "pooling" resources. It seems not, however, to be the whole explanation of what occurred. There was in the very nature of the fur trade an inherent need of monopoly because of its seasonal character, its dependence on the seeming whims of a primitive and uncommercial people, the easy depletion of the numbers of fur-bearing animals by hunting or disease, and the difficulty of carrying the loss of a year's outfit. There were probably also reasons of management in the field, involving the control and distribution of goods, the giving of credit, and the collection of furs.[14] Competition was not the life of the fur trade, but its death.

However that may be, the very name North West Company points to the subsequent political division of the fur country of central North America after the Treaty of Versailles in 1783. More and more there was a southwest and a northwest fur trade from Montreal. After the final implementation of Jay's Treaty in 1795 the southwest trade was increasingly surrendered to Americans. The North West Company grew in importance to the fur trade of Montreal, and the Canadian trade was pressed back upon the uninhabitable and permanently primitive wilderness of the Canadian Shield and the northern forest.

The gradual forcing of the Canadian fur trade toward the northwest intensified the need for large-scale organization. Supply bases were necessary, and with the beginning of the new century the posts on the Red River, the Assiniboine, and the Saskatchewan, along the line where the northern forest and the plains merged in the long grass and the park belt country, became more and more supply centres and less and less fur posts. The buffalo hunt and the *métis* buffalo hunter began to emerge as an institution and a type. Their function was to obtain from the plains the dried meat and pemmican that would provision the Saskatchewan and Athabasca brigades in the long reaches from Bas de la Rivière on Lake Winnipeg to the Methy Portage into the Athabasca country.

In these developments lay the beginning of strain on the loose-jointed organization of the company, particularly in the relations between "wintering" and Montreal partners. In them lay the need to shorten the continental haul of furs to Montreal, either by shifting the *entrepôt* from Montreal to Hudson Bay, or by seeking a western outlet on the Pacific. In them also lay an ever-increasing dependence on the labour of the Indians and the *métis*, a dependence that required the carrying of a rapidly growing number of *métis* families.

The greater the strain, the greater was the need for monopoly and the need at last to take seriously the competition of the much smaller and less effective but enduring, stable, and slowly-learning Hudson's Bay Company. The longer the canoe haul and the larger the labour force, the greater was the necessity of provisions from Red River. The clash between the two remaining fur organizations of the Northwest would seem to have been inevitable even had it not been precipitated by two external factors, namely, the War of 1812 and the Earl of Selkirk's passion for colonization.

Both these factors put pressure on the North West Company at tender and vital points: the main supply area at Detroit-Michilimackinac, from which came corn for the Montreal canoe brigades; and the Red River, from which came pemmican for the canoes bound for the far Northwest. The Astor venture on the Pacific Coast was regarded by Canadians as part of the War of 1812, in that it challenged the formation of a western outlet and supply base at the mouth of the Columbia River.

Because of early British military successes, the alliance with the Indians, and the isolation of the Astorians, the War of 1812 was a means of alleviating the pressures on the Montreal and Columbia routes. There remained the pemmican base at Red River. As the Nor'Westers saw it, the character and the seriousness of Selkirk's part in the new aggressiveness of the Hudson's Bay Company might not by themselves have led to a clash had it not coincided with the War of 1812. Nor'Westers had, after all, dealt successfully with competition before by cultivating the loyalty of their Indian and *métis* hunters with liquor and blandishments, and by the use of their bullies (*batailleurs*) to harass competitors. Despite their suspicion of Selkirk's purposes from the first, the Nor'Westers behaved with exemplary patience from 1811–13. But by the spring of 1814, under the influence of the war temper, they had come to think strategically and to act drastically. By the spring of 1815 they knew they had lost the territorial gains of the war to the United States in Michigan and perhaps in the Columbia Valley. In the winter of 1814–15, because of the action of Miles Macdonnell, Governor of Assiniboia, in first prohibiting and then limiting the export of pemmican from Red River, they became convinced that Selkirk's colony was an immediate and intolerable threat to the supplying of their northwestern posts and brigades. They resolved, therefore, to remove or destroy the colony. Thus the return of peace elsewhere saw the beginning of "war" on the Red River.

The struggle on the Red River in 1815 and 1816, and in the law courts of Canada from 1817–21, reveals little that is new about the North West Company. It fought with all the resources it could command—commercial, primitive, and legal—against a rival who used all these in return and added to them a small army of mercenaries hired after their discharge from service in the late war. In every field the company at least held its own, and beyond doubt deserved to. It could not, however, overcome the inherent weaknesses of its own loose organization, of dependence on a labour force that was constantly growing in size and unruliness, and of the high costs of its extended transportation routes. The aroused Hudson's Bay Company, still a David to the North West Company's Goliath, needed only to keep on fighting to have the giant collapse of his own weight.

The final union of the rivals was at once a victory and a defeat for each. The Hudson's Bay Company was victorious in that its supply route by the bay triumphed over that by the St. Lawrence as did its charter over the partnership of the North West Company. It was defeated in that it won only when it had adopted in large part the techniques and methods of its rivals inland. The North West Company lost its name and legal entity, but not before it had forced on its great competitor the mode of operation and the labour force which it had developed and by which it had flourished. The united company was very much the old North West Company operating out of Hudson Bay.

The North West Company was the first successful combination of European capital and business enterprise with Indian skills. As such, it holds a special place in the history of the North American fur trade and in the history of Canada. Its distinctive character arose from the fact that it came to grips with the unique conditions prevailing in Canada—conditions of climate, distance, and resources, which prevent a large proportion of the country's area from sustaining a pattern of economic and social life like that of Europe or the United States.

The company faced for the first time the fundamental question of how to maintain a western-oriented society in a severely northern, largely uninhabitable land. For much of Canada can be exploited only by extremes: by a primitive culture like that of the Eskimo, skilled in the special techniques of survival and content with merely maintaining life for a tiny population; or by a civilization with a technology so highly developed that it can overcome almost any obstacle of environment if the necessary expenditure is justified on grounds of private profit or state policy.

The effort to deal with this permanent northern frontier makes Canada what it is, and the influence of the effort can be traced all through Canadian history and contemporary society, most obviously in the comparative lack of both people and wealth in a country territorially so vast. The successful solution reached by the North West Company would seem to point toward the two channels through which a sophisticated culture and economy may exploit the North to its own best advantage and with the least detriment to the primitive culture of the people dwelling there. These channels are private monopoly or state development.

Notes

1. The history of the North West Company has now been reconstructed with sufficient completeness both to establish the character of the company as a business organization and to explain its role in the North American fur trade. This has been done despite the lack of documentary evidence for most of its business affairs. The historical task has been carried so far chiefly by two recent and massive works: Paul Chrisler Phillips, *The Fur Trade* (Norman, Oklahoma, 1961); and E. E. Rich, *The History of the Hudson's Bay Company 1670–1870* (London, 1958, 1959).

2. Maple sugar is rarely taken into account by fur trade historians; yet note the frequent references in Elliott Coues, ed., *New Light on the Early History of the Greater Northwest: The Manuscript Journals of Alexander Henry and of David Thompson, 1799–1814*, 1:4, 25, 30, 101, 112, 122, 130, 162, 170, 192, 196, 211, 244, 259, 275, 281; 2:492, 629, 681 (New York, 1897); and in Charles M. Gates, ed., *Five Fur Traders of the Northwest*, 32, 37, 44, 165, 234, 236, 270, 273 (St. Paul, 1965).

3. The necessity for this movement is brought out with painful clarity in Edwin James, ed., *A Narrative of the Captivity and Adventures of John Tanner* (Minneapolis, 1956). On the importance of fruit, see, for example, Henry, in Coues, ed., *New Light on the ... Greater Northwest*, 2:485.

4. This is one of those self-evident facts which, if not made explicit, is sometimes seriously neglected. The importance of Indian manpower was drawn to my attention by Mr. Jan Kupp and will be developed by him in his doctoral dissertation for the department of history, University of Manitoba.

5. See Henry, in Coues, ed., *New Light on the ... Greater Northwest*, 1:44–77; 2:452; Richard Glover, ed., *David Thompson's Narrative, 1784–1812*, 229 (Toronto, 1962).

6. Quoted in J. B. Tyrrell, ed., *Hearne: A Journey from Prince of Wales's Fort in Hudson's Bay to the Northern Ocean*, 102 (Toronto, 1911).

7. See Henry, in Coues, ed., *New Light on the ... Greater Northwest*, 1:282; 2:516, 522, 530.

8. For a discussion of these attitudes, see E. E. Rich, "Trade Habits and Economic Motivation Among the Indians of North America," in *Canadian Journal of Economic and Political Science*, 26:35–53 (February, 1960). Mr. Rich emphasizes the Indian's lack of a "sense of property" rather than a lack of a commercial sense.

9. See W. Kaye Lamb, ed., *Sixteen Years in the Indian Country: The Journal of Daniel Williams Harmon, 1800–1852*, lxxxv (Toronto, 1957).

10. How much of this was actually French practice, and how much developed from French practice it is difficult to state in our want of detailed knowledge of the organization of the French fur trade. There is a revealing though brief description of the resumption of activity by French traders after 1760 in a forthcoming volume by Hilda Neatby of the University of Saskatchewan, to be published under the title "Quebec: The Revolutionary Age," as one of the *Canadian Centenary Series*.

11. See David Thompson's comments on this point in Glover, ed., *Thompson's Narrative*, 41.

12. This aspect of the fur trade is discussed in Margaret Macleod and W. I., Morton, *Cuthbert Grant of Grantown: Warden of the Plains of Red River* (Toronto, 1963).

13. This thesis has been given its classic statement by Harold A. Innis in *The Fur Trade in Canada* (New Haven, Connecticut, 1930).

14. See Matthew Cocking's comment on the need to prevent "Confusion of Goods" among separate traders in one place, in W. Stewart Wallace, ed., *Documents Relating to the North West Company*, 45 (Toronto, 1934); also Alexander Mackenzie, *Voyages from Montreal ... to the Frozen and Pacific Ocean*, 18 (Toronto, 1927).

THE MIDDLEMAN ROLE IN THE FUR TRADE: ITS INFLUENCE ON INTERETHNIC RELATIONS IN THE SASKATCHEWAN-MISSOURI PLAINS

Susan Giannettino

The entrance of European fur traders into the northeast coastal woodlands of North America in the mid-sixteenth century most likely had a profound effect on the intertribal trade networks that criss-crossed the northern interior. In striving to acquire trade goods that the Europeans offered in exchange for furs—primarily the guns, knives, axes, brass kettles, blankets, and metal for projectile points—the native peoples became involved in two distinct economic systems. Jablow (1950:12) notes in relation to the Upper Missouri area that, "On the one hand they functioned in a system of intertribal trade, while on the other, they were producers and traders in furs in the European mercantile system." With time, the native peoples became increasingly dependent on the White trade goods for their survival, and hence became more deeply involved in the fur trade.

From *The Western Canadian Journal of Anthropology*, 7, no. 4 (1977), 22-33. Reprinted by permission of the Department of Anthropology, University of Alberta.

Those Indians who were in closest contact with the European traders found themselves in a lucrative position as middlemen. The profit-minded Whites had established a coastal toehold on the North American continent and had begun immediately to pursue their acquisition of furs. Eager to amass as many valuable pelts as possible, they traded assorted goods with the proximate natives in exchange for furs. These Indians, in turn, traded their recently acquired White goods for the furs of the more isolated natives of the interior. Richard Slobodin (1960:88) writes that such people were

> ... in circumstances which have been experienced by a number of non-urban peoples in relation to the expanding economy of an urban civilization. They were between the civilized traders and more distant aborigines.

The middlemen served as intermediaries in the indirect trade between the White traders and more distant native groups. In the trade there was little or no direct contact between the two peripheral groups. As the natives realized the superiority of many of the White trade goods, especially guns and ammunition, they increased their efforts to obtain them.

Because of the obvious advantages accruing to those groups holding the middleman position, ethnic groups sought to gain and then retain total control over direct trade with Whites. This enabled them not only to make a profit in the redistribution of goods to groups located farther into the interior, but also to control the types of items made available to those groups. In this manner, they limited arms distribution, while keeping the superior White weaponry for themselves. Hence, the middleman role was extremely desirable, since through a superiority in firearms the middlemen were assured greater success in intergroup conflicts.

Intertribal conflict was an important characteristic of the interrelationships of North American native people. Combat was frequent, being a result of a group's desire or need for horses, women, better hunting grounds, or increased status. Alliances between ethnic groups were transitory and fragile. The European fur trade, thrust into the aboriginal trade complexes, added a new dimension to the "status quo" of conflicts and alliances. The magnitude of the profit and power held by the middlemen prompted the development of a new pattern of conflicts and alliances that soon came to dominate interethnic relations. In addition to the traditional reasons for conflicts and alliances, conflict began to occur as a direct response to the middleman trade position. Native groups fought to maintain and exploit a middleman position; or in efforts to rise from a subordinate position and assume the middleman role. Native groups united to maintain and protect their middleman position; for protection against the groups holding the middleman role; or to rise from a peripheral position and become the middlemen themselves. The process involved in trading through middlemen, and the associated interrelationships of the participating ethnic groups, I term the "middleman role complex."

The conflicts engendered by competition for trade goods were sometimes carried over to the White trade sources. Groups unable to obtain sufficient arms through the middlemen attacked the Whites both in attempts to arm themselves and in retaliation for the Whites having dealt with the middlemen. Conversely, those holding the middleman position, anxious to maintain that role, opposed—on occasion with violence—fur traders' attempts to initiate direct trade relationships with the peripheral peoples.

The native middleman role and its effect on interethnic relations in the North American fur trade has been recognized and described by several anthropologists whose studies focus on various areas of the continent. The Eastern Kutchin apparently acted as middlemen to the Eskimo trade. According to Slobodin (1960:90–91), the Kutchin had no tradition of aggression with any peoples other than the Eskimo, and in fact there might be some truth to their folk tales of friendly relations with the Eskimo prior to Kutchin involvement in the fur trade. The repeated instances of Eskimo-Kutchin hostilities reported by early fur traders and explorers, and the efforts of the Kutchin to prohibit Eskimo expeditions from reaching the fur trading posts were motivated by the desire to retain middleman dominance in the fur trade.

McClellan (1975), in an ethnographic survey of the southern Yukon, describes a series of middleman positions extending inland from the Pacific coast fur trade outlets. The coastal Tlingit dominated native trade with the seafaring American, British, and Russian traders. "However, the tribes closest to them in the interior—the southern Tuchone, Tagish, and the inland Tlingit—were in turn able to dominate Athabascans living farther inland" (McClellan 1975:501). According to McClellan's informants, the only motives for warfare between these groups were "the capture of women, the desire for blood vengeance, or the attempts to control access to goods brought by the whites" (*ibid*:518).

Jablow (1950) found extensive evidence illustrating the existence of the middleman trade pattern and related conflicts on the Missouri River:

> The tribes all along the length of the Missouri invariably attempted to prevent the progress of the White traders further than their own villages. Each tribe wished as far as possible to retain control of the White trade and to prevent the goods, especially guns, from flowing freely into the coffers of other tribes.... So long as they retained the trade advantage and a superiority over other tribes and they could dispose of the goods as they saw fit, they were willing to share the bounty unequally.
>
> ... each tribe wanted to prevent guns from falling into the hands of their enemies, and this undoubtedly was the most important interest the Indians had in attempting to control the trade. [*ibid*:35–36]

Thus, it is apparent that the native middleman was an integral element in the expansion of the North American fur trade and a major determining factor in native interethnic relations during that period.

The conflicts and alliances in the plains area between the North Saskatchewan and Missouri rivers during the early historic period have generally been thought of as relatively unstructured, and with little perceivable significant pattern or organization. The result in the literature has been a general hodgepodge of interethnic encounters and relationships. To better interpret interethnic relations in this region, I have used the fur trade and the middleman role complex as an analytical focus for viewing the region's interethnic social network.

As the middleman role complex moved across the North Saskatchewan-Missouri plains from northeast to southwest, the major ethnic groups, one after another, became involved—first in a subordinated role as they traded with more easterly middlemen, then in a dominant role, as the contact zone in which there was direct trade with Whites moved westward and they became the middlemen themselves. Successively, the Assiniboine, Cree, Northern Blackfeet, Blood, Piegan, Atsina, and the Rocky Mountain Plateau groups—the Kutenai, Pend d'Oreille, Nez Perce, and Flathead—were peripheral subordinates and then middlemen. The pattern of alliances which developed assumed a form similar to the process of complementary opposition, or the "massing effect" described by Marshall Sahlins (1961:332): "In any opposition between parties A and B all those more closely related to A than to B will stand with A against B, and *vice versa*." On the North Saskatchewan-Missouri plains, the "haves"—those with privileged access to guns and ammunition—united in defence of or extension of their shared interests, while the "have nots" joined in efforts to attain the middleman role.

The alliance pattern that occurred as part of the middleman complex is summarized in the schematic diagram in Fig. 1. This diagram necessarily is a very generalized, overall interpretation of interethnic relations. Interrelations were not always precisely along these lines, and dates for changes in alliances overlapped, but the basic pattern can be seen here. The active trade complex consistently moved southwestward, with little trade occurring to the northeast because the fur-bearing animals were usually harvested more rapidly than they could successfully reproduce. Solid lines in the diagram signify direct White trade contact, while broken lines signify trade filtered through the middleman.

The reports of Hudson's Bay Company emissaries and French Jesuit missionaries (e.g., see Ray 1974) clearly document the early fur trade involvement of the eastern groups of the region, the Assiniboine and Cree. By the late 1700s the Assiniboine and Cree were allies in warfare and trading partners seeking French goods through Ottawa middlemen (Ray 1974:12). As the fur companies expanded operations westward in the 1770s, the Assiniboine and Cree began to trade directly with Whites for guns and ammunition.

In the 1770s and 1780s, Hudson's Bay Company and the French Canadian traders established trading posts all along the North Saskatchewan River. With the construction of these inland trading posts, the Assiniboine and Cree became the peoples with whom the Europeans dealt directly. Though each company and

FIGURE 1 The Middleman Pattern

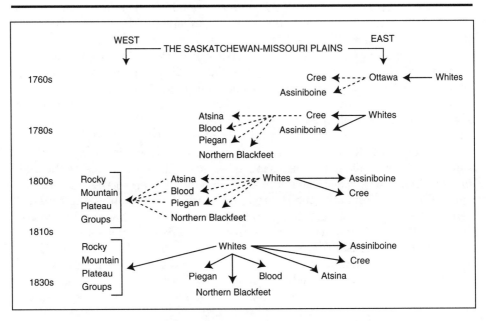

individual trader had a different relationship with the natives, the very existence of each post as an outlet for armaments was of primary importance to the Indians. The Assiniboine and Cree found the traders of the North Saskatchewan posts eager to trade guns for their abundant supplies of pelts. They rapidly built up a profitable trade relationship—the Whites obtaining the furs they desired, and the Indians gaining possession of the coveted guns and ammunition. With the development of this relationship, the middleman complex moved in its entirety into the North Saskatchewan-Missouri plains.

The Blackfeet groups (Northern Blackfeet, Blood, and Piegan) and the Atsina, who lived to the west of the Cree and Assiniboine, had farther to travel to reach the trading posts, and at this time traded only the less valuable skins of wolves and foxes. Duncan M'Gillivray and Alexander Henry, both employees of the North West Company, recorded that trade with the Blackfeet and Atsina was not worth the time or effort (Morton 1929:31, Coues 1897:541). For example, M'Gillivray, stationed at Fort George in 1794, wrote:

> ... Blackfeet, Gros Ventres [Atsina], Blood Indians, Piedgans, etc., are treated with less liberality, their commodities being chiefly Horses, Wolves, Fat and Pounded meat which are not sought after with such eagerness as the Beaver. [Morton 1929:31; brackets mine]

Consequently, there was not a significant direct flow of guns and ammunition to these groups. The Assiniboine and Cree exploited their advantage to the fullest.

As middlemen in the trade of the area, the Assiniboine and Cree came to dominate the North Saskatchewan-Missouri plains social network. They attempted to prohibit access of other ethnic groups to the posts, and filtered the westward and southward distribution of trade goods so as to prevent the Blackfeet groups, the Atsina, and other peoples from acquiring a supply of guns. Most conflicts in the area revolved around the Assiniboine-Cree attempts to maintain the middleman position, and the efforts of other groups to reach the trading posts and acquire weapons through direct trade. The documents of this period (e.g., the journals and correspondence from Edmonton and Chesterfield Houses (Johnson 1967), the journals of Duncan M'Gillivray (Morton 1929), and the journals of Alexander Henry (Coues 1897), and David Thompson (Tyrrell 1915) give ample testimony to conflicts between the allied Assiniboine and Cree on the one hand, and the three Blackfeet groups, the Atsina, and, to some extent, the western Plateau peoples on the other. Strife was a frequent occurrence and battles often resulted in massacres. For example, John MacDonald of Garth reported at Fort George in 1793 that a war had broken out that summer between the Plains Cree and the Atsina in which several had been killed on both sides (MacDonald in Morton 1929:xlix). In 1801 a party of Blood Indians informed Peter Fidler of Hudson's Bay Company that the "Southern Indians [Cree] from below and the Stone Indians had killed fourteen men and sixty women and children of the Fall Indians [Atsina] thirty-four days ago" (Johnson 1967:293; brackets mine). Still other fur traders, among them Daniel Harmon (1911:55) and Duncan M'Gillivray (Morton 1929:156), reported numerous instances of large-scale conflicts between the armed Assiniboine and Cree and their less effectively armed, more westerly enemies. Alexander Henry cites repeated attempts of Assiniboine and Cree to prevent their enemies from obtaining ammunition in the early 1800s (e.g., Coues 1897:540,558), a pattern which is repeated until as late as the 1810s as recorded by John Franklin (1824:133,166) who also noted:

> The Stone Indians [Assiniboine] keep in amity with their neighbours the Crees from motives of interest; and the two tribes unite in determined hostility against the nations dwelling to the westward, which are generally called Slave Indians [Blackfeet]—a term of reproach applied by the Crees to those tribes against whom they have waged successful wars. [1824:166; brackets mine]

White traders became involved in the native conflicts and alliances from two perspectives. On the one hand, they were perceived by the outlying ethnic groups as enemies since they were suppliers and allies of the dominant Assiniboine and Cree. Duncan M'Gillivray wrote in 1795 that the Atsina, considering the traders to be allies of their enemies the Cree, had decided to attack the fur trading posts. "For this purpose a Strong party endeavoured to plunder

Pine Island Fort [Fort de l'Isle] the ensuing Winter, but the attempt was fortunately unsuccessful ..." (Morton 1929:63; brackets mine). The Atsina plundered Manchester House on the Saskatchewan River in 1793, and attacked and burnt to the ground South Branch House in 1794, in both instances attempting to get weapons with which to defend themselves against the raids of the Assiniboine and Cree (Johnson 1967:xvii).

On the other hand, from the perspective of the Assiniboine and Cree, the westward advancing White traders were adversaries, intent on toppling them from the dominant middleman position by opening direct trade relations with the Blackfeet, Atsina, and western Plateau groups. Alexander Henry recorded in the fall of 1808 that a large assembly of Crees had gathered at Battle River, determined to halt his trade expedition to the Blackfeet. They wished "to prevent the Slaves from receiving arms and ammunition." They feared, he continued, that a serious war would result (Coues 1897:495).

The Assiniboine and Cree shared a dominant social position based on privileged direct access to White traders. The more western groups were allied against both the Assiniboine and Cree, and the Whites who supplied the Assiniboine and Cree with the weaponry which enabled them to dominant interethnic relations in the area.

Throughout the 1780s, 1790s, and early 1800s, the peltry trade companies and the free traders expanded their activity even farther into the North Saskatchewan-Missouri plains, along the South Saskatchewan River, and in the early 1830s along the upper Missouri River. The more central location of these posts in the North Saskatchewan-Missouri plains, as well as the change in White demand from beaver pelts to buffalo meat and robes, made it much easier for the Northern Blackfeet, Blood, Piegan, and Atsina to obtain guns and ammunition through direct trade. In 1820 Franklin noted that the Crees were no longer a dominant force on the plains because their enemies were now as well armed as they (1824:107–108).

The Piegan were the first of the Blackfeet groups to establish direct relations with the peltry traders. Alexander MacKenzie wrote, "They are the beaver hunters of their nation" (Lewis 1942:32). Living near the foothills of the Rocky Mountains, they had both the opportunity and the incentive to develop their trapping skills. Because of preferential treatment by the Whites, the Piegan assumed the middleman role before their neighbours the Atsina, Blood, and Northern Blackfeet. Through direct trade, they rapidly acquired a supply of guns and ammunition. As the dominant group in the area, they sought to exploit and maintain their influence while other peoples allied in attempts to topple them. Prince Maximilian, while at Fort McKenzie in 1832, recorded an example of the hostilities between the once allied Blackfeet groups. The traders, he wrote (Thwaites 1906:127–131), treated the Piegan preferentially, encouraging jealousy among the Blackfeet peoples. On an occasion when a new uniform and gun were presented to a Piegan chief in an attempt to make an example of him for the other groups, the Blood Indians were offended and spoke loudly of their plans for slaughtering the Piegan and the White traders. A few days later when a relative of the Piegan chief was shot by some Bloods, the Piegan attacked the Bloods in retaliation (Thwaites 1906:139–142). At a later date, once the demand for furs had changed to one for bison robes, the Blood, Northern Blackfeet, and Atsina were able to obtain guns and ammunition through trade at the posts, and through raids and interethnic trade. They came to share the middleman position with the Piegan.

And so, the balance of power had shifted. Through the early 1800s, the Blackfeet groups and their allies, the Atsina, occupied the role of middlemen in the complex trade relations of the fur trade. The trade pattern evident in the previous decades during which the Assiniboine and Cree were in a dominant position was repeated with only a few minor alterations. The Northern Blackfeet, Blood, Piegan, and Atsina allied against the more peripheral peoples to the north and west as they exploited their temporary, advantageous position. As early as 1795 Duncan M'Gillivray observed this exploitation. While at Fort George he wrote:

> The most general news among the natives at present is.—that the Coutonées [Kutenai] a tribe from the Southwest are determined to force their way this year to the Fort or perish in the attempt ... The Gens du Large [the Blackfeet and perhaps the Atsina] and all the other nations in this neighbourhood wishing to retain an exclusive trade among themselves, have hitherto prevented the Intentions of this Band, of commencing a friendly intercourse with the Fort, in order to exclude them from any share of our commodities, which they are well aware would put their enemies in a condition to defend themselves, from the attacks of those who are already acquainted with the use of arms.—The Coutonées have already made several attempts to visit us, but they have been always obstructed by their enemies and forced to relinquish their design with loss. [Morton 1929:56; brackets mine]

In 1798 Peter Fidler observed much the same restrictions.

> They [the Kutenai] was never near any of the Trading Settlements altho they much wish it. But the Muddy River [Piegan], Blood, Blackfeet, and Southern Indians always prevents them, they wishing to monopolize all their skins to themselves, which they do giving the Poor Indians only a mere trifle for .... [Johnson 1967:112; brackets mine]

The western Plateau peoples in turn allied in their struggle to acquire guns, for their own protection and to overcome the imposed subordinate role. Oscar Lewis (1942:21) makes the appropriate observation that, "The differences in the rate of arming the various tribes was crucial in determining the balance of power in this area."

As middlemen of the North Saskatchewan-Missouri plains, the Blackfeet groups exploited their military advantages over their neighbours. The Plateau peoples were often raided by the Blackfeet groups, particularly by the Piegan and the Atsina (Young 1899:190, Ross 1956:213–214, Lewis and Phillips 1923, Ewers 1944, Parker 1840). The Reverend Samuel Parker (1840:232) wrote in the 1830s:

> The Indians west of the great chain of mountains, have no wars among themselves, and appear to be adverse to all wars ... except in self-defense.... Their only wars are with the Blackfeet Indians, whose country is along the east border of the Rocky Mountains, and who are constantly roving about in war parties on both sides, in quest of plunder.

Captain Nathaniel J. Wyeth, while conducting a government exploration of the Rocky Mountains in the 1830s, wrote in his journal of a mountain battlefield, "where 200 Flatheads, Conterays, Ponderays and other Inds. were killed by the Blackfeet Inds." (Young 1899:190). Hell's Gate—a narrow canyon on the Clark Fork River leading into present day Missoula, Montana—was in the 1820s the pass or "great war road" by which the Blackfeet entered the mountain valleys to raid the Flathead. Alexander Ross (1956:213) noted that, "the spot has therefore often been the scene of many a bloody contest between these two hostile nations."

As middlemen, once the Blackfeet groups and the Atsina had obtained dominance through possession of the gun, they sought to maintain their position through regulation of the goods allowed to filter through them to the west and south. In their efforts to accomplish this, they, in their turn, came into conflict not only with the peripheral groups trying to procure the guns, but with the Whites who were trying to extend their trade networks into the mountains. The attitude of the Blackfeet groups was one of "unremitting enmity" toward the White traders and trappers, both English and American, who threatened to cross the mountain passes and trade with the Plateau groups (Galbraith 1957:85). David Thompson, while attempting to establish trade relations with the Flathead in 1807 wrote of the Piegans' attempts to prevent his crossing the mountains into Flathead territory. They feared, he said, his "arming the Natives on that side" (Tyrrell 1915:375). The Blackfeet warned the traders that all Whites found by them west of the mountains would be dealt with as their enemies. Alexander Ross and his trapping parties who frequented the Rocky Mountain foothills in the early 1820s were constantly harassed by the Blackfeet groups. In his journals Ross (1956) uses the terms Blackfeet and Piegan interchangeably as an equivalent to the word "enemy."

In 1810 David Thompson reported that the Piegan suffered their first defeat at the hands of the Kutenai and Flathead. The latter were apparently sufficiently well-armed at this point to defeat the heretofore dominant middlemen, although it is doubtful that, at this time, all the Plateau peoples had or could operate guns (Tyrrell 1915:424–425). In any case, this was the beginning of the end of the Blackfeet and Atsina's power dominance. The apprehensions the Piegan, Blood, Northern Blackfeet and Atsina had felt toward the peripheral groups obtaining guns were well founded. The Plateau peoples—the Kutenai, Flathead, Pend d'Orielle, Nez Perce, and others—once the easy prey of the Plains Indians, upon becoming well armed became formidable enemies (Murray 1930:15–16). Through the decade of 1810s the Plateau peoples obtained more guns and ammunition from the ever-increasing number of Whites in the area. Aware of their new-found and rapidly growing strength, they were no longer intimidated. In a March 1810 incident reported by David Thompson this bravery is illustrated:

> ... while at the Saleesh [Flathead] Camp, an alarm came of the tracks of Peeagans being seen near the Camp, everything was now suspended ... About one hundred Men now mounted their Horses proud of their Guns and iron headed Arrows to battle with the Enemy; they soon returned, having found these Cavalry to be the Kootanaes ... but it gave me, as well as the old Men, great pleasure in seeing the alacrity with which they went to seek the enemy, when before, their whole thoughts and exertions were to get away from, and not to meet, their enemies. [Tyrrell 1915:420, brackets mine]

As late as the 1830s the plains groups were trying to retain some vestige of their former position as middlemen to the Plateau groups. Prince Maximilian noted that an expedition sent from Fort McKenzie to the Kutenai in August 1832 was cut off by the Blackfeet when but a few days out of the fort. The Blackfeet's vigilance was still active but not effective (Thwaites 1906:153–154). The Blackfeet and the Atsina lost their dominant position as the gun was acquired by the peripheral groups. The pattern established with the Assiniboine-Cree was repeated: the subordinate peripheral groups eventually managed to acquire guns and ammunition and equalize the discrepancy in power.

The middleman phenomenon was for the most part defunct in the North Saskatchewan-Missouri plains by the mid 1830s, and so too was the patterned series of interethnic relations that had been part of the middleman role complex from 1785 to 1830. Following this period, the base of interethnic conflicts reverted to what they had been before the 1790s, centring around hunting ground disputes, and raids for women and horses (Bradley 1900:207–211, Lewis and Phillips 1923:122, 127–128). No longer were conflicts and alliances centred around an ethnic group's desire to exploit the possession of firearms while restricting distribution to others, for all peoples had relatively equal access to White trade outlets.

References

Bradley, James H.
1900   "Affairs at Fort Benton, from 1831 to 1869; from Lieut. Bradley's Journal," *Contributions to the Historical Society of Montana*. 3:201–287.

Coues, Elliot, ed.
1897   *New Light on the Early History of the Greater Northwest: The Manuscript Journals of Alexander Henry and of David Thompson, 1799–1814*. 3 vols. New York: F.P. Harper.

Ewers, John C.
1944   "The Story of the Blackfeet," *Indian Life and Customs Pamphlet #6*. Washington, D.C.: Education Division of the United States Indian Service.

Franklin, John
1824   *Narrative of a Journey to the Shores of the Polar Sea*. London: J. Murray.

Galbraith, John S.
1957   *The Hudson's Bay Company*. Berkeley: University of California Press.

Harmon, Daniel Williams
1911   *A Journal of Voyages and Travels in the Interior of North America, 1800–1819*. Toronto: Courier Press Ltd.

Jablow, Joseph
1950   "The Cheyenne in Plains Indian Trade Relations, 1795–1840," *Monographs of the American Ethnological Society*, 19, New York: J.J. Augustin.

Johnson, Alice M., ed.
1967   *Saskatchewan Journals and Correspondence*. London: Hudson's Bay Record Society.

Lewis, Oscar
1942   "The Effects of White Contact upon Blackfoot Culture," *Monographs of the American Ethnological Society*, 6, New York: J.J. Augustin.

Lewis, William S. and Paul C. Phillips, eds.
1923   *The Journal of John Work*. Cleveland: Arthur H. Clark Co.

McClellan, Catherine
1975   "My Old People Say—An Ethnographic Survey of Southern Yukon Territory," *National Museums of Canada Publications in Ethnology*, 6, Ottawa.

Morton, Arthur, S., ed.
1929   *The Journal of Duncan M'Gillivray of the North West Company*. Toronto: Macmillan Company of Canada, Ltd.

Murray, Genevieve
1930   "Marias Pass," *Studies in Northwest History*, 12, Missoula: State University of Montana Press.

Parker, Samuel
1840   *Journal of an Exploring Tour Beyond the Rocky Mountains*. Ithaca, N.Y.: Samuel Parker.

Phillips, Paul C.
1969   "The Fur Trade in Montana," *in* Michael P. Malone and Richard B. Roeder, eds., *The Montana Past*, pp. 35–60. Missoula: University of Montana Press.

Ray, Arthur
1974   *Indians in the Fur Trade*. Toronto: University of Toronto.

Rich, E.E.
1959   *The History of the Hudson's Bay Company*, 2 vols. London: Hudson's Bay Record Society.

Ross, Alexander
1956   *The Fur Traders of the Far West*. Norman: University of Oklahoma Press.

Sahlins, Marshall D.
1961   "The Segmentary Lineage: An Organization of Predatory Expansion," *American Anthropologist*. 63:2.

Slobodin, Richard
1960   "Eastern Kutchin Warfare," *Anthropologica*, 2:76–93.

Thwaites, R.G., ed.
1906   "Maximilian: Prince of Wied, Travels in the Interior of North America, 1832–34," *Early Western Travels*, 1748–1846, 23.

Tyrrell, J.B., ed.
1915   "David Thompson's Narrative of his Explorations in Western America: 1784–1812," *Publications of the Champlain Society*, 12, Toronto.

Young, F.G., ed.
1899   "The Correspondence and Journals of Captain Nathaniel J. Wyeth, 1831–36," *Sources of the History of Oregon*, 1, Eugene: University of Oregon Press.

WAGE-LABOUR IN THE NORTHWEST FUR TRADE ECONOMY, 1760–1849

Glen Makahonuk

Although the history of the fur trade has experienced something of a renaissance over the past decade with the publication of studies on such topics as demographic patterns, women and family relationships, and Indian/trader economic relations, there has been relatively little done on the wage-labour situation. In fact, except for a few articles on the subject there seems to be a general assumption that a capitalist labour relations system is not applicable to the Canadian fur trade.[1] In a recent review of H.C. Pentland's *Labour and Capital in Canada 1650–1860,* however, Allan Greer argues that the study is "fundamentally incoherent" in the treatment of the transition to capitalism. He suggests that because Pentland confined himself to a very "narrow range of class relations" he was unable to distinguish between "different modes of production," or address the concept of "free" labourers working for wages during a period of primitive accumulation.[2] In other words, what may appear to be contrary to popular opinion, the Northwest fur trade economy of the period 1760 to 1849 operated within an emerging capitalist labour relations system.

I

The Northwest fur trade economy operated during an early stage in the development of capitalism in North America. The Marxist economic historian Maurice Dobb writes that "the development of Capitalism falls into a number of stages, characterized by different levels of maturity and each of them recognizable by fairly distinctive traits."[3] The distinctive traits of the Canadian economy prior

From *Saskatchewan History*, 41, no. 1 (Winter 1988), 1-18. Reprinted by permission of *Saskatchewan History*.

to 1850 were *petit bourgeois* farmers or *habitants*, family units of independent commodity producers, land and transportation companies, and commercial enterprises involved in the trade of fish, furs or timber.[4] The fur trade economy was based on what may be termed merchant capitalism.

The two main fur trade companies prior to their merger in 1821 were the Hudson's Bay Company (HBC) and the North West Company (NWC). Although both were in competition with one another, they still held a monopoly of the fur trade in which they could pursue their wealth and profits. The NWC had established a large inland trading empire from its base in the St. Lawrence region, while the HBC had been operating from the shores of Hudson Bay since the late seventeenth century. The HBC had both economic and political objectives: the economic one was "to make a sustained profit or gain through trade" and the political one was to maintain the interests of the Crown by carrying out exploration, territorial expansion and law-making. As was explained by a contemporary writer and critic:

> ... the Hudson's Bay Company enjoys a right of exclusive trade with the Indian population. This right of exclusive trade is, practically and positively, a right of exclusive property in the labour, life and destines of the Indian race. It is an absolute and unqualified dominion over their bodies and their souls—a dominion irresponsible to any legal authority—a despotism, whose severity no legislative control can mitigate, and no public opinion restrain. It knows but one limit, and obeys but one law,—"Put money in thy purse."[5]

A similar opinion was held of the NWC. From its beginning the NWC was a monopoly which sought "higher profits for the merchants and more ruthless exploitation of the native trappers."[6] Indeed, the NWC proved to be an extremely profitable organization in comparison to the HBC and commanded the lion's share of the fur trade by the end of the eighteenth century. Roderick Mackenzie, a Company partner, estimated that "the value of the adventure in 1787 was £30,000 Halifax currency and that this had trebled in eleven years. The profits from 1784 to 1798 totalled £407,151 Halifax currency."[7] The wealthy partners of the NWC, according to historian Stanley Ryerson, "wielded a power equivalent to that of rulers of the colony" and were to become "the precursors of the modern Canadian capitalist class."[8]

II

The profit motive of the fur trade companies had a direct impact on their labour relations policies. It has been argued that their labour relations policies were based on paternalism, or to use H.C. Pentland's term, "personal labour relations," that is, relations that were characterized by the employer's obligation to provide for the welfare of the labourer in exchange for a loyal and reasonably efficient labour force.[9] Historians like Jennifer Brown and Sylvia Van Kirk have used the model of paternalism and patriarchal society developed by Peter Laslett in *The World We Have Lost* to describe the organization and structure of fur trade company posts. But it is the renowned Canadian working class historian Bryan Palmer who has developed a definition of paternalism to include a class conflict relationship.

> Paternalism defined relations of superordination and subordination in an age of commercial capital and nascent industrialism, paternalism grew out of the necessity to justify exploitation and mediate inherently irreconcilable interests. It rationalized inequality and provided for a hierarchical order ... In its historical manifestations, it included kindness and affection of superiors toward subordinates, as well as cruelty, harshness and gross insensitivity. But paternalism's ultimate significance ... lay in undermining the collectivity of the oppressed by linking them to their "social superiors." This did not necessarily imply an absence of social, even overtly class, conflict ... Paternalism was one part self-conscious creation by the merchants, independent producers, and landed gentry, and one part negotiated acceptance by the various plebeian subjects of the producing classes. But these two parts did not constitute the whole. Paternalism was reinforced by the material constraints of the social formation that had spawned it. For much of paternalism's sustaining power lay in the unique economics, politics and culture of each locality in early Canadian society.[10]

In carrying out their labour relations policies, the companies used a hierarchical and authoritarian management structure. In the case of the HBC, councils were established in the Northwest to regulate the local concerns of the company. A council was composed of chief factors who met each year usually at Red River to audit the accounts of the preceding year, to place orders with London suppliers for the goods required for the ensuing year's trade, to station company servants at various posts, to make recommendations in the filling of vacancies and to discipline or suspend any of the Company's servants.[11] After the chief factors came the chief traders, traders (who actually engaged in trade with the Indians), chief clerks and the clerks and postmasters. The apprentice clerks were at the very bottom of what Jennifer Brown has termed a "white collar" personnel structure.[12] The system operated in such a way that no upper position could be filled without passing through an apprenticeship of at least several years.[13] It was also possible for clerks to be promoted to the ranks of the factors and traders on the basis of "good conduct and seniority."[14] And at the very bottom of the company, what may be termed the "blue collar," were the interpreters who were described as "intelligent labourers" knowledgeable in "a smattering of Indian" and the labourers (both Native and European), "who [were] ready to turn [their] hands to anything; to become ... trapper[s], fishermen, or rough carpenter[s], at the shortest notice."[15]

Management's power and authority were based on the requirement that all company employees had to follow a code of established rules and to "yield due obedience to such authority in all cases in which [the Governor, Chief Factor or

Chief Trader] may find necessary to exercise it."[16] Any employee who did not follow these rules was subject to discipline, which in some cases reached the point of "tyrannical exploitation." For example, John Feeny, a vagabond boy at Red River, was "tied to a tree and flogged on the posteriors" for refusing "to assist in cooking."[17] In an attempt to eradicate private trade in 1773 Humphrey Marten, the factor at Severn Fort, put one of his workers in irons and gave him eighteen strokes of the cat for trading one skin.[18] The Governor at Churchill Fort, according to Edward Umfreville, was so despised by his employees for his cruel behaviour that Orcadian labourers refused to work for him. In one case Umfreville wrote about the woes of a tailor who had to quit and go back to his Orkney Islands' home because of the cruel treatment he received.

> From thence he wrote to the Company, representing in the most humiliating ... manner, the cruel treatment he had received from the Bay Governor; he informed them that the blows he had received would be the cause of unhappiness to him to the latest period of his life, as he was thereby unable to get a livelihood at his business; upon which account he humbly solicited a small consideration, to compensate in some measure for the injury he had undeservedly sustained in their service. Though it would have been an act of the greatest charity to have listened to the prayer of this poor man's petition, yet, so great is the partiality of the Company to their chief officers in the country, that no attention was paid to the petition; and, indeed, an inferior servant, may apply for redress till he is tired, before any notice will be taken of his complaints, or the slightest reprimand given to the authors of his misery.[19]

The NWC was not that much better; James Sutherland, an HBC servant, reported in 1793 that a number of employees of the NWC complained about the frequent beatings they received from the so-called "mad man," Mr. La Tour.[20] An apologist of the HBC justified "the exercise of strict discipline" on the grounds that it would prevent not only "anarchy among [the employees]," but also "neighbours" from "sowing discontent and rebellion among [them]."[21]

The economic historian H.A. Innis points out that by the late 1700s the personnel policies of the HBC, especially the discipline, actually discouraged Company employees from working harder or expanding the fur trade in the interior to counter the competition from the North West Company.[22] The NWC had labourers and traders who were quite willing to seek the rich harvest of furs in the interior regions. Many of the HBC employees, on the other hand, were loath to exert themselves because they had nothing to expect from the Company in terms of fringe benefits. In testimony before the Select Committee on the HBC in 1857, Governor George Simpson was asked: "Is there any provision made for your servants in case of sickness or old age?" His reply was "There is no provision made for them."[23] And in the case of Indian labourers who were no longer valuable to the Company because of old age or sickness, they were "driven to the woods, to seek a lingering death by famine, with all the honour and dignity of British liberty."[24] Such policies and treatment created a lack of *ésprit de corps* and thus forced a number of employees like David Thompson and Edward Umfreville to leave the HBC and join the NWC, which seemed to have more flexible personnel policies. These policies provided for upward mobility and profit sharing, which, according to the explorer and trader Alexander Mackenzie, "excited among them a spirit of emulation in the discharge of their various duties, and, in fact, made every agent a principal who perceived his own prosperity to be connected immediately with that of his employers."[25] By the early 1800s, however, the NWC changed its policy on hiring ex-HBC employees, because there was no longer a need to win the affection of Indians who were willing to trade furs. And most important the NWC had more than enough employees to contest the bitter trade rivalry with the HBC. At a company meeting held at Fort William in July 1811, it was decided "that none of the Hudson's Bay Servants should in future be received into any of the Company's Forts except in cases of Starvation—and on *no account* to be engaged to the N.W. Co."[26] In a word, then, both companies had personnel policies to control their respective employees.

III

The recruitment of a suitable labour force to produce furs and make profits was a major personnel problem for both the HBC and the NWC during the period under study. To solve the problem the companies set up a two-part labour process at each factory or post.[27] The first part involved the actual production of furs—a topic that has been subject to considerable scholarly debate. Historians such as E.E. Rich, H.A. Innis and Arthur J. Ray have clearly articulated the traditional role of Indians in the fur trade as that of hunters, trappers and middlemen.[28] Both companies vied with each other for the trade of the Indians inhabiting the Western Interior. The HBC, in particular, relied on the Indians to do the hunting and trapping. But as the hunting areas dried up the former Indian hunters turned into middlemen in order to control the trade and transportation routes from the new fur areas to the European posts. Furthermore, in their economic relationship with the fur trade companies the Indians, especially those acting as middlemen, were concerned with getting "good measure" in order "to satisfy their immediate needs, to maintain their political alliances, and to gain access to reliable sources of European arms."[29] The *métis* researcher Ron Bourgeault, on the other hand, has a different interpretation to explain how the fur companies used the trading system to conquer economically the Indian people and turn them into a dependent labour force which would produce a profit. The companies did this by

> trading the products of European technology, such as guns, traps, hatchets, knives, in exchange for fur. These tools of work were more developed or advanced than the tools then being used in Indian society. These goods were introduced and traded to the people. Once the people had learned how to use them, they were able to reduce the amount of time and labour needed to provide for themselves (necessary-labour). They now had more time and better

tools to produce more surplus (surplus-labour production). In other words, it became much easier and quicker to hunt food, cut wood and skin animals with the new European technology than with the old technology or work tools. What the European wanted from the Indians' labour was the ability to produce a surplus ...[30]

The second part of the labour process needed European workers to operate and maintain both the fur trade posts and the transportation system. These workers were recruited from Lower Canada in the case of the NWC and from Europe in the case of the HBC. The NWC hired *hommes-du-nord* who were described as

> rough and simple men, and though used to doing hard work they preferred doing nothing at all and would not even hunt or fish for themselves unless told to do so by their employers. The work that they did while travelling was amazing. On the river at first light and going until dark, their usual respite from the hard work of paddling was the even harder work of portaging. The portages were many and difficult and everything had to be carried over them. Shouldering two or more ninety-pound bales of goods or fur, the *voyageur* set off a trot across the portage, and later returned for more.[31]

They looked down on the "goers and comers" from Montreal and referred to them as the *mangeurs-du-lard* (pork-eaters). The so-called pork-eaters were employed for four or five months to transport supplies to Grand Portage and then to bring back the cargoes of furs to Montreal; at this point their seasonal contract was at an end and they were laid off. The NWC usually employed about 1,280 workers in a season: fifty clerks, seventy-one interpreters and under-clerks, thirty-five guides and the remainder canoemen.[32] Most of them were French-Canadians (with some Iroquois) and they formed a labouring class which, according to Sylvia Van Kirk, was ethnically and occupationally separate from the British officer class.[33]

The HBC, on the other hand, had a different labour market. The HBC had established regular recruiting policies as early as the 1680s and had relied on common labourers, tradesmen and urban workers from the London area and on some occasions from Ireland and Scotland. By the early eighteenth century, however, the HBC changed its policy of hiring Londoners because of the recommendation of Joseph Myatt, Governor of Albany. In 1727 Myatt had written to the London Committee that Londoners were becoming better "acquainted with the ways and debaucheries of the town" rather than the hard work necessary in the fur trade economy.[34] Myatt believed that young Orkneymen, who had a reputation for hard work and sobriety, could replace the unsuitable urban workers from London for a wage of only "£6 per annum."[35] Another eighteenth-century writer, Edward Umfreville, had a good opinion of Orkneymen, for he described them as "a close, prudent, quiet people, strictly faithful to their employers ..."[36] As a consequence the HBC started recruiting its labourers and some of its craftsmen from the Orkneys by the late 1730s.

In his important quantitative study of the recruitment patterns of Orkneymen in the HBC, the historian John Nicks points out that most of the HBC employees prior to 1821 came from the middle and lower ranks of Orkney society. Most of them could be classified as plebeians for "they were young, unmarried sons of small tenant farmers, craftsmen, and cottagers."[37] The tradesmen, on the other hand, could be classified as proletarians, for they were recruited from the urban centres like Kirkwell and Stromness in which a Scottish working class was in the making.[38] Although by the end of the eighteenth century English labourers were becoming a rarity, most of the skilled tradesmen positions and the so-called "white collar" positions like writers, clerks and officers still continued to be held by Englishmen.

The Orcadians were useful employees at the HBC posts on the coast lines, but seemed to show little initiative to become *voyageurs* when the need to expand the trade to the interior developed in the late eighteenth century. The HBC was quite concerned that its employees might not be able to counter the NWC's push inland. The Orcadians were reluctant to move inland because they received no extra wage for a job that offered more toil, more misery, more hardship and the possibility of starvation.[39] As a consequence the HBC had to rely on Indian *voyageurs* to do the inland work until the Company could hire skilled Orcadian canoeists and canoebuilders who would be willing to do it. To speed the process along Samuel Hearne made the following proposal to the London Committee:

> All persons that may perfect themselves, so far as to be capable of steering a canoe up and down will in my opinion greatly embrace the value of their Services; if such person were to meet with some little gratuity it would not only be the means of inducing them to a longer continuance in the Service but would be a great inducement to other young fellows to make themselves qualify for that Station.[40]

The London Committee accepted the proposal and offered extra wages for skilled Orkney canoemen. It seems their skills developed to the point that they became specialists at being "Bowsmen," "Middlemen" or "Steersmen."

The lack of skilled canoemakers was another labour problem. Because of the competition with the NWC for the Western Interior, the HBC needed a greater number of large canoes which could carry as many men and goods as those of the NWC. Since the Orcadians were not skilled in the art of canoemaking, the HBC had to rely on the Indian labouring class to build canoes.[41] However, Indian labourers, according to both Hearne and Turnor, were not reliable in keeping up the production of canoes. And even those canoes that were built were often unsatisfactory because they were too small in comparison to the *canots de maître* and *canots du nord*. Turnor noted that it took ten HBC men with five canoes to carry as much as five Canadians with one canoe.[42]

Realizing the advantages of the Canadians over the HBC, Matthew Cocking, a company writer and commander at York Fort, proposed that "Vessels in Canoe form made of Fir might be contrived of a small Draught of greater burden than the Indian Canoes, and Yet of such a Weight as to be carried occasionally by those who go in them, and the Company's Servants will probably sooner learn the Management of these as they will be much steadier than Indian Canoes, which are dangerous to unskillful Persons."[43] If his proposal failed, Cocking suggested that it might be necessary to hire Canadians who could build canoes in "the Pedlers manner." The HBC's solution to its problems with the canoe was to have its own employees trained in the art of canoe building and canoe handling. In 1792 both Charles Isham, "a noted half-breed," and Robert Longmoor, who had joined the HBC as a sailor in 1771, became the first employees to "attain any degree of Proficiency in Bowing or Sterring Canoes" and "to perfect [themselves] in the Art of Canoe Building."[44]

A different type of personnel problem developed in the early 1800s when a number of managers filed complaints about the laziness and lack of productivity of their Orkney workers. In fact, Governor Miles Macdonell's opinion of Orcadians had become quite negative:

> There cannot ... be much improvement made in the country while the Orkneymen form the majority of labourers; they are lazy, spiritless, and ill-disposed-wedded to old habits, strongly prejudiced against any change, however beneficial ... It is not uncommon for an Orkneyman to consume six pounds or eight pounds of meat in a day, and some have ate as much in a single meal. This gluttonous appetite, they say, is occasioned by the cold. I entirely discredit the assertion, as I think it rather to be natural to themselves. All the labour I have seen these men do would scarcely pay for the victuals they consume.[45]

As a consequence the HBC decided to recruit workers from Glasgow, Island of Coll, Ireland, Lower Canada and, on some occasions, even the jails of Norway.[46]

In a letter to William Auld, superintendent of Northern Department, Governor Miles Macdonell reported that the Orcadians working for the HBC did not like "the arrival of strangers among them" because "they have enjoyed the exclusive advantages of the Trade for a long time unmixed with any others; which might induce them to suppose that no people ought to be employed but themselves."[47] Macdonell was of the opinion that the HBC would be better off to hire workers from other parts of the United Kingdom and get rid of the Orcadians whom he claimed have become prone to insubordinate behaviour and disobedience:

> ... the Company can get abundance of men from other parts of the United Kingdom and experience can be acquired. With regard to settling a Colony, people from other parts would I think ... serve the purpose better than these from Orkney, particularly such of them as have already been in this Country, whose habits of insubordination, idleness, and inactivity will be very difficult to eradicate. One or two old hands is enough to poison any party—they tell the others that they ought to have this thing and that other thing,—make the whole discontented and keep themselves in the back ground. William Finlay has already occasioned a little difficulty, laying down *Factory Law* (as he explained it) and disobedience ...[48]

It seems that Macdonell's suggestion of controlling the labour supply and eliminating the potential bargaining power of the Orcadians was soon adopted. Indeed, the establishment of Selkirk's colony and the introduction of the HBC's new employment policy started to diminish slightly the number of Orcadians and increase the number of French-Canadians, Scots, Irish, *Métis* and English, especially in the period between 1812 and 1821.[49]

The HBC's attempt at controlling the labour supply was made much easier after the union with the NWC in 1821. The merger meant that much of the existing manpower and the fur trade posts were both redundant and superfluous. Locations that at one time had both a NWC post and HBC post could now do with only one. It was also obvious to Governor George Simpson that if labour costs or the wage bill was reduced by 25 per cent, then profits could be increased.[50] Consequently 250 workers were laid off; the first being the older ones with larger families and "the leading turbulent characters," who had carried out various protests and strikes against the companies. Simpson was criticized for being too zealous in dismissing family men and retaining only those who were in debt to the company. It was pointed out to Simpson that the Company could not operate with "inadequate personnel."[51] Simpson, however, dismissed the warning claiming that he could always get new recruits when needed and explained the HBC's new hiring philosophy:

> The relative qualifications and merits of Canadians and Orkneymen have been duly weighed and the preference is given to the former in so far as regards the duties and services to be performed, but in point of expense which is likewise a very important consideration the opinion is in favour of the Orkneymen. The Canadians, generally speaking are a volatile inconsiderate race of people, but active, capable of undergoing great hardships and easily managed by those who are accustomed to deal with them; the Orkneymen on the contrary are slow and do not possess the same physical strength, and spirits necessary on trying occasions ... If brought young into the Country, however, say from eighteen to twenty-two years of age they may be greatly improved; and upon the whole we consider it good policy to have about an equal proportion of each, which will keep up a spirit of competition and enable us to deal with them on such terms as may be considered necessary and proper. Scotch and Irish in any considerable numbers we have strong objections to being quarrelsome independent and inclined to form leagues and cabals [i.e., a secret organization and overthrow authority] which might be dangerous to the peace of the Country.[52]

The policy was to keep a balance between Orcadians and Canadians, especially those from Lower Canada in the regions of Sorel, Maskinonge and Montreal in the period between 1823 and 1849. Simpson's policy also recognized the value of the Indians and *métis* in the Red River colony as an important reserve of labourers in this same period.[53]

IV

The determination of wages in the fur trade economy was based not only on a fixed contract rate or social custom, but also on the buying and selling of labour power. Workers had an understanding of the operation of the labour market and would try to increase their wages when the demand was greater than the supply. For example, John Ballenden reported in June 1799 that the workers at Gordon House wanted to negotiate new wage rates. In his report to the Company, Ballenden stated:

> the chief point I had for visiting the Settlement [Gordon House] was to settle terms with the men respecting their contracts which was the most difficult task I ever undertook—from time to time they have hitherto been only engaged for one year—now their times being all expired at once. They did not hesitate to think and tell me that they would get their own terms or leave the service. So one and all declared for home or extraordinary wages which I was determined not to comply with, finding me not to deviate—several came afterwards and entered into Contracts at what your Honours offered them ...[54]

In the buying and selling of labour power Marx states that the "interests of capital and the interests of wage-labour are diametrically opposed to each other."[55] The workers (sellers of labour power) depend on their wages for their subsistence and are therefore forced to maximize them, while the buyers (employers) treat the wages as a cost and are perpetually trying to minimize them. The eighteenth-century economic philosopher Adam Smith had the same conclusion:

> the common wages of labour, depends every where upon the contract usually made between those two parties, whose interests are by no means the same. The workmen desire to get as much, the masters to give as little as possible. The former are disposed to combine in order to raise, the latter in order to lower the wage of labour.[56]

In *A Sketch of the British Fur Trade,* the Earl of Selkirk pointed out that the NWC was able to maintain a monopoly and earn profits by the wage policy it administered. This policy involved the payment of wages in "Grand Portage currency" or "North-West currency," which meant that a dollar in Montreal was only worth 50 cents in Grand Portage, and that goods transported from Montreal to Grand Portage were sold at double the price.[57] The company also encouraged its employees to drink because the profits on rum reduced wages in proportion. To support his argument, Selkirk referred to a description made by Count Paolo Andreani, who had travelled in the Upper Country in 1791.

> It is ... considered as an essential point of duty in the master of a trading post, to take care that the men ... shall have as little as possible of their wages to receive in cash at the end of the year ... Whenever any of their servants begin to indulge in habits of expense, credit is allowed him with unbound facility, till he is deeply involved in debt to the Company. When this has been accomplished he is in complete bondage; and no alternative is left him but absolute submission to his employers, or a gaol. He must therefore submit to every imposition, which his superiors may think fit to practice upon him.[58]

The worker, as a result of this practice, was always in debt to the company and in "a degree of poverty seldom to be met with in other parts of America..."[59] While visiting Canada in 1797 Francois Alexandre Frederic la Rochefoucault Liancourt, a French nobleman and philanthropist interested in the abolition of slavery, had come to a similar conclusion about the NWC's wage policy and truck payments:

> As the men employed in this trade are paid in merchandize which the Company sells with an enormous profit, it is obvious at how cheap a rate these people are paid. They purchase of the company every article they want; it keeps with them an open account, and as they all winter in the interior of the country and beyond Lake Winnipeg, they pay as a consequence excessively dear for the blankets and the cloths which they bring with them for their wives. These servants of the Company are in general extravagant, given to drinking ... and these are exactly the people whom the Company wants. The speculation on the excesses of these people is carried so far, that if one of them happened to lead a regular sober life, he is burdened with the most laborious work, until by continual ill-treatment he is driven to drunkenness and debauchery, which vices cause the rum, blankets and trinkets to be sold to greater advantage. In 1791, nine hundred of these menial servants owed the Company more than the amount of ten or fifteen years pay.[60]

This policy stayed in effect until the merger with the HBC in 1821.

The HBC did not have a so-called special currency but did have what Rich calls "the Canadian System" and describes it as "vicious and extravagant."[61] In essence the system was based on the London Committee's instructions to reduce all wages as much as possible, similar to what was being practised by employers in the British Isles. One way to prevent wage increases was to charge high prices for company goods, while commissioned officers paid only 33.5 per cent.[62] This policy seemed effective; for example, the wage bill for the Northern Department in 1825–26 was cut by approximately £5,000. Another way of carrying out the "Canadian System" was merely to cut wages and post a new scale, despite protests from the servants. On one occasion in August 1822 James Bird, acting on behalf of the clerks, wrote a letter to Governor Simpson protesting the cut in their wages. Simpson's response was to dismiss their so-called "trifling grievances" because they did not "have a right to expect much relief." Simpson also warned the London Committee that "if you once begin to give way there will be no end to their demands and some of those useless old people will never think of withdrawing from the concern but keep more enterprizing young men in the background."[63]

The "Canadian System," however, did not always work to the advantage of the HBC. Changes in labour market conditions and the bargaining strategies of HBC employees, as Simpson notes in his *Athabasca Journal,* contributed to a movement in (exorbitant) wages.[64] Simpson's reference to exorbitant wages was made in response to the Company being forced to pay higher wages than those in the British Isles in order to attract workers. For instance, prior to 1800 labourers, bowsmen and canoemen from the Orkney Islands received wages from £6 to £12 per annum plus room, board, and a basic set of clothing, which was two to three times greater than what they would have received as labourers on Orkney farms.[65] Skilled labourers or tradesmen, on the other hand, usually received a wage which ranged from £20 to £40, depending upon the craft and the market demand. For example, Nicholas Spence from Stromness, Orkney Islands was hired in 1793 as a boatbuilder at the rate of £25 per year on a three-year contract. On the renewal of his contract in 1796 his wage was increased to £36 per year because of the shortage of skilled boatbuilders.[66] And when Indians and *métis* were in great demand as hunters, they could earn as much as £30 per year, which was the equivalent of some skilled labour rates.[67] The wages of clerks ranged between £75 and £100 during the early nineteenth century.[68] And by the 1840s the Council minutes of the Northern Department were listing wages as follows:

> the following Servants be engaged for the Northern Department on 5 years Contracts Viz
>
> From Europe
>   2 Blacksmiths @ from £25 to £30 per an.
>   2 Coopers (Fishcurers) @ from £25 to £30 per an.
>   3 Masons @ from £25 to £30 per an.
>   2 Joiners @ from £25 to £30 per an.
>   6 Sloopers @ £20.
>   <u>30</u> Labourers @ £16.
>   45
>
> From Canada 3 years Contracts
> 50 Voyageurs @ prix du Poste or £17 per an.[69]

In comparison to the wage rates paid in the Orkney Islands, the above listed HBC's wages were at least £5 to £10 greater. In fact, the higher wage rates made it possible for some tradesmen to save enough money in order to return home and set up their own shop or farm.[70] But before these tradesmen could return home they were often required to provide instruction in the HBC's apprenticeship program. Chief Factors and Chief Traders were authorized "to engage strong healthy half-breed lads not under fourteen years of age as apprentices to be employed with those tradesmen with the purpose of acquiring of their business on a term not less than seven years ..." The wages were £8 per annum for the first two years, £10 for the next two years, £12 for the following two and £15 for the last year.[71] The apprenticeship system was designed to get skilled work done at a cheap price.

V

The adversarial labour relations system in the Northwest fur trade economy created a significant number of disputes. These disputes were part of what both Marx and Adam Smith would call the continuous struggle between capital and labour. The noted French economic historian Paul Mantoux argued that "the disputes between capital and labour afford the best possible illustration of the economic evolution prior to the coming of the factory system."[72] Many British Marxist historians, in particular E.P. Thompson, have also examined this ongoing relationship and have referred to it as class-struggle.

> That we choose to continue to employ the heuristic category of class (despite this ever-present difficulty) arises not from its perfection as a concept but from the fact that no alternative category is available to analyse a manifest and universal historical process. Thus we cannot (in the English language) talk of "estate-struggle" or "order-struggle," whereas "class-struggle" had been employed, not without difficulty but with signal success, by historians of ancient, feudal and early modern societies ...[73]

Thompson further argues that far too little attention has been placed on the concept of class struggle. As he explains it:

> ... people find themselves in a society structured in determined ways (crucially, but not exclusively, in productive relations), they experience exploitation (or the need to maintain power over those whom they exploit), they identify points of antagonistic interest, they commence to struggle around these issues and in the process of struggling they discover themselves as classes, they come to know this discovery as class-consciousness.[74]

In a series of articles on *métis* history in *New Breed*, Ron Bourgeault points out that it was in "the late 1700s that class formations within the economy of the fur trade became distinct."[75] The class formations, according to Bourgeault, led to class struggle between the fur trade companies and the Indian and European labouring class. Although the concept of class struggle in the Canadian fur trade company is subject to debate, it still may be used in the context of what E.P. Thompson has described as "fragments of proto-conflict." This proto-conflict marked a transition period in which the fur trade labour disputes were being carried out in both the cultural tradition of plebian struggles and the new class relations created by capitalism. One Canadian working class historian has come to the conclusion that:

> These eighteenth-century disputes were but the opening skirmishes in a class war that would grow in both extent and intensity. In the years ahead workers would gather their forces for organized battle against an enemy grown more vicious in defense of their increase of wealth and power ...[76]

The labour disputes focused on two major issues which were also common in European society: one involved the lack of adequate provisions, and the second involved insufficient wages.[77] Between 1767 and 1769 Andrew Graham, an employee of the Hudson's Bay Company, observed a number of disturbances caused when the company failed "to keep up a stock of cheese, beef, pork or any other ... commodities ..."[78] Samuel Hearne noted in his Journal of 8 February 1775 that "the very scanty allowance of Provisions" has caused "many grumblings among some of the men ..."[79] In a letter to Joseph Colen, resident at York Factory, dated 10 July 1798 William Tomison, Inland Master, describes the dangerous grumblings that his men had about the lack of adequate provisions in their trip from Gordon House to Trout River. He believed that unless a "larger stock of each article" was served to each worker, it "would create animosities disention among the people."[80] And a year later Tomison was still experiencing difficulties with his men when they discovered that he had tried to cut their provisions and brandy by one-half.

A series of these disputes broke out in the Red River region in the 1812–14 period. In most cases the workers carried out short work-stoppage protests; they immediately stopped working when provisions were inadequate or when treatment from their overseer was too harsh. Both on 14 September and 6 November 1812 Miles Macdonell reported in his Journal that his "men refused to work under Mr. O.K." because of "bad advise." It seems that their problem was solved, for they "resumed work" the next day and "appeared satisfied."[81] On 11 December 1812 the workers walked off the job protesting the lack of provisions and demanding that more be given. Macdonell refused to give them any. Two days later their hunger forced them to send "one of their number to apologise ... and promise never to quit work again without orders."[82] The promise was short-lived for on 14 January 1813 another incident broke out in which three labourers refused to obey their overseer. Macdonell found them guilty of insubordinate behaviour and fined them £2 each.[83] Another similar incident occurred on 1 February 1813 when the men did not work because of the lack of provisions.[84] Approximately one year later in April 1814 Fort Daer was the site of a protest led by James Toomy and Mr. Delorme, who used "inflammatory language" in their demand "for an augmentation [of] their daily rations." They held out a week before capitulating; Toomy and Delorme were dismissed and the others were reprimanded with a warning about their "future behaviour."[85] The warning had little impact because on 8 June 1814 fifteen labourers once again struck for more provisions. Two days later they returned to work after "paying a fine of 5 [shillings] per day while they were off."[86] And as a final example, in the summer of 1836 we find "a state of mutiny," as Thomas Simpson refers to it, breaking out in Red River. In a letter to James Hargrave, Simpson demanded that the "mutineers" never "be employed by the Company again."[87] Such discontent and protests continued throughout the period under study and became most acute when the HBC could not provide enough provisions to keep body and soul together.

It was the wage issue which generated the most discontent and heightened the conflict between the fur trade companies and their workers. Andrew Graham observed that much of the "grumblings and discontents" among the labourers, especially at York Fort, was caused by low wages. The labourers would show their unhappiness by getting drunk and then becoming "so haughty and impudent that they will dispute an officer's orders to do any duty but what they term their own business."[88] And another way to show their discontent was to strike.

A number of strikes broke out between 1760 and 1849. The first major one to involve the HBC was the great seamen's strike of 1768 on the Thames. The seamen had gone on strike because of a reduction in their wages. The HBC seamen had notified the Company that its three ships would be prevented from sailing until it agreed to raise their wages to 40s per month. Because of the critical shipping season, the Company agreed to the demand and the ships were allowed to sail.[89] Although combinations were illegal, workers did attempt to form combinations in order to raise wages by means of a strike if necessary.[90] For example, in July 1777 the Orkney labourers at Cumberland House, under the leadership of James Batt and William Taylor, formed "a kind of Combination" and struck for a wage of £15 per year, which was approximately £9 above the existing rate. Humphrey Marten, the Factor, retaliated by threatening the labourers with a forfeit of all of their wages if they did not return to work.[91] Even though the initial strike was defeated, E.E. Rich points out that the Company later responded to the labourers' wage problems by setting up a system of incentive-payments for those who made inland voyages.

Meanwhile the NWC also had its share of labour disputes. A number of them broke out in 1789 on the issue of insufficient wages. On 10 July 1794 the French-Canadian *voyageurs* at St. Helen formed a combination and struck against the Company's attempts to reduce wages. The magistrates were called in to punish the leaders by having them pilloried. The *voyageurs*, however, showed their defiance of the law by freeing their leaders and escaping. A month later on 3 August 1794 the *voyageurs* at Lac La Pluie formed a combination and went on strike for higher wages. Unfortunately, they lost both the strike and their jobs. And in March 1814 a group of *voyageurs* carried out a protest by going to Montreal to prosecute the NWC for failing to pay their full wages. They were unsuccessful in their case and were subsequently dismissed.[92]

Another major strike broke out again at Cumberland House on 1 August 1799 when canoemen formed a combination and refused to comply with orders to go to Beaver River until they received "additional wages." James Bird warned them that their strike was a "flagrant breach of contract" and they would be punished for it. The workers disregarded the warning and continued the strike. Tomison then wrote a letter to the Governor requesting that an example be made of these men which would "ensure obedience from all the rest on this establishment for the future: for should these escape with impunity the little subordination that has been (but very lately) ... established will be entirely subverted, and it will consequently be utterly impossible to carry on your Honours' concerns in this part with any degree of vigour."[93] Management, in other words, did not view the strike as a mere economic dispute, but rather as a test of power over the control of work. Indeed James Bird argued that it was a challenge to management authority:

which of the two is esteemed the more probable method of advancing the interest of our Honourable Employers: whether to carry into execution a plan suggested by an experienced and vigilant officer undertaken by one not less active and enterprising aided by the prompt obedience of his men; or whether it be an implicit submission to the will of the servants and supinely to adopt or relinquish such schemes as they may think proper to approve or reject. Now will all know whether for the future the servant is to comply with the orders of his master to act under the immediate direction and control of his servant.[94]

The strike finally came to an end on 30 August 1799 when Joseph Howse notified the strikers that "they were no longer on duty or considered as the company's servants ...." The strikers responded by abandoning the strike and then deciding to join the NWC.

Another example of a strike that actually became a challenge to management authority occurred at Nelson Encampment in February 1812. Governor Miles Macdonell reported that fourteen men under the leadership of William Finlay formed a combination "against the authority of the officers set over them."[95] It seems that the labourers were supporting Finlay who had "refused to conform ... to regulations ... established for the health of the people" and to orders "to resume work." Macdonell had Finlay brought before a magistrate and charged with a number of misdemeanours. Finlay was found guilty and sentenced to "confinement as a refractory servant" and jailed in a small hut. The combination came to Finlay's rescue by burning the hut to the ground and "triumphantly shouting in the most audacious manner ...." Macdonell was unable to get them to return to work, despite threats of having them tried for mutiny. The strikers carried out a more defiant act when they armed and fortified themselves in a nearby house. In retaliation, wrote Macdonell,

> we ... armed ourselves and went down with some of the Gentlemen to prevent insult being offered to the three officers who had first gone. These we met returning without having got any of the arms, and suffered gross abuse with threats of violence. We proceeded onto the Insurgent's authority to deliver up their arms immediately ... and were further informed of the serious consequences of refusal, that they must be treated as people in open hostility who set all order at defiance; they not withstanding remained inflexible.[96]

The Company finally decided to starve them into submission. By June 1812 the strikers were unable to carry on any longer and surrendered. They were sent to Montreal for trial. They were found guilty and dismissed from service.

These disputes and strikes, then, were a clear expression of the disharmony and class tensions in the fur trade economy. Labourers, servants and *voyageurs* were quite prepared to challenge the authority and power of the Company in order to achieve their demands.

VI

In conclusion, this paper has attempted to examine the unique capital-wage-labour relationship in the fur trade economy between 1760 and 1849. It has tried to argue that even though this period has been considered by a number of historians as pre-industrial Canada, the fur trade workers, both Indian and European, were starting to operate under a capitalist labour relations system. Many economic and social historians would claim that this labour relations system was paternalistic or patriarchal. But "no thoughtful historian," writes E.P. Thompson, "should characterize a whole system as paternalistic or patriarchal."[97] Evidence has been provided to show that both fur trade companies and their workers had an astute understanding of the operation of the labour market, especially as it applied to the buying and selling of labour power. And it was this particular relationship which resulted in class tensions as expressed by the various disputes and strikes. More research, however, is still needed on labour-capital relations and the actual number of disputes in the fur trade economy in order to get a better understanding of this period in working class history.

Acknowledgement

I would like to thank Professors W. A. Waiser of the History Department of the University of Saskatchewan and Frank Tough of the Native Studies Department for reading earlier drafts of this paper and providing many useful comments.

Notes

1. These examples are: Philip Goldring, "Labour Records of the Hudson's Bay Company, 1821–1870," *Archivaria,* 11 (Winter 1980–81), 53–86; John Nicks, "Orkneymen in the HBC, 1780–1821" and C. M. Judd, "'Mixed Bands of Many Nations:' 1821–70" in *Old Trails and New Directions: Papers of the Third North American Fur Trade Conference,* edited by C. M. Judd and A. J. Ray (Toronto, 1980) and Allan Greer, "Wage Labour and the Transition to Capitalism: A Critique of Pentland," *Labour/Le Travail,* 15 (Spring 1985), 7–22.

2. Allan Greer, "Wage Labour and the Transition to Capitalism ...," 8–10.

3. For a more detailed explanation see Maurice Dobb, *Studies in the Development of Capitalism* (New York, 1973), 17–32.

4. George Heriot, *Travels through the Canadas, containing a description of the picturesque scenery on some of the Rivers and Lakes; with an Account of the Productions, Commerce and Inhabitants of those Provinces* (Rutland, Vermont, 1971) (reprint), 208–233, and H. A. Innis, *The Fur Trade in Canada* (Toronto, 1977), Section II.

5. James E. Fitzgerald, *An Examination of the Charter and Proceedings of the Hudson's Bay Company* (London, 1849), 135–136.

6. Stanley Ryerson, *The Founding of Canada: Beginnings to 1815* (Toronto, 1975), 244.

7. For a more detailed account of the returns on the capital of the company, the value of shares and rate of profit see H. A. Innis, *The Fur Trade in Canada,* 258–259.

8. Stanley Ryerson, *The Founding of Canada,* 250.

9. For a more detailed discussion see chapter 2 in H. C. Pentland, *Labour and Capital in Canada, 1650–1860* (Toronto, 1981).

10. Bryan Palmer, *Working-Class Experience: The Rise and Reconstitution of Canadian Labour, 1800–1980* (Toronto, 1983), 14, 19.

11. Canada. House of Commons. Report from the Select Committee on the Hudson's Bay Company; Together with the Proceedings of the Committee, Minutes of Evidence ... 1857. Evidence of E. Ellice, p. 325.

12. Jennifer S. H. Brown, *Strangers in Blood: Fur Trade Company Families in Indian Country* (Vancouver, 1980), 30.

13. R. M. Martin, *The Hudson's Bay Territories and Vancouver's Island with an Exposition of the Chartered Rights, Conduct and Policy of the Hon. Hudson's Bay Corporation* (London, 1849), 67.

14. B. Willson, *The Great Company, being a history of the Hon. Company of Merchant-Adventurers, trading into Hudson's Bay* (Toronto, 1899), 434.

15. R. M. Ballantyne, *Hudson's Bay; or Every-Day Life in the Wilds of North America, during six years' residence in the Territories of the Honourable Hudson's Bay Company* (Edinburgh, 1848), 32.

16. The Minutes of the Council of the Northern Department of Rupert's Land, 1830 to 1843, being the Transaction and Enactment of the Rulers of the Country during that period ... 3 July 1830, 656.

17. Morton MSS C505/1/2.3 Selkirk's Papers. Miles Macdonell's Journal, April 22, 1813 to Feb. 11, 1815, p. 17.

18. E. E. Rich, *The History of the Hudson's Bay Company. Vol. II: 1763–1870,* 103.

19. Edward Umfreville, *The Present State of Hudson's Bay containing a Full Description of that Settlement, and the Adjacent Country; and Likewise of the Fur Trade with hints for its Improvement* (Toronto, 1954), 58.

20. A. S. Morton, *A History of the Canadian West to 1870–71* (Toronto, 1973), 429.

21. R. M. Martin, *The Hudson's Bay Territories ...,* 73.

22. H. A. Innis, *The Fur Trade in Canada,* 155.

23. Minutes of Evidence Select Committee on the HBC ... 1857, 61.

24. J. Fitzgerald, *An Examination of the Charter and Proceedings of the HBC,* 139.

25. Alexander Mackenzie, *Voyages from Montreal through the continent of North America to the Frozen and Pacific Oceans in 1789 and 1793 ... Vol. I* (Toronto, 1911), xlviii.

26. Minutes of the deliberations and transactions of the North West Company assembled at Fort William at their regular meetings in ... July 1811 in *Documents Relating to the North West Company,* edited by W. S. Wallace (Toronto, 1934), 275.

27. Morton MSS C505/1/2.2 Selkirk Papers. Miles Macdonell's Journal Sept. 6, 1812 to April 22, 1813, p. 270; Morton MSS C510/1/2 Journal of Robert Campbell,

1808–1851, pp. 11–12 discusses the division of labour at the HBC experiment farm at Red River in 1831; and David Thompson, *Travels in Western North America, 1784–1812,* edited by V. Hopwood (Toronto, 1971), 73.

28. See E. E. Rich, *The Fur Trade and the Northwest to 1857,* H. A. Innis, *The Fur Trade in Canada,* and A. J. Ray, *Indians in the Fur Trade* (Toronto, 1974).

29. See Arthur J. Ray and D. Freeman, *'Give Us Good Measure': An Economic Analysis of Relations Between the Indians and the Hudson's Company Before 1763* (Toronto, 1978), 5, and A. J. Ray, *Indians in the Fur Trade.*

30. Ron Bourgeault, "Metis History," *New Breed, 13,* 4 (April, 1982), 8.

31. W. Sheppe, ed., *First Man West: Alexander Mackenzie's Journal of His Voyage to the Pacific Coast of Canada in 1793* (Montreal, 1962), 18–19.

32. The Earl of Selkirk, *A Sketch of the British Fur Trade in North America; with Observations relative to the North West Company of Montreal* (London, 1816), 33 and George Heriot, *Travels through the Canadas,* 242.

33. Sylvia Van Kirk, "Fur Trade Social History: Some Recent Trends," in *Old Trails and New Directions: Papers of the Third North American Fur Trade Conference,* edited by Carol M. Judd and A. J. Ray (Toronto, 1980), 163.

34. G. F. K. Davies, ed., *Letters from Hudson Bay 1703–40* (London, 1965), 123.

35. *Ibid.,* 116.

36. E. Umfreville, *The Present State of Hudson's Bay ...,* 109.

37. John Nicks, "Orkneymen in the HBC 1780–1821," in *Old Trails and New Directions...,* 122.

38. For a discussion about the making of the Scottish working class in the period 1770 to 1820 see James D. Young, *The Rousing of the Scottish Working Class* (London, 1979), 41–47.

39. See R. Glover, "The Difficulties of the Hudson's Bay Company's Penetration of the West," *Canadian Historical Review* (hereafter *CHR*), XXIX, 3, (Sept., 1948), 245 and "North Western Explorations," *Report on Canadian Archives 1890,* 51.

40. *Ibid.,* 191–192.

41. Norman Zlotkin and Donald R. Colborne point out in "Internal Canadian Imperialism and the Native People," *Imperialism, Nationalism and Canada: From the Marxist Institute of Toronto,* edited by Craig Heron (Toronto, 1977), 163, that as the Indians were being replaced as middle men in the fur trade, they were being turned into pro-letarians. Also see Ron Bourgeault, "The Indians, the Metis and the Fur Trade: Class, Sexism and Racism in the Transition from Communism to Capitalism," *Studies in Political Economy: A Socialist Review,* 12, (Fall, 1983), 45–86.

42. Turnor estimated that in 1779 the HBC lost 18,000 Made Beaver on the Saskatchewan alone because of the lack of adequate canoes. *Hearne and Turnor Journals,* 154.

43. Cocking's account of his proceedings June 27, 1776 in *ibid.,* 47.

44. HBCA. A. 11/116, fos. 6d., 13d. Journal of George Sutherland 1796–1797 in *Saskatchewan Journals and Correspondence 1795–1802,* edited by Alice M. Johnson (London, 1967).

45. Cited in B. Willson, *The Great Company,* 381.

46. R. Glover points out that Norwegian convicts were hired to build Norway House; see "The Difficulties of the Hudson's Bay Company's Penetration of the West," *CHR,* 253.

47. National Archives of Canada (NAC). *Report on Canadian Archives 1886* (Ottawa, 1887). Miles Macdonell to William Auld, 25 Dec. 1811, p. cc.

48. *Ibid.,* cci.

49. Also see Minutes of Evidence Select Committee on the Hudson's Bay Co. 1857. Evidence of Sir. G. Simpson, p. 61; and Eric Ross, *Beyond the River and the Bay. Some Observations on the State of the Canadian Northwest in 1811* (Toronto, 1973), 18–19.

50. HBCA. D4/1, 20; D4/85, 3, Simpson's Official Reports, 1822 in C. M. Judd, "'Mixt Bands of Many Nations' ...," 130.

51. John Galbraith, *The Hudson's Bay Company,* 21.

52. HBCA. D4/86, 14f-14 cited in C. M. Judd, "'Mixt Bands of Many Nations'...," 130–31.

53. A. J. Ray, *Indians In The Fur Trade,* 218–219.

54. Journal of William Tomison 1798–1799 in *Saskatchewan Journals and Correspondence 1795–1802,* 173.

55. K. Marx, *Wage-Labour and Capital* (New York, 1977), 39.

56. Adam Smith, *An Inquiry into the Nature and Causes of the Wealth of Nations* (New York, 1937), 66.

57. W. S. Wallace, ed., *Documents Relating to the North West Company,* 272.

58. Earl of Selkirk, *A Sketch of the British fur trade in North America, with observations relative to the North-West Company of Montreal* (London, 1816), 40–41.

59. *Ibid.,* 37.

60. Francois A. F., duc de La Rochefoucault-Liancourt, *Travels through the United States of North America, the Country of the Iroquois, and Upper Canada* ... translated by H. Newman (London, 1799), 330–331 cited in A. S. Morton, *A History of the Canadian West,* 353.

61. E. E. Rich, *The History of the HBC Vol. II,* 482.

62. Appendix No. 8 George Gladman, Chief Trader, Report from the Select Committee on the Hudson's Bay Company ... 1857, 393.

63. G. Simpson to A. Colvile 16 Aug. 1822 in *Fur Trade and Empire: George Simpson's Journal,* edited by F. Merk (Cambridge, 1931), 186.

64. *Journal of Occurrences in the Athabasca Department by George Simpson, 1820 and 1821, and Report,* edited by E. E. Rich (Toronto, 1938), 2.

65. Numerous examples of labourers hired at between £6 and £10 are contained in *Andrew Graham's Observations on Hudson's Bay 1767–91,* 247; Journal of William Tomison 1795–96 in *Saskatchewan Journals and Correspondence 1795–1802,* 34–35, 42, 167; E. E. Rich, *The History of the HBC, Vol. II,* 268; E. E. Rich, ed., *Cumberland House Journals and Inland Journal 1775–82* (London, 1951), 19.

66. HBCA. A. 30/7, fos. 27, 8/; A. 32/8, fo. 49 Journal of George Sutherland, 71.

67. Morton MSS C505/1/2.2 Selkirk Papers. (16746–16818). Miles Macdonell's Journal Sept. 6, 1812 to April 22, 1813, 255.

68. Minutes of the Council Northern Dept. 29 June 1831, 677–678.

69. Minutes of the Council of the Northern Dept. of Rupert's Land, 1830 to 1843, 790.

70. John Nicks, "Orkneymen in the HBC ...," 119.

71. Minutes of the Council Northern Dept. 3 July 1830, 660–661.

72. P. Mantoux, *The Industrial Revolution in the Eighteenth Century* (London, 1970), 74.

73. E. P. Thompson, "Eighteenth-century English Society: Class Struggle without Class?" *Social History, 3,* 2, (May, 1978), 149.

74. *Ibid.*

75. Ron Bourgeault, "Metis History," *New Breed, 13,* 8, (Sept., 1982), 4. Also see L. Bergeron, *The History of Quebec: A Patriote's Handbook* (Toronto, 1971), 12–38 for an interesting discussion of the chain of exploitation in the fur trade and the pyramid class structures in Canadian society during this period. And John Lambert defines the different classes of society in *Travels through Lower Canada, and the United States of North America in the Years 1806, 1807 and 1808* Vol. I (London, 1810), 277–278.

76. Jack Scott, *Sweat and Struggle: Working Class Struggles in Canada. Vol. I: 1789–1899* (Vancouver, 1974), 18.

77. For an excellent account of the European example see E. P. Thompson, *The Making of the English Working Class* (New York, 1968); John Rule, *The Labouring Classes in Early Industrial England 1750–1850* (London, 1986) and George Rude, *The Crowd in History, 1730–1848* (New York, 1964).

78. G. Williams, ed., *Andrew Graham's Observations on Hudson's Bay 1767–91* (London, 1969), 306.

79. *Journals of Samuel Hearne and Philip Turnor,* 136–137.

80. W. Tomison to J. Colen, 10 July 1798 in *Saskatchewan Journals and Correspondence 1795–1802,* 177.

81. Morton MSS C505/1/2.2 Selkirk Papers. Miles Macdonell's Journal Sept. 14, 1812, p. 253 and Nov. 6, 1812, p. 271.

82. *Ibid.,* Dec. 11-13, 1812, 280.

83. *Ibid.,* Jan. 16, 1813, 287–288.

84. *Ibid.,* Feb. 1, 1813, 291.

85. Morton MSS C505/1/2.3 Selkirk Papers. Pp. 16819–16957. Miles Macdonell's Journal April 22, 1813 to Feb. 11, 1815, pp. 73–75.

86. *Ibid.,* June 8-10, 1914, 86–87.

87. G. P. de T. Glazebrook, ed., *The Hargrave Correspondence 1821–1843* (Toronto, 1938), 241–242.

88. *Andrew Graham's Observations on Hudson's Bay 1767–91,* 306.

89. For an account of the strike see B. Willson, *The Great Company,* 295–297.

90. Adam Smith notes that even though there were laws prohibiting the formation of trade unions, workers still combined to either increase wages or prevent a reduction, *The Wealth of Nations,* 66–67. And Marx and Engels wrote that "the collisions between individual workmen and individual bourgeois take more and more the character of collisions between two classes. Thereupon the workers begin to form combinations ... in order to keep up the rate of wages ...," *The Manifesto of the Communist Party* (Moscow, 1975), 55.

91. HBCA. A. 11/116, fo. 22, H. Marten to the Governor and Committee, Aug. 25, 1777 in *Cumberland House Journals and Inland Journal 1775–82,* edited by E. E. Rich (London, 1951), 142–143.

92. For an account of these disputes see C. Lipton, *The Trade Union Movement of Canada 1827–1959* (Montreal, 1966), 1; H. A. Innis, *The Fur Trade in Canada,* 241–242; A. S. Morton, *A. History of the Canadian West,* 348–350; and E. Coues, *New Light on the Early History of the Greater Northwest* (New York, 1897), 860–861.

93. Journal of James Bird in *Saskatchewan Journals and Correspondence 1795–1802,* 196–197.

94. *Ibid.,* 199.

95. NAC, *Report on Canadian Archives 1886,* M. Macdonell to William H. Cook, 14 Feb. 1812, ccvi.

96. *Ibid.,* M. Macdonell and William Hillier to William Auld, 15 May 1812, ccxiii.

97. E. P. Thompson, "Eighteenth-century English Society: Class Struggle without Class?" 137.

CHAPTER

10 1837–1838: REBELLIONS, OR REVOLUTIONARY CRISIS IN CANADA?

Historian R.G. Collingwood's dictum that "every new generation must rewrite history in its own way" is well-demonstrated by the 1837–38 rebellions in Upper and Lower Canada, perhaps because the questions raised by them are so varied. Were they isolated British North American events, or part of a larger, transatlantic revolutionary phenomenon? If the former, were they the consequence of long-term, structural problems, or merely responses to immediate, localized difficulties? Were they fundamentally political, economic, social, or nationalist in nature, or some combination thereof? Were they the products of an élitist few, or did they have a much broader base of support within the British North American population? What were their short- and long-term consequences?

As Allan Greer notes in the most recent revisionist article on the subject and the third of those reprinted here, until well into the twentieth century the diverse and contradictory answers to these questions proffered by historians of all ideological and nationalistic stripes tended to share a common historical perspective: "...the rebels of 1837 were quite literally on the wrong track. They lost because they *had* to lose; they were not simply overwhelmed by superior force, they were justly chastised by the god of History." For example, Donald Creighton, the acknowledged English-Canadian authority on the nineteenth-century Empire of the St. Lawrence, argued that the rebellions arose mainly from economic conflict between backward-looking, rural agrarians and pro-gressive, urban-based mercantile interests in the Canadas. Abbé Lionel Groulx's Catholic nationalistic view of the rebellion in Lower Canada was equally teleo-logical, as, in its own way, was that of Stanley Ryerson, one of the first Marxist historians of Canada, who claimed 1837–38 marked the failure of a "national-democratic revolution" in the Canadas. In "1837–38: Rebellion Reconsidered," Greer undertakes a major reappraisal of the subject by eschewing all such his-torical imperatives and focusing on what he terms the "complexity and contingency" of these events.

A second notable dimension of Greer's reappraisal is his examination of the commonalities and interconnectedness of the rebellions in Upper and Lower Canada, something that few of his contemporaries or immediate predecessors have attempted. Indeed, to find an approximate parallel to Greer's article it is necessary to jump back more than half a century to the relevant chapters of Creighton's *The Empire of the St. Lawrence*. Historians of the generation between Creighton and Greer, for the most part, have limited their scope to one or other of the Canadas. The strengths and weaknesses of doing so are reflected in the two other articles reprinted here, one on each of the Canadas. Representing the literature on the Lower Canadian rebellion is a piece by Fernand Ouellet, one of the most prolific and important writers on the history of pre-Confederation Quebec. In "The Failure of the Insurrectionary Movement, 1837–1839" ex-cerpted from his *annaliste* study, *Economic and Social History of Quebec, 1760–1850: Structures and Conjunctures*, Ouellet nicely summarizes his socio-economic interpretation of the events of 1837–38. More traditionally political in focus but nonetheless informative for that is Gerald M. Craig's analysis of the rebellion in Upper Canada, "Conservatives and Rebels 1836–37" taken from *Upper Canada: The Formative Years*. Students should assess the extent to which Ouellet and Craig manifest the shortcomings identified by Greer, as well as the advantages their more narrowly focused approach brings to the general understanding of the rebellions.

Suggestions for Further Reading

Bergeron, L., *The History of Quebec: A Patriot's Handbook*. Toronto: NC Press, 1971.

Craig, Gerald M., *Upper Canada: The Formative Years*. Toronto: McClelland and Stewart Limited, 1963.

Creighton, D.G., "The Economic Background of the Rebellions of Eighteen Thirty-Seven," *Canadian Journal of Economics and Political Science*, III, no. 3 (August 1937), 322–34.

_____, *The Empire of the St. Lawrence*. Toronto: Macmillan of Canada, 1956.

Groulx, Abbé Lionel, *Histoire du Canada français depuis la découverte*. Montreal: Fides, 1960.

Keilty, Greg, (ed.), *1837: Revolution in the Canadas*. Toronto: NC Press Limited, 1974.

Manning, H.T., *The Revolt of French Canada, 1800–1835*. Toronto: Macmillan of Canada, 1962.

Ouellet, F., *Economic and Social History of Quebec 1760–1850 Structures and Conjunctures*. Ottawa: The Carleton Library, 1980.

_____, *Louis Joseph Papineau: A Divided Soul*. Ottawa: The Canadian Historical Association, 1964.

_____, *Lower Canada, 1792–1841*. Toronto: McClelland and Stewart, 1980.

Parker, W.H., "A New Look at Unrest in Lower Canada in the 1830's," *Canadian Historical Review*, XL, no. 3 (September 1959), 209–17.

Read, Colin, *The Rising in Upper Canada, 1837–38: The Duncombe Revolt and After*. Toronto: University of Toronto Press, 1982.

_____, *The Rebellion of 1837 in Upper Canada*. Ottawa: The Canadian Historical Association Booklet No. 46, 1988.

Ryerson, S., *Unequal Union: Confederation and the Roots of Crises in the Canadas, 1815–1837*. Toronto: Progress Books, 1968.

THE FAILURE OF THE INSURRECTIONARY MOVEMENT, 1837–1839

Fernand Ouellet

> *I verily believe that the almost total destruction of the wheat crops by the wheat fly, which was the case for six or seven years, and just about the period of the rebellion in 1836 and 7, was in one respect an incidental cause of the rebellion. The French-Canadian peasantry had always been in the habit of consuming a great deal of wheaten bread in their families. But by the wheat fly they were obliged to feed up on the inferior grain, oats and potatoes. I have myself observed among them the discontent this at first occasioned....*
>
> W. Sutherland, On the Present Condition
> of United Canada as regards to Agriculture,
> Trade and Commerce (1849), p. 7.

The insurrection of 1837–38 has been presented in many ways. Some historians have seen it as a sudden outburst of anger and indignation, evidently without premeditation, unleashed by the resolutions of Lord Russell, which violated a constitutional principle. This view seems somewhat out of tune with the French-Canadian mentality. Spontaneous recourse to arms has never been the favoured means used by the French Canadians to realize their collective objectives or assert their demands. Lafontaine, who knew them well, said that their principal weapon was inertia and, let us add, verbal agitation. The insurrections cannot be primarily explained either as a spontaneous reaction or as a defence of principles—political or constitutional. The peasant mass was not yet living in an age of liberalism or democracy.

From *Economic and Social History of Quebec, 1760–1850: Structures and Conjunctures*, Carleton Library no. 120 (Ottawa: Gage and Institute of Canadian Studies, 1980), 420–47, 635–36.

Other historians, sometimes the same ones, have spoken of a logical outcome to a long political and constitutional conflict, accordingly non-nationalist in its main dimensions, but ultimately of national import. Some, however, such as Filteau, are quick to postulate the nationalist character of the disturbances of 1837–38. Some have also spoken of an explosion of reform, comparing it with the English Chartist movement and with Jacksonian democracy, and, finally, have seen the insurrections of the two Canadas as part of the same reality. They have tried to show in this way that it was, in the end, a matter of overthrowing colonial oligarchies in order to promote a colonial system built on a more liberal basis. The insurrectionary phenomenon, in short, as far as its real origins, its nature, its extent, and its consequences are concerned, has been simplified in the extreme. We must not overlook either the systematic pronouncements, based on canon law and moral precepts, of which this movement has been the object for numerous historians. In this regard, Chapais is the model. He has succeeded in outclassing the clerical historians on their own ground, that is, in his moralizing fervour. That many of these interpretations are partially just, we readily admit. But what, on the whole, is most lacking is a total perspective which restores to this phenomenon its meaning and its complexity.

It seems evident that if the insurrection had only political roots, even remote ones, it would not have taken place. It is no less clear that if it had involved only abstract principles, it would have in no way mobilized the rural masses, any more than the liberal professions. As we believe we have shown, the crisis which prepared the way for the insurrectionary upheaval was first and foremost economic and social before being political. The agricultural crisis, the demographic and social tensions, the particularly critical situation of the liberal professions were the principal foundations of the nationalist reaction, which mobilized certain élite groups and rallied a large part of the masses. Nor can the influence of ideologies other than nationalism be denied. We have already pointed out why they intruded into French-Canadian society and what functions they assumed there. French and English liberalism, British radicalism, Jeffersonian and Jacksonian democracy, in turn and in varying degrees, influenced the political élites according to their particular needs. But these ideological currents never reached the rural masses or the working-class minority. On the whole, we can say that these systems of values and thought remained dependent on the aims pursued by the dominant ideology, *nationalism*. Furthermore, because it aimed at control of the political structures to the advantage of the liberal professions and the French-Canadian nationality, the nationalist reaction asserted itself at the political level before it found expression in two successive insurrections. After 1806, political conflicts took hold at the same time as economic difficulties, demographic pressures, and social tensions. From time to time, as temporary improvements occurred in one sector or another, there was a relative reduction of the conflicts. Although the major initiator was economic, the interdependence of the different levels of activity becomes obvious at every turn. It was the same with the mental outlook and the fluctuations of collective psychology, which operated within this overall context. The time was given over to pessimism, tragic visions, and aggressiveness. In 1852, G.J. de Lotbinière wrote: "It seems to me that we are in an age when we feel things more sharply than before. Our Fathers knew how to maintain their liveliness and cheerfulness right to the very end, despite all of life's vicissitudes, while now we take everything seriously: private life and public life. Our wounds no longer heal. Who is to blame?"[1]

We must not overlook either the essential role of the dominant personalities, especially that of Papineau. He was at once the reflection of the situation, one of its principal definers, and the instrument through which the nationalist reaction was expressed. His ambitions, his interests, and above all his personality made him the key figure of this reaction. Having reached the head of the nationalist movement for a variety of reasons, he managed to direct it for nearly twenty-five years. After 1830, he even conceived the plan of becoming the president of a French-Canadian republic, independent or attached to England by very tenuous ties. But Papineau was a man of opposition, of systematic obstruction, and of verbal agitation. He was not cut out for action. Idealistic, doctrinaire, indecisive, deeply torn between contradictory tendencies, his kingdom was the House of Assembly. He was more a symbol than the instigator of a revolutionary movement. In short, there was nothing, unless it was his ambition and faithfulness to the myth which he embodied, predisposing him to be the leader of an insurrection and to remain so in spite of everything. His political attitudes, however, were directly conducive to an armed uprising. The systematic obstruction that he practised after 1831–32 and the intransigence of his demands could have no other result unless England and the British minority of Lower Canada agreed to a number of total concessions. The latter, however, refused categorically to consider such an option. At the beginning of the year 1837, political conflicts seemed insoluble. Briefly, the insurrections of 1837–38 were the logical conclusion to a whole complex of factors, some of which had been at work since the first years of the nineteenth century. But was this enough to guarantee the success of the operation?

I. THE *CONJUNCTURE* DURING THE REVOLUTIONARY PERIOD

As early as the beginning of 1837, the economic *conjoncture* was very bad, worse even than in 1834. The British economic crisis now had repercussions in the St. Lawrence Valley. It should be noted that in England this was not an ordinary contraction affecting only a few sectors of the economy, but rather a widespread crisis. There was thus a serious decline in most areas, particularly in finances. In November 1836, H. Bliss notified the president of the Quebec Chamber of Commerce of the difficult situation of the English banks.[2] In February, the crisis had taken on more serious proportions. Bliss recorded several bankruptcies.

He wrote then: "The state of foreign exchanges still continues unfavourable and the Bank Directors are supposed to be contemplating some more energetic means of turning the current of Gold inward to this country, a measure only to be accomplished by a further considerable contraction of the issues of paper."[3] By April, the prospects were still less encouraging. Bliss wrote:

> the continued and still-continuing depression of the Money Market had involved the commerce of this country in the greatest difficulty and despondency. The Bank has lessened the circulation by above 2 millions, notwithstanding some advances of considerable amount to several American Houses. Prices have consequently declined...while to make this depression still more severe the Corn Market has actually advanced. In fine the reckoning for the excessive issues of Paper in the later half of 1835 and the early part of 1836 has come attended with backward spring after a severe winter and deficient harvest. The merchants who have entered into extensive contracts based upon the high prices which those excessive issues had caused, have now to sell such purchases at the low rates which the present contraction of the currency imposes; and as that contraction is rendered necessary by the foreign exchanges, it must continue and be carried still further, until the price of gold rises or which is the same thing the price of other commodities falls enough to make *specie* the best remittance which the foreigner can send us. The severe loss in which all and the utter ruin in which many of the commercial classes have been thus already involved and have yet further to sustain, will probably compel the public and Government to make some more thorough enquiry into the cause.[4]

The rash of speculation which had prevailed in England since 1835 reached its outcome in the form of a general economic crisis complicated by poor crops. But, as usual, bad crops in Britain did not constitute a disaster for Canada, providing, of course, that they corresponded to high production in the Canadas. But in 1837, neither Lower nor Upper Canada was in a position to profit from the high prices commanded on the British market.

As the crowning misfortune, a very serious financial crisis broke out in the United States, where the *conjoncture* was to be most unfavourable until 1842. The American banks stopped cash payments in May 1837. The combined effects of these two financial panics, the English and the American, had their repercussions in Canada. The Quebec Chamber of Commerce immediately recommended the suspension of payment in cash by the banks. "That in consequence of the suspension of *specie* Payments in the United States, this Committee deem it expedient that a Public Meeting of the Merchants be immediately called to adopt such measures as may be considered necessary to prevent a drain of *specie* in the present alarming crisis."[5] The merchants were not content with asking the Governor to permit the banks to stop cash payments, they requested permission to defray their customs duties by means of "vouchers issued by the Banks." To support their request, they pointed to the unusual scarcity of *specie*. Although these decisions were inspired by a desire to avoid greater evils, they did not prevent the monetary difficulties from tightening their grip. In June 1837, an observer wrote:

Many difficulty results from the derangement that the suspension of payments in *specie* by our banks has produced in trade, owing to the general suspension of these payments by Banks in the United States. There is a shortage of small change and a lack of fixity in values so that industry cannot count on its income with security and uncertainty and hesitation have been created in business everywhere.[6]

The American financial crisis subsequently carried over into Great Britain. On 5 June, Bliss wrote:

The Bank of England I regret to say had lately receded from the conduct that it had so wisely adopted of succouring the embarrassments, and mitigating the evils, brought upon all commercial classes, by its own reckless enlargement of the circulation. The American merchants are now left to their fate. The failures consequent upon this change must soon reach the Manufacturing districts and their distress will probably compel at least inquiry into its cause.[7]

It was only in the month of September 1837 that Bliss was able to announce a reversal of the British situation: "the basis on which the industry and trade of the whole country is founded and will probably lead to a further extension of every enterprise and to an improvement of prices."[8]

Altogether, the year 1837 was a particularly severe one in England. When we are aware of the strict sensitivity of the Lower Canadian economy to the *conjoncture* prevailing in the mother country, we can be sure of finding a similar situation in the St. Lawrence Valley. Lower Canada, moreover, was already deeply affected by an agricultural crisis.

The poor crops of 1836, which correspond to a more or less deficient harvest in the West and an increased demand in England, had provoked a rise in agricultural prices. Thus, at the beginning of 1837, the shortage of products and money was the order of the day. On 4 January, an editor gave an account of some of the difficulties which existed on the market of Quebec City:

Abundance has not reigned on our markets these past days, as we might have expected it would; this is owing to the lack of communication with the south sides of the River. Today the market is mediocre to fair. With the exception of butter, all provisions have experienced a considerable rise; grains especially have increased and it seems that they will not remain there....We have already several times warned those who frequent the markets not to inflate the price of the meats they bring there; this disgusting habit, however, continues. Several quarters of lamb belonging to farmers have been confiscated this morning by the market clerks for the benefit of the poor and sent to the workhouse. The prices quoted in the table given below have been verified by the clerk of the markets; their accuracy can be relied on.[9]

In short, there was in 1837 an appreciable rise in agricultural prices. Table 1 illustrates the behaviour of prices during the revolutionary period.

The inflation which existed in January 1837, was not solely attributable to the factors listed below, it depended also on the speculation in produce and agricultural commodities. On 16 January 1837, an observer wrote: "We have for

TABLE 1   **Average Price Increase (in livres tournois)**

	1835–39	*1835–39 / 1830–34*	*1837 / 36*	*1838*	*1839*
Flour (Quebec)	21.97	61%	83%	11%	0
Wheat (Quebec)	9.66	28%	51%	8%	13%
Wheat (Montreal)	7.5	22%	38%	-5%	-5%
Moving average	6.8	3%	—	—	—
Oats (Quebec)	3.13	11%	20%	3%	5%
Moving average	2.7	-3%	—	—	—
Oats (Montreal)	—	—	26%	—	—
Beef (Quebec)	0.50	28%	53%	0	8%
Moving average	0.44	7%	—	—	—
Beef (Montreal)	—	—	high of 10% in 1836		
Butter (Quebec)	1.32	30%	39%	6%	23%
Moving average	1.17	-1%	—	—	—
Butter (Montreal)	—	—	8%	—	—
Silberling	112.4	4%	0	6%	4%
Peas (Montreal)	—	—	42%	—	—

a long time on various occasions spoken of the drawbacks caused by the absence of laws concerning bakers and of a tariff on bread. Again this food item has just risen in price, which can hardly be explained in view of the previous high price except by the facility with which the bakers can raise their profits to the levels which suit them. Flour in New York is a dollar more expensive than here, and yet bread costs four cents less per six pounds."[10]

In Montreal, the crisis raged with almost as much force as in the District of Quebec. "The ice on the river," declared one observer, "is now furrowed with tracks crossing in all directions; and the people from the south have easy access to the city. The roads, however, are still bad, the wind fills them up as soon as people have passed by. Few people come to the market, and the price of supplies is always increasing and money grows ever more scarce. Without the aid that the poor receive in the workhouse, there is no doubt that many of them would die of hunger and cold in the long and rigorous winter season. The distress may not be as great in our districts as in Quebec, there are none the less many who are destitute. The crops have been very mediocre in many parishes. The shortage of money is the order of the day almost everywhere in the country."[11]

In some areas, the famine was such that there was a real fear a large part of the population would die of hunger. At Trois-Pistoles, 1,200 people were in this tragic situation. "A letter from Trois-Pistoles, dated the thirtieth of Dec.," reported one observer, "paints a frightening picture of the misery which prevails in this area. It is so bad that several farmers are eating their horses. There have been no crops for four years and many people haven't even a potato. The most well-off barely have enough for themselves and their families, even living very sparingly. What will become of all these poor unfortunates from now until May? It is torture to think about it. It is certain that many of them will die of hunger, unless aid comes at once."[12]

In February, nothing occurred to modify this desperate situation, apart from the intervention of private charity organizations. Moreover, since 1833, a lasting conflict had existed with the principal *patriote* leaders, who refused to consider the social responsibilities of the State. Some asked the government to create public granaries and others demanded funds to help the unfortunate. In 1833, Papineau unwillingly agreed to some concessions, but subsequently refused to encourage, as he phrased it, a spirit of dependence among the peasants. An article in *Le Canadien* is especially indicative of these problems:

> You know that for four years, almost all the parishes below Quebec have been afflicted by the destruction of their grain. Are not the great destitution of the lower, but most numerous, class, and I might add the noticeable decrease of resources among the other classes of Quebec society, the result of the distress in the country areas which form the territory around the capital and to which they should give support?[13]

This document, then, sums up the situation of the countryside of the District of Quebec since 1833. In 1834, owing to government subsidies, the farmers had been able to sow their crops. In 1835, despite pressing needs, the farmers had made no requests for help: "They prefer to sell their animals and go into debt to the *seigneurs*, parish priests, and merchants. But today, these influential people can give no more without putting their own possessions in danger.... Should the virulent declarations of Papineau and some members from Montreal, who have always been opposed to such assistance, be able to paralyse the nerves of the chief of the Executive out of mere apprehension, and prevent him from doing what all his predecessors have done in similar cases?"

The harvest of 1836 had therefore been a complete failure in the Quebec region, while in the Montreal area it had scarcely been better. "It has been part of the system," added the same analyst, "to cultivate a little of everything and a lot of potatoes since the great scarcity of 1816; but what can they do against a climate which at times, like this year and the preceding years, despite the most favourable appearances, destroys everything in one night, even the potatoes."[14] Thus the wheat crisis had been coupled since 1833, by reason also of bad weather conditions, with a serious crisis in alternative crops. Hence the particular seriousness of the agricultural malaise at the time of the adoption of the Russell Resolutions.

In 1837 complaints broke out everywhere. F. Papineau wrote from Petite-Nation: "There is neither straw, nor hay, nor wheat, nor meat in the area. Animals and people are destitute."[15] Some days later, in *Le Canadien*, the misery of the people in the Beauce was evoked:

The distress goes on increasing in the parishes of St. François and St. Georges and even all through the Beauce. The roads, having become impassable because of the flooding rivers, have reduced the people to the most extreme want. The least afflicted, i.e., the best *habitants*, are themselves exhausted. They have done everything in their power to help the others and prevent them from starving by selling or lending the little bit of wheat or flour which they were setting aside for themselves, hoping to get some soon from Quebec. Our poor farmers are disconsolate, not only from enduring hunger this year, but from seeing themselves exposed to the same distress next year, since a large part of the two parishes will have to remain without crops. Most have no food at all except a little sugar which they dissolve in water. There are even those who have no other means of avoiding death from hunger than by eating the dead animals found along the roadsides.... Add to this the measles and scarlet fever which have struck these unfortunate families, and imagine if you can, the state of the poor people of the Beauce.[16]

Thus, in 1837, destitution and discontent prevailed everywhere. The meagre hopes that might have been entertained regarding the next harvest were to be disappointed, so that the situation instead of improving continued to get worse. Moreover, the crisis of 1837 did not affect only agriculture; it was general. In February, Lafontaine wrote: "Possibly the almost total distress, in business as much as in agriculture, is bringing discouragement to the peoples' hearts. I confess that in Canada the poverty is great and the misery complete."[17]

The critical *conjoncture* of this period is revealed in the movement of exports.

The crisis thus struck all sectors, even the timber industry and shipbuilding. The agricultural crisis had repercussions in the towns, while the decline in lumbering and shipbuilding provoked unemployment. A document of 1837 very clearly illustrates the situation in the urban areas, especially among the workers of Quebec:

St. Roch, District of: contains from 95 to 110 widows who earn their livelihood by the day and a large part of whom very often have difficulty in finding work at this season. With them are around 200 orphans. Age, sickness, and infirmity make a large number of these poor women unable to work for part of the winter. And since these same causes stop them from entering the Workhouse, which moreover can take no more people for lack of space, they will perish with their children unless the public comes to their aid. In St. Roch, there are also 100 to 110 poor families. A certain number of them, it is true, have been brought to poverty because of drink, whose use is so deadly and widespread among our working-classes.... Besides these families which suffer so much through the fault of their Head, there is a large number whose misery comes only from the contagious sicknesses which thrive almost continuously in the midst of our poor population, or, again, only from the sad results of the accidents to which the workmen who labour in the shipyards are daily exposed.[18]

TABLE 2

	EXPORTS		INCREASE		
	1838–42	*1833–37*	*1837/36*	*1838/37*	*1839/38*
Shipping: Quebec and Montreal (Tonnage)	403,048	21%	-7%	3%	9%
Shipping: Canals (Total tonnage)	265,662	4%	-21%	-3%	14%
Grain: Quebec (Barrels)	216,791	202%	-100%		
Grain: Deficit in Lower Canada (Barrels)	169,935	63%	?		
Grain: Total imports: Lower Canada	409,373	133%	-100%		
Boards and deals (Number)	2,732,645	8%	1%	3%	5%
Staves (Number)	6,083,686	1%	-7%	-11%	10%
Squared pine (Tons)	310,982	17%	-11%	6%	21%
Squared oak (Tons)	24,980	14%	stable	32%	15%
Potash, total (Barrels)	25,823	-17%	stable	-12%	-13%
Potash, Lower Canada	9,345	-12%	5%	-17%	-39%
Shipbuilding (Tonnage)	17,122	99%	-6%	-12%	80%

Obviously, the decreased production in the sectors linked to the export trade particularly influenced imports, whether from Great Britain, the United States, or the West Indies.

On the whole, the economic crisis of 1837 was a central event which could be felt more keenly each day. It did not equally affect the whole province. It was in the District of Montreal that it reached its maximum intensity. Indeed, the Montreal region depended above all on local and western agriculture. Then the malaise spread to the district of Trois-Rivières. Here, it was the direct result of shortages in agricultural production and overpopulation. There existed, nevertheless, in these two parts of the province some areas relatively shielded from the crisis. These were the areas, such as the Ottawa Valley, where the timber industry predominated, and partially neutralized the consequences of the difficulties which agriculture was experiencing.

This is a basic observation for the understanding of the insurrectionary movement: namely that the restlessness in men's minds and the inclination towards revolt largely reflected the agricultural context and the demographic pressures. On the other hand, despite the very marked falling off recorded in the timber sector and in shipbuilding, it seems evident that these two sectors continued to play, even in 1837, a moderating role, especially in Quebec City and in certain rural centres in this district. In June 1837, an observer noted this important phenomenon:

Moreover, the port trade which is maintained and the employment which timber continues to supply to part of the population contributes strongly to neutralizing the effect of the seasons and other unfavourable circumstances.[19]

These are not the only factors explaining the geographical distribution of the revolutionary thrusts; but, in our opinion, they had considerable importance. We are tempted to assert without fear of error that on the eve of 1837, the rural population in almost every locality where the timber industry did not have a hold was psychologically prepared to attempt the insurrectionary venture. But certain moderating influences and other circumstances prevented them from taking part in revolutionary action.

TABLE 3

	IMPORTS			*INCREASE*	
	1838–42	*1838–42 / 1833–37*	*1837 / 1836*	*1838 / 1837*	*1839 / 1838*
Value: Quebec and Montreal	1,943,854	35%	-26%	-6%	43%
Value: Quebec, Montreal, and St.-Jean	2,147,314	17%	-17%	-21%	50%
Value: St.-Jean	131,717	40%	-17%	2%	124%
Volume: Quebec and Montreal (Tonnage)	401,343	24%	-8%	5%	7%
Volume: Gaspé and New Carlisle	10,384	2%	-23%	-24%	97%
Molasses (Gallons)	104,265	18%	36%	-2%	27%
Sugar (Lbs.)	8,778,441	45%	-10%	28%	6%
Wine (Gallons)	335,465	-2%	-23%	67%	46%
Salt (*Minot*)	378,550	47%	-16%	28%	57%
Coffee (Lbs.)	236,207	127%	-38%	-4%	54%
Tea (Lbs.)	1,054,952	24%	-6%	62%	-6%
Rum, spirits (Gallons)	678,113	-36%	-33%	118%	-18%
Tobacco (Lbs.)	836,925	13%	38%	-23%	0.6%
Butter and Cheese (Lbs.)	450,436	10%	-13%	38%	12%
Pork and Beef (Barrels)	31,948	-6%	-15%	-24%	51%
Lard (Lbs.)	225,884	-16%	-65%	234%	-40%
Rawhides (Number)	40,870	73%	-23%	-12%	63%
Rice (Lbs.)	277,122	30%	-47%	74%	-56%
Cattle (Number)	799	-82%	-34%	-42%	-54%

To conclude, we can say that the year 1837, as much in England as in Quebec, was marked by a profound economic crisis, a situation eminently favourable to a pronounced aggravation of the social and political conflicts. While the crisis in England unleashed the Chartist movement, in Canada, there occurred the conclusion of a long struggle which went back to the years around 1806. The economic crisis precipitated this *denouement*.

In Great Britain, the *conjoncture* reversed in the autumn of 1837. A recovery got underway which lasted until the last quarter of 1839 and was brought to an end by another financial crisis. These circumstances, theoretically most favourable to the Canadas, did not have immediate repercussions, so that the year 1838 was just as hard for the people of Lower Canada, who were already shaken by the recession of 1837 and the uprising of the *patriote* forces. In 1838, another armed rising occurred in the Montreal region. Shortly after the miscarriage of this uprising, the Quebec region, in its turn, threatened to come into the insurrectionary movement. But the plot failed.

In practice, the poor harvest of 1837 still determined the general situation. Destitution persisted in the countryside; money and supplies were scarce. Prices continued, in most cases, to rise. Speculation, the strong demand on the British market, and local poverty forced prices up. Luckily, Upper Canada had large surpluses at its disposal which it could sell either in Britain or in Quebec. But the poverty of consumers and producers, who were always in debt, was an obstacle to the satisfaction of needs. In April, Joseph Papineau mentioned the powerlessness of individuals who wished to obtain money and open up business.[20] In the autumn of 1938, extreme poverty still prevailed in the rural areas. The cities, in turn, were suffering the consequences of the agricultural disasters.

In the other sectors, moreover, despite partial improvements, circumstances were far from encouraging. Exports of squared timber (pine, 6 per cent; oak, 32 per cent) and lumber (3 per cent) increased in an appreciable fashion, but shipments of staves and potash declined by 11 and 17 per cent respectively. In shipbuilding the decline was still sharper than in 1837 (12 per cent). To complicate the situation, the banks again closed their doors after November 6. All this explains the new drop which incurred in import levels. For Quebec and Montreal, the decrease was 6 per cent, but for the ports of entry as a whole, it was 21 per cent. An itemized analysis of imports proves that the importers, stimulated by the encouraging prospects in England at the beginning of 1838, had bought excessively. This was particularly true for rum, lard, tea, rice, butter, and cheese. It should be added that the requirements of the timber industry and the troops explain these purchases.

The year 1838, in short, was also dominated by the crisis. In the timber industry, some very definite signs of recovery appeared, while the movement of grain from the West was more vigorous. But this was not enough to make up for the magnitude of the agricultural crisis, or to limit the consequences of the crisis which raged in shipbuilding.

In 1839, Lower Canadian agriculture was in a deplorable state. It was suffering from the consequences of the preceding year's failures and the plundering of the soldiers and "Loyalists" in certain parishes of the Montreal region. In April, the seigneuress of St. Hyacinthe wrote:

> We are beginning to feel strongly the ill-effects that the pillaging has had here. Not enough meat is brought to the market for half of the village's needs and the little that does come is extremely dear and of the worst quality, and we have not the advantages, as in other years, of finding in the farmyard what the market lacks. They have killed, carried away, and destroyed my cattle, cows, pigs, sheep, and poultry of every kind, and I am the least to be pitied. To how many others has the same thing happened, who now are stripped of resources for obtaining the basic necessities of life, who are responsible for families or are aged or infirm, or who are unable to find work because most of those who have some resources do not dare to undertake any improvements in such precarious times.[21]

Another warning came from Ottawa, more precisely from the *seigneurie* of Petite-Nation:

> We thought here would have the earliest spring in three or four years; the warm weather came almost at once, and not make a quarter of the sugar taken in former years. The weather now, however, is languid, cool and often overcast, the trees have only begun to bud. The garden here is completely finished, dug, seeded, etc., there are still some flowers. Summer, however, is coming in with some bad symptoms. We fear that there will be great poverty, everything is very costly. We can hardly obtain any beef, too often doing without it for eight or ten days or even fifteen days. Also, thefts are beginning to occur....[22]

Thus, poverty was the lot of a large number of rural folk throughout the year 1839. It was the most severe in the parishes where the timber industry only constituted a minor activity. In these cases, almost nothing happened to stimulate local economic life. The following testimony, applicable to these agricultural areas, clearly reveals their distressing situation: "It's very sad in Canada. Nobody is doing business in the countryside. They have been pillaged. They will have a winter destitution. In short, it is a disaster."[23]

But in 1839, Lower Canada began to feel some movement in certain sectors which had been influenced by the British economy. Aside from the potash trade which was in difficulties, all other sectors which were connected with the timber industry indicated definite progress. The most spectacular expansion occurred in shipbuilding, with an increase of 80 per cent. From then on, Quebec experienced full employment. The increase in exports of staves and lumber reached 10 and 5 per cent; the increase in squared timber was still more remarkable: pine, 21 per cent; oak, 15 per cent. It is very obvious that such a growth in foreign sales could only stimulate imports. At the ports of Quebec and Montreal, the growth in import values was 43 per cent; and 50 per cent, if we add the arrivals at the inland port of St. Jean.

Thus, the *conjoncture* in 1839 was not comprised of solely discouraging elements. In the sector of timber and shipbuilding, the revival had been very great and coincided with the liquidation of the political crisis. The refugees in the United States little by little gave up their last plans for the invasion of Canada, and those least compromised took one by one or in small groups the road back to Lower Canada.

The insurrections of 1837–38 corresponded therefore with an economic crisis which affected not only agriculture but also the protected sectors of the economy. This crisis constituted the background to the insurrectionary venture. It suddenly sharpened the discontents and the social tensions, and hardened political attitudes. It was in this climate, charged with hostility, that the famous Russell Resolutions appeared in March 1837. In allowing the Governor to draw on the treasury, and in rejecting the principal demands of the *patriotes*, the Resolutions forced the latter to adopt a firm position. Because of the challenge presented to them, they could only submit or rebel. Unconditional surrender was obviously impossible. Hence, from March 1837 on, they moved towards an armed uprising.

II. THE FAILURE OF THE INSURRECTIONS

The tactless resolutions of Russell were thus presented to the Imperial Parliament at a time when the atmosphere was particularly explosive in Lower Canada. That is why they marked a turning point in the political situation. From that time on, events followed one another at an increasing tempo until the day of armed confrontation. It was very clear that the *patriotes*, although several of them had long considered the need for an armed revolt, were not immediately prepared to undertake such action. Public opinion needed further preparation and a revolutionary organization had to be set up. Spring, moreover, seemed an unfavourable time for successful insurrection. It was better, they believed, to wait for "the ice to set in."

It would be wrong to suppose that all the *patriote* leaders were sworn to armed revolution. In this regard, two distinct groups existed within the *patriote* movement. Some, above all, believed in the efficacy of force. As for the others, they wished it only as a last resort. They advocated resistance through systematic agitation. A compromise was finally reached between the two factions. The plans drawn up in the spring of 1837 reveal that the two factions, for different motives, had united around a single solution. This plan contained two main aspects: a phase of agitation which would remain within legal limits and another, in the event that England refused to yield to *patriote* pressures, of a revolutionary character. The Papineau group, which believed in the intrinsic merits of verbal agitation, was convinced that Britain would give way in time. The radical elements were not so optimistic. They considered armed confrontation to be inevitable. They, therefore, looked upon the first phase as a preparatory stage for an armed uprising. We should thus not be surprised to find them working toward this final outcome. Moreover, as events unfolded, the influence of the extremist group continued to grow, until from October on these elements held the initiative in the movement.

In short, behind agitation that was "constitutional" or within legal limits, the *patriotes* pursued truly revolutionary ends. The series of great parish and county assemblies which began in May and culminated in the Assembly of the Six Counties responded to intentions which were not entirely peaceful. When Papineau, on 10 May 1837, made two wills in favour of his wife and children in turn, he understood perfectly the risks in the decisions taken by the *patriote* leaders. Almost to the end, he might be deluded as to the efficacy of verbal protests, but he could not escape the exigencies of the revolutionary movement. The contradictions in his behaviour prove that he was not equal to the task before him; they do not show that he acted in good faith when he claimed that no *patriote* had thought of or wished for an armed insurrection. Likewise, the obvious lack of preparation among the *patriote* forces in November at the outbreak of the conflict was not the infallible sign of a single-minded intention; it simply demonstrated the weakness of leadership in a movement which was under the direction of orators rather than men of action. In this regard, Wolfred Nelson was an exceptional figure.

In the evolution towards armed confrontation, the Assembly of the Six Counties marked a veritable turning point. The moderate elements were overrun by the extremists. The declaration of the rights of man issued on this occasion and modelled on the American Declaration of Independence, like the decisions adopted at this time, indicated a new direction. The unrest which had prevailed since spring in the country areas acquired a new importance. The peasants systematically blamed the British and the "Loyalists." Meanwhile the *"Fils de la liberté"* were organized in Montreal. This society was designed not only to promote political education in a democratic and national perspective, but also to train the military forces necessary for a successful revolution. In short, starting in October 1837, the second phase of the plan outlined in the spring was set in motion. The armed uprising was to occur during the first week of December.

It is at this time that the government intervened. The government, during the second week of November, placed the principal *patriote* leaders under arrest. This unexpected act threw the *patriote* leaders in Montreal into disarray, and they hastened to take refuge in the countryside. Some made for St. Denis and St. Charles, others headed for St. Benoit and St. Eustache. Papineau himself, after several days of indecision and an interview with the emissaries from Upper Canada, made for St. Denis, where a gathering of the *patriote* forces had already commenced.

After an initial incident on the road to Longueuil between the constables and a group of *patriotes*, the government finally decided to attack. On 23 November the battle of St. Denis took place, and the *patriotes* were victorious. Two days later, they were crushed at St. Charles. Barely ten days were needed to pacify the Richelieu region. In the meantime, Colborne arrived with his troops. His orders were to put down the resistance of the *patriote* forces billeted at St. Eustache. Despite the fierce resistance of Chénier, the *patriotes* were defeated.

The overthrow of this first attempt at insurrection did not discourage the *patriote* leaders who had fled to the United States. Relying on the Americans and the Lower Canadian population, they sought to organize a new uprising. But internal dissensions, and the break between Papineau and the radicals of the revolutionary group made the task of setting up an organism capable of taking charge of a military venture particularly difficult. A first unsuccessful attempt was made in February 1838 under the direction of Robert Nelson, who managed in the end only to issue a declaration of Canada's independence. Subsequently, plans multiplied, without any consistent policy. During the summer of 1838, the *patriotes* finally succeeded in creating and spreading the *Société des Frères-Chasseurs*. The purpose of this secret organization was to gather all the individuals capable of taking part in a revolution. The date of the uprising was fixed for the third of November. The plan of invasion contained a certain number of immediate objectives: first, to seize St. Jean and Chambly; next, to attack Montreal and, from there, to go on to occupy Quebec. The commander-in-chief, Robert Nelson, successfully gathered together almost 5,000 peasants at Napierville. But there ended the success of the insurgents. For a variety of reasons, the rebels were unable to start off, still less to display any degree of unity, energy, and readiness to fight. The suppression of the uprising by Colborne's troops was that much easier.

While the government troops were pacifying the Richelieu region, the Quebec region was the object of an organizational effort on the part of the revolutionary elements. This movement, moreover, did not seem to have direct connection with that in Montreal. The local leaders, those that we know, were Morin, Huot, and Blanchet. But the movement also involved some Americans who acted as the principal instigators: "Don Philippie," and Foster. This organization relied on two groups: the rural dwellers and the workers of St. Roch. The insurrection was to begin with the establishment of a camp at Ste. Anne de la Pocatière and another at Mont Ste. Anne. It was here that the gathering of the peasant forces was to take place. At the same time, the *Frères-Chasseurs* of Quebec were to attempt a surprise attack, carefully prepared, on the citadel of Quebec. Unfortunately, a police agent called Hutton, who had managed to infiltrate the organization, exposed the plot. Things went no farther.

This portrayal of the revolutionary events still leaves some problems. The first concerns the geographical extent of the revolutionary agitation. How can we explain why the events affected only the Montreal region? We have already shown that in 1837 Quebec City, because of the stabilizing impact of the timber industry and shipbuilding, had formed a "Loyalist" island in the midst of a rural region which was, however, awake to the revolutionary phenomenon. The research which we have carried out in the archives of the period prove this. Furthermore, the city of Quebec was the seat of government, so that a large part of the élite, lay and ecclesiastic, gravitated towards the Château. On the other hand, the famous Quebec-Montreal rivalry had exercised considerable influence on the relations between the political leaders of the two cities. Since 1835, a split had occurred between the two. Conflicts of interest, personal rivalries, and the opposition between the two cities explain, as much as the economic differences, the lack of solidarity among the French-Canadian political leaders in these two strategic areas. But, still in this perspective, there is another basic observation: Montreal was the centre of the *patriote* movement. The *patriote* party was essentially a **Montreal phenomenon. Its principal leaders and its minor chiefs were Montrealers,** just as its objectives were defined in terms of the realities of the rural world and the Montreal region. The party leaders had never succeeded in making the Quebeckers forget that after 1815 the direction of the nationalist movement had passed from Quebec to Montreal. Equally as important, the leadership of the group was a sort of family coterie with Papineau as the leader. In short, there was no deep unanimity between Quebec and Montreal. Since the split between Papineau and Neilson, other ruptures had occurred to break the ideological accord as well as the agreement among individuals.

Thus, when a movement that appeared insurrectionary began to take shape, there were no grounds to hope that the Quebec elements would participate. Centred too much around the Montreal region, it was almost impossible for the leaders of the *patriote* movement to organize revolutionary action in the rural areas of Quebec and Trois-Rivières. Moreover, no serious effort was made in this direction, although these rural localities had responded well to the message delivered by the great assemblies. The concentration of the insurrectionary movement in the Montreal region ensued from this situation. But in 1838, the economic context changed. The crisis in timber and shipbuilding accentuated the difficulties in the city of Quebec, while certain political events helped to awaken part of the élite to the insurrectionary phenomenon. The Quebec leaders then organized their own plot, which woefully miscarried.

With a Montreal character, the revolutionary phenomenon united the social groups which, since the beginning of the nineteenth century, had supported, each in its turn, the *parti canadien* and the *patriote* party. That is why we find at the head of the movement members of the groups which were most keenly attuned to the nationalist venture. First, the notaries, the lawyers, and the doctors. If, in Montreal, the lawyers played a more important role, the notaries carried more weight in the country. Then came the country merchants who, from being political organizers, became very active in the insurrections. Even here a distinction is necessary according to the financial status of these individuals. Generally, the revolutionary elements were recruited from among those who were least favoured, which was a very large number throughout this period. As for the shock forces, they were drawn from the rural setting: peasants exasperated by the agricultural crisis and the demographic pressures, day labourers in search of land and work. In Montreal, it seems clear that the small shopkeepers and the craftsmen would have been ready to take a more active part in the movement than they did.

How can we explain the rather lamentable failure of these uprisings? Some have attributed the defeat of the two insurrections to the clergy's intervention, particularly to the formidable condemnations of Mgr. Lartigue. We can be sure that the fierce opposition of a very large majority of the clergy posed a serious moral problem for the population, which in many ways found itself torn between its religious allegiance and its nationalist beliefs. The refusal of a Christian burial to those who died in the fighting was a measure designed to create very strong fears in the masses. The fear of eternal, as much as temporal, punishments had indeed a powerful influence on the peasants, and one can also say on the revolutionary leaders themselves. In some cases, this distress could be acknowledged, in others, it could not. We know, for example, what relief there was among the people of Ile Perrot when their priest, until then an opponent of the *patriotes*, announced to them from the pulpit that he had had a vision which revealed to him that in less than a year the French Canadians would march up to their ankles in the blood of their enemies, the English. It is true that, owing to the intervention of government officials and the Bishop of Montreal, this worthy priest was later forced to repudiate his sources. But the fact is worth considering as additional proof, if it were needed, of the efficacy of the prohibitions or encouragements delivered by the clergy in these dramatic circumstances. Whatever may have been the influence of the clergy, which was the defender of the divine right of monarchy and of the union of Church and State, no one can, however, see it as the major reason for the revolutionary failures of 1837–38. In this context of a nationalist crisis, in which the clergy appeared as the collaborator of the English, other more decisive factors better account for the destiny of the separatist choice.

Thus, the contradictory behaviour of a man like Papineau is an important explanatory factor. The man himself was the object of a particularly vivid myth in the rural areas. Because he embodied the nationalist cause, he appeared to the peasant mass as the strong man without equal who, for more than twenty-five years had led a desperate battle against the conqueror. Eloquent, energetic, honest (it was thought), he raised awareness, aroused admiration, and excited the popular imagination. After the setback of 1837, the people still hoped for the triumphant return of the Messiah, whom they considered to be their eventual saviour. Witnesses of the time relate that the peasants saw him invading Lower Canada at the head of 50,000 negroes, cyclops into the bargain, armed with repeating rifles. Others, it is said, saw him flying through the air, sitting in a large bark canoe drawn by several white horses. The paradoxical fact for those impressed only by sound and fury is that this man who, they claimed, was the very person to undertake the regeneration of the French Canadians, and the one who symbolized the national struggle, did not have the qualities that they attributed to him.

When we analyse Papineau's behaviour from the spring of 1837, until his flight in disguise on the morning of the St. Denis engagement, we cannot but be struck by the split between the individual and the demands of his role. He was constantly torn between contrary choices, he displayed chronic indecision and, in the final analysis, he showed himself incapable of truly assuming his responsibilities as leader. The task was too heavy for him, and yet, he was just as incapable of withdrawing from a movement whose direction he maintained in spite of everything. We cannot emphasize too strongly the disastrous influence of such conduct. His action, instead of stimulating and inspiring his subordinates, was rather inclined to throw the revolutionary organization into a state of anarchy. The difficulty encountered in setting up a solid cadre and a suitable organization of supply resulted in large measure from the hesitancy of the supreme leader and from the tensions which this situation encouraged. A man good for speaking but not for acting, said Robert Nelson in reference to Papineau. But it was not only Papineau in whom the propensity for endless deliberation and the disposition for passively witnessing events were to be deplored; a large number of those who gathered around him displayed the same characteristics. There were, fortunately, some exceptions to this rule: W. Nelson and Chénier are the best-known. For others, heroism was to come later, namely at the time of the executions that followed the 1838 uprising. Such a patent lack of forceful *leadership* could only fall back on everyone, provoke anarchy and inefficacy, and encourage outbursts of fear. According to the documents of the period, it is obvious that fear prevailed among all the revolutionary elements and sparked the most absurd behaviour. Papineau's flight was not an isolated case; it was the expression of a much wider phenomenon.

But when we examine this failure, we are necessarily led to connect the insurrectionary movement with its objectives and origins. The experience of 1837–38, as we have said, was of a nationalist character. Some historians, especially Mason Wade, have proclaimed that it was reformist and liberal in character, because some Anglo-Saxons had taken part in it. It must be pointed out that these elements were far too small in number ever to influence the philosophy of the movement. It would be even surprising, moreover, if the Irishman O'Callaghan had been particularly motivated by the reformist ideal. As for Brown, a small businessman in financial difficulties, the real motives at the source of his decisions are not known. There remain the Nelson brothers, who although they had been closely connected with the French-Canadian milieu, nonetheless pursued liberal ends. But we must say here that during the whole of the revolutionary period, the authentic liberal and democratic members of the *patriote* group had always been in conflict with those who accorded unquestionable priority to nationalist objectives. The resulting break was primarily the product of these ideological confrontations.

The major objective of the *patriotes* was Lower Canada's independence. Independence aimed at making the liberal professions the only élite in French-Canadian society, an élite which would henceforth be responsible for defining and directing the fulfilment of the common objectives of this society. Independence would allow the development of the restoration of a purely agricultural economy, of a society enclosed in the framework of the *seigneurie* and governed by the old French customary law. At all costs, they wished to prevent capitalism from establishing what they called inequality of conditions. We find here an unconscious quest for political and cultural isolation and for "feudalism." This society, furthermore, was to be democratic and liberal, to the extent, however, that no outside force threatened it. The future of individual liberties and of the secular structures was thus dependent on this fundamental need of defence. In fact, the external peril was unconsciously exaggerated in order to hide an internal danger which was much more effective. The anxiety felt in the face of the demands of progress and the fear of giving up the old securities offered by the traditional order and its taboos, formed the basis of this internal peril. The projection of the collective misfortunes onto the English served above all to hide the need for a complete recasting of the traditional social structures and outlook. When the cause of all trouble was outside, there was no need to give priority to a questioning of traditions.

Independence, in fact, was not aimed at resolving any of the important problems facing French Canada. Whereas the only solution to the agricultural crisis was through a technical revolution, the *patriotes* sought only palliatives, such as the expansion of land areas and the seigneurial territory. In this perspective, it is clear that the rapid exhaustion of the soil threatened as much the new territories of colonization as the old seigneurial lands. This was a faulty response to the demographic question. The extremely rapid growth of the French-Canadian population implied an increase in agricultural activity through improved techniques and, at least as much, the maintenance of the other economic sectors. Equally as serious, independence would mean an immediate severance of economic relations with the Empire. It implied the abandonment of the preferential system which, for other supplementary reasons, would bring about the fall of the timber industry and shipbuilding. According to the French-Canadian leaders, these activities were ladened with a whole past of immorality. Finally, independence would serve to give free reign to the real aspirations of the liberal professions towards feudalism, or at least, towards the old economic regime. On the other hand, the supremacy of agriculture, with its virtues of self-sufficiency, would be ensured by the mass of *censitaires*; on the other, the direction of society would be assumed by the landlords, the clergy, the lay *seigneurs*, the liberal professions. Because of their obligations in the matter of religion, education, and hospitals, the clergy would derive its revenues from tithes, seigneurial rents, gifts, and various assessments for the construction of churches and rectories. The seigneurial system would provide for the subsistence of the lay *seigneurs* as it did for the ecclesiastics. There remained the liberal professionals who, in their normal activities, collected what amounted to an indirect rent, and who also could be considered rentiers in the political sphere.

A political élite protecting the nation's interests, such were the justifications given. In short, the liberal professions unconsciously saw themselves as an aristocratic élite in a hierarchical society. Despite the rationalizations based on liberal and democratic ideologies, their real intention was to preserve a society like the *ancien régime* on the banks of the St. Lawrence. All this was illusory, but it is partly explained by the negative reactions which the *conjoncture* of the time had engendered among the liberal professions. It was as if the event and the drama of the Conquest had belatedly invaded the collective consciousness to inhibit it, and to trigger a whole series of defensive reflexes. Thus, under the guise of democracy and liberal aspirations which had a certain authentic character, we witness the search for an impossible isolation leading to a "feudal" and theocratic society. Under these conditions, a democracy and a liberal State were inconceivable.

The nationalist venture of 1837–38 was too tightly linked to the ambitions of specific individuals, to the immediate interests of the liberal professions, and to the particular difficulties to the period to succeed. It was not based on the elements which would have allowed the building of a better future. The economic weakness of the French Canadians was due above all to their mental outlook, their level of technical skills, their traditions, and their institutions. There certainly, for there is no need to believe that they were totally blameless, is the major reason for the failure of the insurrectionary movement.

More than anything, this lack of justification in regard to long-term interests and progressive values accounts for the behaviour of the majority of the revolutionary leaders. They were prevented from entering wholeheartedly into their venture by a sort of bad faith. This was also true of the leaders of the Banque de Peuple who, at the last moment, refused to invest in independence.

In fact, the economic crisis of 1837–38 had not seriously disrupted the structures which served to support the bourgeoisie of Lower Canada and relations with the Empire. The crisis in timber and shipbuilding was only temporary and, in 1839, expansion once again characterized the *conjoncture*. The extent of the recovery, as it appears in the averages for the years 1837–42, indicates the vigour of the sectors which helped to cushion the effects of the agricultural crisis. Nevertheless, the difficulties of those years had been great enough to make glaringly apparent an overall situation which had become intolerable. Durham, who carried out his studies during this critical period, was certainly deeply influenced by the particular events of his stay.

III. DURHAM AND HIS VIEW OF THE PROBLEMS OF LOWER CANADA

Instructed to inquire into the nature of the conflict which existed in the North American colonies, especially in Lower Canada, and to propose long-term, viable solutions, Lord Durham arrived in Quebec on 27 May 1838. Already, however, through the view of his radical and liberal friends, he had been able, before his arrival in Canada, to form an idea of the troubles which were poisoning political life in the Canadas. From a distance, the struggles seemed to him to be of a reformist, liberal, or probably a democratic nature. Hence, at the beginning of his Report he wrote: "I looked on it as a dispute analogous to those with which history and experience have made us so familiar in Europe—a dispute between a people demanding an extension of popular privileges, on the one hand, and an executive, on the other, defending the powers which it conceived necessary for the maintenance of order."[24] But Durham would not be slow to realize his assessments were premature, indeed, erroneous, especially as they related to Lower Canada.

In fact, the Lord Commissioner arrived during a *conjoncture* which was particularly favourable for the understanding of the strong tensions which had paralysed Lower Canadian politics since the beginning of the century. Indeed, the insurrection had pulled off many masks, entirely or in part. Papineau, for example, had never had an interest in placing his political action under the sign of nationalism. What would have become of his external supports and even his English support if he had openly hoisted the nationalist banner? The English radicals and the reformers of Upper Canada and Quebec would certainly not have continued to back or collaborate with his movement. Thus, the break between Papineau and Neilson had its source in the discovery by Neilson of the real objectives of the *patriote* group much more than in any opposition between reformer and democrat. Politically, nationalism needed a cover. Can we believe that Britain, while knowing as early as 1820 the motives by which the French-Canadian leaders were impelled, might have sought to maintain an equilibrium between the opposing factions? Within the political context of the period, nationalist ideology was to a large extent avowable. Papineau either understood or felt this. Durham was to grasp the nuance very quickly, or at least the exact relations which existed between the nationalism and the liberalism of the *patriotes*.

On the nature of the Lower Canadian conflicts, Durham wrote:

> The same observation had also imposed on me the conviction, that for the peculiar and disastrous dissensions of this Province, there existed a far deeper and far more efficient cause—a cause which penetrated beneath its political institutions into its social state—a cause which no reform of constitution or laws, that should leave the elements of society unaltered, could remove; but which must be removed, ere any success could be expected in any attempt to remedy the many evils of this unhappy Province. I expected to find a contest between a government and a people; I found two nations warring in the bosom of a single state: I found a struggle, not of principles, but of races; and I perceived that it would be idle to attempt any amelioration of laws or institutions until we could first succeed in terminating the deadly animosity that now separates the inhabitants of Lower Canada into the hostile divisions of French and English.[25]

As the basic principle in all other confrontations, Durham discovered this conflict of nationalities manifested at all levels of society. In mental outlook, institutions, traditions, social classes, and political life, the national cleavage appeared to pervade strongly everywhere, and to give rise to the fundamental conflicts. Two national groups, he said, extremely hostile to each other, were in close contact within the same State, and sought to dominate it without hindrance from the other. At the economic level, an equally irreducible incomprehension existed. Within this State, there were not only two different "racial" groups, but two national entities at different stages of evolution. There was, on the one hand, rural French-Canadian society which had not moved beyond the stage of the *ancien régime*: "They remain an old and stationary society in a new and progressive world. In all essentials they are still French; but French in every respect dissimilar to those of France in the present day. They resemble rather the French of the provinces under the old regime."[26] Durham's judgement coincides in every way with that of Ambassador Pontois, who came to Canada on the eve of the 1837 insurrection. On the other hand, Lower Canada was inhabited by another community made up of the British: "They have developed the resources of the country; they have constructed or improved its means of communication; they have created its internal and foreign commerce. The entire wholesale, and a large portion of the retail trade of the Province, with the most profitable and flourishing farms, are now in the hands of this numerical minority of the population."[27]

This British superiority in the economic domain, and an undoubted favouritism in the administration which benefited a clique of civil servants, aroused jealousy among the French Canadians, whose élite was inferior to the English merchants in practical intelligence but, stated Durham, superior in speculative intelligence. From this, the product of the total context and especially of "social feelings," came an almost insoluble political confrontation. The British wanted a government designed to promote "the increase of population and the accumulation of property."[28] On the other hand, the French-Canadian leaders "looked on the province as the patrimony of their race; they viewed it not as a country to be settled, but as one already settled."[29] In all their legislative efforts, they therefore sought to preserve their interests and feelings of their own collectivity without regard for the demands of progress.

After grasping these realities, Durham did not hesitate to declare that the official labels of the political parties meant almost nothing compared to what actually existed.

> It is not indeed, surprising that each party should, in this instance, have practised more than the usual frauds of language, by which factions, in every country, seek to secure the sympathy of other communities....The French Canadians have attempted to shroud their hostility to the influence of English emigration, and the introduction of British institutions, under the guise of warfare against the government and its supporters, whom they represented to be a small knot of corrupt and insolent dependents; being a majority, they have invoked the principles of popular control and democracy, and appealed with no little effect to the sympathy of liberal politicians in every quarter of the world. The English, finding their opponents in collision with the government have raised the cry of loyalty and attachment to British connection, and denounced

the republican designs of the French, whom they designate, or rather used to designate, by the appellation of Radicals. Thus the French have been viewed as a democratic party, contending for reform; and the English as a conservative minority, protecting the menaced connection with the British Crown, and the supreme authority of the Empire....But when we look to the objects of each party, the analogy to our own politics seems to be lost, if not actually reversed; the French appear to have used their democratic arms for conservative purposes, rather than those of liberal and enlightened movement; and the sympathies of the friends of reform are naturally enlisted on the side of sound amelioration which the English minority in vain attempted to introduce into the antiquated laws of the Province.[30]

In the Commissioner's mind, it was the racial conflicts which were responsible for the main deviations of the political and constitutional machinery. Each group entrenched itself behind one or several governmental organizations, whose operations it glorified to the maximum. Each tried to strengthen and set up its own system of patronage. The British relied especially on the Executive and the Legislative Council and the French Canadians on the Assembly, which eventually, thanks to the control it obtained over highway and school policy, set up a system of strictly political patronage. The judicial institutions were also hotly disputed by the two national groups.

This analysis of Lower Canadian problems made by Durham, despite its incomplete and partial nature, carries conviction. The Commissioner had exerted considerable effort to discover, behind the subterfuges of policy and official attitudes, the real nature of the oppositions which were then at work in Lower Canada. Many historians, who claim that the passage of time makes for a fairer view, have been less clear-sighted. Durham's judgements, nevertheless, do often call for modification and more precision. For example, the liberal and democratic ideal, despite its utilitarian and subordinate functions, surely answered something authentic, though very difficult to assume responsibility for, in the consciousness of the bourgeoisie of the liberal professions.

If Durham's analysis seems fair enough on the whole, this is not the case, in our opinion, with several of his conclusions and recommendations. When he states, for example, that revolt was almost permanently ingrained in the French-Canadian spirit, he reveals that he was too influenced by the particular *conjoncture* prevailing in 1838. He seized upon the ethnic conflicts at a time when they appeared to be almost insoluble, namely at the very heart of the revolutionary period.

> Nor does there appear to be the slightest chance of putting an end to this animosity during the present generation. Passions inflamed during so long a period cannot speedily be calmed. The state of education which I have previously described as placing the peasantry entirely at the mercy of agitators, the total absence of any class of persons, or any organization of authority that could counteract this mischievous influence, and the serious decline in the district of Montreal of the influence of the clergy, concur in rendering it absolutely impossible for the Government to produce any better state of feeling among the French population.[31]

Thus, for Durham, French-Canadian nationalism, which now implied independence, had become a major obstacle to the development of the St. Lawrence Valley. The almost characteristic inferiority of the French group, its basic attitudes, in a word, he said, its culture, like the options that it was now and henceforth committed to, were in contradiction with North American realities. "The language, the laws, the character of the North American Continent are English; and every race but English...appears there in a condition of inferiority. It is to elevate from that inferiority that I desire to give the Canadians our English character."[32]

The policy of assimilation proposed by Durham was as illusory as similar fleeting notions produced in the past. No more than before would the idea of assimilation succeed in becoming a coherent and sustained policy. In advocating the union of the Canadas in order to submerge the French Canadians in a British majority, Durham displayed an excessive confidence in the virtues of politics. Moreover, the establishment of the Union regime and, shortly after, the abandonment of the assimilation policy proved the faulty basis of the Commissioner's predictions. Durham's fundamental error was to have thought that the French Canadians' inferiority was congenital and that the only possible objective of their nationalism was henceforth independence. The Lord Commissioner did not know how to get beyond the particular circumstances which surrounded his mission. Had he been able to do so, he would have understood that the insurrectionary phenomenon was transitory. That is why, as the principal result of the reflections arising from the revolutionary experience, French-Canadian nationalism took other directions as early as the years 1840–41. New circumstances commanded everyone's attention; after the fall of the old heroes, new men would grasp the needs of the new situation and find answers better adapted to the challenges and problems posed by the coexistence of the two cultural groups.

Notes

1. APQ, P.-B., letter of January 13, 1852.
2. APQ, QBT, Minute Book (1832–42), H. Bliss to the president of QBT (November 12, 1836).
3. *Ibid.* (1832–42), the same to the same (February 2, 1837).
4. *Ibid.* (1832–42), the same to the same (April 20, 1837).
5. APQ, QBT, Minute Book (1832–42). Decisions adopted from May 16 to 18, 1837.
6. *Quebec Gazette*, June 6, 1837.
7. APQ, QBT, Minute Book (1832–42), H. Bliss to the president of QBT (June 5, 1837).
8. *Ibid.* (1832–42), the same to the same (September 1, 1837).
9. *Le Canadien*, January 4, 1837.
10. *Ibid.*, January 16, 1837.
11. Extract from *La Minerve*, idem.

12. *Le Canadien*, January 9, 1837.

13. *Ibid.*, February 20, 1837.

14. Idem.

15. RAPQ (1951–53), pp. 288*ff.* F. Papineau to L.-J.P. (May 16, 1837).

16. *Le Canadien*, May 26, 1837.

17. APQ, P.-B., Lafontaine to Chapman (February 17, 1837).

18. *Le Canadien*, January 23, 1837.

19. *Ibid.*, June 6, 1837.

20. RAPQ (1953–55), p. 290, J.P. to L.-L.-A.P. (April 27, 1838).

21. APQ, P.-B., unclassified, letter from R. Dessaulles (April 13, 1839).

22. *Ibid.*, unclassified, letter from Emery Papineau (May 2, 1839).

23. *Ibid.*, unclassified, letter from J.-B.-N. Papineau (April 13, 1839).

24. *Report on the Affairs of BNA from the Earl of Durham, Her Majesty's High Commissioner* (1839), p. 8.

25. *Ibid.*, p. 8.

26. *Ibid.*, p. 12.

27. *Ibid.*, p. 14.

28. *Ibid.*, p. 18.

29. *Ibid.*, p. 19.

30. *Ibid.*, p. 10.

31. *Ibid.*, p. 22.

32. *Ibid.*, p. 105.

CONSERVATIVES AND REBELS: 1836–37

Gerald M. Craig

I

At the end of 1835 the British government concluded that a powerful movement of political discontent had arisen in Upper Canada and that it represented majority opinion in the province. As embodied in the reform party, that movement had captured the Assembly in 1834 and in the Seventh Grievance Report had called for sweeping changes in the provincial Constitution, notably an elective legislative council, an executive council responsible to the Assembly, and severe limitations on the Lieutenant-Governor's control over patronage. In consequence, the Colonial Office believed that redoubled efforts must be made to

From *Upper Canada: The Formative Years* (Toronto: McClelland and Stewart, 1963), ch. 12, 226–251, 292–93.

conciliate provincial opinion. Although demands for fundamental constitutional changes could not be met, every effort must be made to remedy practical grievances if the province was to retain its British allegiance. It was in this spirit that instructions were written to Sir Francis Bond Head, Colborne's successor, in December 1835.

On the other hand, it was the view of the Family Compact that the British government wholly misjudged the political state of Upper Canada. The leaders of the Compact believed that conservative forces in the province were far stronger than the forces of innovation, and that they would prevail if given firm leadership and provided with unwavering support from London. Although the political scene was in fact chaotic, and subject to wild fluctuations, the Compact leaders were correct in placing a high estimate on the strength of the conservative forces.

To be sure, there had been a time in the early 1830s when the Compact leaders were seized with the darkest pessimism. The reform spirit in Britain raised the danger, in their minds, that the mother country might cut loose from its moorings and sail out into the uncharted seas of innovation and even anarchy. They believed that the Whig government's policy of conciliating the colonies encouraged agitators to redouble their efforts. In Lower Canada the campaign led by Papineau not only slowed economic progress in the two provinces but threatened the very existence of British rule. In Upper Canada much of the population was unreliable and growing more republican in outlook. In his first years in the province, the Lieutenant-Governor, Sir John Colborne, seemed to the Compact to show little grasp or firmness. In a fit of extreme exasperation John Strachan cried out that the British Ministry should be told that "if they continue to attend to such persons as Ryerson & McKenzie & break down the Constitution the Conservative party will turn round upon them & first trample on the necks of these miscreants and then govern ourselves."[1]

Nevertheless, the conservatives were never people to confine themselves to hand-wringing and futile denunciation. While they continued to fight vigorously against their political opponents, they had good reason to think that reinforcements were on the way. The Solicitor General wrote hopefully of "the influx of British Emigrants" that would save them from the "'Canadian Native' or the neighbouring republic." He noted that the province was "filling with people of wealth and intelligence" who would not be gulled by "such fellows as Ryerson and McKenzie." When "thinking people" of this type began to exert an influence on their neighbours, the "overthrow of these miserable factionists" would be certain. The future security of the province, then, lay with emigrants whose "predilections will be English" and who would "strenuously adhere to the Unity of the Empire." Efforts must be made "to conciliate the Emigrants by every act of kindness in our power" and to warn them constantly of "the mischievous designs of such fellows as Bidwell, Ryerson and McKenzie."[2] Such was the conservative strategy of counter-attack against the reformers. As events were to show, it proved to be remarkably successful.

Sir John Colborne consciously adopted this strategy from the beginning of his term as the only way to make Upper Canada "a really British Colony," and to combat the influence of "Settlers from the United States," who were "generally active, intelligent and enterprising."[3] Consequently, he undertook to do everything in his power to assist the emigrants who were now pouring out of Britain in unprecedented numbers, a great many of them indigent and destitute. He posted agents along their route from Montreal westward to give emigrants information and advice. He placed superintendents in the townships open for settlement, who were to provide temporary shelters and to assign indigent settlers fifty-acre lots on which no payment was to be made for three years. The government undertook to build access roads to new settlements which, incidentally, provided much-needed employment to the able-bodied among the newcomers. In addition, Colborne encouraged the formation of emigrant societies throughout the province to draw local authorities and individuals into the work of relieving and assisting those who came. This work took on enormous and fearful proportions in the summer of 1832 when a cholera epidemic raged among the emigrants and was carried to many in the province. But all fell to with a will, and although hundreds died, the crisis was surmounted. Altogether, it was a magnificent effort, an epic in the province's history.

Within three years, from 1820 to 1833, population increased by nearly 50 per cent. After that the influx fell off somewhat but continued at a substantial rate until 1837. All of the settled parts received a share of the increase, but townships around Lake Simcoe, north of Rice Lake, in the south-west between Colonel Talbot's domain and the Huron Tract, and up the Ottawa River received a major part of the new settlement. Colborne tried to steer some of the most reliable emigrants to the western parts of the province, where American settlers were numerous. A Presbyterian minister learned from a recent visitor to York that "it is the intention of the government to raise up such a body of persons attached to the Constitution of Great Britain as may counteract the influence of Yankeeism so prevalent about St. Thomas and along the lake shore," while John Langton had to resist Colborne's urging that he go to the western townships.[4]

The great contribution of the tens of thousands of new settlers lay in their work in further opening of the province. No one could be sure what impact they would have on its political life, and whatever it might be it would take time to be felt. They were necessarily almost entirely uninformed about provincial affairs, and since most of them had been too low in the social scale at home to be politically active there, they would be slow in learning an unaccustomed role. Some of them belonged to religious communions that discouraged any concern with politics. Moreover, they were ineligible to vote until they received patents for their freeholds. Most important, they were too busy getting established to be able to look much beyond their own clearings for some time. Their letters home reflected this concern with immediate things: "... we have plenty of good food and grog... we dine with our masters.... We have no poor rates nor taxes of any consequence.... We shall never want timber nor water.... Bricklayer is a good trade here... a poor man can do a great deal better here than he can at home....I do not like Canada so well as England; but in England there is too many men, and here, there is not enough; there is more work than we can do, here... our dogs... live better than most of the farmers in England."[5] And there were heartaches and disappointments that were not written about.

Nevertheless, interested observers in the province often speculated on what political part they would play. Reformers hoped that men from the middle and lower classes, who had felt the mighty reform surge in Britain, would turn naturally to their ranks. Yet they were disturbed by the influence which the governing group was able to exert in teaching "Emigrants from the old Countries... to regard the Reformers of Upper Canada" with a "spirit of enmity." "From the moment an Irishman or an Englishman sets foot upon our soil, his ears are stunned by the cry of Treason and Rebellion which is constantly kept up... to deceive the ignorant and unwary." They were taught to view the old American settlers with suspicion, and to call them "Yankees, Republicans, &c., by way of reproach.... Hence the supercilious deportment of Europeans towards Canadians when they first come amongst them."[6] In a lengthy letter addressed to his newly arrived countrymen a writer of Protestant Irish origins and reform sympathies, who had long resided in the province, sought to show that the same aristocratic "high church and tory system" from which they had fled was growing up in the province. He pleaded with them not to be deceived by demagogues who tried to convince them that they should take up their shillelaghs to defend "a British colony from Yankees, mosquitoes, bullfrogs, or something or other they knew not what."[7]

But conservatives were confident that they would win over the new settlers. One of their leading newspapers observed that the political conflicts in Upper Canada differed essentially from those in Britain. In the latter, Whigs and Tories disagreed over the powers of the Lower House of Parliament, but both were "alike ardently attached to a Government of Kings, Lords and Commons." In the province, however, the contest was between "monarchical government" and "Democratic Republicanism"; in consequence, "every acceptable individual of the Whig, and even the Radical party in England, with scarcely a solitary exception, becomes what the disaffected party term a 'tory,' the moment he comes to Canada."[8] Looking more deeply, Christopher Hagerman, as well as many other observers, counted on the change that the possession of property and a new economic security would effect: "however turbulent or discontented individuals may have been prior to their arrival in the province, comfort and plenty soon work wonders on those who are of industrious habits, and loyalty and good-humour speedily follow."[9] And in discussing the elections of 1834, Colborne noted that it was too early to expect them to "be generally affected by the recent Emigration," but that better results could be expected in the future.[10] This proved to be an accurate prophecy.

One important consequence of the immigration was a great strengthening of the Orange Order in Upper Canada. For several decades this fervently Protestant organization had been fighting vigorously against the Catholics in Ireland, so vigorously that by the 1830s the British government, as a contribution to the peace of that strife-ridden island, was striving to disband the Order. But Orangemen were always more British than the king, and they paid little attention to official discountenance. When Protestant Irish came to Canada they brought the Order with them.

The first lodges were formed in the early 1820s. In 1824 the Assembly deplored their existence and advised the public to treat them "with silent disregard." Sir Peregrine Maitland publicly expressed his opposition to them.[11] For several years they were few in number and confined largely to the eastern counties. With the large influx of Protestant Irish in the late 1820s and following, however, their numbers grew rapidly, especially after the arrival in 1829 of Ogle Robert Gowan, who became the leading figure in the movement. He was untiringly zealous in the cause, an effective organizer, and at once at home in the rough and tumble of provincial journalism.

In Ireland, Orange devotion to the British Empire required constant vigilance against the subversive schemes of Roman Catholics, but in Upper Canada for a time it took a different form. In Upper Canada, to be sure, there were the usual riots and broken heads on the Glorious Twelfth as their Papist brethren tried to break up their parades. And good Orangemen could not but be alarmed at the thought of so many French-Canadian Catholics just down the river. But for the time being, in the 1830s, the task of keeping Canada British required a different tack. The French Canadians were outside the province, and the Catholics within posed little immediate threat. In later years Orangemen returned to their traditional campaign of keeping the country alive to the dangers of Catholic power, but for the present there was a more threatening enemy: the reformers, with their supposed separatist and republican tendencies.

An order that so loudly proclaimed its loyalty to the Empire was naturally welcome to conservatives and to people who felt that the British connection was in peril. Many residents, including descendants of United Empire Loyalists, who knew nothing of the controversies back in Ireland, gladly joined this militant organization. To be sure, others joined it simply because, like good North Americans everywhere, they had a natural affinity for fraternal orders. Such members often retained previous reform sympathies for a time, but if they remained they usually became convinced that it was disloyal to go on voting for a party labelled as pro-American and anti-British. As we shall see later, the Orange Order played an important role in deciding the crucial election of 1836. By providing, as it often did, the shock troops of Upper Canadian toryism, it proved to be one of the most important consequences of the recent British immigration. An element had been introduced into Canadian life that was to have remarkable durability over the next century and more.

But apart from the ordinary people in the new immigration, who could be expected to remain loyal to their British heritage, Colborne and his government placed especial reliance on the much smaller but still sizable number of men of quality who were arriving at the same time. These men had been far from destitute at home, but had concluded that they could no longer maintain or improve their existing status, or provide adequately for their often numerous families. Among them were professional men, substantial farmers, and of particular importance, military and naval officers who were languishing in the long peace following Waterloo. Many of them brought considerable amounts of money with them. Very often they carried letters of introduction from prominent men in Britain addressed to the Lieutenant-Governor. The latter received them cordially, and advised them fully on the opportunities available in the various sections of the province. It was hardly an accident that they often received the choice lots in new townships and other advantages. Within a very short time they were likely to receive appointments as Justices of the Peace, militia commissions, and other local posts.

Neither political group in the province ever had any doubt of what the influence of these men would be. A conservative paper, for instance, predicted that when the country had "received over its wide expanse even a slight sprinkling, so to speak, of such incomers,... we may rest pretty well assured that the vocation and the importance of the demagogue will soon be both at a very small discount." On the other hand, one reformer, referring to the half-pay officers, complained that the "curse of Canada is an *unprincipled* aristocracy, whose pretensions to superiority above other settlers would disgust a dog... getting possession of a few hundred acres of wild land [they think] themselves Lords of Canada."[12]

Some of them may have looked like lords to the average settler, because they had enough capital to hire labourers to clear land and to employ house servants, while they engaged in gentlemanly sports and attended balls and dinners in the provincial capital. But most of them were not so circumstanced, and these did their share of hard work. And it was work done at the edge of settlement, without the amenities by then enjoyed in the older townships at the front. Somewhat self-consciously, perhaps, Mrs. Traill, the wife of a half-pay officer, spoke of her kind as "the pioneers of civilization in the wilderness, and their families, often of delicate nurture and honourable descent, are at once plunged into the hardship attendant on the rough life of a bush-settler." Yet into the bush the half-pay officer went, "bringing into these rough districts gentle and well-educated females, who soften and improve all around them by *mental* refinements." In Canada, where property was so easily acquired, it was only "education and manners that must distinguish the gentleman."[13]

And so it happened that the most polite and cultivated society to be found anywhere in Upper Canada flourished in some of the most primitive settlements of the backwoods. There the newcomers of this type preferred to be, where servants were "as respectful, or nearly so, as those at home" and the "lower or working class of settlers" were "quite free from the annoying Yankee manners that distinguish many of the earlier-settled townships."[14] There in the bush one might "meet with as good society, as numerous and genteel, as in most of the country parts of Ireland," consisting not only of "ex-officers of the army and navy" but also of "young surgeons, Church of England clergymen, private gentlemen, sons of respectable persons at home, graduates of the colleges, &c."[15] But not all of these people succeeded; certainly their hopes of becoming gentleman farmers were nearly always disappointed. Some of them returned home, either disappointed or satisfied to have had a brief experience of a novel but essentially dull existence. Others escaped to provincial towns to take up more rewarding and less back-breaking activities. But enough of them remained to strengthen greatly the British cast of the Upper Canadian back country.

In summary, then, while the reformers were improving their political organization in the early 1830s, the conservative side was also being greatly reinforced by immigration from the British Isles. It need hardly be said that the immigrants were not necessarily supporters of the Family Compact, about which in fact they knew relatively little. Probably the great majority of them were quite hospitable to the idea of moderate reform. When, however, the issue appeared to be reduced to a vote for or against the British connection, there was no question where they would stand. They were forerunners of those young men from Britain who filled up the first Canadian contingent in 1914.

II

Despite previous efforts of conservative leaders to emphasize the overriding importance of the loyalty issue, it had never yet been possible to focus all attention on it in a provincial election. This fact was first accomplished by the new Lieutenant-Governor, Sir Francis Bond Head, who arrived in the province at the beginning of 1836.

Historians, with their eyes on the sequel, have usually regarded Head's appointment as one of the strangest ever made by the Colonial Office. He had had no previous experience in colonial government and, indeed, none in politics, as he was the first to admit and proclaim. After a career as a military engineer, which took him to several parts of Europe, he retired from the army as a half-pay major. Later he had an adventurous but not very successful experience as the manager of British silver mines in South America. From this and other journeys he acquired some reputation as the author of sprightly travel books; already he had revealed a facile pen. He was an assistant poor-law commissioner in Kent when the sudden call to Upper Canada reached him; perhaps his vigorous administration of the new Act had brought him to the attention of the Whig government. Following their irritation with Colborne they wanted a new man who would make a fresh start, yet they could not aspire much higher than to a person of Head's attainments. Upper Canada was not an attractive post to qualified civilians, and it had been decided not to appoint another high-ranking military officer.

In an attempt to demonstrate the British government's sincere intention of conciliating provincial opinion, Lord Glenelg provided Head with a long dispatch instructing him on the course to follow.[16] Most of the dispatch took the form of comments on the Seventh Report on Grievances. Although he disputed the Report's extreme charges on the matter of the Crown's control of patronage, he ordered Head to review the whole subject, to limit and reduce its amount where possible, and to make appointments on the basis of qualification, not politics. Regarding other complaints Head was to do everything possible to meet the wishes of the Assembly, and Glenelg reiterated the British government's determination not to interfere in the internal affairs of the province. The reformers' demand for an executive council responsible to the Assembly could not be conceded, however. True responsibility lay in the Lieutenant-Governor's accountability to the British government which always stood ready to receive and to investigate complaints coming from the province. In short, without promising any basic change in the system of government, Glenelg was ready to support the reform of all concrete and specific grievances and to defer to provincial opinion in every practicable way. No one could have been more well-meaning. But Glenelg apparently assumed that after vigorous debate the provincial legislature would reach agreement on outstanding issues, something that was quite impossible, given the composition of the two houses. Moreover, in Sir Francis Bond Head, he had chosen a strange instrument to accomplish his laudable purposes.

How strange was not long in becoming apparent. Soon after his arrival in Toronto Sir Francis divulged his instructions to the legislature, not just their substance, as Glenelg had ordered, but the full text, which contained material certain to embarrass Lord Gosford, who had come out to Lower Canada a few months before as the head of a conciliating royal commission. Apparently Sir Francis felt very little sense of obedience to his superiors in London. At about the same time he was forming his impressions of provincial politics, which he did with amazing quickness. Taking an immediate dislike to Mackenzie and Bidwell, and being much impressed by Chief Justice John Beverley Robinson, he soon decided that "strong Republican Principles [had] leaked into the country from the United States," and were predominant in the Assembly, whose majority did not represent "the general Feeling and Interests of the Inhabitants." The "Republican Party," as he henceforth described the Reformers, were "implacable" and would never be satisfied by concessions.[17] It was an unpromising beginning for Glenelg's policy of conciliation.

Nevertheless, Head did take one important step that was within the spirit of his instructions. Finding it essential to make additions to the membership of the executive council, he asked informed observers for the names of qualified men who would serve to make the council a more balanced body and one more representative of political opinion. As a result of these inquiries he offered appointments to Robert Baldwin, John Rolph, and J.H. Dunn, the Receiver General. The last named was a member of the administrative group, and had long been active in Welland Canal affairs, but was not directly identified with the Family Compact. The first two were well-known as reformers but had been politically inactive in recent years. At first, Baldwin refused the offer, saying that he could not accept office unless his well-known views on a responsible executive council were acceded to. Head, however, argued that he should come in, and then speak for his views from within the council. With much foreboding, Baldwin agreed.

It was not long before he felt his apprehensions to be fully justified, since he was soon quite dissatisfied with the extent to which the Lieutenant-Governor consulted the council. Thereupon, he convinced his colleagues, the old tory members as well as Rolph and Dunn, to unite in a formal complaint which, by coincidence, was very much in the spirit of Strachan's letter to James Stephen of five years earlier. The Council asked to be consulted on all general matters relating to the conduct of government; if this were not to be done, they thought that the public should know how little they had to do with affairs.[18] Head flatly rejected this proposal. With both precedent and Glenelg's instructions to back him up, he argued that the responsibility for carrying on the government was his alone, and could not be shared with the council, although he would consult it whenever he saw fit to do so. All six councillors then resigned, the old members being forced out as well as the new, although they were not ready to draw back.

These resignations fell like a thunderclap upon the reform majority in the Assembly, already disgruntled and irritated by other events. After calling on Head for more information, in which step they were joined by all but two conservative members, they then set up a select committee, chaired by Peter Perry, to investigate and report on the incident. After Head had appointed a new council, made up of men of conservative views, the Assembly, in a straight party vote, passed a motion of want of confidence.[19] As well, reformers throughout the province quickly wheeled their formidable political organizations into line of battle. Meetings were organized. Petitions and addresses were adopted and forwarded to the provincial capital.

The conflict reached a new intensity after Perry's committee made its report in the middle of April. During its deliberations the committee, and the province, had learned a new fact, not directly related to the current controversy, that drove reformers into a fury, and for a time brought all elements of the party together in outraged opposition to the government. The new fact was that Sir John Colborne, in his last important act before leaving the province, had set up fifty-seven rectories as endowments for Anglican clergymen. (Actually, he had had time to sign only forty-four patents, and these were all that were established.) In Colborne's view, this was a perfectly defensible step. Glebe lands for this purpose had been set aside, partly from the Clergy Reserves and partly from Crown Lands, from time to time over the previous forty-five years. Altogether, they amounted to some 20,000 acres. On more than one previous occasion Colborne and his predecessors had received explicit approval from the Colonial Secretary to take the step, but the rising tide of provincial opposition to the exclusive claims of the Church of England had hitherto delayed action. Now it had been taken, in flat defiance of this opposition, and in a secretive, midnight fashion.

Indignation at this action did much to heighten the language of the committee's report, which was a bitter attack upon Sir Francis Bond Head. His appointment of Baldwin, Rolph, and Dunn was termed "a deceitful manoeuvre to gain credit with the country for liberal feelings and intentions where none really existed," while he continued to act "under the influence of secret and unsworn advisers." The committee could not understand why "a Lieutenant-Governor, at a distance of more than 4,000 miles from his superiors, is so much more immaculate and infallible than his royal master," who always acted on the advice of his councillors. With a government resorting to "arbitrary principles" and with conditions in sad contrast to the prosperity, activity, and improvement "in the adjacent country," it was clear that the state of public affairs was growing steadily worse. The last straw was the knowledge that "fifty-seven government parsons" had been established, "in contempt of all our humble remonstrances"; final proof, if it were needed, of "the necessity of having a responsible Government." All other measures having failed, the committee advised the Assembly to stop the supplies.[20]

Events now moved rapidly to a climax. On 15 April the Assembly approved the committee's report and voted to stop the supplies. Tension was further increased when four days later Mr. Speaker Bidwell laid before the House a letter sent to him by Papineau, which denounced the British ministers and asserted that "the state of society all over continental America requires that the forms of its Government should approximate nearer to that selected... by the wise statesmen of the neighbouring Union, than to that into which chance and past ages have moulded European societies." On the next day Sir Francis prorogued the legislature, letting it be known that in retaliation for the stoppage of supplies, he would refuse his assent to money bills already passed, a measure that was far more crippling to provincial prosperity than was the Assembly's rather empty gesture. He also took the opportunity to make an appeal to the "backwoodsman" and to "every noble-minded Englishman, Irishman, Scotchman, U.E. Loyalist"; clearly, he knew where to look for support. In the same breath he assured the province that the best hope for genuine reform lay in cleaving to him, not to a selfish faction.[21]

A month later, he dissolved the legislature and the province was soon in the midst of a bitterly fought election campaign, with Sir Francis boldly assuming the leadership of the conservative forces. He had already concluded that he "was sentenced to contend on the soil of America with Democracy, and that if I did not overpower it, it would overpower me."[22] In vigorous, colloquial, or as he put it, "homely" language, he never missed an opportunity to pin the republican label on his opponents or to assert that all who stood for the British Constitution and the British connection would throw their weight against Bidwell and his party. The reformers also tried to take this ground, arguing that all they wanted was the Constitution as applied in Britain, but they were never able to seize the initiative from the Lieutenant-Governor. When the smoke had cleared early in July, it was at once obvious that the reformers had been routed. Although the vote was close in several constituencies, they would be outnumbered more than two to one in the next house. Bidwell, Perry, and

Mackenzie were only the most notable of the party to suffer defeat; only Rolph among leading reformers had survived the landslide.

Many factors combined to produce so striking a political reversal. For many voters, economic considerations bulked large. With the boom in the neighbouring states reaching its peak, just before the crash of the next year, Upper Canada seemed to be losing in the race for prosperity and development. While people were leaving the province for the western states, reformers argued over abstract principles of government, complained about the Welland Canal and the banks, and seemed not to welcome an inflow of British capital. To be sure, in the last Assembly they had voted money for roads, bridges, and other local improvements, but much of it went to their own constituencies in the older settled districts rather than to the struggling townships in the back country. Moreover, in an attempt to provide themselves with some patronage and to keep the money voted out of the hands of the executive, the reformers had set up commissionerships to supervise its expenditure and had distributed these among themselves. This device could easily be made to appear as a political job. It was also well-known that the reformers regarded themselves as the protectors of the interests of the farmers, the "honest yeoman." In the last Assembly they had passed a bill, killed in the legislative council, to impose higher duties and other restrictions on agricultural imports from the United States. This measure undoubtedly pleased many established farmers, but in newer areas, which still needed to import food, and in the lumbering centres of the Ottawa Valley it was disliked. It was especially disliked by all who were engaged in mercantile pursuits, and who lived by forwarding goods down the St. Lawrence. If to these is added the reformers' often-expressed opposition to the Canada Company and the lukewarm attitude of many of them to British immigration, it is apparent that they had offended important economic interests in the province.

The reformers were also more vigorously opposed than in any previous election. Conservative forces were alerted as never before, although now they called themselves Constitutionalists. They believed that the British connection—to which the province "principally owe[d] its rapid advancement"—was in danger, and they believed that the provincial Constitution was threatened with innovation. They were seeking to prevent revolution, not to impede honest reform. Indeed, reform would be accelerated by a "Constitutional House": the land-granting system would be improved, the Clergy Reserves would be returned to the Crown, immigration would be encouraged, "capital and wealth" would flow in from the mother country "like a fertilizing stream," and "Sir Francis Head would be enabled to carry into effect those Reforms and improvements for which he has been expressly sent here by our good KING."[23] Appeals such as this combined with increasing political activity roused intense feeling against the "Bidwellian Party."

The victory also owed something to the Lieutenant-Governor's skill as a campaigner. He never wavered from one simple theme: that the contest was between a loyal people and a disloyal faction. He sought, with much success, to sweep away all previous distinctions between tories and radicals, conservatives and reformers. He announced frequently that he himself was a reformer, and that the best way to achieve true reform was to support him. Conservative leaders were delighted by his firm opposition to the radicals and by the support which he brought to their cause. He knew how to strike responsive chords in the breasts of many residents. For instance, on one occasion he denounced the letter from Papineau recently placed on the Assembly's journal, suggested that there were "one or two Individuals" in Lower Canada who welcomed the prospect of foreign interference in the provinces, and then concluded with the rousing challenge, "In the name of every Regiment of Militia in Upper Canada I publicly promulgate—*Let them come if they dare!*"[24] To the reformers this was ludicrous bombast, and they did their best to pour ridicule upon it. But to all, and there were many, who disliked the course of the French-Canadian extremists, and who had memories of the War of 1812, the challenge had a reassuring sound.

As already suggested, Sir Francis made a special appeal to the recent British immigrants, and it was one which most of them enthusiastically answered. With the election approaching, some of them made hurried efforts to secure their land patents, and hence the franchise, in which efforts the government was very cooperative. John Langton wrote of how he and his friends brought voters in a steamer down the Otonabee River to the polling-place, remarking, "There was astonishingly little fighting considering the number of wild Irishmen we brought down, but they were altogether too strong for the Yankees...."[25] Another resident, recently from Britain, stated that the men in his settlement, "to the number of nearly a hundred, marched in procession to the polling booths," in order to make a demonstration "on the side of religion, order and true liberty."[26]

A remarkable feature of the campaign was the ready cooperation of Orangemen and Roman Catholics to defeat the reformers. The Orange Lodge in Toronto and Bishop Macdonell publicly complimented each other's loyalty. Orangemen voted for Roman Catholic conservative candidates, and Roman Catholics similarly supported Orange candidates. It has been calculated that from one-third to one-half of the reform defeats were caused by this uniting of the Orange and the Green. The Orangemen even abstained from their annual parades on the Glorious Twelfth, just after the election, to show their appreciation of Catholic loyalty. Mackenzie, who had probably been defeated by this joint effort, denounced the "Orange Papists," but the two groups continued to cooperate until after the Rebellion.[27]

The Methodist leaders were also in the field against the reformers in this election. The gulf between the Mackenzie wing of the party and the Methodists had widened after the publication of the Seventh Report, while the denomination had grown more conservative under British Wesleyan influence. When the issue was narrowed to one of loyalty, there was no question where its leaders would stand. The *Guardian* staunchly supported the Lieutenant-Governor and the Constitutional party, with Egerton Ryerson publishing several letters in criticism of the reformers in general and Peter Perry in particular. Some months after the election John Ryerson informed his brother that "Not one Radical was returned from the bounds of the Bay of Quinty Districts. The preachers & I laboured to the utmost extent of our ability to keep every scamp of them out & we succeeded. And had the preachers of done their duty in every place, not a *ninny* of them would have been returned to this parliament."[28]

Undoubtedly, then, the Methodists made their contribution to the defeat of the reformers but, as Professor Sissons has noted, it was probably not as decisive as has sometimes been claimed. Many of the rank and file again voted the reform ticket, as they had always done.[29] Reformers at the time complained more about Orangemen than about Methodists, and put particular emphasis on the role of the new voters. Although the St. Thomas *Liberal*, for instance, referred generally to the "unholy exertions of the State-paid Priests," in which group it probably included the Methodists, it also spoke of the "exhibition of ruffianism, club-law and intimidation" put on in every constituency. The editor continued:

> Above all... heaps of new Deeds, *the ink scarcely dry on them*, were sent in all directions, not only the week preceding, but absolutely the very week of the Elections.... The honest and legitimate constituency of the Province—the old— the peaceable—the respectable settlers were thus overwhelmed, in almost every County, by pensioners and paupers, who never before exercised the elective franchise, who did not know any more about the Constitution of Canada or about the subjects in dispute, between the late House of Assembly and Sir Francis Head, than the man in the moon.[30]

Acting on this last complaint, Charles Duncombe, a leading reformer from the western part of the province, took a petition to England which stated that the Lieutenant-Governor had favoured tory candidates in various ways, and in particular had overwhelmed "legally registered voters" by illegally issued patents.[31] This petition was referred back to a select committee of the newly elected Assembly which, not surprisingly, found no truth in it. The committee was able to show convincingly that patents issued just before the elections could not have influenced the results.[32]

The charge of fraud, as drawn by Duncombe, was clearly exaggerated, but he and his reform colleagues had good reasons for complaining that it had not been a fair election. In 1836, as in previous elections, they suffered from the fact that the election machinery was in the hands of their opponents. Above all, it was intolerable that they should have a recently arrived Lieutenant-Governor openly in the field against them, accusing them of treason. Undoubtedly there was a real shift of opinion in the provincial electorate in 1836, intensified by the activity of new voters. Many voters genuinely felt that the reformers sought dangerous changes in the Constitution, and that a victory for them would imperil the British connection. Yet, not without some cause, a great many reformers drew the conclusion that a free expression of public opinion was impossible under existing circumstances. Their feeling that the scales were tipped against them was heightened when the newly elected conservative Assembly passed a bill providing that it should not be automatically dissolved at the king's death, which was expected soon. Reformers were quite convinced that this measure would never have been accepted by the Legislative Council, the Lieutenant-Governor, and the Colonial Office, or any of them, if they had been in a majority.

Disheartened by the nature and results of the election campaign, many reform leaders of moderate outlook turned their backs on political life. Bidwell, smarting from defeat after twelve years of representing his county, wrote to Robert Baldwin in bitter tones of the practice of "denouncing every man as disloyal, a revolutionist, a secret traitor, etc., who happens to differ from the Provincial government, on questions of expediency or constitutional principles."[33] He returned to his law practice. Baldwin himself had gone to England before the elections to warn the Colonial Secretary that the province's connection with Britain was being endangered by Sir Francis Bond Head's actions. Although refused a personal interview, Baldwin stated his views in a lengthy memorandum, which fully set out his conception of responsible government as the one means of bringing harmony and stability to Upper Canada. If this "English principle" were denied, the people of the province might be driven to turn "to another Quarter" and "call for the power of electing their own Governor, and their own Executive," but they would never "abandon the object of obtaining more influence than they now possess, through their Representatives, in the administration of the Executive Government of the Colony."[34] Baldwin, too, stayed in private life upon his return.

For the time being, however, the province enjoyed harmonious government, with an Assembly that had confidence in Sir Francis Bond Head and his executive council. In the first session of the new legislature, a large number of bills easily passed through both houses providing for overdue changes in the judiciary, amendments to the University Charter and, especially, internal improvements. In the latter category there was not only more money for the Welland Canal and for roads and harbours but the first railroads for the province were projected. Sir Francis gladly approved all of these bills, although his instructions required him to reserve several banking bills that were also passed.[35] The constitution of 1791 could work fairly effectively when there was a conservative Assembly.

For some months after the election, then, the province was relatively quiet in contrast to the furious political debate of the previous months. Attempts were made by some reformers to rebuild their shattered organizations, but with limited results. Mackenzie, who had returned to journalism with a newspaper entitled *The Constitution* which began publication, somewhat symbolically perhaps, on 4 July 1836, attacked the government and all its works as bitterly as ever, but he seemed to be shouting into the wind. The province as a whole seemed to be more concerned to participate in the prevailing boom that was sweeping North America than to revive the sterile debates of earlier years. Conservatives congratulated themselves on having brought the people to their senses by the firm stand taken against radicalism.

Yet these appearances were deceiving. Farmers had little opportunity to benefit from the commercial boom; instead they were suffering from low prices and lack of good markets. Opponents of the government were suffering from a kind of emotional exhaustion, but they nursed the old complaints as much as ever. Shortly after she arrived from England, at the end of 1836, Anna Jameson, the wife of the Attorney General recently appointed from England, found "among all parties a general tone of complaint and discontent—a mutual distrust—a languor and supineness.... Even those who are enthusiastically British in heart and feeling ... are as discontented as the rest: they bitterly denounce the ignorance of the colonial officials at home...."[36] Sir Francis Bond Head's glorious victory had not really cleared the air very much.

Sir Francis was in fact throwing away the fruits of victory as rapidly as possible. Having defeated the forces of democracy and republicanism, he was then determined to disperse and destroy them. He proceeded to dismiss from office certain men accused of showing sympathy for the reform side in the recent election, including a judge who flatly denied the charge. He urged upon the Colonial Office an end of the policy of conciliation, and its replacement by stern and decisive measures. Not only did he begin to lose some of the support of moderate men in the province, but his action and views met with diminishing acceptance in Downing Street. From the end of 1836 onward he was engaged in an increasingly acrimonious correspondence with Lord Glenelg that led eventually to his resignation. Despite the Lieutenant-Governor's coup the Colonial Office could no longer entrust Upper Canada to this erratic and insubordinate "damned odd fellow," as Lord Melbourne dubbed him on his return to England. Sir Francis had no answer to the problems facing the province.

But these problems, real though they were, did not drive Upper Canada to rebellion. If the province could have been insulated from outside pressures it would have had every prospect of a peaceful political evolution. The British government had no desire to interfere in its internal affairs; instead, it was fully prepared to approve of and assist in the transition to a broadened political structure. And with the gradual rise of effective political parties within the province that transition was inevitably and inexorably coming. A rebellion was not needed to solve Upper Canada's political problems; the rebellion that did come complicated rather than eased the transition.

Upper Canada, however, was not insulated or immunized from outside pressures. Instead, it was caught up in a severe financial crisis that reached in from the larger Anglo-American world of which it was a part and that greatly disturbed its economic life. In addition, and at the same time, it was directly affected by the bitter struggle coming to a head in Lower Canada. And now more than ever, political differences were exacerbated by proximity to the neighbouring republican states. Alternately goaded and inspired by these outside pressures, Mackenzie and a small group of followers determined on their ill-starred plan to overthrow by force a nearly unprotected government.

Of these outside pressures the most clearly disruptive was the financial crisis. After several years of unprecedented business expansion in both Britain and America, the bottom suddenly fell out of the boom at the end of 1836, and conditions became steadily worse during the following year. The causes of the downturn in the business cycle were essentially the same on both sides of the Atlantic—excessive speculation and optimistic expansion by businessmen, and indeed the public at large, who were eager to seize the opportunities made available by a rapidly growing economy—but the effects were felt with particular sharpness in the young debtor communities of the New World. The latter were heavily dependent upon the British money market for capital. When they could no longer borrow there, when indeed British investors began to liquidate their holdings in America, the western communities found themselves in an intolerable position. That position, moreover, had already been made highly precarious by the policies adopted by the Jackson administration in the United States. By destroying the Bank of the United States the administration had removed the one agent that might have restrained the headlong speculation of the 1830s. Then, in his own attempt to halt the speculation, Jackson issued, in July 1836, a *Specie Circular*, ordering that henceforth only hard money would be received in payment for the public lands. This measure drained *specie* away from the banking centres of the eastern seaboard, which were soon also suffering from insistent British demands. By the spring of 1837 business failures and unemployment were followed by the decision of banks throughout the United States to suspend *specie* payments.

The province of Upper Canada, inevitably affected by business conditions across the line, as well as in Britain, was in a very poor condition to weather the resulting storm. Following the prevailing pattern, the provincial legislature had also borrowed heavily, in an attempt to speed up economic progress, and was in no position to meet its commitments. Bankers in the province were suffering from the same drain of *specie* as across the line, but because of the Lieutenant-Governor's belief that suspension would be dishonourable, they were unable to protect themselves, unless they met very difficult requirements. This quixotic attitude of Sir Francis soon lost him much of the popularity among conservatives that he had earlier enjoyed. It was W. H. Merritt's view, expressed after the event, that Head's policy of placing obstacles in the way of *specie* suspension, which was persisted in "*against the expressed opinion of the Inhabitants and their Representatives,*" had done more "to create a feeling in favour of *Responsible Government* than all the essays written or speeches made on the subject."[37]

Few voices had been raised in opposition to the orgy of bank bills and borrowing that reached its climax in the session of 1836–37. Most reformers were just as enthusiastic for this course as were conservatives. Indeed, it was only at the extremes of the political spectrum that doubts and antagonism were expressed. At one end were some tories who wanted strict regulation of the note-issuing powers of banks, perhaps following a recent New York law on the subject.[38] At the other end was William Lyon Mackenzie who opposed the craze for banks root and branch.

As we have seen, Mackenzie had always opposed the banks. He had followed with the closest sympathy the efforts of Jackson and the hard-money men to break the power of the banks in the United States, and he was determined to follow their example in Upper Canada. Needless to say, he was not deterred by the fact that most reform leaders did not agree with him, any more than Jackson had been deterred by the fact that many in his party had campaigned against the Bank of the United States in order to open the way for an expansion of local banking. When the provincial banks found themselves in difficulties in the spring of 1837, because of the heavy drain on *specie* reserves, Mackenzie made every effort to mount a campaign against them. He warned the "Farmers of Upper Canada" that they would be "richer and happier" if these "vile Banking Associations" were swept away. He advised them to *"Get Gold and Silver for your Bank Paper, while it is yet within your power."* In particular, he denounced the Bank of Upper Canada for having "controlled our elections, corrupted our representatives, depreciated our currency, obliged even Governors and Colonial Ministers to bow to its mandates, insulted the legislature, expelled representatives, fattened a host of greedy and needy lawyers, tempted the farmer to leave his money with it instead of lending it to his worthy neighbour, shoved government through its hands, sent many thousands of hard cash to foreign lands as bank dividends, taxed the farmers and traders at £18,000 a year for the use of this paper, and supported every judicial villainy and oppression with which our country has been afflicted." In Mackenzie's mind, Upper Canada suffered just as much from the money power as did the United States, but with a vital difference. In that country Jackson, and now Van Buren, were "purging the nation of vile rotten cheating bank folks," while these were still all-powerful in the province.[39] Considering the difficulties that bankers had with Sir Francis in the summer of 1837, they must have been astonished to learn how much power they had.

With the bank power ruling Upper Canada and ruining its farmers, Mackenzie was more than ever impressed with the contrast between this sad picture and the glorious scene across the lakes. His paper was once again filled with glowing accounts of the virtuous simplicity of American state governments. Michigan, newly arriving at statehood, had a "government by farmers" while Upper Canada had "a government by strangers from beyond the great sea, who do not intend to become permanent settlers," and were paid salaries five to ten times as high as those of their opposite numbers across the Detroit River.[40] With blithe inconsistency Mackenzie also pointed repeatedly to the rapid progress of the western states, ignoring the fact that this progress was inseparably connected with the banking expansion and business speculation which he so vehemently opposed. Instead, he was secure in his simple faith that Upper Canada, too, could achieve such utopian bliss if it could only achieve a pure agrarian polity, which in fact nowhere existed across the line except in Mackenzie's imagination.

A final factor was needed to turn Mackenzie's thoughts in the direction of armed uprising, and that was the abrupt reversal of British policy toward Lower Canada. Following the failure of Lord Gosford's mission of conciliation,

Lord John Russell announced a return to firmness in his Ten Resolutions of 2 March 1837. These Resolutions rejected the demands of the Papineau party and allowed the Governor to take funds from the provincial treasury that the Assembly had refused to vote. When the Lower Canadian radicals learned that these Resolutions had been approved by Parliament they immediately intensified a campaign of agitation and organization that led to rebellion within six months.

The passage of the Ten Resolutions brought Mackenzie to new heights of furious indignation. He denounced "the mercenary immoral wretches" who had supported resolutions "more suitable for the Meridian of Russia in its dealing with Poland." He was soon in correspondence with Wolfred Nelson, perhaps the most militant radical leader in the lower province, and he was soon preaching the doctrine of non importation. "Buy, wear, and use as little as you possibly can of British manufactured goods or British West India merchandise or liquors."[41] Mackenzie now agreed with his Lower Canadian friends that a bold attack must be made against British authority, not simply against the local oligarchy.

By the beginning of July 1837 he was seeking to convince his readers that the Lower Canadians had both the will and the means to make good their independence; moreover, he asserted, "There are thousands, aye tens of thousands of Englishmen, Scotchmen, and above all, of Irishmen, now in the United States, who only wait till the standard be planted in Lower Canada, to throw their strength and numbers to the side of democracy."[42] Two weeks later he began to reprint Tom Paine's *Common Sense*, which had sparked the movement for independence in 1776.[43] At the same time he set forth in great detail a scheme for local reform organizations, some features of which had distinct military overtones. One of his subscribers reported finding a note from Mackenzie folded in his paper, asking him to accompany the editor to Lower Canada "to assist the french" and then return and conquer the upper province.[44] At the end of July he met with a group of radicals in Doel's brewery in Toronto to adopt a Declaration closely modelled on the famous document proclaimed at Philadelphia on 4 July 1776. It ended by asking the reformers of Upper Canada to make common cause with Papineau and his colleagues, to organize political associations and public meetings, and to select a convention of delegates to meet at Toronto "as a Congress, to seek an effectual remedy for the grievances of the colonists."[45] A Committee of Vigilance was named, with Mackenzie as agent and corresponding secretary.

Mackenzie then set out on a tour of the country north of the capital to organize public meetings and to superintend the adoption of the Toronto Declaration and other inflammatory resolutions. More than a score of such meetings were held, and there was similar though less intense activity in other parts of the province.[46] Orangemen and other opponents of the radicals attempted to break up the meetings by force; in turn, the radicals armed themselves with clubs and other weapons. Soon they were drilling and shooting at targets, although with no clear idea in their minds why they were doing these things. Mackenzie sought to convince them, however, that everything was within their grasp if they should move against the government. "... Britain has no power here if opinion be concentrated against the measures of her agents. We are far from the Sea—for five months our shores are ice-bound—the great republic is on one side of us, the Lower Canadians on another; Michigan and the wilderness, and lakes are to the west and north of us. The whole physical power of the government, the mud garrison, redcoats and all, is not equal to that of the young men of one of our largest townships."[47] This line of argument became all the more persuasive in October when Sir Francis, who was prepared to rest the fate of his government entirely upon the loyalty of the people of Upper Canada, denuded the province of regular troops in order to strengthen the garrisons in Lower Canada.

Meanwhile, Mackenzie and his lieutenants sought to convince their followers that a display of physical force was both justified and necessary. A rising tone of nationalism marked their appeals. Reformers were asked to be "more Canadian" in their "habits and feelings," to throw away their "lip-loyal feelings and sayings of other countries," and to "substitute the word patriotic for the word loyalty."[48] "Foreign" colonial ministers and "foreign" governors were vigorously denounced, while at the same time the advantages of membership in the American Union were set forth in attractive terms. As a state in the Union, the people of Upper Canada would enjoy complete local self-government, universal suffrage, and vote by ballot.[49] Mackenzie's nationalism was now a North American nationalism. With the same grievances that the old thirteen colonies had suffered from, the Canadian people had the same right to rebel;[50] their logical haven after successful rebellion was in the Union that had emerged from the earlier Revolution.

From this rising campaign of agitation, which looked to cooperation with the Lower Canadian radicals and to separation from the mother country, the main body of reformers in Upper Canada kept themselves increasingly aloof. None of the party's prominent leaders, Perry, Bidwell, or of course the Baldwins, had any part in it, although John Rolph's private attitude was somewhat equivocal. In effect, these men abdicated their responsibility to give a lead to public opinion, leaving the field to Mackenzie and his radical associates. And the moderate rank and file of the party also withdrew from political activity rather than follow Mackenzie's leadership. They still believed firmly in the reform objectives but also believed, as one correspondent informed Mackenzie, that they must "be attained in peace." This man asserted that Mackenzie's extremism had nearly wrecked the cause by driving Methodists, Catholics, and Presbyterians in to the ranks of toryism and by making it almost impossible for the British government to continue its policy of conciliation.[51]

These were accurate observations, but Mackenzie was past heeding them. Let the old-line politicians stay on the sidelines and frown; he did not need them or want them. Instead, he was now working closely with a number of men who were ready for action. In the main, these men were drawn from among the old American settlers north of Toronto, who had lived in the province for a generation. They were well-established farmers and artisans, but they had never become reconciled to a government which, they were convinced, discriminated against them at every opportunity, and went out of its way to favour British immigrants at their expense. Notable among them were Samuel Lount, born in Pennsylvania in 1791, Silas Fletcher, born in New Hampshire in 1780, and Jesse Lloyd, born in Pennsylvania in 1786.[52] Working with these men, and in conjunction with the American-born Charles Duncombe in the London district, Mackenzie convinced several hundred supporters that a demonstration of physical force would easily, indeed peacefully, sweep away the oligarchy, the banks, the land-grabbers, and the state-paid priests, and inaugurate a democratic government controlled by the plain people, under which all would prosper.

The blueprint for the new order was published in Mackenzie's paper on 15 November 1837, in the form of a draft constitution for the State of Upper Canada. In presenting it to the public Mackenzie invoked the names of Henry Grattan, John Locke, Algernon Sydney, Benjamin Franklin, John Hampden, William Pitt, Charles James Fox, Oliver Goldsmith, Henry Brougham, J.A. Roebuck, Jospeh Hume, and George Washington in support of the course he was taking. The document itself closely followed the outlines of the Constitution of the United States, although many of its individual clauses were related directly to Mackenzie's long-standing complaints against the provincial government. In particular, he would require that money bills and bills of incorporation be passed only after a three-fourths vote of each House, while the agrarian purity of the new commonwealth was to be protected by a total prohibition against bank charters.

A month before publishing this constitution Mackenzie had sought to convince his associates in Toronto that Head's removal of the troops gave them the perfect opportunity to seize the arms and ammunition in the City Hall and capture the government in one bloodless and decisive move. These more cautious men had backed away from the fatal step at that time, but in subsequent weeks Mackenzie had convinced them that he had the men needed to bring off a successful *coup*. The more respectable members of the conspiracy, particularly John Rolph and Dr. T.D. Morrison, now agreed to join the movement at the appropriate time. In every way they tried to cover their tracks in the event of failure. By the middle of November, however, Mackenzie was determined to force the hands of his timid colleagues. On a trip north of the city he set a date for the uprising, December 7, and put plans in motion that could not easily be reversed. The news, toward the end of November, that the Lower Canadian *patriotes* had risen, was the final proof for Mackenzie that the time to act had come.

On a last trip north of the ridges at the end of November Mackenzie distributed a handbill calling on the "Brave Canadians" to strike for "Independence," and made final arrangements with his trusted friends. But with plans in their last stages everything began to go wrong. First, there was a worried call from

John Rolph that the authorities in Toronto were alerted to the uprising—in fact, they refused almost to the last moment to take seriously the possibility of rebellion—and that the date must be advanced in order to retain the element of surprise. This eleventh-hour change threw out of line arrangements for assembling, arming, and victualling the men. Then the disheartening news arrived that the *patriote* uprising in the lower province had been put down. Rolph now tried to convince Mackenzie that the project was hopeless, but the latter had crossed his Rubicon. In any event the men were already marching.

During the evening and night of December 4–5 some seven to eight hundred of them gathered at Montgomery's Tavern, about two miles north of Toronto. Rebel guards were posted down Yonge Street to prevent any movement into the city, and a well-known tory, Colonel Robert Moodie of Richmond Hill, was mortally wounded as he tried to ride past them. Coming up from the city to reconnoitre, an alderman, John Powell, was captured, but escaped after shooting dead the rebels' most capable military leader, Anthony Anderson. Powell got back to the city with conclusive proof that long-rumoured rebellion was a fact. Now all chance of surprise was gone.

Even so, the rebels were a larger force than any that was ready to meet them as they set off down Yonge Street about noon on December 5. After moving a little more than a mile they stopped to reform their ranks at the brow of Gallow's Hill. There they were presently met by a truce party, sent out by Sir Francis, consisting of Robert Baldwin and John Rolph, men whom the rebels would know and presumably trust. (Rolph was still not identified with the conspiracy.) The rebels were offered a full amnesty if they would go home. Mackenzie asked for the promise in writing, and marched on another mile. Then the government withdrew its offer when it learned that militiamen were on the way. Rolph, however, secretly sent word that the city was still poorly defended, and that an attack would succeed.

And so the last act of the little tragicomedy was enacted. In the gathering darkness of the late December afternoon the rebel army trudged on down Yonge Street, with a few dozen riflemen at its front. The rest were armed only with pikes, pitchforks, and cudgels. As they neared the northern outskirts of the city they were observed by a small picket of some two dozen men, commanded by the sheriff. When the front ranks of the oncoming band were within musket range the sheriff gave his men the order to fire. Fire they did, but having done so, they promptly dropped their weapons and took to their heels, to avoid being crushed by the much larger force opposing them. Samuel Lount, commanding the rebel riflemen, ordered the fire returned. The front ranks then fell to their knees to allow their companions behind to continue the fusillade. But the smell of gunpowder in the fearful darkness brought as much confusion to the rebels as it had to the loyal picket. When the men behind saw the tall hats of the front riflemen disappear from the skyline, they at once concluded that these men had been shot down. Not knowing what hordes of well-armed tories were about to charge them they, too, turned and ran, carrying most of the army with them. Lount and his few riflemen had no choice but to follow them. One rebel had been killed, and two died later of wounds.

With the retreat of the rebel army up Yonge Street to Montgomery's Tavern went the last flickering chance of scattering the government. On that same evening reinforcements led by Colonel Allan MacNab reached the capital by steamer from Hamilton, and by the next morning confusion and near-hysteria had given way to confident determination. A day later, with bands playing and with a couple of pieces of artillery, a force of more than a thousand men marched north to attack Mackenzie's men. Contact was made south of the Tavern, and within half an hour the outnumbered, poorly armed, and almost leaderless rebels were put to demoralized flight. Through a combination of good luck and the help of many sympathizers Mackenzie managed to work his way round the lake to safety on the American side. A slight western phase of the rebellion came to nothing. Dr. Charles Duncombe raised the standard of revolt in the country between London and Brantford, but his little band quickly fell away before militia advancing from several sides.

There is no certain way of knowing how much potential support there may have been for the uprising. An initial success might well have enlarged the movement somewhat. Some men who were marching to support Mackenzie quickly changed sides to become rebel-chasers when they saw how events were going. Mackenzie was often identified while escaping, as were other leaders, and yet they were not stopped despite a price on their heads. Nevertheless, the uprising had no broad following. Mackenzie and his associates managed to dupe only a few hundred farm lads and other rather simple people, many of whom paid a bitter price for their adventure, into believing that an armed uprising would cure the province's ills. The vigour with which people from one end of Upper Canada to the other rose to support the government showed that in no sense was Mackenzie the leader of a popular movement. His later admission that resort to force had been a mistake was cold comfort to the men and their families whose lives he had helped to ruin and to the reform cause which he had greatly injured.

Mackenzie's attempt to use force against the government, coinciding with the much more formidable rebellion in Lower Canada, was bound to disturb the political and social life of the province. Nevertheless, it had been a very small affair, engaging the support of only a fraction of the population. Within a few days all was quiet, with no possible chance of renewed disorder of any consequence originating within the province. If Upper Canada had been left free to absorb the consequences of the December rising a normal atmosphere might well have been restored in a relatively short time. But it was not left alone. Intervention from across the American border, lasting over several years, was to bring far more alarm, expense, and bloodshed than the rebellion itself produced, and was to complicate seriously the process of political and social transition.

The reasons behind this intervention were many, varied, and changing, and here they can be alluded to only briefly. To many Americans the fact that the Canadas still maintained a political tie with Great Britain was in itself proof that they must be suffering from tyranny and oppression; now they had imitated the patriots of '76 by rising to strike off their shackles. Assuming that the rebellions represented a widespread popular movement that had been put down by British regulars, and that the provinces still yearned to be free, Americans instinctively extended their sympathy and many of them saw a duty to give their active support to the downtrodden Canadians. And these sentiments were reinforced by other considerations. A mood of Manifest Destiny was seizing the United States, and one of its aspects was the belief that Americans had a moral obligation to extend the "area of freedom" throughout the North American continent. Yet such feelings were general and vague; more was needed to bring action. In particular, there was an unstable border population, made restless by the panic of 1837, and ready for adventure especially if it was coupled with the promise of free land in Upper Canada. More substantial elements in the American population were ready to see the rank and file so occupied, and also ready to take advantage of anything they might accomplish. The recent history of Texas, and its emerging importance in American politics, could never be far from people's minds at this time.

Thus it was that Mackenzie received an enthusiastic welcome when he arrived in Buffalo on December 11. After he had spoken of the bitter oppression under which the people of Upper Canada were labouring, many volunteers offered to join his cause, and a campaign to collect weapons and supplies was soon under way. Within two or three days a motley little band had established themselves on Navy Island, on the Canadian side of the Niagara River, where Mackenzie proclaimed a provisional government for Upper Canada and offered land in the province to all who would join him.

At first, the government and the people of Upper Canada watched these events with some calmness, assuming that American authorities would soon stop these hostile actions against a neighbouring province. But federal power was distant and ineffectual, and local and state officials showed little desire to act. When Colonel Allan MacNab of the militia saw that the American-owned steamer *Caroline* was openly and without hindrance engaged in ferrying men and supplies from the American side to Navy Island, to build up power for a raid on Upper Canada, he instructed Commander Andrew Drew, R.N., to destroy the ship. Not finding her at Navy Island, Drew's naval party continued across the river, where they set fire to the *Caroline*. She was sent down the river, and broke up before reaching the Falls. In the boarding operation an American citizen was killed and others were injured.

This incident greatly heightened tension along the border. The Assembly of Upper Canada applauded the action, while many Americans were outraged at this violation of their territory. To the existing motives for filibustering against Upper Canada that of retaliation was now added. Moreover, the *Caroline* affair darkened Anglo-American relations for several years to come.

By the spring of 1838 "patriot" preparations were in full swing all along the border of the two provinces. Mackenzie and other refugee Canadians had little part in these activities, which were led and supported almost entirely by American citizens. The favourite form of organization was the secret society, of which the Hunters Lodges came to be the largest and best known. It was only gradually that official American action against these offensive preparations became effective. For many contemporary Upper Canadians the outstanding consequence of the Rebellion of 1837 was the threat, which on several occasions became a reality, of further invasion from the United States, in a time of Anglo-American peace and of quiet within the province.

Notes

1. O.A., Macaulay Papers, Strachan to John Macaulay, 12 March 1832.

2. *Ibid.*, C.A. Hagerman to John Macaulay, 17 April 1832.

3. C.O. 42/394, pp. 177–78, Colborne to Hay, 25 Nov. 1831.

4. "Proudfoot Papers," *Transactions of the London and Middlesex Historical Society*, VIII (1917), 23; W.A. Langton, ed., *Early Days in Upper Canada* (Toronto, 1926), p. 11.

5. Martin Doyle, *Hints on Emigration* (Dublin, 1831), p. 100; *Emigration: Letters from Sussex Emigrants* (Petworth, 1833), pp. 7, 10, 42, 45.

6. St. Thomas *Liberal*, 4 April, 19 Sept. 1833.

7. Quoted in *The Advocate*, 27 March 1834.

8. *Courier*, 15 June 1833.

9. Adam Fergusson, *Practical Notes Made During a Tour in Canada, and a Portion of the United States in MDCCCXXXI* (London, 1833), p. 115, quoting a conversation with Hagerman.

10. C.O. 42/418, p. 135, Colborne to Hay, 7 March 1834; C.O. 42/43, p. 202, Colborne to Spring Rice, 20 Nov. 1834.

11. O.A., *Eleventh Report*, 1914, Journals of the Assembly, 1824, p. 620, Resolution of 7 Jan. 1824; P.A.C., U.C. Sundries, William Morris to Colborne, 27 May 1830, refers to Maitland's statement.

12. *Patriot*, 24 Oct. 1834; Robert Davis, *The Canadian Farmer's Travels*, p. 9.

13. Catherine Parr Traill, *The Backwoods of Canada* (London, 1836), pp. 3–4, 81–82.

14. *Ibid.*, p. 271.

15. *Canada in the Years 1832, 1833, and 1834... By an ex-settler* (Dublin, 1835), p. 23.

16. *P.A.C.R.*, 1935, pp. 381–97, Glenelg to Head, 5 Dec. 1835.

17. C.O. 42/429, pp. 118–20, Head to Glenelg, 5 Feb. 1836.

18. *Report of the Select Committee to which was referred the answer of His Excellency...* (Toronto, 1836), Appendix A. pp. 1–4, Executive Council to Sir F.B. Head, 4 March 1836.

19. Journals of the Assembly, 1836, pp. 289, 303.

20. *Report of the Select Committee...* pp. 7, 39, 80–81, 87, 99.

21. Journals of the Assembly, 1836, pp. 469, 499, 524 ff.

22. F.B. Head, *A Narrative* (London, 1839), p. 65.

23. *The Patriot*, 17 May, 17 June 1836.

24. C.O. 42/430, pp. 92–93, Reply of His Excellency... to an Address... from the Electors of the Home District.

25. Langton, *Early Days*, pp. 168–70, John Langton to his father, 13 July 1836.

26. Thomas Need, *Six Years in the Bush...* (London, 1838), p. 119.

27. W.B. Kerr, "When Orange and Green United, 1832–39," *O.H.S.P.R.*, vol. 34 (1942), 34–42; same, "The Orange Order and W.L. Mackenzie in the 1830s," *The Sentinel*, 1939.

28. Sissons, *Ryerson*, I, Chapter IX, *passim*, and p. 361, John Ryerson to Egerton Ryerson, 25 Sept. 1836.

29. *Ibid.*, I, 350–53.

30. Quoted in *The Correspondent and Advocate*, 3 Aug. 1836.

31. G78, pp. 39–47, Duncombe's petition to the House of Commons, enclosed in Glenelg to Head, 8 Sept. 1836.

32. Journals of the Assembly, 1836–37, Appendix 5, Report of the Select Committee on Charles Duncombe's Petition, 23 Jan. 1837.

33. T.P.I., Robert Baldwin Papers, A92, M.S. Bidwell to Robert Baldwin, 29 July 1836.

34. *P.A.C.R.*, 1923, p. 332, Robert Baldwin to Glenelg, 13 July 1836.

35. This conservative Assembly, like its predecessor in 1834, protested against the reservation of banking bills that were "purely local in their nature." Journals, 1836–37, pp. 321–22, Resolution of 20 Jan. 1837.

36. Anna Jameson, *Winter Studies and Summer Rambles* (London, 1838), I, 76–77.

37. P.A.C., U.C. Sundries, Merritt to Sir George Arthur, 11 Feb. 1839.

38. P.A.C., Durand Papers, vol. III, J.W. Macaulay to Alexander Hamilton, 17 Jan. 1837.

39. *Constitution*, 24 and 31 May, 14 June 1837.

40. *Ibid.*, 11 Jan. 1837.

41. *Ibid.*, 19 April 1837; O.A., Lindsey collection, Mackenzie section, Wolfred Nelson to Mackenzie, 4 May 1837.

42. *Constitution*, 5 July 1837.

43. *Ibid.*, 19 and 26 July, 2 Aug. 1837.

44. P.A.C., U.C. Sundries, R. Coate to Sir F.B. Head, 17 July 1837.

45. *Constitution*, 2 Aug. 1837.

46. The places of the meetings are conveniently listed in S.D. Clark, *Movements of Political Protest in Canada* (Toronto, 1959), pp. 379–80.

47. *Constitution*, 13 Sept. 1837.

48. *Ibid.*, 2 Aug. 1837.

49. *Ibid.*, 4 Oct. 1837.

50. Charles Lindsey, *The Life and Times of William Lyon Mackenzie* (Philadelphia and Toronto, 1862), II, 53.

51. *Constitution*, 18 Oct. 1837, letter from James Hunter, dated 29 Sept. 1837.

52. John Barnett, "Silas Fletcher: Instigator of the Upper Canadian Rebellion," *Ontario History*, XLI (1949), 7–35.

1837–38: REBELLION RECONSIDERED
Allan Greer

There was a time when historians thought they understood the events of 1837–38. They did not much *like* the Rebellion, and their accounts of the event itself were often sketchy in the extreme, but they knew where it belonged in the broad sweep of Canadian history; they could explain why it happened and what it meant. For the generation of academic historians writing before the deluge of the 1960s, the less said about the illegal machinations of Louis-Joseph Papineau, William Lyon Mackenzie, and their followers the better.[1] And yet, curiously, the Rebellion formed a major—I think it would be fair to say, *the* major—focal point in their writings about the pre-Confederation century. Like the ghost of Hamlet's father, it brooded over a stage that historians proceeded to furnish with political backgrounds, social and economic causes, and imperial results. Developments converged on 1837, and then moved off in novel directions after 1838, but the tumultuous turning-point itself did not seem a worthy object of research once its essential character had been identified.

Donald Creighton saw the Rebellion as the climactic episode in the long-term struggle of "commerce and agriculture."[2] Reformers, rebels and *patriotes* represented a narrow-minded agrarianism opposed to the expansionist commercialism of the Montreal merchants and their Tory political allies. This second, capitalist/conservative camp was the one that grasped Canada's potential for greatness, promoted economic development, and, more or less unconsciously, laid the foundations of a transcontinental nation. Their conflict with the carping radicals came to a violent head in 1837, but, fortunately, things turned out for the best: rebellion was crushed and the empire of the St. Lawrence gained a new lease on life. The defeat of the rebels is hardly surprising, for, in Creighton's account, they had set their faces against the forward march of History itself.

Creighton's liberal-minded contemporaries had a somewhat different view of the subject.[3] Sympathetic to moderate reform and critical of the colonial oligarchy, they believed that a few extremists had temporarily hijacked a perfectly legitimate political movement. The ascendancy of Mackenzie and the radical *patriotes* had come about partly because of Tory intransigence, and the result was a revolt misguided in its principles and disastrous in its results. The liberal historians, too, had their view of the overarching thrust of Canadian history. It was a story of the gradual and peaceful development of British liberty within a framework of growing colonial autonomy. What was so deplorable about the

From *Canadian Historical Review*, Vol. LXXVI, no. 1, March 1995 (Toronto: University of Toronto Press, 1995), 1–18.

rebels of 1837 was not only their violence but also their republicanism, their failure to appreciate the wonders of the British constitution. And yet, in the grand scheme of things, the role of the radicals and their revolt was ultimately positive, for, by their foolish actions, they unwittingly summoned up a saviour in the form of Lord Durham. Durham set in motion the liberalizing machinery that, in the fullness of time, brought forth Responsible Government, Confederation, and dominion autonomy. "The Rebellions," wrote A.R.M. Lower, "were blessings in disguise, the cornerstones of Canadian nationhood."[4]

While liberal and business/conservative interpretations held sway in English Canada, French-Canadian historiography was dominated by a Catholic nationalist school best represented by Abbé Lionel Groulx.[5] Papineau and the *patriotes* (like most Quebec historians then and now, Groulx had little to say about the Rebellion crisis outside the borders of Lower Canada) posed vexing problems for Groulx. Quite clearly, they were defenders of the nation, and that role gave them a major claim on the sympathies of a historian whose central preoccupation was the struggle of his people to maintain their ever-threatened cultural identity. But French Canada was, at its core, a Catholic and conservative society, as far as Groulx was concerned, and it was difficult to ignore the democratic, anti-clerical, and, in the end, revolutionary character of the *patriote* movement. To some extent, the historian contrived to reconcile his divided reactions by downplaying the *patriotes'* radicalism and by arguing that, strictly speaking, they were innocent of the crime of rebellion since it was the government that attacked them. Yet, insofar as the "mistakes" of the insurgents could not be ignored, Groulx was quite prepared to condemn them; consequently, his account featured a moral dissection whereby readers were advised to admire the *patriotes'* good points (their nationalism) and reject their bad points (their deism and republicanism). There are some striking affinities here with the liberal anglophone historians. Groulx's pulpit-style language may be more overtly judgmental than theirs, but in both the liberal and the Catholic versions of the Rebellion, resistance to constituted authority was seen as an understandable, though nonetheless egregious, error.

All these interpretive schemes that dominated Canadian historical writing through the middle decades of the twentieth century were built on the assumption that history had a discernible direction and flow. Canada was moving towards a goal in the nineteenth century; whether this end point was the construction of a transcontinental, commercial, and political union, the development of parliamentary government, or the preservation and resurrection of French Canada, it was certainly a Good Thing. Thus the rebels of 1837 were quite literally on the wrong track. They lost because they *had* to lose; they were not simply overwhelmed by superior force, they were justly chastised by the god of History. (The narrative structure in these older accounts resembles the revolutionary triumphalism then prevalent in American, French, and Soviet historiography, though, in the Canadian case, the form is inverted.) The Rebellion was the necessary anomaly in this providential account of the past, the sorry fate of the insurgents serving to validate the larger pattern, as well as providing Canadians with powerful moral and political lessons.

These teleological modes of explanation continue to resound down to the present day, even though historians long ago abandoned the confident overview genre favoured by Creighton, Groulx, and the rest. Original scholarship in the last few decades has veered in the opposite direction, away from overarching theses and towards specialized research on down-to-earth particulars. Moreover, since conflict and violence have ceased to be taboo subjects, empirical research on the Rebellion itself has made great strides since the 1960s. Military specialists have told us about troop movements and casualties;[6] imperial historians have shown us how Whitehall viewed the affair.[7] Meanwhile, research on the economy has revealed the financial and agrarian distress that helped to poison the atmosphere of the times.[8] A rich social-history literature has concentrated attention, as never before, on the ordinary people who formed the great majority of those caught up in the Rebellion;[9] even the religious background to 1837 has been explored.[10] The result has been a great advance in empirical knowledge: myths have been punctured, generalizations have been qualified, and a wealth of factual data has been accumulated.

However, reflection at the conceptual level has not kept pace with the progress of empirical and microscopic research. One can only pity the poor student or non-specialist reader who wanders into this historiographical terrain in search of answers to fairly basic questions about the Rebellion: what exactly was it? Was this a single phenomenon with various aspects and phases—the Rebellion—or were there two or more distinct rebellions? Why did it (they) occur and why did it turn out as it did? Was it a minor disturbance or an important event with lasting consequences? The student or reader will encounter a literature that seems more concerned with interpretive fine points than fundamental issues. Data abound on the rebels—the number who were Methodists, or the percentage who owned more than four cows—but what exactly makes someone a rebel? Books and articles enumerate the regiments involved in the battles of St. Denis and St. Eustache, but they say little about the effects of the British military presence on Lower Canadian politics.

This is not to say that the recent works lack conclusions, only that little thought seems to have gone into them. When it comes time to sum up, the discussion becomes crude and schematic; in many cases, historians fall back on the shopworn formulae of the traditional accounts. Even more pervasive is the "police officer's" conception of just what constitutes rebellion: it is essentially a crime, according to conservative historians, an illegal deed concerted in advance by ill-disposed traitors. More modern, liberal-minded writers try to avoid loaded vocabulary and strive to bring out the mitigating circumstances, but they still portray the revolt as a simple, unilateral *act*, something that rebels did—for whatever combination of social, economic, and political reasons. The behaviour of the government and of other actors is, in most accounts (though not those of the French-Canadian nationalists), merely reactive: normal, unremarkable, unproblematic.

This police officer's view of the subject underlies many of the implicit definitions of rebellion currently favoured in the literature. For many historians, particularly those who concentrate on Upper Canada and on Mackenzie, a rebellion seems to be a sudden and forcible attempt to unseat a government, something virtually indistinguishable from a *coup d'état*. But if Mackenzie's attack on Toronto is the Rebellion, what term do we apply to the all-important *context* of that exploit, a situation in which Upper Canadian radicals believed legitimate government had already ceased to exist? Violence seems to be a defining feature of rebellion in many accounts, and it is usually associated with the rebels, even though the violence of the government and its supporters was far more extensive and deadly. There is even a tendency to assimilate the fighting of 1837–38 with the various riots and brawls that punctuated the history of pre-Confederation Canada. Conservative commentators thus find confirmation of their view that the Rebellion was simply the most dramatic of many cases of lower class hell-raising, while writers on the left, seduced by a vision of the toiling masses in arms, find this a cheering instance of popular resistance. (Resistance to what? To whom?) Missing again is an appreciation of context, of the exceptional political circumstances which brought conflict to a bloody climax, and which gave the fighting an importance quite different from that of a canal workers' riot or an Orange-Green brawl.

The time has come, I believe, for some basic rethinking about the Rebellion of 1837–38, and I will suggest lines on which such a reconsideration might proceed. In my view, we should pause in the search for causes and effects and concentrate first on identifying more clearly the phenomenon that is to be explained. Surely the "what" question is prior to the "why" question. We can best approach this definitional problem, I would argue, by looking more closely at the crisis of 1837–38 as a complex series of events, one involving the actions and interactions of several parties, not just those identified as rebels. Rather than focusing on a one-dimensional act of revolt, we should recognize the contingency of events. Choices were made, actions taken, not as the inevitable result of metaphysical forces or of rigidly determining structures, but in response to rapidly changing circumstances. Placing the accent on complexity and contingency may seem a recipe for chaos rather than definitional clarity; nevertheless, as I hope to show, this is the only way to achieve an integrated view of the Rebellion and to grasp its essential nature.

Two major obstacles stand in the way of any synthetic initiatives of the sort outlined above: the comparative isolation of Canadian historiography from larger international currents, and the yawning chasm separating studies of Lower Canada and works on Upper Canada. The historiography of this country, strong in many other areas, lacks precisely the language and conceptual tools needed to make sense of revolutionary matters. Given Canada's history, as well as the historiographic traditions mentioned earlier, this is hardly a cause for wonder; what is surprising is the failure of Rebellion specialists to make fuller use of the enormous literature, empirical and theoretical, on revolutionary episodes in Europe and the Americas in the late eighteenth and early nineteenth centuries.[11] Not that the Canadas had the same experience as Belgium and Poland in 1830, or as Argentina and Venezuela in 1808. Naturally, there were numerous points of contrast, as well as similarities, but we cannot even begin to identify elements that are peculiarly and specifically Canadian in the absence of a comparative framework. Indeed, we can hardly find the words to describe the events of 1837–38 without drawing on the histories of other revolutionary outbreaks.

While a broader international view might provide useful concepts and points of comparison, any attempt to construct an integrated account of the Canadian Rebellion is still bedevilled by a particularly advanced case of historiographical apartheid. Creighton was quite prepared to encompass Upper and Lower Canada in his classic work, but since his time, researchers on the two sides of the Ottawa River have been pursuing different issues using different methods and, on the whole, ignoring one another.[12] The Canadian Historical Association, following the prevailing trends but also awarding them a sort of official stamp of approval, commissioned two Historical Booklets on the Rebellion: one devoted to Upper Canada, the other to Lower Canada. This gap, mirroring the separation of French- and English-Canadian historiographies, greatly magnifies the effects of fragmented views and specialized research—a situation prevailing in almost all fields of history—and makes consideration of larger questions particularly difficult. Above all, it tends to obscure the links connecting developments in the two provinces.

These days, it appears that only the authors of textbook syntheses are forced to examine both rebellions. Drawing of necessity on a bifurcated monographic literature, these writers often seem, quite understandably, at a loss as to how to integrate the diverse materials on the two provinces. Those writing in French tend to solve the problem by simply ignoring Upper Canada altogether and concentrating on the historical ancestor of the province of Quebec.[13] English textbook writers do their best to present a pan-Canadian view of the Rebellion, but the results are still disjointed—in most instances the two rebellions are covered in separate chapters—and rather cockeyed owing to the effects of an anglophone and Ontario bias. In four recently published histories of Canada, I found roughly equal space allotted to the Upper and Lower Canadian phases of the Rebellion, in spite of the fact that the crisis in Lower Canada was far deeper and, by any standard, much more significant. Three of the books placed the Upper Canadian rising *before* the Lower Canadian, even though the chronological and logical order of events was just the opposite.[14] The remaining work gets the sequence right, but recognizes no connection between the two rebellions, as if it were pure coincidence that Mackenzie attacked Toronto just after fighting broke out in the Montreal region.[15]

My own view, as should be apparent by now, is that events in the two provinces were indeed connected; in fact, I believe they can best be understood as various elements of a single phenomenon. It is quite true that conflict took different forms in Upper Canada and Lower Canada, and that the populations involved came from dissimilar backgrounds, but the Canadas are not the only British possession where revolts occurred in dispersed locations and involved people of different religions and languages. The Irish Rebellion of 1798 saw risings in various areas of the north and the south; Protestants and Catholics, English-speakers and Irish-speakers, all clashed with the existing order (and with one another as well) in a complicated eruption of violence.[16] The Indian Rebellion of 1857 (formerly known as the Mutiny) was just as multidimensional: there were agrarian insurrections as well as military revolts; various provinces, ethnic groups, religions, and castes were involved.[17] And yet, in both the Irish and the Indian cases, historians seem to have no difficulty applying the singular term "rebellion" to events that were actually far more plural than the Canadian crisis.[18] In other words, there is no reason to consider dispersal over space and diversity in form to be, in themselves, grounds for denying the basic unity of a revolt.

Although my point is mainly about the integrity of the events of 1837–38, I might also observe that the structural antecedents of revolt in the two Canadas were not as dissimilar as has often been supposed. Both provinces had essentially pre-industrial economies and a preponderance of independent farming families. Everywhere there was widespread anxiety about procuring new lands to settle the rising generation, and so government policies that threatened to restrict access to wilderness lands were naturally a matter of grave concern in these settlements. Tensions between town and country were as much apparent in the Toronto region as in Montreal's hinterland, and, as a consequence, conflict tended to follow a rural-urban pattern when fighting broke out in 1837. Seigneurial tenure, on the other hand, was unique to Lower Canada, and with it went landlord-*habitant* friction, a dynamic of rebellion in that colony. Lower Canada was, in general, an older settlement with a larger population that was in majority French-Canadian; in contrast, its neighbour was expanding rapidly, thanks to the effects of agricultural prosperity and massive immigration from the British Isles. Some immigrants also settled in Lower Canada, with the result that a linguistic minority of British origin shared the province with the old-stock *canadiens*.

According to Lord Durham and a long succession of historians after him, tensions between English and French in Lower Canada lay at the root of the civil strife of 1837–38. The Rebellion in Lower Canada, we are often told, was "racial" and, as a consequence, it was sharper than—indeed fundamentally different from—the milder strife that disturbed "English" Upper Canada. But, in fact, Upper Canada was also a divided society with friction between British immigrants and older settlers of Canadian and American origin, as anyone who has read Susanna Moodie can attest. Furthermore, research by Ronald Stagg and Colin Read reveals that the North American-born and the recent immigrants tended to gravitate to opposing camps when civil strife broke out in this "racially" homogeneous colony.[19] The language of race suits the purposes of those wishing to emphasize distinctions between the Upper and the Lower Canadian rebellions and to denigrate the latter (a matter of prejudices rather than principles), but it does so by concealing an important similarity. The civil strife of 1837–38 saw an ethnocultural polarization on both sides of the Ottawa River—long-established settlers tending to come to blows with unassimilated newcomers. The fact that immigrants were, in relative terms, so much more numerous in Upper Canada goes a long way to explaining the weaker showing of insurrection in that province.

The constitutions of the two provinces were identical, though politics had developed along somewhat different lines. Without delving into the complex particulars of ideologies, grievances, and programs, we might simply note the existence in both Canadas of polarizing tendencies that produced, by the mid-1830s, two basic political camps: on one side, office-holding oligarchies loosely affiliated to more broadly-based "Tory parties," composed mainly of British immigrants, and, on the other, a "Reform" opposition, critical of existing power structures. Because of the larger proportion of immigrants in the Upper Canadian population, Tories in that province, and not Lower Canada, enjoyed considerable electoral strength. The *patriote* opposition in Lower Canada was marked by its origins as a French-Canadian ethnic movement, though its nationalism was far less narrow by 1837 than it had been earlier. An outlook that might, for shorthand purposes, be labelled masculine-democratic-republican predominated among *patriotes*, their rhetoric dwelling on the rights of the people (read propertied men), the dangers of corruption, and the need to defend the independence and prerogatives of the colonial Assembly.[20] Mackenzie spoke for those who took a similar radical line in Upper Canada, though most Reform politicians in that province favoured a more moderate approach.

This, very roughly, was the situation in the Canadas on the eve of the Rebellion. I am quite aware that this compressed sketch of the social and political background could be debated in almost every one of its particulars. Indeed, my hope is that brave souls will someday come forward to examine these issues in some depth and from an integrated point of view encompassing both Canadas. Meanwhile, I am anxious to get on to the events of 1837–38. The potted history that follows pays particular attention to the linkages connecting developments in Upper Canada and Lower Canada in an attempt to gain a better grasp of the essential nature of the Rebellion crisis as a whole.

If we place ourselves at the beginning of 1837, almost a year before armed struggle erupted, we find the Canadas already embroiled in a serious political crisis. The legislative business of Lower Canada had by then ground to a complete halt, owing to acute conflict between the elected and the appointed elements of the legislature. City councils and school boards no longer existed because the statutes creating them had expired and could not be renewed. No budgets were approved, and funds for routine state operations had to be raised by extraordinary means. In Upper Canada, the situation was superficially normal; harmony reigned between the executive and a Tory-dominated Assembly. However, the legitimacy of that Assembly was by no means universally accepted; it was a matter of notoriety that the 1836 election had been marked by poll violence, fraud, and gubernatorial interference, and, whether or not these factors had truly determined the defeat of Reform, many Upper Canadians certainly thought they had. The Tories clearly had doubts about their popularity for, knowing that the king did not have long to live and that consequently a new election would have to be called soon, they passed a bill extending the life of the Assembly in disregard to the established practice of dissolving the House upon the death of a monarch. Reform politicians concluded that traditional parliamentary politics were at an end; the moderates among them retired from public life, while Mackenzie used his newspaper to propound the view that the current Assembly was not simply of the wrong political complexion, but was illegal and illegitimate.

Many *patriotes* and radical Reformers seem to have looked forward to the day when Canada would be free of the "baneful domination" of Great Britain. However, this was a blessing they expected in the distant future; meanwhile, the threat of secession could be employed to extract concessions from the Colonial Office. Historians are quick to warn us that, at this stage, and even later when the crisis deepened, most Upper Canadians did not want a revolution. Insofar as revolution was associated with lawlessness and bloodshed, this observation is of course perfectly correct, and it applies to Lower Canadians as well. But they did not want tyranny, oppression, and injustice either. The fact that most Canadians lacked what might be called a revolutionary consciousness in 1837 is quite unremarkable; it simply puts them in the same category as most French people in the spring of 1789, most Russians in early 1917, and most Europeans at the beginning of 1848. Revolutions are almost never launched in consequence of some prior shift of public opinion in favour of revolt. Of course, the development of widespread alienation from the existing order does frequently play a role in precipitating a crisis of government, but the populace need not have insurrection on its mind at the outset. It is when the authorities are unable to co-opt, channel, or crush opposition, or when they are overwhelmed by financial collapse (France, 1788) or military failure (Russia, 1905 and 1917), that the situation becomes explosive. In other words, revolutions occur when governments find themselves unable to govern, and this was just the situation facing the colonial administration of the Canadas as the spring of 1837 approached.

Dangerous political gridlock could not be allowed to endure indefinitely; His Majesty's government, claiming ultimate authority over British North America, therefore had to find a way out of the impasse. After years of vacillation and repeated attempts to conciliate irreconcilable colonial parties, the cabinet now opted for a crackdown on the Lower Canadian *patriotes*. Lord John Russell's Ten Resolutions were not exactly draconian in their specific provisions, but they did constitute a clear rejection of *patriote* demands for democratic constitutional reform. Furthermore, they allowed the colonial Governor power to spend funds without the approval of the Assembly, and this violated the sacred principle of "no taxation without representation" proclaimed since the time of the American Revolution. In the strained atmosphere of the day, these measures were bound to provoke angry reactions; the Colonial Office understood this clearly and immediately ordered additional troops to Lower Canada. Sure enough, as soon as news of the provocative Russell Resolutions reached Quebec, radical newspapers began howling with indignation about "despotism" and "robbery" of the public purse.

Only the lower province was directly implicated in these developments, but Upper Canadians of all political stripes followed them with the closest attention. In Lower Canada's ongoing crisis, they not only saw a more vivid and starkly drawn coercion of their own debates and conflicts, but they discerned unmistakable portents for the future of their corner of British North America. Thus, in the furore over the Russell Resolutions, Upper Canadian Tories fulminated against "treason" and "French republicanism," while an increasingly anti-British Mackenzie sounded more and more like the leader of a Lower Canada solidarity campaign. Paranoid Tory fantasies notwithstanding, this was not the product of any interprovincial revolutionary conspiracy. Indeed, communications with the *patriotes* were limited, and personal relations between Mackenzie and Papineau were less than cordial, but when the British moved to provoke a confrontation with their neighbours, Upper Canadian radicals knew that their own future was hanging in the balance. The famous declaration (28 July) of the Toronto Friends of Reform put it this way: "The Reformers of Upper Canada are called upon by every tie of feeling, interest, and duty, to make common cause with their fellow citizens of Lower Canada, whose successful coercion would doubtless be in time visited upon us."[21]

Meanwhile the *patriotes* were mobilizing a wider public for a massive campaign of protest. Local committees were established and, between May and September, rallies were held in towns and villages across Lower Canada. Upper Canada followed suit beginning in July. Mackenzie was the driving force, using the pages of his newspaper to urge the creation of local "political unions" and touring the outlying settlements to rouse audiences with his fiery oratory. The speeches and the resolutions passed at these Upper Canadian meetings naturally dwelt on the familiar litany of Family Compact abuses and other grievances of strictly local interest. The occasion of the campaign, unprecedented in its intensity, was nevertheless the confrontation between the Lower Canadian *patriote* movement and the government of British Empire. "We earnestly recommend every township to form political unions," editorialized the St. Thomas *Liberal*, "to hold meetings and to express boldly and above board their determination to rise or fall with their brethren in Lower Canada."[22]

Through the summer and fall, conflict in Lower Canada only intensified. The Governor, in a vain attempt to stem the agitation, had outlawed "seditious assemblies" in June; they continued unabated, in spite of government efforts to get local officials to enforce the ban. The administration's next recourse was to dismiss "disloyal" militia officers and Justices of the Peace, but this action politicized local government and precipitated *patriote* countermoves against "loyal" magistrates and officers. The upshot was that, by late October, early November, large sections of the rural District of Montreal had set up their own revolutionized local regimes.[23] Such a state of affairs constituted a clear challenge to the sovereignty of the British Empire and so, with ever larger numbers of soldiers arriving in Montreal, it became increasingly apparent that armed force would soon be used against the *patriotes*.

These new and graver developments had a double impact on Upper Canada. First of all, they provided an opportunity for action by stripping the province of British troops. The military build-up in the District of Montreal took place at the expense of other colonial garrisons with the effect that, by early November, not a single soldier remained in Upper Canada. Power relations accordingly tilted in favour of the anti-government forces, though not to the degree that Mackenzie, greatly underestimating the loyalist militia, thought. The Lower Canadian drift towards war provided an impulse, as well as an opportunity, to Upper Canadian radicals. Facing a major military onslaught, the *patriotes* stood in obvious need of support: not just support in the customary form of speeches and encouraging resolutions, but substantial diversionary action. "Let me advise every friend of the people," Mackenzie wrote on the eve of the Battle of St. Denis, "to provide himself with a rifle, or a musket or gun... *keep your eyes on Lower Canada*."[24] In early December, shortly after news would have reached Upper Canada of the outbreak of armed conflict in the District of Montreal, insurgents marched down Yonge Street in their ill-fated attempt to capture Toronto. Word quickly spread westward to the London District and there, in a tertiary reaction, radical forces assembled in support of their colleagues but dispersed without firing a shot when it became clear that the game was up and that resistance was futile. The fighting in 1837 had been far more extensive and intense in Lower than in Upper Canada; the casualty figures reflect the disparity: about 250 men killed in battle in the former, four in the latter.[25] Yet it was only a matter of weeks from the time the bullets began to fly until the government and its supporters had triumphed decisively in both provinces.

The crisis was by no means at an end, however. Hundreds, perhaps thousands, of refugees fled to the United States in the wake of the first round of fighting and, in the process, they helped to keep the revolution alive while widening its geographic scope. There was tremendous public support for the Canadian rebels, especially in the borderlands of northern Vermont, New York, Ohio, and Michigan. However, the United States government, a major actor in the crisis of 1837–38, decided to preserve peace with Great Britain at the expense of revolution in the Canadas, and this decision eventually sealed the fate of the latter. Yet, for a time, the federal government had difficulty imposing its will on the turbulent northern frontier. "Patriots," American as well as French- and English-Canadian, launched a series of border raids in 1838; these culminated in November of that year in a comparatively large-scale invasion of Lower Canada, coupled with a rising of Lower Canadian rebels. Cross-border actions against Upper Canada tended increasingly to be the work of U.S. citizens, locked now in conflict not only with the British colonial regime but also with their own government, which quickly expanded its army by about 50 per cent in order to take active measures to preserve American neutrality and bring northern Patriots to heel.[26]

By the end of 1838, the colonial regime had completely mastered the situation from a military point of view; politically, far-reaching changes were under way, all designed to consolidate the victory and strengthen government. For the Rebellion was not exclusively—or even primarily—a military affair, nor was it only the work of "rebels." The seriousness of the crisis can be gauged not only in the far-reaching challenges to the existing order, but also in the extraordinary measures taken to preserve British rule. In addition to mounting military assaults against its Lower Canadian foes, the government also effected an unprecedented juridical revolution to guarantee its victory. Martial law was imposed, *habeas corpus* suspended, and arrests were carried out on a massive scale and largely without charges being laid. Legal surgery was less radical in Upper Canada where the revolutionary threat was less serious, but even here the right of *habeas corpus* was abridged: an unorthodox system was established of summary conviction and attainder of prisoners who petitioned for pardons. Finally, legislation passed in March 1838 gave immunity from prosecution to loyalists who may have broken the law in apprehending rebels.[27] This last provision points us in the direction of the unofficial but very real actions taken against opponents of government in the Rebellion years. Both Canadian provinces provide dozens of instances of assault, theft and destruction of property, and arbitrary arrest committed by loyalist forces. Of course, such irregularities are almost inevitable in times of civil strife, but they do constitute an additional dimension to the abandonment of the rule of law.

In the years following the fighting, the British colonial regime was not so much restored as reconstituted. The state, in its administrative and executive aspects, grew enormously in size, scope, and power. In the short run, soldiers and police proliferated, but, before long, more peaceful agencies of regulation came to predominate: schools, prisons, asylums, and above all, bureaucracies. (By the end of the 1840s an arrangement known as Responsible Government had been worked out to help coordinate executive, legislature, and electorate.) The provincial Assembly of Lower Canada was gone for good; in its place, an appointed Special Council (1838–41) was free to pass unpopular measures in fields such as the law, property, and municipal government.[28] The two Canadas were united, as is well known, in order to allow the resumption of the parliamentary system without letting the French Canadians have the degree of power their numbers would otherwise entitle them to. A punitive forced marriage, the Act of Union attempted to solve the "French-Canadian problem" through repression, and, as such, it represented the negation of the insurgent spirit of 1837–38 with its implicit commitment to self-determination and mutual support. (Successor regimes would be paying the price for that authoritarian solution for many years to come!) All in all, the decisive defeat of republican opposition in the Canadas paved the way for a major transformation of imperial rule.

No matter how paltry the military contests of the Rebellion may seem, this had been a political turning-point of the first magnitude. From the summer of 1837 until the end of 1838, the central part of British North America underwent a thoroughgoing crisis of sovereignty, one in which the very framework of state power was in danger of collapse. Fundamental questions came to the fore, not as abstract debating points but as real problems requiring immediate answers: who would rule the Canadas? How would that rule be carried out? Its legitimacy contested in theory and challenged in practice, the state could hardly carry out its normal function as ultimate arbiter; instead of containing and channelling political contention, it was now the actual object of conflict. Wherever there are parties and factions one finds competition for power and influence, and, in parliamentary systems, for the right to form a government; but, in 1837–38, the actual framework of politics was at stake: that is what made this a revolutionary crisis.

Much has of necessity been left out of the compressed account of the crisis of 1837–38. However, I hope that its inadequacies can be overlooked in keeping with the spirit of the exercise. I have tried to bring out the contingency of events and to dispense with the metaphysical forces of Fate, Destiny, and capital-h History; also absent are master-plotters scripting their revolutionary scenarios in advance of events. Almost every action, whether by rebels, loyalists, or government, was also a reaction: developments were interconnected and reciprocal, repression and resistance provoking one another in dialectical fashion. A spatial dynamic is also apparent, with the effects of conflict radiating outward from an epicentre in the District of Montreal. Each succeeding political or military explosion there sent out shockwaves that detonated secondary upheavals, first in the Toronto area, then around London, and finally across adjacent regions of the United States. Clashes took different forms in each of the widely dispersed areas affected; moreover, the people involved in the two Canadas and in the United States spoke different languages, partook of different political cultures, and cherished a variety of aspirations. Yet, for all its internal diversity, this was a single historical phenomenon, and no phase of it can be fully understood in isolation from the whole.[29]

Notes

1. For the sake of brevity, I am confining my attention here to influential works belonging to what might be called the academic mainstream. Dissenting interpretations that never received the attention they deserved include S.D. Clark, *Movements of Political Protest in Canada, 1640–1840* (Toronto: University of Toronto Press 1959), and Stanley B. Ryerson, *Unequal Union: Confederation and the Roots of Conflict in the Canadas, 1815–1873* (Toronto: Progress Books 1973). My own approach owes much to these writers, particularly Clark.

2. Donald Creighton, *The Empire of the St. Lawrence* (Toronto: Macmillan 1956), 255–320.

3. See, for example, A.R.M. Lower, *Colony to Nation: A History of Canada* (Toronto: Longmans, Green 1946), 213–56; J.M.S. Careless, *Canada: A Story of Challenge* (Toronto: Macmillan 1963), 164–87; Kenneth McNaught, *The Pelican History of Canada* (Harmondsworth: Penguin 1969), 85–89.

4. Lower, *Colony to Nation*, 256.

5. Lionel Groulx, *Histoire du Canada français depuis la découverte*, 2nd ed., 2 vols. (Montreal: Fides 1960), 2; 162–77. For an excellent overview of the historiography of the Rebellion in Lower Canada, see Jean-Paul Bernard, "L'évolution de l'histo-riographie depuis les événements (1837–1982)," in *Les Rébellions de 1837–1838: Les patriotes du Bas-Canada dans la mémoire collective et chez les historiens* (Montreal: Boréal 1983), 17–61.

6. Elinor Kyte Senior, *Redcoats and Patriotes: The Rebellions in Lower Canada, 1837–38* (Ottawa: Canada's Wings 1985); Mary Beacock Fryer, *Volunteers and Redcoats, Rebels and Raiders* (Toronto: Dundurn 1987). Please note that, in this note, and in those which follow, only a few of the more significant recently published books are included. This is not a comprehensive bibliographic essay.

7. Peter Burroughs, *The Canadian Crisis and British Colonial Policy, 1828–1841* (Toronto: Macmillan 1972); Phillip A. Buckner, *The Transition to Responsible Government: British Policy in British North America, 1815–1850* (Westport, Conn.: Greenwood 1985), 205–49. Imperial history of a different sort can be found in George Rudé, *Protest and Punishment: The Story of the Social and Political Protesters Transported to Australia, 1788–1868* (Oxford: Clarendon Press 1978).

8. The relevant literature is vast, but the works of Fernand Ouellet are particularly noteworthy: *Economic and Social History of Quebec, 1760–1850: Structures and Conjunctures* (Toronto: Macmillan 1980), and *Lower Canada 1791–1840: Social Change and Nationalism*, translated by Patricia Claxton (Toronto: McClelland & Stewart 1980). See also the highly perceptive discussion by Douglas McCalla in *Planting the Province: The Economic History of Upper Canada, 1784–1870* (Toronto: University of Toronto Press 1993), 187–93.

9. In addition to the works by Ouellet cited above, see Leo A. Johnson, *History of the County of Ontario, 1615–1875* (Whitby: County of Ontario 1973), 95–127; Colin Read, *The Rising in Western Upper Canada, 1837–87: The Duncombe Revolt and After* (Toronto: University of Toronto Press 1982); Bryan Palmer, *Working-Class Experience: Rethinking the History of Canadian Labour, 1800–1991* (Toronto: McClelland & Stewart 1992), 69–75; Allan Greer, *The Patriots and the People: The Rebellion of 1837 in Rural Lower Canada* (Toronto: University of Toronto Press 1993).

10. Richard Chabot, *Le curé de campagne et la contestation locale au Québec de 1791 aux troubles de 1837–38* (Montreal: Hurtubise 1975); Gilles Chaussé, *Jean-Jacques Lartigue, premier évêque de Montréal* (Montreal: Fides 1980); Albert Schrauwers, *Awaiting the Millennium: The Children of Peace and the Village of Hope, 1812–1889* (Toronto: University of Toronto Press 1993).

11. A qualification is in order: on particular themes, Rebellion specialists have indeed drawn on a comparative literature covering such matters as riots in eighteenth-century Britain or the agrarian economy on the eve of the French Revolution, but they have shown hardly any interest in revolutionary episodes *per se* and in their integrity.

12. *Mea culpa*!

13. An exception is Denis Vaugeois and Jacques Lacoursière, eds., *Canada-Québec: synthèse historique* (Montreal: Éditions du Renouveau pédagogique 1976), 306–18, which integrates a good, though very brief, account of Upper Canadian events into a chapter devoted primarily to the Rebellion in Lower Canada.

14. R. Douglas Francis and Donald B. Smith, *Origins: Canadian History to Confederation* (Toronto: Holt, Rinehart and Winston 1988), 227–31, 249–53; David J. Bercuson et al., *Colonies: Canada to 1867* (Toronto: McGraw-Hill Ryerson 1992), 219–24, 236–39; J.M. Bumsted, *The Peoples of Canada: A Pre-Confederation History* (Toronto: Oxford University Press 1992), 248–57.

15. Margaret Conrad, Alvin Finkel, and Cornelius Jaenen, *History of the Canadian Peoples*, vol. 1: *Beginnings to 1867* (Toronto: Copp Clark Pitman 1993), 412–24.

16. Gearoid O'Tuathaigh, *Ireland before the Famine, 1798–1848* (Dublin: Gill and Macmillan 1972); Thomas Pakenham, *The Year of Liberty: The Story of the Great Irish Rebellion of 1798* (London: Hodder and Stoughton 1969).

17. Christopher Hibbert, *The Great Mutiny: India 1857* (London: Penguin 1978); Eric Stokes, *The Peasant Armed: The Indian Rebellion of 1857* (Oxford: Clarendon 1986).

18. I am on record as favouring the term revolutionary crisis rather than rebellion (Greer, *Patriots and the People*, 4). I still think the former phrase applies, but consideration of the Irish and Indian cases makes me more inclined to go along with the prevailing usage which prescribes the word "rebellion" for colonial revolts that do not culminate in the overthrow of the imperial regime.

19. Ronald J. Stagg, "The Yonge Street Rebellion of 1837: An Examination of the Social Background and a Reassessment of the Events" (Ph.D. thesis, University of Toronto 1976), chaps 6 and 8; Read, *The Rising in Western Upper Canada,* 164–204.

20. Affinities in the rhetoric, tactics, and political styles between the colonial radicals and analogous elements in Britain have yet to be explored in depth. The term "reform" had rich and varied connotations in the early 1830s, and Mackenzie's use of the term "political unions" would have had powerful Old-Country resonances. See John Belcham, "Republicanism, Popular Constitutionalism and the Radical Platform in Early Nineteenth-Century England," *Social History* 6 (Jan. 1981): 1–32.

21. Colin Read and Ronald J. Stagg, eds., *The Rebellion of 1837 in Upper Canada: A Collection of Documents* (Ottawa: Carleton University Press 1985), 54. Compare 62, 70, 77, 87, 104, 105, 107, 316.

22. Read and Stagg, eds., *1837 in Upper Canada*, 65. Mackenzie even announced his initial plans to organize an extra-parliamentary network halfway through an article describing the progress of the anti-government campaign in Lower Canada. Clark, *Movements of Political Protest*, 375.

23. For further details see Greer, *The Patriots and the People*, 219–26.

24. *The Constitution*, 22 Nov. 1837, quoted in Anthony W. Rasporich, ed., *William Lyon Mackenzie* (Toronto: Holt, Rinehart and Winston 1972), 69 (emphasis in original).

25. Senior, *Redcoats and Patriotes*, 213; G.M. Craig, *Upper Canada: The Formative Years, 1784–1841* (Toronto: McClelland & Stewart 1963), 247–48. Note that these figures apply to the first phase of the Rebellion crisis only. My thanks to Colin Read for guidance on this subject.

26. See especially Albert B. Corey, *The Crisis of 1830–1842 in Canadian-American Relations* (New Haven: Yale University Press 1941), 44–69, but also Oscar A. Kinchen, *The Rise and Fall of the Patriot Hunters* (New York: Bookman 1956); Orrin Edward Tiffany, *The Relations of the United States to the Canadian Rebellion of 1837–1838* (Buffalo 1905); Edwin C. Guillet, *The Lives and Times of the Patriots* (Toronto: University of Toronto Press 1968); John Duffy and H. Nicholas Muller, "The Great Wolf Hunt: The Popular Response in Vermont to the *Patriote* Uprising of 1937," *Journal of American Studies* 8 (Aug. 1974): 153–69.

27. Read and Stagg, *The Rebellion of 1837 in Upper Canada*, lxxxvii–viii.

28. Brian Young, "Positive Law, Positive State: Class Realignment and the Transformation of Lower Canada, 1815–1866," in Allan Greer and Ian Radforth, eds., *Colonial Leviathan: State Formation in Mid-Nineteenth Century Canada* (Toronto: University of Toronto Press 1992), 50–63.

29. Certainly the Rebellion was multifaceted and, as a consequence, historians of ethnicity or of class struggle, gender formation or popular violence, can find ample material in 1837–38 for research and reflection. I hope it is understood that, far from disparaging inquiries of this sort, I welcome them. Similarly, there is no reason to object to the study of the Rebellion in the context of Ontario history or Quebec history, as long as neither province is treated as a completely self-contained entity.

The author wishes to thank an anonymous *Canadian Historical Review* assessor for helpful comments, and the Social Science and Humanities Research Council of Canada for research funding.

CHAPTER

11 THE IRISH COME
TO CANADA

The Irish immigrants who came to British North America in the decades before Confederation not only altered the composition of the population and its religious make-up, but also served as a catalyst for innumerable other changes. The absorptive capacity of Canadian society was severely tested by that unprecedented inundation of Irish who were attempting to escape from the economic devastation wrought in their homeland by the potato famine of the 1840s. Since then there has been sharp disagreement over the nature of the Irish experience. The early literature, which dominated for almost one hundred years, exaggerated the "paddy" stereotype. In the 1960s, however, the "Irish" in Canada were reinvented by a growing army of academics. It is usually the Catholic Irish who are studied, for it was they who shattered the Protestant monopolies in the Maritimes and Canada West. The impact of that sudden and massive influx of largely destitute souls affected both the society and those who wrote about it. The "Irish" riots, strikes and parades jump out of the pages of the newspapers of the 1840s and 1850s, and while the stereotypes of the early writers have been rejected by all but the most determined, there is no consensus on the "new Canadian Irish."

There are professional Irish apologists, and they have their critics. To a certain extent, this was influenced by modern multiculturalism and the desire to recapture the fading of the green. There are ideological splits over class, religion, contribution, and politics. The most significant disagreement centres on the rural/urban roles and occupations of the Irish. For some years, the question which seemed to require an answer was why the Irish, deriving as they did from a rural, peasant culture, evolved into an urban proletariat ghetto in Canada. The debate over the nature of the urban proletariat and rural yeomanry became as rancorous as it was indecisive, and some might add tedious.

The two readings selected here concentrate on the dramatic, the riot and the parade, but in each case the events merely provide the backdrop for an analysis on the nature of the whole society. The first reading is by Scott W. See on "The Orange Order and Social Violence in Mid Nineteenth-Century Saint John." The centrepiece of this article is the Saint John riot of 12 July 1849, one of the most violent in Canadian history, but one that See finally explains. See does not pretend to be a detached observer, however, and students should speculate on the implications of that. A later article by See on "Mickeys and Demonds *vs.* Bigots and Boobies: The Woodstock Riot of 1847" in the autumn *Acadiensis* of 1991 extends his argument on Protestant bigotry beyond Saint John.

If the See article is characterized by an undercurrent of rage, then a very different spirit prevails in Michael Cottrell's "St. Patrick's Day Parades in Nineteenth-Century Toronto: A Study of Immigrant Adjustment and Élite Control." Like the parades of July 12, those of March 17 frequently ended in violence, yet as Cottrell shows it is a mistake to dismiss them as unimportant. The hierarchy of the Roman Catholic Church certainly did not dismiss them, and instead manoeuvred to exploit and control them. Cottrell demonstrates the complexity and ameliorativeness of the St. Patrick's Day Parades. He also shows, as See does not, the change that comes with the passage of time.

Suggestions for Further Reading

Akenson, Donald, "Ontario: Whatever Happened to the Irish?," in *Canadian Papers in Rural History*, vol. III, 1982, pp. 204–205, 217–56.

Elliot, Bruce S., *Irish Migrants in the Canadas: A New Approach*. Kingston and Montreal: McGill-Queen's University Press, 1988.

Duncan, Kenneth, "Irish Famine Immigration and the Social Structure of Canada West," *Canadian Review of Anthropology and Sociology*, February 1965, pp. 19–40.

Houston, Cecil J. and William J. Smyth, *The Sash Canada Wore: A Historical Geography of the Orange Order in Canada*. Toronto: University of Toronto Press, 1980.

Kealey, Greg, "The Orange Order in Toronto: Religious Riots and the Working Class," in Greg Kealey and Peter Warrian, eds., *Essays in Canadian Working Class History*, Toronto: McClelland and Stewart, 1976.

Lockwood, Glen J., "Irish Immigrants and the 'Critical Years' in Eastern Ontario: The Case of Montague Township, 1821–1881," *Canadian Papers in Rural History*, IV, 1984.

Nicolson, Murray, "The Irish Experience in Ontario: Rural or Urban?," *Urban History Review*, 14, 1, June 1985, pp. 37–46.

Senior, Hereward, *Orangism: The Canadian Phase*. Toronto: McGraw-Hill Ryerson, 1972.

THE ORANGE ORDER AND SOCIAL VIOLENCE IN MID NINETEENTH-CENTURY SAINT JOHN

Scott W. See

In March 1839, the St. Patrick's, St. George's and St. Andrew's societies held a joint meeting in Saint John, New Brunswick. Delegates noted and condemned the Protestant-Catholic confrontations that appeared to be endemic in Boston and other unfortunate American cities. In a spirit of congeniality, they applauded themselves on the good fortune of living in a British colony free of such acrimonious religious strife. Generous toasts were proposed to young Queen Victoria, Lieutenant-Governor Sir John Harvey and, most effusively, to each other.[1] A short eight years later, after Saint John and neighbouring Portland had experienced a series of bloody riots involving Protestant Orangemen and Irish Catholics, those sentiments would be recalled with bitter irony. Sarcastic comparisons would then be drawn between Saint John and New Orleans, a tumultuous city with a reputation for collective violence.[2]

What happened to shatter the calm, and why would the toasts of 1839 turn out to be so farcical in the light of events during the 1840s? Why would Saint John and Portland, relatively stable communities that escaped major incidents of social violence prior to the 1840s, become ethno-religious battlegrounds involving natives and immigrants?[3] The growth of Irish Catholic immigration to Saint John and Portland before mid-century was accompanied by the expansion of the Orange Order as an institutionalized nativist response to those unwelcome settlers. Confrontations between the two groups began with relatively mild clashes in the late 1830s and culminated in the great riots of 1847 and 1849. The Ireland-based Orange Order, fuelled originally by British garrison troops and Irish Protestant immigrants, attracted significant numbers of native New Brunswickers and non-Irish immigrants because of its anti-Catholic and racist appeal. By mid-century it functioned as a nativist organization whose purpose was to defend Protestantism and British institutions against Irish Catholic encroachment. The clashes in Saint John and Portland were not primarily the result of transplanted rivalries between Protestant and Catholic Irish immigrants, as was commonly believed by contemporaries and historians.[4] Rather they represented both a vehement rejection of certain immigrants because of cultural and religious differences, as well as a symbolic struggle to protect Protestant jobs against competitive Irish Catholic famine victims during a decade of severe economic hardship. Thus as Irish Catholic immigration burgeoned, so did the nativist Orange Order.

From *Acadiensis*, Vol. XIII, no. 1 (Autumn 1983), 68–92.

Saint John was New Brunswick's most populous city in the nineteenth century.[5] Settled by Loyalists in 1783 and incorporated two years later, it rapidly developed into the province's primary port for the export of staple timber goods and the import of manufactured products and foodstuffs. Lying in its northern shadow was the shipbuilding and mill town of Portland, now annexed into greater Saint John. The localities were connected by several roads, the busiest thoroughfare being a dilapidated bridge spanning an inlet on the harbour's northern extremity.[6] Both communities bustled in mid-century; along the narrow streets and wharves sailors rubbed shoulders with tradesmen, merchants, lawyers, mill workers and itinerant labourers. Moreover, both gained their economic focus almost entirely from New Brunswick's timber staple. Sawn lumber and deals were shipped to the British Isles from their wharves, while numerous sawmills and shipyards dotted their skylines. In turn, the two communities received the bulk of New Brunswick's imports, inducing immigrants.[7]

Despite their industriousness, Saint John and Portland had fallen on hard times in the 1840s. Indeed all of New Brunswick suffered from the worst sustained downturn since the colony's inception.[8] Several factors accounted for this. First, the colony had enjoyed decades of timber trading privileges with Great Britain due to a combination of preference subsidies and high tariffs for foreign imports. But starting in 1842, England began to shift toward a policy of free trade in an attempt to curtail its soaring deficits. Subsequently it lowered or dropped its foreign tariffs and increased colonial duties. News of England's policy change created chaos in New Brunswick. Fears of the ramifications of such a move led to a decade of lost confidence among investors and merchants. Although New Brunswick would experience a slight recovery in 1844, due primarily to speculation that Great Britain's railroad fever would stimulate timber trade, the decade would be marked by high unemployment, rising commodity prices, commercial bankruptcies and legislative indebtedness.[9] Second, a worldwide glut of lumber and the over-exploitation of New Brunswick's forests caused a severe export slump.[10] Later in the decade, moreover, hundreds of workers were displaced as the province's sawmills abandoned labour-intensive operations in favour of steam-driven machinery.[11] These factors combined to create a decade of commercial distress that crippled Saint John and Portland, especially in the years 1842–43 and 1845–49.

During this decade of financial hardship, these communities experienced dramatic changes in immigrant patterns. Prior to the 1840s, both were relatively homogeneous. Indeed New Brunswick in general consisted primarily of the descendants of Loyalists and pre-Revolutionary War New England settlers, plus a moderate number of immigrants from England, Scotland and Ireland. The only significant non-Protestants were the Acadians, who populated the northern and eastern shores and the north-western interior. Moreover, the immigrant flow throughout the 1830s was strikingly consistent: for example, 1832 and 1841 differed in raw totals by only twelve.[12] This fairly uniform influx brought an increasingly large proportion of Irish, a trend that would continue to mid-century.[13]

Prior to the 1840s the majority of these Irishmen came from the Protestant northern counties. Most were of Scots or English ancestry, reflecting the British colonization of Ireland. They were artisans and tenant farmers with modest savings who sought a better life within the British colonial system. Most importantly, they shared cultural and ideological views with the native New Brunswickers and other British emigrants they encountered. They adhered to Protestantism and supported the English constitutional and political domination of Ireland. Thus they made a relatively smooth transition to their new lives in New Brunswick.[14]

During the 1830s, however, emigrant patterns within Ireland shifted and thereby profoundly altered the demographic face of New Brunswick. The more skilled, financially-solvent Protestant Irishmen from northern counties began to be replaced by more destitute Catholics from Ireland's poorer southern and western regions. The percentage of Irish Catholics who emigrated to New Brunswick before 1840 was small, yet ever-increasing. The trickle became a flood as a tragic potato famine decimated Ireland's staple crop from 1845 to 1848.[15] New Brunswick's immigration rate would increase yearly by at least 150 per cent from 1843 until 1847, when the Irish famine tide finally crested. For the mid-1840s, the province would receive virtually all of its immigrants from the Catholic districts of Ireland. For example, of the 9,765 immigrants arriving in 1846, 99.4 per cent were from Ireland. Of these, 87 per cent landed in Saint John, clearly underscoring the city's role as the province's chief immigration port. The overwhelming majority were poor Catholic agricultural labourers.[16] New Brunswick in the 1840s, and particularly Saint John, was bombarded with thousands of non-Anglo-Saxon Protestants.

The influx of Irish Catholics dramatically altered the ethno-religious faces of Saint John and Portland. Although perhaps half of the incoming Irish used the ports as temporary shelters, earning enough at manual labour along the docks for the fare on a coastal vessel heading for the United States, thousands of the poor agrarian peasants remained.[17] By mid-century, more than one-third of the residents of Saint John and Portland were born in Ireland. More profoundly, Catholicism mushroomed. Roman Catholics were as large as any Protestant sect in Saint John by the mid-1840s; when the 1861 census appeared, the first to include religious data, both localities had populations almost 40 per cent Catholic. Since the Acadians, who were New Brunswick's only other substantial Catholic population, were practically nonexistent in the Saint John region during mid-century, Irishmen accounted almost entirely for the high Catholic population.[18]

The Irish Catholics settled primarily in two sections of Saint John and Portland. They clustered in overcrowded squalour in York Point, a district of north-western Saint John bounded roughly by Union Street to the south, George's Street to the east, Portland Parish to the north and the bay to the west.[19] In Portland, they huddled in the busy wharf area on the harbour's northern shore. The two districts, connected by the "Portland Bridge," grew into twin ethno-religious ghettos during the 1840s.[20] They were so strongly identified with Irish Catholics that they would play host to virtually all of the major episodes of social violence between Orangemen and Irishmen during the decade.

The influx of thousands of Celtic Catholics into the Protestant Anglo-Saxon bastions of Saint John and Portland triggered a nativist response among the more entrenched residents. A useful paradigm for interpreting nativism was pioneered by John Higham, and while his model concerned American movements, it applies equally well for any nativist response. Higham's nativism was the "intense opposition to an internal minority on the ground of its foreign... connections," or a "defensive type of nationalism." Though Higham cautioned that the word "nativism," of nineteenth-century derivation, has become pejorative, his definition provides a valuable intellectual foundation for analysing people's reaction to immigrants.[21] In the context of the British colonial experience, nativists tended less to focus on place of birth than to draw inspiration from the virtues of Protestantism and British institutions.[22] From this perspective, the local response to incoming Irish Catholics may clearly be considered as a nativist response. Protestants who wanted to discourage Catholic settlement and block further immigration began to channel their energies into an institutionalized counter-offensive during the 1840s. As Saint John's *Loyalist and Conservative Advocate* explained:

> The necessity... for Protestant organization in this Province, arose not more from the many murderous attacks committed upon quiet and unoffending Protestants, by Catholic ruffians, than from the dreary prospect which the future presented. The facts were these: several thousands of immigrants were annually landing upon our shores: they were nearly all Catholics, nearly all ignorant and bigotted, nearly all paupers, many of them depraved... What have we to expect but murder, rapine, and anarchy? Let us ask, then, should not Protestants unite? Should they not organize?[23]

The call to battle was dutifully answered by an organization with a history of responding to similar entreaties in Ireland and England—the Loyal Orange Order.

The Orange Order became the vanguard of nativism in mid nineteenth-century New Brunswick, yet the organization was neither new nor unique to the province. After a violent birth in Loughgall, Ireland in 1795, Orangeism quickly spread throughout Northern Ireland and England. As a fraternal body tracing its roots to a feuding tradition between Protestant and Catholic weavers and farmers, the Orange Order paid ideological homage to the British Crown and Protestantism. Group cohesion was provided by a system of secret rituals, an internal hierarchy of five "degrees" and the public celebration of symbolic holidays such as July 12, the anniversary of the victory of the Prince of Orange (King William III) over Catholic King James II at the Battle of the Boyne in 1690. In the early nineteenth century the Orange Order was firmly entrenched in the British Isles, where its members fervently combated the growth of Jacobinism and Roman Catholicism.[24]

Given the ideological foundations of the Orange Order, it transferred well within the British Empire. British garrison troops who joined the organization while stationed in Ireland carried warrants for new lodges when they transferred to new posts. Irish Protestant immigrants who settled in England and British North America also brought Orange warrants as part of their "cultural baggage." By the early nineteenth century, British regulars in Halifax and Montreal were holding formal Orange meetings. Lodges mushroomed as they found support among Loyalists and the swelling ranks of Irish Protestant immigrants. In 1830 a Grand Orange Lodge, headquartered in Upper Canada, obtained permission from Ireland to issue lodge warrants for all of British North America except New Brunswick.[25]

New Brunswick's organized lodges, dating from the turn of the century, clearly reflected a similar pattern of garrison troop and Irish immigrant conveyance. The earliest known lodge, formed among soldiers of the 74th Regiment in Saint John, met regularly by 1818. Six years later they obtained an official Irish warrant.[26] After several abortive efforts to establish civilian lodges in the mid-1820s, Orangeism became rooted among Saint John's Irish Protestants in 1831. Initial growth was sluggish. Fifteen local, or "primary" lodges existed by 1838, representing ten in Saint John and Portland. Membership tended to be small, with some lodges having only a handful of regular participants. Even the establishment of a provincial Grand Orange Lodge in 1837–8, under the mastership of James McNichol, failed to generate widespread growth and attract significant numbers. With the advent of the 1840s New Brunswick's Orange Lodges, particularly in Saint John and Portland, were staffed primarily by small numbers of recent Irish Protestant immigrants and British troops.[27]

A catalyst appeared in the 1840s to spur growth in the fledgling organization. The rising tide of famine immigration brought concerned Protestants to the organization's doorstep, seeking action and viable solutions to the Irish Catholic "menace." By the close of 1844, when the transition from Protestant to Catholic emigrant was well under way in Ireland, New Brunswick had twenty-seven lodges. Of these, ten were less than a year old. As Irish Catholics arrived and filtered throughout the province, Orange Lodges burgeoned to lead the counter-offensive. Buttressed by a network of primary, county, district and provincial lodges, Orangeism swept up the St. John River Valley hard on the heels of the Catholic immigrants. Mid-century found 123 primary lodges across the province, representing a five-year growth of 455 per cent.[28] Together with its smaller Nova Scotia affiliates, New Brunswick's Orange Order boasted an estimated 10,000 members. Yet despite its impressive expansion, the Orange Order's seat of power and membership base remained firmly rooted in Saint John and Portland.[29]

The traditional membership pools did not account for the explosive growth of Orangeism. Irish Protestant immigration dropped dramatically during the 1840s, becoming negligible by mid-century. Moreover, Britain reduced its garrison troops because of budgetary constraints. What, then, explained the Orange Order's meteoric rise? How did the organization broaden its attraction to ensure its survival? The answers were to be found in the Order's ideological appeal to native New Brunswickers and non-Irish Protestant immigrants.

Evidence of Orange membership in the 1840s clearly proved that initiates came from various cultural groups and classes. While the organization may have been rooted among British garrison troops and Irish Protestant settlers, it succeeded only because it found a willing supply of Loyalist and New England descendants and non-Irish immigrants who shared its philosophical tenets. In other words, to tell the story of Orangeism in mid nineteenth-century New Brunswick is to trace the growth of an indigenous social movement. At least half of all identified Orangemen in mid-century were born in New Brunswick. They came from all walks of life, including legislators, barristers, magistrates, doctors, ministers, farmers, artisans and unskilled labourers. Motivated primarily by locally-defined problems and prejudices, many New Brunswick natives and immigrants found the Orange Order both philosophically and socially attractive.[30]

In the Saint John region, some natives participated in Orange activities when lodges first appeared in the early nineteenth century. Indeed, several of the nascent city lodges drew their membership exclusively from transplanted New Englanders and Loyalists from America's mid-Atlantic and southern regions.[31] When the provincial Grand Orange Lodge organized in 1844, prestigious native Saint John residents were there. They included W.H. Needham, a Justice of the Peace, H. Boyd Kinnear, a lawyer, and Thomas W. Peters, Jr., a city official. Each would assume an Orange leadership role at some point in his career.[32] During the period of intensified social violence, from 1845–49, Saint John and Portland residents embraced the Orange Order because of its campaign to protect Protestantism and British hegemony against the bewildering and oftentimes frightening effects of Irish Catholic immigration.[33] For example, Portland's Wellington Lodge welcomed its largest initiate group since its inception in the meeting following the great Orange-Catholic riot of 12 July 1849.[34]

Membership lists also illuminated the Orange Order's effective appeal to native-born in Saint John and Portland. Data gleaned from official lodge returns, trial transcripts, Orange histories and newspapers yielded the names of eighty-four active Orange members in the late 1840s. When matched against the available 1851 manuscript census returns from Saint John County, they showed significant native involvement in Orangeism: 56 per cent were not Irish-born, including 43 per cent native and 13 per cent other Protestant immigrants.[35] Moreover, the entrenchment of Irish Protestants in the Orange Order was evident because 80 per cent of them had emigrated to New Brunswick prior to 1840. The occupational range already noted for provincial Orangemen was corroborated by the Saint John evidence, though a higher proportion of members could be classified as skilled or unskilled labourers. Finally, the portrait of Saint John Orangemen revealed a youthful organization: almost three-quarters of those traced were less than forty years old in 1851.[36] Clearly, the Orange Order in Saint John and Portland in mid-century represented a mixture of native-born and Protestant immigrants.

The essential ideological glue of the Orange Order was unquestioning loyalty to the Crown and an emphatic rejection of Roman Catholicism. With these concepts codified in the initiation oaths, Orangeism guaranteed itself a philosophical continuum that transcended the divergent social appeals and emphases of individual primary lodges.[37] In New Brunswick, lodges exercised a great deal of independence. Several accepted only temperate men; others attracted members by offering burial insurance plans; still more touted their commitment to charitable endeavours.[38] New Brunswick's Orange Lodges had disparate social and functional appeals, and many men gathered under the symbolic Orange banner. Except in the rare case where evidence exists, individual motives for joining the organization are a matter for speculation. Nevertheless, the philosophies and goals of Orangemen may be justifiably construed from organizational rhetoric and collective behaviour.

Orange rhetoric in the 1840s strikingly resembled the propaganda campaigns carried out by American and British nativists during the same period. New Brunswick Orangemen charged an elaborate counter-offensive to combat Irish Catholic immigration and permanent settlement. The organization's views were stated succinctly in two documents from the late 1840s. In a welcoming address to Lieutenant-Governor Edmund Head, Orangemen explained:

> Our chief objects are the union of Protestants of the several denominations, to counteract the encroachments of all men, sects or parties, who may at any time attempt the subversion of the Constitution, or the severance of these Colonies from the British Empire; to bind Protestants to the strict observance of the Laws, and to strengthen the bonds of the local authorities, by the knowledge that there is ever a band of loyal men ready in case of emergency, to obey their commands, and assist them in the maintenance of order.[39]

Thomas Hill, the zealous Orange editor of the *Loyalist and Conservative Advocate*, was more direct in his appraisal of the fraternity:

> Orangeism had its origins in the *necessity* of the case; it has spread in this Province, also from *necessity*, for had not the country been infested with gangs of lawless ruffians, whose numerous riots, and murderous deeds compelled Protestants to organize for mutual defence, Orangeism would have been scarcely known. And whenever the *Cause* shall disappear, Orangeism may retrograde.[40]

Underscored in the above quotations was the unique philosophical framework which Orangemen operated within: unquestioning loyalty, exclusive Protestantism and the threat to carry out their policies with vigilante force.

New Brunswick's Orangemen, in an effort to check the Irish Catholic invasion, fought a rhetorical battle on several fronts. The overarching goal was to maintain the colony as a Protestant and British bulwark against Catholicism. The Orange Order directly appealed to all Protestants who feared that the ethno-religious supremacy enjoyed by Anglo-Saxons would be permanently undermined or destroyed by the swelling numbers of Celtic Irishmen. Orangemen even advocated the repeal of legislation giving Catholics the franchise and the right to serve in the Legislature.[41]

Anti-Catholic diatribes grew in part from a Papal conspiracy myth that enjoyed a North American vogue in the mid nineteenth century.[42] New Brunswick's Orangemen claimed the famine immigration was but a skirmish in a global battle, masterminded in the Vatican, to expunge Protestantism from the earth. A Saint John editor who supported Orangeism warned that "A great, perhaps a final, conflict is at hand between Protestant Truth and Popery leagued with Infidelity."[43] Orangemen embarked on a propaganda campaign to educate Protestants about the Pope's despotic control over Catholics—in church, the home, the workplace and on the hustings. Only by removing the insidious network of priests, Orangemen argued, could papal control over the "uncivilized minds" of the Irish Catholics in New Brunswick be broken.[44]

Another vital weapon in the Orangemen's arsenal rested upon the assumption that the Celtic Irish were inherently an unruly and violent race. The stereotype had a measure of truth. As a subjugated people under English rule, Irish Catholics often resorted to disruptive tactics to achieve their goals.[45] As poor Irish Catholics crowded into squalid quarters in York Point and Portland, Orangemen bandied stereotypes of the Celtic propensity for strong drink and villainy. After all, they argued, "no one can deny that the lower orders of the Roman Catholic Irish are a quarrelsome, headstrong, turbulent, fierce, vindictive people."[46] Petty crime did increase dramatically as Saint John and Portland absorbed thousands of the famine immigrants, but it is more plausible to suggest that factors such as overcrowding, poverty and hunger were more responsible for creating a crucible for crime than were cultural idiosyncrasies.[47] Tragically, Orangemen painted all Catholics with the same nativist brush. Though even the most scurrilous propagandists recognized that not all immigrants participated in this orgy of crime, they nevertheless called for Orange vigilantism in York Point and Portland. Moreover, they suggested dispersing the immigrants among loyal Protestants. The theory was that such a dilution would facilitate social control and the assimilation of those immigrants who chose to remain. For the Orangemen of mid nineteenth-century Saint John, every Celtic Irishman was a potential criminal.[48]

New Brunswick's Orange rhetoric was also laced with racism, mirroring the contemporary British philosophy of Anglo-Saxon superiority.[49] Ethnicity was mingled with class as Orangemen railed against the "ignorant Mickie" hordes who formed a substandard "class of people." The destitution of famine immigrants as they disembarked in Saint John, and the squalour of their ghettos in York Point and Portland, appeared to corroborate Orange assertions of Celtic inferiority. Here was positive proof that the Protestant Anglo-Saxon must remain firmly in legislative and judicial control in order to assure the colony's peaceful survival.[50] The more zealous Orange propagandists, believing that assimilation was a bankrupt concept, called for the deportation of all Celtic Catholics.

One might as well, they argued, "attempt to change the colour of the Leopard's spots, or to 'wash the Ethiope white,' as to attempt to tame and civilize the wild, turbulent, irritable, savage, treacherous and hardened natives of the Cities and Mountains of Connaught and Munster."[51] The editors of the *Loyalist and Conservative Advocate*, the *Weekly Chronicle* and the *Christian Visitor*, all either Orange members or openly sympathetic to the organization's policies, regularly exposed their readers to racist editorials, Irish jokes, and vignettes pointing out the sub-human proclivities of the Celtic immigrant. Through their efforts, the argument of Anglo-Saxon racial superiority fell convincingly upon the ears of native Protestants who feared the demise of peace, order and good government in New Brunswick.[52]

Yet another focal point for Orange propagandists was the tangible threat that the poor Irish Catholic immigrants represented a formidable and willing pool of cheap labourers.[53] The famine victims, thrust into the severely depressed economy of the 1840s, were greeted as pariahs by Saint John's working classes. The destitute Irish Catholics eagerly accepted the most demanding and lowest-paying jobs, which in a healthy economic environment would be vacant. But during the "hungry forties," unemployed native labourers were forced to compete with the immigrants for these undesirable jobs.[54] In an attempt to combat the debilitating effects of immigrant competition, such as a general lowering of wage scales, Orangemen sounded the call for economic segregation. They suggested that Protestant merchants and employers should hire and do business only with co-religionists. By ostracizing Roman Catholic labourers, Orangemen hoped to persuade entrenched immigrants to leave and to discourage incoming Catholics from settling in the community.[55]

While Saint John's Orangemen fought a rigorous rhetorical battle, perhaps their most effective campaigns involved physical engagements with Irish Catholics. Indeed, collective social violence grew in direct proportion to the rising levels of famine immigration and Orange membership during the 1840s. In the aftermath of each confrontation, Orangemen enjoyed even greater Protestant support from natives and immigrants alike. The number of local lodges and engorged memberships at mid-century were tributes to the Orange Order's successful appeal. The persuasive rhetorical campaigns may have won converts, but the bloody riots gave concerned Protestants tangible "proof" of the Irish Catholics' uncivilized behaviour.

The first clearly identifiable incident of collective violence between Orangemen and Catholics in Saint John occurred on 12 July 1837. Small Catholic crowds forced entry into two merchants' stores and attempted to burn them.[56] In later years such incendiarism was eclipsed by more traditional rioting. The spring of 1841 found Irish Catholics clashing with Orangemen in the streets of Saint John. At issue was an Orange commemorative arch erected to celebrate the visit of a dignitary.[57] Catholics reacted similarly the following year on 12 July, when a crowd of several hundred gathered outside a Saint John home flying the Union Jack festooned with orange ribbons. Their jeers and taunts brought Orange reinforcements from across the city; by evening a general riot prompted Major William Black to swear in 150 special constables. The all-Protestant volunteer squad arrested several Irish Catholics, most of whom were ultimately found guilty of rioting.[58] Although these early disturbances paled when compared to subsequent riots, they established important patterns that would be repeated throughout the decade. While Irish Catholics would be deservedly or incorrectly labelled the aggressors, the Orangemen would invariably be perceived as the defenders of Saint John's Protestant and Loyalist traditions. Moreover, an exclusively Protestant constabulary and judiciary would consistently arrest and convict only Irish Catholics for disturbing the peace.

The next three years, coinciding with the first substantial waves of Irish Catholic immigrants and the attendant surge of Orangeism, brought several important episodes of social violence. The Twelfth of July in 1843 witnessed clashes between religious crowds in Saint John and Portland, though an official Orange procession was not held.[59] A more serious incident occurred in March of the following year. Squire Manks, Worshipful Master of the recently-established Wellington Orange Lodge, shot and mortally wounded a Catholic Irishman during a dispute at York Point. Angry residents poured into the streets and demanded revenge. Rather than being arrested, however, Manks was placed into protective custody and expeditiously exonerated by an examining board of city magistrates. The verdict was self-defence.[60] The year closed with sporadic riots from Christmas until after New Year's. Crowds of up to 300 Irish Catholics roamed throughout York Point and Portland's wharf district, attacking Orangemen and their property. The Orangemen enthusiastically reciprocated. Two companies of British regulars finally succeeded in quashing the disturbances, but not before one Catholic had died and dozens more from both sides had received serious injuries. Although uninvolved residents bemoaned the apparent state of anarchy, the rioting was neither indiscriminate nor uncontrolled. Catholics and Orangemen carefully picked fights only with "certain... obnoxious individuals."[61]

The tensions of the winter of 1844–45 culminated in a St. Patrick's Day riot that eclipsed all earlier Orange-Catholic conflicts in its violence. On 17 March 1845, Portland Orangemen fired without provocation upon a group of Catholic revellers. The incident touched off a wave of reprisals. By nightfall general rioting between Orangemen and Irish Catholics had spread throughout the wharf district and York Point. The fighting was most intense at the foot of Fort Howe Hill in Portland.[62] The rioters dispersed when British troops positioned an artillery piece near Portland's wharves. The ploy was at best symbolic, for the concentrated fighting abated in the evening when the well-armed Orangemen gained a measure of control over the streets. The riot killed at least one Catholic, although several bodies were probably secreted away for private burials. The tally of wounded was correspondingly high, with dozens of combatants being hurt seriously enough to warrant medical attention.[63]

The examinations and trials in the riot's aftermath followed the patterns established in 1842. Although authorities arrested several Orangemen, including two suspected of murder, Saint John's all-Protestant Grand Jury pre-emptively threw out their bills before the cases could be brought to trial. Instead the jury returned bills for several Irish Catholic rioters, two of whom were ultimately found guilty and sentenced. The swift vindication of Orangemen by the Grand Jury, despite an abundance of damaging testimony, illustrated the reluctance of Protestant authorities to condemn Orange violence and their continuing propensity to convict only Irish Catholics.[64]

Saint John and Portland escaped collective social violence for the next two years, but the hiatus did nothing to diminish enmity or foster peaceful linkages between Orangemen and Irish Catholics. The latter abstained from public displays on the St. Patrick's Days of 1846 and 1847. Orangemen quietly observed July 12 in their lodges in 1845; the following year they took a steamer to Gagetown for a procession with their brethren from Queens, Kings and York Counties.[65] For 1847's Twelfth of July, when famine immigration was reaching its zenith, city Orangemen invited neighbouring brethren and staged the largest procession since the organization's inception. On 14 July a Saint John newspaper trumpeted the now-familiar requiem for the Orange holiday: "Dreadful Riot! The Disaffected District [York Point] Again in Arms—Shots Fired—Several Persons Dreadfully Wounded—the Military Called Out."[66] The two-year truce had yielded only larger numbers of Catholic immigrants and nativist Orangemen, and a more sophisticated network for the combatants in both groups to utilize in battle.

July 12 started quietly enough in 1847, but as Saint John's and Portland's Orangemen began to make their way to their lodges, crowds of wary Irish Catholics spilled into the streets. One of the larger Portland lodges, probably Wellington, entertained the amateur band from the local Mechanic's Institute. All of the band members were Orangemen. In the early evening, the group led a procession of Orangemen and onlookers through the streets of Portland, across the bridge, and into the heart of the Roman Catholic ghetto at York Point.[67] The tunes they played, like most Orange favourites, were clearly offensive to Irish Catholics.[68] At the foot of Dock Street, the crowd attacked the procession with sticks and bricks, smashing many of the band's instruments and forcing the revellers to flee back across the Portland Bridge. Gathering reinforcements and firearms from their lodges and homes, the undaunted Orangemen quickly returned to their enemy's stronghold.[69]

The Irish Catholic crowd, which by now had grown to several hundred, also made use of the respite and collected weapons in the event of a reappearance of the humiliated band members and Orangemen. The buttressed Orange legions did attempt to revive the procession and music when they reached York Point. A battle was inevitable. Volleys of shots from both parties shattered the summer air, leaving scores of wounded lying in the streets along the procession route. The melee continued throughout the evening, with most of the bloodshed occurring along Dock and Mill Streets and the bridge. At midnight detachments of the 33rd Regiment, dispatched at the mayor's request, converged upon York Point only to find the streets deserted. Rather than chance an engagement with the military, both sides ceased hostilities.[70] Aided by the darkness, the Irish Catholics escaped capture and returned to their homes. The constabulary failed to make any arrests after the riot, and the grand jury issued no warrants.[71]

Assessment of the riot's severity is hampered due to the secretive removal of the dead and wounded by both parties, particularly the Irish Catholics. Official tallies included only one Catholic killed and several seriously wounded, but everyone involved knew that many had died during the encounter.[72] The significance of the conflict, however, emerged unclouded in the following months. Both sides were organized, well-stocked with weapons and clearly prepared to kill for their beliefs. Catholics had gathered hours before the Orange procession had entered York Point; they were motivated by a desire to "defend" their "territory." Orangemen consciously provoked the enemy by twice marching in procession and playing obnoxious songs through the most Catholic district of Saint John. An undeniable linkage also emerged between the Orange Order and the Mechanic's Institute, which was symbolic of the nativist attraction that Orangeism had to the economically beleaguered Protestant workers facing stiff competition from famine immigrants. Finally, the riot underscored the Orange belief in vigilante justice. The procession's return to York Point represented a "heroic" action to remove a dangerous Catholic "mob" from Saint John's thoroughfares. According to Orange sympathizers, the anaemic state of the city's constabulary justified the vigilantism.[73] In retrospect, the riot of 1847 illuminated the entrenchment of social violence as a perennial method of interaction between Orangemen and Catholics.[74]

A year of bloody skirmishes was the riot's true legacy, for neither side had emerged with a clearcut victory on the Twelfth. A wave of assaults and murders swept Saint John and Portland during the weeks that followed; Orange and Catholic vengeance was the motive for all of them.[75] A sensational series of witness examinations after the murder of a suspected Orangeman in September brought religious antipathy to a fever pitch. Dozens of testimonials exposed paramilitary networks operated by militant Orangemen and Catholics. Personal revenge on a small scale appeared to be the favourite tactic of the weaker and outnumbered Catholics. Orangemen, enjoying the support of a Protestant majority, preferred a collective vigilantism whereby they dispensed extralegal justice while acting as an unofficial watchdog of the Irish lower orders.[76] By the year's end, it was apparent that the Orange-Catholic struggle had not diminished. Both sides habitually armed themselves if they ventured into unfriendly districts; each tried desperately to identify its most virulent enemies, and in many cases, both were prepared to kill for their causes.

The religious conflict of the 1840s peaked two years later in Saint John's worst riot of the nineteenth century. The city was quiet in 1848, much as it had been in 1846, because local Orangemen travelled to Fredericton to participate in a massive demonstration.[77] But as the Twelfth approached in 1849, Saint John's Orangemen advertised for the first time their plans for hosting provincial brethren and sponsoring an elaborate procession.[78] Motivated by vivid memories of the inconclusive 1847 conflict, Orangemen and Irish Catholics grimly prepared themselves for battle. On the eve of the holiday, Mayor Robert D. Wilmot met with local Orange officials and asked them to voluntarily abandon their plans to march. But the Orangemen, well-versed on their rights, rejected the suggestion because no provincial statute gave civilian officials the authority to ban public processions.[79] The march, they insisted, would proceed as planned.

With a measure of fatalism, Saint John prepared for the occasion. While Orangemen from Carleton, York, Kings and Queens Counties were boarding steamers and carriages for Saint John, Irish Catholics were buying arms and ammunition. Shopkeepers along Prince William Street, King Street and Market Square boarded their windows and decided to declare the day a business holiday.[80] Early on the morning of the Twelfth, hundreds of Orangemen from Saint John and Portland collected at Nethery's Hotel on Church Street and marched to a nearby wharf to greet the Carleton ferry. Among the disembarking brethren was Joseph Corum, the Senior Deputy Grand Master of the New Brunswick Grand Lodge. As the procession leader, Corum would have the honour of representing King William by riding a white horse. The Orangemen came heavily armed with pistols, muskets and sabres. After assuming a military file, they began the march to the Portland suburb of Indiantown where they would meet the steamer bringing reinforcements from the northern counties. Their planned route would take them through both Irish Catholic bastions—York Point and Portland's wharf district.[81]

Upon reaching York Point they encountered a large pine arch, symbolically green, which spanned the foot of Mill Street. Several hundred jeering Irish Catholics clustered near the arch's supporting poles; they implored the Orangemen to continue. Outnumbered for the moment, the Orangemen accepted the humiliation and dipped their banners as they passed under the arch. While a few stones were hurled at the Orangemen, and they responded with warning shots, no fighting broke out.[82] Without further incident, the procession reached Indiantown where it gratefully welcomed scores of reinforcements. Among the newcomers was another pivotal Orange leader. George Anderson, a Presbyterian grocer and primary lodge master, was a veteran of several disturbances in his home town of Fredericton. Anderson, bedecked with a sword that indicated his rank, assumed a position next to Corum at the column's head. The procession now numbered approximately 600 people. The men were heavily armed, the majority carrying muskets on shoulder straps. A few clutched axes that would be used to destroy the green bough when they returned to York

Point. Finally, a wagon filled with weapons and supplies took up a station at the rear of the procession. As the Orangemen made their way back to York Point, Portland inhabitants observed that the procession resembled a confident army about to engage in battle.[83]

In the meantime, authorities attempted to alleviate the growing tensions with three separate plans, all of which would ultimately fail to prevent a conflict. Mayor Wilmot's first scheme was to defuse the powder keg by removing the pine arch and dispersing the Catholic crowd in York Point. Wilmot, accompanied by a magistrate and a constable, was physically rebuffed in this endeavour by a cohesive, territorially-minded crowd that chanted "Stay off our ground!" He then dispatched Jacob Allan, the Portland police magistrate, to intercept the Orangemen before they reached York Point.[84] Allan asked Corum and Anderson to bypass the Catholic district by using the longer Valley Road on their approach to Saint John. After conferring with their followers, the leaders rejected Allan's suggestion. Their men had suffered humiliation during the morning's passage under the Catholic arch; now they insisted on "Death or Victory."[85] Wilmot borrowed the third and final plan from Saint John's history of dealing with riots. At his request, sixty British soldiers stationed themselves in Market Square to prevent general rioting. While the choice of location would do nothing to prevent a conflict, for Market Square lay to the south of York Point and the Orangemen would enter from the north over the Portland Bridge, it would serve to contain the battle to the Catholic ghetto. The detachment's failure to position itself between the advancing Orangemen and the offensive arch, when it had ample time to do so, raised questions about the sincerity of the authorities' attempts to prevent bloodshed.[86]

General rioting broke out along Mill Street before the procession arrived at the bough. The Catholic crowd now numbered approximately 500, and like the Orangemen, many had armed themselves with muskets. Reports of who fired the first shots varied, but roofers working on a Mill Street building agreed that Orangemen opened fire after being met with a volley of stones and brickbats.[87] Several Catholics lay wounded or dying after the barrage, and then their guns answered the Orangemen's. A heated battle ensued. Men and women along Mill Street threw anything they could at the better-armed Orange contingent. Some engaged in fistfights with individuals that they were able to pull from the Orange ranks. Corum struggled to free himself after a handful of Irishmen grabbed his horse's tether. A dozen Catholics captured the wagon filled with arms and gave its driver a sound thrashing. Hundreds of shots were fired, and at least twelve combatants lost their lives. The Irish Catholics suffered most of the casualties. After several minutes of furious fighting, the Orangemen emerged from York Point. As they headed for the safety of the troops, their procession was still intact.[88]

The British garrison, after remaining stationary in Market Square throughout the heat of the battle, went into action as soon as the Orangemen left the Irish Catholic ghetto. Without firing a shot, the soldiers marched past the procession and positioned themselves on Dock Street to seal off the Catholic district. This manoeuvre effectively doused what remained of the conflict.[89] It also gave the Orangemen the opportunity to continue their procession unmolested, for any Catholics wishing to leave York Point in pursuit would have to contend first with the soldiers. The Orangemen, heady with their successful assault on the enemy's territory, proceeded through Market and King Squares and made a circle through the city's centre. Only when they entered Market Square again, with the intention of parading through York Point for the third time, were the troops commanded to impede their progress. Being satisfied with their efforts, the Orangemen agreed to disband. With the Orange threat finally removed, the Irish Catholics waiting in York Point also dispersed. The great Saint John riot of 1849 was over.[90]

The riot's judicial aftermath followed patterns well-established by 1849, although there was one notable exception. At Lieutenant-Governor Edmund Head's insistence, the Saint John Grand Jury served warrants on Orange participants as well as the Catholics. This attempt at impartiality was severely undermined, however, by a prejudiced investigative team that included the prominent Orangeman W.H. Needham.[91] Ultimately, all but five of the bills against Orangemen, including those for Corum, Anderson and eighteen others, were dropped before the defendants reached trial. The five Orangemen who actually stood in the dock were swiftly declared innocent by a jury that remained seated. Much to the prosecution's dismay, the jury ignored recent provincial legislation that clearly outlawed armed public processions.[92] For the Irish Catholics, on the other hand, the judicial pattern of the 1840s remained intact. Of the twenty-four implicated, six were tried on assault charges, one for attempted murder and four for unlawful assembly. Two were eventually found guilty, including the alleged "ringleader" who led the defence of the green arch. John Haggerty, immigrant labourer and father of three, would spend his sixty-third birthday in the provincial penitentiary while serving his one-year sentence for assault.[93]

The 1849 riot signalled an end to collective social conflict between Orangemen and Catholics, although small skirmishes would continue for years.[94] Various factors brought about this extended truce, the most important being the hegemony established by Orangemen in Saint John and Portland. In a sense, Orangemen had won the battle of the 1840s. The Irish Catholics' attempts to check the growth of Orangeism with counter-demonstrations had failed. They undeniably suffered the most casualties in the course of the riots. Moreover, a fusion between all levels of authority and the Orange Order had taken place. Orangemen, constables and British soldiers had combined to contain every major disturbance within the Irish Catholic ghettos of York Point and Portland. The Orange Order became an acceptable accomplice for the maintenance of social control. A double standard had clearly emerged: authorities found Orange vigilantism preferable to "mob rule" by the Irish Catholic "lower order."[95] During the 1840s Orangemen served as constables, magistrates and legislative representatives.

Excepting one active magistrate in Saint John, the Irish Catholics were excluded from power. This inequity profoundly shaped law enforcement during the riots and trials. No Catholic would be allowed to sit on juries; moreover, only Irish Catholics would be found guilty of rioting offences. Even when Orangemen stood in the dock, such as after the York Point riot of 1849, they were expeditiously exonerated.[96] Ethnicity and religion targeted the Irish Catholics for suppression during the 1840s; meanwhile Orangeism developed into an unofficial arm of social control to protect the Protestant majority.

New Brunswick's improved economic environment after mid-century contributed to the demise of collective conflict by alleviating some of the fierce competition between immigrants and natives. The "Hungry Forties" had indeed been more than a historical cliché to many colonists. A sustained depression had brought scarcities of goods, food and services. Natives had competed with Irish Catholic immigrants for limited jobs, a factor that had contributed to the rapid growth of Orangeism. Economic variables alone did not cause the Orange-Green riots, but they certainly helped to account for a foundation of social tension.[97] As the province successfully weathered the English transition to free trade in the 1850s, investment capital increased and jobs became more available.[98] Thus Orangemen found one of the key elements of their rhetorical campaign against Irish Catholics undermined. Ultimately, fuller employment fostered better relations between Protestant and Catholic workers.

Another factor in the disappearance of perennial disturbances between Protestants and Catholics was the Orange Order's discontinuance of July 12 processions while it fought for provincial incorporation. Saint John and Portland Orangemen wisely decided not to risk any negative publicity that might accompany collective violence with Irish Catholics while the bill was being debated in the New Brunswick legislature. The process lasted 25 years, but eventually the trade-off of abstention for legitimacy proved fruitful.[99] Not until after the bill finally passed in 1875, in the midst of the emotional separate schools issue, would Orangemen again take to Saint John's streets to display their fervent brand of loyalty and Protestantism.[100]

Finally, a drastic reduction in the number of Irish Catholic immigrants after 1848 helped to subdue the nativist impulse. The tide of famine immigrants had dropped as precipitously as it had risen. Improving conditions in Ireland accounted for a general reduction in emigrants, especially from the poorer Catholic counties. In addition a discriminatory immigration policy, instituted at the behest of Lieutenant-Governors Sir William Colebrooke and Sir Edmund Head, curtailed Catholic immigration while it increased the number of more desirable Protestant settlers from the British Isles.[101] The results were striking: between 1851 and 1861 the percentages of Irish compared to the total immigrant population dropped dramatically in both Saint John and Portland. This decrease also reflected the continuing out-migration of transient Catholics to the "Boston States" and to other British North American provinces.[102] Finally, it indicated the beginnings of a process of acculturation; the sons and daughters of Catholic and Protestant immigrants would be listed as New Brunswickers in the 1861 census. The "soldiers" of the 1840s—both Orange and Green—would be supplanted by generations to whom the violent experiences of the "Hungry Forties" would be historical anecdotes.

The Orange Order was New Brunswick's institutionalized nativist response to Irish Catholic immigration during the 1840s. Prior to this decade, the organization was a small and mostly invisible fraternal order dominated by Irish Protestant immigrants and British garrison troops. As Irish Catholic famine victims poured into Saint John and Portland during the 1840s, however, Protestant natives and non-Irish-born immigrants joined the Orange Order. Orangemen spearheaded a rhetorical campaign to combat the famine immigration, using anti-Catholic and racist propaganda to discourage the Irish from settling permanently in the city. Additionally, the Orange Order increasingly acted as a paramilitary vigilante group that freely engaged in riots with bellicose Irish Catholics. The combination of nativist rhetoric and a mutual willingness to engage in armed conflict provided a decade of collective social violence that culminated in the tragic riot of 12 July 1849. Thus Saint John and Portland, like several eastern seaboard cities in the United States, experienced a strong nativist impulse and several destructive episodes of social violence.

Notes

1. *Weekly Chronicle* (Saint John), 22 March 1839.

2. *Morning News* (Saint John), 24 September 1847.

3. For this study, social violence is defined as "assault upon an individual or his property solely or primarily because of his membership in a social category." See Allen D. Grimshaw, "Interpreting Collective Violence: An Argument for the Importance of Social Structure," in James F. Short, Jr. and Marvin E. Wolfgang, eds., *Collective Violence* (Chicago, 1972), pp. 12, 18–20.

4 Sir Edmund Head to Lord Grey, 15 July 1849, Colonial Office Series [CO] 188, Public Record Office [PRO], London: *Royal Gazette* (Fredericton), 19 September 1849; D.R. Jack, *Centennial Prize Essay on the History of the City and County of St. John* (Saint John, 1883), pp. 136–37; Reverend J.W. Millidge. "Reminiscences of St. John from 1849 to 1860," *New Brunswick Historical Society Collections*, Vol. IV (1919), pp. 8, 127.

5. Its mid-century population stood at 23,000, making one in every 8.5 New Brunswickers a Saint John resident. Portland, with 8,500 inhabitants, was roughly one-third the size of Saint John. See New Brunswick Census, 1851, Provincial Archives of New Brunswick [PANB].

6. Presentment of the Saint John Grand Jury, 27 October 1847, Minutes, Saint John General Sessions, PANB.

7. *Morning News*, 8, 11 September 1843; Abraham Gesner, *New Brunswick: With Notes for Emigrants* (London, 1847), pp. 122–24: Reverend W.C. Atkinson, *A Historical and Statistical Account of New Brunswick, B.N.A. with Advice to Emigrants* (Edinburgh, 1844), pp. 28–29, 36–37.

8. The 1840s was a particularly depressed decade, but as Graeme Wynn eloquently pointed out, the colony was already a veteran of the nineteenth-century boom and bust "bandalore"; in 1819, 1825 and 1837, New Brunswick suffered trade depressions due to financial downturns and the erosion of speculation capital in Great Britain: *Timber Colony: A Historical Geography of Early Nineteenth Century New Brunswick* (Toronto, 1981), pp. 3–33, 43–53. See also P.D. McClelland, "The New Brunswick Economy in the Nineteenth Century," *Journal of Economic History, XXV* (December, 1965), pp. 686–90.

9. W.S. MacNutt, *New Brunswick, a History, 1784–1867* (Toronto, 1963), pp. 283–84, 296: MacNutt, "New Brunswick's Age of Harmony: The Administration of Sir John Harvey," *Canadian Historical Review, XXXII* (June 1951), pp. 123–24; D.G.G. Kerr, *Sir Edmund Head: The Scholarly Governor* (Toronto, 1954), pp. 39–54; Wynn, *Timber Colony*, pp. 43–44, 51–53.

10. *Colonial Advocate* (Saint John), 14 July 1845; MacNutt, *New Brunswick*, p. 285; Wynn, *Timber Colony*, pp. 51–53.

11. *New Brunswick Reporter* (Fredericton), 13 October 1848, 24 August 1849; *Morning News*, 28 May 1849; Wynn, *Timber Colony*, pp. 150–55; MacNutt, *New Brunswick*, p. 320.

12. Immigration Returns, New Brunswick Blue Books, 1832–50. Public Archives of Canada [PAC]: "Report on Trade and Navigation." *Journal of the House of Assembly of New Brunswick*, 1866.

13. Only in 1853, after the famine abated in Ireland, would English immigrants once again become the largest group. See New Brunswick Census, 1851: "Report on Trade and Navigation," *Journal of the House of Assembly of New Brunswick*, 1866; William F. Ganong, *A Monograph of the Origins of Settlements in the Province of New Brunswick* (Ottawa, 1904), pp. 90–120.

14. Cecil Woodham-Smith, *The Great Hunger: Ireland 1845–9* (London, 1962), pp. 206–9; Lawrence J. McCaffrey, *The Irish Diaspora in America* (Bloomington, Ind., 1976), pp. 59–62; William Forbes Adams, *Ireland and Irish Emigration to the New World* (New York, 1932); Donald Akenson, ed., *Canadian Papers in Rural History*, Vol. III (Gananoque, Ont., 1981), pp. 219–21.

15. Woodham-Smith, *Great Hunger*, pp. 29, 206–13; John I. Cooper, "Irish Immigration and the Canadian Church Before the Middle of the Nineteenth Century." *Journal of the Canadian Church Historical Society*, II (May 1955), pp. 13–14; Adams, *Ireland and Irish Emigration*; McCaffrey, *Irish Diaspora*, pp. 59–62; Oliver MacDonagh, "Irish Emigration to the United States of America and the British Colonies During the Famine," in R. Dudley Edwards and T. Desmond Williams, eds., *The Great Famine: Studies in Irish History 1845–52* (Dublin, 1956), pp. 332–39.

16. Immigration Returns, New Brunswick Blue Books, PAC; M.H. Perley's Report on 1846 Emigration, in William Colebrooke to Grey, 29 December 1846, CO 188.

17. *Ibid.: Royal Gazette*, 17 March, 7 July 1847; *Saint John Herald*, 12 November 1845; James Hannay, *History of New Brunswick* (Saint John, 1909), Vol. II, p. 70; MacDonagh, "Irish Emigration," pp. 368–73; Adams, *Ireland and Irish Emigration*, p. 234; Woodham-Smith, *Great Hunger*, pp. 209–10.

18. New Brunswick Census, 1851, 1861; *Morning News*, 8, 11 September 1843; Alexander Monro, *New Brunswick: With a Brief Outline of Nova Scotia, and Prince Edward Island* (Halifax, 1855), p. 125; James S. Buckingham, *Canada, Nova Scotia, New Brunswick, and the Other British Provinces in North America* (London, 1843), pp. 409–10.

19. Kings Ward, which included all of York Point and was roughly equal in size to the other Saint John wards, had twice the population of any ward in the 1851 New Brunswick Census. For descriptions of York Point, see Grand Jury Reports, 16 December 1848. Minutes, Saint John General Sessions, PANB, and D.H. Waterbury, "Retrospective Ramble Over Historic St. John," *New Brunswick Historical Society Collections*, Vol. IV (1919), pp. 86–88.

20. Colebrooke to Grey, 28 January 1848, CO 188; Gesner, *New Brunswick*, p. 124.

21. John Higham, *Strangers in the Land: Patterns of American Nativism 1860–1925* (New Brunswick, N.J., 1955), pp. 3–4; Higham, "Another Look at Nativism," *Catholic Historical Review*, XLIV (July 1958), pp. 148–50.

22. For examples of Canadian nativist studies, see Howard Palmer, *Land of the Second Chance: A History of Ethnic Groups in Southern Alberta* (Lethbridge, 1972); Palmer, "Nativism and Ethnic Tolerance in Alberta: 1920–1972," Ph.D. thesis, York University, 1974; Simon Evans, "Spatial Bias in the Incidence of Nativism: Opposition to Hutterite Expansion in Alberta," *Canadian Ethnic Studies*, Vol. VI, Nos. 1–2 (1974), pp. 1–16.

23. *Loyalist and Conservative Advocate* (Saint John), 13 August 1847. See also issues from 20, 27 August 1847.

24. For histories of the Orange Order, see Hereward Senior, *Orangeism in Ireland and Britain 1765–1836* (London, 1966), especially pp. 4–21, 194–206; Senior, "The Early Orange Order 1795–1870," in T. Desmond Williams, ed., *Secret Societies in Ireland* (Dublin, 1973); Peter Gibbon, "The Origins of the Orange Order and the United Irishmen," *Economy and Society*, I (1972), pp. 134–63.

25. Canadian Orange Order histories include Cecil Houston and W.J. Smyth, *The Sash Canada Wore: A Historical Geography of the Orange Order in Canada* (Toronto, 1980); Hereward Senior, *Orangeism: The Canadian Phase* (Toronto, 1972); Senior, "The Genesis of Canadian Orangeism," *Ontario History*, LX (June 1968), pp. 13–29.

26. James McNichol's report, *Loyal Orange Association Report, 1886* (Toronto, 1886), *Sentinel*, 3 July 1930; J. Edward Steele, comp., *History and Directory of the Provincial Grand Orange Lodge and Primary Lodges of New Brunswick* (Saint John, 1934), p. 11.

27. Miscellaneous Orange documents, courtesy of Professor Peter Toner, University of New Brunswick at Saint John; James McNichol's report, *Loyal Orange Association Report*, 1886; Steele, *History of the Orange Lodges of New Brunswick*, pp. 11, 17–21; Houston and Smyth, *The Sash Canada Wore*, pp. 69–70.

28. Lodge returns, in *Minutes of the Grand Orange Lodge of New Brunswick* (various publishers, 1846–53); *Annual Reports of the Grand Orange Lodge of the Loyal Orange Association of B.N.A.* [various publishers, 1846–50]; *New Brunswick Reporter*, 10 May 1850; *Loyalist*, 8 June 1848; *Carleton Sentinel* (Woodstock), 15 July 1854; *Sentinel*, 3 July 1930; Steele, *History of the Orange Lodges of New Brunswick*, pp. 11–13, 37–39, 53–55, 59.

29. Because Nova Scotia's lodges, who received their warrants directly from New Brunswick, were only two years old in mid-century, the vast majority of the 10,000 members resided in New Brunswick. See "Minutes of the Grand Orange Lodge of New Brunswick and Nova Scotia," in *Weekly Chronicle*, 6 July 1849; Orange Order documents, Peter Toner; *Minutes of the Grand Orange Lodge of New Brunswick*, 1846–50; *Sentinel*, 3 July 1930.

30. Correspondence from John Earle in *Annual Report of the Grand Orange Lodge of the Loyal Orange Association of B.N.A.*, 1851; *New Brunswick Reporter*, 26 April 1850; Head to Grey, 7 September 1847, CO 188; *New Brunswick Courier* (Saint John), 25 July 1840; Steele, *History of the Orange Lodge of New Brunswick*, p. 11.

31. Houston and Smyth, *The Sash Canada Wore*, pp. 70–72; Steele, *History of the Orange Lodges of New Brunswick*, pp. 115–18.

32. "Minutes of the Organizational Meeting of the Grand Orange Lodge of New Brunswick, 1844," in Steele, *History of the Orange Lodges of New Brunswick*, p. 11; New Brunswick Census, 1851.

33. James Brown letters to *New Brunswick Reporter*, 28 April, 5, 12 May 1848; *Morning News*, 18 July 1849; John Earle's correspondence in *Annual Report of the Grand Orange Lodge of the Loyal Orange Association of B.N.A.*, 1851.

34. Minute book, Wellington Orange Lodge, Portland. New Brunswick Museum (NBM), Saint John.

35. 1851 manuscript census returns from Saint John County are incomplete. Returns from only four of the city's wards are extant: Kings, Dukes, Sydney and Queens. Records from Portland Parish and Carleton are missing.

36. Returns for Saint John County, New Brunswick Manuscript Census, 1851, PANB; Orange documents, including dispensations and lodge returns, Peter Toner; *Minutes of the Grand Orange Lodge of New Brunswick*, 1846–55; Evidence, Saint John Riot Trials, Documents, New Brunswick Executive Council Records, PANB; New Brunswick Supreme Court Documents, PANB. The newspapers consulted were the *Loyalist, Weekly Chronicle* and *Morning News* for the 1840s, as well as the *Daily Sun* (Saint John), 13 July 1897, and Steele, *History of the Orange Lodges of New Brunswick*.

37. *Laws and Ordinances of the Orange Association of British North America* (Toronto, 1840), p. 11; *The Orange Question Treated by Sir Francis Hincks and the London "Times"* (Montreal, 1877).

38. For example, Portland's Wellington Lodge attempted to combat negative publicity after a decade of social violence by declaring itself a "benefit" organization in 1851. See Minute Book, Wellington Orange Lodge, NBM. See also *Rules and Regulations of the Orange Institution of British North America* (Toronto, 1838), p. 5; Steele, *History of the Orange Lodges of New Brunswick*.

39. *Morning News*, 24 January 1849; *Headquarters* (Fredericton), 24 January 1849.

40. *Loyalist*, 1 October 1847.

41. *Minutes of the Grand Orange Lodge of New Brunswick*, 1852; Rev. Gilbert Spurr's address to Orangemen, in *Loyalist*, 15 October 1847; Head to Grey, 26 July 1848, CO 188; *New Brunswick Reporter*, 26 October 1849; *Carleton Sentinel*, 2 July 1850; *Weekly Chronicle*, 15 July 1842, 4 February 1848; *Christian Visitor* (Saint John), 8 March 1848; Steele, *History of the Orange Lodges of New Brunswick*, pp. 13–15, 21.

42. For discussions of the papal conspiracy theory in North America, see S.M. Lipset and Earl Raab, *The Politics of Unreason* (New York, 1970), pp. 47–59. David B. Davis, "Some Themes of Counter-Subversion: An Analysis of Anti-Masonic, Anti-Catholic, and Anti-Mormon Literature," *Mississippi Valley Historical Review*, XLVII (September, 1960), pp. 205–7, Higham, *Strangers in the Land*, pp. 5–6.

43. *Church Witness* (Saint John), 21 September 1853.

44. *Minutes of the Grand Orange Lodge of New Brunswick*, 1846–55, particularly S.H. Gilbert's sermon in 1854; Grand Orange Lodge of New Brunswick's address to Queen Victoria, in Head to Grey, 28 April 1851, CO 188; *New Brunswick Reporter*, 9 April 1850; *Carleton Sentinel*, 16 July 1850; *New Brunswick Reporter*, 1 October 1847; *Weekly Chronicle*, 31 August 1849, 18 July 1851; *Loyalist*, 24 September 1847; *Church Witness*, 16 July, 13 August 1851, 6 July 1853.

45. Adams, *Ireland and Irish Emigration*, pp. 363–64; Carl Wittke, *The Irish in America* (Baton Rouge, La., 1956), pp. 46–47; Kenneth Duncan, "Irish Famine Immigration and the Social Structure of Canada West," *Canadian Review of Sociology and Anthropology*, II (February, 1965), pp. 33, 39.

46. *Loyalist*, 6 April 1848.

47. Alexander McHarg Diary, NBM; *Morning News*, 8 January, 8 December 1841, 6 January, 14 June 1843, 5 January 1848; *Weekly Chronicle*, 5 January, 28 June 1844, 26 November 1847; Queen vs. David Nice, New Brunswick Supreme Court Documents, PANB.

48. *Loyalist*, 30 March 1848; *New Brunswick Reporter*, 20 April 1850; *New Brunswick Assembly Debates*, 8 March 1850, PANB; *Morning News*, 24 January 1849; *Loyalist*, 16 July, 15, 28 October, 4 November 1847; *New Brunswick Reporter*, 19 November 1847, 15 March 1850; *Morning News*, 11 August 1847.

49. For excellent studies of racism in the British Isles, see L.P. Curtis, Jr., *Anglo-Saxons and Celts: A Study of Anti-Irish Prejudice in Victorian England* (Bridgeport, Conn., 1968), pp. 8–9, 24–26, and *Apes and Angels: The Irishman in Victorian Caricature* (Devon, England, 1971), *passim*.

50. *Weekly Chronicle*, 31 August, 28 September 1849; *Loyalist*, 24 September 1847.

51. *Loyalist*, 1 October, 11 November 1847.

52. *New Brunswick Reporter*, 10 May 1850; *Loyalist*, 16 July, 17 September, 15 October 1847; *Weekly Chronicle*, 29 July 1842.

53. The theme of competition between immigrant labourers and nativists in North America is explored in Oscar Handlin, *Boston's Immigrants* (Cambridge, Mass., 1959), pp. 180–87. Higham, *Strangers in the Land*, p. 57. Adams, *Ireland and Irish Emigration*, p. 353.

54. M.H. Perley's Report on 1846 Emigration, in Colebrooke to Grey, 29 December 1846, CO 188; *Royal Gazette*, 17 March, 7 July 1847; Wynn, *Timber Colony*, pp. 155–56; Kathryn Johnston, "The History of St. John, 1837–1867: Civic and Economic," Honours thesis, Mount Allison University, 1953, pp. 24–28.

55. *Loyalist*, 24 March 1845, 17 September, 28 October, 4 November, 9, 23 December 1847; *New Brunswick Reporter*, 10 September 1847; *New Brunswick Reporter*, 19 November 1847.

56. Joseph Brown to R.F. Hazen, 11 July 1837. R.F. Hazen Papers, NBM: *Weekly Chronicle*, 14 July, 1837.

57. *New Brunswick Reporter*, 26 April, 10 May 1850.

58. *Morning News*, 13 July, 5 August 1842; *Weekly Chronicle*, 15 July, 12 August 1842; *New Brunswick Courier*, 16 July, 13, 27 August 1842; Minutes, Saint John General Sessions, 9, 10, 17 December 1842, 25 March 1843, PANB; *Sentinel*, 29 October 1891.

59. *New Brunswick Reporter*, 26 April 1850.

60. Mayor Lauchlan Donaldson to Alfred Reade, 8 March 1844, New Brunswick Supreme Court Documents, PANB; McHarg Diary; *Morning News*, 5 April 1844.

61. *Weekly Chronicle*, 3 January 1845; *Morning News*, 3 January 1845; *Headquarters*, 8 January 1845; McHarg Diary.

62. Donaldson to Reade, 29 March 1845, Saint John Grand Jury to Colebrooke, 27 March 1845, "Riots and Disasters." New Brunswick Executive Council Records [Executive Council Records], PANB; *Loyalist*, 24 March 1845; *Weekly Chronicle*, 21 March 1845.

63. Minutes, New Brunswick Executive Council, 7 April 1845, PANB; Report of Doctors Robert and William Bayard, 17 March 1845. "Riots and Disasters." Executive Council Records: McHarg Diary; *Weekly Chronicle*, 21 March 1845; *Morning News*, 19 March 1845; *Observer* (Saint John), 18 March 1845; *New Brunswick Reporter*, 21 March 1845; *New Brunswick Courier*, 22 March 1845; *Loyalist*, 24 March 1845.

64. Minutes, Saint John General Sessions, 20, 22, 26 March, 14 June 1845; Donaldson to Reade, 22 March 1845. "Riots and Disasters." Executive Council Records: *New Brunswick Courier*, 5 July 1845; *Saint John Herald*, 2 July 1845.

65. *Minutes of the Grand Orange Lodge of New Brunswick*, 1847; *Weekly Chronicle*, 17 July 1846.

66. *Morning News*, 14 July 1847.

67. Orange supporters tried to disassociate the Orange Order, the Mechanic's Institute Band and the crowd that followed the procession. *The Loyalist*, 16 July 1847, claimed that the band had nothing to do with the Orange procession, while Clarence Ward made the dubious assertion that the Orange entourage consisted of "children." See "Old Times in St. John—1847." *Saint John Globe*, 1 April 1911, p. 8. Yet an article in the *Orange Sentinel*, 29 October 1891, proudly revealed that all the band members were Orangemen.

68. For examples of these songs, see *The Sentinel Orange and Patriotic Song Book* (Toronto, 1930?) and R. McBride, ed., *The Canadian Orange Minstrel for 1860. Contains Nine New and Original Songs, Mostly All of Them Showing Some Wrong that Affects the Order or the True Course of Protestant Loyalty to the British Crown* (London, 1860). Note particularly "Croppies Lie Down," a nineteenth century favourite of Orangemen in Europe and North America.

69. *New Brunswick Courier*, 17 July 1847; *Morning News*, 14 July 1847; *Loyalist*, 16 July 1847; *Sentinel*, October 1891; McHarg Diary.

70. *Morning News*, 14 July 1847; Colebrooke to Grey, 30 July 1847, Documents, Executive Council Records, PANB; McHarg Diary *New Brunswick Courier*, 17 July 1847; *Loyalist*, 16 July 1847; Ward, "Old Times in St. John—1847."

71. *New Brunswick Courier*, 7 August 1847.

72. Colebrooke to Grey, 30 July 1847, CO 188; *Morning News*, 14 July 1847.

73. *Loyalist*, 16 July 1847; Ward, "Old Times in St. John—1847."

74. One newspaper referred to it as a "civil war," *Morning News*, 14 July 1847.

75. *New Brunswick Courier*, 24 July 1847; *Morning News*, 14, 21, 23, 28 July 1847; *Loyalist*, 23 July 1847; *Weekly Chronicle*, 30 July 1847.

76. Queen vs. Dennis McGovern, 7–17 September 1847. New Brunswick Supreme Court Documents, PANB. Note especially the testimonies of Thomas Clark, James Clark, Ezekiel Downey and Edward McDermott. See also *Morning News*, 24 January 1848, *Weekly Chronicle*, 10 September 1847, *New Brunswick Courier*, 11 September 1847; *Loyalist*, 10 September 1847; *Morning News*, 8 September 1847.

77. *Weekly Chronicle*, 14 July 1848. Fredericton's Orangemen invited provincial brethren to celebrate the anniversary of their successful 1847 battle with Irish Catholics: *New Brunswick Reporter*, 10 May 1850.

78. *Weekly Chronicle*, 6 July 1849.

79. Head to Grey, 15 July 1849, CO 188. The question of the legality of public processions, especially armed ones, would become a hotly debated topic in the House of Assembly after the riot, yet no restrictive legislation would emerge from the debate.

80. Testimonies of Thomas Paddock and Francis Jones, "Riots and Disasters," Executive Council Records; *New Brunswick Reporter*, 13 July 1849; Head to Grey, 15 July 1849, CO 188.

81. *Morning News*, 13 July 1849; *New-Brunswicker* (Saint John), 14 July 1849; *New Brunswick Courier*, 14 July 1849; Testimonies of Francis Jones, George Noble, Jacob Allan, Charles Boyd, Squire Manks and George McKelvey. "Riots and Disasters," Executive Council Records; Head to Grey, 15 July 1849, CO 188.

82. Testimonies of Josiah Wetmore, Jeremiah McCarthy, George Nobel and Jacob Allan. "Riots and Disasters." Executive Council Records; Head to Grey, 15 July 1849. CO 188; *Sentinel*, 3 July 1930.

83. Testimonies of Jacob Allan, George Mason, Samuel Dalton, Samuel Gordon and Francis Jones. "Riots and Disasters," Executive Council Records; Head to Grey, 15 July 1849, CO 188; *Weekly Chronicle*, 13 July 1849; *New Brunswicker*, 14 July 1849; *Sentinel*, 3 July 1930.

84. Head to Grey, 15 July 1849. CO 188; Testimonies of James Gilbert, Henry Gilbert, John Nixon, John Fitzpatrick, Joseph Wetmore and James Clark. "Riots and Disasters," Executive Council Records.

85. Testimonies of Jacob Allan, Francis Jones and Squire Manks, "Riots and Disasters," Executive Council Records; Head to Grey, 15 July 1849, CO 188; *Sentinel*, 29 October 1891, 3 July 1930.

86. Head to Grey, 15 July 1849, CO 188; Jacob Allan testimony, "Riots and Disasters," Executive Council Records; *Morning News*, 13 July 1849; *Temperance Telegraph* (Saint John), 19 July 1849.

87. Testimonies of James McKenzie, William Smith, Francis Wilson and Francis Jones, "Riots and Disasters," Executive Council Records; *Temperance Telegraph*, 19 July 1849; *Weekly Chronicle*, 13 July 1849; *Morning News*, 13 July 1849.

88. Testimonies of Squire Manks, James McKenzie, William Smith, Francis Wilson and Jeremiah Smith, "Riots and Disasters," Executive Council Records; *Morning News*, 13 July 1849; *Christian Visitor*, 14 July 1849; *Weekly Chronicle*, 13 July 1849.

89. Head to Grey, 15 July 1849, CO 188; Charles Boyd testimony, "Riots and Disasters," Executive Council Records; *Morning News*, 13 July 1849; *New-Brunswicker*, 14 July 1849; *Weekly Chronicle*, 13 July 1849.

90. Testimonies of Charles Boyd and Jacob Allan, "Riots and Disasters," Executive Council Records; *Morning News*, 13 July 1849; Head to Grey, 15 July 1849, CO 188.

91. Head to Grey, 15 July 1849, CO 188; *Morning News*, 23 July 1849; *New Brunswick Courier*, 21 July 1849.

92. William B. Kinnear to Head, extract, 6 September 1849, in Head to Grey, 7 September 1849, CO 188; Recognizances, July-September 1849. "Riots and Disasters," Executive Council Records; Documents, Saint John Justice Court, 1849, PANB; Inquests, 1849, New Brunswick Supreme Court Documents, PANB; 12 Victoria, c. 29, 1849, *New Brunswick Statutes*, 1849; *Morning News*, 30 July 1849; *New Brunswick Courier*, 21, 28 July 1849; *Temperance Telegraph*, 23 August 1849.

93. Documents, Saint John Justice Court, 1849; Kinnear to Head, extract, 6 September 1849, in Head to Grey, 7 September 1849, CO 188; John Haggerty petition to Head, September 1849, in Judicial Documents, Executive Council Records; *Weekly Chronicle*, 24 August 1849; *New Brunswick Courier*, 18, 25 August 1849.

94. *New Brunswick Courier*, 19 July 1851, 16, 23, 30 July 6, 13 August 1853; *Weekly Chronicle*, 18 July 1851; *Morning News*, 15, 20 July 1853; *New Brunswick Reporter*, 15, 22 July 1853; *Freeman* (Saint John), 14 July 1855; McHarg Diary.

95. *Loyalist*, 30 March 1848; *New Brunswick Reporter*, 20 April 1850. Irish immigrants in the United States experienced a similar double standard: see Theodore M. Hammett, "Two Mobs of Jacksonian Boston: Ideology and Interest," *Journal of American History*, LXII (March 1976), pp. 866–67.

96. Documents, Saint John Justice Court, 1849: "Riots and Disasters," Executive Council Records.

97. W.W. Rostow explored the linkages between social unrest and economic downturns in *British Economy of the Nineteenth Century* (Oxford, 1948) pp. 123–25.

98. Wynn, *Timber Colony*, pp. 84–86, 166–67; MacNutt, *New Brunswick*, p. 329; James R. Rice, "A History of Organized Labour in Saint John, New Brunswick, 1813–1890," M.A. thesis, University of New Brunswick, 1968, pp. 33–34.

99. *Journal of the House of Assembly of New Brunswick*, 1850–51, 1853–54, 1857–60, 1867, 1872–75; 38 Victoria, c. 54, 1875, *Statutes of New Brunswick*, 1875.

100. Saint John's Orangemen sponsored a massive procession on the first Twelfth of July following the bill's assent. See *Freeman*, 13, 15, 18 July 1876; *Morning News*, 14, 17 July 1876.

101. Colebrooke to Grey, 30 July 1847, Head to Grey, 15 July 1849, CO 188; Colebrooke Correspondence, 1847. Head Correspondence, 1849. PANB.

102. New Brunswick Census, 1851, 1861; Immigration Returns, New Brunswick Blue Books, 1850–55, PAC: "Report on Trade and Navigation," in *Journal of the House of Assembly of New Brunswick*, 1866.

ST. PATRICK'S DAY PARADES IN NINETEENTH-CENTURY TORONTO: A STUDY OF IMMIGRANT ADJUSTMENT AND ÉLITE CONTROL

*Michael Cottrell**

Irish immigrants brought to nineteenth-century British North America a rich and diverse cultural heritage which continued to flourish in the areas they settled. A particular fondness for parades and processions was part of this inheritance, and annual demonstrations commemorating the Battle of the Boyne and the feast of St. Patrick were soon commonplace throughout the colonies. In the charged sectarian climate of Ireland, however, "parades were at the very centre of the territorial...political and economic struggle" and these connotations were also transplanted.[1] Especially in Toronto, where Catholic and Protestant Irish congregated in large numbers, parades frequently became the occasion of violent confrontation between Orange and Green.[2] But while the July 12 activities of the Orange figure prominently in Canadian historiography, little attention has been paid to St. Patrick's Day celebrations or their significance for Irish Catholic immigrants. This study seeks to redress this imbalance by tracing the evolution of St. Patrick's Day parades in nineteenth-century Toronto, beginning with a close examination of the 1863 celebration which was one of the largest and most impressive on record.

The tone was set the previous evening by the garrison drums beating "St. Patrick's Day in the Morning" and this was followed by the Hibernian Benevolent Society band's late-night promenade, "discoursing some of the choicest [Irish] national airs." Crowds began to gather at St. Paul's Church on King Street early the next morning and at ten o'clock, the procession began marching towards St. Michael's Cathedral. About 2,000 strong, the assemblage was drawn largely from the "humbler elements," some of whom had reportedly journeyed to the city from surrounding districts. The Cathedral was "filled to its utmost capacity" for the mass which was celebrated by Bishop John Joseph Lynch, assisted by over a dozen other Irish priests from the Toronto diocese. The high point of the service was undoubtedly the sermon delivered by the Bishop on the exploits of the "glorious saint," concluding with an exposition on the providential mission of the Irish diaspora to spread Catholicism to the four corners of the world.[3]

Religious obligations having been fulfilled, the procession then reformed and paraded through the principal streets of the city. Led by the Hibernian band, whose repertoire seemed to consist of nostalgic and militant tunes in equal measure, the procession swelled even further as it slowly returned to

---

From *Histoire sociale / Social History*, Vol. xxv, no. 49 (May 1992), 57–73.

*Michael Cottrell is professor of history at the University of Saskatchewan in Saskatoon.

St. Paul's Church. Here, a platform had been erected for the occasion and various notables, including the Bishop, members of the clergy, prominent Catholics and officers of various Irish organizations addressed the crowd. The obvious favourite, however, was Michael Murphy, president of the Hibernian Benevolent Society. Murphy's oration was received with "loud cheers and applause," especially when he denounced British government in Ireland as "radically wrong" and compared it to the suffering of the Polish people under a "powerful military despotism." But he prophesied that Irish deliverance was at hand from an organization rapidly growing among her exiles. In Canada alone, he claimed, there were 20,000 Irishmen ready to rally to the cause:

> ...three-fourths of the Catholic Irish of this country would offer themselves as an offering on the altar of freedom, to elevate their country and raise her again to her position in the list of nations. Nothing could resist the Irish pike when grasped by the sinewy arm of the Celt.[4]

Murphy then commended the Hibernians for keeping the spirit of Irish nationality alive in Canada, despite the opposition and hostility which this evoked from the host society. But he ended in a more conciliatory tone by expressing "perfect satisfaction" with the laws of Canada because, here, the people "were their own law-makers."[5] When the speeches were over, the procession broke up into smaller parties and soirées which lasted late into the night. And "thus passed away one of the most pleasant St. Patrick's Days we have ever spent in Toronto."[6]

For those who participated, almost exclusively Catholic Irish immigrants, the St. Patrick's Day celebration was obviously an extremely important event. On a social level, it provided a holiday from work and an occasion to parade about the city dressed in their Sunday best. Those who lived outside the city could visit friends and relatives, shop at the large stores and partake of the excitement of city life for a day. This influx undoubtedly provided a welcomed boost for the many Irish cabmen, storekeepers and tavernkeepers who lived a normally precarious existence. For the pious, it was an occasion to worship, for the notables an opportunity to speechify and revel in a stature which rarely extended beyond that day. But the event also had a deeper significance, for it was, in essence, a communal demonstration, an annual and very public assertion of Irish Catholic presence and solidarity in Toronto. It was perhaps the one day in the year on which Irish Catholics could claim the city as their own and proudly publicize their distinctiveness on the main streets. The ritualistic nature of the celebrations—with parades, masses and speeches being constants—obviously played a vital role in rekindling tribal memories and inculcating the collective consciousness necessary for reforging a group identity in a new environment. St. Patrick's Day parades were therefore central both to the emergence of Irish Catholic ethnicity in Toronto and to the communication of identity to the host society.[7]

The celebrations also reflected the interests and aspirations of those who assumed direct responsibility for organizing them. Since high visibility and prestige were the rewards, control of the event allowed different elements to establish supremacy within the Irish Catholic community, to impose their stamp on the group's corporate image and thereby to decisively influence its relations with the larger society. Thus, the intermittent struggle both for control of the celebrations and over the form which they should take revealed a great deal about the experience of Irish Catholic immigrants as they adjusted to an unfamiliar and often hostile environment. Like most ethnic groups, the Irish oscillated between the extremes of separation and integration, persistence and assimilation; and the celebration of the feast of St. Patrick was central to the resolution of these internal tensions for Irish immigrants in Toronto.[8]

Yet, to the host society comprising largely Loyalist and British settlers, the event had a very different significance. An annual reminder of the existence of a substantial alien Irish presence, it also demonstrated the determination of these immigrants, once settled into the country, to preserve aspects of their traditional culture. More ominously, speeches such as that delivered by Michael Murphy in 1863 evidenced a continued Irish obsession with the problems of their homeland, and the frequent violence which accompanied the parades demonstrated that the importation of these problems to British North America could prove extremely disruptive. Hence, the Canadian press was less than enthusiastic in its coverage of the event, expressing the wish that such celebrations, and the Old World orientation which they represented, would shortly be abandoned.[9]

The establishment of the Toronto St. Patrick's Society in 1832 attested to the growing Irish presence in the city and by 1861, Irish Catholics constituted over one-quarter of the population. However, a sharp increase in immigration and steady out-migration contributed to their decline as a percentage of the population thereafter.[10] Early St. Patrick's Day celebrations were usually low-key affairs—concerts, balls and soirées—which brought together the Irish élite to honour their patron saint and indulge their penchant for sentimental and self-congratulatory speeches.[11] Largely free from the sectarian biases so evident in the 1860s, they suggested a cordiality between early Catholic and Protestant immigrants. But while the St. Patrick's Society survived into the 1850s, the inclusive definition of Irish ethnicity which sustained it was undermined by the Famine immigration of the late 1840s. Since Catholics predominated among those who settled in Toronto, this influx shattered the virtual Protestant consensus which had previously existed, and the destitution of many of these Famine victims further contributed to a nativistic backlash from the host society.[12] This prejudice prompted Irish Protestants to dissociate themselves from their unpopular Catholic counterparts and instead to look to the Protestant, loyalist values of the Orange Order as the focus of their identity.[13] But since Catholics found themselves largely consigned to the lowest ranks of the occupational hierarchy and excluded from the emerging British Protestant colonial consensus, their response was to withdraw into an exclusive and essentially defensive form of ethnicity.[14] By the 1860s, the polarization of Irish immigrants along religious and cultural lines was complete and observers noted that the "Irish constitute in some sort two peoples: the line of division being one of religion and...one of race."[15]

These changes were reflected in the way in which St. Patrick's Day was celebrated, as the seventeenth of March became increasingly identified with Irish Catholicism. Partly a response to rejection by the host society and dissociation of the Protestant Irish, this development was also encouraged by elements within the Irish Catholic community. After the Famine, the Roman Catholic Church created a network of social and religious institutions to assist the adjustment of Irish immigrants and re-establish clerical control over their lives.[16] After a few small-scale and generally disorganized parades in the late 1840s, the clergy soon enlisted St. Patrick in their campaign and by the early 1850s, the annual celebration revolved primarily around the Catholic Church. Organized and led by Church-sponsored societies, processions to the Cathedral

TABLE 1   Population of Toronto, 1848–1881

Date	Irish	Catholic	Total
1848	1,695	5,903	25,503
1851	11,305	7,940	30,775
1861	12,441	12,125	44,821
1871	10,336	11,881	56,092
1881	10,781	15,716	86,415

Source: Census of Canada, 1848–1881.

TABLE 2   Irish Catholic Occupational Profile, 1860

Unskilled	45.0%
Semi-skilled	13.5%
Skilled	12.1%
Clerical	2.8%
Business	16.7%
Professional	3.3%
Private means	6.6%

Source: B. Clarke, "Piety, Nationalism and Fraternity: The Rise of Irish Catholic Voluntary Associations in Toronto, 1850–1895" (Ph.D. dissertation, University of Chicago, 1986), 33.

now became a regular feature and the clergy assumed a prominent role throughout.[17] But though the celebrations became larger and more public, the mass was clearly the focus of the event, and the sermons preached on these occasions had the effect both of strengthening the association between Irishness and Catholicism and of fostering a sense of ethno-religious particularism among Irish Catholic immigrants. The heroic figure of St. Patrick provided an easy continuity between the Irish history of persecution and their current experience as unwelcomed exiles in a strange land, and served as a rallying symbol for Irish Catholics in the New World, as Father Synnott's exhortation of 1855 indicates:

> Go on then, faithful, noble and generous children of St. Patrick, in your glorious career...keep your eyes ever fixed on the faith of St. Patrick which shall ever be for you a fixed star by night and a pillar of light by day—forget not the examples and memorable deeds of your fathers—be faithful to the doctrines of your apostle. A voice that speaks on the leaf of the shamrock—that speaks in the dismantled and ruined abbeys of lovely Erin—yea a voice that still speaks on the tombstones of your martyred fathers and in the homes of your exiled countrymen—be faithful to the glorious legacy he has bequeathed to you.[18]

In the early 1850s, then, the Roman Catholic Church was instrumental in transforming St. Patrick's Day into an essentially religious event, to establish Catholicism as the primary identity of Irish immigrants and thereby strengthen clerical authority. For by encouraging Irish immigrants to see themselves first as Catholics and to hold themselves aloof from the Protestant majority, the clergy reinforced their claim to leadership and control. But the Catholic Church was unable to satisfy all the needs of Irish immigrants. Under the French-born Bishop Armand de Charbonnel, it was unable to express the cultural or political nationalism which these immigrants transported as baggage.[19] Moreover, the group's organizational infrastructure was so tightly controlled by the clergy that it frustrated the desire for leadership and initiative among the Irish Catholic laity, especially the small but ambitious middle class which began to emerge in the mid-1850s.[20]

Irish nationalism provided one of the few rationales for lay initiative independent of the clergy, and it also served both as a catalyst and a vehicle for expressing the growing ethnic consciousness among Irish Catholics in Toronto.[21] Indicative of this was the establishment, in 1855, of the exclusively Catholic Young Men's St. Patrick's Association, an ethnic organization which sought to provide a social life for Irish immigrants, based on their traditional culture, and to secure their collective advancement in Toronto.[22] Animated by the Irish Catholic middle class, it quickly moved to put its stamp on what had become the group's leading communal event, and in the late 1850s, the new lay élite assumed responsibility for organizing the St. Patrick's Day celebrations.

Under their auspices, the event changed dramatically. Parades, which had previously been merely a prelude to the mass, now increased in size and colour to become major public demonstrations. In 1857, over 1,000 people, their faces animated by "a sacred patriotic fire," marched behind 400 members of the Young Men's St. Patrick's Association.[23] Religious hymns were replaced by popular tunes and secular emblems such as shamrocks, harps and wolfhounds were now more prominent than Catholic icons. As the clergy lost their previous stature in the extra-Cathedral festivities, the whole tone of these events also changed. Clerically-induced temperance gave way to alcoholic good cheer, and instead of the expressions of loyalty and three cheers for the Queen, which had previously characterized the proceedings, mildly anglophobic speeches were now heard.[24]

Alienated from the larger society by a growing "No Popery" crusade which was expressed through the mainstream press and the hostile activities of the Orange Order, Irish Catholics in the late 1850s used St. Patrick's Day parades to assert their ethno-religious distinctiveness and protest their marginalized position within the city. But changes in the parade also reflected a shift in the internal dynamics of the group, as a struggle was clearly developing between the clergy and members of the laity for leadership and control of the Irish Catholic community. While the latter agreed that Catholicism defined the parameters of Irish ethnicity, they emphasized a secular and cultural dimension to this identity which went beyond the clergy's narrowly religious vision. These tensions were demonstrated by Bishop de Charbonnel's refusal, in 1856, to hold mass to coincide with the parade, but the events of St. Patrick's Day 1858 healed this rift, at least temporarily.[25]

The growth of the Catholic population in the city, its increasing visibility and public assertiveness on occasions such as St. Patrick's Day were all seen as evidence of a growing menace by Upper Canadian Protestants already inflamed by the British Papal aggression crisis and the American Know-Nothing movement.[26] The parades, especially, were seen as unduly provocative by the Orange Order which had become the most popular vehicle for expressing militant Protestantism in Upper Canada.[27] This tension boiled over in 1858 when Orange attempts to disrupt the parade resulted in widespread violence during which one Catholic was fatally stabbed with a pitchfork.[28]

Coming at a time of growing self-confidence and rising expectations among the Catholic Irish population, this debacle was a sobering experience, for it demonstrated both the continued hostility of their traditional Orange enemies and the vulnerability which Catholics faced as a consequence of their minority position in Toronto. Moreover, the blatant partisanship of the police and judiciary indicated where the sympathies of the authorities lay, and served notice that the triumphalist behaviour involved in the parades was out of place in a community subscribing to a British and Protestant consensus.[29] As a result, both lay and clerical Irish leaders concluded that a lower public profile would have to be adopted if the acceptance, recognition and prosperity which they desired were to be achieved. This new spirit of conciliation and moderation was expressed most clearly by the decision to forego public processions on St. Patrick's Day for an indefinite period. The suspension of the parades for the next three years followed a conscious decision of the Irish élite to relinquish their right to the streets in the interests of public harmony. Yet, while this moderation forwarded the desires of the clergy and middle class for an accommodation with the Canadian establishment, it did not meet acquiescence from all elements within the Irish Catholic community, and it was soon challenged by rumblings from below.

The murder of Matthew Sheedy by Orangemen on St. Patrick's Day 1858 was symptomatic of the growing hostility experienced by Irish Catholics in Toronto. Prejudice, harassment and attacks on Catholic priests and Church property all contributed to the growth of a siege mentality among Catholics. While this beleaguerment produced the above-mentioned conciliatory stance from the Irish élite, it also generated a more militant response in the form of the Hibernian Benevolent Society. Established after the 1858 debacle to protect Catholics from Orange aggression, the Hibernians invoked the traditional Irish peasant prerogative of self-defence in the face of the failure of the authorities to secure their rights or redress their grievances. But they soon rose above these Ribbonite roots and by the early 1860s, had evolved into a full-fledged ethnic voluntary organization.[30] As well as rendering Toronto safer for Catholics, the Hibernians took over, from the Young Men's St. Patrick's Association, the tasks of generating an extensive social life and material benefits for its largely working-class male members. In keeping with the values of the latter, the organization also sought to inject a more aggressively nationalistic spirit into the Irish community to engender pride and self-confidence, thereby strengthening the demand for recognition and respect for the Irish in Toronto.[31]

One of their first steps in this direction was to reassert the Irish Catholic right to the streets of the city by resuming parades on St. Patrick's Day. Unlike the Young Men's St. Patrick's Association which had openly flouted the authority of the clergy, however, the Hibernians showed great deference to the new Bishop of Toronto, John Joseph Lynch. When the Hibernians sought clerical permission to revive the parades, in 1862, Lynch supported their decision despite strong opposition from "the most respectable Catholic inhabitants of the city." Led by members of the now-defunct Young Men's St. Patrick's Association, they argued that a resumption of public processions would inevitably provoke a confrontation with the Orangemen, and since Catholics would automatically be depicted as the aggressors, the good feelings which developed from their suspension would be lost. Lynch was thus implored to ban the parade or at the very least to "hold mass at such an hour as not to suit the procession."[32] But the Bishop chose to ignore their warnings and not only granted his approval, but addressed the parade from the steps of the cathedral and commended the Hibernians for their "noble efforts on behalf of faith and fatherland."[33]

This dispute over the resumption of the parades suggested an ongoing conflict within the Irish Catholic community about the appropriate response to their countries of origin and of adoption, and acute divisions on the strategy which would best secure them a comfortable niche in the latter. Upwardly-mobile middle class immigrants argued that the best route to success lay in winning the confidence of the host society by quietly discarding those aspects of their traditional culture which were found objectionable and by working through the political system to redress outstanding grievances. But the organized Irish working class, in the form of the Hibernians, rejected the timidity and abandonment of cultural distinctiveness which this policy entailed, and instead demanded a more vigorous assertion of the Irish Catholic presence in the city.[34] For symbolic effect, the St. Patrick's Day parade surpassed all else, since it represented both a commitment to the preservation of Irish culture and an insistence on the right to advertise this distinctiveness on the streets of Toronto.[35]

This conflict between strategies of accommodation and protest constitutes the typical dilemma faced by ethnic groups in a new environment and is frequently related to economic adjustment. Ironically, it was the Irish middle class which had first resorted to protest in the mid-1850s, only to retreat from ethnic militancy once it became obvious that this jeopardized its attainment of social acceptance and economic prosperity. Control of the parades had now changed hands and since this event provided one of the major opportunities for lay initiative, it seems that leadership of Irish-Catholic ethnicity in Toronto was passing from the moderate and accommodationist middle class to the militantly separatist lower class. The power and prestige of the Roman Catholic clergy were also demonstrated by this embroglio, however, for Bishop Lynch's moral role as adjudicator between the warring lay factions was clearly recognized. On this occasion, he sided with the Hibernians, primarily because their uncompromising nationalism reinforced the Church's attempt to foster religious particularism and strengthened the hierarchy's claim to communal leadership.[36] But the limits of this control would soon be tested and the alliance between clergy and nationalists severely strained in the process.

Unknown to Bishop Lynch, the Hibernians established contact with the revolutionary American Fenian Brotherhood in 1859, and the Hibernian president, Michael Murphy, became head-centre of the Fenian organization in the Toronto area. Although sworn Fenians were always a minority of the Hibernians' membership, the organization became more militant under their influence. The establishment in January 1863 of the weekly ethnic newspaper, the *Irish Canadian*, further evidenced their increasing sophistication, for this mouthpiece augmented their influence within the Irish-Catholic community and enabled the Fenians to articulate their concerns to the larger society. Under the editorship of Patrick Boyle, the *Irish Canadian* sought to "link the past with the present, the old country with the new," and propagated the simple message that religion, patriotism and support for the liberation of Ireland were all inseparably linked with the demand for Irish recognition and the achievement of prosperity, success and respect in their new environment.[37]

The prominence which the Hibernians established within the Irish Catholic community was demonstrated by their complete control of St. Patrick's Day celebrations in the early 1860s. As statements of Irish protest and radicalism, they surpassed all previous efforts. The years 1863 and 1864 saw the largest parades on record and in keeping with Hibernian membership, those who led and those who followed were increasingly drawn from the Irish Catholic lower class. A new militancy was apparent in the playing of martial tunes such as "The Croppy Boy," "God Save Ireland" and "The Rising of the Moon," and changes in the route of the parade also suggested a spirit of confrontation previously lacking. These two parades covered a wider territory than ever before and while this was obviously designed to assert their right to the entire city, the provocation involved in marching past so many Orange lodges could not have been lost on the organizers. Even more ominous was the proliferation of Fenian sunburst banners among the crowd and the open expressions of support for Fenianism which concluded both of these parades.[38]

Bordering on treason, Murphy's speeches incurred the wrath of the host society and also alienated many Irish Catholics who feared the new radicalism he represented. Led by Thomas D'Arcy McGee, moderates argued that the Fenian-sympathizing Hibernians would confirm the stereotype of Irish disloyalty held by the host society, inevitably prompting a violent reaction from the Orange Order. Even sympathetic Protestants would be alienated by this extremism, he suggested, and the resulting backlash would obliterate all of the tangible gains made by Irish Catholics since the bitter era of sectarian warfare in the 1850s.[39] The situation was particularly embarrassing for the Catholic Church since Lynch's presence alongside Murphy on the podium on both occasions gave rise to allegations that the clergy sanctioned these treasonous sentiments. As rumours of a Fenian invasion mounted, Bishop Lynch came under increasing pressure to denounce the Hibernians and he finally bowed to internal and external pressure. In August of 1865, he condemned the Hibernians and called on all Catholics to quit the organization since they had "fallen away from Catholic principles."[40]

Once again, a struggle for leadership and control of the Irish community was apparent, but the internal alliances had shifted since the early 1860s. Now the clergy were supported by the middle class élite, as moderate Irish Catholics sought to rein in a working-class organization whose radicalism threatened their interests. This clash, essentially one between strategies of protest and accommodation, came to a head in March 1866 amid rumours that the long-anticipated Fenian invasion was to coincide with a huge St. Patrick's Day parade organized by the Hibernians.[41] As tension within the city mounted in the preceding weeks, Irish moderates sought to distance themselves from the Hibernians to reassure the Protestant majority that the latter's extremism was not shared by all. Having supported and even encouraged the extremists, Bishop Lynch found himself at the centre of the storm, as moderates appealed to him to control the Hibernians. "Everything depends on Your Lordship," D'Arcy McGee warned the Bishop, and he insisted that the future of the entire Irish Catholic community in Canada was at stake: "The position of our Church and race in Canada for the next twenty-five years, will be determined by the stand taken, during these next six weeks."[42]

In this situation, Lynch clearly had no choice but to ban the parade, which he did shortly thereafter by advising all Catholics to spend the day either in Church or at home. By this point, however, the Hibernians had moved beyond the control of the clergy. Having foregone the procession at the Bishop's insistence the previous year, they were less amenable on this occasion, and insisted on their right to take to the streets regardless of the consequences. Clearly, the Hibernians were determined to push the strategy of protest and their strident assertion of ethnic persistence to its extreme. But they had by now left the bulk of Irish Catholics behind in this respect. While a great many supported their call for Irish liberation and fervently resented the domestic prejudice which the Hibernians sought to counter, very few were willing to provoke the wrath of the host society or flout the authority of their bishop to express these sentiments. Thus, only the die-hard Hibernians turned out to march in the smallest parade in years, and the anti-climax was completed by the failure of the Fenian invasion to materialize.[43]

This caution was even more forcibly demonstrated when the Fenian raids finally occurred in June of 1866. For despite a widespread expression of sullen resentment, an overwhelming majority of Irish Canadians were induced to hold themselves aloof from the Irish American "liberators" by a combination of clerical and lay pressure, instincts of self-preservation and the desire for acceptance in their new homeland.[44] The Fenian raids, nevertheless, cast a shadow of suspicion over the entire Irish community in Canada. The inevitable Protestant backlash produced what one individual described as a "reign of terror," confirming McGee's dire predictions of the consequences of flirting with treason.[45] In this hostile climate, Catholics naturally reverted to a low profile and there was no suggestion of holding a public celebration on St. Patrick's Day 1867.

Once boisterous and triumphant, the Hibernians found their influence and prestige within the Toronto Irish community greatly undermined, and the round-up of suspected Fenian sympathizers further decimated the radical leadership. Control of the organization now reverted to relative moderates, such as Patrick Boyle, editor of the *Irish Canadian*; and while he followed Murphy's old lead in some respects, marked changes soon became apparent. Nationalism had proven its effectiveness as a vehicle for mobilizing the ethnic consciousness of Irish Catholic immigrants and focusing their resentment against the marginalization they experienced in their new home. But unlike the American situation, where republican nationalism placed Irish immigrants within the ideological mainstream, in Canada these sentiments clearly isolated them from the larger British population.[46] As well as separating the

Irish from their neighbours, it also had the effect of alienating Catholics from their Church, which was the only institution in Canada the Irish could claim as their own. To rehabilitate themselves, therefore, nationalist leaders had to reforge the link between nationalism and Catholicism; develop a variation of nationalism which integrated rather than isolated Irish Catholics from Canadian society; and make their message more relevant by addressing the material needs of Irish Catholic immigrants in Toronto and Ontario. As with many other shifts within the Irish community, these developments would be reflected in the way St. Patrick's Day was celebrated.

After the Fenian fiasco, the Hibernians reverted to their former deference towards the Catholic Church and the first public sign of this rapprochement came in 1868 when Bishop Lynch approved a resumption of the St. Patrick's Day parades. Although 400 Hibernians turned out to lead the procession, both the attendance and the tone were far cries from the massive demonstrations of the early 1860s. A subdued atmosphere pervaded the celebrations and this was clearly reflected in the speech delivered by Patrick Boyle which focused on the plight of Fenian prisoners in Canadian jails, but avoided more contentious issues.[47] This uncharacteristic moderation of the Hibernians stood in sharp contrast to the obsession which the nationalist press began to exhibit in provincial and federal politics. Obviously a more practical and effective means of improving the position of the Irish than the Utopian promises of the Fenians, this new focus also facilitated a growing cordiality between nationalists and members of the middle class who were determined to transform Irish Catholics into an influential political pressure group in Ontario.[48] The politicization of Irish nationalism received public expression on St. Patrick's Day 1869 when John O'Donohoe, a former member of the Toronto corporation and veteran political activist, was invited to deliver the keynote speech to the procession from the steps of St. Michael's Cathedral.[49] Although he paid lip-service to the traditional nationalist shibboleths, O'Donohoe focused primarily on the political situation and the social inferiority suffered by Irish Catholics because of their lack of political influence. In the Legislature of Ontario, he lamented, "we find our body as completely excluded as if we formed no portion of the body politic," and he insisted that the only means of improving their standing within the province was by putting aside their internal differences and demanding their rightful share of power and the spoils of office: "Let us practice unanimity and in cordial cooperation form a united phalanx, determined to live in harmony with all men—but determined for our right."[50]

A consensus clearly existed within the Irish community concerning its subordinate status in Ontario and on the efficacy of political activity as a means of overcoming it. With the new moderation of the nationalists paving the way for closer cooperation with the clergy and the lay élite, all were soon working together within the Catholic League, a political pressure group established in 1870 to forward the political interests of the province's Catholics.[51] The League soon became the focus of Irish organizational activities and this new concern with politics was reflected in the prominence which these matters received in subsequent St. Patrick's Day celebrations. Long an occasion for reaffirming religious or nationalist solidarity, the parades in the early 1870s also became a vehicle for disseminating political propaganda—indicating once again the flexibility of Irish immigrants to adapt traditional cultural practices to the needs of a new environment.[52]

This concern with politics reflected a very important change in the celebration of St. Patrick's Day, a change which manifested a wider shift within the Irish Catholic community in Toronto. Rather than emphasizing religious or ethnic exclusivity and separatism as had been the practice in the past, both the sermons and the outdoor speeches now focused on the need to carve out for Irish Catholics an acceptable place in Ontario society.[53] These new integrationist tendencies may be seen as by-products of the growing adjustment of Irish immigrants to Ontario and the increasing acceptance and respect which they were receiving from the host society.[54] Moreover, the success of the Catholic League in attracting attention to Irish grievances and securing the election of an increasing number of Irish candidates suggested that they were gradually coming to wield the power and influence they felt they deserved within the political structures of their adopted home.[55]

By the mid-1870s, therefore, the collective fortunes of Irish Catholics in Toronto had improved considerably, and these changes were reflected in the celebration of St. Patrick's Day. While it was still felt necessary to advertise their presence and distinctiveness by taking to the streets on the feast of their patron saint, the event differed radically from the boisterous nationalist demonstrations of the early 1860s. The Hibernians were still present, but they attracted nowhere near the numbers they previously commanded. Their once splendid banners were now dilapidated and the speeches in support of Home Rule and constitutional solutions to the Irish problem, while compatible with their presence in a self-governing colony, were a far cry from Michael Murphy's fiery harangues of an earlier time.[56] Increasingly anachronistic, the Hibernians no longer exercised a stranglehold over the celebrations and they were forced to share the podium with organizations such as the Father Matthew Temperance Society, the Emerald Benevolent Association and the Sons of St. Patrick.[57] The values which the latter sought to impress both on their audience and on the host society—sobriety, temperance, self-help and thrift—in short mid-Victorian respectability—represented the new collective identity of the Irish Catholic community.[58] Indeed, the primary function of St. Patrick's Day celebrations now seemed to be to put lingering stereotypes to rest by demonstrating that Irish Catholics were worthy of full citizenship and total acceptance from a host society that had once expressed reservations about their fitness.[59]

Distance and time were gradually weakening the attachment of Irish immigrants to the Old Country and militant nationalism was giving way to nostalgic sentimentality. Increasingly prosperous and secure both economically and socially, and with a new generation growing up for whom Ireland had very little relevance, Irish Torontonians were in fact becoming Canadianized.[60] On a personal level, it was no longer necessary to rely on the ethnic support group for survival, and collective self-respect no longer depended upon a constant assertion of distinctiveness. Their efforts, instead, were directed towards downplaying the differences between themselves and their neighbours and, in this, the St. Patrick's Day celebration was an obstacle rather than an asset. Commenting on the extremely poor turnout at the 1876 parade, Patrick Boyle suggested that the time had come to re-evaluate the annual celebrations. These demonstrations perpetuated the isolation of Irish Catholics, he concluded, for of all the ethnic groups in Canada, they alone insisted on "placing before the public their persons and sentiments in a more or less ridiculous drapery."[61] More important than the ridicule of their neighbours, however, was the fact that such displays were increasingly incompatible with their higher duty as citizens of Canada:

> Their abandonment is demanded by many considerations of good citizenship. They serve to maintain in this land, to which we have all come for quiet rather than broil, the miserable dissension and violence of a past which the present generation has outlived and outgrown. As a duty to the concord of society, to peace and order, to industry and steadiness, to that perfect unity which proves strength to the State, those processions which were instances of bad citizenship in this country...ought to be abandoned.[62]

With even the remnants of radical nationalism losing interest, the future of the event was obviously in doubt, and it came as no surprise that 1877 saw the last public St. Patrick's Day celebration in Toronto for over a century.[63]

While it lasted, the event was the most visible demonstration of Irishness in the city and, as such, provided an important continuity between the Old World and the New for Irish immigrants. The parades, however, can only be understood in the context of the needs of the Irish Catholic community in their new environment. The unfurling of the green banners on St. Patrick's Day asserted the Irish Catholic right to the streets and constituted both a "ritualized demand for recognition and an affirmation of ethnic solidarity in a predominantly Protestant city."[64] The parades thus allowed Irish immigrants to define their collective identity, to advertise their distinctiveness and, in the process, to demand corporate recognition for their presence. The two decades after the Famine were crucial to the first of these goals, as Catholicism and nationalism were established as the parameters of Irish ethnicity and served as the focus of the celebrations until the 1870s. Resolving the appropriate response to the host society was much more contentious, however, as evidenced by the struggle for control of the celebrations by different elements within the Irish community. Protest and accommodation were ultimately the alternatives offered by those vying for ethnic leadership, and by the mid-1870s, the issue had been resolved in favour of the latter. Thus, nationalism was largely discarded because of its fundamental incompatibility with the prevailing English-Canadian ideology, and religion became the primary identity for a group who increasingly defined themselves as English-speaking Catholic Canadians.

The abandonment of the parades in the mid-1870s may therefore be seen as a crucial indice of Irish assimilation, but also points to an important relationship between ethnic persistence and structural integration. For as long as Irish Catholics found themselves outside the Canadian mainstream, elements within the group insisted on preserving and advertising their distinctiveness, especially on St. Patrick's Day. When the political and economic structures began to embrace them, and Irish Catholics were afforded the same social acceptance as other groups, however, the need for displaying such distinctiveness was no longer perceived to exist. Thus, public celebrations of St. Patrick's Day, which had once served the interests of Irish immigrants recently arrived in a strange environment, were abandoned when they became an impediment to the group's subsequent and natural desire to become Canadian.

Notes

1. S.E. Baker, "Orange and Green: Belfast, 1832–1912," in H.J. Dyos and M. Wolff, eds., *The Victorian City: Images and Realities*, Vol. II (London and Boston: Routledge and Keegan Paul, 1973), 790; D.W. Miller, "The Armagh Troubles, 1784–87," in S. Clark and J.S. Donnelly, Jr., eds., *Irish Peasants: Violence and Political Unrest, 1780–1914* (Madison: University of Wisconsin Press, 1983), 174–76.

2. G.S. Kealey, "The Orange Order in Toronto: Religious Riot and the Working Class," in R. O'Driscoll and C. Reynolds, eds., *The Untold Story: The Irish in Canada* (Toronto: Celtic Arts of Canada, 1988), 841–47.

3. This report was taken from the *Irish Canadian*, 18 March 1863; the *Canadian Freeman*, 19 March 1863; and the *Globe*, 18 March 1863.

4. *Irish Canadian*, 18 March 1863.

5. *Ibid.*

6. *Canadian Freeman*, 19 March 1863.

7. St. Patrick's Day celebrations as an institution within the Irish diaspora have received surprisingly little attention. *See* C.J. Fahey, "Reflections on the St. Patrick's Day Orations of John Ireland," *Ethnicity*, Vol. II (1975), 244–57; O. MacDonagh, "Irish Culture and Nationalism Translated: St. Patrick's Day, 1888 in Australia," in O. MacDonagh, W.F. Mandle and P. Travers, eds., *Irish Culture and Nationalism, 1750–1950* (London: Macmillan, 1983), 69–82.

8. J. Higham, ed., *Ethnic Leadership in America* (Baltimore and London: The Johns Hopkins University Press, 1978), 1–18.

9. *Leader*, 18 March 1863; and *Globe*, 18 March 1863.

10. For a demographic profile of Irish Catholics in Toronto, *see* Table 1.

11. *Mirror*, 19 March 1841, and 24 March 1843.

12. G.J. Parr, "The Welcome and the Wake: Attitudes in Canada West Toward the Irish Famine Migration," *Ontario History*, Vol. LXVI (1974), 101–13; K. Duncan, "Irish Famine Immigration and the Social Structure of Canada West," *Canadian Review of Sociology and Anthropology*, Vol. II (1965), 19–40; D. Connor, "The Irish Canadians: Image and Self-Image" (M.A. thesis, University of British Columbia, 1976), 50–92.

13. D.S. Shea, "The Irish Immigrant Adjustment to Toronto: 1840–1860," *Canadian Catholic Historical Association. Study Sessions* (1972), 55–56; C. Houston and W.J. Smyth, "Transferred Loyalties: Orangeism in the United States and Canada," *American Review of Canadian Studies*, Vol. XIV (1984), 193–211; G.S. Kealey and P. Warrian, eds., *Essays in Canadian Working Class History* (Toronto: McClelland and Stewart, 1976), 13–34.

14. For an occupational profile of Irish Catholics in Toronto, *see* Table 2.

15. *Leader*, 25 January 1862.

16. M.W. Nicolson, "The Catholic Church and the Irish in Victorian Toronto" (Ph.D. dissertation, University of Guelph, 1981); *idem*, "Irish Tridentine Catholicism in Victorian Toronto: Vessel for Ethno-Religious Persistence," *Canadian Catholic Historical Association, Study Sessions*, Vol. L (1983), 415–36; B.P. Clarke, "Piety, Nationalism and Fraternity: The Rise of Irish Catholic Voluntary Associations in Toronto, 1850–1895" (Ph.D. dissertation, University of Chicago, 1986), Vol. I.

17. *Mirror*, 7 March 1851; 14 March 1852; and 11 March 1853.

18. *Mirror*, 23 March 1855.

19. For the complex relationship between Catholicism and nationalism in Irish culture, *see* L.J. McCaffrey, "Irish Catholicism and Irish Nationalism: A Study in Cultural Identity," *Church History*, Vol. XLII (1973), 524–34.

20. The best evidence for the existence of this middle class was the proliferation of advertisements for wholesale establishments and professional services in the Irish ethnic press. *See* the *Mirror* or *Canadian Freeman*, 1850s.

21. The emergence of lay voluntary organizations revolving around Irish nationalism is explored in detail in Clarke, "Irish Voluntary Associations, Vol. II."

22. *Mirror*, 30 November, and 21 December 1855.

23. *Mirror*, 20 March 1857.

24. *Ibid.*

25. *Mirror*, 28 March 1856.

26. J.R. Miller, "Bigotry in the North Atlantic Triangle: Irish, British and American Influences on Canadian Anti-Catholicism, 1850–1900," *Studies in Religion*, Vol. XVI (1987), 289–301.

27. The power of the Order was perhaps best demonstrated by its virtual stranglehold on municipal politics for much of the nineteenth century. *See* G.S. Kealey, "The Union of the Canadas," in V.L. Russell, ed., *Forging a Consensus: Historic Essays on Toronto* (Toronto: University of Toronto Press, 1984), 41–86.

28. P. Toner, "The Rise of Irish Nationalism in Canada" (Ph.D. dissertation, National University of Ireland, 1974), 27–35; Clarke, "Irish Voluntary Associations," 305–7.

29. *Globe*, 18 and 19 March 1858; *Leader*, 18 and 19 March 1858.

30. For an introduction to the Ribbonite tradition, *see* T. Garvin, "Defenders, Ribbonmen and Others: Underground Political Networks in Pre-Famine Ireland," *Past and Present*, Vol. LXXXXVI (1982), 133–55; and J. Lee, "The Ribbonmen," in T.D. Williams, ed., *Secret Societies in Ireland* (Dublin: Gill and Macmillan, 1973), 26–35.

31. Clarke, "Irish Voluntary Associations," esp. 289–329; G. Sheppard, "God Save the Green: Fenianism and Fellowship in Victorian Ontario," *Histoire Sociale/Social History*, Vol. XX (1987), 129–44.

32. Archives of the Archdiocese of Toronto (henceforth A.A.T.), Archbishop Lynch Papers, Rev. G.R. Northgraves to Lynch, 4 March 1865.

33. *Leader*, 18 March 1862, and *Canadian Freeman*, 20 March 1862.

34. Occupational profiles of Hibernian membership demonstrate it was "predominantly a working-class organization." Clarke, "Irish Voluntary Associations," 365–66.

35. *Canadian Freeman*, 20 March 1862; *Irish Canadian*, 18 March 1863 and 23 March 1864.

36. A.A.T., Lynch Papers, Bishop Lynch to Bishop Farrell, 12 August 1865 and Bishop Lynch to Archbishop T. Connolly, 1 February 1866.

37. *Irish Canadian*, 7 January 1863.

38. *Irish Canadian*, 18 March, 25 March 1863 and 23 March 1864; *Canadian Freeman*, 19 March 1863, 24 March and 31 March 1864; *Leader*, 18 March 1864.

39. *Canadian Freeman*, 31 March, 14 April and 21 April 1864.

40. A.A.T., Archbishop Lynch Papers, Bishop Lynch to Bishop Farrell, 12 August 1865; *Canadian Freeman*, 17 August 1865.

41. *Globe*, 9 March 1866.

42. A.A.T., Archbishop Lynch Papers, T.D. McGee to Bishop Lynch, 7 March 1866.

43. *Globe*, 18 March 1866; *Irish Canadian*, 21 March 1866.

44. W.S. Neidhardt, *Fenianism in North America* (Pennsylvania: Pennsylvania State University Press, 1975), 50–80.

45. National Archives of Canada, J.L.P. O'Hanley Papers, Vol. 1, J.L.P. O'Hanley to J. Hearn, 4 May 1868.

46. For the role of Irish nationalism in the integration of Irish immigrants into American society, *see* T.N. Brown, *Irish-American Nationalism, 1870–1890* (New York: J.P. Lippincott, 1966.)

47. *Leader*, 18 March 1868 and *Irish Canadian*, 18 March 1868.

48. M. Cottrell, "Irish Catholic Political Leadership in Toronto, 1855–1882: A Study of Ethnic Politics" (Ph.D. dissertation, University of Saskatchewan, 1988), 225–312.

49. For O'Donohoe's career, *see* M. Cottrell, "John O'Donohoe and the Politics of Ethnicity in Ontario," *Canadian Catholic Historical Association, Historical Papers*, forthcoming.

50. *Irish Canadian*, 24 March 1869.

51. M. Cottrell, "Irish Political Leadership," 225–312.

52. *Irish Canadian*, 23 March 1870, 20 March 1872, 19 March 1873 and 22 March 1876; *Canadian Freeman*, 23 March 1871.

53. *Irish Canadian*, 22 March 1871 and 18 March 1874.

54. M. McGowan, "We Endure What We Cannot Cure: J.J. Lynch and Roman Catholic-Protestant in Toronto, 1864–75. Frustrated Attempts at Peaceful Co-Existence," *Canadian Society of Church History Papers*, Vol. XV (1984), 16–17.

55. M. Cottrell, "Irish Political Leadership," 313–454; D. Swainson, "James O'Reilly and Catholic Politics," *Historic Kingston*, Vol. XXI (1973), 11–21.

56. *Irish Canadian*, 20 March 1872 and 18 March 1874.

57. *Ibid.*, 22 March 1876.

58. Clarke, "Irish Voluntary Associations," 433–38.

59. *Irish Canadian*, 22 March 1876 and 21 March 1877.

60. For the transformation of Toronto's Irish Catholics into an English-speaking Canadian Catholic community, *see* M. McGowan, "We Are All Canadians: A Social, Religious and Cultural Portrait of Toronto's English-Speaking Roman Catholics, 1890–1920" (Ph.D. dissertation, University of Toronto, 1988).

61. *Irish Canadian*, 5 April 1876.

62. *Ibid.*, 5 April 1876.

63. *Ibid.*, 20 March 1878.

64. Clarke, "Irish Voluntary Association," 460.

CHAPTER
12 RESPONSIBLE GOVERNMENT, THE EMPIRE AND CANADA

Responsible government was the most written-about and, in the view of some, most important subject in Canadian history until as recently as the mid-twentieth century. It was "the crowning achievement of the second empire," according to the doyen of Canadian historians, Chester Martin, the "Great Experiment" in British North America that demonstrated how a colony could evolve into a nation yet remain within the British Empire. The centrepiece of this thesis was Lord Durham's *Report* with its suggestion of colonial self-government. The multiracial British Commonwealth, a significant international institution, was a product of the recommendations in Lord Durham's *Report* and their celebrated application in British North America.

In Canada, as well as in Great Britain, the notion of the brilliance of responsible government had served several generations of politicians and historians. In Canada it formed the essential link in the Whig-Liberal interpretation of a past divided into forces of light and forces of darkness. The 1848 success of Robert Baldwin and L.H. Lafontaine against the philistine Tories was but the first in a series that led through George Brown, Edward Blake and Wilfrid Laurier to William Lyon Mackenzie King, the grandson of William Lyon Mackenzie, the Upper Canadian leader of the Rebellion that helped to precipitate Durham's *Report* and responsible government.

In Great Britain Durham's *Report* and the concept of self-government played an essential role in the justification of Empire. This idea is traced in the first selection, "The Influence of the Durham Report," by Ged Martin. He examined far more than the title indicates, for he discussed responsible government in Canada as part of Imperial history and indicated how several myths or traditions were invented, especially the notion that the *Report* was the "Magna Charta for the empire." As Martin stated in his conclusion of this highly critical paper, it is time for "more realistic perspectives," since "the British empire is all but an episode of the past."

That process had been underway in Canada for some time. Chester Martin's *Foundations of Canadian Nationhood* (1955), quoted above, was almost the last study of its type. The relevance of the Empire was in sharp decline as he wrote, and Canadians were already reconstructing a past with less emphasis on Britain. Nowhere was this more obvious than in Quebec. Separatist historians denounced all accommodation with the English, including responsible government. Others, such as Jacques Monet, sought to understand rather than condemn the generation of the 1840s that turned its back on rebellion. In "French-Canadian Nationalism and the Challenge of Ultramontanism" Monet provided a convincing analysis of the unlikely alliance of political nationalism and conservative Catholicism in Canada East that would survive for a century. "A funny thing indeed," he concluded, "had happened to French-Canadian nationalism on its way to responsible government."

A more recent examination of responsible government by S.J.R. Noel, the third selection, is almost exclusively political. In "Brokerage and the Politics of Power Sharing" he offered a Canadian "politics of byzantine complexity," in which "almost everything was legitimate grist to a political mill." Noel did not ignore the role of the British nor that of the ultramontane nationalists, but in his analysis the key was brokerage politics, the product of astute politicians in a unique Canadian situation.

Suggestions for Further Reading

Buckner, Phillip A., *The Transition to Responsible Government: British Policy in British North America, 1815–1850*. Westport, Conn.: Greenwood Press, 1985.

Careless, J.M.S. (ed.), *The Pre-Confederation Premiers: Ontario Government Leaders, 1841–1867*. Toronto: University of Toronto Press, 1980.

————, *The Union of the Canadas: The Growth of Canadian Institutions, 1841–1857*. Toronto: McClelland & Stewart, 1972.

MacNutt, W.S., *The Atlantic Provinces: The Emergence of Colonial Society, 1712–1857*. Toronto: McClelland & Stewart, 1965.

Monet, Jacques, *The Last Cannon Shot*. Toronto: University of Toronto Press, 1969.

THE INFLUENCE OF THE DURHAM REPORT

Ged Martin

"It has long been recognized as the greatest state document in British imperial history." Thus in 1945 Sir Reginald Coupland described the Durham Report. Few works can have had such a chequered career as Lord Durham's *Report on the affairs of British North America.* Largely rejected by contemporaries and ignored for half a century, it became the most revered of texts for the Edwardian empire and continued to be regarded as the Magna Charta of the Commonwealth until the 1960s. As late as 1971 Ward could complain of "what ought to be known as the great Durham illusion," and the myth was still strongly enough entrenched in standard works to provoke two strong and independently inspired assaults.[1] Although the old orthodoxy is by no means universally rejected, it is strange that it should have remained unchallenged for so long. The case for the Report's significance was riddled with logical fallacies. For instance, the celebratory generation of imperial historians recognized that the Report made little impact on influential contemporaries, yet never wholly explained how its initial failure could be reconciled with their claims for its formative influence. Second they failed to see how far Durham's two main aims were contradictory. The Report recommended both the Anglicization of the French and the introduction of a form of local self-government in which the French themselves would take part. These historians never explained how a powerful French minority could be persuaded to commit communal suicide, and failed to understand that the Report was intended as a Utilitarian "package" of interdependent points. Durham's hostility to the French was apologetically downgraded by Coupland to "the only first-rate blunder in his *Report,"* when arguably it was an inaccurate diagnosis of the Canada he so briefly visited and it certainly proved to be no prediction for its future. Third, although admitting that the scheme of local autonomy sketched in the Report would have been highly restricted, historians have tended to excuse Durham by their own speculation about his posthumous reactions to imperial change. Sir Charles Lucas in 1912 gave a good example of this technique:

> it is of course a vain thing to ask what a man would have said or done many years after his death, in altered conditions or with fuller knowledge. A broad-minded man moves with the times, and Lord Durham would never have stood still....

although in this case Lucas implicitly forbade Durham's shade to move further into the twentieth century by hurriedly adding that the Report offered "a British prescription for a British community," and not "a recipe for non-British communities."[2] The point remained, however, that historians were prepared to

---

From Ronald Hyam and Ged Martin (ed.), *Reappraisals in British Imperial History* (Toronto: Macmillan, 1975), 75–87. Reprinted by permission of the author.

measure Durham's contribution to the development of the empire not by the limitations of what he actually wrote, but by how his ideas might have changed had he outlived his generation. No one ever thought of allowing this indulgence to Lord North or Sir Francis Bond Head. Durham actually considered allowing British North America to elect members to Parliament at Westminster, which suggests that in 1838 at least he did not contemplate further extensions to colonial autonomy. No doubt this charity was largely inspired by Durham's untimely death—a parallel would be the apologia for John F. Kennedy's Vietnam policy, just as Campbell-Bannerman's death earned him a reputation for "solving" the South African problem. Benevolent as it may be, it is a misleading argument. It is easy to overstress the extent of Durham's radicalism. He was not in general politics the most single-mindedly radical or adaptable of his contemporaries, and he was certainly not the most prescient in colonial affairs. Others wanted Canada to have more freedom than he proposed—men like Howick, Roebuck and H.S. Chapman, whose involvement in the subject was deeper than Durham's own: as late as August 1837 he dismissed Canada as an "unfortunate business" in which he did not intend to be involved. By concentrating on "the great Durham illusion" historians have succeeded in conveying the impression that no serious thought had been given to the Canadian problem until he offered his brilliantly simple device of responsible government. In fact the problem of reconciling colonial autonomy with metropolitan supremacy was a good deal more complicated than the Report's superficial analysis allowed, and contemporaries were unimpressed by it precisely because they knew how much detailed and fruitless consideration the problem had already received. Historians, however, allowed themselves to be dazzled by Durham's confident prose, and took for perspicacity what infuriated contemporaries dismissed as arrogance. The *Morning Herald,* for instance, attacked the Report as a device for

> representing John George Lambton Earl of Durham as the only wise, discreet, virtuous, and truly intelligent statesman that ever cast a glance at Canadian affairs.[3]

The Report had its background in a mission flawed in many respects. One major weakness lay in Durham's poor relations with the ministers he served and with Melbourne the Prime Minister in particular; in a mission in which mutual confidence was vital, neither side really trusted the other. Opportunities for misunderstanding were increased by Durham's vanity. He certainly laid great stress on his own magnificence, and arguably an imposing front was necessary for the success of his mission. His mistake was to delay his departure for nearly four months while assembling his equipment and retinue. While Canada was in crisis, the High Commissioner made apparently leisurely arrangements for his journey, including the dispatch of his racehorses, plate and an orchestra. Durham's vanity was in itself a source of amusement, but coupled with his poor judgement of men and issues it became a fount of disaster. His most obvious blunder was the appointment of Thomas Turton and Edward Gibbon Wakefield, the first a central figure in a sensational divorce case, the second a former inmate of Newgate prison as a result of his abduction of an under-age heiress. Parliamentary attacks on the appointments helped to widen the breach between Durham and Melbourne. Yet damaging as these associates were, Durham's fundamental error of judgement was his reliance on his kinsman Edward Ellice, a great Canadian landowner and an influential figure in politics. Ellice was regarded by French Canadians as "one of their bitterest, most indefatigable, and most powerful enemies." From the outset Durham adopted Ellice's view of the Canadian problem and consulted closely with him. Even before the High Commissioner had left Britain, he had adopted the francophobic view which was a fundamental weakness in the mission. In the short term he missed a great opportunity. French Canadians did in fact welcome him as a deliverer, and Durham alone among British statesmen at the time had the stature to rally moderate leaders into the communal partnership which Elgin presided over a decade later. By dashing French hopes, and adding the insult of Anglicization to the injury of repression, Durham made subsequent reconciliation of French and British more difficult. And in the long run no Canadian settlement could be made which involved the mastery of one over the other.[4]

The major weaknesses of the Durham mission—his authoritarian behaviour, his lack of sympathy for French Canada and his poor choice of advisers—were all united in the affair of the Bermuda Ordinance. This dealt with his proposed exile of leading rebels. Overruled on a technicality, Durham responded by an abrupt and spectacular resignation. Resignation in itself seemed bad enough— an abandonment of a difficult post—but the timing was unfortunate, and Durham's behaviour was widely criticized. Durham now intended to adopt a dignified and tenable position by writing a report giving his views on Canada— although from the government's point of view a report in London was a poor second to a settlement in Quebec.

Writing a report on Canada increased Durham's dependence on Edward Ellice, both for his influence in politics and for his interest in Canada, and who noted: "Ld. Durham is going to produce a plan & hopes & intends to redeem himself thereby." Subsequent events suggest that Durham or his staff intended the Report to appeal over the heads of the ministers to the Crown and the people. For most of December a haughty feud continued between Durham and the Whig leaders. There is little sign that ministers intended to give much weight to Durham's opinions. The hostile Melbourne bluntly said: "I do not expect much from Durham's suggestions." Thus at the time the Durham Report was being written, there was no question of guilty ministers eagerly awaiting the pronouncement of a triumphant High Commissioner. The government was united in condemning Durham's behaviour, and Durham himself was hoping to re-establish his position in politics.[5]

In January 1839 work on the Report progressed rapidly and, as the Tories had cynically predicted, Durham and the ministers patched up their feud to avoid open conflict when Parliament met. Naturally, as the Report was produced hurriedly, it contained mistakes. But its fundamental error was much more one of analysis. In 1836–37 the government, under the prompting of Howick, aided by James Stephen of the Colonial Office, had been moving towards the idea of British North American federation. This was broadly the plan which Durham took to Canada. Not the least unfortunate aspect of his resignation was that it aborted an intercolonial convention about to meet in Quebec to discuss the possibility of a federal union with the Maritimes. But a second French rebellion, late in 1838, seemed to rule out any federal solution. After two revolts in a year, a French Canadian unit in a federation had become unthinkable. Under Ellice's influence, Durham turned instead to a legislative union, in which the French would be outvoted centrally but without the nuisance of their own local legislature. Poor communications made a legislative union with the Maritimes virtually impossible, although Durham hoped they would eventually be incorporated. Circumstances, then, dictated a union of the Canadas alone: a solution which Ellice and the Lower Canada British minority had advocated as far back as 1822. Durham concluded that the French identity would have to disappear altogether. A Canadian Union would have an English-speaking majority, which immigration would reinforce. As a result, the French would be Anglicized.

Durham had thus shifted from the idea of a locally autonomous federation based on some accommodation between French and British colonists, to proposing a locally autonomous legislative union, in which immigration was to be used to swamp and absorb the French. As a solution it contained several basic weaknesses. To give the united province any measure of self-government was tantamount to inviting the French, who formed about two-fifths of the population, to acquiesce, if not cooperate, in their own demise. So open an avowal of an Anglicizing policy could be expected to unite the French in self-defence. Furthermore, in attempting to define the scope of local self-government, Durham reserved to British imperial control not only foreign relations, but the local constitution, tariffs and public lands. The limitation of colonial autonomy had been and remained an almost insoluble problem. Durham had simply drawn up an agenda for disagreements, while giving little indication how imperial supremacy in the disputed areas could be upheld. As Sir George Arthur pointed out, Durham had never had to handle a colonial legislature. At one and the same time he wished to thrust the British imperial government into Canadian affairs, while driving the French into opposition. It pointed to a period of instability for, as Bagot was to complain in 1842, it was one thing to rely on the Anglicizing effects of immigration in the long term, but quite another to keep the government going in the short term.[6]

The Report was not well received. Praise from liberal journals was hardly enthusiastic, and several promised "due attention to this important document hereafter" and then abandoned the subject. Only the radical *Spectator* and the *Colonial Gazette,* both influenced by Wakefield, loudly defended the Report. It was certainly not "greeted with public acclamation by Englishmen of liberal sympathies," as Burroughs has claimed. The *Morning Chronicle* contented itself with saying "that great good will be effected by the mere circulation of this Report." Even the radical *Leeds Mercury* was less enthusiastic than it had expected to be. The field was left virtually clear for the opposition press to denounce the Report for "its mass of verbiage and its scantiness of fact," and to dismiss it as a "fatiguing mass of impertinent trifling and newspaper trash." It was widely noted that one of its major recommendations, the Canadian Union, was "whether good or bad, practicable or impracticable, not a *new* scheme," and one which Durham had adopted, "without giving it any very profound consideration." Many thought the Report superficial, containing nothing which "any man of third-rate abilities who had visited Canada for three or four months might have written just as well." In February 1839 the Durham Report was certainly not recognized as the charter of the colonies.[7]

A recent writer has confused press reception of the Report with its influence on the cabinet. However, there is independent evidence that ministers were little more impressed than journalists. Howick criticized the limitations Durham wished to place on colonial self-government. Russell, although listing the Report in a cabinet memorandum as one of the authorities for union, rejected Durham's portrait of communal hostility and thought his restrictions on self-government unenforceable. Normanby, who succeeded Glenelg as colonial secretary in February 1839, argued that the government should check "whether Durham speaks the opinions of the Representative Men of the English Party in Lower Canada." To Normanby, Durham's own recommendation was not important. What mattered was whether union was supported by the Lower Canadian minority: "If so this would decide the point of attempting to form a Legislative Union." Other ministers cared even less for Durham. When Normanby wished to tell him what policy was to be adopted, the cabinet refused its permission. Ministers had already decided not to consult Durham during their own deliberations. It seems unlikely, then, that the cabinet decided "to adopt in principle Durham's proposal for a legislative union of the Canadas," as Burroughs has restated the myth. Overall, they realized, as Durham had realized, that there was no real alternative to union. Following the rebellions, the French could not be allowed to control Lower Canada. Yet equally a liberal government could not indefinitely deprive a North American colony of a constitution. Union with English-speaking Upper Canada was the only way out. Nor did the principle of union come from Durham. Ellice had drawn up a complicated scheme of his own in December 1838, but as part of his policy of rehabilitating Durham, he did not submit it to the cabinet until February, when "Durham had paved the way by giving his report." When ministers accepted the principle of union, they decided to draw up a bill "mainly founded on Ellice's project." Its provisions were rewritten in detail several times in the next year, but the Report offered little guidance about the mechanics of Union. In its final form the government's scheme differed from Durham's on one important point, by giving Upper Canada equal representation with the lower province. Above all, it is difficult to see what other scheme the cabinet could have adopted. As Russell said, it was "the best principle of a settlement, not because the principle of a union did not in itself contain very great difficulties, but rather from the difficulties attending every other plan." When they did adopt it, they began with Ellice's scheme, not Durham's.[8]

Nor is there much evidence from parliamentary debates on Canada in 1839–40 that the Report had many supporters. It seemed, as Greville noted, "enormously long," and even Stanley, a leading opposition spokesman on colonial affairs, did not have time to *"skin"* it until June 1839. It seems unlikely that ministers or anyone else had "got it almost by heart" as Brougham emphasized, in what was ironically one of the more favourable references to the Report—apart from those of Durham's secretary, Buller. Durham did not prove a good parliamentary authority. In the summer of 1840 Melbourne quoted parts of the Report, arguing that "whatever opinions might be entertained of some parts of it," it was still "a very able and impartial view of the matter." A week later he found it necessary to qualify even that endorsement:

> There were unquestionably many things in that report which he did not praise, and which he did not think were prudent matters to be brought forward, and which he thought it would have been wise to have omitted, and he therefore did not say, that the report was an important authority.

Nevertheless he still thought "it contained much which was of very great value, and which was well deserving of consideration and attention. A month later the sympathetic *Colonial Gazette* complained that the Report was "well-nigh forgotten" in Britain.[9]

It may of course be argued that the impact of the Report either on the British government or British opinion is only a secondary question, and that the important issue is its reception in the colonies. It might also fairly be objected that British policy stemmed less from prescript than from reaction to events in the colonies, and hence Durham's Report could have had a major round-about effect in shaping the empire. Among French Canadians Durham's impact was traumatic, though hardly in line with his intentions. His advent inspired a burst of optimism in a beaten people: all would be well at last, it was felt, for if the British really wished French Canada ill, how could they have sent their most liberal statesman to start a new chapter in its government? Disillusionment was rapid and brutal, as Durham moved openly into the arms of the franco-phobe British minority in Lower Canada, and excluded the French from all but minor appointments. The satirical journal, *Le Fantasque,* which had applauded Durham's firmness in July 1838, was by October lamenting that they had regarded him as a god when he was only a man after all. The Report's cold dismissal of French Canadians as a people without history or literature helped to spur on a local renaissance, paradoxically helping to ensure that within a couple of decades French Canadians had a more self-consciously local culture than the still derivative British colonials. Durham's relations with the French were doubly disastrous. They had trusted him almost alone among British statesmen, and he might have been able to draw them into a British American federation based on a new chapter of communal cooperation. Instead he chose to trumpet a policy of assimilation which was threatening enough to reinforce French bitterness, but never in fact consistently enough adopted to destroy French identity. A good opportunity for statesmanship was discarded in favour of an unreal project of social engineering. When M-P. Hamel edited a French edition of the Report in 1948, he made it clear that the suspicions remained.

In Upper Canada the Report was mainly important for its effect on parties. The reformers, previously split into factions, were able to rally behind "responsible government," and Durham flags appeared at their meetings. Egerton Ryerson, the Methodist leader, was able to cover his tracks by insisting that Durham's view of responsible government differed from previous conceptions which he had opposed. Yet the unity which the Report gave the party was one of tactics rather than of intellectual revelation. Leading reformers differed in their responses to Sydenham's blandishments in 1841, and Ryerson himself broke with them in defending Sir Charles Metcalfe in 1844. Nor was this surprising. Responsible government was hardly a novel issue in colonial politics. Indeed, reformers had to make this point in order to defend themselves against the charge that they wished to abandon established constitutional forms in favour of the crochet of a visiting English peer. Nova Scotia's Joseph Howe denied in 1840 that the responsible government cry had been "learned from the Earl of Durham.... I am glad to have such an authority in support of my argument; but it was not learned from him." The Nova Scotian Assembly had been asking:

> for a government responsible in local affairs, before his lordship saw this continent.... I am happy to have the concurrence of so celebrated a man; but I think it right to show that we are not mere followers of his report, but had asked for responsible government before that document appeared.

Taking a wider perspective, it may be noted that the Report made less impact in New South Wales, despite extravagant claims by Wakefield. Few newspapers there seemed even to realize the full import of Durham's proposals. The *Sydney Herald* dismissed the Report as "not of very great interest," and the *Australian* thought it lacked "the least pretension to originality, or grandeur of thought." D. Beer concludes that in 1839 at least, the Report "had no significant effect on public opinion in New South Wales," and he indicates that the same was probably true of other Australian colonies. The English language press in South Africa was more enthusiastic. The *Graham's Town Journal* thought it:

> one of the most massy, and the same time one of the most lucid, documents which we have been privileged to read. Every thing like ornament has been discarded; and yet, as a whole, it is extremely beautiful.

It predicted that Durham's mission would be a landmark "in the future history not alone of Canada, but of all the British colonies." The *Commercial Advertiser* in Cape Town went further: "Nor will the mere colonist alone discover his face as in a glass looking into this Report." It would shake the foundations of the peerage and of the established church. Yet when it came to deciding how far Durham's lessons from the two communities in Canada applied to multiracial South Africa, there was less certainty. The *Commercial Advertiser* published thirteen extracts from the Report over two months, but never delivered its promised article on the Report's application to the Cape. The subject faded quietly away.[10]

What influence then did the Durham Report have on the Victorian empire? Conventionally it has been seen not only as the blueprint for colonial self-government, but also as a general picture of colonial affairs which made it, in Craig's phrase, "a document of enduring value and interest." There is a logical problem in arguing for the informative value of the Report. Lucas admitted that it contained "one or two instances of direct mis-statement, and more numerous instances of obvious exaggeration," while Coupland pointed to "some palpably unfair judgements in it and one or two small mistakes of fact." The real informative value of an inaccurate report may be doubted. Furthermore, even where the Report provided a mass of evidence, it understandably arranged it to make a particular point. MacDonagh has commented that the Report's evidence on emigration, although sensational enough to administer "a very healthy jolt" to the government machinery involved, was largely "high-purposed manipulation of evidence to antecedently determined ends," amounting to "an unprincipled indictment." The Report was anything but the "first-rate piece of research" which G.S. Graham asserted as recently as 1970. Nor should the Durham Report be considered in isolation. It had been preceded by two major inquiries into Canadian affairs, the parliamentary committee of 1828 and the Gosford commission of 1836–37, both of which had produced lengthy and less-hurried reports. Admittedly, Durham had the burden of administration to cope with, but it is none the less true that the amount of enquiry on which his findings were based fell far short of that given to other major reports. Compare Durham's mission, for instance, with that carried out upon penal settlement by J.T. Bigge as special commissioner in Australia between 1819 and 1821. Durham spent five months in Canada; Bigge spent seventeen in Australia. Durham's impressions of the 400,000 people of Upper Canada were based on a ten-day steamboat tour; Bigge took six days to inspect a few hundred convicts at Port Hunter. Durham did not visit the Atlantic colonies at all, and confessed to "no information whatever, except from sources open to the public at large" about Newfoundland; Bigge spent three months in Van Diemen's Land. Not surprisingly, Durham's account was often superficial. Unfortunately, it was some of his more sensational comments which lingered. The Whig government was embarrassed by his description of "two nations warring in the bosom of a single state." Russell labelled the description as "highly coloured," since if hostility between the two communities were so bitter it hardly made sense to unite the provinces. Similarly, Durham's picture of a striking difference between American prosperity and Canadian stagnation seems to have been occasionally referred to in the 1840s and 1850s.[11]

These peripheral references make all the more striking the absence of extended reference to the Report during discussions of the painful emergence of Canadian self-government in the 1840s. Exactly how Canada achieved a system of parliamentary self-government in 1847–48 remains a matter for debate. One quaint suggestion, recently made, is that "it was the apparent resolution of the French question in 1840 that made British ministers willing to concede greater self-government"—which makes nonsense of the political crises under Bagot and Metcalfe. The concession of virtual tariff autonomy to the colonies in 1846 made possible a wider measure of self-government than Durham had contemplated, and the adoption by the USA of an expansive policy under the presidency of Polk made a Canadian settlement more vital. The British concession of responsible government to the mainland colonies of North America in 1847–48 represented a timely realization that Canada at least could not be retained in any other way. Durham's idea of local self-government had involved the quasi-presidential rule of an Anglicizing Governor, controlling a wide field of reserved topics, including land policy and tariffs. Canada in the late 1840s evolved a cabinet system explicitly based on Anglo-French partnership, and evading a close definition of local and imperial powers. When the first contentious legislation of the LaFontaine-Baldwin ministry was attacked in the British parliament, Brougham alone quoted Durham, and quoted his view of the "war of races" to criticize the idea of partnership with the French. In fact as early as 1842, when Bagot was forced to admit the French to office, it was clear that Durham's mixture of autonomy and Anglicization had gone astray. In the *Morning Chronicle,* Charles Buller was unwise enough to hail the new ministry as the triumph of Durham's policy. *The Times* took up the subject:

> It is not a little curious, and reflects no great credit on the penetration of the late Lord Durham, to compare the working of the new union of the Canadas, adopted in accordance with his report, with the purposes for which he recommended it.

Subsequent events had not inspired "implicit reliance on the predictions of that well-known, and certainly very interesting Report." A year later it returned to the theme, blaming Durham for the "strange combination of blunders" by which a union designed to end French influence had given them control of the province.

> He it was ... who contrived to revive and set the seal upon the worst suspicions of the French Canadians by the same act which conferred upon them an unlimited power of avenging themselves—to unite the evils of provoking tyranny with those of the most dangerous concession.

Yet few of the many detailed press discussions of the problem of colonial self-government in the 1840s mentioned Durham's views. Perhaps the reason was revealed by a journalist reviewing one of Sir Francis Head's books in 1846, who said of Durham's Canadian mission, without any trace of hostility: "It has been hinted that mental malady afflicted his Lordship at this period of his political career, and it is but fair to think so."[12]

How then did the Report become an imperial symbol? Its rediscovery came late in the nineteenth century. Historians trained in the Whig tradition found in its clear and vigorous style an equivalent of Magna Charta for the empire. Durham's career, both heroic and tragic, added to the Report's stature as an imperial testament. Moreover, with hindsight it was easy to minimize the theoretical weaknesses of Durham's idea, and credit him with prophecy. Irish and South African problems seemed to give the Report a continuing relevance. In the latter case, those who wished to Anglicize the Afrikaners and those who wished to reconcile them could equally appeal to his authority. The South African crisis of the 1890s marked, however, a rediscovery, if not a rescue, of a largely forgotten document: the republication of the Report in 1902 was the first reprinting since 1839. This process is notably evident in the case of John X. Merriman of Cape Colony. Although born in England, Merriman had opposed British intervention in South African affairs from his entry into its politics in the 1870s, and consequently disapproved of the Anglo-Boer War. In 1900 he argued strongly in favour of clemency for Cape rebels who had risen in support of the Afrikaner armies, and he began to read about the Canadian rebellions of the 1830s in order to seek precedents. Admiration for Durham's policy led him to read the Report, finding in the picture of communal hostility "much that applies to this country, but much that is so different." He was struck by the fact that he should have known so little about it.

> Lord D's Report is, of course, the Magna Charta of Colonial Government much talked about but seldom if ever read or looked at, and I say this with a guilty blush as being a very tardy reader myself of this particular document.

In 1902 he observed that Elgin and Durham had established the British Commonwealth. "Yet how few even know their names?"[13]

Within a few years this complaint could no longer be made. A mammoth biography by Reid in 1906 and a magisterial edition of the Report by Lucas in 1912 enshrined Durham firmly in the imperial pantheon. The report thus became the symbol of the empire's success in solving one of its problems, namely relations with the colonies of settlement. In the twentieth century, it had less relevance than ever. For the empire as a whole, the central problem was with non-European peoples, to whom Durham's Anglocentric remedies could hardly be applied. In Canada, national status was replaced by cultural partnership as the major issue, and here the Report became a positive embarrassment. Historians' references gradually faded from the passionate to the merely polite, a process which ironically helped to shield the Durham myth from basic challenge. Consequently "what ought to be known as the great Durham illusion" continued to be enshrined in general histories and respected textbooks. Probably the myth was a benevolent one in the twentieth-century empire, stressing some of its more liberal elements and incidentally making its demise less painful. Now that the British empire is all but an episode of the past, we should discard the Durham myth in order to seek more realistic perspectives on the imperial experience.

Notes

1. For editions of the Report, C. P. Lucas (ed.) *Lord Durham's Report on the affairs of British North America* (1912); R. Coupland (ed.) *The Durham Report* (1945), and quotation from cxlvi; G. M. Craig (ed.) *Lord Durham's Report* (1963). For biographies: S. J. Reid *Life and letters of the first Earl of Durham 1792–1840* (1906); C. W. New *Lord Durham* (1929). For criticisms: J. M. Ward in *HS* xiv (1969–71) 592; R. S. Neale "Roebuck's constitution and the Durham proposals" ibid. 580–90; Ged Martin *The Durham Report and British policy* (1972), on which this essay is based. For recent strong affirmations of the importance of the Report: N. Mansergh *The Commonwealth experience* (1969) 30ff; and G. S. Graham *A concise history of the British empire* (1970) 152–4.

2. Coupland (ed.) *Durham Report* clxi; Lucas (ed.) *Lord Durham's Report* I 311, and cf. Craig (ed.) *Lord Durham's Report* vii.

3. C. R. Sanderson (ed.) *The Arthur Papers* (1957–9) I 274; for Head *The Times* 28 Aug 1869; Lord Esher *The girlhood of Queen Victoria* (1912) I 280; New *Lord Durham* 78; *The life and times of Henry Lord Brougham* (1871) III 502 Durham to Brougham 7 Dec 1827; Reid *Life and letters* II 143–4 Durham to Ellice, 27 Aug 1837; *Spectator* 17 Nov 1838, 1084–5; *Morning Herald* 11 Feb 1839.

4. L. C. Sanders (ed.) *Lord Melbourne's Papers* (1889) 428–9 Melbourne to Durham 18 Jul 1838; *The Times* 21 Sep 1863; *Spectator* 17 Nov 1838, 1084–5; National Library of Scotland, Ellice Papers E30, Durham to Ellice, private, [Jan 1838] 43–4; J. Monet *The last cannon shot* (1969) 19–20; PAC, Chapman Papers, O'Callaghan to Falconer, Apr 1838; W. Ormsby "Lord Durham and the assimilation of French Canada" in N. Penlington (ed.) *On Canada: essays in honour of Frank H. Underhill* (1971) 37–53.

5. Buller to Mill (most private) 13 Oct 1838, A. G. Doughty (ed) *Report of the Public Archives for the year 1928* (1929) 74–6; Ellice Papers, Lady Durham to Ellice [1 Dec 1838] 151–2; Russell to Ellice 24 Dec 1838, 24–5; Russell Papers (microfilm B-970), Russell to Melbourne 9, 12 Dec 1838; University of Durham, Grey Papers, Howick Journal 5 Jan 1839; Melbourne to Russell 19 Dec 1838, Sanders (ed.) *Lord Melbourne's Papers* 443–4.

6. Ellice Papers, E30, Durham to Ellice 18 Jan 1839, 79–80; Melbourne to Russell 11, 23 Dec 1838, Sanders (ed.) 441–2, 444; Lucas II 168–73; Arthur to Colborne 6 Apr 1839, Sanderson (ed.) *Arthur Papers* II 110–11; PAC, Derby Papers (microfilm A-30), Bagot to Stanley (private) 10 Jun [Jul] 1842.

7. H. E. Carlisle (ed.) *A selection from the correspondence of Abraham Hayward, Q.C.* (1886) I 68–70; *Leeds Mercury* 8 Dec 1838; *Globe* 8 Feb; *Examiner* 10 Feb, 90–1; *Manchester Guardian* 9 Feb 1839; P. Burroughs (ed.) *The colonial reformers and Canada 1830–1849* (1969) 128; *Morning Chronicle* 9 Feb; *Leeds Mercury* 16 Feb; *Morning Herald* 9, 11 Feb; *Morning Post* 9, 18 Feb 1839.

8. P. Burroughs *CHR* LV (1974) 320–2; Howick to Durham 7 Feb 1839; A. G. Doughty (ed.) *Report of the Public Archives for the year 1923* 338–40; Russell Papers, memo, 28 Mar 1839, Normanby to Russell [misdated 1841]; *3PD* XLVII 3 Jun 1839, 1254–75; Grey Papers, Howick Journal 2, 24 Mar, 13 Apr 1839; P. Burroughs *The Canadian crisis and British colonial policy, 1828–1841* (1972) 107; PRO CO. 880/1, Ellice to Melbourne (private) 24 Feb 1839, enclosing plan of 21 Dec 1838, 10–12; *3PD,* XLIX 11 Jul 1838, 174–5.

9. H. Reeve (ed.) *Greville memoirs—the second part* (1885) I 162; Graham Papers, microfilm 31, Stanley to Graham 6 Jun 1839; *3PD* XLIX 26 Jul, 852, and LV 30 Jun, 7 Jul 1840, 232, 515; *Colonial Gazette* 12 Aug 1840, 529.

10. M-P. Hamel (ed.) *Le Rapport de Durham* (1948) 16, 26, 50–1; Monet *Last cannon shot* 17–20, 24–33; M. Wade *The French Canadians* (1968 ed.) I 284–5; G. W. Brown "The Durham Report and the Upper Canadian scene" *CHR* XX (1939) 136–60; G. M. Craig *Upper Canada: the formative years 1734–1841* (1963) 264–71; D. C. Harvey "Nova Scotia and the Durham mission" *CHR* XX (1939) 176; D. Beer "A note on Lord Durham's Report and the New South Wales press, 1839" *JRAHS* LIV (1968) 205–7; *Graham's Town Journal* 23 May 1839; *South African Commercial Advertiser* 8 May 1839.

11. Craig ix; Lucas I 116; Coupland xlviii; O. MacDonagh *A pattern of government growth 1800–60* (1961) 135, 131; Graham *Concise history of the British empire* 152; J. Ritchie *Punishment and profit: the reports of Commissioner John Bigge* (1970); *Lucas* II 202, 16 and cf. *3PD* XLVII 3 Jun 1839, 254–75. Durham's comments on Canadian economic backwardness were cited by *The Times* 12 Aug 1848, and in a speech by Elgin, *Daily News.*

11. Jan 1855.

12. P. Burroughs *CHR* LV (1974) 320–2; *3PD* LVI 19 Jun 1849, 455–7; *The Times* 29 Oct 1842, 16 Dec 1843, 5 Dec 1846.

13. P. Lewsen (ed.) *Selections from the correspondence of J. X. Merriman* (1960–69) III 196–9. When the Report appeared in 1839, Abraham Hayward, a lawyer and journalist sympathetic to Durham, noted that it was thought to be "well-written, but all well-informed people say that it is superficial and one-sided." This verdict remains closer to a balanced judgement than Graham's recent claim that the Report was "a great, if not the greatest landmark in the history of the British Empire." (Carlisle *Correspondence of Hayward* I 68–70; Graham 153.)

FRENCH-CANADIAN NATIONALISM AND THE CHALLENGE OF ULTRAMONTANISM

Jacques Monet

A funny thing happened to French-Canadian nationalism on its way to responsible government. It became ultramontane.

At the end of the 1830s French Canada was in ferment. Under British domination for some seventy-five years, the French had succeeded in surviving, but not in developing by themselves a full, normal, national life. They had kept the essentials: their ancestral land, their French language, their Catholic Faith, their time-honoured and peculiar jurisprudence, and their long family traditions. But they needed a new life. The seigneurial system could no longer hold the growing population, the economy lagged, the problems of education had reached such an impasse that the schools were closed, and the old civil code no longer applied to modern circumstances. Above all, the upward thrust of the growing professional middle class created a serious social situation of which the rebellions of 1837–38 were only one expression. Clearly, if the struggle for national survival were to hold any meaning for the future, French-Canadian nationalists needed new solutions.

They were divided, however. Inspired by the ideology of Louis-Joseph Papineau some considered *la survivance*[a] could be assured only by political isolation in a territory over which French-Canadians would be undisputed masters. Militant idealists, they were led by John Neilson and Denis-Benjamin Viger until Papineau returned to politics in 1847. Others, broader-minded and more practical, held to a doctrine of which the Quebec editor Etienne Parent was the clearest exponent, and which Louis-Hippolyte LaFontaine translated into politics. They reasoned that it was the flexibility of the British constitutional system that could best assure not only their acquired rights, but also (by means of self-government) the certain hope of a broadening future for their language, their institutions, and their nationality.

Before achieving responsible government, however, LaFontaine needed to accomplish two things. He had to forge the unity of his people in favour of British parliamentary democracy and, along with this, form a united political party with the Upper Canadians. Neither was easy. In the years immediately following the rebellion French Canada's strongest sympathies belonged to the leaders of the Viger-Neilson group, believers neither in responsible government nor in union with Upper Canada. After the election of 1841, for instance, out of some twenty-nine members elected by French-Canadian ridings, LaFontaine could

---

From Canadian Historical Association, *Annual Report* 1966, pp. 41–55. Reprinted by permission of the author and the Canadian Historical Association.

[a] survival

count on only six or seven to be sympathetic to his views. By 1844, he had succeeded in persuading many more—at least he could then count on some two dozen. But not before the end of the decade could he be certain of victory, for until then Papineau, his followers, and especially his legend remained one of the strongest forces in the country. Still, after a decade of fistfights on electoral platforms, scandals, riots, and racial fury; after a brilliant, dynamic, and flexible partnership with Robert Baldwin, LaFontaine became in 1848 the first Canadian Prime Minister in the modern sense and, by means of the British Constitution, the first French-Canadian to actually express and direct the aspirations of his people.

He had also gradually, and all unwittingly perhaps, presided over the marriage of ultramontanism with the practical politics and the nationalist ideology of his party. At the beginning of the decade, the hierarchy and priests of the Roman Catholic Church in French Canada hardly conceived that practical party politics could be their concern, nor did they think of adding significantly to the nationalist theme. They worked behind the scenes; and, in 1838, for instance, after deciding to oppose the Union, they composed and signed an unpublicized petition which they sent directly to London to be presented to the Queen. But in 1848, during the crisis which consecrated the practice of responsible government, they openly took sides with LaFontaine's party, and allowed their newspapers to give approval to his administration. Likewise, at the time of the rebellions, most of the priests, and especially those among the hierarchy, had officially disassociated themselves from what seemed to be the main preoccupations of the leading French-Canadian nationalists. *"Des mauvais sujets ... prétendus libéraux, attachés à détruire dans nos peuples l'amour de la religion,"*[b][1] Bishop Jacques Lartigue of Montreal called the *Patriotes,* while Archbishop Signay of Quebec tried to explain to his flock that Colborne's devastating march against the rebels had been undertaken *"pas à dessein de molester ou maltraiter personne, mais pour protéger les bons et fidèles sujets, pour éclairer ceux des autres qui sont dans l'erreur et qui se sont laissés égarer."*[c][2] Within a decade later, however, they openly wrote and talked of the doctrine that the Catholic Faith and French Canada's nationality depended one upon the other. *"Tous les rapports qui nous arrivent des divers points du diocèse,"* the *Mélanges Religieux* reported on 7 July 1843, about the Saint-Jean-Baptiste day celebrations, *"prouvent combien sont vifs et universels les sentiments de religion et de nationalité de nos concitoyens. Partout ces deux sentiments se sont montrés inséparables dans les coeurs: la pompe et les cérémonies religieuses ont accompagné les démonstrations civiles et patriotiques ... C'est parce que nous sommes catholiques que nous sommes une nation dans ce coin de l'Amérique, que*

---

[b] "Some evil subjects..., claiming to be liberal and determined to destroy our people's love of religion."

[c] "not with the intent of bothering or molesting anyone but to protect true and loyal subjects, to enlighten those others who are in error and have allowed themselves to wander from the correct path."

nous attirons les regards de toutes les autres contrées, l'intérêt et la sympathie de tous les peuples ... Qu'on nous dise ce que serait le Canada s'il était peuplé exclusivement d'Anglais et de Protestants?"[d] Of course, much happened between 1838 and 1848 to change the thinking of both nationalists and Catholic clerics.

One very important thing was the advent of Ignace Bourget. A short time after succeeding to the See of Montreal in 1840, this earnest and authoritarian Bishop made it clear how much he intended to renew the face of Catholicism in French Canada. During his first year—incidentally, after successfully reasserting in an interesting conflict with Poulett Thomson the doctrine of Papal supremacy and of episcopal independence of civil authority—he had organized a great mission throughout his diocese, preached by Bishop Forbin-Janson, one of France's foremost orators. Between September 1840 and December 1841, the French Bishop travelled across Lower Canada, visiting some sixty villages and preaching rousing sermons—two of which Lord Sydenham attended in state at Notre-Dame—before crowds sometimes estimated at 10,000. Bishop Bourget thus initiated close and large-scale religious contacts with France.

Indeed, while Forbin-Janson was still in Canada, the new Bishop of Montreal left on the first of some five voyages to France and Rome, a trip from which he would return carrying with him the reawakened energies of the Catholic revival. While in Europe, he held discussions with a cluster of interesting and influential Catholic ultramontane leaders. At this time, European ultramontanes—whose intellectual roots reached as far back as the quarrels between Philippe LeBel and Boniface VIII, the pope "beyond the mountains"—had outgrown the traditional belief that the Pope held doctrinal and jurisdictional supremacy over the whole Church. Brought up on DeMaistre's *Du Pape*, a book that urged Papal dominion over temporal rulers in all Church matters, and feverish with romanticism's revival of all things medieval, they urged the subservience of civil government to the papacy, of State to Church. They had not understood that there was a difference between the surrender of all men to God's will, and the obedience of civil society to the Pope. They were mistaken—but they were, perhaps because of this, all the more dogmatic, energetic, aflame with zeal: they directed newspapers, notably Louis Veuillot's *L'Univers*, entertained crucial political polemics over education, censorship, and "secret organizations"; by the 1840s, they had founded hundreds of pious societies for desirable ends, collected a multiplication of relics from the Roman catacombs, covered Europe with imitation Gothic, and filled their churches and parlours with Roman *papier-maché* statuary.

---

[d] "All the reports that we receive from all over the diocese... prove how alive and widespread are religious and national feelings among our fellow citizens. These two sentiments have shown themselves to be inseparable in hearts everywhere: ceremony and religious rites have always been part of lay and patriotic demonstrations... This occurs because we are Catholics and a nation in this corner of America. As a result, we draw the attention of all other lands, the interest and sympathy of all peoples... We would like to know what Canada would be like if it were populated only with English and Protestants."

Bishop Bourget fell under their spell as soon as he arrived. In Paris he had long conversations with the Abbé Desgenettes, *curé* of the ultramontane cenacle at Notre-Dame-des-Victoires, and the founder of the Archconfraternity of the Most Holy and Immaculate Heart of Mary; he met Théodore de Ratisbonne, a convert from Judaism and the founder of the Daughters of Sion, Jean-Marie de Lamennais, the founder of the Brothers of the Christian Schools, and the most noted of them all, Louis Veuillot, who attended a sermon of Mgr Bourget's at Notre-Dame-des-Victoires and gave it a rave review in *L'Univers*. At Chartres, he was entertained by the compelling personality of the Abbé, later Cardinal, Louis-Edouard Pie, the future exponent of Papal infallibility at the Vatican Council. In Marseille, he was impressed by Bishop de Mazenod, another staunch defender of the Vatican; and in Rome, he was greeted by Fr. John Roothaan, the General of the Jesuits, with whom he spent eight days in retreat and meditation. Finally, several audiences with the kindly Gregory XVI crowned the series of discussions that made him the most ultramontane churchman of his generation in Canada.[3]

In Chartres, the Bishop of Montreal also had a long conversation with Bishop Clausel de Montals. The latter was a strong Gallican, but nonetheless the acknowledged champion in the fight for Catholic institutions against the State University. He doubtless recited for his Canadien colleague a long list of the dangers and evils of the *école laïque*.[e] For from that day onwards Mgr Bourget would battle tirelessly to keep the Church in control of education in Lower Canada. And all Canadian ultramontanes would follow him in this.

Back in Montreal, Mgr Bourget began injecting into the *Canadien* mood the full fever of his Roman creed. With a crusader's singleness of purpose, he arranged for the immigration from France of the Oblate and Jesuit Orders, of the Dames du Sacré-Coeur and the Sisters of the Good Shepherd; he founded two Canadian religious congregations of his own, established the Saint Vincent de Paul Society; carried out an extensive canonical visitation of his diocese, and pressed Rome to establish an ecclesiastical Province that extended within a few years to new dioceses in Toronto, Ottawa, British Columbia, and Oregon, *"une vaste chaîne de sièges épiscopaux qui doit s'étendre un jour de la mer jusqu'à la mer: a mari usque ad mare."*[f][4] He also organized a whole series of Parish revivals and religious ceremonies superbly managed to stir the emotion of all classes. At Varennes on 26 July 1842, for example, before a huge crowd of several thousand, surrounded by some sixty priests and in the full pontifical splendour of his office, he presided over the crowning of a holy picture of Saint Anne, according to *"le cérémonial usité à Rome pour de semblables solennités."*[g] (The end of the day was, perhaps, more *Canadien: "Tous ces feux,"*

---

[e] non-religious schools

[f] "a long chain of episcopal sees that one day must stretch from sea to sea: a mari usque ad mare."

[g] "the rites used in Rome on similar solemn occasions."

reported the *Mélanges,* "*des salves d'artillerie ou de mousquetterie au milieu du silence d'une nuit profonde, après toutes les cérémonies de la journée, faisaient naître des émotions nouvelles inconnues.*"[h] [5]) Another time, in November 1843, he presided over a huge demonstration in honour of the transferral to the chapel of the Sisters of Providence of the bones of Saint Januaria, ancient Roman relics which he had negotiated away from the custodian of one of the catacombs. At this service, the golden reliquary was carried by four canons of the cathedral surrounded by eight seminarians bearing incense, and "*la foule eut peine à se retirer, tant était grande son émotion.*"[i] [6] Throughout the 1840s, he ordered many more such occasions. For the blessing of the bells for the new towers of Notre-Dame Church, "*on exécuta parfaitement le jeu du God Save the Queen—Dieu sauve notre reine auquel la bande du régiment fit écho de toute la force de ses instruments.*"[j] [7] (Yes, the ultramontanes were also strong royalists. The *Mélanges* often published articles on royalty, one of which began by praising "*les principes d'honneur, de devoir, d'ordre, de générosité, de dévouement, qui dérivent de l'idée monarchique.*"[k] [8]) A not untypical reaction to this type of demonstration was that of the politician Joseph Cauchon who wrote to a colleague about the funeral of Archbishop Signay in October 1850: "*Le deuil de l'Eglise était grandiose et solennel à l'extrême. L'installation du nouvel archevêque s'est faite avec une égale solennité. Il y a quelque chose de grand, de sublime dans ce développement des cérémonies soit lugubres soit joyeuses du Catholicisme.*"[l] [9]

The new Orders naturally aided Mgr Bourget with his ultramontanism—especially the Jesuits who began in 1843 to lay the foundation of Collège Sainte-Marie, an institution that would train so many energetic young nationalist Catholics. The *Mélanges Religieux* also helped. In this bi-weekly newspaper, the priests from the bishopric published over and over again long articles of praise for the papal states, and copious excerpts from the works of leading ultramontanists: speeches by the Spanish conservative Donoso Cortés, Montalembert's famous oration on the Roman question, Mgr de Bonald's pastoral letter "*contre les erreurs de son temps,*"[m] and long book reviews such as the

---

[h] "After all the ceremonies during the day, all these artillery salutes and rifle-fire breaking the deep silence of the night stirred up strange new emotions."

[i] "the crowd could hardly hold back so greatly was it stirred."

[j] "we performed *God save the Queen — Dieu sauve notre reine* perfectly accompanied by the regimental band playing its instruments very loudly."

[k] "the principles of honour, of duty, of order, of generosity and of devotion that derive from the idea of the monarchy."

[l] "The mourning of the Church was great and solemn in the extreme. The installation of the new archbishop was carried out with equal solemnity. There is something great and sublime when Catholic ceremonies occur, be they sad or joyful."

[m] "against the errors of the present time."

one condemning Eugène Sue's salacious *Les Mystères de Paris* for trying to *"répandre sur la religion et ses pratiques tout l'odieux possible."*[n] [10] They also issued vibrant appeals to Canadian youth to join their movement: *"Vous voulez être de votre siècle jeunes amis, vous voulez marcher avec lui? ... Avez-vous trouvé mieux où reposer votre âme que dans les oeuvres immortelles des DeBonald, de Maistre, de Chateaubriand, de Montalembert, du Lamartine catholique, de Turquety?"*[o] [11] They also gave news of Catholicism throughout the world, concentrating especially on the independence of the papal states and the university question in France. *"Pour parvenir à remplir leur mission,"* the *Mélanges* noted on 31 March 1846, *"les Éditeurs n'ont rien épargné; ils ont fait venir à grands frais les meilleurs journaux d'Europe, L'Univers, L'Ami de la Religion, Le Journal des Villes et des Campagnes de France, le Tablet de Londres, le Freeman's Journal de New York, le Cross d'Halifax, le Catholic Magazine de Baltimore, le Catholic Herald de Philadelphie, le Propagateur Catholique de la Nouvelle-Orléans."*[p] In a word, the *Mélanges* opened a window on the Catholic world. And through it there blew in the high winds of ultramontanism, which, for the *Canadiens*, felt so much like their own aggressive and assertive nationalism.

Through it there also came for the clergy a novel regard for the layman. Since the Restoration in Europe, the Catholic Bishops and priests had achieved some success there in reintegrating the Church into educational life and social services. Very often they had done this with the assistance of influential laymen. Through the *Mélanges* publication of articles and speeches by these European ultramontane politicians, the *Canadien* priests gradually developed a fresh respect for their own lay politicians. They began to think of new ideas on how they could work with them. In fact, with the coming of responsible government the old ways which the priests had grown accustomed to were passing into history forever. The Union had marked the end of the courteous and courtly style which the Bishops and the British Governors had so carefully devised over the years to fuse the good of the throne with the good of the altar. Now, effective political power was passing from the hands of Governors-General to those of the *Canadien* electors. And if the Church was to exercise the influence which the priests felt in conscience it must, then the clergy must begin to deal directly with the politicians and the people.

---

[n] "spread as much filth as possible on our religion and practices."

[o] "Young people, do you wish to be part of your century and march with us? ... Have you found a better spot to find comfort for your souls than in the immortal works of DeBonald, Maistre, Chateaubriand, Montalembert, of the Catholic Lamartine or Turquety?"

[p] "In order to carry out their mission ... the Publishers have spared nothing; they have brought in at great expense the best newspapers from Europe: *L'Univers, L'Ami de la Religion, Le Journal des Villes et des Campagnes de France,* the *Tablet* from London, the *Freeman's Journal* from New York, the *Cross* from Halifax, the *Catholic Magazine* from Baltimore, the *Catholic Herald* from Philadelphia, the *Propagateur Catholique* from New Orleans."

Besides, they were finding nationalist politicians whom they liked. Indeed, by the middle of the decade, it was becoming obvious how much LaFontaine's followers and the priests seemed made to understand each other. The debate on the Union, during which they had been on opposite sides, was settled. And since then, they had forged new personal friendships. In Quebec, politicians such as René-Édouard Caron, Étienne-Pascal Taché, and especially Joseph-Édouard Cauchon, the editor of the influential *Journal de Québec,* enjoyed frequent hospitality at the Séminaire. Taché and Cauchon were also close correspondents of the Archbishop's secretary, the talented and ubiquitous *abbé* Charles-Félix Cazeau. In Montreal, LaFontaine's close friend, Augustin-Norbert Morin, also received a cordial welcome at the bishopric, especially from Mgr Bourget's *Grand-Vicaire,* Mgr Hyacinthe Hudon. So did other partisans like Lewis Thomas Drummond and Joseph Coursol. Indeed, as these priests and politicians grew to admire each other, a new esteem was also developing between their leaders, between the new Bishop of Montreal and the man who in 1842 had become French Canada's Attorney-General. Despite initial suspicion on both their parts, Bourget and LaFontaine were by temperament made to understand each other. Both were heroes to duty, strong-willed leaders, unyielding in their principles, and expert at manoeuvring within the letter of the law. Especially they had this in common that each one thought in absolute terms that he was in total possession of the truth. Neither could accept from an adversary anything but complete conversion.

Thus it was that slowly within the womb of LaFontaine's party, despite appearances, the pulse of the clerico-nationalist spirit began, faintly, to beat.

None of these things—Bishop Bourget's trip to Europe and its effects in Montreal, the historical turn in Canadian politics caused by responsible government, the new intimacy between ultramontanes and nationalists—none could weigh enough to bring the priests officially into LaFontaine's party. But they did prepare the way. Then, in 1846, the public discussion over a new Education Bill and over the funds from the Jesuit Estates revealed to the clergy which politicians were its natural allies and which were not. The Education Bill of 1845, proposed by Denis-Benjamin Papineau, the great tribune's brother, who was Commissioner of Crown Lands in the Viger-Draper administration, did not satisfy the clergy. Although it provided for the *curés* being *ex officio* "visitors" to the schools, it did not give them the control they wished. They therefore began a campaign to have the project amended in their favour.

The *Mélanges* took the lead, repeatedly emphasizing the close connection between education and religion. *"Nous ne comprenons pas d'éducation sans religion, et conséquemment sans morale,"* it had written back in 8 November 1842, in words which could easily have been inspired by Bishop Bourget's conversation with Clausel de Montals, *"et nous ne voyons pas ce qui pourrait suppléer à son enseignement dans les écoles. Que sera donc l'instruction et l'éducation des enfants sans prières, sans catéchisme, sans instruction religieuse et morale quelconque?"*[q] Even as the Bill was being debated, the *Mélanges* kept up the pressure, receiving great assistance from A.-N. Morin, *"ce monsieur dont le coeur est droit,"*[r] as one *curé* wrote.[12] From his seat on the Opposition benches, with the aid of his colleagues Taché, Drummond, and Cauchon, Morin proposed amendment after amendment to bring about a system which would happily unite clerical authority on the local level with centralized control by the Superintendent at the Education Department. *"M. Papineau, auquel j'ai eu le plaisir d'administrer quelque dure médecine pour lui faire digérer son Bill d'Éducation, ne veut pas que l'éducation soit religieuse,"* Cauchon reported to the *abbé* Cazeau. *"J'ai dit, moi votre ouaille, qu'une éducation dépouillée de l'instruction religieuse mènerait à de funestes résultats."*[s] [13] Finally, in mid-1846, Denis-Benjamin Papineau bowed to the pressure, and accepted the Morin amendments.

If the Bishops accordingly felt happy about the Act in its final form, they owed it in great part to the support of politicians like Morin and his friends. At the same time, they were receiving support from LaFontaine's friends on another critical issue: the Jesuit Estates.

The problem of these lands which had been granted by a succession of French Kings and nobles to serve as an endowment for education, had definitely passed to the British Crown in 1800 at the death of the last Jesuit. Their revenues were used by the Colonial Office for any number of Government sinecures until 1832 when as a gesture of conciliation it agreed that they be administered by the Lower Canadian Assembly. Then there began another struggle with the Catholic Bishops who claimed that they and not the Assembly were the true heirs of the Jesuits. By 1846 the controversy had reached the floor of the House, and the Provincial Government, led by Denis-Benjamin Viger, refused the Bishops' claim. As in the debate over Papineau's Education Bill, LaFontaine and his party supported the priests. LaFontaine, Morin (who had been acting as confidential advisor to the clergy on the question), Drummond, and Taché each delivered an impassioned speech against the "spoliation" of French Canada's heritage; Morin himself proposing that the funds be transferred entirely to the Church. Viger defended the Government's action on the grounds of precedent and Parliamentary supremacy. He won the vote. But in appealing to Parliamentary supremacy, he began a disagreeable discussion

---

[q] "We cannot understand education separate from religion and therefore from morality ... and we don't see what could take the place of religious teaching in schools. What would the education and instruction of children be without prayers, without catechism, without religious and moral instruction at all?"

[r] "this gentleman whose heart is true,"

[s] "Mr. Papineau, to whom I had the pleasure of giving a nasty dose of medicine to help him digest his Education Bill, does not want education to be religious, ... As a member of your flock, I said that education that does not include religious instruction would lead to fatal results."

which continued in the press for over three months. At the end, it was clear how wide a division had taken place among French-Canadian nationalists: a division as explicit as the opposing doctrines of liberalism and ultramontanism.

While traditionally nationalist papers such as *Le Canadien*, and *L'Aurore des Canadas*, defending Viger, assailed the Church's position, *La Minerve, Le Journal de Québec*, and *La Revue Canadienne*, all LaFontaine papers, became like the *Mélanges* defenders of the Faith. In a series of articles probably written by Viger,[14] *L'Aurore* insisted that the Bishops had at most a very tenuous claim to the Jesuit funds which had never, in fact, belonged to them, and which, if the intentions of the donors were to be respected, should be applied to the whole territory of what had been New France. Since they were being spent exclusively in Lower Canada, as the Bishops themselves agreed was correct, then the revenues derived their title from the Imperial decision of 1832 which put them at the disposal of the "*volontés réunies des pouvoirs exécutif, législatif, administratif*"[t] of the Lower Canadian Assembly, and hence of the union government which was its heir. When the LaFontaine press generally replied that the taking of the property from the Church in the first place had been a sacrilege, the argument rose to a higher level.[15] Running through precedents that went back to Justinian, La Régale, and the *coutumes*[u] of pre-Revolutionary France, *L'Aurore* retorted that since the Church's possession of property derived from the State's civil law, any change by the government could hardly be a sacrilege. To which, in best scholastic manner, the *Mélanges* retorted that since the Church possessed property by divine and natural right, civil recognition added nothing. And to this *L'Aurore,* in best liberal tradition, asserted that since nature knew only individuals, no corporate body such as the Church could claim existence by natural law.[16]

And so the controversy proceeded. It was one which could not easily be resolved. For while the *Mélanges* was reasserting the doctrine so dear to the nineteenth-century ultramontane that the Church, by natural and divine right, was autonomous with respect to the State, Viger, brimming with the liberal's faith in the individual, denied any natural right to a corporate body. It was an argument that could not be settled for generations; indeed not until both the liberals and the ultramontanes, in the face of other problems, would come to modify their intransigence.

This was not the first difference of opinion that had brought Viger's party and the *Mélanges* into conflict. Back in 1842 they had measured paragraphs against each other over the interpretation of Bishop Lartigue's famous *Mandement* against rebellion in 1837; and at that time also they had been quarrelling from the viewpoint of opposing ultramontane and liberal doctrines.[17] Yet somehow that discussion had not caused any overt split. The 1846

---

[t] "combined intentions of the executive, legislative and administrative powers"

[u] legal ordinances

one did—and soon with the re-emergence of Louis-Joseph Papineau into political life, all bridges were broken between his party and the clergy. By 1849, the priests had become one of the great forces on the side of responsible government in Canada.

Having returned from his exile in liberal, anticlerical France, the great rebel found little to encourage him in Canada. He was disgusted by LaFontaine's politics, repelled by the growing power of the priests. Especially he suffered at being forced to witness his people's growing commitment to the British Connection. In the late fall of 1847 he issued what Lord Elgin called "a pretty frank declaration of republicanism,"[18] reviving his dreams of the 1830s for a national republic of French Canada. Around himself he rallied Viger's followers and a group of enthusiastic young separatists who edited the radical newspaper *L'Avenir*. They shared the rebel leader's philosophy: if it only depended on them they would win through the sharpness of their minds what he had not by sharpness of sword.

What struck the ultramontanes about Papineau and *L'Avenir* was of course not so much the attacks against LaFontaine and responsible government. It was their anticlericalism. As things turned out the republicans would hurt their own cause more than they would the Church: on the subject of responsible government, Papineau might conceivably weaken LaFontaine, especially if he concentrated on nationality and the defects of the Union. But by challenging the Church, the *rouges* merely helped to cement the alliance between LaFontaine and the priests.

On 14 March 1849, *L'Avenir* created quite a stir by publishing large extracts from the European liberal press on the Roman revolution which had forced Pius IX into exile and proclaimed Mazzini's republic. The articles were bitter: and the Lower Canadian republicans left little doubt where their own sympathies lay. The *Mélanges* took up the challenge. Through several series of learned front pages, it tried to show *"les Messieurs de l'Avenir"* how serious were *"l'injustice et la faute qu'ils ont commises."*[v] [19] But the young editors did not understand. They continued to insult the Pope; and at their Société Saint-Jean-Baptiste banquet that year, they replaced their traditional toast to the Sovereign by a defiant speech on *"Rome Régénérée."*[w] *"Les journaux socialistes et anti-religieux sont sans cesse à vanter les hauts faits de MM.-les rouges à Rome,"* the *Mélanges* complained,[20] adding sadly that *"la manie d'aboyer contre la soutane semble être à la mode."*[x] [21]

Indeed it was. On 21 July 1849, *L'Avenir* led another attack which would lock the journalists in another discussion for two months: this time on tithing.

---

[v] "the gentlemen of the future ... the injustice and the errors that they caused."

[w] "renewed Rome."

[x] "The socialist and anti-religious newspapers continually praise the great deeds of the left-wing gentlemen in Rome, ... The craze for barking at cassocks seems to be in style."

"*La dîme,*" it pronounced, "*est un abus encore bien plus grand que la tenure seigneuriale.*"[y] Then later, when it began to campaign for the abolition of seigneurial tenure, the radical paper again attacked the Church for its ownership of seigneurial lands. In fact, it averred, one of the very reasons against the system was the amount of revenue which accrued from it to the Séminaire de Québec and other religious institutions.

On 14 September 1849, the *Mélanges* warned the republican youngsters at *L'Avenir:* "*Nos adversaires ne doivent pas se dissimuler que par leur conduite et leurs écrits ils se font plus de tort qu'ils nous en font à nous-mêmes.*"[z] True enough. For as the priests were being attacked by their own political enemies, LaFontaine's publicists naturally came to the clergy's rescue. Thus, all during 1849, the *Journal de Québec, Le Canadien,* and *La Minerve,* defended the Church as if they themselves had been directly concerned.

While the dispute raged about the Pope's temporal sovereignty, for instance, Cauchon's *Journal* featured a serial on the subject by the French Bishop Dupanloup of Orleans, and another series covering several instalments by "*Un Canadien Catholique*" assailed *L'Avenir* for "*la prétention qu'il entretient de catéchiser le clergé sur ses devoirs.*"[aa] So also on the issue of tithing: Cauchon spread an article defending the Church over the front page of three issues in October 1849, and underlined the connection between anticlericalism and the republicans: "*Ce sont les aimables procédés du passé, la haine entre le peuple et ses chefs religieux pour assurer le triomphe des doctrines pernicieuses et anti-nationales.*"[bb] [22] When the *rouges* criticized the clergy's role in the schools, Cauchon answered by giving the clergy credit for *la survivance:*

> D'où vient cette haute portée d'intelligence, ce caractère si beau, si noble, si grand de franchise, d'honneur, de grandeur d'âme et de religieuse honnêteté qui distingue nos premiers citoyens et qui contraste si étonnamment avec cette populace de banqueroutiers qui soudoient les incendiaires, les parjures, les voleurs et la lie des villes pour commettre en leur nom, pour eux, et à leur profit des crimes dignes de Vandales? Du clergé national, sorti des rangs du peuple, identifié avec tous ses intérêts, dévoué jusqu'à la mort, initié à tous les progrès des sciences modernes, des arts et du génie, aux tendances des sociétés actuelles.[cc] [23]

---

[y] "Tithing ... is a much greater abuse than the seigneurial land-hold system."

[z] "Our opponents must admit that their conduct and articles have done them more harm than us."

[aa] "A Catholic Canadian ... the claim of the newspaper to instruct the clergy on its duties."

[bb] "These are the friendly actions of the past, stirring up hate between the people and their religious leaders in order to guarantee the triumph of destructive and anti-national doctrines."

[cc] Where does this great amount of intelligence come from, these beautiful and noble traits of character filled with openness, honour, high-mindedness and religion that contrast so amazingly with the qualities of the bunch of bankrupts who bribe the arsonists, the perjurers, the thieves and the scum of our towns and cities to commit crimes worthy of the Vandals in their name, for them and for their gain? These virtues come from the national clergy issuing forth from the ranks of the people, at one with its interests, devoted for life, aware of all the progress made in modern science, the arts and knowledge as well as of the trends in today's societies.

Finally, when the *rouges* hurled insults, the editor of the *Journal* answered flamboyantly:

> Détrôner le Dieu de nos pères et lui substituer l'infâme idole du sensualisme, voilà leur but; vilipender le prêtre, calomnier son enseignement, couvrir d'un noir venin ses actions les plus louables, voilà leur moyen ... Quel but, quelle fin vous proposez-vous en livrant à l'ignominie le prêtre du Canada, votre conci-toyen, votre ami d'enfance, l'ami dévoué de notre commune patrie! Aurez-vous relevé bien haut la gloire de notre pays lorsque vous aurez avili aux yeux de l'étranger ses institutions les plus précieuses, couvert de boue ses hommes les plus éminents dans l'ordre religieux et civil, enseveli sous un noir manteau de calomnies le corps le plus respectable de la société comme un cadavre sous un drap mortuaire?[dd] [24]

Le Canadien wrote less lyrically, but like the *Journal,* it too came to the defence of the priests, and struck back at *L'Avenir.* It found that the republicans' articles *"représentent trop de passion et par conséquent une notable injustice envers les hommes en qui le pays a confiance."*[ee] [25] And at the height of the temporal power dispute, it noted how the same republicans who praised Mazzini had also supported those who burned down the Canadian Parliament buildings, and signed the manifesto demanding annexation to the United States.

In return, of course, the priests supported LaFontaine. At the time of Papineau's Manifesto at the end of 1847, during the general election that swept LaFontaine to the final achievement of responsible government, reports from different parts of Lower Canada came in to Montreal that *"certains prêtres, même à Montréal, ont prononcé en chaire des discours presqu'exclusivement politiques."*[ff] [26] But more important still than such electoral advice was the increasing involvement in party politics of the *Mélanges Religieux* and its junior associate in Quebec, the weekly *Ami de la Religion et de la Patrie.* Edited by Jacques Crémazie, *L'Ami* first appeared in early 1848 under the interesting motto: *"Le trône chancelle quand l'honneur, la religion, la bonne foi ne l'environnent pas."*[gg] It endorsed LaFontaine's ideas so unequivocally that Cauchon was glad to recommend it to his party leader for patronage:

[dd] Casting down the God of our ancestors and raising up the foul idol of self-indulgence in His place—such is their aim; vilifying the priest, slandering his teaching, covering his most praise-worthy actions with black poison—such are their methods.... What end, what goal do you intend by bringing to shame the priest of Canada, your fellow citizen, your friend since childhood, the devoted friend of our common fatherland! Will you have raised the glory of our country when you have debased its most valuable institutions in the eyes of foreigners, covered with mud the most eminent men in religious and civil life, buried under a black coat of slander the most respectable part of society like a corpse in its shroud?

[ee] "contain too much passion and, as a result, a great amount of injustice towards the men in whom the country has confidence."

[ff] "some priests, even in Montreal, have preached sermons from the pulpit that were almost en-tirely political."

[gg] "The throne trembles when it is not surrounded by honour, religion and good faith."

> Il ne faudra pas oublier quand vous donnez des annonces d'en donner aussi
> à l'*Ami de la Religion* ... qui montre de bonnes dispositions et fait tout le
> bien qu'il peut.[hh] [27]

As for the *Mélanges,* since mid-1847 it had practically become a LaFontaine
political sheet. In July 1847, the clergy had handed over the editorship to a
twenty-one-year-old law student who was articling in the offices of A.-N. Morin:
Hector Langevin, whose religious orthodoxy they felt well-guaranteed by his
two brothers (and frequent correspondents) in Quebec: Jean, a priest professor at the *Séminaire,* and Edmond who in September 1847 became secretary to
the Archbishop's *Grand-Vicaire* Cazeau.

With mentors like Morin, the youthful editor soon threw his paper into the
thick of the political fight. In fact he became so involved that at last the priests
at the Bishopric felt they had to warn him (they did so several times) to tone
down his enthusiasm for LaFontaine. He did not, however. His greatest service was perhaps the publicizing of the clergy's support for LaFontaine at the
time of the trouble over Rebellion Losses. At the height of the crisis, on 5 May
1849, he issued the rallying call:

> En présence de cette activité des gens turbulents et ennemis de la Constitution,
> on se demande ce qu'ont à faire les libéraux [i.e. LaFontaine's supporters] ...
> Regardons nos Évêques, regardons nos prêtres, regardons notre clergé; il vient
> de nous montrer l'exemple en présentant lui-même des adresses à Son
> Excellence Lord Elgin, et en en envoyant d'autres à notre gracieuse souveraine.
> Après cela hésiterons-nous à agir avec vigueur, promptitude et énergie?
> Hésiterons-nous à suivre la route que nous trace notre épiscopat, que nous
> trace notre clergé tout entier?[ii] [28]

Half a year later he spelled out his full sentiments in a letter to his brother
Edmond:

> Si les rouges avaient l'autorité en mains, prêtres, églises, religion, etc., de-
> vraient disparaître de la face du Canada. Le moment est critique. Il faut que le
> ministère continue à être libéral tel qu'à présent, ou bien on est Américain, et
> puis alors adieu à notre langue et à notre nationalité.[jj] [29]

[hh] When you place advertisements, you mustn't forget to give some of them to the *Ami de la Religion*
... It shows that it is inclined in your favour and is doing all the good that it can.

[ii] Faced with the actions of these troublemakers and enemies of the Constitution, we can only wonder what the Liberals [i.e., LaFontaine's supporters] have to do. ... Behold our bishops, our priests,
our clergy; they have just shown us a good example by presenting addresses to his excellency
Lord Elgin and sending others to our gracious sovereign. Will we hesitate to act with vigour,
speed and energy after this? Will we hesitate to follow the path that our bishops, that all our
clergy have traced out for us?

[jj] If the *rouges* had power in their hands, priests, churches, religion and so on would have to disappear
from the face of Canada. The moment is critical. The ministry must remain liberal as it is at present. If it doesn't, we will become Americans and then good-bye to our language and nationality.

Perhaps it was inevitable that during the closing years of the decade the French-Canadian clergy would come to play an increasingly political role. For with responsible government the *Canadiens* had, for the first time in their long national life, taken over the direction of their own destiny. And as the Catholic Church had long played an important part in fashioning their thought, it was natural for most of those on the political stage to welcome the support of the priests. Yet, would it have happened as effortlessly if Bishop Bourget had not fallen in with the *Veuillotistes?* If LaFontaine and Morin had not supported clerical schools in 1846? If Hector Langevin had not articled in Morin's office? If *L'Avenir* had not attacked the papal states? Would it have happened at all if Denis-Benjamin Viger had won the election of 1844? If the Papineau legend had persisted? Be that as it may, the *bleu* alliance of priest and politician (since we can now give it its name) radically transformed LaFontaine's party and French-Canadian nationalism.

Except when the rights of the Church were in question, ultramontanes tended to consider politics as secondary. They concentrated rather on Church-State problems, thus gradually moving away from areas of cooperation with Upper Canada—especially at a time when the "voluntary principle" was converting Baldwin's party as ultramontanism was LaFontaine's. Gradually they came to appeal almost exclusively to ideas and feelings which were proper only to French Canada. When he began in the late 1830s LaFontaine aimed at political and economic reforms in which both Canadas would share. In his famous *Adresse aux Électeurs de Terrebonne*,[kk] he described the problems of French Canada in political and economic terms alone. As the decade moved on, however, under pressure from his opponents and his followers, he found himself becoming more and more involved with ultramontanism and a narrower nationalism. Reluctantly, it seems. Late in 1851, several weeks after his resignation, he recalled to Cauchon, who had bragged about rallying the priests, how he had cautioned him about the faith-and-nationality theme. *"Je me rappelle ce que vous m'avez dit,"* Cauchon admitted, *"par rapport à la question nationale. Mais je vous répondais que c'était la seule corde qu'il était possible de faire vibrer avec succès."*[ll] [30] Later, to another admonition from the former premier, the editor of the *Journal de Québec* admitted that *"la question de nationalité était délicate,"* but protested again that *"c'était la corde qui vibrait le mieux. J'espère que vous avez en cela parfaitement compris ma pensée et que vous êtes convaincu que je n'ai pas voulu employer un moyen malhonnête pour atteindre mon but."*[mm] [31]

---

kk Speech to the Voters of Terrebonne

ll "I recall what you told me ... concerning the national question. But I told you that it was the only string that could be made to vibrate with success."

mm "the nationality question was tricky ... it was the string that vibrated the best. I hope that you have completely understood my opinion in this matter and that you are certain that I did not intend to use dishonest means to attain my goal."

LaFontaine had wanted to break with Papineau's particularist and republican nationalism. He appealed to a more general, open point of view, founding his hopes on cooperation with Upper Canada and in the British political system. Yet, in the end, he found himself the head of a party which tended to be as particularist as Papineau's (although for different reasons).

His party also turned out to be one which did not understand parliamentary institutions. The ultramontanes were not rigid republicans like Papineau, but they were rigid Catholics, used to "refuting the errors of our time," with a doctrine which they proudly wanted as *"toujours une, toujours sublime, toujours la même."*[nn][32] They were accustomed to think in an atmosphere rarified by unchanging principles. Instinctively they reacted in dogmatic terms, pushing ideas to their limits—and students of the absolute make poor parliamentarians. The ultramontanes could not really understand parliamentary practice as LaFontaine and Parent had. They lacked political flair and skill in manoeuvring. They could not adapt to the gropings and costs of conciliation. To them, "rights" were an objective reality which could not be negotiated, only acknowledged. "Toleration" could not mean respect for an opposing opinion; at best it was a necessary evil. Applied to theology, their attitude might have had some validity (although not for ecumenism!) but transferred to politics and nationalism—as inevitably it was—it could not but extinguish LaFontaine's hopes for a broadening democracy of the British type.

For years the *bleus* and their Upper Canadian colleagues supported the same men, but as the French party gradually concentrated so dogmatically on Faith and Nationality, there could be no true meeting of minds. Outwardly, LaFontaine's and Parent's wider nationalism seemed to have prevailed: responsible government and British Parliamentary institutions were secured. Also, a political party uniting Upper and Lower Canadians continued to govern the country for over a generation. But this was external appearance only: in reality, the party from which LaFontaine resigned in 1851 was assiduously becoming less concerned with the larger perspective than with the particular Church-State problems of French Canada; it was becoming decreasingly parliamentarian, increasingly authoritarian.

A funny thing indeed had happened to French-Canadian nationalism on its way to responsible government.

Notes

1. Archives de l'Archevêché de Montréal, Mgr Lartigue à G.A. Belcourt, 24 avril 1838.
2. Archives de l'Archevêché de Québec, Mgr. Signay à A. Leclerc, 25 novembre 1837.

[nn] "always united, always noble, never changing."

3. I want to thank Fr. Léon Pouliot, author of *Mgr Bourget et son Temps* (2 vols., Montréal, 1955–56) and of *La Réaction Catholique de Montréal* (Montréal, 1942) for pointing out to me the importance of this trip in the formation of Mgr Bourget's thinking.

4. *Mélanges Religieux* [henceforth *MR*], 13 mai 1842.

5. *MR*, 28 juillet 1842.

6. *MR*, 14 novembre 1843.

7. *MR*, 4 juillet 1843.

8. *MR*, 27 janvier 1843.

9. *Archives de la Province de Québec* [henceforth *APQ*], Papiers Taché A50. Joseph Cauchon à E.-P. Taché, 9 octobre 1850.

10. *MR*, 20 novembre 1849.

11. *MR*, 26 novembre 1842.

12. *APQ*, Fonds de l'Instruction Publique. Lettres reçues. P. Davignon à J.-B. Meilleur, 23 novembre 1843.

13. Archives de l'Archevêché de Québec, DM H-245. Joseph Cauchon à C.F. Cazeau, 24 février 1845.

14. *L'Aurore des Canadas,* 3, 6, 13, 16 juin 1846.

15. *L'Aurore des Canadas,* 13 juin 1845.

16. *MR*, 26 juin 1846, *L'Aurore des Canadas,* 30 juin 1846.

17. Cf. F. Ouellet, "Le Mandement de Mgr Lartigue de 1837 et la Réaction libérale," *Bulletin des Recherches historiques,* 1952 (58), pp. 97–104.

18. Elgin-Grey Papers I, 102. Elgin to Grey, December 24, 1847.

19. *MR*, 30 mars 1849.

20. *MR*, 6 juillet 1849.

21. *MR*, 21 septembre 1849.

22. *Journal de Québec,* 2 octobre 1849.

23. *Journal de Québec,* 2 mars 1850.

24. *Journal de Québec,* 6 décembre 1849.

25. *Le Canadien,* 31 mai 1848.

26. *MR*, 14 décembre 1847.

27. Public Archives of Canada, MG 24, B-14. LaFontaine Papers. Joseph Cauchon à LaFontaine, 24 octobre 1849.

28. *MR*, 5 mai 1849.

29. *APQ*, Collection Chapais, 253. Hector à Edmond Langevin, 25 janvier 1850.

30. LaFontaine Papers. Joseph Cauchon à LaFontaine, 11 novembre 1851.

31. *Ibid.,* décembre 1851.

32. *MR*, 15 décembre 1843.

BROKERAGE AND THE POLITICS OF POWER SHARING

S.J.R. Noel

> *You are, of course, aware how strongly LaFontaine holds to the principle of the two majorities ... I think this quite absurd, and I am inclined to think so do you. Nevertheless I would have no objection to see it tried. I am sure it would strengthen us materially as a party ... [and] it would drive the Tories here mad...*
> —Francis Hincks to Robert Baldwin, 23 September 1844

I

The general election of 1847 brought LaFontaine and Baldwin triumphantly back to power, each with clear majority support in his own province.[1] The inauguration of their ministry marked the full and unambiguous acceptance by all concerned, including the British government, of the Baldwinian version of responsible government. In effect, the control of patronage that had been so completely exercised by Draper could no longer be withheld from the reformers. Theirs was seen as a party victory, and it was assumed that they would function in office as a party government; that is, it was assumed that they would have the right to allocate patronage as they saw fit. The new Governor General, Lord Elgin,[2] who had replaced Metcalfe in 1846, would do nothing to upset this assumption. Unlike his predecessor, he had no mandate, and no desire, to be a "partisan Governor." Instead, he aimed to establish "a moral influence," which, he hoped, would "go far to compensate for the loss of power consequent on the surrender of patronage."[3] The age of "Governor Generalities" had arrived. In fact, there was no sweeping introduction of an American-style spoils system, as the opponents of party government had feared. LaFontaine and Baldwin simply picked up where Draper had left off; that is to say, they dispensed the usual patronage in the usual way, but there was no wholesale turnover of public officials. Over the next few years, however, the public service was considerably expanded as the reform ministry pressed ahead with policies that expanded the role of government generally, and the newly created posts naturally went mainly to supporters of the winning side.[4]

Yet in the long run it was not the final establishment of responsible government that mainly distinguished the LaFontaine-Baldwin administration, nor even its record of progressive and reformist legislation in such areas as education and municipal government, but rather its entrenchment of a unique system of power-sharing. This was basically the system that the two leaders had successfully introduced in 1842–43, only now their positions were more secure, for not only had the British government decided not to intervene, but the whole course of the Draper administration had served to underline the essential practicality, even the necessity, of their approach. They were thus free to extend their system, refine it, and pragmatically adapt it to fit the political circumstances of the time. To satisfy Baldwin—who insisted that the conventions of Westminster-style responsible government could not be stretched to include a dual premiership—LaFontaine was nominally Prime Minister.[5] But in reality the ministry was a dual one in which they functioned as co-premiers, with each responsible for filling his allotted share of cabinet posts, the one in effect leading the government in matters pertaining to Lower Canada and the other in effect leading it in matters pertaining to Upper Canada.[6] Within the Assembly, their respective parties retained their separate identities; that is to say, it was a genuine coalition and not a blending or amalgamation of the two.

Given the notoriously unstable nature of Upper Canadian party alignments, however, the question was bound to arise of whether, or to what extent, such a system of government required adherence to the principle of "concurrent" or "double" majorities. In other words, in addition to the ministry's maintaining the confidence of the Assembly as a whole—which was now totally accepted as the basic principle of responsible government—did each *section* of the ministry (the Lower Canadian under LaFontaine, the Upper Canadian under Baldwin) have to maintain majority support *within its own section of the Assembly?* There could be no doubt that the ministry would enjoy a considerable advantage if each of its sections could do so. But there could also be no doubt that it was not a constitutional requirement. The real question, therefore was whether it was an *operative* requirement. And if it was, what were its implications? Did it mean, for example, that "sectional legislation should be the exclusive concern of the representatives from the affected section, and the majority from each section should govern only that section?"[7] Or did it mean only that the ministry should in general maintain the confidence of both sections of the House, but that on a day-to-day basis sectional exclusivity in the passage of legislation was not required? Also, considered more broadly, did it mean that, in future, whichever party won a majority in its own section would automatically be entitled to claim all of the ministerial seats for that section?

Both LaFontaine and Baldwin rejected the extreme sectionalist position, but otherwise their viewpoints diverged widely. LaFontaine supported the double majority principle in theory but recoiled from accepting its practical implications. In particular, as he had shown by his rebuffing of Draper's overtures in 1845, he was not prepared to participate in a coalition with the Upper Canadian conservatives. But it was only with great difficulty that he had been able to restrain some of his colleagues from doing so (for, following his own logic, they could see no reason why they should be deprived of lucrative ministerial positions for the sake of an alliance with the Upper Canadian reformers, who were plainly a minority in their own section.[8]) At the time, however, responsible government had not been conceded; now that it had been, it was unlikely that LaFontaine would be able to prevent such a coalition from being formed should the situation arise again. Baldwin, by contrast, consistently denied the validity of the double majority principle in theory but, as it turned out, was prepared to accept its implications in practice. Hence, when in June 1851 he failed to secure majority support in his own section in a division on a strictly sectional issue—an opposition motion to abolish the Upper Canadian Court of Chancery—he promptly resigned.[9]

On the face of it there could hardly have been a more stunning demonstration of the practical force of the double majority principle: Baldwin still had the confidence of the House as a whole, since the motion had been defeated by a margin of thirty-four to thirty, yet had regarded a defeat in one section as sufficient to compel his resignation from the ministry. But beyond that obvious fact the matter remained shrouded in ambiguity. The other Upper Canadian ministers did not resign with him, nor did he ask them to, and in giving reasons for his resignation he cited almost everything *except* the double majority principle—including the rise of "mere demagogue clamour," which he blamed for the defection of his former supporters.[10] The principle remained, as Stephen Leacock put it, "the will o' the wisp of the rival politicians."[11] But it was a will o' the wisp that would haunt every ministry that followed.

As LaFontaine and Baldwin had shown, however, if a ministry possessed majority support in both sections of the Assembly, it could enjoy the luxury of appearing to comply with the double majority principle without having either to define it or declare undying adherence to it. Not surprisingly, this was Hincks' preferred approach. And since no realistic alternative was ever found, it remained a convenient evasion to the end of the Union era. The trouble arose, as it did for Baldwin, when a ministry lost its majority in one section or the other, for to do so was to advertise weakness, nearly always to invite trouble, and frequently to compel resignation.

Finally, the double majority principle itself was in many respects less important, and less influential in the long run, than the assumptions and understandings on which it rested. This was something the Upper Canadian tories understood perfectly, which explains their persistent inclination to view it purely in instrumental terms. For them it was a means of combating the centralizing tendencies of the Union and of maintaining the essential separateness of Upper Canada. In this attitude, ironically, they were closer to the Lower Canadian French than to any other group.[12] Hence, in spite of the apparent absence of consensus, the Union of the Canadas was not ungovernable. What was required to make it work was above all a tacit acknowledgement by each ministry of the validity of the old provincial boundaries, for once that acknowledgement was made, other political arrangements became more readily negotiable—such as the operation of government on a double majority basis as far as possible; the sharing of executive power on a mutually acceptable basis; and the distribution of patronage within each section by the members of the cabinet drawn from that section.

II

To maintain such a system required continuous attention to the art of brokerage politics, especially in the Upper Canadian section of the coalition. Baldwin's party, for example, was never as cohesive and disciplined as LaFontaine's. Many of its moderate reform members were in fact quasi-independents whose support generally had to be secured issue by issue—perhaps in this respect accurately reflecting the view of their constituents, who likewise tended to show little consistent attachment to reform principles. In consequence, in addition to dealing with their French colleagues, the Upper Canadian ministers had also constantly to deal with their own loose assemblage of supporters—a collection of local patrons, aspiring brokers, disappointed claimants for office, individualists, and political mavericks, among whom there were also potentially disruptive differences of region, religion, and business connections. As Donald Swainson observes: "Backbenchers might be simple tools of powerful regional leaders; often, however, they were men of substance and local power who could and did challenge their party leaders, sometimes successfully."[13]

Moreover, the reformers' appetite for patronage was insatiable. As James Morris (who would later be appointed postmaster-general) wrote to Baldwin: "Now that we have fully assumed the helm of state you will feel no surprise at the numberless missives which reach you asking for all sorts of favours, reasonable and unreasonable."[14] Little wonder, therefore, that Baldwin attached such importance to brokerage skills in the filling of the Upper Canadian ministerial posts. Francis Hincks was of course indispensable, becoming in effect Minister of Finance (Inspector-General), and in short order places were found for two more of the ablest brokers of their time, William Hamilton Merritt (who thus completed his passage across the political spectrum from tory to reform) and the young John Sandfield Macdonald,[15] the leading reform politician of Glengarry and the eastern counties—and the political heir of the old tory grand patron, Alexander Macdonnell, a line of succession that accurately reflected the evolution of the Upper Canadian clientele system as a whole in this period.

In its main features, the form of power-sharing that became entrenched in Union politics was of a type that has since become fairly common in culturally segmented societies and is now generally identified in the literature of political science as "consociational democracy." Its basic premise, as a theory, is that stable, electorally-based political systems can function successfully in societies that are not culturally homogeneous as long as the following conditions are met: (1) at the top, power must be shared through some form of coalition, either formally or informally; (2) the political leaders of each cultural segment must be willing (and sufficiently trusted by their respective communities) to make the deals and compromises necessary to maintain the system (a process of brokerage usually labelled "elite accommodation"); (3) proportionality must be observed in the legislature and in the distribution of government benefits, including patronage; and (4) in general the principle of "mutual veto" must take precedence over the principle of rule by simple majority. The first three of these conditions obtained, if not perfectly, at least to a considerable extent in the political system of the United Canadas as it took shape during the LaFontaine-Baldwin era; and while more problematical, the fourth, in the form of the double majority principle, was at least honoured in the breach in that the political cost of contravening it was shown to be high. Though the LaFontaine-Baldwin coalition foundered in 1851, the system itself proved durable. Thereafter every administration more or less was modelled on theirs, and, though over the years deadlocks grew more frequent and effective coalitions harder to achieve, no practical alternative emerged until the idea of forming a federation of all the British North American colonies found currency in the 1860s—but that federation, too, would retain certain strong consociational features.[16]

III

That the Union of the Canadas came to operate in a manner different from that intended by its imperial architects, reinforcing and entrenching cultural particularisms instead of obliterating them, is perhaps not in itself very remarkable; after all, the consequences of constitutional change were as unpredictable then as they are now. But that it operated in a manner so diametrically at odds with that intended, and yet on the whole so peacefully and constructively, is very remarkable indeed and requires further explanation.

Part of the answer undoubtedly lies in the economic context, for the period of the Union also happened to be a period of sustained and at times even exponential economic growth. The working out of a new set of political arrangements and understandings thus took place within a generally favourable economic environment. This was not something for which LaFontaine and Baldwin, or for that matter any administration, could claim responsibility. The immensely productive agriculture of Upper Canada and the forest resources of Lower Canada and the Ottawa Valley needed only the right combination of external factors to produce a booming economy, and with the rising cycle of world trade after 1850, fuelled by British and American industrial growth, new steam technology, and the Crimean War (which removed competing Russian grain and Baltic timber from British markets), that combination had arisen. For example, exports of wheat and flour via the St. Lawrence grew from 3,645,000 bushels in 1849 to 4,547,000 in 1850 and to 6,597,000 in 1853. By 1856 it had reached 9,391,531 bushels. There was a similarly rapid increase in timber exports, both to the United States and Britain.[17] Ironically, insofar as government played a role, it was the public investment policies of the old Family Compact regime in Upper Canada, especially in improvements to the St. Lawrence waterway, that had now come to fruition—largely to the benefit of their reform opponents. But by the time the Hincks-Morin coalition lost power in 1854 it was abundantly clear that the Union of the Canadas, for all its peculiar anomalies, was a goose with a demonstrable capacity for laying golden eggs. Thereafter, for all but the most extreme sectionalists, it was the underlying premise of politics that whatever changes might be contemplated, nothing ought to be done that might risk killing that goose. And since it was also clear that the two Canadas were, and for the foreseeable future would probably remain, effectively separate entities, there was thus a strong incentive for the politicians of each to seek to maintain the Union through the processes of brokerage and accommodation, processes that success had endowed with an undeniable legitimacy.

A second factor that no doubt contributed to the distinctive *modus operandi* of the Union is more problematical but perhaps ultimately no less important: namely, the capacity of each subculture to produce political leaders who possessed a sure grasp of the mechanics of brokerage politics. This was most crucial in the early formative years, for the Union began as a constitutionally complex entity, unnecessarily burdened with hostilities and with an enormous potential for disaster. That it also began with two extremely able and creative political élites suggests that the old pre-1841 provinces of Upper and Lower Canada—of which those élites were the product—possessed more sophisticated political cultures than is generally realized.

Arend Lijphart has remarked on the extraordinary development of consociational devices in the United Canadas in spite of the fact that "not even a trace of prior consociational traditions can be detected." While this is obviously true, in the sense that neither Upper nor Lower Canada displayed the sense of cultural pluralism of the smaller European states that were once part of the Holy Roman Empire, and subsequently evolved consociational political systems, it is misleading to conclude (as Lijphart does) that there must therefore have occurred a "spontaneous development of a series of key consociational devices arising from the necessity of ruling a plural society in the United Province,"[18] *for that development arose out of a significantly different historical experience.* In Upper Canada, as we have seen, brokerage politics evolved out of an indigenous clientele culture and directly reflected the transition of the society as a whole towards more complex, triadic forms of economic and social interaction. So far from being "spontaneous," then, the growth after 1841 of consociational arrangements was but a natural extension of brokerage politics. It was not by accident that a key role was played by Francis Hincks, the broker *par excellence*. And though brokerage norms might have been relatively weaker

484 CHAPTER 12 Responsible Government, the Empire and Canada

in French-Canadian political culture (though that has by no means been established—they might only have been less commercially oriented), the shrewd understanding of them on the part of LaFontaine, A.N. Morin, and their successors suggests that they were by no means alien or unfamiliar. Moreover, there clearly existed in that culture, even more strongly than in Upper Canada, another of the important prerequisites for the success of a consociational system: a bond of trust between the élite and the mass of the people such that the élite were free to make the deals and accommodations necessary to ensure the system's survival. It was that bond of trust that allowed LaFontaine, for example, to work so effectively with Baldwin, A.N. Morin with Hincks, and later, George-Etienne Cartier with John A. Macdonald.

None of these embraced consociationalism as a doctrine or practised it as a matter of rigid convention. Instead, in practising it they usually trod (and occasionally crossed) the fine line that separates the pragmatic from the cynical. And even those who attempted at times to enunciate and defend the "double majority" principle, such as John Sandfield Macdonald, would not themselves be absolutely bound by it when circumstances dictated otherwise.[19] The result was a political system that was full of anomalies and inconsistencies. Some ministries, for example, were split down the middle along Upper Canadian-Lower Canadian lines, from top to bottom; others were partially split in a variety of ways; some maintained a semblance of administrative unity; others did not; and some actually were fairly well unified. Within the legislature, governing coalitions invariably formed across segmental lines, but their actual composition, in detail, was always subject to negotiation. Within each section of a ministry, moreover, the allocation of portfolios and the determination of who would be inside the cabinet and who outside it in practice involved a good deal of political horse-trading. Even the location of the capital was settled in a supremely realistic (and roughly consociational) way: Kingston was chosen first, but proved too much of a backwater to make a suitable capital; Montreal was next, but proved too volatile when an English mob rioted and set fire to the legislative chambers. Thereafter, from 1849 to 1865 the capital rotated between Toronto and Quebec City. This curious arrangement worked surprisingly well until, with Confederation in the air, Ottawa became the capital in 1866.

IV

That the Union of the Canadas was an economic success is undeniable, and indeed the visible signs of that success are still very much in evidence in such things as the splendid heritage of Union-era architecture and in the many contemporary institutions, both public and private, that arose originally out of its burgeoning growth. But what is less commonly acknowledged, perhaps because the evidence is less materially visible, is that the Union was also a political success. To view it merely as a prelude to the greater political act of Confederation, or as a "problem" that Confederation solved, is grossly to undervalue its very real and very great achievements, not only legislatively in specific areas of public policy such as education, municipal government, social services, and communications, important though these were, but above all in its evolution of a unique political system that was in some respects in advance of any other in the world at that time.

It is useful to view the Union of the Canadas in comparative perspective. It was not without its defects, but no other form of government anywhere was conspicuously more successful in providing its people with a framework of peace and order, or in maintaining their rights and freedoms as individuals and as communities, or in generally supporting conditions favourable to the growth of economic, social, and religious institutions. It must be remembered that in the mid-nineteenth century the United States, for all its commitment to the idea of liberty, allowed nearly 4 million of its people to be held in slavery, a contradiction that would shortly tear the republic apart; in Europe for the most part the price of peace was still acceptance of autocratic rule, while in Britain it was deference to an aristocracy (except in Ireland, where submission was required). No student of European politics, especially, can fail to be struck by one startling feature of the political system of the United Canadas: virtually everything was open to negotiation. In contrast to the bi- or multi-ethnic European states and empires, where the forces of popular democracy were either suppressed or kept under tight rein and inter-élite bargaining restricted to a limited range of traditional rights and privileges, in the United Canadas the combination of responsible government and brokerage politics produced a system in which practically all the important areas of public policy (with the exception of external relations, which remained in the hands of the imperial government) were dealt with through the processes of bargaining, deal-making, and compromise; in other words, almost everything was legitimate grist to the political mill.

The result was a politics of byzantine complexity. At its worst it was flagrantly cynical, utterly scurrilous, and more than a little corrupt. But at its best it was innovative, practical, and wonderfully civilized. Such were its intricacies and so finely balanced were its mechanisms that almost invariably among the leading politicians, both French and English, those who were winners and held power had also at some point been losers and sat in opposition, and *vice versa*. And those who were on opposite sides of the House had always to keep in mind that in the next coalition they might well become allies; they were thus naturally disinclined to treat politics as a winner-take-all proposition, a zero-sum game. Moreover, the quality of decision-making does not appear to have suffered unduly: there were fewer stalemates than might reasonably have been expected, and the overall record of governmental accomplishment compares favourably with that of any other era, either before or since.

Notes

1. Paul G. Cornell, *The Alignment of Political Groups in Canada, 1841–1867* (Toronto 1962), 22–5, 100. LaFontaine was returned at the head of a party of thirty-three, including nine English members. Baldwin's supporters numbered twenty-three, to eighteen for the Conservatives. Hincks was later declared the winner of a disputed election in Oxford, increasing the Reform total to twenty-four and reducing the Conservative total to seventeen.

2. *Dictionary of Canadian Biography,* IX, 89–93.

3. Quoted in J.M.S. Careless, *The Union of the Canadas* (Toronto 1967), 116.

4. J.E. Hodgetts, *Pioneer Public Service: An Administrative History of the United Canadas* (Toronto 1955), 56–7; and J.M.S. Careless, "Robert Baldwin," in J.M.S. Careless, ed., *The Pre-Confederation Premiers: Ontario Government Leaders, 1841–1867* (Toronto 1980), 133–4.

5. George E. Wilson, *The Life of Robert Baldwin* (Toronto 1933), 243.

6. Careless, "Baldwin," 132; and R.M. and J. Baldwin, *The Baldwins and the Great Experiment* (Toronto 1969), 215–18.

7. M.E. Nish, "Double Majority: Concept, Practice and Negotiations, 1840–1848," MA thesis, McGill 1966, 146.

8. See R.S. Longley, *Sir Francis Hincks* (Toronto 1943), 144–9.

9. To add insult to injury, the author of the motion was Baldwin's old enemy, William Lyon Mackenzie. See Wilson, *Baldwin,* 284–90.

10. Ibid., 289.

11. *Baldwin, LaFontaine, Hincks* (Toronto 1907), 259.

12. Nish, "Double Majority," 141–2.

13. "Sir Henry Smith and the Politics of the Union," *Ontario History* 66 (1974): 161.

14. Quoted ir Longley, *Hincks,* 276.

15. *DCB,* X, 462–9.

16. See S.J.R. Noel, "Consociational Democracy and Canadian Federalism," *Canadian Journal of Political Science* 4 (1971): 15–18.

17. Careless, *The Union,* 133–4.

18. *Democracy in Plural Societies* (New Haven 1977), 128–9.

19. The Macdonald-Sicotte ministry remained in office, to the derision of the opposition, after sustaining a defeat in the Upper Canadian section in 1863. See Bruce W. Hodgins, "John Sandfield Macdonald," in Careless, ed., *Pre-Confederation Premiers,* 274–7.

CHAPTER

13 GROWING UP IN PRE-INDUSTRIAL CANADA

Glimpses of the family and children growing up rarely emerge from the pages of Canadian history. Stereotypes do exist such as the *habitant* flock on the *seigneurie*, or the street urchins in the industrial cities. These are rare and atypical, yet the most characteristic of Canadian institutions was the family unit, either nuclear or extended, and the majority of Canadians for much of the past were children and teenagers. The preoccupation of Canadian historians with political developments largely explains their aloofness from numerous topics. With the broadening of content areas in the 1960s, the family and childhood were discovered. The sources, unfortunately, are always difficult and the concept of family itself has divergent meanings at various times and places. Insights have been borrowed from sociologists, psychologists, educationalists and demographers. Approaches to the subject have been diversified as well, ranging from the traditional impressionistic study to advanced statistical analysis.

In the summer of 1995, Statistics Canada released a study called *Family Over the Life Course*. It concluded that the "typical" family no longer existed because of the dramatic changes in modern society. It was apparently assumed that the "typical" family had been universal. In her introduction to *Childhood and Family in Canadian History* in 1982, Joy Parr stressed the changing nature of concepts such as childhood and family, which are formed by historical rather than biological phenomena. She also saw them as social rather than natural associations, being moulded by economic and cultural forces. The readings included here confirm her observations, and make the observations of Statistics Canada less startling than readers might think. During the pre-industrial era, the nature of the family and ideas about children in Canada were fluid. Whether it was on the farm, in the fur trade, in urban shops, or in the family mansion, children were essential participants.

In this unit, three strands of the study of growing up in Canada are presented. The first by John F. Bosher on "The Family in New France" is a thoughtful reappraisal of an aspect of the Canadian past where history is presumed but obviously misunderstood. The second selection, by anthropologist Jennifer S.H. Brown on "Children of the Fur Trades," clearly demonstrates the fluid nature of "family" over the long and unstable history of the fur trade. She recreates those atypical families over time, especially for the children of the Northwesters who "experienced some shocks, cultural, psychic, and even physiological" when at the approximate age of six they left one or both parents to move to strange cultures. According to Brown, that between-culture crisis was stressful indeed. The third reading, by social workers Patricia T. Rooke and R.L. Schnell, "Childhood and Charity in Nineteenth-Century British North America," offers yet another version of what it was like to be a child in pre-industrial Canada. No typical family existed for the "poor, uncared-for, destitute children," and this article examines some of the alternatives such as the Protestant Orphans' Homes. The role of such agencies in their offer of "protection, segregation and dependency" was more complex and encompassing than might be expected.

Suggestions for Further Reading

Bradbury, Bettina (ed.), *Canadian Family History: Selected Readings*. Toronto: Copp Clark Pitman Ltd., 1992.

Brown, Jennifer S.H., *Strangers in Blood: Fur Trade Families in Indian Country*. Vancouver: University of British Columbia Press, 1980.

Davey, I., "The Rhythm of Work and the Rhythm of School," in *Egerton Ryerson and His Times*, ed. N. McDonald and A. Charter. Toronto: Macmillan of Canada, 1978, 221–53.

Gaffield, C., "Canadian Families in Cultural Context: Hypotheses from the Mid-Nineteenth Century," CHA *Historical Papers* (1979), 48–68.

Houston, Susan E. and Alison Prentice, *Schooling and Scholars in Nineteenth-Century Ontario*. Toronto: University of Toronto Press, 1988.

Mattingly, Paul H. and Michael B. Katz (eds.), *Education and Social Change: Themes from Ontario's Past*. New York: New York University Press, 1975.

Mays, Herbert J., "'A Place to Stand': Families, Land and Permanence in Toronto Gore Township, 1820–1890," CHA *Historical Papers* (1980), 185–211.

Medjuck, Sheva, "Family and Household Composition in the Nineteenth Century Case of Moncton, N.B. 1851–1871," *Canadian Journal of Sociology* (Summer 1979), 275–286.

Parr, Joy (ed.), *Childhood and Family in Canadian History*. Toronto: McClelland and Stewart, 1982.

Rooke, Patricia T. and R.L. Schnell (eds.), *Studies in Childhood History: A Canadian Perspective*. Calgary: Detselig, 1982.

THE FAMILY IN NEW FRANCE

John F. Bosher

One of the fundamental changes in Quebec since the 1940s is a marked decline in the birth rate which has lately become the lowest in Canada.[1] The large family is quickly disappearing, but until recently it was, as is well known, characteristic of French-Canadian society. Furthermore, if we go back to the history of that century-and-a-half before 1763, when Quebec was a French colony, we find that the family, large or small, was a stronger and more prominent group than it is now. It was, indeed, one of the main institutions in New France. The study of it may help to explain how early Canadian civilization is so different from our own.

The typical family of New France may be described in figures drawn from statistical histories, making a sort of statistical portrait.[2] In the early eighteenth century, families had an average of five or six children, but this average includes families in which one of the parents had died and so stopped its growth. Those "arrested" families had, on the average, four or five children, whereas the complete family, in which neither parent had died, had eight or nine. These averages conceal the variety, of course: some 16 percent of all families had from ten to fourteen children and 2.8 percent had no less than fifteen children. Death among the children also kept numbers down, and to a degree staggering in comparison with our present-day infant mortality. We now lose twenty or twenty-one babies out of every thousand; but in New France 246 out of every thousand died during the first year of life, and that was normal in the eighteenth century. What the figures suggest is that the small families at the bottom of the statistical scale were made so by the hazards of death, not by the habits or wishes of the parents. If no parents or children had died, most families would have numbered a dozen or more children. These figures are for the early eighteenth century, it should be added, after the immigration from France had fallen off; and an analysis of the population in 1663 shows it at an earlier stage when four-fifths of all families had no more than from one to six children. But at every stage the family was enormous compared to the average Quebec family in 1951 which had only 2.2 children.

Taken by themselves, the statistical facts for New France may seem to confirm two common traditions about the family habits of all our ancestors: first, that women married very young; and second, that they tended to be eternally pregnant thereafter and to have a baby every year. Yet the facts for New France—as for Old France and England also—contradict both those traditions.

From *In Search of the Visible Past*, Barry M. Gough, ed. (Waterloo: Wilfrid Laurier University Press, 1975), 1–11.

The average age of women at their first marriage was nearly twenty-two in New France and about twenty-five in Old France. There are, of course, some well-known cases of girls being married at twelve, which was the youngest a girl might legally marry in New France. In 1637, the explorer, Jean Nicollet, set an extreme example by marrying an eleven-year-old girl, Marguerite Couillard, who was Champlain's god-daughter. Not many girls followed that example, it appears, because on 12 April 1670 the royal government ordered the Intendant to pay a premium—or a bounty, perhaps—to every girl under sixteen who found a husband, and to every man who married under twenty. The Crown thought it necessary to encourage people to marry younger. For the same purpose, the Crown also decided to help poor families with the dowries for their girls, and this brings to our notice one of the impediments to an early marriage: the dowry, often a struggle for a father to find for a numerous family of girls. For this and other reasons, too, no doubt, some 18 percent of women did not marry until they were thirty or more; 10 percent waited until they were thirty-five or over; and 6 percent until they were over forty. Women married later than tradition and a few famous examples have led us to believe. Men, too, married older—on the average at nearly twenty-seven.

As for the frequency of births in a family, we learn that in New France women tended to have babies about every two years, not every year as legend has held. The demographic effects of such a difference were, of course, enormous; and one historian has concluded that the reason for this pause between babies, a pause of some twenty-three months from birth to birth or fourteen months plus nine months of pregnancy, was that women tended to remain temporarily sterile during the period of breast-feeding.[3]

To sum up, a typical "complete" family, which had not lost a parent, might consist of a father just over forty, a mother in her middle thirties and about eight children ranging from fourteen years of age down to a few weeks old. This may seem to be a very simple conclusion, disappointingly obvious, but it has the great merit of some basis in historical fact.

It leaves us wondering how to account for the phenomenal rate of the population's growth. In 1663, there were just over 3,000 people in New France, and a century later there were perhaps 70,000.[4] The population had multiplied by more than twenty-three. During that century, it appears that less than 10,000 immigrants came from the mother country. The remaining 57,000 people had all been born to the 3,000 Canadian families or to immigrant families as they came in, in less than five generations. If the French population had multiplied at that rate during the same century there might have been some 400 million Frenchmen by 1763, whereas there were, in fact, only 22 or 23 million. Lest we should be tempted to dismiss the figures for New France as improbable, we should glance at the increase during the two centuries after 1763 which amounts to an even more staggering rise of from 70,000 to 5.5 million, or an eighty-fold increase. If the French had multiplied as quickly as the French

Canadians since 1763 there would be nearly 2 billion Frenchmen by now, or more than half the population of the entire world. In this context, the figures for the twenty-three-fold increase in New France during the century before 1763 do not seem improbable. But they are nevertheless in need of explanation.

Leaving the mathematics of the problem to the demographers, we may sum up in general terms as follows: if women did not marry so young as we thought; if they had babies half as often as we thought; if nearly one-quarter of those babies died before they were a year old and nearly another fifth of them died before the age of ten; and if the annual crude death-rate for the country was somewhere between twenty and forty per thousand; then why did the population increase so quickly? Why was the crude birth-rate so much higher than the crude death-rate or from forty-eight to sixty-five per thousand? The answer (and the missing fact in the problem as I have posed it) is that the people of New France had a high propensity to marry. They were exceptionally fond of the married state.

People in Quebec today marry at an annual rate of about seven or eight per thousand, which is below our national average. The French during the eighteenth century used to marry at the rate of about 16.5 per thousand. But in the colony of New France, the marriage rate was between 17.5 and 23.5 per thousand. The result of this high marriage rate was that from 30 percent to 40 percent of the total population were married or widowed, and this proportion seemed to be increasing in the first half of the eighteenth century.[5]

In addition to this, we find a marked tendency to remarry. Nearly one-fifth of married men married twice, and nearly one-fifth of families had fathers who had been married before. Widows were not snapped up quite so quickly as Peter Kalm and other travellers like to think, but the average widow remarried after three years of widowhood. One way or another very few women reached the age of forty without having married and even remarried. The remarriage rate was 163 per thousand or nearly twice as high as in 1948.

Another figure that may reflect the strong propensity to marry is the low rate of illegitimacy: it seems to have been not more than ten or twelve per thousand whereas in 1969 the average in Quebec was seventy-six per thousand. We are, I think, obliged to conclude from all the evidence that Canadians were fond of the married state and that this is one reason for the high birth rate. For all that the frontier, like any frontier, had large numbers of single young men, and for all that many Canadians were attracted by the adventurous life of the *coureur de bois*, the society as a whole consisted mainly of married people with families. After all, the *coureurs de bois* were not very numerous and not many girls went into religious orders. There were forty-one women in religious orders in 1663 and in 1763 all seven of the orders of nuns numbered only 190 women altogether, a large number of them from France.

The marriage ceremony which these early Canadians went through in such large numbers left people in no doubt about what their main duty was as a couple. Immediately after the couple had been blessed by the officiating priest, the marriage bed was blessed with the sprinkling of holy water, prayers, and exorcisms. The exorcisms were intended to ward off the evil effects of an especially dangerous curse which some enemy of the couple might put on the marriage to make it barren. This curse was known as the *nouage de l'aiguillette*, and on occasion the Church would dissolve a marriage which produced no children on the grounds that this evil magic had made it barren, so important was the procreation of children in that society. And yet the bed in which children were to be conceived and born was not supposed to be a place for pleasure, as the official ceremony for Quebec, *Le Rituel du diocèse de Québec*, made very clear. The priest was to say to the newlyweds,

> Remember that your wedding bed will some day be your death bed, from whence your souls will be taken to be sent before God's Tribunal....[6]

When we come to consider why the people of New France married so willingly and in such large numbers we may at first be tempted to think that the Church forced them into it. Marriage was, after all, a Christian institution, one of the seven sacraments of the Church. There was no civil marriage, nor any civil status at all, in New France. All marriages had to be Catholic marriages and priests were forbidden to marry anyone who was not a Catholic. Very few Canadians married Indians, baptized or not, and very few married Protestants. Priests had to make sure that people who wanted to marry were satisfied that God had called them to marriage; that they had been instructed of the duties and religious principles of marriage (for instance, that it was for having children and for no other purpose); that they had made a full and true confession and communion in their parishes; and that they intended to appear and to behave decently on their wedding day, not to give way to the Devil's temptation to dress vainly or to eat and drink too much. In 1682, Bishop Laval spoke out against women coming to church "in scandalous nakedness of the arms, of the shoulders and the throat or being satisfied to cover them with transparent cloth which often serves only to give more lustre to these shameful nudities."[7] We might be inclined to conclude that it was as good and faithful Catholics in a theocracy that the people of New France were drawn to marriage.

However, we do not have to look very far to see that marriage in that society was not only a religious sacrament, but much else besides. For one thing, weddings were one of the main social events, famous for celebrations lasting several days or even weeks together. That was why most marriages were held in November, January or February, the idle months of the year between the labours of autumn and the labours of spring. Marriage was also set about with pagan customs like the *charivari*, a ritual gathering of young people who made a disturbance outside the house of a widow who had just been married soon after being widowed, or of people of very unequal ages who had married. The crowd shouted until the newlyweds came out and either explained their actions or else paid a fine.[8] Another folk custom, brought from France, like nearly all Quebec customs, was for young people who wished to marry without their parents' consent, or without a proper wedding, to attend a regular church service and announce at the end of it that they regarded themselves as married. This was called *mariage à la gaumine* and was based on a strict and (said the clergy) illegitimate interpretation of the Papal ruling that marriage required the Church's blessing. Although it died out in the eighteenth century, this custom showed that some people viewed the Church's rules as hindrances to marriage. But all these things are only small clues to the irreligious side of marriage. Much more importantly marriage was an act of the family as a business and social enterprise. It was only rarely an act of two free individuals.

In New France, and in Europe at the time, the family was truly the fundamental unit of society and not the frail and limited group we know today. But in New France, the family was particularly important because some of the other French social groups had not taken root here. The typical French peasant lived in a close-knit village with common lands, common taxes, and a collective or communal life reflected in the word "commune" still used in France more or less as a synonym for "village."[9] However, the *habitants* of New France were not peasants, for the most part, and they lived dispersed across the countryside without common lands or duties in a pattern of rural settlement known as *le rang*.[10] Again, tradesmen in France were organized in guilds or *corporations* which governed most aspects of their working lives, but in New France they worked in a much freer and more independent way. The family was therefore a relatively more important social unit.

In both France and New France, however, as Guy Fregault writes, "The ties of family relationship had extraordinary strength at that time."[11] Four of its basic features will show what I mean. First, the family tended to be a business or agricultural unit with every member expecting to live on the family wealth and in turn expected to take part in the family enterprise. It was also a social enterprise in which every member tried to assist in the advancement of the whole. Families climbed socially like ivy up a wall. The mentality of social advancement at the time may be glimpsed in, for instance, some statements by an eighteenth-century Governor whose attitudes may be taken as exemplary in the colony. This is Vaudreuil, who wrote to the minister at Versailles on 15 November 1703: "We have chosen the Honourable Chevalier de Courcy to carry these letters ... to you because he is the nephew of Monsieur de Callieres. We have been pleased to give him this honour to let him know the respect we have for the memory of his late uncle." A year later, Vaudreuil wrote to the Minister on behalf of his own children: "I have eight boys and a girl who need the honour of your protection. Three of them are ready for service. I entered the musketeers when I was as young as my oldest. I hope you will have the goodness to grant me for him the company of the Sieur de Maricourt who has died." He then discusses his wife's relations and concludes, "On my side [of the family] I have only one relation, to whom the late Sieur Chevalier de Callieres gave a small office as ensign. I beg you to grant him a lieutenancy...."[12]

Of course patronage extended beyond the family, but the strongest claims were on blood relations and for them. We cannot read very far in any official correspondence of the time without encountering such claims, for there was almost no other way of getting ahead in life. The system of patronage is revealed in a vocabulary all its own, peculiar to the *ancien regime* whether in France or in Canada: *protection* meant patronage; *grâce* referred to a post, a promotion, a pension or a title conferred by a patron or at his request; *estime* was the attitude of the patron towards his *créature* and it was the reason they both alleged for the *grâce*. And *crédit* was the power a friend or relation had to obtain a *grâce* from someone else; whereas *faveur* expressed the power he had to obtain something for himself.

A second feature of the family is that the act of marriage was in part a business event. In particular, the family had to find a dowry for a girl or else she would probably never find a husband. Trying to marry a girl off without a dowry would have been like fishing without bait on the hook. To use another image, the dowry was a sort of marriage "scholarship," and this metaphor seems all the more true when we remember that Talon gave the *filles du Roi* dowries of fifty *livres* in linen and other goods, and that in 1711 the government of New France set aside the sum of 3,000 *livres* to be distributed as dowries among sixty girls. In New France, dowries varied a good deal and they reflect roughly the social level of the family. Here is an example of a modest dowry which Magdeleine Boucher brought to her husband, Urbain Baudry Lamarche:

> Two hundred *livres* in silver; four sheets; two table-cloths; six cloth and hemp napkins; a mattress and a blanket; two plates; six pewter spoons and six pewter plates; a pot and a cauldron; a table and two benches; a flour bin; a chest with a lock and key; one cow; two pigs, male and female. The parents gave the bride a suit of clothes and as much underwear as she wanted.[13]

This was an *habitant* family affair, of course. A rich shipping merchant's daughter, at the other end of the scale of commoners, might bring thousands of *livres* to her marriage. Denis Goguet, who retired to La Rochelle after making his fortune in Canada, put up dowries of 50,000 *livres* for his daughters.[14]

The main point about such dowries is that they were family property transferred by legal contract. At the time of the marriage a contract was drawn up before a notary stating this transfer of property and other business terms pertaining to the marriage. Marriage thus had a business side to it and the business negotiations were usually between the families rather than the betrothed couple. As a rule, the families signed these contracts in large numbers; we find the signatures of uncles, aunts, cousins and so on scrawled on the last page. One of the interesting effects of this system is that the wife, represented by her family and bringing considerable property to the marriage, tended to have a greater material equality with her husband than most wives in our time.

Needless to say, therefore, both families were very much interested in arranging the marriage in the first place, and this brings up my third point about the family as enterprise: marriage was a major theatre of the family struggle for social advancement or for security. To marry above the family station was a triumph, a step upward for the entire family. The new link with a grander or more noble family was a source of benefit through the influence it afforded. If the daughter of a successful merchant married a government official or his son, the assumption was likely to be that henceforth they were allies in a common struggle for advancement.

Why, we may wonder, would a family ever allow a marriage with a lesser family? The answer is that wealth attracted the poor but respectable; and respectability attracted the rich but low-born. Or else a powerful merchant or clerical family might be glad to marry into a large family of military officers with strong connections in the army. The benefit would still be mutual. Professor Cameron Nish has shown with many examples how the various social spheres intermarried in New France, there being only one ruling class and no such thing as purely military, purely seigneurial or purely administrative families.[15]

The fourth feature of the family was its hierarchy with the father in command, captain of the family enterprise. It is all too easy these days to imagine that paternal authority was merely a rank injustice or a quaint superstition. Far from it. Every enterprise in a competitive world must be under the command of someone or some group with authority to make decisions: a manager, a president, a ship's captain, a general in the army, a board in a company, and so on. The family enterprise in New France and Old France was nearly always under the father, though there were no impediments to a widow taking over her husband's family firm. In France, especially, there were many firms with "widow" in their titles: *La Veuve Charly* of La Rochelle, *La Veuve Augier et fils aîné* of Tonnay-Charente; *La Veuve Courrejolles et fils* of Bayonne, and so on.

It has been said that circumstances in Canada tended to put women and children much higher in the social scheme of things than French women and children and to make them more equal with the husband and father.[16] Yet such a difference was not sanctioned either by custom or by law, and normally the father's authority extended to most things, unless he died in which case his widow might assume some, though by no means all, of his authority. Parental authority over children may be seen very clearly in the field of marriage. No child could marry without his father's or widowed mother's consent until the age of twenty-five for girls and thirty for men. Until those ages, the children were considered minors. And in a world where life was shorter than it is now, we must add several years to those ages in order to appreciate the significance of that law. Marriage was primarily the family's business and by law as well as by custom the children were expected to make their marriages according to the best interests of the family.

French law provided that if a son, for example, wanted to marry a girl of whom his father did not approve, he might draw up three "respectful applications" (*sommations respectueuses*) at a notary's office, one after the other at a few weeks' intervals. Let me read to you the first respectful application that a certain Jean-Claude Louet made to his father in January 1733. He was then thirty years old and wanted to marry a shoemaker's daughter, but the father did not approve of the marriage.[17]

> My Very Dear Father,
>
> I am in the throes of misery at finding myself deprived of the kindnesses that I was used to receiving from you. I am extremely pained that your tender impulses which have moved me so often and so deeply are entirely extinct. However, dear father, if I withdraw the obedience and submission that I owe you it is out of an indispensable obligation to restore the reputation of the one whom I have lost, without which there is no salvation for me.
>
> Finally, dear father, I entreat you in your paternal love, and by all that is dearest to you of your own blood, to let yourself be touched and persuaded by the pitiable fate of the poor girl and the lamentable state to which I have been reduced for so long. You have spoken; I have obeyed. You have sent me away to a place where I have nothing but tears and sighs to console me and keep me company.
>
> I believe, however, that today you will be moved by my woes and will grant me the favour I am asking of you.
>
> > From he who is,
> > My Dear Father,
> > Your most humble and submissive son,
> >
> > C. Louet

After the third such letter, the son was then legally entitled to marry because he was thirty years old. Under thirty, if his father still refused to consent the son would have had to wait.

We see in all this that the family was engaged in a collective struggle for survival or advancement, and children could not usually please themselves as individuals but had to act as members of the family team. This state of affairs was not merely a quaint custom, but enforced by the law of the kingdom. The law in New France, as in Old France, was prepared to punish children who disobeyed and defied their fathers; for the government, the Church and the society saw the family in that age as though it were itself a tiny kingdom in which the father, like a king, had almost total authority to rule, reward and punish. In other words, in that society the family appeared as the smallest political cell in the kingdom, modelled on the kingdom itself.

This metaphor is, however, reversible, and if we reverse it we find that the family in that eighteenth-century society served as a general pattern of organization and authority. The Church, for example, appeared to the people as a sort of family because God was presented as a father to be obeyed as one obeyed one's own father. The letter of Claude Louet above reads a little like a prayer. And not only was God a father-like figure, but beneath him there was a whole hierarchy of fathers in authority: the archbishops, the bishops and the priests. Catholic priests were addressed as "father" while the lay brothers were "brothers." The head of an order of nuns was, of course, a "mother superior," and the nuns were either "mother" or "sister." Girls first entering religious orders were expected to bring dowries as though they were being married, and a nun's dowry was not merely a symbol but a substantial sum of money, a piece of land or a parcel of goods. Records of dowries brought to Quebec orders are a useful guide to the wealth of the girls' families: some brought several thousand *livres* in cash, others came with a dowry of annuities or planks, barrels of wine, linen, furniture, wheat and so on.[18] When a Canadian girl chose to go into a monastery, she and her family prepared for the event in somewhat the same way as if she were going to be married, for they saw her as marrying into the Church. She joined the Church just as she might have joined a husband's family. Of course there were differences, but the similarities are striking.

Listen to the following ecstasies of love written by a woman who spent most of her life in New France: "Oh, beloved of my soul! Where are you and when shall I possess you? When shall I have you for myself and entirely for myself? Ah, I want you, but I do not want only half of you. I want all of you, my Love and my Life.... Come, then, come Oh my Love! The door of my heart is open to you ..." and so on. Now who was this passionate woman? And who was the fortunate man to whom she was so passionately drawn? She was none other than Marie de l'Incarnation, a nun in the seventeenth century and now a saint in the Canadian Catholic calendar, and all these emotional outpourings were addressed to God. She was expressing her vocation, her call to a life in New France in God's service to which she devoted herself passionately. The point is that as these and other such passages show she saw herself as in some sense married to God or to Jesus and in her writings often referred to him as "my dear Husband."[19]

The image of the family was also present in the army. When a soldier wanted to marry, he needed the consent of his captain or other senior officer and of the Governor of New France. These two consents, which were not merely perfunctory, were duly registered by the officiating clergy. Military authority was thus in some measure paternal authority. But all authority which is not defined by clear regulations must inevitably appear as paternal in the sense that it has no limits and may extend, like a father's authority, into personal and family matters.

The political hierarchy, too, was organized on the family plan. What was the King in the Bourbon kingdom but a great father with paternal care for his subjects and paternal authority over them? Under him, the Governor and Intendant were also father figures expected to enforce not the law, but the King's paternal will. They themselves had paternal rights and duties; and this explains why they used their authority in many matters great and small which astonish us. Paternal authority had very different limits from those of men in authority in our world. "You must maintain good order and peace in families," the minister at Versailles wrote to one Canadian Governor, "refrain from joining in private discussions except to bring them to an end and not join in them if you cannot settle them, never listen to women's talk, never allow anyone to speak ill of someone else in front of you and never do so yourself...." As the Intendant Raudot said, the colony was supposed to be managed "as a good father of a family would manage his estate."[20] When, for instance, the Minister happened to hear of an officer who was not supporting his impoverished mother, he arranged to have the officer punished and part of his pay withheld for the mother.[21]

There were, then, a number of hierarchies of authority in Canada all patterned on the family and all helping to reinforce one another in the Canadian mind. To introduce the rule of law into such a society, as the British tried to do after 1763, was a difficult task. How could it be introduced in a society where all authority was regarded as personal and paternal? Still, under British rule, the change began in New France a quarter of a century before it began in Old France during the French Revolution. Since then the French have reverted frequently to the paternal authority of a father figure such as the Bonaparte emperors and General de Gaulle, not to mention Marechal Petain whose regime used the motto, *Famille, Patrie, Travail.* Let us hope that in Quebec the rule of law has taken a firmer hold on the minds of the people during the past two hundred years, and that the ancient vision of the polity as a family has faded away.

Notes

1. *The Canda Yearbook for 1972,* 241–42.

2. Jacques Henripin, *La Population canadienne au début du XVIIIe siècle* (Paris, 1954); Henripin, "From Acceptance of Nature to Control: The Demography of the French Canadians since the Seventeenth Century," in M. Rioux and Y. Martin, *French-Canadian Society,* vol. 1 (Toronto, 1964), 204–216; Marcel Trudel, *La Population du Canada en 1663* (Montreal, 1973); J.N. Biraben, "Le Peuplement du Canada français," *Annales de démographie historiques* (Paris, 1966), 104–139.

3. Jacques Henripin, "La Fécondité des ménages canadiens au début du XVIIIe siècle," *Population,* vol. 9 (Paris, 1954), 74–84.

4. Trudel, 11. Professor Trudel lists 3,035 people, but admits that he is not sure of 221 of them. On immigrants, see Biraben, and Henripin, *La Population canadienne,* chap. II, quoting Georges Langlois, *Histoire de la population canadienne française de Montréal* (1934).

5. Trudel finds that in 1663, the proportion was nearly 50 percent (p. 74).

6. Robert-Lionel Seguin, *La Vie libertine en Nouvelle-France au XVIIe siècle,* vol. 2 (Ottawa, 1972), 365–66.

7. Paul-Andre Leclerc, "Le Mariage sous le régime français," *Revue d'histoire de l'Amérique française,* 13 (1959): 525.

8. *Ibid.,* 229ff. On "mariage à la gaumine," see *Le Rapport de l'Archiviste de la Province de Quebec* (henceforth cited as R.A.P.Q.), 1920–21, 366–407.

9. Marc Bloch, *Les Caractères originaux de l'Histoire rurale française* (Paris, 1952) [first published in 1931], chap. V.

10. Pierre Deffontaines, "The Rang—Pattern of Rural Settlement in French Canada," in Rioux and Martin, *French-Canadian Society*, 3–18.

11. Guy Fregault, *Le XVIIIe siècle canadien* (Montreal, 1968), 179.

12. *R.A.P.Q.*, 1938–39, 21–22 and 49–50.

13. Leclerc, 59.

14. Archives départementales de la Charente maritime (La Rochelle), minutes of the notary Delavergne, 10 December 1760 and 4 June 1770.

15. Cameron Nish, *Les Bourgeois-Gentilshommes de la Nouvell-France, 1729–1748* (Montreal and Paris, 1968), chap. X, "La Bourgeoisie et le mariage."

16. Philippe Garigue, *La Vie familiale des canadiens français* (Montreal and Paris, 1962), 16–17.

17. *R.A.P.Q.*, 1921–22, 60–63.

18. Micheline d'Allaire, "L'Origine sociale des religieuses de l'Hôpital-général de Québec," *Revue d'Histoire de l'Amérique française* 23 (March 1970): 559–83.

19. Dom Albert Jamet, ed., *Le Témoignage de Marie de l'Incarnation, Ursuline de Tours et de Québec* (Paris, 1932), 70–72.

20. Guy Fregault, *Le XVIIIe siècle canadien*, 162–63.

21. *Ibid.*, pp. 163–64.

CHILDREN OF THE FUR TRADES

Jennifer S.H. Brown

Many thousands of people in North America can trace their ancestry to the French and British fur traders of the seventeenth to nineteenth centuries and the Indian women who befriended, tolerated, or endured these European strangers. The descendants of fur trade alliances have followed many different paths, sometimes remembering and emphasizing their distinctive parentage, and sometimes establishing white or Indian identities that minimize their bi-racial origins.[1]

Such identity-building begins in the small and circumscribed context of an individual's immediate family and community. Children born in the fur trade country experienced family and community relationships that varied considerably according to the time, place, and company setting in which they matured, and depending on the social standing and ethnic identity of their parents.

From *Childhood and Family in Canadian History*, Joy Parr, ed. (Toronto: McClelland and Stewart, 1982), 44–68.

These patterns reflected the history of the fur trade itself and its complexities. Socially and organizationally, it was not one monolithic entity, although its European participants all pursued the same or similar resources with similar motives. The northern fur trade was dominated early by the French, and later by English and Highland Scottish entrepreneurs who drew on French expertise and labour to build the businesses that eventually coalesced into the North West Company. The Hudson's Bay Company began with English employees and later took on large numbers of Lowland and Orkney Scots; its servants' social origins and home affiliations thus contrasted with those of the Scots of the North West Company, although both were British and anglophone.[2] European traders' relationships with their native-born children, and the mothers of those children, were correspondingly diverse.

The early days of both the French and the British fur trades were characterized by trader bachelorhood. New France in its first decades contained a preponderance of young males, many of whom engaged in the fur trade. Much to colonial administrators' concern, traders were slow to establish stable family units. White women and potential wives were few. Indian women were not, and many from among the Huron and other tribes became involved in alliances with French traders.[3]

Such unions, usually temporary and unsanctioned by European norms, were not acceptable within New France. There, marriage was a Roman Catholic ritual that required a commitment for life. The traders who turned to Indian women, then, sought short-term personal gratification and trade advantages and did not expect their familial obligations to be permanent. In so doing, they did not necessarily violate Indian values. Missionaries who accompanied traders inland found to their dismay that the relatives of Indian women usually encouraged these relationships.

The Huron perceived ties between Frenchmen and Huron women as bases for personal kinship alliances that converted trader strangers into relatives and led to mutual trust and goodwill. Thus French priests as well as traders were offered Huron wives from motives of hospitality and trade-related friendship. The possibility that such unions might not be permanent did not surprise the Huron, for in their own society divorce was an accepted occurrence. Huron courtship customs, too, were relaxed. Young men and women accepted premarital sexual relations as normal, and marriages were stabilized as such only when children were born.[4] As long as they accepted Huron codes of politeness and proper behaviour among kin, French traders could ally themselves with Huron women without causing offence to any but their own churchmen.

The paths of such unions were probably smoothed by the fact that the French traders' occupational roles approximated those of Huron husbands in certain respects. Huron males, like their French allies, were absent from their homes for considerable periods, to pursue trading, provisioning, and political activities. The women remained at home, tending their crops and maintaining their matrilineal and familial ties and traditions. The children born to them, whether to Huron or French husbands, were readily absorbed into the female-centred extended families that resided in the large longhouses of Huron villages.[5] Half-French children became Huron, members of their mother's matrilineage. If orphaned, they still had a broad network of relatives who accepted them as kin, without raising the questions of legitimacy and morality that troubled the French authorities and clergy. The Huron themselves would doubtless have resisted yielding orphaned youngsters to French care if that option arose. Maternal descent placed them in the mother's line, not the father's. And children, in the Huron view, were happier and better-treated in their society than among the French. Huron children never suffered corporal punishment as discipline, and the Huron were shocked by the French advocacy and use of that method, just as the French were perturbed at its absence among the Huron.[6]

The destruction of the Huron confederacy and its dispersal in 1649 disrupted the formation of new kinship ties between French and Huron. But traders' own inclinations, in combination with widespread Indian interests in alliance through kinship, continued to foster trader-Indian intermarriage. In later periods, unknown numbers of fur trade children continued to be assimilated as members of northern Algonkian and other Indian groups, as long as their maternal relatives' communities were able and willing to absorb them.

After 1650, as the French trade reached farther inland, some of its participants loosened their ties with New France and formed more lasting bonds with each other and with their Indian associates, at a distance from the restricted and regulated life of their home colony. Officials wrote with concern about how attracted these young men were to "this Indian way of life" and how increasing numbers were living in the Indian country for years at a time.[7]

A major base for these men's activities was Michilimackinac at the junction of Lakes Huron and Michigan. It served as a depot for supplies from Montreal and a departure point for establishing outposts that eventually spread from the Ohio River to Lake Winnipeg and the Hudson Bay drainage. Clergy saw Michilimackinac as a den of sin, where informal and unsanctified liaisons flourished between French and Canadian-born white men and Algonkian women. Traders, however, welcomed Indian women as companions and helpmates on inland expeditions, as well as at remote winter outposts and at the major posts. Fur trade families arose as domestic units in which children matured, at least for a time, with both parents present. By 1695, sixty or so bark-covered dwellings were said to be housing such families in the vicinity of Michilimackinac.[8]

The continuing campaigns of the clergy against such relationships probably encouraged many traders to separate themselves still further from New France and its moral and legal strictures. The Jesuits, who urged that traders and Indians be kept as separate as possible, and the Governor-General of New France, who forbade mixed marriages at the post of Detroit in 1709, had few means to enforce compliance from people who by choice had removed themselves from respectable colonial society. The Detroit prohibition gave Governor-General Vaudreuil occasion to note the distinctiveness of these traders and to generalize about their offspring: the former were *"libertins fenéans, et d'une independence insuportable,"* ("lazy libertines and insufferably independent,") and the latter, *"d'une fenéantise aussy grande que les sauvages mesmes* ("as bone-lazy as the Indians themselves.")[9]

Details about these men's family lives and their children are hard to come by. But we can infer certain things about the fur trade parents and children of the late 1600s and early 1700s. From the numbers of their descendants and the diversity of their French names, we may conclude that a substantial proportion of early traders around Mackinac and elsewhere had such families and that many fathers were remaining sufficiently in touch to transmit their surnames to their offspring.

The mission registers of later years are also informative. From 1670 until the end of the French regime a mission priest was resident at Mackinac, and the registers of that place, which are relatively intact after the 1720s, preserve details on numbers of families who, sooner or later in their domestic cycles, accepted marriage or baptismal sacraments, in some instances while visiting Mackinac from outlying points such as Green Bay, Chequamegon, and Prairie du Chien, Wisconsin. On 22 July 1747, for example, the priest married Jean Baptiste Tellier de la Fortune and Marie Josephe, a Nipissing woman baptized that morning, and thereby legitimized their children, aged nineteen, fourteen, ten, six, three and six months. On 4 February 1748, "former *voyageur*" Charles Hamelin married Marie Athanasie, "a Sauteux [northern Ojibwa] woman Savage recently baptized." The marriage of Jean Manion l'Esperance to his Sauteux wife on 30 August 1749 legitimized their three children, aged about eight, six and three. Numerous other entries are similar in content.[10]

These registers are only a partial record but, in combination with other data on later fur trade families, they suggest the development of certain demographic patterns. Indian families, according to historical descriptions, were usually small, and children were commonly born three, four, or more years apart, owing to long periods of nursing that reduced the mothers' fecundity and sometimes to post-partum taboos on sexual relations. In times of hardship, infanticide and starvation might take their toll on newborns. Indian women's alliances with whites, however, tended to produce more children, more closely spaced, if the couple lived together fairly constantly. Children's survival chances were perhaps enhanced by access to fur trade centres and supplies, and European males were probably intolerant of long nursing and post-partum sexual restrictions. Whatever the importance of these various factors, fur trade families, once established as ongoing units, grew at rapid rates equalling those of New France and other expanding European colonies in North America.[11]

As the numbers and sizes of these families grew, they formed their own communities around the Great Lakes and westward in the direction of Red River. Mothers and children who became separated from their trader husband-fathers continued to rejoin their Indian relatives, but local Indian bands, by the mid-1700s, had difficulty absorbing all their progeny. Fathers who continued to reside in the Indian country retained their native kin around them. They supported themselves and their families by continuing in the direct employ of the fur trade, or by becoming *coureurs de bois*—outlaw traders, or *gens libres*—freemen who made an independent living by supplying the trade and subsisting on country resources, eventually to retire and die in the North-west.

Their early unplanned communities lacked visibility as recognized political entities, and their land titles were problematic. Owing to environmental and subsistence limitations the communities of the Great Lakes *métis* remained small, usually consisting of no more than a few hundred persons. Dependent mainly on local furs, game, and other resources shared cooperatively with Indian kinsmen nearby, *métis* populations were obliged to disperse into scattered nuclei. But unlike the Indians' more seasonal and temporary shelters, their clusters of upright-log, bark-covered cabins with high-pitched roofs might last many years. Several became the foci of later towns. Reflecting the importance of water transport, their homes were strung out along a lake or river with small, narrow, fenced gardens cut into the woods behind.

Children grew up with a mixed Indian-French heritage—a blending of languages, customs, and foods, for example, crêpes and maple sugar. They matured to wear distinctive apparel combining moccasins, leggings, pantaloons, ruffled shirts, and decorative feathers. Neither Indian nor French, yet both, some moved into major broker roles between New France to the east and Algonkian and Siouan groups to the west. Interpreting, guiding, transporting goods, messages, and people, they learned to function "not only as human carriers linking Indians and Europeans, but as buffers behind which the ethnic boundaries of antagonistic cultures remained relatively secure."[12]

Some of the sons became well-known personages, and yet they charted an independent course with respect to both their parental cultures. Charles Langlade was the son of a French trader and officer and of the sister of an Ottawa chief. Charles alternated in youth between wintering with his maternal kin and being tutored by Jesuits at Michilimackinac where his father was commandant. Believed by the Ottawa to possess a powerful manito, he might have become prominent among them but instead became a trader and military leader. Married first to an Ottawa Indian woman and later to a Detroit trader's daughter, he had his son schooled in Montreal and his daughters tutored at home. His children's marriages repeated the pattern of his own—Indian-*métis* alliances and *métis* endogamy, reinforcing Indian-*métis* ties around the western Great Lakes and swelling the ranks of the *métis* themselves.[13] With the rise and spread of the Langlades and countless other similar families, a new ethnically and culturally distinctive population had become an established presence around the Great Lakes by the end of the French regime.

The British conquest of New France in 1763 opened a new chapter in the Canadian fur trade and in fur trade family history. In the next years, political and economic control of the colony passed to anglophone leaders, among whom Highland Scots were conspicuous.

The mainly Scottish takeover of the higher echelons of the French fur trade and its related Montreal businesses in this period has been well-documented.[14] The process was accelerated by the Highlanders' tendency to reinforce and expand their commercial partnerships by recruiting Scottish kinsmen and friends from home or from among those who had migrated to New York and New England. Partners first formed strong competing networks in the fur business and later tended to combine forces as costs of rivalry grew and as the networks themselves spread and intersected. The North West Company was a group of partnerships that joined forces in 1784 and expanded rapidly thereafter. In 1804, it combined with its major remaining rival, the New North West or XY Company, to gain an effective monopoly of the Montreal fur trade.[15]

The North Westers formed a unified superstructure built on a foundation of French trade expertise, labour, and organization. Its winterers followed the old French trade routes, using Canadians and *métis* of French descent as guides, interpreters, and *voyageurs*. A two-tiered social system developed. French fur trade society had been truncated by the conquest, and its leadership had been removed or demoted. Its upper levels were taken over by newcomers who assumed prominent roles not only as winterers in the fur trade country but also in the higher social ranks of the growing business centre of Montreal. Even after long absences inland, these partners had incentives to return to Montreal where they could rejoin their kin and consolidate their fur trade gains and their social standing. Remaining active in the business, they also participated in the Beaver Club, their own society of former winterers, and in churches and other organizations.

As partners and company directors, the British North Westers also had opportunities to recruit and train their own successors. The young men whom they chose as clerks and possible future partners were, like themselves, predominantly British, usually being kinsmen or personal acquaintances. Collateral relationships extending among active and prospective colleagues were significant links for this purpose. Thus, for example, Simon McTavish, one of the leading merchant partners in Montreal, brought three of his sister's sons, William, Simon, and Duncan McGillivray, from Scotland and also introduced John George McTavish, the son of his clan chief, into the business; all four became important figures in the fur trade.[16]

The emphasis that the North Westers placed on these wider kin ties sometimes detracted from their marriages and immediate families. Simon McTavish married the daughter of a distinguished old French fur trading family, Marie Marguerite Chaboillez—an alliance that fostered good relations with those few French Canadians who still maintained standing in the fur business. But this late marriage, contracted when he was forty-three, did not become the sole focus of his life. Before his death in 1804, he made a will whose provisions paid as much attention to his Scottish kin as to his wife and four children. And he made it clear that Marie Marguerite and her relatives were not to have the management of the children; rather, they were to be given a proper British education.[17] Their deaths at early ages left unanswered the question of how their own ties and allegiances might have developed.

When the British North Westers travelled into the Indian country, they carried their loyalties, mutual connections, and familial attitudes with them. Like the French before, and like the Indians with whom they traded, they were receptive to unions with women who would cement alliances with native trading partners. Yet, unlike many French, most British North Westers were too well-placed in their home society to develop permanent attachments in the Indian country.

Additionally, unlike the French traders among the Huron and westward, they lacked the constraint of being observed and reported upon by the churchmen resident in the Indian country; after the British conquest of Canada, the clergy rarely made visits even as far as Mackinac, and mission activity in the North-west practically ceased until the 1820s.[18] The private partnerships whose interests these Britishers served were not concerned to convert or civilize the fur trade country; nor did they undertake to build up governmental or legal structures beyond those supervisory functions required by the trade.

The result was that formal European legal and moral constraints in the Montrealers' North-west were weaker than they had been in the areas penetrated by the French. Among North Westers and their Canadian and *métis* employees as they extended their activities to the Athabasca country and beyond, codes of conduct with regard to native families varied depending on local circumstances and the individuals concerned. Most became involved, sooner or later, in what were known as marriages "according to the custom of the country" (*en façon du pays*). But "marriage" could mean several different things. It was sometimes a transitory union, lasting only while a man was engaged in local trade with the woman's relatives. It might be longer-term like William Connolly's, with the woman and her children accompanying a trader to different posts, perhaps far away from her Indian kin. Or it might prove to be lifelong, as did some—notably the well-recorded marriages of Daniel Williams Harmon and John Macdonell.[19] But alongside these relationships were others that were more exploitative and abusive, involving seizures of women or their sale among traders. Fur trade marriages could be matters of "custom and ceremony" or alternatively involve few or no ritual or social sanctions. One woman from the fur trade country testified in the Connolly court case in Montreal that she knew nothing of marriage rituals in such unions: "The custom is that one sleeps with men."[20]

The children of these alliances had diverse experiences. Those who, like the early French *métis*, were absorbed into Indian societies, generally left little trace in the historical record. We know more about the offspring of men whose long attachment to their native families drew their children away from their maternal relatives. A number of their histories have been published elsewhere.[21] One useful source concerning some of them has not been systematically investigated before, however, and makes an interesting focus for discussion here.

Some North Westers were Roman Catholics and Anglicans; but others were Presbyterians who by the 1790s were actively supporting their own church in Montreal, the St. Gabriel Street Presbyterian Church. The registers of this church for the years from 1796 to 1821, when the North West Company and the Hudson's Bay Company merged, list the baptisms of seventy-five children born of alliances between North Westers and women of the Indian country.[22] The entries are revealing and yet also curiously elliptical about the familial relationships behind them.

A North Wester who sent his native children back to Montreal for baptism assumed certain paternal obligations and expenses. He did not necessarily thereby establish an ongoing "nuclear family" of co-residing parents and children. With occasional exceptions, the mothers of children listed in the St. Gabriel Street records were absent from the ceremony and left unnamed; the standard description included the child's name and age, and then read "son" (or "daughter") of, for example, "Roderick McKenzie of the North West Company Esquire by a woman of the Indian Country." The mother's invisibility in this context was no proof that she was unknown or that her alliance with the child's father had terminated: some, such as Roderick McKenzie's with Angelique,[23] became lifelong; some had ended; some would end later as North Westers set aside old liaisons for respectable white marriages. But plainly at that time such relationships were rarely accepted or made permanent in Montreal. The clergy were willing to baptize the native children of North West Company gentlemen, but most mothers, unbaptized and unmarried by Christian rite, remained unacknowledged.

Of fifty-seven baptismal entries listing parentage, seven did name mothers, and these families have some special interest. On 25 July 1796, Charles Phillips, "Indian Trader," presented two sons and a daughter for baptism. Their mother was "Jenny the Red Bird of the tribe of the Hurons," whom he married that day. Phillips had been a North Wester, for many years in charge of Rivière Dumoine (Quebec). But by the time of his marriage he had left the company, under criticism for mismanagement of his charge, and was trading independently at Point St. Claire.[24] He was evidently a marginal figure both among company colleagues and in his decision to marry Jenny the Red Bird in Montreal.

The noted explorer David Thompson and his family are another exception. Thompson entries account for three of the seven in which mothers are named. On 30 September 1812, Thompson and his country wife, Charlotte, daughter of North Wester Patrick Small and a Cree woman, presented three sons and a daughter for baptism; on 30 October, the parents were married by minister James Somerville. Later entries record part of the history of this large family:

in 1813, a son was baptized at the age of one month; in early 1814, two of the children baptized earlier were buried; and in 1815, a daughter, aged eight weeks, was baptized. During this period, the family was living at Terrebonne, where several other old North Westers, notably Roderick McKenzie, may have offered congenial company. Yet Thompson, like Phillips, was in some respects a marginal North Wester. A product of the charitable Grey Coat School in England, he had been apprenticed in 1784 to the Hudson's Bay Company, which he served until 1797 when he joined the North West Company. Certainly he lacked, both in England and Canada, the broad kinship and friendship networks in which so many North Westers were intertwined. This absence of competing ties and his strong sense of morality constrained him from setting aside his native wife and children for other allegiances. Unrecognized for his great fur trade explorations once he left the North West Company, he and his family lived a penurious and obscure existence for many years thereafter, in Terrebonne and later in Williamstown (Ontario), another centre of retired traders.[25]

Two other North Westers named lifelong companions as the mothers of their children, although they did not marry them in the St. Gabriel Street Church. John Thomson and Frances Boucher presented a son and two daughters, aged nine, eleven, and two, for baptism in May of 1811; the mother, aged about twenty-five, was also baptized. The family was long-lasting. Françoise Boucher and John Thomson "cohabited together for many years in the Indian Territory, by which they had a family of six children and on their arrival in Lower Canada, married, having previously executed before Seguin and his confrere Notaries a contract of Marriage bearing date 8 March 1822 at Terrebonne in the District of Montreal." A seventh child was born after Thomson's death in 1828 causing the estate to be divided into eight equal shares.[26]

In 1812, the same year that David Thompson married Charlotte Small, John McDonald of Garth brought her sister, Nancy (seemingly misnamed Catharine in the register), and two children to the St. Gabriel Street minister for baptism; an older daughter had been baptized in 1810. Their familial ties also were lifelong. Possibly McDonald's attachment to Nancy was reinforced by the fact that his mother was a relative of her father, Patrick Small, through family connections going some distance back in Britain.[27]

The final mother named in the register is most notable for her description; nothing more is known of her or her son. Whether by disguise or by some arrangement, she became the only woman known to have served as an employee of the North West Company. Her son's entry, dated 13 December 1818, reads, "Charles Grant, Esqr., North West Company, and Lizette or Elizabeth Landry, an Engage formerly in the service of the North West Company had a son born at Athabaska, about five years ago." Neither parent signed the register; the boy was presented by two members of other families active in the fur business.

Slightly more often than not, twenty-eight instances of a possible fifty-four, the fathers of children baptized were not present at the ceremony (two fathers were deceased). Absences of fathers, like non-naming of mothers, held varying significance. Some fathers were able to coordinate their Montreal leaves from the Indian country with their children's journeys east; others could not manage to do so and entrusted to eastern relatives or friends the baptisms and perhaps also the care and schooling of their offspring.

Children experienced some shocks, cultural, psychic, and even physiological, as at an average age of six[28] they left one or both parents and the informal, isolated life of the North-west to face uncertain welcome among the strangers who were their father's city kinsmen and friends. The strain of the transition told on some. Eight of the seventy-five children surveyed here died within a few days to a few years after their baptisms. Another five native-born children were buried from the church without having been baptized there.

The St. Gabriel Street Church baptismal entries yield other information about familial relations among the North Westers. The father's surname was invariably conferred, affirming paternity in cases in which traders might have ignored or denied it. North Westers baptizing their children thus made explicit an immediate personal commitment whatever their subsequent actions.

The North Westers' children presented for baptism were, however, a selected group. Two-thirds of the St. Gabriel's fur trade children (fifty-one of seventy-five) were boys. Given the costs involved, North Westers usually sent east sons who could be educated and carry on their father's name in some suitable occupation, usually assumed to be the fur trade. Daughters more often remained in the fur trade country, marrying Indians, traders, or native-born sons of traders, often at early ages. Some found homes in the *métis* communities around and beyond the Great Lakes. But a North West Company ruling of 1806, one of few dealing with social and moral matters, suggests that a high proportion of traders' daughters remained around the posts and required some consideration; it dictated that North Westers henceforth were to choose their fur trade mates only from among the daughters of white men.[29]

Not much is known about the life histories of most of the North Westers' children baptized on St. Gabriel Street. Some, such as Alexander William McKay (b. 1802) and Benjamin McKenzie (b. 1805), matured to take company positions. But there was little prospect of advancement for "half-breeds" once the North West and Hudson's Bay Companies merged in 1821 and the labour retrenchments of the 1820s and 1830s set in. Cuthbert Grant (b. 1793), being found politically useful in Red River Settlement, was better rewarded than some.[30]

The case of George, son of Duncan McDougall, reveals persisting childhood ties with a father, although the son's later life is obscure. During 1803–06, Duncan McDougall and a party of North Westers were established on James Bay to compete with the Hudson's Bay Company. They were assisted by one Jack Hester, "Indian," probably a son or grandson of HBC officer James Hester who had retired from Albany in 1767. Jack's sister or daughter, Nancy, became

McDougall's companion during that time. A few years after McDougall had left the area, George Gladman, officer at Eastmain, baptized George and Anne, children of "Duncan McDougall and Nancy Hester"; presumably they and their mother were dependents of that post.

The father, in this period, left the North West Company, joined the Pacific Fur Company in 1810, helped to found Fort Astoria on the Columbia River in 1811, and rejoined the North West Company when it took over Astoria in 1813. He was known particularly for contracting a temporary but helpful fur trade alliance with the daughter of the Chinook chief Concomly, who acquired in exchange for "this precious lady" fifteen guns and fifteen blankets, "besides a great deal of other property." Yet his Hudson Bay children, or at least the son, were not completely forgotten. George, aged eight, was brought to Montreal by an unknown party by the fall of 1812 and baptized there on 26 October, with Alexander McDougall and Mary Anne McDougall as sponsors. Doubtless he remained with his Montreal relatives while his father (who died in the Northwest in 1818) continued in the company. His sister Anne evidently stayed with her maternal relatives around Eastmain.[31]

This evidence sustains some general observations about the children of the British North Westers. Montreal or Scottish and company attachments loomed large in their fathers' lives, and allegiances to native wives and children could be correspondingly weak. Alternatively, fathers might draw on their kinsmen and friends in the fur business to care for those children, usually sons, whom they particularly favoured but with whom they were unable to remain. This pattern is traceable both in eastern Canadian records and in the fur trade country, for example, when Daniel W. Harmon became temporary tutor to the son of Archibald Norman McLeod and an Indian woman in 1801.[32]

Daughters were more likely to remain with their maternal relatives in the Indian country. There they raised families of mixed ancestry, some of whom came to assert the importance of their maternal heritage and later expressed pride in their Indian ancestry by supporting Louis Riel's *nation métisse*. Those women who separated from their trader fathers or husbands and rejoined subarctic Indian societies may have found themselves especially in harmony with and may also have reinforced the "matri-organizational" emphasis of some of these societies.[33]

Most British North Westers did not form permanent nuclear families with their native mates; decisions to retire, to go on leave, or to change location severed bonds with some or all of their children and with their children's mothers. Such familial ties and responsibilities were individual affairs, individually interpreted. Although some social pressures existed to maintain country wives, to look after native families, or to place them in another's care, these were private matters in which the company hardly interfered, except for the regulation of 1806. If the North Westers had not merged with the Hudson's Bay Company in 1821, they probably would have begun to provide more regularized care and formal education for their native children; in 1820 partners and clerks in both the Indian country and Canada were said to have subscribed "several thousand dollars toward the establishment of a school, either at the Rainy Lake, or at Fort William, for the instruction of the children, connected with their establishments."[34] But this plan emerged relatively late, more than a decade after similar projects had been advanced for the native children of Hudson's Bay. Hudson's Bay children were not necessarily possessed of more supportive fathers than their North West counterparts. But their formative social and company context was different.

To compare the Hudson's Bay Company posts and personnel with those of the Montreal fur trade is a little like comparing greenhouse vegetation with what develops in the garden outside it. Both were subject to regulation and supervision—but to very different degrees and in different ways. The Hudson's Bay Company was founded by a royal charter that granted power and ownership to a London-based committee of shareholders or "Adventurers" who typically never travelled to Hudson Bay. Their concerns were to maintain their monopoly against French interlopers, to control their employees, and to establish cordial diplomatic ties with Indian groups who were expected, unrealistically, to share European understandings about such formalities. The posts on the Bay were fortified residential enclaves organized in accord with military and rather monastic ideals. Disciplined, celibate men, serving the company for years at a time, were to conduct its business in orderly fashion and protect its interests, by force if needed.

This rational model for behaviour proved unrealistic. HBC traders were not skilled or successful as military men or builders of fortifications. The occasional French attacks on their posts were usually successful. Still more problematic was the company effort to maintain discipline and chastity among its men. The distance between London and the Bay was great, and the periods of isolation endured by the Bayside employees were long. Most early recruits were bachelors, many being young apprentices who signed for seven-year terms. Older men who had families were after one unsuccessful experiment in 1683, forbidden to bring them to the Bay. Having few social ties at home and scant opportunity to reinforce those that they had, the lives of Bay men, which initially centred on their posts and colleagues, later came to include Indians as trading partners, familiar acquaintances, and kin.[35]

Company rules forbade the free admission of Indians, especially women, into the posts, and urged formal circumspection in interactions with them. But the Cree along the Bay, like their earlier counterparts among the French to the south, saw kin ties as a natural basis of friendly trading partnerships. HBC traders were often subject and frequently susceptible to offers of female companionship. The chief officers of the posts, being recognized by the Indians as men of power and privilege, were most frequently approached. Some took advantage of their high standing to claim Indian wives while enforcing the company's rules against women upon sometimes resentful subordinates.

These women were sometimes abused; and in at least one instance, the attack on Henley House in 1755, the Indians vigorously retaliated.[36] But more often HBC traders formed relatively stable familial relationships. Despite the old restrictions, these attachments were less covert after the 1740s and were receiving considerable company attention by the 1790s.

Fathers were concerned for their country wives and children in the event of their own deaths, dismissals, or retirements from the Bay. Unlike its Montreal counterparts, the HBC forbade former employees to remain in the country either as pensioners or free traders who could become burdens or rivals to its own commerce. Nor would it normally allow native dependents a passage in its ships to England. For many decades, then, the families of HBC men were left behind, typically to rejoin their maternal relatives, usually Cree "Home" or "Homeguard" Indians, around the posts. Increasingly, traders provided families with legacies and annuities to be dispensed by the local HBC factors. Distinct mixed-descent communities could not develop freely and maintain themselves as they had around the Great Lakes; children of Hudson's Bay families remained or once again became Indian, though they might bear a former trader's name or visit a post regularly to trade and claim an annuity.

Some men, admitting that their native dependents would face severe adjustment problems in Britain, left their families behind as a matter of practical kindness. Others sought a middle ground, bringing one or two male children to England if the company could be persuaded to grant them passage and returning their wife and perhaps daughters to Indian relatives. Several such daughters, for example those of Matthew Cocking, William Pink, Isaac Batt, and Humphrey Marten, became the country wives of traders. A few sons, after visiting England or receiving some education there, returned to the Bay as company employees. Early classed as English (for example, James Isham's son, Charles), they later became numerous enough to acquire their own label in the books as "natives of Hudson Bay." The families of George Atkinson and William Richards were known in this way.[37]

As the numbers of these mixed-blood offspring grew, the daughters among them matured to found new fur trade alliances whose progeny were tied more closely to company than to Indian life. Neither the company nor its traders wished an ungoverned, dependent, and possibly troublesome mixed-blood population to develop around the posts; nor did many fathers wish their family ties severed. For these dilemmas, diverse solutions arose between 1790 and 1810. Some officers began systematic efforts to train and educate "factory boys," including their own sons, as a "colony of very useful hands" for permanent company service. They pressed for local education of both sons and daughters with some modest success; company schools were founded at several bayside posts in 1807–10. Finally, in Lord Selkirk's colony at Red River, the company provided a place where former employees and their native families might remain together and find new livelihoods in the North-west while still under company monopoly and governance.[38]

The rising aspirations and growing attachment of many HBC men for their families are especially clear in the Moose Factory register of families. Chief officer John Thomas began the register in 1808, following the company request for records of the names and ages of employees' children at the post. Thomas took the duty as a personal opportunity to note far more data about his nine children than the company required to plan its school for Moose. His entries give an unusually full picture of a family that spanned three decades and had become closely interconnected with other James Bay traders and their offspring. Most of the children had not been baptized, but spaces were left for christening dates to be entered, in the event that the rite became available. The Thomas entries are worth quoting as a sample of these early records and their format:

John Thomas Sen.ʳ declares that he has the following children:

Eleanor Thomas born Old Brunswick House the 22ᵈ Nov.ʳ 1780 Christened the _____ now Married to William Richards of this Factory.

John Thomas born at this Factory 25ᵗʰ Sept.ʳ 1784 Christened _____ now resident at Kenogumesee House.

Margaret Thomas born at this Factory 25ᵗʰ Sept.ʳ 1784 Christened _____ in England she is now resident.

Elizabeth Thomas born at this Factory July _____ 1785 (relict of the late Richard Story Robins) now married to Jas. Russell of this Factory, Christened the _____.

Charlotte Thomas born June 2ᵈ 1788 at this Factory Christened the _____ now married to Peter Spence of this Factory.

Charles Thomas born at this Factory 9ᵗʰ Sept.ʳ 1793 Baptized in St. Benedicts Church, Fenchurch Street 11th Dec.ʳ 1800, his Father John Thomas & Alex.ʳ Lean [HBC Secretary] Godfathers Mrs. Lean Godmother, now resident at this Factory.

Ann Thomas born at this Factory the 29ᵗʰ Dec.ʳ 1795 Christened the _____ now married to Thomas Hodgson of Albany Factor.

Frances Thomas born at this Factory 17ᵗʰ Dec.ʳ 1798 Christened the _____.

Henry Thomas born at this Factory 20ᵗʰ June 1807 Christened the 5ᵗʰ July 1807.

Several details of these entries are of interest. The baptism of Charles was sponsored by his father and an important company official in London. The entry for Henry Thomas, and many thereafter, indicates that the traders themselves began to conduct lay baptisms at Moose Factory, clergymen being absent; compare the baptisms of the Hester-McDougall children at Eastmain, noted earlier. Margaret's residence in England, evidently permanent (she was still there when her mother died at Moose in 1813), was unusual for a daughter of the time. The absence of reference to the children's mother is at first glance reminiscent of the North Westers' St. Gabriel Street baptisms. But when Thomas, as a "disconsolate Husband," recorded her death in the register on 31 December

1813, he left no doubt about her name and standing as "Mrs. Margaret Thomas." Similarly, although no clergy were present to sanctify their unions in Christian terms, he described his daughters as married.[39] In this he followed an increasingly visible Hudson's Bay convention that was reflected in the register after 1814; baptismal entries after that year almost invariably named both parents.

Of eighty offspring whose sex was indicated (it is undetermined for two), forty-six were girls and thirty-four were boys, a proportion of 57.5 per cent to 42.5 per cent, which suggests that the selectivity evident in the St. Gabriel Street entries was not operative here. This bias toward girls, not extreme for a sample of this size, may, however, have reflected two factors: the general tendency of more females than males to survive birth, and the possibility that some traders' sons were not mentioned because they had been sent to Britain.

Numbers of the people mentioned between 1808 and 1821 were members of families that had been linked with Moose and other James Bay posts for two or more decades previously—the Thomases, the Richardses (later Rickard?), the Turnors (later Turner), the Moores, the Gills, and Sarah Good, the daughter of eighteenth-century officer Humphrey Marten. Some branches of these families have continued to live in the Moose area until the present day.[40]

Other company families from HBC posts began in the early 1800s to move southwards as families when their husband-fathers retired or were dismissed, rather than face separation or the strain of making new homes in Britain. Some moved to Red River, particularly after 1820 when the settlement seemed safely established. Others, beginning in about 1810, went to eastern Canada, and some traces of them are found in their company rivals' territory—along the Ottawa River and in the Montreal area. When John Hodgson was dismissed for mismanagement of Albany in 1810, he and his family travelled south to Lac des Chats where they took up land and lived for a number of years, quite inelegantly, according to some later Ottawa River travellers who visited them.[41]

In the same year, a company family from farther inland made a similar journey, to settle at Vaudreuil by the mouth of the Ottawa River. Robert Longmoor, who had entered the company as a labourer in 1771, retired "to enjoy the fruits of his labours; he is now worth about £1,800," as a contemporary reported. Thanks to the St. Gabriel Street Church registers in Montreal, we know that about eight family members were with him. On 29 March 1813, Jane Longmoor, aged about twelve, "daughter of Robert Longmoor of Vaudreuil by a woman of the Indian country," was baptized, with Robert and Andrew Longmoor as witnesses. On 11 June 1813, daughters Catharine, aged about twenty-five, and Phoebe, aged about seven, were baptized, as were Catharine's four young children, "born to James Halcro of Vaudreuil farmer (formerly of the Northwest)," with Halcro as witness. Halcro, an Orkneyman, had joined the Hudson's Bay Company in 1789 and served on inland rivers as Longmoor's pilot. By this date, Longmoor had died; Catharine and Phoebe were identified as "daughters of the late Robert Longmoor ... and Sally Pink spinster."

Sally was doubtless the native-born daughter of William Pink, inland explorer from York Fort in the 1760s and 1770s. Now a widow in Hudson's Bay if not in Montreal church terms, she was baptized on 1 July 1813 as Sally Pink, with James Halcro as witness. And on that day, minister James Somerville married Halcro and Catharine Longmoor.[42] Their success as a farming family in Vaudreuil is not known, but their familial ties, stretching back many years in the Hudson's Bay territories, were evidently strongly maintained in their new setting.

Another contingent of Hudson's Bay families, whose names already appear in this text, travelled to Vaudreuil the next year. The Moose Factory journal of 24 June 1814 recorded that John Thomas, who had just resigned his position there, departed that day for Canada, accompanied by his son Charles with wife and child, his daughter Charlotte and her husband (Peter Spence) and their three children, and three other grandchildren, Henry and Richard Thomas and Richard Robins. Three children of Thomas Knight, a surgeon at Eastmain who had died there in 1797, travelled with the party. The beginnings of their new life were evidently shaky; in November, 1815, John Thomas asked the company if he might return to Moose. This request was rejected, but the London committee offered Thomas land at Red River and his sons employment at Moose. Charles Thomas returned north and served the company for some years. But the other Thomases remained at Vaudreuil for at least some time and were joined by more kin. On 23 February 1819, Elizabeth, daughter of John Thomas, was formally married in the St. Gabriel Street Church to "James Russell of Vaudreuil merchant," her husband at Moose Factory since 1808. On the same day, she and her son Richard, "by the late Richard Story Robins of Hudson's Bay," were baptized. On 4 March, Catherine, aged eighteen, daughter of HBC surgeon Thomas Thomas, was baptized with James Russell as witness. Plainly these Hudson's Bay families remained together after leaving their company posts and supported relatives and other HBC offspring in their new environment.[43]

The St. Gabriel Street Church and Moose Factory registers overlap closely in time, and record a similar number of fur trade children from two different contexts—seventy-five from the North Westers' "Indian Country" and eighty-two from Hudson's Bay. These two sources are unique to their respective companies. No document comparable to the Moose Factory register survives from a North West Company post. No Canadian and probably no British church served so conspicuously as a centre for Hudson's Bay men as St. Gabriel Street did for the North Westers (although more records of Hudson's Bay offspring doubtless await discovery in various churches in London and elsewhere). The two registers reveal the differing family and company settings which affected the fur trade children before 1821. Plainly the policies and attitudes of the two companies regarding fur trade dependents differed widely, and fur trader fathers were constrained by different company and home settings as they made decisions about their native offspring.

The North Westers relied in both their occupational and personal lives upon networks linking kinsmen and friends sometimes over broad distances—from Scotland to Montreal and western Canada. These ties seemed to compete with nuclear family bonds, particularly where native families of unproven legitimacy and doubtful standing were involved. White relatives were unwilling to concede inheritance rights to these families and some North Westers' estates, most notably William Connolly's, were subject to intense court disputes. Connolly made specific testamentary provisions for his mixed-blood children after he set aside his Cree wife of many years to marry a Montreal cousin, but these provisions faced stiff resistance from other claimants.[44] Thus Montreal and Scots networks often posed strong challenges to the position and welfare of fur trade families.

Yet eastern connections also helped traders with their country families. A father seeking to secure the future of particular children, most usually males, might place them with colleagues in eastern Canada. Old mutual ties gave some assurance that these guardians would carry out their duties with care, although some fathers found their confidence misplaced.[45]

From the children's viewpoint, these placements posed graver problems. The children faced a traumatic move away from both parents into a foreign setting where adults' interest might be diffuse and shallow. Certainly some children proved unable to meet their fathers' aspirations. The involvement of some North Westers' sons in a short-lived native independence movement, the Indian Liberating Army on the Great Lakes in 1836, reflected their sense of rootlessness in eastern Canada and their persisting attachment to the Indian country.[46]

Most HBC traders did not have the extensive interlocking social ties of the North Westers. Their legacies to native dependents were not challenged in courts. But their children were not easily brought to Britain for care and education. Even if the company were persuaded to give passage, many traders had no English kin who could take their children. The result was that, especially before Red River was established, many HBC offspring were assimilated by the Indians. As an alternative, their fathers by the late 1700s pressed the company to provide education, training, and employment for their children at the main posts, allowing the formation of distinct company communities.

When such families ended their post life—when a husband-father retired or was dismissed—they increasingly relocated as families, as did the Hodgsons on the Ottawa River, the Longmoors and Thomases at Vaudreuil, and others at later dates at Red River. The persistence of these Hudson's Bay Company families as integral units, even in eastern Canada (a persistence mirrored also in the family of former HBC man David Thompson), reflects the distinctiveness of their company origins and suggests that their familial attitudes, priorities, and decision-making patterns differed in important ways from the North Westers' more open, diffuse, and far-reaching kin relationships.

The 1820s brought drastic changes to the lives of fur traders' offspring in the North-west—the Great Lakes *métis*, the "half-breed" descendants of the British North Westers, and the "Indian" or "Hudson's Bay native" offspring of the Hudson's Bay Company. Around the southern and western Great Lakes, American government and courts sought to organize and civilize the mixed communities whose antecedents lay in the old French fur trade. In a one-week court session in 1824 in La Baye (Green Bay), Michigan Territory (now Wisconsin), a newly-arrived judge declared that the long-standing customary marriages of most of that community's principal inhabitants were invalid. To avoid penalties, most couples agreed to be (re)married by a Justice of the Peace, although a few defended the *de facto* legitimacy of their unions as being based on "the customs of the Indians."[47] The incident was a token of impending developments—the incursions of officialdom, new legal standards, and settlers and missionaries who would overshadow and eventually submerge the small *métis* fur trade settlements they encountered.

To the north, parallel developments modified the old ways of traders and their families. The Hudson's Bay and North West Companies merged in 1821, bringing a unified governance and control to the North-west. The first Anglican and Roman Catholic clergy reached Red River by 1820 and attempted to enforce Christian marriage as a necessary rite to legitimize customary alliances and their progeny. Traders found themselves obliged to make conscious decisions about their commitments. Some yielded to clerical pressure and married in church. A few, like the die-hards of Green Bay, asserted that local custom, long-term co-residence, and mutual affection had already validated their marriages and that the Christian ritual was superfluous. And some, notably former North Westers, saw in clerical non-recognition of customary marriages an excuse not to recognize their own. Leaving behind old country entanglements, they found white brides in their home social circles, following the example of their new company Governor, George Simpson, whose fur trade liaisons were not permitted to interfere with his marriage to his cousin Frances in 1830.[48]

These developments, along with post-merger reductions in fur trade employment opportunities, meant that fathers, more than before, had to assume an active role if their children's futures were to be secured. Many men took their children from the growing social and economic strains of the fur trade country to secure them gentlemanly eastern livelihoods. As means of communication and transport improved, more Hudson's Bay and old North West Company families found new homes in eastern Canada or Britain, hoping to ease their offspring into white society, toward what one father aptly called "ultimate respectability."[49]

Many fur trade children had more difficulty finding work and a secure identity. Few could find success within the new monopoly, and the prejudices of Governor Simpson against "half-breeds," particularly evident in his personnel records of the early 1830s, dimmed the prospects of those sons who did maintain company positions. The political agitations that surfaced among some fur trade sons in the Guillaume Sayer free-trade trial of 1849 and again in the Louis Riel risings of 1869 and 1885 were understandable responses to hardships imposed by economic monopoly and lack of opportunity. They were also reactions to the incursions of new governmental structures and controls and new settlers into a country the *métis* viewed as their inheritance through both their fathers and their mothers.

These movements came mainly from native sons of North West Company origin who developed a distinctive sense of identity in Red River and beyond—in lands which most of their fathers had been quite willing to leave behind when they retired. Old Hudson's Bay families, in contrast, seemed more content to settle together in Red River and, later, in other western communities where their descendants retained identities as members of company families or "Rupertslanders" and showed little affinity for *métis* causes.[50]

Farther east, in the original heartland of the Hudson's Bay Company territories, the term *métis* as an ethnic category appeared relatively late. Many company descendants of mixed ancestry continued living as Indians through the nineteenth century and into the twentieth and were officially classed as Indian, for example by the Treaty No. 9 commissioners who visited James Bay in 1905. But that year several families at Moose Factory "were refused treaty by the Commissioners on the grounds that they were not living the Indian mode of life," and some, describing themselves as halfbreeds, petitioned the government of Ontario for attention, noting that "scrip has been granted to the Halfbreeds of the North West Territory." The Ontario government, however, had no provisions for issuing scrip to halfbreeds; and a government proposal to issue 160-acre land patents instead was never acted upon.[51] Some descendants of the people thus left in limbo, without distinctive rights or recognition, have in recent years become active in local *métis* associations or in the Ontario *Métis* and Non-Status Indian Association.

Choices of career paths and ethnic identities remain problematic for many descendants of the fur trade who still reside in the North-west. Their distinctive fur trade contexts—French, British North Wester, and Hudson's Bay—have been blurred by a century and a half of radical social, economic, and government pressures that have changed and challenged older ways of life. Current generations seek to reconcile their distinctive pasts with the overbearing demands of the present. At the same time, numerous descendants of families who early left the fur trade are reclaiming that portion of their heritage, discovering the ways that their own family histories and Canadian history have intersected in the last two to four centuries.

Notes

1. Fur trade social historians are often reminded that identity-building is a dynamic process continued from generation to generation, as they try to answer the genealogical queries of traders' descendants pursuing and rediscovering their origins. Some descendants have themselves contributed actively to fur trade scholarship—for example, Elaine Allan Mitchell, *Fort Timiskaming and the Fur Trade* (Toronto: University of Toronto Press, 1977); Jean Murray Cole, *Exile in the Wilderness: The Life of Chief Factor Archibald McDonald, 1790–1853*, (Seattle: University of Washington Press, 1979).

2. For a detailed discussion of these differences and their implications, see Jennifer S.H. Brown, *Strangers in Blood: Fur Trade Company Families in Indian Country* (Vancouver: University of British Columbia Press, 1980), Chapters 1 and 2.

3. On demographic patterns in early New France, see Marcel Trudel, *The Beginnings of New France, 1524–1663* (Toronto: McClelland and Stewart, 1973), 260–61.

4. Bruce Trigger, *The Children of Aataentsic: A History of the Huron People to 1660* (Montreal: McGill-Queen's University Press, 1976), vol. 1, 365, 49–50.

5. *Ibid.*, 40–41, 45.

6. *Ibid.*, 47, 263; vol. 2, 762.

7. W.J. Eccles, *The Canadian Frontier 1534–1760* (New York: Holt, Rinehart and Winston, 1969), 90, quoting the Marquis de Denonville (1685) and Intendant Jean Bochart de Champigny (1691).

8. *Ibid.*, 109–10, 90–91; Jacqueline Peterson, "Prelude to Red River: A Social Portrait of the Great Lakes *Métis*," *Ethnohistory*, 25, 1 (1978), 47–48.

9. Eccles, *The Canadian Frontier*, 91, 199, n. 11.

10. Reuben G. Thwaites (ed.), *Collections of the State Historical Society of Wisconsin*, vol. 18, 1908 (Mackinac Register of Marriages—1725–1821); vol. 19, 1910 (Mackinac Register of Baptisms and Interments—1695–1821).

11. On later fur trade demography, with special reference to the higher ranks of traders, see Jennifer S.H. Brown, "A Demographic Transition in the Fur Trade Country: Family Sizes and Fertility of Company Officers and Country Wives, ca. 1751–1850," *Western Canadian Journal of Anthropology*, 6, 1 (1976), 61–71. On birth rates in New France, see Jacques Henripin, *La population canadienne au debut du XVIIIᵉ Siècle: Nuptialité, Fécondité, Mortalité infantile* (Paris: Presses Universitaires de France, 1954). In 1828, Major Anderson, Indian agent, "computed the number of Canadians and mixed breed married to Indian women, and residing on the north shores of Lake Huron, and in the neighbourhood of Michilimackinac, at nine hundred. This he called the *lowest* estimate." Anna Jameson, *Winter Studies and Summer Rambles in Canada* (New York, 1839), vol. 2, 141n.

12. Peterson, "Prelude to Red River," 55.

13. *Ibid.*, 57–58.

14. For extensive biographical data on the British North Westers, see the appendix to W.S. Wallace (ed.), *Documents relating to the North West Company* (Toronto: Champlain Society, vol. 22, 1934).

15. See Marjorie Wilkins Campbell, *The North West Company* (New York: St. Martin's Press, 1957).

16. Brown, *Strangers in Blood*, 40.

17. Wallace, *Documents*, 134–43.

18. Thwaites (ed.), *Collections of the Wisconsin State Historical Society*, vol. 18, xiii. The founding of Red River Colony brought both Roman Catholic and Anglican clergy into that area by 1821.

19. Brown, *Strangers in Blood*, 100–7.

20. Johnstone *et al.* v. Connolly, Court of Appeal, 7 September 1869, *La Revue legale*, 1, p. 287.

21. For some examples, see Brown, *Strangers in Blood*, 171–72.

22. St. Gabriel Street Presbyterian Church registers, 1796–1821, Provincial Archives of Ontario, Toronto, microfilm.

23. M. Elizabeth Arthur, "Angelique and her Children," *Thunder Bay Historical Museum Society Papers and Records*, 6 (1978), 30–40.

24. Mitchell, *Fort Timiskaming and the Fur Trade*, 38, 62.

25. James K. Smith, *David Thompson, Fur Trader, Explorer, Geographer* (Toronto: Oxford University Press, 1971), 105–6.

26. Hudson's Bay Company Archives (hereafter HBCA), A. 36/13, fo. 192.

27. Brown, *Strangers in Blood*, 98–99.

28. Baptismal ages ranged from under one year to thirteen for the seventy-one children whose ages were given.

29. Wallace, *Documents*, 211.

30. Glyndwr Williams (ed.), *Hudson's Bay Miscellany 1670–1870* (Winnipeg: Hudson's Bay Record Society, 1975), 219 (McKay), 233 (McKenzie), 209–11 (Grant).

31. K.G. Davies (ed.), *Northern Quebec and Labrador Journals and Correspondence 1819–35* (London: Hudson's Bay Record Society, 1963), 263–64, 281. HBCA, A. 1/43, fo. 156, on James Hester. HBCA, B. 59/Z/1, fo. 92, baptisms of George and Anne McDougall. Elliott Coues, *New Light on the History of the Greater Northwest. The Manuscript Journal of Alexander Henry ... and of David Thompson* (New York, 1897), vol. 2, 901. The diary of George Nelson from Tete au Brochet in 1818–19 (Provincial Archives of Ontario) for 16 December 1818 records that McDougall's death occurred at Fort Alexander on 25 October 1818.

32. W. Kaye Lamb, *Sixteen Years in the Indian Country, the Journal of Daniel Williams Harmon 1800–1816* (Toronto: Macmillan, 1957), 50.

33. Charles A. Bishop and Shepard Krech III, "Matriorganization: The Basis of Aboriginal Social Organization," *Arctic Anthropology*, 17, 2 (1980).

34. Lamb, *Sixteen Years in the Indian Country*, 6 (Rev. Daniel Haskel's preface to Harmon's edited journal).

35. Brown, *Strangers in Blood*, 6–22, discusses the social organization of the early Hudson's Bay Company.

36. Charles A. Bishop, "The Henley House Massacres," *The Beaver* (Autumn, 1976), 36–41.

37. *Dictionary of Canadian Biography* (Toronto: University of Toronto Press, vols. 4 [1981] and 5 [forthcoming]) contains biographical information on most of the families named. On William Pink's daughter, see the discussion of the Longmoor family later in this text.

38. Brown, *Strangers in Blood* , 162–69.

39. Moose Factory register of baptisms, marriages, and burials, Provincial Archives of Ontario, microfilm.

40. Data from cemetery records and Moose Factory residents, 1980.

41. For example, the accounts of Colin Robertson in E.E. Rich (ed.), *Colin Robertson's Letters, 1817–1822* (Toronto: Champlain Society for the Hudson's Bay Record Society, 1939), 52, 220.

42. See Coues, *New Light*, vol. 2, 599, for Alexander Henry the Younger's description of Longmoor. On James Halcro, see Alice M. Johnson (ed.), *Saskatchewan Journals and Correspondence 1795–1802* (London: Hudson's Bay Record Society, 1967), xlvii, n; 189. On William Pink, see E.E. Rich, *History of the Hudson's Bay Company 1670–1870* (New York: Macmillan, 1961), vol. 2, 17, 19, 22, 32.

43. E.E. Rich and A.M. Johnson (eds.), *Moose Fort Journals, 1783–1785* (London: Hudson's Bay Record Society, 1954), 370; St. Gabriel Street Church registers.

44. The court case of William Connolly and that of his colleague, Alexander Fraser, are discussed in some detail in Brown, *Strangers in Blood*, 90–95.

45. For examples, see letters of John McDonald le Borgne and Donald McIntosh quoted in *ibid.*, 180–82.

46. *Ibid.*, 190–92.

47. Peterson, "Prelude to Red River," 41–42.

48. Sylvia Van Kirk, "Women and the Fur Trade," *The Beaver* (Winter, 1972), 11–21.

49. Brown, *Strangers in Blood*, 181.

50. *Ibid.*, 218–19.

51. John S. Long, *Treaty No. 9: The Half-Breed Question, 1902–1910* (Cobalt, Ont.: Highway Book Shop, 1978), 7–8.

CHILDHOOD AND CHARITY IN NINETEENTH-CENTURY BRITISH NORTH AMERICA

Patricia T. Rooke and R.L. Schnell

> *From six in a bed in those mansions of woe,*
> *Where nothing but beards, nails and vermin do grow,*
> *And from picking of oakum cellars below,*
> *Good Lord, deliver us![1]*

In *Children in English-Canadian Society,* Neil Sutherland argued that the transformation of attitudes and institutions that came to characterize modern child welfare had occurred by the 1920s. It will be demonstrated in this paper that Sutherland's focus on the period 1880–1920, with a look at the

From *Histoire sociale / Social History,* XV, no. 29 (May 1982), 157–79. Reprinted by permission of *Histoire sociale / Social History.*

1870s as an introduction and the 1920s as a conclusion, placed severe constraints on the possibility of an adequate historical understanding of the development of modern, scientific and professional child welfare in Canada.[2] It will be argued further that child welfare underwent several substantial and influential changes between 1800 and 1900 and that a careful examination of the establishment and transformation of that most Canadian of child-rescue institutions, the nineteenth-century Protestant Orphans' Home, provides a useful means of explicating those changes.

In an earlier article based on trans-Atlantic studies, one of the authors formulated a theoretical framework for analyzing the development of the concept of "childhood," which demonstrated that it entailed the criteria of protection, segregation, dependence, and delayed responsibilities. It was further argued that childhood as a concept implied rescue and restraint, that is, child rescue and childhood are synonymous.[3] The four criteria will be used to map the history of child rescue sentiment and institutions by examining their manifestations in provisions for dependent and neglected children and youth in British North America. In order to establish the colonial and imperial context out of which late nineteenth-century Canadian child welfare developed, the Old World background and implementation of poor relief in the New World will be examined.

The paper consists of three parts. The first part is an explication of the dominant themes of pre-Victorian child rescue in Great Britain. Although customarily acknowledging the influence of Victorian evangelicals on social action in the slums of Great Britain, the United States and Canada, scholars less frequently note the institutional development of the late seventeenth and eighteenth centuries that provided the base for Victorian activism.[4] The arguments behind the establishment of these early orphan asylums, schools and houses of industry, and other charitable institutions and the debate over boarding-out and general policies of relief, intervention, and prevention in trans-Atlantic anglophone communities will introduce the study. The second part describes the mixed forms of relief and rescue available in British North America in the early nineteenth century.

The third and most developed section will demonstrate that, contrary to Sutherland, the first significant shifts in Canadian sentiment toward dependent child life had occurred well before the 1880s and that the transformation is best understood by examining the establishment and growth of children's homes.

I — British Models of Child Rescue

The eighteenth-century charity school movement was a major extension of ideas concerning character development to the children of a class deemed a potential threat to the civil and religious stability of British society. As children's institutions, the schools were the first substantial "modern" attempt to use formal education to instruct children in a protective environment, and as means of child rescue they were the prototypes of nineteenth-century pedagogical experimentation that culminated in the common schools.[5]

The charity schools with their concern for children were supplemented by older mixed forms of relief such as houses and schools of industry that included adults and children and the worthy and unworthy poor. Aware that indiscriminate association of inmates was "destructive of industry, order, and decency," the acting governors of the Dublin House of Industry in 1798 sought to classify them according to age, qualities, conduct and abilities so that a "class of merit"—based on superior industry, moral conduct and obedience to House rules—would be lodged and fed separately from their less worthy fellows.[6] The belief in the value of employment and the danger of idleness was succinctly put in 1756 by the founders of the Ladies' Charity School (Bristol), who observed that "when youth, idleness, and poverty meet together, they become fatal temptations to many unhappy creatures."[7]

In *An Essay Toward the Encouragement of Charity Schools,* Isaac Watts asserted that it would "be a great and unspeakable advantage to these Schools ... if ... some methods whereby all the children of the poor might be employed in some useful labours one part of the day" could be contrived. Watts recommended that children sufficiently instructed and improved should "be placed out, and fixed either in country-labours, in domestic services, in some inferior post in a shop, or in mechanical trades, that so they may not run loose and wild in the World."[8]

The insistence on useful employment and religious training as fundamental elements in the rescue of children and adults is a major theme in the reports of all the societies. In 1813, the Edinburgh Society for the Suppression of Beggars argued that its object required that "a great portion of their attention must be devoted to the education of the children of the poor in habits of morality and industry." In one of the earliest discussions of the contamination of children by their parents, the Edinburgh Society cited the expense of residential care and hoped that, given a proper day school, "the injury they will sustain from the society of their parents will not be so great as is apprehended." Although much of the interest in schools and houses of industry was aroused by the presence of sturdy beggars and other undeserving objects of charity, tract writers and philanthropists were equally attracted by the educational cure for pauperism promised by institutionalizing and instructing children. The schooling provided children lodged in houses of industry was in most cases very limited. The 1759 rules of a house of industry in Suffolk required a school "where all children above three years of age shall be kept till they shall be five years old, and then set to spinning and such other proper and beneficial work as they are able to perform."[9] The Ladies' Charity School (Bristol), much affected by the danger of idleness, had said little about learning and much about spinning.

It is not until the nineteenth century that the more subtle possibilities of education were recognized by those seeking to promote a spirit of independence or self-reliance among the poor. Charitable institutions were to be an essential means of impressing on them that "it is upon their own exertions, habits of economy, and prudent foresight alone, that they and their families, must depend for their comforts, as well as their daily bread." That the poor were not unaware of such possibilities for self-help is shown in the complaint of the Bath Society that when "the children can earn something for themselves exclusive of clothing, and contribute towards defraying the expenses [of the school], they are taken away by their parents." Such calculative self-interest, later observed in Canada also, was not the kind of self-reliance that the patrons of the poor had in mind. Many societies such as the St. James School of Industry, limited parental visits to Sundays to diminish family influence over the children, a practice followed in nineteenth-century Canada.[10] The Shrewsbury House of Industry sought to prevent the children of depraved families from "inevitably imbib[ing] the contagion by a *total and complete separation of [children and youth] from the abandoned and depraved* [that would] place them out of the way of temptation, and prevent the fatal contagion of profligate discourse, and vicious examples."[11]

The conditions that had given rise to the eighteenth-century efforts at childsaving continued into the nineteenth century. In 1846, a Manchester committee originally formed to found a ragged school established instead the Manchester Juvenile Refuge and School of Industry. The society aimed "to rescue a large class of destitute and neglected children from the paths of vice, misery, and degradation, and to train them to honesty, industry, and virtue." Rejecting confinement as an inadequate means of reformation, the committee stressed prevention through an education that would "render them better fitted to endure and overcome the necessary hardships and temptations of a poor man's lot." The required education included three elements: first, reading, writing, and arithmetic, which were both useful and an excellent means of keeping the mind engaged; second, moral and religious training which were pre-eminently suited to exercise a "purifying, restraining and elevating influence" on children; and finally, industrial training to prepare the boys for a self-supporting occupation.[12] Unlike earlier emphases on habituation as a means of ensuring a decent life in the midst of appalling poverty, the new view saw education as a double rescue from immorality and incompetence. On the other hand, the Aberdeen industrial schools organized in 1841 saw the protection of children from their "debased" families in terms of separating them and binding them in order that they might have the advantages of family life while ensuring that they be made dependent through such surveillance.[13]

In addition to private philanthropic ventures, the poor laws provided a wide variety of indoor and outdoor relief. With the 1834 Poor Law Act Amendment, the process of unionization and rationalization of public charity created the reformed workhouses as the central institution of relief. The new workhouse allowed, at least theoretically, the classification and provision of special facilities for inmates. Education and other services for children offered the possibility of depauperization of future generations; the 1850s, however, witnessed the controversy over the results of institutionalization and the effectiveness of workhouse schooling. Advocates of boarding-out, drawing on Irish and Scottish experience, argued for the superiority of rearing poor law children in families over the stultifying atmosphere of the workhouse.[14]

Thus, with those precedents, sentiments and attitudes toward dependent children clearly established in Great Britain by the eighteenth and early nineteenth centuries, such institutional models and ideas were often transplanted by reformers involved in Canadian efforts at child rescue.

II — British North American Child Rescue

Information about the care of children who were neglected, abandoned or destitute is spotty in early colonial records; however, it seems clear that protection, segregation, dependence, and delayed responsibilities were not generally part of child life. The care of these children was considered part of the general provision for the poor.

The Atlantic colonies of Newfoundland, Nova Scotia, New Brunswick, and Prince Edward Island were typical of the extension of poor law ideas and practices to the New World. In Newfoundland, public relief was distributed on a casual basis by commissioners of public roads, who provided minimal funds during the colony's periodic and endemic seasons of distress. Nova Scotia, the most progressive and prosperous colony, had a flourishing number of private institutions and societies to relieve the misery of its inhabitants as well as a system of poor relief. New Brunswick also closely approximated the earlier British model in both its system of poor relief and religiously connected orphan asylums. Prince Edward Island with its predominantly rural population and parsimonious ruling class resembled a rural English parish.[15]

The Halifax Orphan House, established in 1752, which bound out its older orphans and engaged the younger ones in carding and spinning of wool, the picking of oakum and "other little offices" around the garden and hospital, was an initial, largely unsuccessful, attempt at a public-supported specialized facility in British North America. According to the earliest nineteenth-century records it was in disarray within a short time and the young public charges were provided for in the Poor Asylum along with aged, diseased, infirm, and degenerate adult paupers.

An inquiry into New Brunswick provincial institutions in 1857 expressed dismay at the young male offenders between ten and under eighteen years incarcerated in the penitentiary for crimes of the "most trivial kind." Since these boys were "without parents or friends to instruct and guide them, and without homes to attract and improve them," the report observed that they were "thrown into circumstances of exposure and temptation, and thus become an easy prey to vice." It recommended a separate facility to be called a "Reformatory School" with a special keeper in charge where the lads would be taught the elementary branches of education for several years instead of the prevailing custom of months, so that "real improvement" could be achieved. This would be done under the 1855 and 1857 acts that provided for juvenile offenders. Young females were recommended to be placed in a segregated section of the almshouse. Similar concerns were being expressed elsewhere about the necessity of segregating and protecting dependent young people.[16]

The 1822 plan of Captain Robert Parker Pelly, the Governor of Assiniboia, for the care of "half breed" children whose parents had died or deserted them was part of the general concern for safety of the trading posts if men with large families were discharged and left in "an uneducated and savage position" to "collect across the country" without "proper superintendence." Using arguments almost identical with Isaac Watts', Pelly concluded that "it will therefore be both prudent and economical to incur some expense in placing these people where they may maintain themselves and be civilized [and] instructed in religion." The expense was only temporary since once the boys had been trained for agriculture and the girls for industry they could be apprenticed. Children were merely part of a larger problem of an unsettled population and were not given any special treatment.[17]

As in the case of the Society for Promoting Education and Industry among the Indians and Destitute Settlers in Canada in 1828, schools of industry were to combine economy and industry along with elementary education and a knowledge of agriculture and the mechanic arts. At Quebec City, for example, "children [were] engaged in some useful branch of labour half of each day, which [the Ladies' branch conceived] ought to be the case in all schools which may be opened for the children of the poor." The plan for a school of industry at Montreal, intended for "the amelioration of the poor and the establishment of honest industry," offered employment for those able to work, instruction in some useful branch of work for the unskilled, relief of the helpless poor in their own dwellings, and instruction in reading to the illiterate.[18]

Although the school of industry was intended primarily to relieve adults, the Society's agent, T. Osgood, on "seeing a number of orphans and poor children out of employment, destitute of bread and the means of instruction," placed them under the care of the superintendent and provided them with bread and clothing in return for their labour. Moreover the agent brought into the institution the blind and the lame who with the help of cheap machinery were employed in sawing and boring holes in stone. The Montreal Society freely mixed the objects of its charity in the school of industry.[19]

Canadian institutional arrangements under the poor laws in the Maritimes and the modified legislation of Ontario, as well as the orphan asylums that sprang up in the second half of the century, were dissimilar in several ways from those of Britain. While using much of the same rhetoric and seemingly transplanting institutional models, the houses of industry and of refuge, even before the segregation of their child inmates, never became the huge, impersonal and architecturally pretentious buildings of the new 1834 British poor laws.

These buildings were mainly showpieces while certainly older buildings like Westminster Asylum for Female Orphans, or the London Orphans' Asylum, could not have been designed with the needs of children or of adults in mind. As bleak as life must have been for the Canadian dependent poor compelled to remain in their parish and municipal "almshouses," they retained more the appearance and organizational patterns of earlier models and bear a striking resemblance to the American colonial buildings discussed by David Rothman in *The Discovery of the Asylum*.[20] Therefore, while being parsimoniously governed, the Canadian poorhouses were frequently ordinary, although decrepit and cheerless, "homes" or farmhouses, and did not exude quite the same forbidding aspect of Britain's "pauper palaces" and congregate systems.

The Toronto House of Industry, founded by a private committee in 1836, aimed at "the total abolition of street begging, the putting down of wandering vagrants, and securing an asylum at the least possible expense for the industrious and distressed poor." Supported in part by a parliamentary grant and the City Council, the House in its first year had relieved 857 persons of whom 638 were children and had forty-six inmates of whom twenty-six were children. By 1853, the House of Industry was giving its "most anxious attention ... to making permanent provision for orphans, deserted children, and those whose parents have rendered themselves liable to legal punishment." A system of apprenticeship was devised by which a "large number of children were placed out with respectable persons in the country" whereby they were removed "from the temptations and vices to which they are exposed in a large city." To encourage training of children in habits of industry and sobriety that "will prepare them for usefulness and competency through life," the House of Industry received children whose parents and friends were unable to support them, placed them at school, and cared for and protected their morals and persons, until suitable country homes could be found.[21]

Still, by the 1850s the need to separate and distinguish children from adults was not general. An interesting example of mixed categories occurred in 1856 with the City of Toronto's purchase of a tract of land to be used as an industrial farm "where offenders (particularly juveniles) may be classified and reformed, while punished, but also where many of the infirm and maimed might be made to assist, in some way, to their support."[22]

Kingston provides a powerful example of the shift in the concept of childhood, which included the growing recognition of children as a special class with particular needs such as protection and segregation. The central charitable institution was the House of Industry founded in 1814 and not closed until 1916. The details of this institution, which are well preserved, give all the appearances of the workhouses under the English poor laws.[23] Children, who were abandoned, orphaned, or destitute, were received by the House which acted *in loco parentis* with regard to placing them out or employing them in household chores. Children remained part of the House of Industry until the Orphans' Home and Widows' Friend Society opened its first building in 1857. Citing the degraded habits, predisposition to idleness, and the dubious health and morality of inmates as an undesirable environment for the young, the Society charged that the children were not "cared for, supervised [or] protected from the vice and degradation" of an institution that offered "no humanizing influences."[24]

Between 1830 and 1860 the first institutionalized care for dependent and orphaned children began to emerge in the form of the Protestant Orphans' Homes in Montreal, Kingston, Toronto and Halifax, to be followed soon after in London, Ottawa, Victoria and Winnipeg. None of these ever sheltered the many hundreds of children at a given time as did the British orphan asylums.

Moreover, although unable fully to create the domestic atmosphere and family spirit their directors idealized, the Protestant Orphans' Homes were able to approximate it more closely than their British counterparts. First, most orphan asylums in Canada were modest undertakings with populations ranging from merely a score or so as in Victoria to several hundred at their height in Toronto, Winnipeg and Saint John.

Secondly, the Canadian institutions exercised remarkable control over the selection of their clients by careful admission procedures which articulated the implicit assumptions made by the ladies' committees regarding who were the "worthy" and "unworthy" poor. In fact, since these institutions largely received custodial cases for nominal fees rather than full orphans, they did not admit the most alarming or desperate situations or the chronic poor as was the case in the large British institutions and the North American Roman Catholic ones. The open-door policy of British homes such as Ashley Down in Bristol, the National Children's Homes, and the Barnardo Homes, was shared in Canada by the Roman Catholic orphanages which subsequently were more crowded.

Thirdly, the debates that resounded in Britain over the psychological consequences of institutional life—the lack of spontaneity and initiative on the part of children—did not apply in the same degree to Canada although in the twentieth century such arguments would be used to advocate fostering practices. True, a matron and superintendent might be harassed by too many children, too many tasks, too little money and too small a domestic staff, but there is little sense of the barracks-like discipline and the anonymity of a militaristic atmosphere that later critics suggested were prevalent. Statements in some annual reports that "regular methodical habits" and "cleanliness, order and good management" were enforced, and that "a spirit of docility and subordination testified to good management" must be interpreted cautiously since the minutes of many asylums testify that such management was not as mechanistically induced or as impersonally imposed as the rhetoric suggests. Indeed, some homes seem as much arguments for confusion and nonchalance as for orderliness and inflexibility and as reflections of the various temperaments of the matrons themselves as any institutional plans.[25]

Finally, repressive religious fervour and the excesses sometimes associated with evangelical enthusiasm as a means to disciplining young and suggestive minds are surprisingly missing, given the "Protestant" origins of the homes, in the Canadian records. Interdenominationalism, even if on pragmatic and economic grounds rather than on principle, it seems, had a neutralizing effect on such fervour. In sum, there appears to be a dissonance between the rhetoric (a rhetoric almost identical to British sentiments) expressed at annual meetings and fund-raising functions, and in annual reports, and the actual conduct, the physical arrangements and the clienteles of the Protestant Orphans' Homes.

If these were the differences between the British congregate systems and the Canadian homes, then what were the similarities? Four aspects seem worth noting: (1) the application of the new awareness for the peculiar needs of children that resulted in actual institutional environments which rendered them objectively and psychologically dependent upon those maintaining them while assuring the inmates of maximum protection and segregation; (2) the ultimate segregation of children from undesirable adult influences by controlling the inmates, *in loco parentis,* even to the point of interfering with parental access by binding children out if fees had not been forthcoming; (3) the segregation of various classes of children from each other, that is, the distinction between "dependent" and "delinquent"; and (4) the training of children into menial occupations through indentures and the regimens of the homes.

The following section will examine these aspects by a survey of the rise of the Canadian Protestant Orphans' Homes as a conscious and concrete articulation of the concept of childhood whose origins can be discerned in the debates and practices of the late eighteenth and early nineteenth centuries.

III — The Rise of Protestant Orphans' Homes

In 1854, the Reverend Mr. William Bond preached an edifying sermon before the ladies' committee of the Protestant Asylum for the Aged and Infirm, which included children among its residents. Pointing out that the home was the only institution in Montreal that accepted children who had not lost both parents, the future Anglican bishop warmed to his subject by praising the ministrations of womankind—"her softening, elevating, purifying, gladdening influence; her fond companionship in the seasons of joy, her devoted tenderness in the hours of sickness." His remarks were intended as a salutary reminder that those ladies who had organized themselves into benevolent societies to found houses of refuge and orphan asylums were gentlewomen of means and respectability with virtues peculiar to their sex and entirely suited to such philanthropic endeavours.[26] Largely through the efforts of such women the first segregated institutions for children were organized. Even in those cases where gentlemen's committees founded such institutions or retained official governance, it was through the ladies' committees that actual management and control were directed.[27]

Founded in 1857 to train "poor, uncared-for, destitute children" in "the habits of virtue and regularity," the Kingston Orphan Asylum reported two years later the condition of many of these children was "more desolate than that of children left wholly orphans, as the very circumstances of their having a parent living prevents their adoption into families that would gladly receive an orphan." The ladies of the Women's and Orphans' Friend Society had decided that a separate institution for children was necessary when their attention was drawn to the numbers of them living in the overcrowded house of industry without suitable supervision and being placed out as household drudges without proper circumspection. From the beginning, fee-paying children who required residential accommodation in times of need or emergency were admitted along with whole or part orphans. To control the admission of children who had guardians, the Kingston Asylum in 1862 stipulated that parents had to agree not to remove their children without consent of the Society or to prevent them from taking a situation if a good one occurred.[28]

As with the Kingston institution, the Toronto Protestant Orphan Home and Female Aid Society (founded in 1851) received children from the house of industry, which had been founded to provide "for the industrious and distressed poor." In that year alone, the house listed in its registry 638 children in addition to thirty-seven deserted women, eighty-seven widows, and ninety-five ill and unemployed. In 1853, the Toronto Protestant Orphans' Home noted that it assisted mothers in service by caring for their children for a minimal fee and provided a custodial service for the poorer members of society as well as for the widowed and orphaned. Fee-paying children were usually returned to their living parent or to relatives rather than being adopted or indentured as happened with the first clients of the Toronto Girls' Home and Public Nursery in 1859. Sarah and Mary Anne Kingwood, aged five and three years, the first entry in the register, were duly adopted because their father was dead and their mother was in a penitentiary. In the case of the Toronto institution, the number of runaways suggests that for fee-paying children the ties of kinship were strong enough to induce them not to remain in the institution.[29]

Managed by males but superintended by women, the Newfoundland Church of England Orphans' and Widows' Aid Society of St. John's was established in 1855 as a thanksgiving for the departure of cholera from the city. John Tunbridge, its first honorary secretary, acknowledged the orphanage's debt to the "deadly pestilence" whose chief victims had been the poor. "It scarcely entered a dwelling of any other class" and its "desolatory presence ... bequeath to us, as it were the widow and the orphan." From the outset, however, the majority of inmates proved to be not full orphans but the children of the fatherless whose mothers were "incapable of providing for them." During its decades, the home received somewhat more unusual objects of charity than elsewhere. Among those of "affecting and interesting circumstances" were children who lost their fathers in the 1855 Sealing Disaster and the survivors of the 1863 shipwreck of the *Anglo-Saxon*. The Methodist Orphanage of St. John's, founded in 1888 but whose first official residence was not purchased until 1901, received mostly the children of the widowed and deserted. The poverty in Newfoundland, particularly in the outposts, was more general, constant and dire than anywhere else in British North America and the dependence of many candidates on the various Protestant and Roman Catholic asylums was frequently the result of tubercular mothers or fathers who had died of this disease which proved an unremitting scourge throughout the colony's history.[30]

Both the Methodist and Anglican homes remained relatively small—the Methodist never having over forty-two girls and the Church of England averaged between seventy and eighty for both sexes at its height. Given the appalling destitution in Newfoundland and the constantly inadequate provisions for relief, such small numbers of children from working-class families are astonishing; however, the rates of child mortality and the frequency of disaster and disease suggests that a calloused colonial administration had such problems repeatedly alleviated by what often amounted to a grim "final solution." Children whose mothers remarried were customarily returned to them, but those whose mothers did not wish to receive them, either through circumstances or through choice, remained in the homes which continued to receive the orphan grant allowed institutions by the commissioners of the poor.[31]

The Halifax Infants' Home is another example of an institution whose function was as useful as it was benevolent. Although infants were received free of charge owing to parental inability to pay for a child's board, many were actually boarded by mothers who visited and nursed their babies, or in cases of weaned children, visited and clothed them, paying for their maintenance and thus using the home as a residential custodial institution. In 1884, the new physician, Dr. Oliver, recommended that it would be preferable for the child if the mother were actually boarded with it and that in order to ensure the character of the home and preserve the privacy of the infants the home ought not to accommodate by the day the children of women who were in daily service.[32]

An interesting small select orphanage, the Wiggins Home for Boys at Saint John, New Brunswick, founded and generously endowed in 1867 for the sons of lost and deceased mariners, also provided similar facilities. The sons of deserted wives and widows were received until their parents were able to provide for them.[33]

The Saint John Protestant Orphan Asylum, founded in 1854, admitted five classes of children which were usually included in the rules of other orphans' homes. In the case of the New Brunswick home, the orphaned were generally in the minority. The majority of inmates consisted of poor and indigent children; children, both or only one of whose parents were dead, insane, inebriate, helpless or confined to penitentiary; children deserted by either or both parents; and destitute children. The orphanage was typical in its exclusion of delinquent youngsters and those with contagious diseases. It admitted children as "nominal boarders or by voluntary surrender" and claimed custody if the terms of the contract were disregarded for over three months after notice had been given to relatives or guardians.[34]

In the founding years of the Protestant Orphans' Homes, these modest schemes were obviously the expressions of a self-indulgent benevolence. Anomalies in admissions sometimes merely reflected the private patronage of members of the ladies' committees as in the case of the deserted Mrs. Stewart who, in April 1860, wanted her three children admitted to the Kingston home. Although her situation was so desperate that she was voluntarily entering the house of industry, the committee decided against the admitting of the children "as both parents were alive." The Stewarts were clearly perceived of as part of the unworthy poor. When Mary Moore's mother, now "remarried and very comfortable," was unwilling to take her home, the ladies' committee acknowledged that the girl was "a favourite with the matron and agreed to keep her at one dollar a month." Such inconsistent policies were common in the first decades of their operations when the institutions are appropriately seen as an extension of the individual women and reflecting their preferences and prejudices. In the face of increasing urban problems, even in relatively small Canadian cities, individual eccentricities diminished and admission became standardized to meet the demands of all types of poverty.[35]

Through its history, the Ottawa Protestant Orphans' Home reflected more faithfully than most institutions the "philanthropic mode." Women such as Lady Macdonald and the wealthy Mrs. Bronson, first and second directresses respectively, seemed impervious to the visible demands of public poverty. Founded in 1865 by the Ladies' Protestant Benevolent Association, the home received widows and women out of place although full and part orphans were seen as "the proper objects for the cure of the institution." In the first months of its mandate eleven ladies were elected to "search for destitute children," which suggests careful selection. Indeed, a year later only twelve orphans were enjoying the ladies' assiduous solicitude. Illegitimate children were not received, as a desperate Mrs. Armstrong of Brockville discovered in 1866 when she was obliged to produce her marriage certificate before her three children were admitted. While the girls assisted in the housework, the ladies' committee was quite cheerfully sending the boys to work in Mr. Bronson's mill during the summer of 1869. One-half of each boy's wages was paid to the home and the other half put aside for the boy's future benefit. The first choice of girls as domestic servants and boys as apprentices was always given to subscribers of the society or to others recommended by the ladies' committee. This policy of first choice was obvious and consistent in all homes examined. The exclusive admission policies of the Ottawa institution did not alter until the late 1890s when it began to receive "transients" from the newly-organized Children's Aid Society. Just as the children of various Sunday schools had not been considered suitable companions on picnics and outings, the original Children's Aid Society cases were judged as being unfit to mix with the Protestant Orphans' Homes children.[36]

The results of epidemics such as ship fever, cholera and typhoid frequently spurred middle-class efforts to found orphanages, refuges and houses of industry in the nineteenth century. The Montreal Protestant Orphans Association, founded in 1822, felt compelled by "an unfortunate, ill-directed immigration from Ireland" to hire a house on William Street for immigrant children. In 1847 during another epidemic, ninety-five children were taken from the ships. Of these, ten died, fifty-four were placed or reclaimed, eight returned to the fever sheds at Point St. Charles, and twenty-three refused to remain in the home. In 1832, the Montreal Ladies' Benevolent Society, organized to counteract the effects of the "most awful visitation of asiatic cholera," founded a refuge for widows and the fatherless.[37]

As early as 1854–56, the Toronto Protestant Orphans' Home publicly appealed to carpenters, joiners, and other members of the working class for aid in adding another floor to its building since the prevailing epidemic caused it to be short of space. The working class responded "nobly, kindly, and cheerfully" with each shop contributing a half-day's free labour to the enterprise. Again in the 1870s, typhoid nearly doubled the number of admissions.[38]

Periodic economic dislocations, by pushing many families into destitution, made the problems of admissions and institutional funding more acute. The depression of the 1890s aggravated poverty and distress and contributed to new problems of indigence and pauperism. The Boys' Home in Toronto placed out many of its children between 1893 and 1896 because relatives could not make support payments and the depression caused a drop in donations for the support of the home. The annual reports lamented "the scarcity of work" and "the hard times" which forced the institution to rescue little ones under the usual required age of five, and that compelled "many unfortunate parents to part with their boys ... until they can take them home again." Preventive help was offered to another class by the Toronto Boys' Home that, beginning in 1861, provided a temporary refuge and lodging for working lads who might otherwise have been convicted of vagabondage. These and many "friendless little orphans" were rescued not only from want and misery but also from being put "among vagabonds, thieves, and burglars—the pests and the curse of the city" in the deplorably squalid city jail. Judging by newspaper accounts five years later the problem of "young thieves and beggars" in Toronto was far from resolved for some of the public was agitating for a law to be passed to round them up and bind them out as the Protestant Orphans' Home and house of industry did, or establish a ragged school to educate them.[39]

Even during good times, the need for day-care facilities that would allow working mothers to leave their children in decent surroundings was apparent in the major cities. Had there been more crèches, day nurseries, and settlement houses, fewer parents would have been compelled to resort to orphanages. The Girls' Home of Toronto had included a public nursery in 1856 but four years later this home began to provide resident services on both a permanent and a daily basis and by 1868 day care was abandoned.[40]

Protestant groups, often working in conjunction with the homes, established lying-in and after-care for unmarried mothers and their infants as well as job placement bureaux with some training for domestic service. The assistance given to this class of needy women was in part a crude attempt to counteract the pernicious effects of "baby farming," which later was the object of the 1914 Ontario Maternity Boarding House Act. The babies of these women were often given over to the orphans' or infants' homes in some cities. The Christian Women's Union of Winnipeg confronted the resentment of inmates of their home by requiring a nine-month stay after confinement. Although there was an insistence on time for "repentance," the stay guaranteed the necessary nursing care for infants before weaning. Without this, the lives of babies were in constant jeopardy unless immediately adopted. Some mothers, not wishing to have their infants adopted, paid a monthly fee of four dollars while they sought employment and a suitable home for themselves and their child. Children remaining in the Winnipeg home past their third birthday became the "property" of the institution.[41]

The Women's Refuge and Children's Home of London, Ontario, required a twelve-month stay during which the mother was to be trained for a "gainful situation, or at least be religiously improved." Four years after its opening in 1876, thirty-two infants under two years were part of its clientele. The London Orphans' Home, which included the aged and friendless when founded in 1874, excluded children under two years. This Protestant Orphans' Home, however, kept mothers and children together on occasion as in 1875 when it maintained Mrs. Noodes and her two little girls for three months while she saved enough money to buy a sewing machine.[42] All the homes were reluctant to receive infants and most stipulated ages of admission over two years because of the dangers to the lives of the very young children, their vulnerability to even the mildest contagion, and inadequate nursing staff.

The reluctance of most homes to receive illegitimate children might be understood as more than punitive moralizing when it is recalled that most of them would be infants. The problems, of course, were where could the unmarried mother go during pregnancy and labour and where could the child be placed once the mother had to seek employment? A deputation from the Christian Women's Union of Winnipeg to the Manitoba legislature in 1890 stated the problem when they pleaded for funds for their essential social service—a female refuge. The refuge was to enable unmarried or recently widowed women "to keep their infants with them until they are old enough to do without a mother's care when they are admitted into the Children's Home or otherwise provided for." The deputation pointed out that infant mortality in institutions was high and the use of wet-nurses unsatisfactory.[43]

In the first year of the Halifax Infants' Home, the managing committee bought "cheap thin cotton" to be made into shrouds. Several months later with scarlet fever in the home, the committee requested from the commissioners of the Poor Asylum the use of their hearse in order to save the expense of cab-hire for funerals. In the three summer months of 1875, thirteen babies died. The home averaged twenty-two boarded children during the time. In 1875, the death rate was 35 per cent and as late as 1890 it was 26 per cent.[44]

Some institutions hired women to live in as wet-nurses. At times, a wet-nurse was guaranteed temporary relief for herself and her children. The desperation and poverty that forced women into homes to engage in an occupation, which traditionally had been delegated to the meanest classes and one which was no longer a common practice, need no elaboration. In 1875, the Halifax Infants' Home required wet-nurses wishing to have their own infants with them to pay three dollars a month for the privilege. Its first wet-nurse was a girl taken from the Poor Asylum.[45]

In addition to the humiliations suffered by these women, regular fee-paying parents customarily had to meet a variety of institutional demands. With wages barely covering their own subsistence, widows, unmarried women, and deserted wives paid nominal fees to keep their children clothed, sheltered and fed in the homes. The fees usually ranged from one to five dollars a month, depending upon the number of children admitted or the actual financial circumstances of parent or guardian. Domestic service often required women to live in, and other occupations took up long hours during which children were unsupervised. The fees were often meagre but the homes found them essential for their survival because of the parsimony and slowness of provincial and municipal grants and unreliable private funding.

An example of the compromising positions in which both parents and the institutions found themselves is provided by Dr. Wishart's demand in 1891 that he be provided with a "perpetual grant of children" from the Toronto Girls' Home for medical demonstrations every Saturday morning. These children, he argued, were "callous both morally and physically and therefore not to be compared with other children." The ladies' committee reluctantly agreed when the good doctor threatened to withdraw his medical services, given *gratis* to the home and worth $400 *per annum*. A month later, an irate mother objected to her children being used in this manner and forced the home not to refuse the doctor's demands but to decide instead that only orphans would be used![46]

The Children's Home of Winnipeg, founded in 1885 by the Christian Women's Union, had been "formerly an adjunct of the maternity hospital but its doors were opened to any destitute child." It finally became of so much importance as to require a board of management and a charter of its own. This Protestant home, the first in the west, was officially separated from the Christian Women's Union in 1887 although the women always retained a special interest in its affairs and management. Initially it included fourteen mothers and children but within four years it housed forty-eight children with a few adults. Although many children were reclaimed by parents once they had established themselves, the indenture rates of children were extraordinarily high as were the delays on the part of employers in finally signing adoption or indenture papers. While all Protestant Orphans' Homes had incidents of legal action over the binding out or adoption of children, which were informal and arbitrary processes before the passage of provincial legislation controlling custody and adoption in the 1920s, the Winnipeg home was particularly beset by such problems until the 1912 Manitoba Children's Act gave the custody of deserted children to the superintendent of neglected and dependent children.[47]

Although the homes usually preferred orphans because rights over them were clearly defined, part-orphans and destitute children constituted a large proportion of their inmates. All the homes under discussion stipulated that older children, usually those over six or seven years, were not to be given out for "adoption" because this frequently was a cloak to use the children as cheap labour without the safety clauses of indenture which included schooling, minimal conditions of food, clothing, and shelter, as well as some remuneration. Until modern legislation, such "adopted" children could not claim the rights of a family member with regard to inheriting property or money. Many "adopted" children were returned sometimes after several years for trivial reasons such as foster parents going on holiday or for irresponsible ones such as a child requiring medical treatment. The wages under indenture, which were always below prevailing rates for usual apprentices, were divided between the institution and an account at the home which was to be given the child at the expiration of the apprenticeship.

Not all parents willingly signed over their children for either indenture or adoption and many objected strenuously to the automatic abdication of parental authority as a result of merely handing their children over to the homes or by failing to pay maintenance fees. Usually such protests were ignored and few incidents ended in litigation. If poverty resulted in children being placed in institutions, it was unlikely that their parents would have the money for a court case. A widely publicized case, Robinson *vs.* Pieper, occurred when Mrs. Robinson, after having placed her infant daughter Alice in the Toronto Girls' Home in 1883, sought to have her returned to her when she was apprenticed with Mrs. Pieper of Owen Sound in 1892. The verdict, upheld in 1896, in the Divisional Court, did not recognize parental rights.

> The learned judge can find no reason whatever for holding that the mother is entitled to have this indenture set at naught and the child returned to her. She was clearly a child having the protection of the Home, when she was apprenticed: her mother was, and had been for years an assenting party to her being at the Home, and under its protection and made no application for her return until she ceased to be helpless.[48]

All the Protestant Orphans' Homes insisted that their rights of *in loco parentis* included not only the wardship of children in the homes but also the right to indenture children at an appropriate age. Since all homes had set ages for demission and since many claimed an absolute wardship, many refused to return children to their families when they reached the age of demission. Indeed, in most cases the homes saw family interest in older children as evidence of greed and self-interest. In 1873, the secretary of the Montreal Ladies' Benevolent Society remarked that twenty-two girls had been reclaimed that year. The girls had been spirited away or blatantly taken by relatives and placed for "the scarcity of servants made them valuable acquisitions to some who had entirely neglected them in their helpless infancy." In 1894, the corresponding secretary of the Toronto Girls' Home decried the too-common occurrence of girls absconding from their places to join their mothers and expressed profound suspicion of "maternal tendencies" that were so "suddenly revived" after several years of "neglect." Although the annual reports cited assistance to all classes as a major aim, the home viewed with a singular lack of sympathy the reuniting of its inmates with their lower-class families. Parents requesting the return of their children were usually identified as part of a certain unscrupulous class of dependent poor willing to fob off their familial responsibilities onto charity.[49]

There can be no doubt that some parents reclaimed their children at the age of indenture when they had rarely visited or paid the slightest attention to them previously. The literature of rescue societies, boy brigades and asylums, all mention the problem. The English child emigration societies wanted to separate children from disreputable families by sending them to Canada. As a result children rescued from potential exploitation by parents or relatives were often subject to actual exploitation by strangers. The enforcement of school attendance laws, which forced poor families to forego additional income needed to maintain family integrity, led to an increased number of children being admitted to charitable institutions.

Although endeavouring to protect the autonomy of their institutions, Protestant Orphans' Homes directors routinely petitioned provincial and municipal governments for funds. Believing in the advantages of private philanthropy with governmental assistance, the ladies of the homes were committed to ideas that saw private philanthropy as the superior means of securing financial support for public charities. At a public meeting of the Ottawa home in January 1887, the Governor-General praised Canadian philanthropic efforts. He told "a large and fashionable audience" that unlike the poor-rate system that perpetuated Old World pauperism such efforts were spontaneous, private, "and almost entirely unaided by the State."[50]

The approval given by the ladies of the homes to such sentiments was matched by civic leaders and Canadian child savers who advocated a policy of private prosperity and public parsimony. In 1894, the Toronto City Corporation, rejecting amalgamation of various charities and any suggestion of a common budget assisted by rates, opposed the city taking over the "entire management of all the different classes of our dependent poor" because the financial burden would fall "upon the rate-payers and private benevolence would be withdrawn."[51]

Writing in the English *Charity Organization Review* of August 1900, J.J. Kelso, Ontario's first superintendent of neglected and dependent children, supported a central associated charities bureau for Toronto while discouraging any tendency to fall back upon charity as typified by British poor law unions. Observing that "there is, unfortunately however a class who, from inherent laziness will not work or make any effort to improve the condition of themselves or their children," Kelso denounced the ticket system of the Toronto House of Industry which provided outdoor relief. Although such schemes assisted families to stay together, which was a prime goal of the new generation of Canadian child savers, Kelso was unable to resolve the basic contradiction in public responsibility for maintaining family stability when it required public funds.[52]

Although the Protestant Orphans' Homes did not share such delicate feelings about family integrity in their efforts to rescue children from pauperism and immorality, such attitudes did not ensure that conservative English Canadians would support the homes as superior to out-door relief schemes. Mr. Goldwin Smith, addressing the fortieth annual meeting of the Toronto home, heartily condemned the "mischief" done by philanthropists. He protested that their very existence removed parental responsibility and that "in many instances this interference tended to have the parents neglect their children so that they could get rid of them or see them reared with greater possibilities than they could furnish."[53]

Throughout the previous discussion it can be seen that the protection of child life from the contaminations of adult improvidence and vicious example was effectively ensured by segregation in specialized asylums. Moreover, in their treatment of children and parents, the Protestant Orphans' Homes represented a transition from the policy of indiscriminate mixing of sexes and ages common in the houses of industry to the growing twentieth-century Canadian commitment to keeping children within a family if not their own. They also represent a significant transformation in British North American child rescue.

No matter how unclear the original policy on eligible subjects for the institutions, the homes soon restricted their inmates to children and their mothers. In time, most of them became segregated institutions for orphaned, abandoned and destitute children between two and fourteen years of age. By removing children from the companionship of degraded adults and inadequate care, which were two common criticisms levelled at houses of industry and other charitable institutions, and by claiming that they exercised a control *in loco parentis* over their inmates, the Protestant Orphans' Homes sought to regulate contacts between children and their parents and kin, and thus reinforced in an extreme manner the criteria of protection, segregation and dependence. Since, other than in exceptional situations, most homes admitted many more non-orphans than orphans, they were compelled to modify their policy with regard to the surrender of parental rights. For those parents and guardians who were able to pay boarding fees, the right to withdraw children was clearly recognized; economic hardship and illness, however, often made even nominal fees a heavy burden, particularly on single parents. Consequently, such children were frequently reduced to a status identical with those who had been surrendered to the homes.

The final criterion of the concept of childhood—"delayed responsibilities"—is less clear in nineteenth-century child rescue. This criterion is best associated with the creation of a new category of childhood, namely "adolescence," which in turn was extended and even objectified through the legal compulsions of schooling for all children in the twentieth century.[54] Before the vertical extension of compulsory schooling, however, the majority of working-class children and those of the dependent poor in Britain and Canada were excluded from this last entry into the world created by a modern concept of childhood.

Nowhere is this denial of entry clearer than in the institutions under discussion, as their attitudes toward indenture along with specific attitudes towards the children and work within the home itself indicate. The children were to assume responsibilities regarding household tasks in the homes and to earn their keep through indentures and apprenticeship, bearing in mind that such responsibilities were directly related to their future employment and status in society. It was thought that the children were peculiarly suited to menial occupations both by social status and by disposition. In this respect, although they were protected, separated, and made dependent in a manner that was more concrete and rigidly enforced than their working-class peers "outside," the expectations regarding their tasks and duties as children and their future roles in the work force were identical with middle-class expectations of the lower class generally.

Keeping such an assumption in mind, we can appreciate the 1875 Kingston report that advocated the "systematic apportioning of household duties" with even little girls being "admitted into the circle of usefulness" as an essential benefit to the children. In the following year, the British Columbia Protestant Orphans' Home insisted that, as an important part of their education, the children were to be taught how to do dishes, wash clothes, scrub floors, attend young children, and do all domestic work.[55] At the Halifax home for the first two decades from its founding, the children did all domestic chores without outside help.[56] The Winnipeg Children's Home perhaps summarizes all those comments made uniformly by the Protestant Orphans' Homes throughout their history regarding such an urgent matter. The ladies' committee agreed that the public was inclined to over-indulge the children with too many "treats" and that in the long run it would spoil them "for their future life." It was strongly urged that "the children be taught to work, and to understand that they have to look forward to work, and that they be made to do it."[57]

IV — Conclusion

Charity children of the last century were not permitted the luxury of forgetting their antecedents or their prospects and were made to bear the burden of their poverty and dependence. The delaying of responsibilities for lower-class children, thus including them in a universal application of the concept of childhood in Canada, was to be postponed until the first decades of the twentieth century.

In his pioneering study, Neil Sutherland suggests a rapid acceptance of the concept of childhood and its consequences by middle-class Canadians between 1880 and 1920. His discussion of child life in the 1870s and 1880s fails to account for the sentiment and practices during the previous thirty years. By the 1850s a substantial number of children's homes had appeared in the major centres of British North America. These institutions, soon to be copied in the Canadian West, ensured for their inmates the beginning of a modern childhood, that is, protection, segregation and dependence.

The debate regarding the appropriate care and control of these children prepared the way for the extension of all aspects of childhood to children in the twentieth century. In particular, Sutherland's excellent explication of the "new education" demonstrates the coming victory of the common school that provides all normal children with a "childhood." In the case of dependent and neglected children, the final triumph of the Canadian consensus had to wait for the beginnings of the welfare state in the decades following 1945.

Notes

1. Joseph A. Chisolm, ed., *The Speeches and Public Letters of Joseph Howe,* 2 vols (Halifax: Chronicle Publishing Co., 1909), 1:67.

2. N. Sutherland, *Children in English-Canadian Society* (Toronto: University of Toronto Press, 1976).

3. R. L. Schnell, "Childhood as Ideology," *British Journal of Educational Studies,* 27 (February 1979): 7–28. Also see P. T. Rooke, "The 'Child-Institutionalized' in Canada, Britain, and the United States," *Journal of Educational Thought,* 11 (August 1977):156–71.

4. Kathleen Heasman, *Evangelicals in Action* (London: G. Bles, 1962): Carroll Smith Rosenberg, *Religion and the Rise of the American City* (Ithaca, N.Y.: Cornell University Press, 1971); and Sutherland, *Children in English-Canadian Society.*

5. M. G. Jones, *The Charity School Movement* (London: Frank Cass, 1964).

6. *An Account of the Proceedings of the Acting Governors of the House of Industry* (Dublin, 1798), p. 10.

7. *The State of the Ladies' Charity School Lately set up in Baldwin Street, in the City of Bristol, in Teaching Poor Girls to Read and Spin* (Bristol, 1756), p. 3.

8. Isaac Watts, *An Essay Toward the Encouragement of Charity Schools* (London, 1728), pp. 8–9.

9. *Society for the Suppression of Beggars; for the Relief of Occasional Distress and the Encouragement of Industry Among the Poor Within the City and Environs of Edinburgh* (Edinburgh, 1813), pp. 13–14; Andrew Gairdner, *A Looking Glass for Rich People and People in Prosperity* (Edinburgh, 1798); and *Rules, Orders, and Regulations ... the House of Industry ... in Suffolk* (Ipswich, 1759), p. 9.

10. *Hints Toward the Formation of a Society for Promoting a Spirit of Independence Among the Poor,* 2nd ed. (Bristol, 1812), pp. 16–17; and *Plans for the Sunday*

Schools and Schools of Industry, established in the city of Bath (Bath, 1789); and *Rules, Orders and Regulations in the Parish School of Industry in King Street* (London, 1792).

11. I. Wood, *Some Account of the Shrewsbury House of Industry* (Shrewsbury, 1791), pp. 3, 8 and 33.

12. *Manchester Juvenile Refuge and School of Industry* (Manchester, 1846), pp. 2, 4, 5 and 6.

13. Alexander Thomson, *Industrial Schools* (Aberdeen, 1847), pp. 7–8 and 11–16.

14. Ursula R. Q. Henriques, *Before the Welfare State* (London: Longman, 1979); Derek Fraser, *The Evolution of the British Welfare State* (London: Macmillan, 1973); and Maurice Bruce, ed., *The Coming of the Welfare State* (London: B. T. Batsford, 1968). For contemporary discussions of boarding-out versus the congregate system, see Mary Carpenter, "What Shall We Do With Our Pauper Children?," Social Science Association (Dublin) pamphlet (London: Longman, 1861); *Reports on the Boarding-Out of Orphans and Deserted Children and Insane belonging to the City Parish, Glasgow* (Glasgow, 1872); and Henry F. Aveling, *The Boarding Out System* (London, 1890).

15. Useful information is found in three typescript studies held by the Centre for Newfoundland Studies, Memorial University of Newfoundland: Stuart R. Frey, "Introduction to Social Legislation in Newfoundland" (1979); Barbara Smith, "The Historical Development of Child Welfare Legislation in Newfoundland from 1832 to 1949" (1971); and Richard Urquhart, "A Survey of the Policies of the Newfoundland Government Towards Poor Relief, 1860–1869" (1973). NEW-FOUNDLAND, *Journal of Assembly* (1848–49), pp. 446–54, Report on the Lunatic Asylum; (1862), pp. 408–11, Rules and Regulations for the Management of the St. John's Poor Asylum; and (1885), pp. 471–72. Report of the Superintendent of Poor Asylum; Public Archives of Nova Scotia, MG 20 214, House of Refuge, Proceedings of Committee (Halifax 1853–57); LEGISLATURE OF NOVA SCOTIA, *Report on Public Charity* (Halifax, 1900); Provincial Archives of New Brunswick, MAL (1853–1963), Saint John Almshouse; NEW BRUNSWICK, *Journal of House of Assembly* (1857), Appendix, pp. DXLIX-DLXI; Provincial Archives of Prince Edward Island, 236/8, Prince Edward Island Poor and Work House Minute Book (1869–1880).

16. Public Archives of Nova Scotia, CO. 217, vol. 18, Report of the State of the Orphan House (circa 1753); NEW BRUNSWICK, *Journal of House of Assembly* (1857), Appendix, pp. DXLIX-DLXI.

17. Provincial Archives of Manitoba, MG2 A5, Pelly Documents, 1816–23.

18. *The Second Annual Report of the Central Auxiliary Society for Promoting Education and Industry Among the Indians and Destitute Settlers in Canada* (Montreal, 1829), pp. 17, 12 and 38.

19. Ibid., p. 40.

20. David Rothman, *The Discovery of the Asylum* (Boston: Little Brown, 1971).

21. Metropolitan Toronto Library (hereafter MTL), MS 385(2), Toronto City Council Papers, 4 May 1837; MS 88(1), Baldwin Papers, 11 July 1837; *Report of the Trustees of the House of Industry* (Toronto, 1853), pp. 5–6.

22. *Report of the Trustees of the House of Industry* (Toronto, 1857), p. 8.

23. Queen's University, Coll. 604, Kingston House of Industry, 1814–1916.

24. Queen's University, Coll. 94, *Kingston Orphans' Home and Widows' Friend Society, Annual Report* (1882).

25. Ibid., *Annual Report* (1859, 1871). Certainly one is never intimidated by such order and industry in the records of the Victoria home founded in 1888. Provincial Archives of British Columbia, British Columbia Protestant Orphans' Home (1888–1942). For a discussion of this aspect of institutionalization, see Patricia T. ROOKE and R. S. Patterson, "The Delicate Duty of Child Saving, Coldwater, Michigan 1871–1896," *Michigan History,* 61 (Fall 1978): 195–219.

26. MTL, BR(S) 361.75 B58, Sermon Preached before Ladies Benevolent Institution in St. George's Church, Montreal, 9 April 1854.

27. Fully discussed by the authors in "Protestant Orphans' Homes as Women's Domain (1850–1930)," presented to the Berkshire Conference on Women's History, Poughkeepsie, N.Y., 18 June 1981.

28. Queen's University, Coll. 94, *Kingston Orphans' Home and Widows' Friend Society, Annual Report* (1859), p. 5; *Constitution* (1862), rule 16.

29. MTL, MS 88(1), Baldwin Papers, 11 July 1837: and Toronto Girls' Home and Public Nursery, Register, 22 June 1859.

30. Anglican Archives, St. John's, Newfoundland, *Church of England Orphans' and Widows' Aid Society, 60th Annual Report* (1914), p. 5, and *First Annual Report* (1855), p. 3. Clayton W. Puddester, "The United Church Orphanage," in *The Book of Newfoundland,* ed.: J. Smallwood (St. John's: Newfoundland Book Publishers, 1937), p. 308.

31. Anglican Archives, St. John's, Newfoundland, *Church of England Orphans' and Widows' Aid Society, Annual Reports* (1855–1929); United Church Archives, St. John's, Newfoundland, Methodist Orphanage, Minutes, Annual Reports, and Correspondence (1855–1952).

32. Public Archives of Nova Scotia, MG 20 177: 13, Halifax Infants' Home, Minute Books (1875–1949).

33. Saint John City Archives, Wiggins Male Orphan Institution, Minute Book (1891–1901), and The Act Incorporating the Governors and Wiggins Male Orphan Institution, 10 June 1867.

34. Saint John City Archives, Max G. Baxter, "New Brunswick Protestant Orphans Home," typescript (1965). The New Brunswick Survey conducted by the Canadian Council on Child Welfare noted as late as 1928 that the home was still claiming the "exclusive and complete control and custody" of such children as if they had been totally surrendered in the first instance. During the previous year only 20 of the 227 children admitted had lost one or both parents while most admissions were the result of unmarried parenthood and desertions (Public Archives of Canada, MG 28 I 10, vol. 38 (1928–29), file 167).

35. Queen's University, Kingston Protestant Orphans' Home, Minutes, 10 April and 18 November 1860.

36. Public Archives of Canada, MG 28 137, vols 1–3, Ottawa Protestant Orphans' Home, Minutes, 18 January 1865, 28 November 1867, 26 April 1869, 28 August 1871, 24 February 1896 and 30 March 1896.

37. *Montreal Protestant Orphan Asylum, Constitution* (1852); *Philanthropy: Care of our Destitute and Criminal Population* (Montreal, 1857); *Historical Sketch of the Montreal Protestant Asylum from its Foundation ... 16th February 1822 to the Present Day ...* (Montreal, 1860), p. 9; and *Montreal Ladies' Benevolent Society, 76th Annual Report* (Montreal, 1909), pp. 2–3.

38. MTL, L30 PCH(E), Toronto Protestant Orphans' Home, Letters and Papers (1854–56).

39. MTL, *Boys' Home for the Training and Maintenance of Destitute Boys not convicted of Crime, 33rd Annual Report* (1893), p. 6; *36th Annual Report* (1896), p. 6; and *2nd Annual Report* (1861), pp. 5–6; *Daily Globe*, 4 January 1866, "The Arabs of the Street."

40. *Protestant Children's Homes of Toronto Milestones (1851–1951)* (Ottawa: Canadian Council on Social Development, 1951), p. 6.

41. *Christian Women's Union, 21st Annual Report* (Winnipeg, 1903); Provincial Archives of Manitoba, Greenway Papers; also, MG10 B24, Children's Home of Winnipeg, Minutes, Correspondence and Annual Reports (1885–1937); RG5 G2, Box 4, Health and Welfare, Welfare Supervision Board, Files 1916–45.

42. Margaret Johnson, *The First One Hundred Years, 1874–1974* (London: Women's Christian Association, 1974); Caroline L. CONRON, *Merrymount Children's Home—A Century in Retrospect, 1874–1974* (London: Merrymount Children's Homes, 1974); University of Western Ontario, VF640, London Protestant Orphans' Home, Minutes, 23 April and 30 July 1875.

43. Provincial Archives of Manitoba, Greenway Papers, 1890.

44. Public Archives of Nova Scotia, Halifax Infants' Home, Minutes, 7 September 1875 and 5 March 1877; *Halifax Herald,* 3 February 1890.

45. Public Archives of Nova Scotia, Halifax Infants' Home, Minutes, 2 March 1875.

46. MTL, Toronto Girls' Home, Minutes, 3 November and 1 December 1891.

47. Provincial Archives of Manitoba, MG10 B24, Children's Home of Winnipeg.

48. MTL, Toronto Girls' Home, Minutes, 12 November 1895.

49. *Montreal Ladies' Benevolent Society, 40th Annual Report* (Montreal, 1873), p. 6. Those attitudes about parental exploitation of similar children in Britain are found in the records of various child-rescue societies who exported juvenile immigrants to Canada. This and the psychological problems of child abandonment and family separation are fully discussed by the authors in "The King's Children in English Canada: A Psychohistorical Study of Abandonment, Rejection and Colonial Response," *Journal of Psychohistory,* 8 (Spring 1981): 387–420.

50. Public Archives of Canada, Ottawa Protestant Orphans' Home, "Clippings," vol. 4 (1884–89), 19 January 1897.

51. MTL, L30 PCH(6), Toronto Protestant Orphans' Home, "Miscellaneous (1895–1915)." The authors have discussed the relationship between the professionalization of charity and the shift from child rescue to child welfare, emphasizing Charlotte Whitton's contribution in "Child Welfare in English Canada, 1920–1948," *Social Service Review, 55* (September 1981): 484–506.

52. *Charity Organization Review,* 7 (August 1900):89–93.

53. Queen's University, *Kingston Protestant Orphans' Home, Annual Report* (1875).

54. Schnell, "Childhood as Ideology," pp. 17–23.

55. Provincial Archives of British Columbia, *British Columbia Protestant Orphans' Home, Annual Report* (1886), File 7, p. 2.

56. Public Archives of Nova Scotia, *Halifax Protestant Orphans' Home, Annual Reports* (1858–77).

57. Provincial Archives of Manitoba, Children's Home of Winnipeg, Minutes, 2 July 1908.

CHAPTER
14 CONFEDERATION

Confederation solved a variety of political, economic, diplomatic and ethnic difficulties that jeopardized British North America's future in the 1860s. Despite early discontent, the union was not seriously threatened in its first century. Not surprisingly, historians have generally treated Confederation as the inevitable unfolding of a scenario stretching back to the American Revolution. The leading Fathers, such as Sir John A. Macdonald, Sir George-Etienne Cartier, George Brown and Sir Charles Tupper, were ascribed heroic qualities in the numerous studies that preceded the Centennial in 1967. Donald Creighton's *Road to Confederation: The Emergence of Canada, 1863–1867* (1964) was the pre-eminent narrative depiction of heroes and villains in a drama that ended with a rising sun on shining faces. His study and others surveyed every conceivable aspect of the happy story. English Canada paid scant attention to naysayers in Quebec, such as Abbé Lionel Groulx and Maurice Séguin, whose disciples drew different pictures and were preparing another agenda.

In "The United States and Canadian Confederation," a paper delivered at the University of Chicago in 1958, Donald Creighton looked back at the abortive British North American union attempt a century earlier, in 1858. That was his starting point in explaining the success of the movement that culminated in Confederation. The paper enunciated several of the themes that Creighton and others would expand upon in the years leading up to the Centennial. Political deadlock, western expansionism, British inducement and American militarism combined to make the era one of "prophetic significance in Canadian history." Canadians "had to build a nation," which "had to be built in the midst of a great war."

In the years since the Centennial in 1967, the imperfections in the Confederation arrangement have, on occasion, eclipsed the advantages and raised questions about its inevitability. Regional alienation, francophone discontent, uncertain leadership and ill-defined national aspirations have forced historians to reappraise the Union movement and those opposed to Confederation in the 1860s. In March of 1990, for example, the *Canadian Historical Review* offered a "CHR Dialogue: The Maritimes and Confederation: A Reassessment." Several disturbing questions were raised, as they were at a seminar at the Centre of Canadian Studies at the University of Edinburgh, Scotland, in May of 1988. Ged Martin, the Director of that Centre, has written several prodding articles on the Confederation movement of the 1860s. The one offered here rejects the notions of inevitability of historians like Creighton. It was presented as a Canada House Lecture on 8 February, 1989 as "History as Science or Literature: Explaining Canadian Confederation, 1857–1867."

Suggestions for Further Reading

Buckner, Phillip, P.B. Waite and William M. Baker, "CHR Dialogue: The Maritimes and Confederation: A Reassessment," *Canadian Historical Review*, LXXI, no. 1 (March 1990), 1–45.

Creighton, Donald, *The Road to Confederation: The Emergence of Canada, 1863–1867*. Toronto: Macmillan of Canada, 1964.

Martin, Ged (ed.), *The Causes of Canadian Confederation*. Fredericton: Acadiensis Press, 1990.

———, "Launching Canadian Confederation: Means to Ends, 1836–64," *Historical Journal*, 27, no. 3 (1984), 575–602.

Morton, W.L., *The Critical Years: The Union of British North America, 1857–1873*. Toronto: McClelland and Stewart, 1964.

Silver, Arthur, *The French-Canadian Idea of Confederation, 1864–1900*. Toronto: University of Toronto Press, 1982.

Smith, Jennifer, "Canadian Confederation and the Influence of American Federalism," *Canadian Journal of Political Science*, XXI, no. 3 (September 1988), 443–463.

Waite, P.B., *The Life and Times of Confederation, 1864–1867: Politics, Newspapers and the Union of British North America*. Toronto: University of Toronto Press, 1962.

Winks, Robin, *Canada and the United States: The Civil War Years*. Montreal, Harvest House, 1960.

THE UNITED STATES AND CANADIAN CONFEDERATION

Donald Creighton

In the next decade both the United States and Canada will face an impressive succession of important centenaries. On 12 April 1961, it will be a hundred years since the Confederate bombardment opened upon Fort Sumter in Charleston harbour. On 22 June 1964, it will be a century since a coalition Government of Reformers and Liberal-Conservatives took office in the Province of Canada with the declared intention of establishing a general federal union of the whole of British North America. Between these two events—the Civil War

---

From *Canadian Historical Review*, XXXIX, no. 3 (September 1958), 209–22. Copyright 1958 by University of Toronto Press. Reprinted by permission of the Estate of Donald Creighton and University of Toronto Press.

in the United States and the federation of British North America—there exists an interesting relationship which I should like to explore with you tonight. It is an important, but also a complex, imprecise, and ambiguous relationship; and it seems to me that there might be more enlightenment in approaching its analysis circuitously than directly. These two famous dates and the national dramas which they recall and commemorate will therefore, for the moment, be set aside; and we can go back a little in time. There is an earlier episode in Canadian history, which could be most appropriately examined on this occasion, for its centenary will be reached, though certainly not enthusiastically celebrated, during the summer of 1958. It is an episode much less well known than the foundation of the coalition Government and the declaration of the coalition Government's purpose in June of 1864; but, for all that, it has its own real significance. And an examination of it may throw some light upon the curious relationship between the American Civil War and the federal union of British North America, upon the influence of the United States on Canadian Confederation.

In the summer of 1858—it was in August, to be precise—the government of the Province of Canada came to a momentous decision. It was, in itself, an important decision, and it was much more important simply because it was the Province of Canada which had reached it. In 1858, the province was only a little over fifteen years old, for it had been formed in 1841 by the union of the two older and smaller provinces of Upper and Lower Canada; but already, in size, ambition, political consequence, and political influence, it was clearly the "empire province" of British North America. From the Gulf of St. Lawrence, it extended westward along the whole long line of the great river and the Great Lakes. On the south, its limit was the international boundary between British North America and the United States; to the north, its frontier was that highly uncertain, vaguely defined line which bounded Rupert's Land, the chartered territories of the Hudson's Bay Company. The other British provinces—Nova Scotia, New Brunswick, Prince Edward Island, and Newfoundland in the east, and Vancouver Island and British Columbia in the far west—were undeniably dwarfed in importance by the Province of Canada. Canada was more prosperous than any of them. Canada was more populous than all of them put together.

It was all true, as the other colonies somewhat enviously admitted; but it was also true that the "empire province" was a socially turbulent and politically agitated community, and that the division between its French-speaking and English-speaking citizens had created a cultural cleavage far more serious than existed elsewhere in the North American Empire. The other northern provinces regarded Canada with a measure of doubt and distrust. The eyebrows of sober Nova Scotians, in particular, were lifted often in pained disapproval at its erratic course. It was always in the throes of some political crisis or other; its citizens were invariably at each other's throats; and it had the highly reprehensible habit of breaking its word in cheerful disregard of the interests of the rest of

British North America. Its whole record, in fact, was simply deplorable. And yet, the unwelcome but inescapable fact was that Canada counted. However violent its actions and however incomprehensible its purposes, they had to be taken seriously. And once again, during the agitated summer of 1858, the Canadian government had given the other provincial administrations considerable food for thought. On August 16, when, after a long and turbulent session, the Governor, Sir Edmund Head, finally prorogued the session of the Canadian legislature, he made a brief formal announcement of the policy which his new Government intended to follow. "I propose in the course of the recess," he told the Houses, "to communicate with Her Majesty's Government, and with the Governments of the sister Colonies, on another matter of very great importance. I am desirous of inviting them to discuss with us the principles on which a bond of a federal character, uniting the Provinces of British North America, may perhaps hereafter be practicable."

What had happened? What had persuaded this most important of British American governments to adopt, as its declared policy, the plan of a British American federal union? Long before this, of course, British Governors and High Commissioners, colonial statesmen, authors, and public speakers had been talking and writing about federal union; but until Governor Head made his famous announcement on the afternoon of 16 August 1858, the whole question had remained almost entirely academic. Why had George E. Cartier and John A. Macdonald, the leaders of the Canadian Administration, decided to commit themselves to an ambitious policy which no other British American government had ventured to espouse before? Nearly six years later, on 22 June 1864, another Canadian Government, as we have already seen, was to make another open profession of faith in a federal plan and, after an interval, was to succeed in carrying it out. Yet these two general declarations of purpose are very similar; and at first sight, the occasion, if not the cause of both of them seem very much alike. Each appears to have arisen out of the chronic weakness and instability of Canadian politics.

The fact was that the Canadian Union of 1841 had been formal, not real. In theory, the province was a unitary state; in fact it was an unacknowledged federal system. Its two sections, Canada East and Canada West, the one largely French and the other overwhelmingly English, were united economically by the St. Lawrence transport system and divided socially by their two contrasting cultural inheritances. They had found it impossible to live apart as the separate provinces of Upper and Lower Canada; they were finding it almost equally difficult to live together as the two divisions of a single government. It was true, of course, that the Union Act had itself helped to make these difficulties almost insuperable. By its terms, Canada East and Canada West had been given equal representation in the provincial legislature, irrespective of population; and this political equality tended to harden the sectional division of the province and to exacerbate its inevitable cultural misunderstandings. The cabinet and several of the important departments of government were organized on a sectional basis. Much of the legislation that was passed had to be sectional in character; and the political parties, although they tried, of course, to win a following in both French- and English-speaking Canada, had an irresistible tendency to become strong in one section of the province and correspondingly weak in the other. They tended also, as a natural consequence, to reach a level of approximate political equality; and thus the public affairs of the province were characterized both by a permanent state of sectional conflict and a persistent condition of political instability.

During the summer of 1858 this chronic political unsettlement reached a sudden, sharp crisis; and it was this crisis which provided the occasion for the Cartier-Macdonald Government's dramatic announcement of its adoption of the federal plan. Earlier in the session, the Assembly had been discussing the constitutional problem which lay at the root of its sectional difficulties. The Assembly was always discussing the constitutional problem. It was always anxiously reviewing a number of contradictory proposals for constitutional reform—including federal schemes—which, it was argued, would remove the province from the inveterate embarrassments of sectionalism; and this painfully familiar exercise was barely over, when there occurred an episode which was, in effect, a preposterous, almost ludicrous, illustration of the political stalemate which everybody was so anxious to end. Its origins were simple and absurdly characteristic of the province's real nature. The political crisis of the summer of 1858 arose out of the endless and agonizing problem of deciding where the capital of this politically united but sectionally divided province was to be.

Ever since the union in 1841, this question had been arousing the most acrimonious dissension. Originally, the seat of government had been fixed at Kingston in Canada West; it had then been transferred to Montreal, in Canada East—a distinctly unfortunate removal, as it turned out, for a few years later, in 1849, the enraged Montreal Conservatives burnt the Parliament Buildings to the ground. For some time after this disgrace, the attempt to find a permanent capital was tacitly abandoned; and the seat of government alternated, at intervals, between Quebec, which was the old capital of Lower Canada, and Toronto, which was the old capital of the upper province. Every few years, the cabinet ministers and a small army of civil servants, together with great masses of official records, government furniture, and personal effects, were laboriously transported, up or down the river valley, in trains and steamships, to their new political headquarters. It is hardly surprising that everybody in politics found these fairly regularly recurring removals an intolerable nuisance; and in 1857 John A. Macdonald had hit upon what was thought to be a most ingenious method of securing permanence. Queen Victoria was invited to name a permanent capital for the united province; and Queen Victoria, duly but privately advised from Canada, decided in favour of a little backwoods town, some distance up the Ottawa River, once called Bytown and now Ottawa.

Ottawa had the advantage of a location on the west bank of the river which formed the boundary between the two sections of the province; but it was definitely in Canada West. Still more obviously, it was neither Quebec nor Montreal; and the French-Canadians in the legislature, even though the great majority of them were members of the Conservative party which had referred the problem to the Queen for final decision, regarded the choice of Ottawa with the darkest disapproval. It was always possible, on a question of such enormous sectional prestige, to persuade some of them, at least momentarily, to forswear their Conservative allegiance; and this was exactly what happened on 28 July 1858. An address to the Queen on the subject of the capital was under consideration. An amendment, declaring flatly that Ottawa ought not to be the permanent seat of government was deliberately moved by the opposition. A small, but sufficient bloc of French-Canadian votes changed sides, and the Government was defeated on this issue.

Macdonald and Cartier decided to resign; and George Brown, the leader of the Liberal Opposition, accepted the Governor's invitation to form a new Government. What followed is of considerable interest in the law and custom of parliamentary institutions in the British Commonwealth. The political crisis of the summer of 1858 anticipates, in some measure, though the circumstances were widely different, the much more famous Canadian constitutional crisis of the summer of 1926 and even finds a faint echo in the speculations and discussions which went on for some time in Canada after the general election of June 1957. Our concern here, however, is not with constitutional issues as such, but with the political instability which resulted in part from the defective constitution of the Province of Canada. Rapidly it became apparent that Brown and his associate French-Canadian leader, Dorion, were in a much more precarious position in the Assembly than their predecessors, Macdonald and Cartier, had ever been. The French-Canadian opponents of Ottawa as the Canadian capital would quickly, if sheepishly, return to the Conservative fold; and, by the law as it then stood, George Brown, Dorion, and the other new ministers would be obliged, on accepting office under the Crown, to resign their seats in Parliament and to seek re-election. With numbers so seriously reduced in such an evenly divided Assembly, the new Government would not be able to meet the inevitable want-of-confidence motion; and Brown, with failure staring him in the face, requested the Governor to grant him a dissolution of Parliament. The request was declined; and on August 4, after having held office for only two days, the Brown-Dorion Administration, "Her Majesty's most ephemeral government," as the Conservatives derisively called it, was obliged to resign, and Macdonald and Cartier were back in power once more.

The crisis had not lasted a long time; it had begun on July 28, and it ended, with the installation of the old ministers, on August 6. Yet this short period of fewer than ten days had provided an almost grotesque illustration of the political instability and futility which was sectionalism's evil gift to the Province of

Canada. The Conservative ministers did not, of course, admit that the episode had taught them a lesson—their own triumphant return to office precluded any such embarrassing avowal; but, at the same time, their subsequent actions proved only too clearly that they had now decided to escape, if possible, from the existing state of affairs. Up to this time, it had been the Liberals or Reformers, not the Conservatives, who had kept suggesting solutions for the sectional problem—who had kept pointing out possible exits from the constitutional impasse in which the province found itself. Now, for the first time, the Conservatives took their stand also upon a new policy. For a colony such as Canada, whose two sections could not afford to be separated and did not want to be too closely united, what could be more suitable than a federal form of government? On August 7, the day after the Ministry was formed, Cartier briefly alluded to the new policy, and on August 16, when he prorogued Parliament, Head formally committed his cabinet to the federal scheme.

II

Undoubtedly the political crisis of the summer of 1858 had precipitated the Canadian Conservatives' adoption of the plan of a general British North American federal union. A way out of the political deadlock of sectionalism had been proved to be peremptorily necessary; and a federal union was surely the solution best calculated to preserve the essential character of the Province of Canada. Yet what kind of a federal union? Why had Macdonald and Cartier declared themselves in favour of a comprehensive scheme which would embrace not only all the Maritime Provinces but also, at some future date, the enormous territories of the British north-west? Why had they not been content with the project of converting Canada into a federation of two provinces? This second, smaller plan, which was actually adopted a year later by the Reform party as its policy, was a much more manageable enterprise. It could have been carried out by Canada herself, at her own convenience, and without the slightest reference to the other colonies. Yet this was not the plan which the Conservative party adopted. Instead it had accepted a vastly more ambitious, vastly more difficult undertaking, which could only be completed with the concurrence of four other colonial governments. Why? The urgent necessity of finding a solution for sectional problems is not a satisfactory explanation, for the sectional problem could have been solved just as effectively, and much more expeditiously, by "applying the federal principle," as contemporaries called it, to the Province of Canada alone. What were the other purposes and intentions which lay behind Macdonald's decision? Why had he and his colleagues conceived the grandiose design of a transcontinental British North American federation?

Now it is quite obvious that Canada, in contrast with the Maritime Provinces, had always held to a tradition of western empire. The Maritime Provinces—

New Brunswick, Prince Edward Island, and, above all, Nova Scotia and Newfoundland—had grown up in a world in which the three words "ships, colonies, and commerce" formed the indissoluble principles, the virtual "holy trinity," of empire. The dominion in which, on the whole, they had been so comfortably adjusted, was an oceanic dominion; but the empire which Canada had sought to achieve through the centuries had been essentially continental in character. From the days of the French explorers onward, all the political and commercial leaders of the community of the St. Lawrence valley had tried to make the Great River and its Great Lakes the basis of an enormous inland empire. The peace treaty of 1783, which cut a line, at that time artificial and almost meaningless, through the centre of this vast region, had transferred its south-west sector to the United States; and it was these tragic losses on their left flank which helped to impel the Montreal fur traders, the real westerners of the period, into the territories north-west of Lake Superior. Here, in a region which could still be made good for the British Empire, the great trader-explorers of the North West Company, Alexander MacKenzie, David Thompson, and Simon Fraser, drove the fur trade across the prairies and through the mountains to the ocean. They clinched the claims of Cook and Vancouver; they helped to give British North America its wide open window on the Pacific. But the terrible struggle with the Hudson's Bay Company, of which these western exploring enterprises were only a part, had exhausted the North West Company; and in 1821 it virtually capitulated to its great rival. From then on, the Hudson's Bay Company held the north-west quarter of the continent in trust for the future Kingdom of Canada; and for a generation the provinces on the St. Lawrence almost forgot their traditional western empire.

Then, fairly suddenly and without much warning, Canadian interest in the region beyond Lake Superior began to revive. The date of the revival is highly significant, for it began just about eighteen months before the Conservatives adopted their federal scheme in the summer of 1858; and this near coincidence in time suggests that, in matters other than its sectional and constitutional problems, the Province of Canada was reaching a species of crisis in its development. It had, in fact, come nearly to the limit of its possibilities of expansion in the circumstances of the moment, and this at the very time when the rule of the Hudson's Bay Company in the north-west was becoming increasingly uncertain and precarious. There was no longer an agricultural frontier in Canada West, for the good lands south of the Precambrian Shield had all been occupied. There was no real prospect of acquiring the bulk of the trade of the international North American west, for the St. Lawrence was obviously losing in its struggle with the American Atlantic ports. The expansive energies of Canada were being held back in frustration and defeat; but far to the north-west, beyond Lake Superior, was an immense and empty territory which lay waiting for both agricultural settlement and commercial exploitation. Why should not the Province of Canada acquire these lands for its own and British North

America's good? Why should it not take over from a moribund seventeenth-century commercial company whose chartered claims were fraudulent, whose rule was baneful, and whose feeble authority was quite incapable of protecting the north-west from encroachment?

Macdonald and his colleagues looked both eagerly and dubiously upon the domain of the Hudson's Bay Company. They were both fascinated and frightened by the thought of acquiring Rupert's Land and the North-west Territories. Inside Canada itself, the popular impulses towards its annexation were very strong; and their strength was powerfully increased by pressures in the same direction which came from outside through both the United Kingdom and the United States. There was no doubt at all that Great Britain was anxious to make new arrangements which would enable her to cut her commitments and reduce her contingent liabilities in North America. In 1857, two years before the Hudson's Bay Company's trading licence was to expire, the British government sponsored a parliamentary committee to consider the state and prospects of Rupert's Land; and although the committee's report made simply a guarded and general recommendation in favour of Canadian settlements in suitable parts of the Red and Saskatchewan valleys, it was quite plain that the imperial government was eager to have Canada take over the responsibility for the north-west.

Yet even this was not all. To the spur of British encouragement was added the stimulus of American rivalry. Canada was determined, sooner or later, to acquire Rupert's Land; the United Kingdom was anxious to arrange a secure British North American future for Rupert's Land; and finally, for both British and Canadians, the irrepressible fear that the United States might succeed in forestalling them lent an additional urgency to their plans for Canadian expansion. This fear was, of course, simply a new western variant of a much older fear, which went back as far as 1775 when, nearly a year before they declared their independence, the Thirteen Colonies launched an attack on Quebec. The armed occupation of Quebec in 1775–76 and the repeated American invasions of the War of 1812 had bred in the British colonies the unshakeable conviction that the United States was the one real threat to their survival on the North American continent. The events which had occurred in the forty years since the Peace of Ghent had, in the main, confirmed rather than qualified this view. At every moment of trouble in British North America, on every occasion of dispute between the United Kingdom and the United States, the threat of American intervention or American attack returned. Only two years before, in 1856, the Crimean War had brought a brief renewal of the old danger. The Nova Scotian, Joseph Howe, with some encouragement and assistance from J.F.T. Crampton, the British Minister at Washington, attempted to secure recruits for the Crimea from among the currently unemployed in the republic. This childishly inept and foolhardy venture was discovered in due course; it was described, a little grandiloquently, by the American Administration as "an act of usurpation against the sovereign rights of the United States." Crampton's recall was demanded; the American newspapers fulminated in indignation. And all this occurred, as similar dangers had occurred so often in the past, when the size of the British garrisons in the northern colonies had been sharply reduced and when Great Britain's hands were tied with a war in Europe.

The fear was an old one, frequently renewed. And now it had taken on a new shape and found a fresh expression. The survival of the existing colonies in a continent dominated by the United States was still not entirely certain; but far more uncertain was British North America's acquisition of the north-west and its expansion to the Pacific Ocean. Would the transcontinental dominion, of which people were already dreaming, ever become a triumphant reality? The Convention of 1818 and the Washington Treaty of 1846 had settled the international boundary, at least on paper; but might not the hard, solid facts of human occupation determine it ultimately in a quite different fashion? There were only three tiny British American communities in the whole north-west— at Red River, on Vancouver Island, and on the mainland of British Columbia; and the tide of American frontier settlement, the network of the American communication systems, were creeping steadily closer to them with every year that passed. Minnesota became a state in 1858, Oregon was to follow in 1859. Hudson Bay had ceased to be the sole centre of the Hudson's Bay Company's transport system; and the Red River settlement was becoming an economic outpost of St. Paul, just as the Pacific colonies were becoming economic outposts of San Francisco.

All this was part of the speculations of informed Canadians in the summer of 1858. All this was inevitably present in the minds of Macdonald and his fellow ministers when they decided to adopt the policy of a general British North American federation. The sectional crisis in the Province of Canada had led them to the idea of federal union; but the shape and scope which they gave to their federal plan had been determined with a view to British North America as a whole. They were eager, not only to reconstruct the constitution of a province, but also to lay the foundations of a nation; and they were convinced that this was the only way in which a transcontinental nation in the northern half of North America could be built. Union with the Maritime Provinces was essential to secure the future nation's Atlantic frontage; but union with the Maritime Provinces was almost equally necessary to provide a base broad and strong enough to support the acquisition of the north-west. Alone, the Province of Canada might not have been sufficiently powerful to bear the responsibility; and even if she had been willing to try, the basic division between her French- and English-speaking citizens would almost certainly have prevented her from making the attempt. Even if only a part of Rupert's Land and the North-west Territories had been added to the united province, the addition would simply have emphasized the already existing preponderance of Canada West. It would probably have forced the adoption of representation by population and led to the abandonment of sectional equality in the provincial legislature. It would, in the eyes of French Canadians, have seriously threatened their distinctive culture; and the union might have broken apart in fear and anger.

British North American federation would prevent all this. British North American federation could transform a provincial crisis into a national triumph. It would provide a framework in which French-Canadian culture would be given the protection of provincial status and in which Rupert's Land and the North-west Territories could be gradually organized as they developed. Only in this fashion, in all probability, could a transcontinental nation be created; and the potential strength of transcontinental nationhood would perhaps alone suffice to ensure the survival of British North America.

III

As one looks back, over the intervening century, at the events of the summer of 1858, one cannot help but be impressed by their prophetic significance in Canadian history. As one regards those three years from 1856 to 1859, one feels almost a sense of astonishment at the closeness of their resemblance to another, much more famous three years which began with the formation of the coalition Government in 1864 and ended with Canadian Confederation in 1867. It is almost as if the period from 1856 to 1859 could be looked upon as a preliminary experiment, a species of dress rehearsal, for successful federal union. Many of the actors have already taken their positions on the stage; some of those with star parts are already clearly discernible. And, as one reads over the letters and memoranda in which the Canadians tried to explain their federal plan to the British Colonial Office during the autumn of 1858, one gets the distinct impression that the dialogue is taking shape and that some of the very best lines have already been written. The situations in the years 1856–59 seem vaguely to anticipate those of 1864–67; and the two plots have an odd family relationship as if, at least, they had been contrived by the same author. The scenery in both cases is identical—a few small, underpopulated, staple-producing provinces, set in the howling wilderness of half a continent, with somewhere in the background, lurking menacingly in the shadow, that sinister villain of all Canadian dramas, the United States.

And yet the dress rehearsal of 1856–59 was not the immediate prelude to a real production. The famous announcement of the summer of 1858 had no direct consequences, while the declared purpose of the summer of 1864 was achieved three years later in Canadian Confederation. How is the success of the one and the failure of the other to be explained? The two episodes lie before us, implying contrasts, inviting comparisons; and one is inevitably tempted to use that method, regarded so fondly by sociologists in general and logical positivists in particular, and, in my opinion at least, so properly distrusted by historians. If we embark on an exercise in the comparative method, we shall probably not discover a general law about movements towards federal union, or even, to narrow the field very sharply indeed, about Canadian movements towards federal union. We may discover that the apparent resemblance between these two examples of the same historical species is a superficial resemblance, observable only from the outside; and that, on closer examination from the inside, the two episodes will turn out to be two separate and quite distinct cases.

One important contrast emerges immediately when one compares the purely parliamentary events of July and August 1858, with those of June 1864. The rapidly changing political situation of the summer of 1858 certainly provided a much better illustration of the governmental instability which sectionalism had brought to the Province of Canada. The constitutional crisis of 1858 was far more dramatic than that of 1864. And yet—and this, surely, is the important point—its parliamentary consequences were a good deal less significant. The federal plan of 1858 was adopted by a Conservative Administration; but it was a coalition Government of Conservatives and Reformers, commanding a large majority in the House and formed with the express purpose of attempting constitutional reform, which, in June 1864, announced that it would seek a federal union of the whole of British North America. There was a good deal of truth in the charge of one of the officials in the Colonial Office that in 1858 the Confederation issue was still in "a crude state of party politics." By 1864 it had been lifted out of the crude state of party politics; and both parties, and all but a small minority of the House, had agreed to end a situation from which everybody had suffered.

The agreement of the Canadian parties was not the only new factor in the situation. The attitude of the United Kingdom had altered in an important and striking fashion in the short period of six years. It was true, of course, that Great Britain's major objectives in the north remained fundamentally much the same. Labouchere and Bulwer-Lytton, the Colonial Secretaries of the late 1850s did not differ materially in purpose from Cardwell and Carnarvon who held office at the time of Canadian Confederation. All of them wished equally to cut British commitments in North America; all of them hoped to persuade the colonies in general, and the Province of Canada in particular, to assume a larger part of the responsibility of government in the new world. Here they were agreed; but Cardwell and Carnarvon realized, as Bulwer-Lytton most emphatically did not, that a British North American federal union would be of immense assistance in achieving these purely imperial objectives. The temperamental Bulwer-Lytton, who, one sometimes suspects, carried the melodrama of his romances into the conduct of the Colonial Office, was at one and the same time hotly insistent that Canada should take over Rupert's Land and the Northwest Territories, and coldly discouraging to the plan of federal union. It was Cardwell and Carnarvon, not Bulwer-Lytton, who understood the essential connection between the west and Confederation. It was Cardwell and Carnarvon who sensibly realized that if Great Britain wished to get rid of some of her burdens in North America, she must help to found a British American state which was strong enough to bear them. From the moment when the new Confederation scheme was first broached in 1864, Cardwell, and later Carnarvon, supported it with conviction and vigour.

British encouragement was much stronger in 1864 than it had been in 1858. And so also, in the eyes of Canadians, was pressure from the United States. The increasing weight of this negative influence, of which British Americans were becoming more and more anxiously conscious during the early 1860s, is attributable largely to the American Civil War. The danger of the encroachment of American settlement and exploitation on the tiny British outposts in the north-west was much as it had been a few years before; it may, indeed, have been developing a little more slowly, as a result, in part, of the republic's concentration on its own desperate domestic struggle. But there was no real reason for assurance here; and there was much cause for disquiet elsewhere. The special peril which threatened Rupert's Land and the new colonies on the Pacific coast might not have increased very noticeably; but the general danger facing British North America as a whole was greater than any of its citizens then living could remember its ever having been before. It is here, perhaps, that we touch upon one of the greatest, if not the greatest of the differences between the situation of 1858 and that of 1864. The Crimean enlistment controversy of 1856 had produced a short, sharp explosion of American annoyance; but the Civil War led to a steady and ominous deterioration of the relations between the United Kingdom and the United States.

British North America was inevitably involved in this mounting antagonism, either directly through the breaches of neutrality which the United States alleged she had committed, or indirectly through the controversies which arose between the United Kingdom and the republic. The *Trent* incident, which led John A. Macdonald to propose a militia force of 100,000 men for Canada alone, provoked the first of these angry quarrels; but the *Trent* incident, for all its seriousness, occurred early, when the hands of the North were more than full and when the outcome of the struggle was still far from certain. In June 1864, when the Canadian coalition Government was formed and when the battle of Gettysburg was nearly a year in the past, the situation had greatly changed. It had changed still more by the autumn of the same year, when a handful of Confederate soldiers launched, from the Province of Canada, their stupid and ineffective raid upon the town of St. Albans in Vermont. By that time the United States was ready and eager for reprisals. It announced the abrogation of the Reciprocity Treaty with British North America; it threatened—and, in the circumstances, no more sinister threat could have been imagined—to suspend the Rush-Bagot agreement limiting naval armaments on the Great Lakes.

It is easy to exaggerate the influence of the American Civil War upon the movement for Canadian Confederation. It is easy, in particular, to overestimate the effects of the St. Albans Raid. The coalition Government of June 1864, was formed and its purpose declared in direct response to a domestic, not an international, crisis. The Quebec Conference, which laid the bases of the federal constitution, met nine days before the St. Albans Raid occurred and the British government's favourable attitude to Confederation had been decided upon even earlier. The American Civil War did not inspire the Canadian desire for constitutional reform or the British wish for retrenchment; but it did help to give both amplitude and urgency to the Anglo-Canadian plans for achieving their objectives. For both Canadians and British it was not enough to do a little constitutional tinkering and make a few budget cuts. They had to build a nation. And their nation had to be built in the midst of a great war which had convulsed the North American continent and threatened to embroil the English-speaking world.

HISTORY AS SCIENCE OR LITERATURE: EXPLAINING CANADIAN CONFEDERATION, 1857–67

Ged Martin

Long ago, there was a controversy among British historians about the nature of their discipline. J.B. Bury's proclamation, in 1903, that "History is a science, no less and no more" led G.M. Trevelyan to complain a decade later that the new school of history was "to the world of older learning what Western Canada is to England today. Settlers pour into the historical land of promise who, a generation back, would have striven for a livelihood in the older 'schools' and 'triposes'."[1] The analogy, underpinned by a disapproving reference to "raw materialism," suggests that Trevelyan did not think much of Canada, and would have been surprised at the notion that it possessed a history at all.

My intention is to explore the idea of history as a science with particular reference to the attempts by historians to explain the differing fates of the two attempts to establish a union of the British North American provinces, the first in 1858–59, and the second between 1864 and 1867. Canadian Confederation, it might be felt, is hardly a subject which calls out for re-examination, for the textbook accounts present an unusually neat and satisfying consensus of historical explanation.[2] For some time, I have been suspicious of the very neatness of this explanation, feeling that Lady Bracknell's famous dictum about truth must apply—that it is rarely pure and never simple. It can hardly be that distinguished scholars and diligent researchers have failed to grasp the events of Canadian Confederation itself. The problem lies much deeper, in the very nature of the way in which history is written—a literary art form which too often poses as an exercise in scientific explanation.

From Canada House Lecture Series Number 41 (1989), 1-33. Reprinted by permission of the author and the Academic Relations Section, Canadian High Commission, London.

History has at least a superficial affinity with the physical sciences in that it seeks to arrange events into ordered explanations. The chemist establishes that compound A causes a reaction, the physicist that particle B breaks a nucleus, the historian that statesman C caused a war. Yet, as Arthur Marwick reminds us, "there *is* a difference, and we all know there is a difference. The physical scientist can repeat his experiments; the historian cannot call for a repeat performance of the past."[3] This does not mean that explanation in the physical sciences is necessarily *better* than that laboriously argued by the historian. Persistent experimentation may enable a medical researcher to establish that a particular drug cures a dangerous disease. The Nobel Prize would not be withheld from such a benefactor of humanity merely because our scientist confessed total inability to explain how the drug actually managed the miracle. Yet there would be little professional acclaim for the historian who announced that there was a correlation between the presence of Bismarck and the outbreak of wars of Prussian aggrandisement, but confessed inability to offer any elucidation of this perceived link. Explanation in the pure sciences, then, is not necessarily *superior* to that offered by historians. It is merely *testable*.

In the case of Canadian Confederation, a very superficial equivalent of the experimental method is offered by the fact that the circumstances of 1858–59, unsuccessful, can be compared with those of 1864–67, successful. The most obvious factor present in the second case but not the first was the American Civil War. Yet although the context of the Civil War—perhaps more narrowly, its impending conclusion in a Northern victory—is undoubtedly important, it does not follow that the Civil War is thereby proven to be a crucial causal element. It may simply be that those who failed in 1858–59 had learned from their mistakes. The only way to test the hypothesis that it is the American Civil War which represents the crucial causal difference between 1858 and 1864 would be to put the 1860s back in the bell-jar of time, where events could be endlessly rerun, with minute variations in endless permutations—this time with no Civil War, then with a Southern victory, a stalemate, European intervention, a negotiated peace, and each of the near-infinite possibilities in combination with millions of alternative developments within the British North American provinces themselves. Of course we cannot do this, but merely to sketch the possibility is to grasp its absurdity. People are not particles. The behaviour of one individual on one occasion is no predictor for the behaviour of another in the same or—more realistically—similar circumstances.

Most historians would probably agree that because the past is not testable and human behaviour cannot be reduced to predictable formulae, Trevelyan was right to protest that "there is no way of scientifically deducing causal laws about the action of human beings in the mass."[4] Yet lurking behind many textbook explanations of the coming of Canadian Confederation, there is the assumption that individual events in the 1850s and 1860s can be given meaning by an appeal to implicit general laws. Occasionally, these assumptions are spelt out as part of a softening-up process to prepare the reader for the inevitability of the outcome. Thus Chester Martin stated: "Nothing but a compelling necessity can reconcile self-governing provinces to the surrender of cherished rights to the exigencies of a distant national state." The "scientific" context is made yet more evident in the elaboration:

> Like chemical reagents which are inert towards one another under normal conditions of pressure and temperature, the most disintegrated provinces may react in a national emergency with unpredictable responsiveness. That reaction at the time may be due to abnormal pressure and temperature but once it has resulted in organic federation, the product may be a permanent chemical compound capable of withstanding the stresses and strains of normal atmospheric conditions with complete organic stability.[5]

We are being prepared here, of course, for an explanation which stresses the hot blast of the Civil War, but at least we are being prepared openly. More recently, Peter Waite began his account of Confederation in the *Canadian Encyclopedia* with the statement:

> The Confederation movement followed Newton's first law of motion: all bodies continue in a state of rest or of uniform motion unless compelled by some force to change their state.[6]

The attractiveness of a bold statement of this kind to historians is demonstrated by the fact that it has been prominently cited in a recent—and indeed excellent—textbook.[7] The problem, of course, comes back to the question of *testability*. A few societies, such as Tokugawa Japan, may have succeeded for a time in walling themselves off from external influences, but most are subject to continual and random buffeting from outside. If we accept Waite's "scientific" dictum, we can indeed easily apply it to the circumstances of British North America in 1864, for the apparently Newtonian pressures for change are obvious. Unfortunately, what we cannot do is discover, by repeated experimentation, whether some or all of these forces might not in reality have bounced harmlessly off the immovable provincial objects.

Chester Martin and Peter Waite are open in their appeal to scientific laws. Other historians deplore the political shortcomings of the province of Canada before Confederation, implying that it was characterized by internal communal divisions and avoidance of real issues to a degree which simply could not be allowed to continue in the face of an overwhelming external threat. Such an assumption could only be valid if it rested upon a general law of political physics, which would mean that it would be as true of the Lebanon in the 1980s as of the Province of Canada in the 1860s. In fact, there is no such law, and the explanation which implies its existence is not logical so much as teleological: it proceeds from the knowledge of hindsight that Confederation is coming just around the corner and brazenly proceeds to conflate *post hoc* with *propter hoc*. The problem, then, as David Hackett Fischer has put it, is not that history is an inexact science but that historians are inexact scientists.[8]

These difficulties are complicated by the fact that history is also a literary art form. My concern is not so much with literary *style,* which is rare enough among historians, as with literary *craftsmanship.* In assembling the construct which we call history from the totality which was the past, we like to think that we get a general idea of what the sources are trying to tell us, before approaching them in more detail with our own hypotheses to test how far the evidence will sustain our theories. The best experimental scientists employ exactly the same approach, and their greatest discoveries stem from just such imaginative leaps. However, the physicist is protected from utter foolishness by the intractability of particles: repeated experimentation will destroy a factually incorrect hypothesis. For the historian, there is a fine distinction between the careful compilation of a case and the outright filtering of evidence in order to impose a pre-conceived crotchet. In a subject which aroused as much long-winded controversy as did Canadian Confederation in the mid-1860s, supporting quotation can be adduced, from somebody, somewhere, to provide the historian's decorative sprig of spurious contemporary endorsement for just about any hypothesis.

In short, we face a problem in the way in which our literary *craftsmanship* builds up a deceptively scientific argument and then triumphantly produces as supporting evidence one or two clinching sentences from a contemporary source. But what of the motives of that source? Peter Stansky has reminded us of an occasion when Gladstone was suddenly threatened by an attack of brevity. As an inexperienced front-bencher charged with the duty of responding to a debate, he turned to his chief, Sir Robert Peel, and asked, "Shall I be short and concise?" "No," replied Peel, "be long and diffuse. It is all important in the House of Commons to state your case in many different ways, so as to produce an effect on men of many ways of thinking."[9] Gladstone managed to resist the temptation to concision for the rest of his career; his colonial contemporaries seem never to have been tested. Some, I am sorry to say, not only advanced arguments in forms designed to appeal to different viewpoints, but were even guilty on occasion of uttering statements which they may not have believed at all. At a banquet in Halifax in August 1864, Joseph Howe seemed to speak warmly of the idea of uniting the British North American provinces—a speech which he was challenged to explain since shortly afterwards he became an out-and-out opponent of Confederation. His indignant explanation of the apparent inconsistency was that he had risen to speak at ten minutes to midnight. "Who ever heard of a public man being bound by a speech delivered on such an occasion as that?"[10] Historians, in their literary personae, may crown their own explanations with the clinching flourish of contemporary evidence. But it may be that the contemporary statement was made by a minister who wished his arguments to chime with the concerns of the Member for Mudville, or that it was advanced by the Member for Mudville in the hope of becoming a minister.

Not surprisingly, most of those who have written about Canadian Confederation have been Canadians, and English-speaking Canadians at that. Understandably, it has stirred their patriotism. Through Confederation, as Careless puts it, "a new Canadian nation was born" and it is not surprising that he should describe it as "one of the most compelling stories in Canadian history."[11] Arthur Lower even regarded Confederation—along with the adoption of the Constitution of the United States—as one of "two political miracles"[12] to have taken place on the North American continent. Provincial politicians are suddenly ennobled to become statesmen, in another continental echo, "Fathers of Confederation." Yet, confusingly, while as *Canadians* the historians have been misty-eyed at the vision so bravely grasped, as inexact scientists they have tended to argue that there was really no alternative. The causes of Confederation are portrayed as being not only overwhelming and above all *interlocking.* "Only a general union, balanced with all the care and precision of a cantilever, was practical in 1864," wrote W.L. Morton in 1963.[13] The apparent contradiction between the inevitability of the solution and the magisterial vision of those who grasped it may owe something to the atmosphere of the 1960s, which saw the publication of both Creighton's *The Road to Confederation* and Morton's *The Critical Year,* when English Canadians finally began to face the need to define a national identity entirely independent of British world power, at a time when a newly assertive French Canadian nationalism in the province of Quebec actually threatened to break the Canadian state apart. Bereft of the empire, it was tempting to laud the wisdom of the Fathers of Confederation as a *national* symbol: in Creighton's biography, John A. Macdonald single-handedly combined Washington's leadership, Jefferson's draftsmanship, Lincoln's melancholic integrity and Grant's fondness for the bottle.[14] Faced with Quebec separatism, it was reassuring to convince oneself that Confederation had been the only possible solution for the northern half of the continent in the 1860s for, by implication, this meant that it was also the inescapable context for the solution of the problems of the 1960s. It is as if the circumstances of 1864 had been fed into a computer which had churned its disks and printed out the single word "Confederation."

The causes cited for the coming of Confederation usually begin with the internal divisions of the province of Canada. Upper and Lower Canada had been ruled by a single legislature and Governor since 1841, but in a curiously quasi-federal union. When the British parliament had enacted the Union, English-speaking Upper Canada had the smaller population, but since the Union was intended both to swamp and to Anglicize French Canadians, each section of the province was given equal representation in the Assembly. By the late 1840s, internal self-government was established in the province of Canada, but the local ministries had a dual character and were usually led by co-premiers, English and French—LaFontaine-Baldwin; Hincks-Morin, Cartier-Macdonald. That was certainly one development which British legislators had not foreseen in 1840. But another was that the principle of equal representation of the sections, originally intended to bolster Upper against Lower Canada, in fact became a grievance in the upper province. By 1851, Upper Canada's population just exceeded that of Lower Canada; by 1861, the figures were 1.4 million to 1.1 million. Increasingly, Upper Canada demanded "rep. by pop.," the majority voice inside the united province. Such a demand was obviously dangerous to a two-headed system, for it risked a confrontation in which one section's major demand was the very concession which the other could not make. Hence the oft-quoted aphorism of Goldwin Smith that "the real father of Confederation was deadlock."

However, the interlocking explanatory package has other attractive elements. The rapid population rise in Upper Canada—numbers trebled in the twenty years from 1841 to 1861—brought a sensation of impending land shortage, especially as new settlement ran up against the intractable barrier of the Canadian Shield. As early as the mid-1850s, the felt need for more land had led various Upper Canadians to cast covetous eyes on the vast and largely empty westward territories of the Hudson's Bay Company. A timely gold rush in the Fraser valley in 1858, which gave birth to the colony of British Columbia, added to the attraction of expansion. But, so the historians argue, the vast western territories could only be absorbed into a wholly new political structure.

If some eyes in the province of Canada were looking west, others were drawn eastward, to the Atlantic seaboard. The 1850s were a time of railway construction, and by 1859 the province of Canada could boast the longest railway line in the world. In fact, few Canadians were tempted to boast about the Grand Trunk. It was at least mildly corrupt, but its real problem was that it ran parallel to the cheap water route of the St Lawrence and petered out about one hundred miles below Quebec City at Rivière-du-Loup. On several occasions from the late 1840s negotiations had been undertaken to extend the Grand Trunk through to the Atlantic ocean, which would give the province of Canada access to the ice-free ports of Saint John and Halifax. Barely half a million people lived in Nova Scotia and New Brunswick, and as a commercial proposition, the Halifax to Quebec or "Intercolonial" railway had little to commend it. From 1851, the Grand Trunk was linked to the Atlantic through a spur line to Portland in Maine, and the American bonding system made it possible to export goods through U.S. territory without payment of duty. The British government was interested in principle in a railway for defence purposes, but the route they favoured naturally ran far from the United States border—and incidentally away from the centres of population and votes. By 1860, the British railway magnate, Edward Watkin, had come to the conclusion that the Grand Trunk should be extended both to the Atlantic and to the Pacific. Watkin's role in the coming of Confederation is shadowy, but his evidence makes it possible for historians to interlock Canada's westward expansion with the need for a railway to the Atlantic seaboard.[15] The urgency of the latter project seemed underlined by the *Trent* crisis of December 1861, which brought Britain and the United States close to war. British troops reinforcing inland positions had to sledge across New Brunswick. The Civil War thus makes its appearance in the web of causation. The argument then reverts to the deadlocked state of the Canadian Union, which in 1862 is seen to be unable to cope with the challenge of either defence or railway construction. It also brings in another element—trade. In 1854, a Reciprocity Treaty had been negotiated between the United States and the British North American colonies, providing for free trade in natural products. During the Civil War, incautiously expressed sympathy for the Southern Confederacy in the provinces played into the hands of Northern opponents of the Treaty, and in 1865, the USA gave twelve months' notice that Reciprocity would end. Thus to the political, settlement and communications aspects of the Confederation package, historians could also add a commercial incentive: if the provinces could not trade with the United States, they could at least unite and trade with each other.

Other causal elements make their appearance in the package. Some proponents talked largely of a "new nationality" in British North America. Historians as various as the socialist Kenneth McNaught, and the undoubtedly Tory Donald Creighton included this element in their analyses,[16] for here, again, the 1860s seemed to be offering reassurance which the 1960s wished to hear. In fact, we need to adapt George Bernard Shaw and recall that the nineteenth century and the twentieth are two eras separated by a common language. Oratorical invocations of a "new nationality" fell a long way short of hoisting a Maple Leaf flag, as the enthusiasts of Canada First sardonically noted when they attempted to build on the rhetorical platform in the decade after Confederation. "The authors of Confederation once appealed to the spirit of nationality," *The Nation* complained in 1875. "Now some of them tell us that their object was limited and that they set the forest on fire only to boil their own pot."[17] But the main framework of the explanatory package starts with rising population in Upper Canada, its paralysing effect on the Canadian Union, its by-product, the demand for westward expansion, and the way in which this came to be interconnected with railway construction to the east at a time when the American Civil War precipitated a defence and trade crisis. To adapt Chester Martin's imagery, the ingredients were there. It needed only the hot blast of the Civil War to bake the cake.

Was the province of Canada really, as J.B. Brebner put it, "on a downward spiral"[18] from the mid-1850s, or does that verdict depend on the fact that we happen to know that Confederation was coming just around the corner? Within a single lecture, there is but little time to discuss such episodes as the "double shuffle" of 1858, the defeat of the Militia Bill in 1862, the collapse of the Intercolonial railway talks later that year, or the passage in 1863 of the Upper Canada Separate Schools Act— forced on the resentful Protestant section by Lower Canadian votes.

The double shuffle was a dodge by which Macdonald and his colleagues avoided having to contest by-elections on re-appointment to portfolios which they had just resigned during an incident which a student of modern Belgian or Italian politics might term a hiccup rather than a crisis. The senior civil servant in the British Colonial Office—usually a rich source of contemporary condemnation of political standards in British North America—merely commented on "the general air of lunacy which hangs over the whole proceedings."[19] By contrast, historians have been mightily disapproving of the double shuffle. "People of all political hues began to wonder how workable was a union that depended upon trickery for its continuation" say J.L. Finlay and D.N. Sprague.[20] It is at least possible that nineteenth-century colonials were less shockable than twentieth-century academics, but in any case, there was nothing illegal about the double shuffle, and even if the law had been broken—as it was, for instance, in the Watergate affair in the United States—that would be to the discredit of the politicians and not of the political system. Canada was to endure murkier political scandals: six years after Confederation, Macdonald was forced to resign in the face of charges that he had given the contract for the transcontinental railway to the man who had funded his election campaign. Imagine the outraged rhetoric with which the historians would condemn the worthless, ramshackle federation which could produce the Pacific Scandal, had the new Dominion broken up in failure after a dozen years! In fact, the admittedly lukewarm element of corruption in the Pacific Scandal is forgiven because villainy may be excused if it is in the interests of Canadian nation-building. Lower was unabashed to admit that the purchase of votes with Canadian money may have played a role in swinging New Brunswickers into line in 1866. "Bribery is a form of consent," he concluded, "and the alternative to consent is force."[21] Confederation, it seems, was not just historically inevitable; it was an offer which could not be refused. In fact, if we abandon the silver trumpets view that Confederation was the beginning of a whole new era, it is possible to perceive that the common element in 1858, 1862 and 1873 was the volatility of members of parliament. Arguably, what Canada needed was not a new political structure but a much firmer system of party government to sustain ministries in difficult times. "Anybody may support me when I am right," Macdonald retorted to a high-minded independent. "What I want is a man that will support me when I am wrong."[22]

The Cartier-Macdonald ministry finally fell over the Militia Bill of 1862. Its replacement, headed by another Macdonald, John Sandfield, is usually regarded as the nadir of the old system. But was the "pawky Highlander"— Morton's dismissive description—really so bad?[23] True, in his two years clinging to office, he consistently sought to evade issues, but so did his more famous and successful namesake—John A. was nick-named "Old Tomorrow"—and so, for a quarter century, did Mackenzie King, an equally unprepossessing physical specimen, of whom it was once said that he did nothing by halves that could be done by quarters.[24] Sandfield Macdonald has been the fall guy of the

Confederation story: we are expected to conclude that any political system which could produce a Sandfield had hit rock-bottom and deserved to be swept away in disgrace. One feels that if Sandfield Macdonald had not existed, the historians of Confederation would have been obliged to invent him. Indeed, it is possible that the Sandfield they portray in the textbooks *was* invented. In 1867, when that great statesman of Confederation, John A. Macdonald, was looking for an ally to instal as premier of the new province of Ontario, on whom did his far-sighted and patriotic choice fall? Joseph Pope, who knew John A. Macdonald, recounted that he "came to the conclusion that John Sandfield Macdonald was just the man to undertake the task."[25] Donald Creighton's great chronicle of Sir John A's nation-building achievements does not mention the selection at all.[26]

If we put aside the unfavourable stereotype of Sandfield Macdonald and look afresh at the question of militia reform in Canada in the 1860s, a less dramatic picture emerges. While acknowledging that it was a complex question, historians have not been very sympathetic in explaining the defeat of the Militia Bill of 1862. Disapproval is evident in Creighton's comment that "Canadians had not as yet become very excited over the alleged danger of the great new military machine which the North was building up"[27] and in Lower's verdict that political rivalry "was so bitter as to cause party advantage to be placed before public necessity."[28] Both comments are fair enough, but they do not tell the whole story. First, the Militia Bill of 1862 contained a contingent element of conscription: if a district did not contribute enough volunteers for training, the shortfall would be made good by ballot. The extent of the continental crisis may well have justified this step, but Canada's historians have been more inclined to assess handling of the conscription issue in terms of the susceptibilities of French Canada than the imperatives of military need.[29] Secondly, the proposed militia reform was to cost almost $1 million, raising expenditure to $12.5 million at a time when revenue was estimated at just over $7 million.[30] No doubt posterity may riposte that it was up to Canadians to face realities and pay their way—but it may be the rejection of the bill proves not that the province of Canada was incapable of responding to challenge, but that parliamentary systems are not very willing to embrace costly defence projects. In Britain, a warning from no less an authority than the Duke of Wellington that the country was wide open to a French invasion by steamships led Lord John Russell's government in 1848 to propose militia reform on a scale similar to that contemplated by Macdonald and Cartier in 1862. Russell proposed to raise and train, over a three-year period, a militia of 120,000 men backed by 80,000 reserves—about four times the force contemplated for Canada, from over ten times the population—coupled with extensive expenditure on ships and fortifications. To pay for this, the income tax—which was actually due to lapse—would have to be increased from seven to twelve pence in the pound. As in 1862, the government's parliamentary exposition of its plan was hampered by the illness of its chief spokesman: Russell had influenza, Macdonald's indisposition was self-inflicted. Despite a decade of often-inflamed relations with France, the House of Commons mutinied at the scale of the plan, which ministers ingloriously withdrew. "The chances of invasion seemed preferable to the certain addition of fivepence to the income tax."[31] Russell's government never fully recovered from the setback, but struggled on for another four years, until Palmerston, his ousted rival, took his revenge—his "tit-for-tat" as he elegantly styled it—by defeating the Militia Bill of 1852.[32] In fairness, Palmerston beat the government after arguing that they had not done enough, but there may have been people in Britain who wondered how long a system of government could continue which made defence the childish sport of parties. If so, their anonymous doubts do not make the textbooks, for not even the shock of the Crimean War could compel constitutional change. Instead, Palmerston himself got into the saddle and between 1859 and 1865 gave a very successful imitation of Sandfield Macdonald, bringing stability to government by the simple expedient of refusing to introduce any major reforms at all.

Yet this comparison may actually be unfair to the abused Sandfield. In 1863, he carried an extensive militia reform, to provide the province with a trained force of 35,000. Actually, Sandfield's reform looked more impressive on paper than on the parade ground, where only a minority of the force ever put in an appearance, but politics—perhaps especially in Canada—is about the possible rather than the ideal. Sir Etienne Taché announced his government's intention of tightening up the 1863 act the day before his minority Conservative ministry was overthrown, to be replaced by the coalition which introduced Confederation. Thereafter, the militia dramatically disappears from the history books. A British officer, Colonel MacDougall, took charge of training, increasing the efficient strength in the province of Canada to 25,000. If the new Dominion was intended to show a larger and more responsible attitude to such questions, it produced a very muted response. Cartier's Militia Act of 1868 seems to have been largely a consolidation of existing forces, and was based on the existing militia laws of the province of Canada—passed in 1863 by Sandfield Macdonald. It aimed at a force of 40,000 men. Of course, the Civil War was over, but the militia was primarily a defence against contingent threats—and there were still Fenians across the border. Cartier's main aim seems to have been to legislate the militia very firmly under the control of the politicians, or—to put it another way—to put patronage before patriotism. When the much-praised Colonel MacDougall argued for the prosecution of men who attempted to leave the militia before the end of their service, Cartier in effect had him fired.[33] The British, who pulled their garrisons out in 1870, continued to allege that Canada did not do enough for its own protection, and in 1874, the impatient nationalists of Canada First included "An improved militia system, under the command of trained Dominion officers" as one of their eleven planks.[34]

In fact, the indictment of the old political system of the Province of Canada rests upon a very few episodes, not all of them shiningly improved upon by the succeeding Dominion. It is surely going too far to compare the Canadian Union with the French Third Republic, as Arthur Lower did. "In the twenty-seven years of the Union there were eight parliaments, innumerable ministries ... and some ten persons who could have been designated 'premier'."[35] By my calculation, there were in fact fourteen, but we should bear in mind that most ministries were double-headed, and that at the very least, we should divide Lower's ten by two to get a fair comparison with other parliamentary systems. In the twenty-two years between 1902 and 1924, Britain had eight Prime Ministers; between 1951 and 1979, there were nine. In any case, what did it matter? Lower's concern appears to reflect an implied scientific law that frequent changes of ministry are in themselves undesirable. Between June 1891 and July 1896, Canada had six Prime Ministers: the decade which followed was one of exploding prosperity and national growth. The province of Canada prospered mightily under the Union. Lower Canada's population virtually doubled under the Canadian Union; Upper Canada's tripled. The political problems were those stemming from success, not failure.

True, in justifying the astonishing union of former enemies to form the coalition of 1864, which launched the successful Confederation initiative, the premier, Sir Etienne Taché, warned that "the country was bordering on civil strife." But a few weeks earlier, the Governor General had opened parliament, reading a ministerial speech which thanked "a beneficent Providence for the general contentment of the people of this province."[36] The notion of a terrifying crisis, within and without, suited the politicians to justify their actions. It suits the historians to quote those politicians to account for the major change which they carried. "Two elections and four ministries in three years!" exclaims Lower. "Everyone recognized that it was impossible to go on."[37] Did they now? Britain had three general elections in under two years between 1922 and 1924. The outcome was not constitutional revolution, but Stanley Baldwin Ireland had three elections in 1981–82: the decade is ending, as it began, with Charles J. Haughey as Taoiscach. For what it is worth, the bell-jar of comparison does not proclaim the same law as the crystal ball of hindsight. But there is a far more crucial weakness in the argument. How was it that after *allegedly* failing to confront a series of crucial challenges—I stress the word "allegedly"—the Canadian Union was suddenly able to carry through the greatest challenge of all, the creation of a new, potentially transcontinental union? Well might Lower call it a "miracle":[38] the logic of his sweeping condemnation of the old system left him with little option. There were certainly contemporaries who asked, on the one hand, why a coalition could not have been formed to work the existing system, or who wanted to know, on the other, how a system of government which had supposedly quarrelled its way to a standstill would work any better when writ large across half a continent.[39] Lower's conclusion that "the two races could not forever be driven in double harness,"[40] is surely a condemnation not of the old province of Canada but of the Canadian experiment as such. If we seek to explain why Confederation was *necessary,* we may indeed be tempted to dwell on the weaknesses of the old province of Canada. If we seek rather to explain why Confederation was *possible,* we are more likely to appreciate the strengths of the Canadian Union.

If the first difficulty in stressing the quarrelsome failure of the Canadian Union is to explain how it managed to sustain the great success of Confederation, the second is to explain why it was possible to persuade the Maritimes to consider climbing into bed at all. According to the textbooks, they were swept along by the interlocking logic of Confederation itself as a solution to the problems of British North America, hammered home by external pressures from the United States and Britain. But how far did the case for Confederation really interlock, cantilever-fashion, from anyone's point of view? And how far did the external pressures compel Confederation, rather than some other solution—or outright and paralysed inaction?

As already noted, railways form the basic ingredient of the interlocking explanation. Canadian duality meant that the Intercolonial railway, needed both for defence and trade reasons, could not be built without counter-balancing expansion to the West—one of those trade-offs which seem so squalid when encountered in the workaday horse-trading of the old province of Canada.

These arguments do not stand scrutiny, either individually or collectively. There is no more reason to assume that political union was an essential precondition for the construction of the Intercolonial than there is to postulate a need for a Franco-British parliament at Calais in order to complete the Channel Tunnel. The outline scheme of 1862 indicated that a railway could have been built by agreement among the separate provinces. The imperial loan guarantee which was invoked in 1867 was the one offered to the separate provinces in 1862. The British government was careful to foster the idea that without Confederation, the House of Commons might rebel against endorsing the guarantee—but even after the passage of the British North America Act in March 1867, the Guarantee Bill had a rough ride. In practice, Confederation and the Intercolonial came to be linked, but it is by no means proven that they had to be.

The argument that the ending of Reciprocity made the provinces draw together is equally unconvincing. There were 31 million Americans, and a little over half a million people in the Maritimes: from the point of view of the province of Canada, the smaller colonies could hardly even rank as a second-best. Even so, as critics pointed out at the time, the logic of the argument, such as it was, pointed not to political union but rather to intercolonial free trade.[41]

But was there any trade to develop? Lower implies that there was: "Oceanic forces towed the Maritime colonies out to sea; continental forces split them in two."[42] Contemporary trade figures would suggest that continental forces barely chipped the Maritimes. New Brunswick in 1863 sent less than one per cent of its exports to Canada, which was the source of under 4 per cent of its imports.

On the other hand, the province of Canada sent 2.2 per cent of its exports to the four Atlantic colonies in 1863, and took 1.1 per cent of its imports from them. Doubters pointed out at the time that since the Maritimes and the province of Canada produced similar staples—timber, potash, fish—they were unlikely ever to become complementary trading zones.[43] Historians may use the purely literary device of claiming that in the 1860s there was enormous potential for the development of trade between Canada and the Maritimes, but by the same token, there is enormous potential for agriculture in the Sahara desert. Nor was the Intercolonial seen as an obvious route for Upper Canadian exports. William McMaster, a Toronto merchant (and academic benefactor), challenged the claim that the line was "an indispensable necessity in order to secure an independent outlet to the sea-board." Rather than use the existing railways to American ports, Upper Canada merchants preferred to pay warehousing, insurance and interest charges to keep wheat and flour in store through the winter "until the opening of the navigation."[44] It is true that by 1874, Ontario manufacturers had captured a large slice of the Maritime market for agricultural equipment, but this owed nothing to the Intercolonial (which was not completed until 1876): goods were sent by steamer to the local railhead at Pictou, Nova Scotia.[45] In any case, the manufacturing sector of the pre-Confederation Upper Canadian economy was far too small to be cited as an explanation for the province's support for intercolonial union.

Weaknesses in individual parts of the explanation of Confederation are glossed over by linking each argument to the overall interlocking package. Whether or not the Intercolonial railway would be useful, its place in the standard account is copper-fastened by arguing that it was a trade-off for westward expansion. Thus Morton, building up to his "cantilever" image:

> A local federation of the Canadas was not enough, for Upper Canada wanted not only freedom from the French majority (sic) in domestic matters; it also wanted, and the Brownite Liberals especially, to annex the north-west and build a Pacific railway. But Lower Canada could scarcely agree to the annexation of the north-west unless this were offset by guarantees of its historic rights in the new union, and by the adherence of the Atlantic provinces to the union to balance the indefinitely growing population of Upper Canada. Neither would Lower Canada and the Atlantic provinces assent to the cost of building a Pacific railway unless they were matched by the building of the Intercolonial.[46]

This statement arouses many questions. If the united province of Canada was not working, why could it not have been reconstructed on federal lines? The Fathers of Confederation themselves saw no necessary objection, for the fall-back position of the Great Coalition of 1864, should the wider union prove unattainable, was a promise to solve "existing difficulties by introducing the federal principle for Canada alone."[47] How urgent was Upper Canada's need to expand westward, and was the campaign focused on the Pacific coast or on the prairies? Was there a straight trade-off between the construction of the Intercolonial and westward expansion, between Upper and Lower Canadian interests? Was Confederation the necessary precondition for annexation of the north-west?

It is possible to overstate the extent to which Upper Canada urgently needed land for expansion. The agitation for the incorporation of the Hudson's Bay Company territories had begun in earnest with the campaign of the *Globe* in 1856, and had a great deal to do with the completion at the end of 1855 of Toronto's Northern Railway to Collingwood, which gave the city easy access to Georgian Bay and consequently an interest in the North-west.[48] While the last blocks of wild land within Upper Canada had been auctioned the previous year, creating what Lower called "a sense of spacial limitation,"[49] it did not mean—as the *Globe* itself acknowledged—that the province had run out of land: there was plenty of room for in-filling of settlement but no new frontiers to open up. As late as 1865, John A. Macdonald told Watkin that the western territories were "of no present value to Canada" for the province had "unoccupied land enough to absorb the immigration for many years."[50] Secondly, there is little to suggest that the kind of westward expansion George Brown hoped for was expected to include a railway to British Columbia—at least not at the outset. In his 1858 lectures, *Nova Britannia,* even the visionary Alexander Morris seemed to locate a Pacific railway up to twenty years in the future.[51] When Edward Watkin embraced the idea in 1860, he accepted that he was perhaps "somewhat visionary for even suggesting it."[52] In one important respect, his vision failed entirely: it was not the Grand Trunk which built the Pacific railway, and from 1872 onwards, the two ventures were to be deadly enemies. The speed with which Cartier was to offer a Pacific railway to the bemused British Columbia delegates in 1870 suggests that the idea was not far below the surface, but Morton is wrong to imply that it formed part of a Confederation package in the 1860s. When George Brown moved a resolution at the Quebec conference providing for the future admission of Newfoundland, the prairies, British Columbia and Vancouver Island, he remarked that the inclusion of the last two was "rather an extreme proposition."[53]

What, then, was being traded off and by whom? Early in 1864, a meeting had taken place between Brown and C.J. Brydges, the manager of the Grand Trunk. Brydges offered Brown the chair of the Canadian Board of the recently reorganized Hudson's Bay Company—a proposition which does not seem to have excited any moral outrage in the textbooks—and went on to convince him "that nothing could be done about the North-west without the Intercolonial."[54] If he had indeed convinced George Brown that the two projects could be traded, subsequent events suggest that—as with the dual aim of British North American union or a federation of the Canadas—Brown was out-manoeuvred in the coalition. Article 68 of the Quebec Resolutions bound the new general government to "secure, without delay" the completion of the Intercolonial. Article 69 spoke more generally of the importance of improving communications with the North-west, and promised that they would "be prosecuted at the earliest possible period that the state of the Finances will permit."[55] Given the state of the finances, complained one critic, this meant that the North-west was "hermetically sealed" for all time to come.[56] There was no trade-off.

In any case, who was doing the trading? It was not "Lower Canada" which wanted the Intercolonial, but *some* Lower Canadians—and by no means all of those francophones, for many of them objected strongly to any further favours for the Grand Trunk. There were also French Canadians who supported the Intercolonial but opposed Confederation on wider cultural grounds.[57] In any case, if the Intercolonial was designed to provide a winter trade outlet, it would presumably be of as much—if not more—benefit to Upper Canada. And if Lower Canadians and Maritimers did indeed purchase the Intercolonial by a tacit agreement to back a counterbalancing line to the Pacific, the bargain was a shaky one, for in the two decades which followed they were at best lukewarm and indeed eventually even hostile to the project.

There are also logical difficulties in accepting the claim that French Canadians felt safer in a union in which the Maritimes would join them in counter-balancing the population of Upper Canada. Cartier indeed advanced the argument—but, then, he would, wouldn't he?[58] Surveys of the Lower Canadian debate on the merits of Confederation by Peter Waite and Arthur Silver do not suggest that French Canadians saw Maritimers as the guarantors of their rights.[59] Joseph Cauchon, one of the most articulate supporters of Confederation, accepted that from the point of view of protecting the basic identity and rights of French Canada, *"la confédération des deux Canadas eût pu être aussi bonne que la confédération de toutes les Provinces de l'Amérique Britannique du Nord"* ["the confederation of the two Canadas could have been as good as the confederation of all the provinces of British North America."[60]] The conventional wisdom of Canadian history is that French Canadians have always resisted annexation to the United States for fear that they would be swamped. Why, then, should they seek union with any more anglophones than were absolutely necessary? One French Canadian opponent argued that his compatriots would be in a four-to-one minority in the federal parliament: "What could so weak a minority do to obtain justice?"[61] French Canadians accepted Confederation because it offered them their own province, in which the local majority could safeguard its educational system and so protect its religion and culture—although some were uneasy that the central government's power of disallowance made the federal structure a legislative union in disguise. What determined the preference of French Canadians was that in 1864–67, a negotiated scheme for local autonomy within British North American Confederation was actually on offer, whereas autonomy within a federation of the two Canadas was not. Yet this is not to say that a similar solution could not have been negotiated, creating a smaller federation confined to the St. Lawrence valley. In this context, we might perhaps recall that in 1867, the very year of Confederation, Austrians and

Hungarians decided to substitute hyphenation for unification as a basis for sharing the Danube valley. In the absence of the bell-jar, we might equate Bismarck's Prussia with the victorious Northern States. Yet no-one, so far as I am aware, seriously argued that the internal stresses of the Austrian Empire could only be solved by federation with Serbia and Moldavia.

Where one argument is weak, appeal is implicitly shifted to some other aspect of the package. A federation of the two Canadas, Morton asserted "could hardly have met the need for expansion."[62] Why not? The British parliamentary enquiry of 1857 had recommended the annexation of the fertile districts of the prairies to the province of Canada, and the gentlemanly legislators of Westminster were not always unstinted in expressions of confidence in the governmental capacity of their colonial counterparts. The internal reconstruction of the province of Canada along federal lines could in fact have made it easier to add the Hudson's Bay territories as an eventual third wheel. Representation for the Red River settlement, which in the 1860s had a francophone majority, coupled with local autonomy for Lower Canada, might have offered just as satisfactory a constitutional settlement as union with the Maritimes. In fact, if Canadians had borrowed from the precedent of territorial government south of the border, the 12,000 people of the Red River might have been incorporated without affecting the balance of representation at all.[63] The United States constitution permitted territories to send a non-voting delegate to Congress, barring them from seeking statehood—and full voting rights—until they had a population of 60,000. Manitoba did not achieve this figure until 1881. Historians rightly inform us that these things *did* not happen, but when they tell us that such things *could* not have happened, they not only pronounce on what they cannot possibly know but distort understanding of what actually occurred.

Some may quibble with an approach which picks holes in this or that part of the postulated causal package. The ingredients may not always be palatable to the fastidious scholar. What matters is the process, the crisis which baked them into the Confederation cake. In a general sense, of course, the historian cannot dismiss the importance of what C.P. Stacey called the "atmosphere of crisis" at the end of the Civil War.[64] It is without doubt the essential *psychological* context for understanding the adoption of Confederation. "The tide of war is rolling towards us," cried a Halifax newspaper. "What do men mean, talking about cents per head of taxation[!]"[65] "Look around you to the valley of Virginia," McGee challenged those who doubted the need for Confederation, "look around you to the mountains of Georgia, and you will find reasons as thick as blackberries."[66] Statements of this kind are a reminder that what we term "arguments" in favour of Confederation were in reality a mixture of inducements appealing to self-interest and threats which fed on fear. Historians delude themselves if they assume that contemporary debate was intended to supply posterity with the pieces of a satisfying intellectual jigsaw.

The beguiling temptation to treat the evidence in this way may be illustrated by Gladstone's memorandum, penned on 12 July 1864 in response to demands for vast expenditure on fortifications in Canada, in which the parsimonious Chancellor of the Exchequer doubted whether Britain could do much to defend the provinces. "Their long and comparatively thin strip of occupied territory extends for 2,000 miles between the States on one side, and the sterility of pinching winter on the other.... I say, nothing can defend them except the desperate energy of a brave, self-relying population, which fights for hearth and home." Assuming, perhaps optimistically, that the "United States can scarcely have a quarrel with Canada for its own sake," he argued that the more provinces were "detached, as to their defensive not less than their administrative responsibilities, from England," the better cross-border relations would become. Consequently, Gladstone opposed the spending of money on any defence projects, with the possible exception of the naval base at Halifax, and argued instead that "the true aim of all our measures at this important juncture should be to bring the people of our British North American Colonies ... as nearly to a national sentiment and position as their relation to the British Crown will permit." Accordingly "efforts should be made, without delay, to ascertain whether it is practicable to establish a Federation or Political Union of these Colonies."[67]

Read in isolation, Gladstone's memorandum makes Confederation seem a mathematical deduction from the circumstances of the defence crisis arising out of the probable end of the Civil War. In fact, it was almost certainly written in the light of the announcement in *The Times* of the previous day of the formation of a new Canadian ministry dedicated to the achievement of precisely that aim of general federation.[68] Gladstone's far-sightedness may be judged by the fact that in July 1864, he still believed that the Civil War would end with the disruption of the United States. He was a consistent opponent of defence projects in Canada: his own Prime Minister, Palmerston, even complained to Queen Victoria that the Chancellor was "troublesome and wrong-headed" on the subject.[69] The only mathematical deduction which motivated Gladstone was the hope of knocking a large item off his expenditure column: Confederation was not so much an alternative as a diversion.

In fact, examined closely, Gladstone's argument was open to serious challenges. The assumption that political unity would strengthen defence is one which appeals to the modern world where the military alliances require sovereign states to accept an element of interdependence. When applied to self-governing colonies in the mid-nineteenth century, the argument was of little relevance: as the duke of Newcastle had written in 1862, "none of the objections which oppose [Confederation] seem to impede a union for defence."[70] Yet even under a unified command, the provinces would remain weak in the face of the United States: the North had put 2.3 million men into the field—almost equal to the entire population of the Province of Canada. Canadian critics could not see how union with the tiny province of New Brunswick—which had one third of the population of neighbouring Maine—could do anything but weaken their already parlous position.[71] As for creating a national community ready to fight to the death for home and hearth, Gladstone's panacea threatened to have exactly the reverse effect. In the Atlantic provinces, critics bitterly objected to the imposition of a government which could order their militia away to distant frontiers—as one Newfoundlander would put it, to leave their bones to bleach "on the desert sands of Canada."[72] British North America would continue to be a narrow corridor between aggressive Yankees and pinching winter. In fact, the rest of the package—massive territorial expansion westward—would actually make Canada's position weaker in relation to its powerful neighbour.

Nor was the Intercolonial Railway an indisputable addition to the defensive capabilities of the provinces. Gladstone certainly did not think so: he had fought bitterly against the Intercolonial guarantee in 1861–62, and his 1864 memorandum opposed any commitment to defend territory not accessible year-round by sea. If the danger of American invasion were so immediate and terrible, the construction of a railway—it was to take nine years to complete—was hardly an appropriate response. In fact, the argument that the Intercolonial would strengthen the provinces at all was open to strong challenge. Even if the New Brunswick section of the line was diverted from the St John valley to the remote Gulf coast of the province, the existing Grand Trunk line still ran very close to the United States—"in some places not more than fifteen or twenty miles from the frontier.... An enemy could destroy miles of it before it would be possible to resist him, and in time of difficulty it would be a mere trap for any troops passing along it, unless we had almost an army to keep it open."[73] Summarizing the argument that Confederation offered a defence against the Americans, a young French Canadian radical called Wilfrid Laurier claimed that it was like being "armed with an egg-shell to stop a bullet ... a wisp of straw in the way of a giant."[74]

It is when we turn to Gladstone's argument that Confederation would be a step in disengagement from Britain—and hence a defensive measure by avoiding American anger—that the fundamental flaw of the interconnecting explanation becomes obvious. Sir Richard MacDonnell, Lieutenant-Governor of Nova Scotia, was not one of the more towering intellects of the colonial service, but it was not simply obtuseness which made him

> unable to see in what way England would be less vulnerable through Canada or Canada less vulnerable through England when a confederated Parliament meets at Ottawa than now. There is not a foot of territory in all these hundreds of thousands of square miles which would become less English than now, so long as the Queen's representative is head of the Federation; nor is there any obligation in regard to these Provinces which now devolves upon Britain that would be diminished by their being thus huddled into one heterogeneous assemblage.[75]

Palmerston refused to admit that there was even a question to be discussed "whether our North American provinces are to be fought for or abandoned."[76] "You can best tell whether the Government at Washington look to unite our provinces to their own Northern Dominion," wrote Lord Russell to the British minister there. "But if they do, they must look to a fight with us."[77] Sir Frederic Rogers, permanent undersecretary at the Colonial Office, felt that, "nothing can be more provoking than to be obliged (if we are obliged) to fight the United States in the place and manner which are most disadvantageous to ourselves, for a colony which is no good to us and has no real care for us. Yet somehow I would not wish England to refrain from doing so; for England would not be great, courageous, successful England if she did."[78] "Let all foreign States know that in touching the North American provinces they touch England," warned a London newspaper.[79] There is abundant contemporary evidence that the British would have rallied to the defence of the Canadians just as they honoured their treaty obligations to Belgium in 1914 and their imperial responsibility to the Falkland Islanders in 1982. As late as 1879, Salisbury referred to the "solid and palpable fact that if they are attacked England must defend them."[80] This is not to deny that there was speculation that the colonial tie might eventually be broken, but this was more speculation than the prediction which Donald Creighton portrayed in his analysis of British press response to the Quebec Conference. "The present status of the federation, *The Times* observed, 'will be only a state of transition, marking the passage of British America from colonial tutelage to national independence'." *The Times* did indeed use those words, but the opening clause of the quotation actually read: "it may be that such a Government will be only a state of transition."[81] Having garbed themselves in the laboratory coat of the scientist to assert that British North American union was necessary, the historians then proceed to use literary sleight of hand to blur three very different concepts: Confederation, independence and neutrality.

In short, it does not follow that a union of the British North American provinces was the logical deduction from the circumstances and problems of 1858–64. Asked to chew upon the continental imperatives so evident in the 1860s, the computer of historical destiny would surely have been far more likely to have anticipated the verdict which Goldwin Smith pronounced ten years later: "Canadian nationality being a lost cause, the ultimate union of Canada with the United States appears now to be morally certain."[82] If French and English really could not co-exist in a single province which shared the mighty common interest of the St Lawrence system, by what logic could they build a transcontinental nation? If the overarching threat was the challenge of the United States, with ten times their population, by what logic could the provinces choose that moment to create a new polity, and one still linked to Britain? This was precisely the kind of ill-timed provocation which lay behind the Mexican empire—as British ministers realised when they vetoed the Canadian wish to style the new union a "kingdom." In bloodless logic, the only enduringly safe solution to the continental crisis of 1864–67 would have been to have sought terms of annexation to the United States. But people are not particles: British North Americans did not wish to become United States Americans. The *logical* alternatives to annexation all involved some kind of neutralisation, either by remaining as separate provinces or by establishing a form of union under explicit United States hegemony. New Brunswick in 1865–66 might well have moved along the first path, had Washington showed any interest in supporting the "westward extension" of its railway system into New England. Joseph Howe feared that Confederation would only be workable in terms of the second alternative. "Inevitably it must succumb to the growing power of the republic. A treaty offensive and defensive with the United States, involving ultimate participation in a war with England, would be the hard terms of its recognition as a separate but not independent state."[83] Some might feel that the terms of the Treaty of Washington of 1871 indicate that Canada had the worst of the muddled bargain. Britain and the new Dominion each continued to be vulnerable through their mutual association, and it was Canada which paid most of the price of appeasing American anger.

Historians and scientists share one important common feature in their method of working: both must master the trick of asking the right question. We can now see that it was pointless for scholars to ponder how it was that leeches managed to cure the sick, or to speculate on the reasons why long-distance mariners avoided sailing over the edge of the world, because we realize that their very assumptions were unfounded. Historians may fall more subtly into a similar trap. There is a world of difference between asking "why did the British North American provinces decide to adopt Confederation in the 1860s?" and identifying the real issue: "why was it that it was the idea of *Confederation* which dominated the British North American response to the crises of that decade, rather than other logically deducible solutions?"

The starting point for explaining Canadian Confederation, then, must be the idea itself.[84] It was not the only solution which could be deduced from the circumstances of 1864; indeed, we are not entitled to assume that it was necessarily the obvious one. (The American Civil War, as opponents of Confederation were fond of pointing out, did not provide strong *prima facie* evidence in favour of the adoption of any form of federal system.) Why then did the idea of Confederation come to dominate in this way? The answer is that it had been around for a long time, always seen as a future aim, an ultimate destiny. But, so it may be retorted, that could also be said of its United States counterpart, Manifest Destiny, which was equally confident in seeing Canada's destiny as part of the American republic. There are important differences. Confederation, in a curious way, had been felt to be coming closer. Even in 1858, the Canadian ministry had defined its policy not so much as Confederation as in terms of an investigation of "the principles on which a bond of a federal character ... may perhaps hereafter be practicable."[85] One participant in the 1862 railway negotiations recalled that it was still regarded as "a matter in the distance."[86]

It was in this context that the elements of the interlocking package had become familiar. In an age of railway building, arguments had been advanced that a line from Halifax to Quebec would increase trade and offer advantages for defence. Since the railway could not be built overnight, these arguments really had no validity when applied to an immediate crisis, such as the imminent ending of Reciprocity or the likelihood of American invasion. However, the importance of the "atmosphere of crisis" of 1864 lay not in the emergence of Confederation as a logical response, but in its adoption as the only measure large enough to provide psychological reassurance. "For the first time we are being brought face to face with the reality," said a New Brunswick newspaper.[87] "Everybody admits that Union must take place sometime," said John A. Macdonald. "I say now is the time."[88] Arguments which had a measure of plausibility when applied to the stately flow of British North American development were nonetheless thrown in, because of their very familiarity, to the Niagara of the 1860s. In practical terms, Confederation was a substitute rather than a centrepiece, a tacit recognition that real and immediate answers could not be forthcoming. "Conscious as we are of our inability to protect these colonies by land in case of war, we must naturally rejoice at any event which seems to place them in a position in which they would be better able to protect themselves," commented *The Times* on the Quebec Conference.[89] The key word, of course, was "seems"; and the substantive point the impossibility of providing effective defence. Anticipating Chester Martin, the Irish journalist W.H. Russell was convinced that "the white heat of American strife" provided the moment for "welding" the provinces together, but he warned against assuming that "any confederation ... would yield such an increase of force as would enable the collective or several members of it to resist the force of the Republic of the Northern American United States—at least, not just now." There might seem to be a contradiction here: Confederation was for defence, but would not provide additional strength. Yet to Russell, it was

> not surprising that the idea of a Confederation for the purposes of common defence ... should have arisen. It is surprising that it should have floated about for so long, and have stirred men to action so feebly. I think it is the first notion that occurs to a stranger visiting Canada and casting about for a something to put in place of the strength which distant England cannot, and Canadians will not, afford.[90]

Confederation, then, was at best a long-term development strategy ingeniously passed off as an emergency response to current crisis. Once launched, the idea seized the centre ground of political debate, and it became easier to go forward than to attempt to fall back. French Canadian *Bleus* would no longer be able to resist "rep. by pop." within the province of Canada after agreeing to the principle in the proposed federal legislature. As the Montreal *Gazette* remarked, it would be highly optimistic to believe "that, after an acknowledgement that Upper Canada ... is entitled to seventeen more members than Lower Canada, the agitation can ever again be quelled."[91] Joseph Cauchon's great fear was that the Lower Canada English minority would crumble under the pressure of a united upper province, preferring to see the issue settled even at the cost of privileged sectional representation: entrenchment of the equal representation of the two sections had been abolished in 1854, and a simple majority would be sufficient to redistribute ridings in favour of Upper Canada.[92] In practice, legislation would involve something much more bitter and protracted than a snap vote, but even so few could welcome a crisis which, as Bishop Laflèche put it, would end either in *"la guerre civile ou la domination du Haut-Canada dans l'Union Législative."*[93] It was better to settle for the local autonomy within a wider confederation which was actually on offer rather than hope to negotiate similar guarantees from an upper province which knew it had the upper hand. For his part, John A. Macdonald equally could not afford to see Confederation fail, since he needed the Maritimes to make good his relative weakness in Upper Canada: at the very least, Confederation as a policy aim was a useful basis for ministerial alliance with former opponents, such as William McDougall, in 1864–66, just as it had been for gaining A.T. Galt in 1858. While significant sections of the province of Canada found it in their interest to keep Confederation at the head of their agenda, their allies in the Maritimes could accept temporary reverses as the price of long-term success. Recent consideration of the issue in Nova Scotia and New Brunswick challenges the pejorative view that all Maritimers were sunk in parochial lethargy, and tends rather to see objections as directed against the terms of the Quebec scheme rather than the aim of union itself, to be ultimately quietened not by "Repeal" but by "Better Terms."[94] Yet even if we embrace the traditional and more censorious view of Maritime hostility to Confederation, we can still see how pressure for the idea from Canada—with or without financial inducements—and from Britain turned it into a juggernaut which politicians had to board unless they wished to be crushed. The very breadth of the opposition coalition made it vulnerable to rupture, both in New Brunswick in 1865–66 and successively in Nova Scotia from 1866 through to 1869.

Thus once Confederation became launched as a practical issue, there is no great mystery in explaining how it managed to occupy the centre ground, marginalizing its critics on all sides. The challenge to the historian is to identify the origins of that idea, which means ceasing to portray it as the necessary product of British North American circumstances. It means moving the starting point of explanation away from the perceived shortcomings of the province of Canada. It means above all abandoning Morton's "cantilever" of interlocking and equally imperative causal arguments, recognizing instead the lesson which Gladstone learned from Peel, that a scheme may be backed by different individuals for different reasons. Of course, this makes the explanation less artistically satisfying, gives it the appearance of being less scientifically watertight, less mathematically complete. It is good to note that at least one distinguished scholar has abandoned the flirtation with basic physics. "One can add up the causes of Confederation and still not get the sum of it," Peter Waite wrote in 1987.[95] Far from being an abandonment of the historian's responsibility of explanation, such a conclusion is in fact a fundamental precondition for interpreting the past in the way that the past actually happened. "One might, indeed, put together a kind of algebraic formula or polygon of forces from the many external and internal elements that converged in pressure upon British North America to unite," wrote J.B. Brebner, "but it would be an inexact thing at best."[96] In seeking to explain Canadian Confederation, it is better for historians to settle for the humility of inexact geometry than to delude themselves with the bombast of inexact science.

Notes

1. Bury's Cambridge inaugural lecture of 1903, "The Science of History," is given in H. Temperley, ed., *Selected Essays of J. B. Bury* (Cambridge, 1930), pp. 3–22, with the quoted phrase at pp. 4, 23; for G. M. Trevelyan's reference to Canada, see his *Clio, A Muse And Other Essays* (London, 1913), p. 141. I am grateful to Dr James Sturgis for discussion of the points at issue, and to Mr Louis A. Delvoie for pointing out that Bury is misquoted in E. H. Carr, *What is History?* (Harmondsworth ed., 1964), p. 57.

2. Especially in D. G. Creighton, *The Road to Confederation: The Emergence of Canada, 1863–67* (Toronto, 1964) and W. L. Morton, *The Critical Years: The Union of British North America 1857–73* (Toronto, 1964). The various textbooks cited below indicate that the consensus of explanation did not simply originate in the Centennial decade: Creighton, for instance, had been an advisor for the 1937–40 Rowell-Sirois Commission whose deliberations were influenced by the idea of a strong central government.

3. Arthur Marwick, *The Nature of History* (London, 1970), p. 99. Marwick's view is endorsed by G. Kitson Clark, *The Critical Historian* (London, 1967), pp. 19–31, but for a very different approach, see Lee Benson, *Toward The Scientific Study of History: Selected Essays* (Philadelphia, 1972). See also Carr, *What is History?*, pp. 56–86.

4. Trevely in, *Clio,* p. 147.

5. Chester Martin, *Foundations of Canadian Nationhood* (Toronto, 1955), pp. 297–98.

6. *The Canadian Encyclopedia* (3 vols, Edmonton, 1985),i, p. 399.

7. R. D. Francis, R. Jones and D. B. Smith, *Origins: Canadian History to Confederation* (Toronto, 1988), p. 378.

8. D. H. Fischer, *Historians' Fallacies: Toward a Logic of Historic Thought* (New York, 1970), pp. xxi-xxii.

9. Peter Stansky, *Gladstone: A Progress in Politics* (New York, 1979), p. 26, and cf. John Morley, *The Life of William Ewart Gladstone* (3 vols, London, 1903), i, p. 192.

10. J. M. Beck, *Joseph Howe: ii, The Briton becomes Canadian, 1848–1878* (Kingston, 1973), p. 182.

11. J. M. S. Careless, *Canada: A Story of Challenge* (Toronto, rev. ed., 1974), pp. 230, 245.

12. A. R. M. Lower, *Colony to Nation: A History of Canada* (Don Mills, rev. ed., 1964), p. 313. Lower believed that the United States constitution was drawn up at Annapolis in 1789. Ibid., p. 314.

13. W. L. Morton, *The Kingdom of Canada: A General History from Earliest Times* (Toronto, rev. ed., 1969), p. 317.

14. Donald Creighton, *John A. Macdonald* (2 vols, Toronto, 1965).

15. E. W. Watkin, *Canada and the States: Recollections 1851 to 1886* (London [1886]).

16. D. G. Creighton, *Dominion of the North: A History of Canada* (Toronto, rev. ed., 1962), esp. pp. 304–5; K. McNaught, *The Pelican History of Canada* (London, rev. ed., 1978), pp. 115, 134.

17. *The Nation* (Toronto), 26 February 1875, quoted F. H. Underhill, *The Image of Confederation* (Toronto, 1964), p. 20.

18. J. Bartlet Brebner, *Canada: A Modern History* (Ann Arbor, 1960), p. 273.

19. National Library of Wales, Harpton Court Collection, C/2028, Herman Merivale to G. C. Lewis, 23 September 1858.

20. J. L. Finlay and D. N. Sprague, *The Structure of Canadian History* (Scarborough, Ont., rev. ed., 1984), p. 170.

21. Lower, *Colony to Nation,* p. 321.

22. J. R. Colombo, ed., *Colombo's Canadian Quotations* (Edmonton, 1974), p. 381, quoting E. B. Biggar, *Anecdotal Life of Sir John A. Macdonald* (1891).

23. Morton, *Critical Years,* p. 112. Morton also damned Sandfield as "an unabashed mediocrity, reckless in speech but cautious in action" whose real offence seems to have been that he aimed "to prolong the life of the Union, and avoid disruption, or confederation." (Ibid., p. 113) Goldwin Smith, no forgiving observer, called him "a thoroughly good fellow, and honest." Goldwin Smith, *Reminiscences* (New York, 1910), p. 436. Professor Roger Hall points out that the "pawky" Sandfield won the hand of a Louisiana beauty.

24. By F. R. Scott, in a famously sardonic poem in 1957.

25. Joseph Pope, *Memoirs of the Right Honourable Sir John Alexander Macdonald* (Toronto, 1894), p. 373.

26. In a bound, Sandfield Macdonald is premier on Ontario on p. 4 of Creighton's second volume. Cf Bruce W. Hodgins, *John Sandfield Macdonald, 1812–1872* (Toronto, 1971), pp. 87–88.

27. Creighton, *Dominion of the North,* p. 290.

28. Lower, op. cit., p. 300.

29. Cf Ged Martin, "Launching Canadian Confederation: Means to Ends 1836–64," *Historical Journal,* xxvii (1984), p. 595 and n.

30. Morton, *Critical Years,* p. III.

31. Spencer Walpole, *The Life of Lord John Russell* (2 vols, London, 1889), ii, pp. 13–30, esp. p. 25.

32. Ibid., ii, p. 144. Cf Donald Southgate, *"The Most English Minister ...": The Policies and Politics of Palmerston* (London, 1966), pp. 308–10.

33. For the militia in this period, see Morton, *Critical Years,* pp. 126–28, 145; Hodgins, *Sandfield Macdonald,* pp. 70–71; Richard A. Preston, *Canada and "Imperial Defense"* (Durham, N.C., 1967), pp. 46–47, 59–62.

34. Quoted, Underhill, *Image of Confederation,* p. 19.

35. Lower, op. cit., pp. 307–8.

36. Henri Joly drew attention to the awkward discrepancy in *Parliamentary Debates on the Subject of the Confederation of the British North American Provinces* (Quebec, 1865), p. 357. [Cited as *CD*].

37. Lower, op. cit., p. 311.

38. Ibid., p. 313.

39. E.g. Thomas Scatcherd and Christopher Dunkin, *CD,* pp. 747, 508.

40. Lower, op. cit., p. 310.

41. The point was made by Henri Joly and A-A. Dorion in *CD,* pp. 356, 528.

42. Lower, op. cit., p. 315.

43. Figures quoted from British Parliamentary Papers, and given in Ged Martin, "The Case Against Canadian Confederation," fn, 86 in Ged Martin, ed., *The Causes of Canadian Confederation: Papers from a Seminar held at Edinburgh May 1988* (Fredericton, forthcoming). For contemporary doubts about trade, see *CD,* pp. 863 (J-B-E. Dorion) and 355 (Henri Joly).

44. *CD,* p. 230.

45. P. B. Waite, *Canada 1874–1896: Arduous Destiny* (Toronto, 1971), pp. 76–77.

46. Morton, *Kingdom of Canada,* p. 317.

47. Pope, *Memoirs,* P. 684.

48. Doug Owram, *Promise of Eden: The Canadian Expansionist Movement and the Idea of the West, 1856–1900* (Toronto, 1980), pp. 38–58; cf. *Weekly Globe,* 14 September 1855, cited J. M. S. Careless, *Brown of the Globe, i: The Voice of Upper Canada 1818–1859* (Toronto, 1959), p. 229.

49. Lower, op. cit., p. 295.

50. Macdonald to Watkin, 27 March 1865, in Pope, op. cit., pp. 397–98. Of course, Macdonald had some motive in talking down the value of the West, since Canada would have to purchase the land it needed for settlement.

51. Alexander Morris, *Nova Britannia* (Toronto, 1884 ed.), p. 78.

52. Letter to unnamed recipient, 13 November 1860, in Watkin, *Canada and the States,* pp. 12–15. "I hope you will not laugh at me as very visionary" began W. H. Draper when he told the parliamentary enquiry of 1857 of his hope that a transcontinental railway might be built, if not in his own lifetime, then in that of his children. British Parliamentary Papers, 1857 (2nd session), xv, q. 4102, p. 218.

53. G. P. Browne, ed., *Documents on the Confederation of British North America* (Toronto, 1969), p. 99.

54. Creighton, *Macdonald, i: Young Politician,* pp. 348–49.

55. Browne, ed., *Documents,* p. 165.

56. *CD,* p. 453 (T. C. Wallbridge).

57. e.g. J. B. B. Pouliot, MPP for Témiscouata.

58. *CD,* pp. 54–55.

59. P. B. Waite, *The Life and Times of Confederation, 1863–67* (Toronto, 1962), pp. 134–160; A. I. Silver, *The French-Canadian Idea of Confederation, 1864–1900* (Toronto, 1982), pp. 33–50.

60. Joseph Cauchon, *L'Union des Provinces de l'Amérique Britannique du Nord* (Quebec, 1865), p. 46.

61. *CD,* p. 624 (Joseph Perrault).

62. Morton *Critical Years,* p. 149.

63. This idea was reflected in a number of questions asked at the British parliamentary enquiry of 1857.

64. C. P. Stacey, "Confederation: The Atmosphere of Crisis," in Edith G. Firth, ed., *Profiles of a Province: Studies in the History of Ontario* (Toronto, 1967), pp. 73–79.

65. *British Colonist,* 7 January 1865, quoted Creighton, *Road to Confederation,* pp. 229–30.

66. Speech at Montreal, 22 October 1864, in E. Whelan, comp., *The Union of the British Provinces* (Charlottetown, 1865), pp. 122–23.

67. Printed in Paul Knaplund, *Gladstone and Britain's Imperial Policy* (London, 1927), pp. 228–42.

68. *The Times,* 11 July 1864, confirmed in an admiring leading article of 12 July.

69. G. E. Buckle, ed., *Letters of Queen Victoria,* 2nd series (London, 1926), i, pp. 248–49.

70. Newcastle's despatch of 21 August 1862 to Lord Monck is widely quoted. Cf Browne, ed., op. cit., p. 32.

71. As A-A Dorion pointed out, *CD,* p. 256–57.

72. James Hiller, "Confederation Defeated: The Newfoundland Election of 1869," in J. Hiller and P. Neary, eds, *Newfoundland in the Nineteenth and Twentieth Centuries* (Toronto, 1980), p. 83. Ct Ged Martin, "The Case Against Canadian Confederation" for similar statements in the Maritimes.

73. Dorion again, *CD,* p. 257.

74. Quoted, J. Schull, *Laurier: The First Canadian* (Toronto, 1966), p. 57.

75. Public Record Office, Co 217/235, MacDonnell to Cardwell, 22 November 1864, fos 187–212.

76. Public Record Office, Russell Papers, PRO 30/22/27, Palmerston to Russell, 29 July 1864. "There may be much to be said for the theory ... that our Colonies are an encumbrance and an expense, and that we should be better off without them, but that is not the opinion of England, and it is not mine." Even Gladstone

reluctantly concluded: "If Canada desires to be British, and to fight for British connection as men fight for their country, I do not think we can shrink from the duty of helping her." Gladstone to Cardwell, private, 23 May 1865, in Knaplund, *Gladstone and Britain's Imperial Policy,* pp. 243–46.

77. Public Record Office, Russell Papers, PRO 30/22/97, Russell to Lord Lyons, copy, 20 October 1864, fos 87–88.

78. Rogers to Taylor [1865], in *Autobiography of Henry Taylor, 1800–1875* (2 vols. London, 1885), ii, pp. 241–42.

79. *Sun,* 25 November 1864. Cardwell, so often cited as the closet separatist, spoke in almost identical terms in the House of Commons on 11 March 1869. J. Mackay Hitsman, *Safeguarding Canada, 1763–1871* (Toronto, 1968), p. 214.

80. Quoted, Creighton, *Macdonald, ii: Old Chieftain,* p. 277.

81. Compare Creighton, *Road to Confederation,* p. 215 with *The Times,* 24 November 1864.

82. Goldwin Smith, "The Political Destiny of Canada," *Fortnightly Review,* cxxiv, 1 April 1877, pp. 431–59, esp. p. 458.

83. Joseph Howe, *Confederation in Relation to the Empire* (London, 1866) printed in J. A. Chisholm, ed. *The Speeches and Public Letters of Joseph Howe* (2 vols, Halifax, 1909), ii, p. 489.

84. Ged Martin, "An Imperial Idea and Its Friends: Canadian Confederation and the British, 1836–64," in G. Martel, ed., *Studies in British Imperial History: Essays in Honour of A. P. Thornton* (Houndmills, 1986), pp. 49–94.

85. Quoted, W. M. Whitelaw, *The Maritimes and Canada before Confederation* (ed. P. B. Waite, Toronto, 1966), p. 128.

86. William Annand, quoted by Waite, *Life and Times,* p. 50.

87. Saint John *Evening Globe,* quoted ibid., p. 63.

88. Speech at Halifax, Whelan, comp., *Union of the British Provinces,* p. 46.

89. *The Times,* 15 October 1864.

90. W. H. Russell, *Canada: Its Defences, Condition, and Resources* (London, 1865), pp. 311–12.

91. Montreal *Gazette,* 3 March 1865, quoted Waite, *Life and Times,* p. 155.

92. Cauchon, *L'Union des Provinces,* p. 18.

93. Laflèche to Boucher de Niverville, 2 March 1864, quoted in Walter Ullmann, "The Quebec Bishops and Confederation," *Canadian Historical Review,* xliv (1963), p. 218.

94. Phillip A. Buckner, "The Maritimes and Confederation: A Reassessment"; James L. Sturgis, "The Opposition to Confederation in Nova Scotia, 1864–1868" and B. D. Tennyson, "Economic Nationalism, Confederation and Nova Scotia," forthcoming in Ged Martin, ed., *Causes of Canadian Confederation.*

95. Peter Waite, "Between Three Oceans: Challenges of Continental Destiny (1840–1900)," in C. Brown, ed., *The Illustrated History of Canada* (Toronto, 1987), p. 314.

96. Brebner, *Canada,* p. 277.

Index

585